DATE DUE

COLLINS
ALBATROSS BOOK OF
LONGER POEMS

COLLINS
ALBATROSS BOOK OF
LONGER POEMS

ENGLISH AND AMERICAN POETRY
FROM THE FOURTEENTH CENTURY
TO THE PRESENT DAY, EDITED
BY EDWIN MORGAN

Granger Index Reprint Series

BOOKS FOR LIBRARIES PRESS
FREEPORT, NEW YORK

GENERAL EDITOR: J. B. FOREMAN

First published 1963
Published in the Granger Index
Reprint Series 1969

STANDARD BOOK NUMBER:
8369-6051-3

LIBRARY OF CONGRESS CATALOG CARD NUMBER:
77-85513

© 1963
William Collins, Sons and Company, Ltd.

PRINTED IN GREAT BRITAIN
COLLINS CLEAR-TYPE PRESS

CONTENTS

ACKNOWLEDGEMENTS

The publishers are indebted to the following authors, publishers and owners of copyright who have given permission for material to be reprinted in this book.

THE SOCIETY OF AUTHORS, DR. JOHN MASEFIELD, O.M. and THE MACMILLAN COMPANY, NEW YORK—for *The Wanderer*, from *Collected Poems*, by John Masefield, copyright, 1930, 1958, by John Masefield.

MRS. GEORGE BAMBRIDGE, MESSRS. METHUEN AND CO. LTD., and THE MACMILLAN COMPANY OF CANADA—for *McAndrew's Hymn* from *The Seven Seas* by Rudyard Kipling.

CHATTO AND WINDUS LTD.—for *Dead Man's Dump* by Isaac Rosenberg.

CITY LIGHTS BOOKS and ALLEN GINSBERG—for *American Change* by Allen Ginsberg, copyright © 1962, by Allen Ginsberg.

J. M. DENT & SONS LTD.—for *Over Sir John's Hill* by Dylan Thomas.

FABER AND FABER LTD.—for *Burnt Norton* and *Gerontion* by T. S. Eliot, *The Quaker Graveyard in Nantucket* by Robert Lowell, and *Spain 1937* by W. H. Auden.

VICTOR GOLLANCZ LTD. and HUGH MACDIARMID—for *Stony Limits* by Hugh Macdiarmid.

GROVE PRESS, INC.—for *The Lordly and Isolate Satyrs* from *The Distances: Poems* by Charles Olson, copyright ©1950, 1951, 1953, 1960 by Charles Olson, published by Grove Press, Inc.

HOLT, RINEHART AND WINSTON, INC.—for *The Axe-helve* and *Paul's Wife* from *Complete Poems of Robert Frost*, copyright 1923 by Holt, Rinehart and Winston, Inc., copyright renewed 1951 by Robert Frost, reprinted by permission of Messrs. Jonathan Cape, Ltd., and Holt, Rinehart and Winston, Inc.

HOUGHTON MIFFLIN COMPANY—for *The Nun's Priest's Tale*, *The Franklin's Prologue and Tale* and *The Pardoner's Prologue and Tale* by Geoffrey Chaucer from *The Works of Geoffrey Chaucer* edited by F. N. Robinson.

THE HUTCHINSON PUBLISHING GROUP—for *The Story of Two Gentlemen and the Gardener* from *Songs* by Christopher Logue.

ALFRED A. KNOPF, INC., and FABER AND FABER LTD.,—for *Sunday Morning* by Wallace Stevens, copyright 1923, 1931, 1954, by Wallace Stevens.

LIVERIGHT PUBLISHING CORPORATION, NEW YORK—for *Voyages I—VI* from *The Collected Poems of Hart Crane*, copyright © R 1961 by Liveright Publishing Corporation.

MACMILLAN AND COMPANY—for *A Song About Major Eatherly* from *Weep Before God*, by John Wain reprinted by permission of John Wain, author, The Macmillan Company of Canada Limited, and Macmillan and Company.

NEW DIRECTIONS—for *Burning the Christmas Greens* from *The Collected Later Poems of William Carlos Williams*, copyright 1944, 1948 and 1950 by William Carlos Williams, and *Tract* from *The Collected Earlier Poems of William Carlos Williams*, both reprinted by permission of New Directions, publishers; for *Near Perigord, I, II, III* from *Personae: The Collected Poems of Ezra Pound*, copyright 1926 and 1954 by Ezra Pound, reprinted by permission of A. V. Moore, literary agent, Princess Mary de Rachewiltz and New Directions, publishers.

MRS. YEATS and MACMILLAN AND COMPANY—for *Meditations in Time of Civil War* from *Collected Poems of W. B. Yeats*.

INTRODUCTION

There is no rigid definition of a ' longer poem '. One might say that its average length would be between 100 and 1000 lines, and that it tended to have a narrative structure; that it came somewhere between the compressed intensity of the lyric and the ambitious grandeur of the epic. Even such loose limits, however, will not go unquestioned. Although a lyrical poem is generally short, the lyrical mood may be sustained by some poets for a considerable period: in the present collection, Spenser's *Epithalamion*, Whitman's *Crossing Brooklyn Ferry*, and Meredith's *The Lark Ascending* are mainly lyrical in feeling, but it is a lyricism which is enriched by ideas, or by fact and action. At the other end of the scale, Milton's *Paradise Regained* has been included, as an ' epic incident ' but not an epic: a poem which deals with great issues and employs certain heroic conventions, but which deliberately restricts its field of operations with a laconism foreign to the voracious inclusiveness of epic proper.

When quantity is being brought into relation with quality, poetic theory is torn in two directions. On the one hand, there is the belief—and it is a natural enough belief—that the shorter the poem the more nearly flawless it can be made. On the other hand, it seems equally reasonable to aver, as Keats did when he was writing *Endymion*, that ' a long Poem is a test of Invention ', and will therefore call forth the highest imaginative powers its writer possesses. The latter view is the more traditional: an early expression of it is given by the 12th century Georgian epic poet Shot'ha Rust'haveli, in the introductory quatrains of his poem *The Man in the Panther's Skin:*

> He who utters, somewhere, one or two verses cannot be called a poet; let him not think himself equal to great singers. Even if they compose a few discrepant verses from time to time, yet if they say, ' Mine are of the best! ' they are stiff-necked mules.
> Secondly, lyrics which are but a small part of poetry and cannot command heart-piercing words—I may liken them to the bad bows of young hunters who cannot kill big game; they are able only to slay the small.
> Thirdly, lyrics are fit for the festive, the joyous, the amorous, the merry, for pleasantries of comrades; they please us when they are rightly sung. Those are not called poets who cannot compose a long work.
> (tr. by Marjory Scott Wardrop, Royal Asiatic Society, 1912)

It is clearly in this spirit that the long poems of Chaucer,

Spenser, Milton, and Wordsworth are written. The long poem is a
challenge which has so much of the weight of the past—of Homer
and Virgil and Dante—pressing behind it as to seem an unavoid-
able encounter. After Wordsworth, however, although the Vic-
torians continued to write poems of formidable length (culminating
in Browning's *The Ring and the Book*), the climate of opinion was
changing, and belief in the value or necessity of the long poem
became less and less automatic. Many people read and enjoyed
the longer poems of the Romantics and Victorians, but more were
beginning to turn to the novel, and some of the most widely read
verse (in Scott, Byron, and Mrs. Browning, for example) was
novelistic in character or effect. The novel itself, in its brilliant
19th century coming-of-age, began to take over many of the
functions—even the most imaginative—which poetry had com-
manded in the past. In addition, there was a growing inwardness
in poetry, a growing distrust of conventional structures of external
action and event—or, where these were not distrusted, an inability
to use them successfully (e.g. Tennyson's *Idylls of the King*).
Matthew Arnold, with his insistence on the importance of choosing
a ' great action ' for one's subject, was soon a lone voice.

Probably the most extreme reaction against the long or narrative
poem came from Edgar Allan Poe when he gave his lecture on
' The Poetic Principle ' in 1848. Basing his argument on the belief
that the psychological excitation produced by a work of art can
only be transient because of its intensity, Poe said:

> I maintain that the phrase, ' a long poem ', is simply a flat
> contradiction in terms . . . The modern epic is of the supposititious
> ancient model, but an inconsiderate and blindfold imitation. But
> the day of these artistic anomalies is over. If, at any time, any very
> long poem *were* popular in reality—which I doubt—it is at least
> clear that no very long poem will ever be popular again.

Despite the apparent contradiction of these remarks in the full-
bodied volumes of Tennyson, Browning, and Whitman, Poe had
struck on a truth in the latter part of the statement. Poe, through
his influence on the French symbolists, became one of the prophets
of 20th century poetry, and modern poetry has been noticeably
spare and fragmented in comparison with the solid over-furnished
Victorian verse interior. Although narrative poetry continued to
be written—with traditional vigour by John Masefield, with a new
obliqueness and subtlety by Robert Frost—there was a decided
movement away from story-telling, and even away from the logical
development of an idea or a theme. This was, in effect, a move-
ment towards shorter poems.

W. B. Yeats, whose best poems are short or of medium length,

felt that the restless times were unpropitious for anything more
sustained. This situation—which he deplored, but thought we
could do nothing about—he described in an essay on ' Art and
Ideas ' in 1913:

> . . . in our poems an absorption in fragmentary sensuous beauty
> or detachable ideas had deprived us of the power to mould vast
> material into a single image. What long modern poem equals the
> old poems in architectural unity, in symbolic importance?

Yet when an older unity and an older kind of organisation are
given up, perhaps a new unity can be created? By concentration
and juxtaposition of disparate material, by hint and suggestion,
by range of reference, by musical strategies of thematic develop-
ment—perhaps by such means it would be possible to compress an
epic intention into a few hundred lines? Modern poets believed
so, and when Ezra Pound returned the final version of T. S. Eliot's
The Waste Land (a poem of 433 lines) to its anxious author in 1921
he said in his letter:

> The thing now runs from ' April . . .' to ' shantih ' without a
> break. That is 19 pages, and let us say the longest poem in the
> English langwidge. Don't try to bust all records by prolonging it
> three pages further.

If *The Waste Land* is 'the longest poem in the English langwidge ',
it is hard to know what to call Pound's own *Cantos* or William
Carlos Williams's *Paterson* or Hugh MacDiarmid's *In Memoriam
James Joyce*. These very lengthy works, however, are not typical
of the modern period. The more typical, and distinctive, modern
poem is of moderate length, articulated in sections, organised not
narrationally but thematically, and often containing within
relatively short compass a variety of tone—lyrical, satiric, medita-
tive, prophetic. Examples are W. B. Yeats's *Meditations in Time of
Civil War*, T. S. Eliot's *The Waste Land* and *Four Quartets*, Hart
Crane's *The Bridge*, and Robert Lowell's *The Quaker Graveyard in
Nantucket*. In some instances the construction sits easy and loose
to the lyricism: Crane's *Voyages* may be considered as a suite of
love-poems related mainly to one central experience in Brooklyn,
just as Yeats's *Meditations* may be taken as a suite of brooding
comments on a changing situation in Irish history. In others—
such as Pound's Browningesque *Near Perigord*—the presentation is
carefully thought out as a series of views of some principal object,
deliberately focused from different angles and with different lenses.
   Methods of compression and unexpected juxtaposition make for
a meaty poetry, but a difficult poetry, and many readers will
continue to prefer ' to know where they are ' by following a

narrative line, as in Masefield's *The ' Wanderer '*. It seems unlikely
on the whole that narrative and 'fable' will not be returned to, and
indeed the second last poem in the anthology indicates a revival (if
perhaps a surprising one) of that very old tradition. A. C. Bradley,
in his interesting essay on ' The Long Poem in the Age of Words-
worth ' (*Oxford Lectures on Poetry*, 1909), said of modern poets:

> They fail to consider, too, that perhaps the business of art is not
> to ignore, but at once to satisfy and to purify, the primitive instincts
> from which it arises; and that, in the case of poetic art, the love of a
> story, and of exceptional figures, scenes, events, and actions, is one
> of those instincts, and one that in the immense majority of men
> shows no sign of decay.

Bradley was writing, of course, before the ' modern movement'
in poetry, as we understand the term, had properly emerged. It is
hoped that the present selection of poems will show some of the
successes of the 20th century longer poem which have been
achieved without recourse to the unfolding of a tale or the paint-
ing of a character or the step-by-step deployment of an idea. At
the same time, we must recognise the line through Whitman and
Williams, emerging strongly in Allen Ginsberg, where Bradley's
' primitive instincts ' have not been ignored.

In poems which are not so short as to be merely lyrical, and not
so long as to be epic, great variety of treatment and effect can be
found, and the aim of the anthology is to present something of
that variety, as well as to represent the hard core of important
longer poems out of which the English and Scottish traditions have
been built up. The friendly urbanity of Jonson's *To Penshurst* and
the agitated atmospherics of Donne's *Storm* and *Calm* are both
enhanced when these poems are compared. Suckling's *Ballad upon
a Wedding* does not suffer when set beside Crashaw's ecstatic *Hymn
to St. Teresa*. Prior's *Jinny*, though only sketched in with a few
darting strokes, is as memorable in her own way as Pope's Belinda.
And the woman who sings the Song of the Shirt shows what the
Lady of Shalott might have become in reality. In one or two cases,
a poem that judged by the highest standards is far from perfect
has been included because it has within it some distinctive quality
which keeps it alive: Hogg's *Kilmeny*, Keats's *Lamia*, and Tenny-
son's *Locksley Hall* are flawed poems, but we don't forget, or want
to forget, the ' still look ' of Kilmeny as she returns from the world
of dream to the world of men, or the shuffling sandals and flicker-
ing shadows of Lamia's Corinth, or the ' pilots of the purple
twilight ' seen in vision from Locksley Hall.

A long poem can of course afford to have within it considerable
variations of poetic intensity, and most readers accept this. Indeed,
when a poem strives to achieve mastery on a continuously high

pitch—Hopkins's *The Wreck of the Deutschland* is an example—the result is often somewhat daunting and uncomfortable, though at the same time a cause of astonished admiration. Edgar Allan Poe's insistence that a ' revulsion ensues ' very soon after we have been deeply moved by a passage in a long poem may have some psychological truth, but this reaction is taken care of by the accomplished poet—by changing the scene, by varying the style, by consciously slackening the reins and yet allowing the next shadowy peak to show over the horizon. Movement is essential, and it is because of this that the narrative structure has been the commonest. Where, as perhaps in a modern poem by Pound or Eliot, the single narrative line has largely disappeared, being replaced by surprising but significant juxtaposition of diverse material, the reader has to accustom himself to an effect which may be static in time (and therefore seem to lack movement) while being extremely active in space and intellectual scope. The difference between *The Nun's Priest's Tale* and *Burnt Norton* is very great. It is not only the difference between a story and a meditation. To Chaucer, cause and effect are so important that to say ' Once upon a time ' is to set the very wheels and delights of the universe in irretrievable motion; motion and change are pleasure and life. To Eliot, ' Once upon a time ' states an isolated absolute—sunlight suddenly filling a dry garden pool—where life concentrates itself in towards stillness and silence, and where time is as much a destroyer as a revealer, since the moment is everything, and cause and effect are equally ' ridiculous '. Yet both of these presentations are arguably true to human experience. Few people are immune to a well-told tale, or think of their lives as other than a kind of tale (though doubtless not so well told); but also, there are few who have not felt the disturbing (disturbing because inexplicable or disproportionate) significance of some isolated momentary event—something which seems not to ' fit in ', but which they can never forget. *Homo sapiens*—but there's nowt so queer as folk. Tolstoy—but Chekhov.

The long poem, it might be thought, is less suited than the short lyric to be the ' moment's monument ', just as it is in Chekhov's short stories rather than in *War and Peace* that we expect to find the greatest human idiosyncrasies and the most startling contingencies. This may be generally assented to, without discounting particular exceptions to the rule. A long poem must often include descriptive passages, where the problem of avoiding blockage of movement rubs shoulders with the opposite problem of maintaining clarity of depiction. It is easy to draw a vivid picture of something that includes motion (like Swift's *City Shower*), but not so easy to carry out James Thomson's intention in *The Seasons* (eventually a poem of some 5500 lines), of conveying essence or quality through minute, full scenic descriptions which must as often be static as progressive. The memorable passages of *The Seasons* nearly always involve movement in nature or human actions—floods and snowstorms, figures moving in a landscape. Fergusson and Crabbe, who are among the best descriptive poets, are adept at imparting that touch of motion or change which brings a scene alive, yet as Crabbe says:

> The best Description must be incomplete;
> But when an happier Theme succeeds, and when
> Men are our subjects, and the deeds of Men;
> Then may we find the muse in happier style,
> And we may sometimes sigh and sometimes smile.

' Men, and the deeds of Men ' are particularly the concern of the longer poem, and this is as true of Wordsworth's delicate but marvellously strong and fresh *To a Highland Girl* as it more obviously is of searing documents like *The Mask of Anarchy* and *Dead Man's Dump*. If the present collection serves to remind its readers of the diversity of human deeds, and of the wonder we must feel when we share a poet's insight into the spirit which activates them and issues from them, it will have fulfilled its purpose.

The text follows, as a general rule, original spelling and punctuation. The older *i/j* and *u/v* spellings (very distracting in Spenser) have been regularised in accordance with modern practice; *than* spelt as *then* in some 16th and 17th century poems has been regularised to *than*; and occasionally a point of punctuation has been changed or added for the sake of clarity. Where, as with some 18th century poems, there are several editions differing in minor points (of spelling, punctuation, use of capitals and italics), a certain freedom of choice has been exercised to present a readable and not too inconsistent text. The initials after notes, e.g. (S.) or (P.), indicate that the note is by the poet himself. All other notes are editorial.

I am grateful to my colleagues of the English Department at Glasgow University for their interest and forbearance, and for many helpful suggestions. My thanks are also due, for assistance on specific points, to Professor T. Neville George, Professor John F. C. Conn, Dr. Michael W. Ovenden, and Mr. Derek R. Diamond; to Mr. Ian C. Bridge of the Royal College of Science and Technology; and to Mr. C. M. Grieve (Hugh MacDiarmid). Lastly, I must thank Miss Irene Elsey for invaluable help with the typing.

EDWIN MORGAN

October, 1962

Geoffrey Chaucer

c. 1340—1400

THE NUN'S PRIEST'S TALE

A povre wydwe, somdeel stape in age
Was whilom dwellyng in a narwe cotage,
Biside a grove, stondynge in a dale.
This wydwe, of which I telle yow my tale,
Syn thilke day that she was last a wyf,   5
In pacience ladde a ful symple lyf,
For litel was hir catel and hir rente.
By housbondrie of swich as God hire sente
She foond hirself and eek hir doghtren two.
Thre large sowes hadde she, and namo,   10
Three keen, and eek a sheep that highte Malle.
Ful sooty was hire bour and eek hir halle,
In which she eet ful many a sklendre meel.
Of poynaunt sauce hir neded never a deel.
No deyntee morsel passed thurgh hir throte;   15
Hir diete was accordant to hir cote.
Repleccioun ne made hire nevere sik;
Attempree diete was al hir phisik,
And exercise, and hertes suffisaunce.
The goute lette hire nothyng for to daunce,   20
N'apoplexie shente nat hir heed.
No wyn ne drank she, neither whit ne reed;
Hir bord was served moost with whit and blak,—
Milk and broun breed, in which she foond no lak,
Seynd bacoun, and somtyme an ey or tweye;   25
For she was, as it were, a maner deye.

A yeerd she hadde, enclosed al aboute
With stikkes, and a drye dych withoute,
In which she hadde a cok, hight Chauntecleer.
In al the land, of crowyng nas his peer.   30
His voys was murier than the murie orgon
On messe-dayes that in the chirche gon.
Wel sikerer was his crowyng in his logge
Than is a clokke or an abbey orlogge.
By nature he knew ech ascencioun   35
Of the equynoxial in thilke toun;
For whan degrees fiftene weren ascended,
Thanne crew he, that it myghte nat been amended.
His coomb was redder than the fyn coral,
And batailled as it were a castel wal;   40
His byle was blak, and as the jeet it shoon;
Lyk asure were his legges and his toon;
His nayles whitter than the lylye flour,
And lyk the burned gold was his colour.
This gentil cok hadde in his governaunce   45
Sevene hennes for to doon al his pleasaunce,
Whiche were his sustres and his paramours,
And wonder lyk to hym, as of colours;
Of whiche the faireste hewed on hir throte
Was cleped faire damoysele Pertelote.   50
Curteys she was, discreet, and debonaire,
And compaignable, and bar hyrself so faire,
Syn thilke day that she was seven nyght oold,
That trewely she hath the herte in hoold
Of Chauntecleer, loken in every lith;   55
He loved hire so that wel was hym therwith.
But swich a joye was it to here hem synge,
Whan that the brighte sonne gan to sprynge,
In sweete accord, " My lief is faren in londe! "
For thilke tyme, as I have understonde,   60
Beestes and briddes koude speke and synge.

29 *Hight:* called.   30 *Nas:* there was not.   32 *Messe-dayes:* mass-
days, feast-days; *gon:* play ('organ' is taken as a plural noun).   33 *Wel
sikerer:* much more reliable; *logge:* lodge, house.   34 *Orlogge:* clock.
36 *Equynoxial:* celestial equator in the old astronomy, making a daily
revolution, so that there was an 'ascent' of fifteen degrees every hour;
thilke toun: that particular town.   38 *That it myghte nat been amended:*
with perfect accuracy.   40 *Batailled:* crenellated.   42 *Toon:* toes.
44 *Burned:* burnished.   46 *Doon:* do.   50 *Cleped:* called.   51
Debonaire: gentle.   52 *Compaignable:* friendly.   55 *Loken in every lith:*
locked in every limb.   56 *Wel was hym therwith:* it made his happiness.
57 *Hem:* them.   59 'My love has gone far away!'

And so bifel that in a dawenynge,
As Chauntecleer among his wyves alle
Sat on his perche, that was in the halle,
And next hym sat this faire Pertelote,   65
This Chauntecleer gan gronen in his throte,
As man that in his dreem is drecched soore.
And whan that Pertelote thus herde hym roore,
She was agast, and seyde, " Herte deere,
What eyleth yow, to grone in this manere?   70
Ye been a verray sleper; fy, for shame! "
    And he answerde, and seyde thus : " Madame,
I pray yow that ye take it nat agrief.
By God, me mette I was in swich meschief
Right now, that yet myn herte is soore afright.   75
Now God," quod he, " my swevene recche aright,
And kepe my body out of foul prisoun!
Me mette how that I romed up and doun
Withinne our yeerd, wheer as I saugh a beest
Was lyk an hound, and wolde han maad areest   80
Upon my body, and wolde han had me deed.
His colour was bitwixe yelow and reed,
And tipped was his tayl and bothe his eeris
With blak, unlyk the remenant of his heeris;
His snowte smal, with glowynge eyen tweye.   85
Yet of his look for feere almoost I deye;
This caused me my gronyng, doutelees."
    " Avoy! " quod she, "fy on yow, hertelees!
Allas! " quod she, " for, by that God above,
Now han ye lost myn herte and al my love.   90
I kan nat love a coward, by my feith!
For certes, what so any womman seith,
We alle desiren, if it myghte bee,
To han housbondes hardy, wise, and free,
And secree, and no nygard, ne no fool,   95
Ne hym that is agast of every tool,
Ne noon avauntour, by that God above!
How dorste ye seyn, for shame, unto youre love
That any thyng myghte make yow aferd?
Have ye no mannes herte, and han a berd?   100

67 *Man:* one; *drecched:* distressed. 71 *Verray sleper:* some sleeper!
73 *Agrief:* amiss. 74 *Me mette:* I dreamed. 76 *Quod:* said; *my swevene
recche aright:* give my dream a favourable issue. 80 *Han maad areest:*
have seized. 85 *Smal:* narrow. 88 *Avoy:* shame; *hertelees:* coward.
92 *Certes:* certainly. 94 *Hardy . . . free:* brave . . . noble. 95 *Secree:*
discreet. 96 *Tool:* weapon. 97 *Ne noon avauntour:* and not a braggart.

Allas! and konne ye been agast of swevenys?
Nothyng, God woot, but vanitee in sweven is.
Swevenes engendren of replecciouns,
And ofte of fume and of complecciouns,
Whan humours been to habundant in a wight.   105
Certes this dreem, which ye han met to-nyght,
Cometh of the greete superfluytee
Of youre rede colera, pardee,
Which causeth folk to dreden in hir dremes
Of arwes, and of fyr with rede lemes,   110
Of rede beestes, that they wol hem byte,
Of contek, and of whelpes, grete and lyte;
Right as the humour of malencolie
Causeth ful many a man in sleep to crie
For feere of blake beres, or boles blake,   115
Or elles blake develes wole hem take.
Of othere humours koude I telle also
That werken many a man sleep ful wo;
But I wol passe as lightly as I kan.
   Lo Catoun, which that was so wys a man,   120
Seyde he nat thus, ' Ne do no fors of dremes? '
   "Now sire," quod she, " whan we flee fro the bemes,
For Goddes love, as taak som laxatyf.
Up peril of my soule and of my lyf,
I conseille yow the beste, I wol nat lye,   125
That bothe of colere and of malencolye
Ye purge yow; and for ye shal nat tarie,
Though in this toun is noon apothecarie,
I shal myself to herbes techen yow
That shul been for youre hele and for youre prow;   130
And in oure yeerd tho herbes shal I fynde
The whiche han of hire propretee by kynde

---

102 *Woot:* knows; *vanitee:* nonsense. 103 *Engendren of replecciouns:*
arise from excess(es) (of one of the four humours, blood, phlegm, black
bile, yellow-red bile). 104 *Fume . . . complecciouns:* vapour from
stomach . . . mixed humours. 105 'When a man has an excess of the
bodily moistures.' 106 *Met to-nyght:* dreamt last night. 108 *Rede
colera:* red choler or bile; *pardee:* by God, indeed. 109 *Hir:* their.
110 *Lemes:* flames. 112 *Contek:* strife; *lyte:* small. 115 *Beres . . .
boles:* bears . . . bulls. 118 'That give many a man a disturbed sleep.'
120 *Catoun:* Dionysius Cato, reputed author of the 4th century
Disticha Catonis, a collection of maxims in Latin verse; *which that:* who.
121 *Ne do no fors of:* attach no importance to. 123 *As taak:* do take.
124 *Up:* upon. 127 *For:* so that. 129 *Techen:* direct. 130 *Hele
. . . prow:* health . . . benefit. 131 *Tho:* those. 132 *By kynde:* natur-
ally.

To purge yow bynethe and eek above.
Foryet nat this, for Goddes owene love!
Ye been ful coleryk of compleccioun;   135
Ware the sonne in his ascencioun
Ne fynde yow nat repleet of humours hoote.
And if it do, I dar wel leye a grote,
That ye shul have a fevere terciane,
Or an agu, that may be youre bane.   140
A day or two ye shul have digestyves
Of wormes, er ye take youre laxatyves
Of lawriol, centaure, and fumetere,
Or elles of ellebor, that groweth there,
Of katapuce, or of gaitrys beryis,   145
Of herbe yve, growyng in oure yeerd, ther mery is;
Pekke hem up right as they growe and ete hem yn.
Be myrie, housbonde, for youre fader kyn!
Dredeth no dreem, I kan sey yow namoore."
  "Madame," quod he, "graunt mercy of youre loore.   150
But nathelees, as touchyng daun Catoun,
That hath of wysdom swich a greet renoun,
Though that he bad no dremes for to drede,
By God, men may in olde bookes rede
Of many a man moore of auctorite   155
Than evere Caton was, so moot I thee,
That al the revers seyn of this sentence,
And han wel founden by experience
That dremes been significaciouns
As wel of joye as of tribulaciouns   160
That folk enduren in this lif present.
Ther nedeth make of this noon argument;
The verray preeve sheweth it in dede.
  Oon of the gretteste auctour that men rede
Seith thus: that whilom two felawes wente   165
On pilgrimage, in a ful good entente;
And happed so, they coomen in a'toun
Wher as ther was swich congregacioun

---

139 *Terciane:* having a crisis every other day. 143 *Lawriol, centaure . . .*
fumetere: spurge-laurel, centaury . . . fumitory. 144 *Ellebor:* hellebore.
145 *Katapuce . . . gaitrys:* caper-spurge . . . buckthorn (?). 146 *Herbe*
yve: buck's-horn; *oure yeerd, ther mery is:* our pleasant yard (?). 148 *For*
youre fader kyn: for the sake of your parentage. 150 *Graunt mercy of:*
thank you for. 151 *Daun:* master, sir. 156 *Mote I thee:* may I
prosper. 157 *Sentence:* judgement, opinion. 163 *Preeve:* test of
experience. 164 Probably Cicero (106-43 B.C.).

Of peple, and eek so streit of herbergage,
That they ne founde as muche as o cotage   170
In which they bothe myghte ylogged bee.
Wherfore they mosten of necessitee,
As for that nyght, departen compaignye;
And ech of hem gooth to his hostelrye,
And took his loggyng as it wolde falle.   175
That oon of hem was logged in a stalle,
Fer in a yeerd, with oxen of the plough;
That oother man was logged wel ynough,
As was his aventure or his fortune,
That us governeth alle as in commune.   180
   And so bifel that, longe er it were day,
This man mette in his bed, ther as he lay,
How that his felawe gan upon hym calle,
And seyde, ' Allas! for in an oxes stalle
This nyght I shal be mordred ther I lye.   185
Now help me, deere brother, or I dye.
In alle haste com to me! ' he sayde.
This man out of his sleep for feere abrayde;
But whan that he was wakened of his sleep,
He turned hym, and took of this no keep.   190
Hym thoughte his dreem nas but a vanitee.
Thus twies in his slepyng dremed hee;
And atte thridde tyme yet his felawe
Cam, as hym thoughte, and seide, ' I am now slawe.
Bihoold my bloody woundes depe and wyde!   195
Arys up erly in the morwe tyde,
And at the west gate of the toun,' quod he,
' A carte ful of dong ther shaltow se,
In which my body is hid ful prively;
Do thilke carte arresten boldely.   200
My gold caused my mordre, sooth to sayn.'
And tolde hym every point how he was slayn,
With a ful pitous face, pale of hewe.
And truste wel, his dreem he foond ful trewe,
For on the morwe, as soone as it was day,   205
To his felawes in he took the way;
And whan that he cam to this oxes stalle,
After his felawe he bigan to calle.

169 *Streit of herbergage:* short of accommodation. 170 *O:* a, one.
176 *That oon:* (the) one. 182 *Ther as:* where. 188 *Abrayde:* started
up. 194 *Slawe:* slain. 196 *Morwe tyde:* morning. 200 'Have that
cart suddenly stopped.' 201 *Sooth to sayn:* truth to tell. 206 *In:* inn.

The hostiler answerede hym anon,
And seyde, ' Sire, your felawe is agon.   210
As soone as day he wente out of the toun.'
⅃his man gan fallen in suspecioun,
Remembrynge on his dremes that he mette,
And forth he gooth—no lenger wolde he lette—
Unto the west gate of the toun, and fond   215
A dong-carte, wente as it were to donge lond,
That was arrayed in that same wise
As ye han herd the dede man devyse.
And with an hardy herte he gan to crye
Vengeance and justice of this felonye.   220
' My felawe mordred is this same nyght,
And in this carte he lith gapyng upright.
I crye out on the ministres,' quod he,
' That sholden kepe and reulen this citee.
Harrow! allas! heere lith my felawe slayn!'   225
What sholde I moore unto this tale sayn?
The peple out sterte and caste the cart to grounde,
And in the myddel of the dong they founde
The dede man, that mordred was al newe.
O blisful God, that art so just and trewe,   230
Lo, how that thou biwreyest mordre alway!
Mordre wol out, that se we day by day.
Mordre is so wlatsom and abhomynable
To God, that is so just and resonable,
That he ne wol nat suffre it heled be,   235
Though it abyde a yeer, or two, or thre.
Mordre wol out, this my conclusioun.
And right anon, ministres of that toun
Han hent the carter and so soore hym pyned,
And eek the hostiler so soore engyned,   240
That they biknewe hire wikkednesse anon,
And were anhanged by the nekke-bon.
Heere may men seen that dremes been to drede.
And certes in the same book I rede,
Right in the nexte chapitre after this—   245
I gabbe nat, so have I joye or blis—
Two men that wolde han passed over see,
For certeyn cause, into a fer contree,

---

212 *Gan fallen in suspecioun:* began to be suspicious. 218 *Devyse:*
describe. 223 *Ministres:* officers. 225 *Harrow:* help (exclamation).
231 *Biwreyest:* revealest. 233 *Wlatsom:* loathsome. 235 *Heled be:* to
be concealed. 239 *Hent:* seized; *pyned:* tortured. 240 *Engyned:*
racked. 241 *Biknewe:* confessed. 246 *Gabbe:* tell lies.

If that the wynd ne hadde been contrarie,
That made hem in a citee for to tarie   250
That stood ful myrie upon an haven-syde;
But on a day, agayn the even-tyde,
The wynd gan chaunge, and blew right as hem leste.
Jolif ard glad they wente unto hir reste,
And carten hem ful erly for to saille.   255
But to t.nat o man fil a greet mervaille:
That oon of hem, in slepyng as he lay,
Hym mette a wonder dreem agayn the day.
Hym thoughte a man stood by his beddes syde,
And hym comanded that he sholde abyde,   260
And seyde hym thus: ' If thou tomorwe wende,
Thow shalt be dreynt; my tale is at an ende.'
He wook, and tolde his felawe what he mette,
And preyde hym his viage for to lette;
As for that day, he preyde hym to byde.   265
His felawe, that lay by his beddes syde,
Gan for to laughe, and scorned him ful faste.
' No dreem,' quod he, ' may so myn herte agaste
That I wol lette for to do my thynges.
I sette nat a straw by thy dremynges,   270
For swevenes been but vanytees and japes.
Men dreme alday of owles and of apes,
And eek of many a maze therwithal;
Men dreme of thyng that nevere was ne shal.
But sith I see that thou wolt heere abyde,   275
And thus forslewthen wilfully thy tyde,
God woot, it reweth me; and have good day! '
And thus he took his leve, and wente his way.
But er that he hadde half his cours yseyled,
Noot I nat why, ne what myschaunce it eyled,   280
But casuelly the shippes botme rente,
And ship and man under the water wente
In sighte of othere shippes it bisyde,
That with hem seyled at the same tyde.
And therfore, faire Pertelote so deere,   285
By swiche ensamples olde maistow leere

253 *As hem leste:* the way they wanted. 254 *Jolif:* cheerful. 255
Casten hem: decided. 258 *Agayn:* just before. 259 *Hym thoughte:* it
seemed to him. 262 *Dreynte:* drowned. 264 *Viage:* voyage; *lette:*
postpone. 271 *Japes:* tricks. 272 *Alday:* continually. 275 *Sith:*
since. 276 *Forslewthen:* lazily waste; *tyde:* time. 280 *Noot I nat:* I
don't know. 281 *Casuelly:* by mischance. 284 *Tyde:* time. 286
Leere: learn.

That no man sholde been to recchelees
Of dremes; for I seye thee, doutelees,
That many a dreem ful soore is for to drede.
  Lo, in the lyf of Seint Kenelm I rede,   290
That was Kenulphus sone, the noble kyng
Of Mercenrike, how Kenelm mette a thyng.
A lite er he was mordred, on a day,
His mordre in his avysioun he say.
His norice hym expowned every deel   295
His sweven, and bad hym for to kepe hym weel
For traisoun; but he nas but seven yeer oold,
And therfore litel tale hath he toold
Of any dreem, so hooly was his herte.
By God! I hadde levere than my sherte   300
That ye hadde rad his legende, as have I.
  Dame Pertelote, I sey yow trewely,
Macrobeus, that writ the avisioun
In Affrike of the worthy Cipioun,
Affermeth dremes, and seith that they been   305
Warnynge of thynges that men after seen.
And forthermoore, I pray yow, looketh wel
In the olde testament, of Daniel,
If he heeld dremes any vanitee.
Reed eek of Joseph, and ther shul ye see   310
Wher dremes be somtyme—I sey nat alle—
Warnynge of thynges that shul after falle.
Looke of Egipte the kyng, daun Pharao,
His bakere and his butiller also,
Wher they ne felte noon effect in dremes.   315
Whoso wol seken actes of sondry remes
May rede of dremes many a wonder thyng.
Lo Cresus, which that was of Lyde kyng,
Mette he nat that he sat upon a tree,
Which signified he sholde anhanged bee?   320

---

287 *To recchelees:* too negligent. 290-2 *Kenelm:* Cenhelm (814-21)
succeeded his father Cenwulf (*Kenulphus*), King of Mercia (*Mercenrike*),
in 821, but was murdered at the instigation of his aunt Cwenthryth.
293 *Lite er:* little before. 294 *Avysioun:* vision; *say:* saw. 295
Norice: nurse. 296 *Kepe:* .guard. 297 *For:* against. 298 'He took
little notice.' 300 *Levere:* rather. 303-4 Macrobius Theodosius
(*fl. c.* A.D. 400) edited Cicero's *Somnium Scipionis* ('The Dream of Scipio
Africanus Minor'). His commentary was widely read in the Middle
Ages. 308 See *Dan. passim.* 310 See *Gen.* xxxvii, xl, xli. 311 *Wher:*
whether. 316 *Seken acts:* search the histories; *remes:* realms. 318
Croesus, King of Lydia (*fl. c.* 550 B.C.).

Lo heere Andromacha, Ectores wyf,
That day that Ector sholde lese his lyf,
She dremed on the same nyght biforn
How that the lyf of Ector sholde be lorn,
If thilke day he wente into bataille.   325
She warned hym, but it myghte nat availle;
He wente for to fighte natheles,
But he was slayn anon of Achilles.
But thilke tale is al to longe to telle,
And eek it is ny day, I may nat dwelle.   330
Shortly I seye, as for conclusioun,
That I shal han of this avisioun
Adversitee; and I seye forthermoor,
That I ne telle of laxatyves no stoor,
For they been venymous, I woot it weel;   335
I hem diffye, I love hem never a deel!
    Now let us speke of myrthe, and stynte al this.
Madame Pertelote, so have I blis,
Of o thyng God hath sent me large grace;
For whan I se the beautee of youre face,   340
Ye been so scarlet reed aboute youre yen,
It maketh al my drede for to dyen;
For al so siker as *In principio*,
Mulier est hominis confusio,—
Madame, the sentence of this Latyn is,   345
'Womman is mannes joye and al his blis.'
For whan I feele a-nyght your softe syde,
Al be it that I may nat on yow ryde,
For that oure perche is maad so narwe, allas!
I am so ful of joye and of solas,   350
That I diffye bothe sweven and dreem."
And with that word he fley doun fro the beem,
For it was day, and eke his hennes alle,
And with a chuk he gan hem for to calle,
For he hadde founde a corn, lay in the yerd.   355
Real he was, he was namoore aferd.
He fethered Pertelote twenty tyme,
And trad hire eke as ofte, er it was pryme.

321 ff. The dream is a medieval addition to the story in Homer's *Iliad*.
322 *Sholde lese:* was to lose. 324 *Lorn:* lost. 334 *Ne telle of . . . no
stoor:* set no store by. 343 'just as truly as the Gospel is true.' (St.
John's 'In the beginning . . .'). 344 'Woman is man's ruin.' 345
Sentence: meaning. 352 *Fley:* flew. 356 *Real:* royal. 357 *Fethered:*
covered. 358 *Trad:* trod; *er it was pryme:* between 6 and 9 a.m.

He looketh as it were a grym leoun,
And on his toos he rometh up and doun; 360
Hym deigned nat to sette his foot to grounde.
He chukketh whan he hath a corn yfounde,
And to hym rennen thanne his wyves alle.
Thus roial, as a prince is in his halle,
Leve I this Chauntecleer in his pasture, 365
And after wol I telle his aventure.
 Whan that the month in which the world bigan,
That highte March, whan God first maked man,
Was compleet, and passed were also,
Syn March bigan, thritty dayes and two, 370
Bifel that Chauntecleer in al his pryde,
His sevene wyves walkynge by his syde,
Caste up his eyen to the brighte sonne,
That in the signe of Taurus hadde yronne
Twenty degrees and oon, and somwhat moore, 375
And knew by kynde, and by noon oother loore,
That it was pryme, and crew with blisful stevene.
" The sonne," he seyde, " is clomben up on hevene
Fourty degrees and oon, and moore ywis.
Madame Pertelote, my worldes blis, 380
Herkneth thise blisful briddes how they synge,
And se the fresshe floures how they sprynge;
Ful is myn herte of revel and solas! "
But sodeynly hym fil a sorweful cas,
For evere the latter ende of joye is wo. 385
God woot that worldly joye is soone ago;
And if a rethor koude faire endite,
He in a cronycle saufly myghte it write
As for a sovereyn notabilitee.
Now every wys man, lat him herkne me; 390
This storie is also trewe, I undertake,
As is the book of Launcelot de Lake,
That wommen holde in ful greet reverence.

359 *Leoun:* lion. 363 *Rennen:* run. 365 *Pasture:* act of feeding.
367 traditionally March, at the vernal equinox. 370 i.e. 3rd May.
374 *Taurus:* sign of the zodiac (in Chaucer, from 12th April–12th
May). 375 A degree of the sun's course round the zodiac is approxi-
mately equal to a day, hence 21 days from 12th April=3rd May.
376 *Kynde:* instinct. 377 *Pryme:* 9 a.m.; *stevene:* voice. 379 The
sun would be about 41 degrees above the horizon by 9 a.m. *Ywis:*
assuredly, indeed. 384 *Hym fil:* befell him; *cas:* happening. 386
Ago: gone. 387 'If an eloquent man could express it properly.'
391 *Also:* as. 392 lover of Queen Guinevere in Arthurian legend.

Now wol I torne agayn to my sentence.
A col-fox, ful of sly iniquitee,   395
That in the grove hadde woned yeres three,
By heigh ymaginacioun forncast,
The same nyght thurghout the hegges brast
Into the yerd ther Chauntecleer the faire
Was wont, and eek his wyves, to repaire;   400
And in a bed of wortes stille he lay,
Til it was passed undren of the day,
Waitynge his tyme on Chauntecleer to falle,
As gladly doon thise homycides alle
That in await liggen to mordre men.   405
O false mordrour, lurkynge in thy den!
O newe Scariot, newe Genylon,
False dissymulour, o Greek Synon,
That broghtest Troye al outrely to sorwe!
O Chauntecleer, acursed be that morwe   410
That thou into that yerd flaugh fro the bemes!
Thou were ful wel ywarned by thy dremes
That thilke day was perilous to thee;
But what that God forwoot moot nedes bee,
After the opinioun of certein clerkis.   415
Witnesse on hym that any parfit clerk is,
That in scole is greet altercacioun
In this mateere, and greet disputisoun,
And hath been of an hundred thousand men.
But I ne kan nat bulte it to the bren   420
As kan the hooly doctour Augustyn,
Or Boece, or the Bisshop Bradwardyn,
Wheither that Goddes worthy forwityng
Streyneth me nedely for to doon a thyng,—

---

394 *Sentence:* subject. 395 *Col-fox:* black-tipped fox. 396 *Woned:* lived. 397 'as foreseen by God' (or perhaps, 'as foreseen in Chauntecleer's dream'). 398 *Nyght:* i.e. early morning; *brast:* burst. 401 *Wortes:* herbs. 402 *Undren:* forenoon. 403 *Waitynge:* watching for. 405 *Liggen:* lie. 407 *Scariot:* Judas Iscariot; *Genylon:* Ganelon, traitor in the *Chanson de Roland.* 408 *Synon:* Sinon, posing as a deserter, introduced the 'Trojan horse' into Troy. 409 *Outrely:* utterly. 411 *Flaugh:* flew. 414 *Moot:* must. 415 *Clerkis:* scholars. 417 *Scole:* philosophy school, university. 420 'I can't sift the flour from the bran.' 421 *Augustyn:* St. Augustine (354-430), Church father. 422 *Boece:* Anicius Manlius Severinus Boethius (*c.* 470/5-*c.* 524), Roman philosopher, author of *De Consolatione Philosophiae; Bradwardyn:* Thomas Bradwardine (*c.* 1290-1349), English archbishop and pro-Augustinian theologian. 423 *Worthy forwityng:* admirable foreknowledge. 424 *Streyneth me nedely:* constrains me of necessity.

" Nedely " clepe I symple necessitee;   425
Or elles, if free choys be graunted me
To do that same thyng, or do it noght,
Though God forwoot it er that it was wroght;
Or if his wityng streyneth never a deel
But by necessitee condicioneel.   430
I wol nat han to do of swich mateere;
My tale is of a cok, as ye may heere,
That tok his conseil of his wyf, with sorwe,
To walken in the yerd upon that morwe
That he hadde met that dreem that I yow tolde.   435
Wommennes conseils been ful ofte colde;
Wommannes conseil broghte us first to wo,
And made Adam fro Paradys to go,
Ther as he was ful myrie and wel at ese.
But for I noot to whom it myght displese,   440
If I conseil of wommen wolde blame,
Passe over, for I seyde it in my game.
Rede auctours, where they trete of swich mateere,
And what they seyn of wommen ye may heere.
Thise been the cokkes wordes, and nat myne;   445
I kan noon harm of no womman divyne.
  Faire in the soond, to bathe hire myrily,
Lith Pertelote, and alle hire sustres by,
Agayn the sonne, and Chauntecleer so free
Soong murier than the mermayde in the see;   450
For Phisiologus seith sikerly
How that they syngen wel and myrily.
And so bifel that, as he caste his ye
Among the wortes on a boterflye,
He was war of this fox, that lay ful lowe.   455
Nothyng ne liste hym thanne for to crowe,
But cride anon, " Cok! cok! " and up he sterte
As man that was affrayed in his herte.
For natureelly a beest desireth flee
Fro his contrarie, if he may it see,   460
Though he never erst hadde seyn it with his ye.
  This Chauntecleer, whan he gan hym espye,
He wolde han fled, but that the fox anon
Seyde, " Gentil sire, allas! wher wol ye gon?

433 *With sorwe:* with an unhappy result. 436 *Colde:* bad, fatal.
447 *Soond:* sand. 449 *Agayn:* in, facing. 451 *Phisiologus:* Latin
collection of animal fables, popular in Middle Ages. 456 'He had no
thought of crowing then.' 461 *Erst:* before.

Be ye affrayed of me that am youre freend?   465
Now, certes, I were worse than a feend,
If I to yow wolde harm or vileynye !
I am nat come youre conseil for t'espye,
But trewely, the cause of my comynge
Was oonly for to herkne how that ye synge.   470
For trewely, ye have as myrie a stevene
As any aungel hath that is in hevene.
Therwith ye han in musyk moore feelynge
Than hadde Boece, or any that kan synge.
My lord youre fader—God his soule blesse!—   475
And eek youre mooder, of hire gentillesse,
Han in myn hous ybeen to my greet ese;
And certes, sire, ful fayn wolde I yow plese.
But, for men speke of synging, I wol seye,—
So moote I brouke wel myne eyen tweye,—   480
Save yow, I herde nevere man so synge
As dide youre fader in the morwenynge.
Certes, it was of herte, al that he song.
And for to make his voys the moore strong,
He wolde so peyne hym that with bothe his yen   485
He moste wynke, so loude he v. olde cryen,
And stonden on his tiptoon therwithal,
And strecche forth his nekke long and smal.
And eek he was of swich discrecioun
That ther nas no man in no regioun   490
That hym in song or wisedom myghte passe.
I have wel rad in ' Daun Burnel the Asse,'
Among his vers, how that ther was a cok,
For that a preestes sone yaf hym a knok
Upon his leg whil he was yong and nyce,   495
He made hym for to lese his benefice.
But certeyn, ther nys no comparisoun
Bitwixe the wisedom and discrecioun
Of youre fader and of his subtiltee.
Now syngeth, sire, for seinte charitee;   500

467 *Wolde:* intended. 468 *Conseil:* secrets. 474 Boethius wrote a
treatise on music. 476 *Of hire gentillesse:* in their courtesy. 479 *For:*
since. 480 *Brouke:* enjoy. 485 *Peyne hym:* exert himself. 486 *Wynke:*
shut his eyes. 488 *Smal:* thin. 492 *Daun Burnel the Asse:* the *Speculum
Stultorum,* or 'Mirror of Fools', a satirical Latin poem of the late 12th
century by Nigel Wireker, a Canterbury monk. 493 *Vers:* verses.
494 *Yaf:* gave. 495 *He:* i.e. the priest's son; *nyce:* foolish. 496 The
cock got its revenge by crowing late and making the young man sleep in
and lose his living. 499 *His subtiltee:* that other cock's cunning.

Lat se, konne ye youre fader countrefete? "
This Chauntecleer his wynges gan to bete,
As man that koude his traysoun nat espie,
So was he ravysshed with his flaterie.
Allas! ye lordes, many a fals flatour   505
Is in youre courtes, and many a losengeour,
That plesen yow wel moore, by my feith,
Than he that soothfastnesse unto yow seith.
Redeth Ecclesiaste of flaterye;
Beth war, ye lordes, of hir trecherye.   510
  This Chauntecleer stood hye upon his toos,
Strecchynge his nekke, and heeld his eyen cloos,
And gan to crowe loude for the nones.
And daun Russell the fox stirte up atones,
And by the gargat hente Chauntecleer,   515
And on his bak toward the wode hym beer,
For yet ne was ther no man that hym sewed.
  O destinee, that mayst nat been eschewed!
Allas, that Chauntecleer fleigh fro the bemes!
Allas, his wyf ne roghte nat of dremes!   520
And on a Friday fil al this meschaunce.
  O Venus, that art goddesse of plesaunce,
Syn that thy servant was this Chauntecleer,
And in thy servyce dide al his poweer,
Moore for delit than world to multiplye,   525
Why woldestow suffre hym on thy day to dye?
  O Gaufred, deere maister soverayn,
That whan thy worthy kyng Richard was slayn
With shot, compleynedest his deeth so soore,
Why ne hadde I now thy sentence and thy loore,   530
The Friday for to chide, as diden ye?
For on a Friday, soothly, slayn was he.
Thanne wolde I shewe yow how that I koude pleyne
For Chauntecleres drede and for his peyne.
  Certes, swich cry ne lamentacion,   535
Was nevere of ladyes maad whan Ylion

---

501 *Countrefete:* imitate. 505 *Flatour:* flatterer. 506 *Losengeour:* liar, flatterer. 508 *Soothfastnesse:* truth. 509 *Ecclesiaste:* either (i) Solomon (cf. *Prov.* xxix. 5) or (ii) *Ecclesiasticus* (cf. *Ecclus.* xxvii. 26). 510 *Beth war:* watch out. 513 *For the nones:* at that moment. 514 *Atones:* at once. 515 *Gargat:* throat. 517 *Sewed:* pursued. 520 *Roghte:* cared. 521-6 Friday was the day of Venus. 527 *Gaufred:* Geoffrey of Vinsauf (*fl. c.* 1200), English author of *Poetria Nova*, a popular rhetorical treatise on poetry. He wrote a Latin elegy on the death of Richard I (1199). 530 *Sentence:* weightiness. 532 Richard was wounded, not killed, on a Friday. 533 *Pleyne:* lament. 536 *Ylion:* Troy.

Was wonne, and Pirrus with his streite swerd,
Whan he hadde hent kyng Priam by the berd,
And slayn hym, as seith us *Eneydos*,
As maden alle the hennes in the clos,   540
Whan they had seyn of Chauntecleer the sighte.
But sovereynly dame Pertelote shrighte
Ful louder than dide Hasdrubales wyf,
Whan that hir housbonde hadde lost his lyf,
And that the Romayns hadde brend Cartage.   545
She was so ful of torment and of rage
That wilfully into the fyr she sterte,
And brende hirselven with a stedefast herte.
  O woful hennes, right so criden ye,
As, whan that Nero brende the citee   550
Of Rome, cryden senatoures wyves
For that hir husbondes losten alle hir lyves,—
Withouten gilt this Nero hath hem slayn.
Now wole I turne to my tale agayn.
  This sely wydwe and eek hir doghtres two   555
Herden thise hennes crie and maken wo,
And out at dores stirten they anon,
And syen the fox toward the grove gon,
And bar upon his bak the cok away,
And cryden, " Out! harrow! and weylaway!   560
Ha! ha! the fox! " and after hym they ran,
And eek with staves many another man.
Ran Colle oure dogge, and Talbot and Gerland,
And Malkyn, with a dystaf in hir hand;
Ran cow and calf, and eek the verray hogges,   565
So fered for the berkyng of the dogges
And shoutyng of the men and wommen eeke,
They ronne so hem thoughte hir herte breeke.
They yolleden as feendes doon in helle;
The dokes cryden as men wolde hem quelle;   570

537 *Pirrus:* Pyrrhus, son of the Greek hero Achilles; *streite swerd:*
drawn sword. 538 *Priam:* King of Troy during the Trojan War with
Greece. 539 *Eneydos:* Virgil's *Æneid*, II. 550-8. 542 *Sovereynly:* very
high, unmatched. 543 *Hasdrubal:* King of Carthage when the city was
burnt by the Romans 146 B.C. His wife committed suicide by throwing
herself into the fire. 548 *Brende hirselven:* burned herself. 549 *Criden:*
cried. 550 *Nero:* (A.D. 37-68), Roman emperor. 555 *Sely:* simple.
557 *Stirten:* rushed. 558 *Syen:* saw. 559 *Bar:* carried. 560 *Harrow*
. . . *weylaway:* help! . . . alas! 563 *Talbot and Gerland:* dogs' names.
566 *Fered:* terrified. 568 'They ran till it seemed to them that their
hearts were bursting.' 569 *Yolleden:* yelled, shrieked. 570 'The
ducks cried as if they were being killed.'

The gees for feere flowen over the trees;
Out of the hyve cam the swarm of bees.
So hydous was the noyse, a, *benedicitee!*
Certes, he Jakke Straw and his meynee
Ne made nevere shoutes half so shrille   575
Whan that they wolden any Flemyng kille,
As thilke day was maad upon the fox.
Of bras they broghten bemes, and of box,
Of horn, of boon, in whiche they blewe and powped,
And therwithal they skriked and they howped.   580
It semed as that hevene sholde falle.
    Now, goode men, I prey yow herkneth alle:
Lo, how Fortune turneth sodeynly
The hope and pryde eek of hir enemy!
This cok, that lay upon the foxes bak,   585
In al his drede unto the fox he spak,
And seyde, " Sire, if that I were as ye,
Yet sholde I seyn, as wys God helpe me,
' Turneth agayn, ye proude cherles alle!
A verray pestilence upon yow falle!   590
Now am I come unto the wodes syde;
Maugree youre heed, the cok shal heere abyde.
I wol hym ete, in feith, and that anon! ' "
    The fox answerde, " In feith, it shall be don."
And as he spak that word, al sodeynly   595
This cok brak from his mouth delyverly,
And heighe upon a tree he fleigh anon.
And whan the fox saugh that the cok was gon,
    " Allas! " quod he, " O Chauntecleer, allas!
I have to yow," quod he, " ydoon trespas,   600
In as muche as I maked yow aferd
Whan I yow hente and broghte out of the yerd.
But, sire, I dide it in no wikke entente.
Com doun, and I shal telle yow what I mente;
I shal seye sooth to yow, God help me so! "   605
    " Nay thanne," quod he, " I shrewe us bothe two.
And first I shrewe myself, bothe blood and bones,

---

571 *Flowen:* flew. 573 *A, benedicitee:* ah, Lord bless us! 574-6 Jack
Straw and his followers (*meynee*), during the Peasants' Revolt of 1381,
attacked Flemish merchants and shopkeepers because they were
prosperous and foreign. 578 *Bemes:* trumpets; *box:* box-tree wood.
579 *Powped:* tooted. 580 *Howped:* whooped. 589 *Cherles:* as we
should say in derogation, 'peasants'. 592 *Maugree youre heed:* in spite of
your marvellous brainwork! 596 *Delyverly:* deftly. 603 *Wikke:*
wicked. 606 *Shrewe:* curse.

If thou bigyle me ofter than ones.
Thou shalt namoore, thurgh thy flaterye,
Do me to synge and wynke with myn ye;   610
For he that wynketh, whan he sholde see,
Al wilfully, God lat him nevere thee! ''
" Nay," quod the fox, " but God yeve hym meschaunce,
That is so undiscreet of governaunce
That jangleth whan he sholde holde his pees."   615
Lo, swich it is for to be recchelees
And necligent, and truste on flaterye.
But ye that holden this tale a folye,
As of a fox, or of a cok and hen,
Taketh the moralite, goode men.   620
For seint Paul seith that al that writen is,
To oure doctrine it is ywrite, ywis;
Taketh the fruyt, and lat the chaf be stille.
Now, goode God, if that it be thy wille,
As seith my lord, so make us alle goode men,   625
And brynge us to his heighe blisse! Amen.

THE FRANKLIN'S PROLOGUE AND TALE

Whether or not one accepts the idea of a ' Marriage Group '
within the *Canterbury Tales,* in which a deliberate discussion of
marriage ideals and realities is carried on from pilgrim to pilgrim,
it is clear that the tale told by the Franklin resolves very finely
the one-sided contributions made by the Wife of Bath, the Clerk,
and the Merchant. In the story of Arveragus and Dorigen,
neither the unnatural convention of courtly love nor a patriarchal
masculine dominance nor a worldly cynicism is allowed to prevail;
instead, we see a marriage based on mutual forbearance and
companionship, where both partners recognise that " love wol
nat been constreyned by maistrye."

PROLOGUE

Thise olde gentil Britouns in hir dayes
Of diverse aventures maden layes,

610 *Do:* cause. 612 *Thee:* prosper. 613 *Yeve:* give. 614 *Govern-*
aunce: self-restraint. 615 *Jangleth:* chatters. 621 See *Rom.* xv. 4.
622 *Doctrine:* edification; *ywrite:* written. 625 *As seith my lord:* an
unexplained reference which may be to Christ or to some contemporary
'lord'—more probably the former. 1 *Gentil:* good, worthy; *Britouns:*
Bretons, inhabitants of Brittany in France; *hir:* their. 2 *Maden layes:*
composed romantic narrative poems.

Rymeyed in hir firste Briton tonge;
Whiche layes with hir instrumentz they songe,
Or elles redden hem for hir plesaunce, 5
And oon of hem have I in remembraunce,
Which I shal seyn with good wyl as I kan.
   But, sires, by cause I am a burel man,
At my bigynnyng first I yow biseche,
Have me excused of my rude speche. 10
I lerned nevere rethorik, certeyn;
Thyng that I speke, it moot be bare and pleyn.
I sleep nevere on the Mount of Pernaso,
Ne lerned Marcus Tullius Scithero.
Colours ne knowe I none, withouten drede, 15
But swiche colours as growen in the mede,
Or elles swiche as men dye or peynte.
Colours of rethoryk been to me queynte;
My spirit feeleth noght of swich mateere.
But if yow list, my tale shul ye heere. 20

TALE

   In Armorik, that called is Britayne,
Ther was a knyght that loved and dide his payne
To serve a lady in his beste wise;
And many a labour, many a greet emprise
He for his lady wroghte, er she were wonne. 25
For she was oon the faireste under sonne,
And eek therto comen of so heigh kynrede
That wel unnethes dorste this knyght, for drede,
Telle hire his wo, his peyne, and his distresse.
But atte laste she, for his worthynesse, 30
And namely for his meke obeysaunce,
Hath swich a pitee caught of his penaunce
That pryvely she fil of his accord
To take hym for hir housbonde and hir lord,
Of swich lordshipe as men han over hir wyves. 35

3 *Rymeyed:* rhymed, versified; *firste:* original. 6 *Oon of hem:* If Chaucer did use one of the Breton lays in this poem, the source has not been discovered. 8 *Burel:* rough, unlearned. 13 *Pernaso:* Parnassus, haunt of the Muses. 14 *Scithero:* Cicero (106-43 B.C.), Roman orator. 15 *Colours:* rhetorical ornaments; *withouten drede:* I assure you. 18 *Queynte:* strange. 20 *If yow list:* if it pleases you. 21 *Armorik:* Armorica, an old name for Brittany. 22 *Dide his payne:* took pains. 24 *Emprise:* undertaking. 26 *Oon:* one of. 28 *Wel unnethes:* scarcely. 31 *Namely:* particularly. 33 *Fil of his accord:* came to an agreement with him.

A.L.P.   B

And for to lede the moore in blisse hir lyves,
Of his free wyl he swoor hire as a knyght
That nevere in al his lyf he, day ne nyght,
Ne sholde upon hym take no maistrie
Agayn hir wyl, ne kithe hire jalousie,   40
But hire obeye, and folwe hir wyl in al,
As any lovere to his lady shal,
Save that the name of soveraynetee,
That wolde he have for shame of his degree.
  She thanked hym, and with ful greet humblesse   45
She seyde, " Sire, sith of youre gentillesse
Ye profre me to have so large a reyne,
Ne wolde nevere God bitwixe us tweyne,
As in my gilt, were outher werre or stryf.
Sire, I wol be youre humble trewe wyf;   50
Have heer my trouthe, til that myn herte breste."
Thus been they bothe in quiete and in reste.
  For o thyng, sires, saufly dar I seye,
That freendes everych oother moot obeye,
If they wol longe holden compaignye.   55
Love wol nat been constreyned by maistrye.
Whan maistrie comth, the God of Love anon
Beteth his wynges, and farewel, he is gon!
Love is a thyng as any spirit free.
Wommen, of kynde, desiren libertee,   60
And nat to been constreyned as a thral;
And so doon men, if I sooth seyen shal.
Looke who that is moost pacient in love,
He is at his avantage al above.
Pacience is an heigh vertu, certeyn,   65
For it venquysseth, as thise clerkes seyn,
Thynges that rigour sholde nevere atteyne.
For every word men may nat chide or pleyne.
Lerneth to suffre, or elles, so moot I goon,
Ye shul it lerne, wher so ye wole or noon;   70

39 'would he take upon himself the right to dominate.' 40 *Kithe hire
jalousie:* show jealousy towards her. 43 *Name:* external title. 44 *For
shame of his degree:* to preserve the respect of his status as a husband.
46 *Gentillesse:* generosity. 47 *Profre:* offer, suggest; *so large a reyne:*
such a liberal rule. 48 *Ne wolde nevere God:* may God never allow.
49 *As in my gilt:* as far as my responsibility is concerned; *were outher:*
that there should be either. 51 *Trouthe:* pledge; *breste:* break(s).
54 *Everych:* each. 60 *Of kynde:* naturally. 62 *Sooth:* truth. 64 *At
his avantage al above:* in a completely superior position. 67 *Rigour:*
hardness. 68 *May nat:* should not. 69 *So moot I goon:* as I hope to go
(on living). 70 *Wher:* whether.

For in this world, certein, ther no wight is
That he ne dooth or seith sometyme amys.
Ire, siknesse, or constellacioun,
Wyn, wo, or chaungynge of complexioun
Causeth ful ofte to doon amys or speken.   75
On every wrong a man may nat be wreken.
After the tyme moste be temperaunce
To every wight that kan on governaunce.
And therfore hath this wise, worthy knyght,
To lyve in ese, suffrance hire bihight,   80
And she to hym ful wisly gan to swere
That nevere sholde ther be defaute in here.

Heere may men seen an humble, wys accord;
Thus hath she take hir servant and hir lord,—
Servant in love, and lord in mariage.   85
Thanne was he bothe in lordshipe and servage.
Servage? nay, but in lordshipe above,
Sith he hath bothe his lady and his love;
His lady, certes, and his wyf also,
The which that lawe of love acordeth to.   90
And whan he was in this prosperitee,
Hoom with his wyf he gooth to his contree,
Nat fer fro Pedmark, ther his dwellyng was,
Where as he lyveth in blisse and in solas.

Who koude telle, but he hadde wedded be,   95
The joye, the ese, and the prosperitee
That is bitwixe an housbonde and his wyf?
A yeer and moore lasted this blisful lyf,
Til that the knyght of which I speke of thus,
That of Kayrrud was cleped Arveragus,   100
Shoop hym to goon and dwelle a year or tweyne
In Engelond, that cleped was eek Briteyne,
To seke in armes worshipe and honour;
For al his lust he sette in swich labour;
And dwelled there two yeer, the book seith thus.   105
    Now wol I stynten of this Arveragus,

73 *Constellacioun:* planetary configuration. 74 *Complexioun:* con-
stitution, disposition. 76 *Wreken:* avenged. 77 'There must be some
moderation in accordance with the circumstances.' 78 *Kan on
governaunce:* knows how to control himself. 80 *Suffrance hire bihight:*
promised her forbearance. 86 *Servage:* subjection. 87 *Above:* exalted.
90 *Acordeth to:* agrees with. 93 *Pedmark:* Penmarc'h, village and head-
land in south-west Finistère, Brittany. 94 *Solas:* comfort. 100
Kayrrud: Kerru is a modern Breton place-name, though not found in the
Penmarc'h district. 101 *Shoop him:* made up his mind. 103 *Worshipe:*
fame, glory. 104 *Lust:* pleasure. 106 *Stynten:* stop (speaking).

And speken I wole of Dorigen his wyf,
That loveth hire housbonde as hire hertes lyf.
For his absence wepeth she and siketh,
As doon thise noble wyves whan hem liketh.   110
She moorneth, waketh, wayleth, fasteth, pleyneth;
Desir of his presence hire so destreyneth
That al this wyde world she sette at noght.
Hire freendes, whiche that knewe hir hevy thoght,
Conforten hire in al that ever they may.   115
They prechen hire, they telle hire nyght and day
That causelees she sleeth hirself, allas!
And every confort possible in this cas
They doon to hire with al hire bisynesse,
Al for to make hire leve hire hevynesse.   120
    By proces, as ye knowen everichoon,
Men may so longe graven in a stoon
Til som figure therinne emprented be.
So longe han they conforted hire, til she
Receyved hath, by hope and by resoun,   125
The emprentyng of hire consolacioun,
Thurgh which hir grete sorwe gan aswage;
She may nat alwey duren in swich rage.
    And eek Arveragus, in al this care,
Hath sent hire lettres hoom of his welfare,   130
And that he wole come hastily agayn;
Or elles hadde this sorwe hir herte slayn.
    Hire freendes sawe hir sorwe gan to slake,
And preyde hire on knees, for Goddes sake,
To come and romen hire in compaignye,   135
Awey to dryve hire derke fantasye.
And finally she graunted that requeste,
For wel she saugh that it was for the beste.
    Now stood hire castel faste by the see,
And often with hire freendes walketh shee,   140
Hire to disporte, upon the bank an heigh,
Where as she many a ship and barge seigh
Seillynge hir cours, where as hem liste go.
But thanne was that a parcel of hire wo,
For to hirself ful ofte, " Allas! " seith she,   145
" Is ther no ship, of so manye as I se,

109 *Siketh:* sighs. 112 *Destreyneth:* torments. 113 *Sette at noght:* account-
ed useless. 119 *Bisynesse:* diligence. 121 *By proces:* gradually; *everichoon:*
each one. 122 *Graven:* engrave. 128 *Duren:* continue; *rage:* violence of
grief. 133 *Slake:* weaken. 135 *Romen hire:* walk, ramble. 141 *Upon the
bank an heigh:* high up on the shore. 142 *Seigh:* saw. 144 *Parcel:* part.

Wol bryngen hom my lord? Thanne were myn herte
Al warisshed of his bittre peynes smerte."
    Another tyme ther wolde she sitte and thynke,
And caste hir eyen dounward fro the brynke.　　　　　150
But whan she saugh the grisly rokkes blake,
For verray feere so wolde hir herte quake
That on hire feet she myghte hire noght sustene.
Thanne wolde she sitte adoun upon the grene,
And pitously into the see biholde,　　　　　155
And seyn right thus, with sorweful sikes colde:
    " Eterne God, that thurgh thy purveiaunce
Ledest the world by certein governaunce,
In ydel, as men seyn, ye no thyng make.
But, Lord, thise grisly feendly rokkes blake,　　　　　160
That semen rather a foul confusion
Of werk than any fair creacion
Of swich a parfit wys God and a stable,
Why han ye wroght this werk unresonable?
For by this werk, south, north, ne west, ne eest,　　　　　165
Ther nys yfostred man, ne bryd, ne beest;
It dooth no good, to my wit, but anoyeth.
Se ye nat, Lord, how mankynde it destroyeth?
An hundred thousand bodyes of mankynde
Han rokkes slayn, al be they nat in mynde,　　　　　170
Which mankynde is so fair part of thy werk
That thou it madest lyk to thyn owene merk.
Thanne semed it ye hadde a greet chiertee
Toward mankynde; but how thanne may it bee
That ye swiche meenes make it to destroyen,　　　　　175
Whiche meenes do no good, but evere anoyen?
I woot wel clerkes wol seyn as hem leste,
By argumentz, that al is for the beste,
Though I ne kan the causes nat yknowe.
But thilke God that made wynd to blowe　　　　　180
As kepe my lord! this my conclusion.
To clerkes lete I al disputison.
But wolde God that alle thise rokkes blake
Were sonken into helle for his sake!
Thise rokkes sleen myn herte for the feere."　　　　　185

148 *Warisshed:* cured. 154 *Grene:* grass. 156 *Sikes colde:* shuddering
sighs. 157 *Purveiaunce:* providence. 159 *In ydel:* in vain. 160 *Feendly:*
fiendish. 166 *Nys:* is not; *bryd:* bird. 167 *To my wit:* as I understand it;
anoyeth: causes harm. 170 *Al be they:* although they are; *in mynde:*
remembered. 172 *Merk:* image. 173 *Chiertee:* affection. 181 *As kepe:*
please look after; *this:* this is. 182 *Lete:* leave; *disputison:* argument.

Thus wolde she seyn, with many a pitous teere.
Hire freendes sawe that it was no disport
To romen by the see, but disconfort,
And shopen for to pleyen somwher elles.
They leden hire by ryveres and by welles,   190
And eek in othere places delitables;
They dauncen, and they pleyen at ches and tables.
So on a day, right in the morwe-tyde,
Unto a gardyn that was ther bisyde,
In which that they hadde maad hir ordinaunce   195
Of vitaille and of oother purveiaunce,
They goon and pleye hem al the longe day.
And this was on the sixte morwe of May,
Which May hadde peynted with his softe shoures
This gardyn ful of leves and of floures;   200
And craft of mannes hand so curiously
Arrayed hadde this gardyn, trewely,
That nevere was ther gardyn of swich prys,
But if it were the verray paradys.
The odour of floures and the fresshe sighte   205
Wolde han maked any herte lighte
That evere was born, but if to greet siknesse,
Or to greet sorwe, helde it in distresse;
So ful it was of beautee with plesaunce.
At after-dyner gonne they to daunce,   210
And synge also, save Dorigen allone,
Which made alwey hir compleint and hir moone,
For she ne saugh hym on the daunce go
That was hir housbonde and hir love also.
But nathelees she moste a tyme abyde,   215
And with good hope lete hir sorwe slyde.
Upon this daunce, amonges othere men,
Daunced a squier biforn Dorigen,
That fressher was and jolyer of array,
As to my doom, than is the month of May.   220
He syngeth, daunceth, passynge any man
That is, or was, sith that the world bigan.
Therwith he was, if men sholde hym discryve,
Oon of the beste farynge man on lyve;

189 *Shopen* (*for*): decided. 190 *Leden:* take; *welles:* springs. 192
Tables: backgammon. 193 *Morwe-tyde:* morning-time. 195 *Maad
hir ordinaunce:* made their arrangements. 196 *Vitaille:* food. 207 *But
if:* unless; *to:* too. 217 *Upon:* in. 218 *Biforn:* before. 220 *As to
my doom:* in my estimation. 223 *Discryve:* describe. 224 'one of the
handsomest men alive' (a mixed construction).

ACKNOWLEDGEMENTS

The publishers are indebted to the following authors, publishers and owners of copyright who have given permission for material to be reprinted in this book.

THE SOCIETY OF AUTHORS, DR. JOHN MASEFIELD, O.M. and THE MACMILLAN COMPANY, NEW YORK—for *The Wanderer*, from *Collected Poems*, by John Masefield, copyright, 1930, 1958, by John Masefield.

MRS. GEORGE BAMBRIDGE, MESSRS. METHUEN AND CO. LTD., and THE MACMILLAN COMPANY OF CANADA—for *McAndrew's Hymn* from *The Seven Seas* by Rudyard Kipling.

CHATTO AND WINDUS LTD.—for *Dead Man's Dump* by Isaac Rosenberg.

CITY LIGHTS BOOKS and ALLEN GINSBERG—for *American Change* by Allen Ginsberg, copyright © 1962, by Allen Ginsberg.

J. M. DENT & SONS LTD.—for *Over Sir John's Hill* by Dylan Thomas.

FABER AND FABER LTD.—for *Burnt Norton* and *Gerontion* by T. S. Eliot, *The Quaker Graveyard in Nantucket* by Robert Lowell, and *Spain 1937* by W. H. Auden.

VICTOR GOLLANCZ LTD. and HUGH MACDIARMID—for *Stony Limits* by Hugh Macdiarmid.

GROVE PRESS, INC.—for *The Lordly and Isolate Satyrs* from *The Distances: Poems* by Charles Olson, copyright ©1950, 1951, 1953, 1960 by Charles Olson, published by Grove Press, Inc.

HOLT, RINEHART AND WINSTON, INC.—for *The Axe-helve* and *Paul's Wife* from *Complete Poems* of Robert Frost, copyright 1923 by Holt, Rinehart and Winston, Inc., copyright renewed 1951 by Robert Frost, reprinted by permission of Messrs. Jonathan Cape, Ltd., and Holt, Rinehart and Winston, Inc.

HOUGHTON MIFFLIN COMPANY—for *The Nun's Priest's Tale*, *The Franklin's Prologue and Tale* and *The Pardoner's Prologue and Tale* by Geoffrey Chaucer from *The Works of Geoffrey Chaucer* edited by F. N. Robinson.

THE HUTCHINSON PUBLISHING GROUP—for *The Story of Two Gentlemen and the Gardener* from *Songs* by Christopher Logue.

ALFRED A. KNOPF, INC., and FABER AND FABER LTD.,—for *Sunday Morning* by Wallace Stevens, copyright 1923, 1931, 1954, by Wallace Stevens.

LIVERIGHT PUBLISHING CORPORATION, NEW YORK—for *Voyages I—VI* from *The Collected Poems of Hart Crane*, copyright © R 1961 by Liveright Publishing Corporation.

MACMILLAN AND COMPANY—for *A Song About Major Eatherly* from *Weep Before God*, by John Wain reprinted by permission of John Wain, author, The Macmillan Company of Canada Limited, and Macmillan and Company.

NEW DIRECTIONS—for *Burning the Christmas Greens* from *The Collected Later Poems of William Carlos Williams*, copyright 1944, 1948 and 1950 by William Carlos Williams, and *Tract* from *The Collected Earlier Poems of William Carlos Williams*, both reprinted by permission of New Directions, publishers; for *Near Perigord, I, II, III* from *Personae: The Collected Poems of Ezra Pound*, copyright 1926 and 1954 by Ezra Pound, reprinted by permission of A. V. Moore, literary agent, Princess Mary de Rachewiltz and New Directions, publishers.

MRS. YEATS and MACMILLAN AND COMPANY—for *Meditations in Time of Civil War* from *Collected Poems of W. B. Yeats*.

"Madame," quod he, "by God that this world made,
So that I wiste it myghte youre herte glade,   260
I wolde that day that youre Arveragus
Wente over the see, that I, Aurelius,
Hadde went ther nevere I sholde have come agayn.
For wel I woot my servyce is in vayn;
My gerdoun is but brestyng of myn herte.   265
Madame, reweth upon my peynes smerte;
For with a word ye may me sleen or save.
Heere at youre feet God wolde that I were grave!
I ne have as now no leyser moore to seye;
Have mercy, sweete, or ye wol do me deye!"   270
   She gan to looke upon Aurelius:
"Is this youre wyl," quod she, "and sey ye thus?
Nevere erst," quod she, "ne wiste I what ye mente.
But now, Aurelie, I knowe youre entente,
By thilke God that yaf me soule and lyf,   275
Ne shal I nevere been untrewe wyf
In word ne werk, as fer as I have wit;
I wol been his to whom that I am knyt.
Taak this for fynal answere as of me."
But after that in pley thus seyde she: 280
"Aurelie," quod she, "by heighe God above,
Yet wolde I graunte yow to been youre love,
Syn I yow se so pitously complayne.
Looke what day that endelong Britayne
Ye remoeve alle the rokkes, stoon by stoon,   285
That they ne lette ship ne boot to goon,—
I seye, whan ye han maad the coost so clene
Of rokkes that ther nys no stoon ysene,
Thanne wol I love yow best of any man,
Have heer my trouthe, in al that evere I kan."   290
   "Is ther noon oother grace in yow?" quod he.
"No, by that Lord," quod she, "that maked me!
For wel I woot that it shal never bityde.
Lat swiche folies out of youre herte slyde.
What deyntee sholde a man han in his lyf   295
For to go love another mannes wyf,
That hath hir body whan so that hym liketh?"
   Aurelius ful ofte soore siketh;

265 *Gerdoun:* reward. 266 *Reweth:* take pity. 267 *Sleen:* kill. 268
Grave: buried. 269 *Leyser:* opportunity. 270 *Do me deye:* make me
die. 273 *Erst:* before. 277 *As fer as I have wit:* as long as I have
control of my thoughts. 283 *Syn:* since. 284 *Endelong:* all along.
286 *Lette:* prevent. 295 *Deyntee:* pleasure.

Wo was Aurelie whan that he this herde,
And with a sorweful herte he thus answerde: 300
" Madame," quod he, " this were an inpossible!
Thanne moot I dye of sodeyn deth horrible."
And with that word he turned hym anon.
Tho coome hir othere freendes many oon,
And in the aleyes romeden up and doun,   305
And nothyng wiste of this conclusioun,
But sodeynly bigonne revel newe
Til that the brighte sonne loste his hewe;
For th'orisonte hath reft the sonne his lyght,—
This is as muche to seye as it was nyght!—   310
And hoom they goon in joye and in solas,
Save oonly wrecche Aurelius, allas!
He to his hous is goon with sorweful herte.
He seeth he may nat fro his deeth asterte;
Hym semed that he felte his herte colde.   315
Up to the hevene his handes he gan holde,
And on his knowes bare he sette hym doun,
And in his ravyng seyde his orisoun.
For verray wo out of his wit he breyde.
He nyste what he spak, but thus he seyde;   320
With pitous herte his pleynt hath he bigonne
Unto the goddes, and first unto the sonne:
He seyde, " Appollo, god and governour
Of every plaunte, herbe, tree, and flour,
That yevest, after thy declinacion,   325
To ech of hem his tyme and his seson,
As thyn herberwe chaungeth lowe or heighe,
Lord Phebus, cast thy merciable eighe
On wrecche Aurelie, which that am but lorn.
Lo, lord! my lady hath my deeth ysworn   330
Withoute gilt, but thy benignytee
Upon my dedly herte have som pitee.
For wel I woot, lord Phebus, if yow lest,
Ye may me helpen, save my lady, best.
Now voucheth sauf that I may yow devyse   335
How that I may been holpen and in what wyse.

301 *Inpossible:* impossibility. 304 *Tho coome:* then came. 309
Orisonte: horizon. 312 *Wrecche:* wretched. 314 *Asterte:* escape.
317 *Knowes:* knees. 318 *Ravyng:* wild talk; *orisoun:* prayer. 319
Breyde: started. 323 *Appollo:* Phœbus Apollo, god of the sun.
325 *After thy declinacion:* according to your distance from the celestial
equator. 327 *Herberwe:* lodging, place. 329 *Lorn:* lost. 331 *But:*
unless. 332 *Dedly:* destined to die. 335 *Devyse:* describe.

Youre blisful suster, Lucina the sheene,
That of the see is chief goddesse and queene
(Though Neptunus have deitee in the see,
Yet emperisse aboven hym is she),   340
Ye knowen wel, lord, that right as hir desir
Is to be quyked and lighted of youre fir,
For which she folweth yow ful bisily,
Right so the see desireth naturelly
To folwen hire, as she that is goddesse   345
Bothe in the see and ryveres moore and lesse.
Wherfore, lord Phebus, this is my requeste—
Do this miracle, or do myn herte breste—
That now next at this opposicion
Which in the signe shal be of the Leon,   350
As preieth hire so greet a flood to brynge
That fyve fadme at the leeste it oversprynge
The hyeste rokke in Armorik Briteyne;
And lat this flood endure yeres tweyne.
Thanne certes to my lady may I seye,   355
'Holdeth youre heste, the rokkes been aweye.'
   Lord Phebus, dooth this miracle for me.
Preye hire she go no faster cours than ye;
I seye, preyeth your suster that she go
No faster cours than ye thise yeres two.   360
Thanne shal she been evene atte fulle alway,
And spryng flood laste bothe nyght and day.
And but she vouche sauf in swich manere
To graunte me my sovereyn lady deere,
Prey hire to synken every rok adoun   365
Into hir owene dirke regioun
Under the ground, ther Pluto dwelleth inne,
Or nevere mo shal I my lady wynne.
Thy temple in Delphos wol I barefoot seke.
Lord Phebus, se the teeris on my cheke,   370
And of my peyne have som compassioun."
And with that word in swowne he fil adoun,

337 *Lucina the sheene:* the bright goddess of the moon. 342 *Quyked:* kindled. 346 *Moore and lesse:* greater and smaller. 349 *Opposicion:* i.e. of the sun and moon, 180 degrees apart. 350 *Leon:* zodiacal constellation Leo, the house or 'mansion' of the sun. 352 *Fyve fadme:* 30 ft. 354 ff. The moon is to move at the same rate as the sun for two years, always at the full, causing endless spring tides. 356 *Holdeth your heste:* keep your promise. 361 *Evene:* continuously. 366 *Dirke:* dark. 367 *Pluto:* god of the Underworld. Lucina, as Proserpina, was abducted by Pluto to be his queen. 369 *Delphos:* Delphi, famous oracle of Apollo on Mt. Parnassus.

And longe tyme he lay forth in a traunce.
His brother, which that knew of his penaunce,
Up caughte hym, and to bedde he hath hym broght   375
Dispeyred in this torment and this thoght
Lete I this woful creature lye;
Chese he, for me, wheither he wol lyve or dye.
Arveragus, with heele and greet honour,
As he that was of chivalrie the flour,   380
Is comen hoom, and othere worthy men.
O blisful artow now, thou Dorigen,
That hast thy lusty housbonde in thyne armes,
The fresshe knyght, the worthy man of armes,
That loveth thee as his owene hertes lyf.   385
No thyng list hym to been ymaginatyf,
If any wight hadde spoke, whil he was oute,
To hire of love; he hadde of it no doute.
He noght entendeth to no swich mateere,
But daunceth, justeth, maketh hire good cheere;   390
And thus in joye and blisse I lete hem dwelle,
And of the sike Aurelius wol I telle.
In langour and in torment furyus
Two yeer and moore lay wrecche Aurelyus,
Er any foot he myghte on erthe gon;   .   395
Ne confort in this tyme hadde he noon,
Save of his brother, which that was a clerk.
He knew of al this wo and al this werk;
For to noon oother creature, certeyn,
Of this matere he dorste no word seyn.   400
Under his brest he baar it moore secree
Than evere dide Pamphilus for Galathee.
His brest was hool, withoute for to sene,
But in his herte ay was the arwe kene.
And wel ye knowe that of a sursanure   405
In surgerye is perilous the cure,
But men myghte touche the arwe, or come therby.
His brother weep and wayled pryvely,
Til atte laste hym fil in remembraunce,
That whiles he was at Orliens in Fraunce,   410

376 *Thoght:* working of the mind. 378 *Chese he:* let him choose.
379 *With heele:* well and happy. 386 *Ymaginatyf:* suspicious. 387
Oute: away. 389 *Entendeth:* pays attention. 390 *Justeth:* jousts.
398 *Werk:* trouble. 402 refers to a medieval Latin poetic dialogue,
Pamphilius de Amore. 405 *Sursanure:* superficially healed wound.
408 *Weep:* wept. 410 *Orliens:* Orléans, university town on river
Loire, France.

As yonge clerkes, that been lykerous
To reden artes that been curious,
Seken in every halke and every herne
Particuler sciences for to lerne—
He hym remembred that, upon a day,   415
At Orliens in studie a book he say
Of magyk natureel, which his felawe,
That was that tyme a bacheler of lawe,
Al were he ther to lerne another craft,
Hadde prively upon his desk ylaft;   420
Which book spak muchel of the operaciouns
Touchynge the eighte and twenty mansiouns
That longen to the moone, and swich folye
As in oure dayes is nat worth a flye,—
For hooly chirches feith in oure bileve   425
Ne suffreth noon illusioun us to greve.
And whan this book was in his remembraunce,
Anon for joye his herte gan to daunce,
And to hymself he seyde pryvely:
" My brother shal be warisshed hastily;   430
For I am siker that ther be sciences
By whiche men make diverse apparences,
Swiche as thise subtile tregetoures pleye.
For ofte at feestes have I wel herd seye
That tregetours, withinne an halle large,   435
Have maad come in a water and a barge,
And in the halle rowen up and doun.
Somtyme hath semed come a grym leoun;
And somtyme floures sprynge as in a mede;
Somtyme a vyne, and grapes white and rede;   440
Somtyme a castel, al of lym and stoon;
And whan hem lyked, voyded it anon.
Thus semed it to every mannes sighte.
  Now thanne conclude I thus, that if I myghte
At Orliens som oold felawe yfynde   445
That hadde thise moones mansions in mynde,
Or oother magyk natureel above,

411 *Lykerous:* eager.   413 *Every halke and every herne:* every nook and
cranny.   414 *Particuler:* strange, recherché.   416 *Say:* saw.   417
Magyk natureel: natural magic, as opposed to black magic, centred on the
study of astrology.   419 *Al were he:* although he was.   420 *Prively:*
half-hidden.   421 *Muchel:* much.   422 *Mansiouns:* 'stations' of the
moon, corresponding to the 28 days of its phases.   423 *Longen:* belong.
425 *Bileve:* creed.   431 *Siker:* sure.   433 *Tregetoures:* magicians,
illusionists.   442 *Voyded it:* made it vanish.   445 *Felawe:* friend.   447
Above: apart from that.

He sholde wel make my brother han his love.
For with an apparence a clerk may make,
To mannes sighte, that alle the rokkes blake 450
Of Britaigne weren yvoyded everichon,
And shippes by the brynke comen and gon,
And in swich forme enduren a wowke or two.
Thanne were my brother warisshed of his wo;
Thanne moste she nedes holden hire biheste, 455
Or elles he shal shame hire atte leeste."
  What sholde I make a lenger tale of this?
Unto his brotheres bed he comen is,
And swich confort he yaf hym for to gon
To Orliens that he up stirte anon, 460
An on his wey forthward thanne is he fare
In hope for to been lissed of his care.
  Whan they were come almoost to that citee,
But if it were a two furlong or thre,
A yong clerk romynge by hymself they mette, 465
Which that in Latyn thriftily hem grette,
And after that he seyde a wonder thyng:
" I knowe," quod he, " the cause of youre comyng."
And er they ferther any foote wente,
He tolde hem al that was in hire entente. 470
  This Briton clerk hym asked of felawes
The which that he had knowe in olde dawes,
And he answerde hym that they dede were,
For which he weep ful ofte many a teere.
  Doun of his hors Aurelius lighte anon, 475
And with this magicien forth is he gon
Hoom to his hous, and maden hem wel at ese.
Hem lakked no vitaille that myghte hem plese.
So wel arrayed hous as ther was oon
Aurelius in his lyf saugh nevere noon. 480
  He shewed hym, er he wente to sopeer,
Forestes, parkes ful of wilde deer;
Ther saugh he hertes with hir hornes hye,
The gretteste that evere were seyn with ye.
He saugh of hem an hondred slayn with houndes, 485
And somme with arwes blede of bittre woundes.
He saugh, when voyded were thise wilde deer,
Thise fauconers upon a fair ryver,

452 *Brynke:* shore. 453 *Wowke:* week. 455 *Biheste:* promise. 457
What: why. 461 *Fare:* gone. 462 *Lissed:* relieved. 466 *Thriftily:*
quickly, confidently. 472 *Dawes:* days. 488 *Ryver:* river-bank used
as hawking-ground.

That with hir haukes han the heron slayn.
  Tho saugh he knyghtes justyng in a playn;   490
And after this he dide hym swich pleasaunce
That he hym shewed his lady on a daunce,
On which hymself he daunced, as hym thoughte.
And whan this maister that this magyk wroughte
Saugh it was tyme, he clapte his handes two,   495
And farewel! al oure revel was ago.
And yet remoeved they nevere out of the hous,
Whil they saugh al this sighte merveillous,
But in his studie, ther as his bookes be,
They seten stille, and no wight but they thre.   500
  To hym this maister called his squier,
And seyde hym thus: " Is redy oure soper?
Almoost an houre it is, I undertake,
Sith I yow bad oure soper for to make,
Whan that thise worthy men wenten with me   505
Into my studie, ther as my bookes be."
  " Sire," quod this squier, " whan it liketh yow,
It is al redy, though ye wol right now."
" Go we thanne soupe," quod he, " as for the beste.
Thise amorous folk somtyme moote han hir reste."   510
  At after-soper fille they in tretee
What somme sholde this maistres gerdon be,
To remoeven alle the rokkes of Britayne,
And eek from Gerounde to the mouth of Sayne.
  He made it straunge, and swoor, so God hym save,   515
Lasse than a thousand pound he wolde nat have,
Ne gladly for that somme he wolde nat goon.
  Aurelius, with blisful herte anoon,
Answerde thus: " Fy on a thousand pound!
This wyde world, which that men seye is round,   520
I wolde it yeve, if I were lord of it.
This bargayn is ful dryve, for we been knyt.
Ye shal be payed trewely, by my trouthe!
But looketh now, for no necligence or slouthe
Ye tarie us heere no lenger than to-morwe."   525
  " Nay," quod this clerk, " have heer my feith to borwe."
  To bedde is goon Aurelius whan hym leste,
And wel ny al that nyght he hadde his reste.

---

511 *Fille they in tretee:* they began to negotiate.   514 *Gerounde:* Gironde'
estuary at Bordeaux; *Seine:* estuary on French north coast. Penmarc'h
was equidistant from both. 515 *Straunge:* difficult. 519 *Fy on a:*
what's a. 522 *Ful dryve:* clinched. 526 *To borwe:* as a pledge.

What for his labour and his hope of blisse,
His woful herte of penaunce hadde a lisse. 530
  Upon the morwe, whan that it was day,
To Britaigne tooke they the righte way,
Aurelius and this magicien bisyde,
And been descended ther they wolde abyde.
And this was, as thise bookes me remembre, 535
The colde, frosty seson of Decembre.
  Phebus wax old, and hewed lyk laton,
That in his hoote declynacion
Shoon as the burned gold with stremes brighte;
But now in Capricorn adoun he lighte, 540
Where as he shoon ful pale, I dar wel seyn.
The bittre frostes, with the sleet and reyn,
Destroyed hath the grene in every yerd.
Janus sit by the fyr, with double berd,
And drynketh of his bugle horn the wyn; 545
Biforn hym stant brawen of the tusked swyn,
And " Nowel " crieth every lusty man.
  Aurelius, in al that evere he kan,
Dooth to this maister chiere and reverence,
And preyeth hym to doon his diligence 550
To bryngen hym out of his peynes smerte,
Or with a swerd that he wolde slitte his herte.
  This subtil clerk swich routhe had of this man
That nyght and day he spedde hym that he kan
To wayten a tyme of his conclusioun; 555
This is to seye, to maken illusioun,
By swich an apparence or jogelrye—
I ne kan no termes of astrologye—
That she and every wight sholde wene and seye
That of Britaigne the rokkes were aweye, 560
Or ellis they were sonken under grounde.
So atte laste he hath his tyme yfounde

532 *Righte:* direct. 534 *Descended:* alighted. 537 *Wax:* grew;
hewed lyk laton: copper-coloured. 538 i.e. during the summer solstice,
in the sign of Cancer. 539 *Shoon:* i.e. had shone. 540 *Capricorn:* sign
of the winter solstice; *adoun he lighte:* he alighted. 544 *Janus:* Roman
god of exits and entrances, represented with two faces (*double berd*);
here, he stands for January, at the threshold of the new year. *Sit:* sits.
545 *Bugle-horn:* drinking-horn made from horn of wild ox or bugle.
546 *Stant brawen:* is set flesh; *swyn:* boar. 547 *Nowel:* celebrating the
period from Christmas to Twelfth Night. 553 *Routhe:* pity. 554
Spedde hym that he kan: applied himself most vigorously. 555 'to watch
out for the ideal moment for his experiment.' 558 *Kan:* understand.
559 *Wene and seye:* imagine and say.

To maken his japes and his wrecchednesse
Of swich a supersticious cursednesse.
His tables Tolletanes forth he brought,   565
Ful wel corrected, ne ther lakked nought,
Neither his collect ne his expans yeeris,
Ne his rootes, ne his othere geeris,
As been his centris and his argumentz
And his proporcioneles convenientz   570
For his equacions in every thyng.
And by his eighte speere in his wirkyng
He knew ful wel how fer Alnath was shove
Fro the heed of thilke fixe Aries above,
That in the ninthe speere considered is;   575
Ful subtilly he kalkuled al this.
     Whan he hadde founde his firste mansioun,
He knew the remenaunt by proporcioun,
And knew the arisyng of his moone weel,
And in whos face, and terme, and everydeel;   580
And knew ful weel the moones mansioun
Acordaunt to his operacioun,
And knew also his othere observaunces
For swiche illusiouns and swiche meschaunces

---

563 *Hise japes and his wrecchednesse:* his wretched tricks.   564 'of such a
diabolical, evil nature.'   565-85 The astrological calculations are
purposely left a little ambiguous or incomplete, to stress the magician's
'mystery.'   565 *Tables Tolletanes:*   Toledan Tables, used in astro-
nomical calculations.   567 *Collect (yeeris):*   computations of planetary
movements for round periods from 20 to 3,000 years; *expans yeeris:*
computations for single years or short periods up to 20 years.   568
Rootes: basic data for a given period; *geeris:*   paraphernalia.   569
Centris: part of astrolabe showing position of fixed star; *argumentz:*
angles or arcs, used as basis for calculations.   570 *Proporcioneles con-
venientz:* tables of proportional parts for computing planetary movements
during fractions of a year.   571 *Equacions:*   allowances for minor dis-
crepancies in motion (?).   572 *Eighte speere:*   sphere of the fixed stars;
wirkyng: calculations (?).   573-5 He is taking into account the pre-
cession of the equinoxes, caused by the slow rotation of the eighth
sphere.   573 *Alnath:*   star in the constellation Aries; *shove:*   moved.
574 *Heed:*   head or beginning of the sign Aries, the true equinoctial
point; *fixe:*   fixed.   575 *Ninthe speere:*   sphere of the Primum Mobile, in
which the true equinoctial point was considered to be situated. Pre-
cession of the equinoxes was measured by observing the distance between
this point and the star Alnath.   577 *Firste mansioun:*   the first mansion
of the moon, named Alnath after the star.   580 *Face:*   third part of a
zodiacal sign; *terme:*   unequal division of a zodiacal sign. Both in-
volved association with particular planets.   582 *Acordaunt:*   best suited.
584 *Meschaunces:*   evil acts.

As hethen folk useden in thilke dayes. 585
For which no lenger maked he delayes,
But thurgh his magik, for a wyke or tweye,
It semed that alle the rokkes were aweye.
Aurelius, which that yet despeired is
Wher he shal han his love or fare amys, 590
Awaiteth nyght and day on this myracle;
And whan he knew that ther was noon obstacle,
That voyded were thise rokkes everychon,
Doun to his maistres feet he fil anon,
And seyde, " I woeful wrecche, Aurelius, 595
Thanke yow, lord, and lady myn Venus,
That me han holpen fro my cares colde."
And to the temple his wey forth hath he holde,
Where as he knew he sholde his lady see.
And whan he saugh his tyme, anon-right hee, 600
With dredful herte and with ful humble cheere,
Salewed hath his sovereyn lady deere:
" My righte lady," quod this woful man,
" Whom I moost drede and love as I best kan,
And lothest were of al this world displese, 605
Nere it that I for yow have swich disese
That I moste dyen heere at youre foot anon,
Noght wolde I telle how me is wo bigon.
But certes outher moste I dye or pleyne;
Ye sle me giltelees for verray peyne. 610
But of my deeth thogh that ye have no routhe,
Avyseth yow er that ye breke youre trouthe.
Repenteth yow, for thilke God above,
Er ye me sleen by cause that I yow love.
For, madame, wel ye woot what ye han hight— 615
Nat that I chalange any thyng of right
Of yow, my sovereyn lady, but youre grace—
But in a gardyn yond, at swich a place,
Ye woot right wel what ye bihighten me;
And in myn hand youre trouthe plighten ye 620
To love me best—God woot, ye seyde so,
Al be that I unworthy am therto.

---

600 *Anon-right:* immediately. 601 *Dredful:* trembling; *cheere:* expression. 602 *Salewed:* saluted. 603 *Righte:* true. 606 *Nere it:* was it not; *disese:* unhappiness. 608 *Me is wo bigon:* I am filled with grief. 610 *For verray peyne:* through my real pain. 612 *Avyseth yow:* think twice. 613 *For:* for the sake of. 615 *Hight:* promised. 617 *Grace:* favour, mercy (as distinct from duty). 619 *Bihighten:* promised.

Madame, I speke it for the honour of yow
Moore than to save myn hertes lyf right now,—
I have do so as ye comanded me;   625
And if ye vouche sauf, ye may go see.
Dooth as yow list; have youre biheste in mynde,
For, quyk or deed, right there ye shal me fynde.
In yow lith al to do me lyve or deye,—
But wel I woot the rokkes been aweye."   630
    He taketh his leve, and she astoned stood;
In al hir face nas a drope of blood. ,
She wende nevere han come in swich a trappe.
" Allas," quod she, " that evere this sholde happe!
For wende I nevere by possibilitee   635
That swich a monstre or merveille myghte be!
It is agayns the proces of nature."
And hoom she goth a sorweful creature;
For verray feere, unnethe may she go.
She wepeth, wailleth, al a day or two,   640
And swowneth, that it routhe was to see.
But why it was to no wight tolde shee,
For out of towne was goon Arveragus.
But to hirself she spak, and seyde thus,
With face pale and with ful sorweful cheere,   645
In hire compleynt, as ye shal after heere:
" Allas," quod she, " on thee, Fortune, I pleyne,
That unwar wrapped hast me in thy cheyne,
Fro which t'escape woot I no socour,
Save oonly deeth or elles dishonour;   650
Oon of thise two bihoveth me to chese.
But nathelees, yet have I levere to lese
My lif than of my body to have a shame,
Or knowe myselven fals, or lese my name;
And with my deth I may be quyt, ywis.   655
Hath ther nat many a noble wyf er this,
And many a mayde, yslayn hirself, allas!
Rather than with hir body doon trespas?
    Yis, certes, lo, thise stories beren witnesse:
Whan thritty tirauntz, ful of cursednesse,   660
Hadde slayn Phidon in Atthenes atte feste,
They comanded his doghtres for t'areste,

628 *Quyk:* alive. 631 *Astoned:* stunned. 632 *Nas:* there was not.
633 *Wende:* expected. 636 *Monstre:* unnatural thing. 648 *Unwar:*
unwary. 652 *Have I levere to lese:* I would rather lose. 655 *Ywis:*
surely. 660 The Thirty Tyrants were appointed by Sparta to rule
Athens in the late 5th century B.C. 661 *Atte feste:* at the feast.

And bryngen hem biforn hem in despit,
Al naked, to fulfille hir foul delit,
And, in hir fadres blood they made hem daunce   665
Upon the pavement, God yeve hem meschaunce!
For which thise woful maydens, ful of drede,
Rather than they wolde lese hir maydenhede,
They prively been stirt into a welle,
And dreynte hemselven, as the bookes telle.   670
    They of Mecene leete enquere and seke
Of Lacedomye fifty maydens eke,
On whiche they wolden doon hir lecherye.
But was ther noon of al that compaignye
That she nas slayn, and with a good entente   675
Chees rather for to dye than assente
To been oppressed of hir maydenhede.
Why sholde I thanne to dye been in drede?
Lo, eek, the tiraunt Aristoclides,
That loved a mayden, heet Stymphalides,   680
Whan that hir fader slayn was on a nyght,
Unto Dianes temple goth she right,
And hente the ymage in hir handes two,
Fro which ymage wolde she nevere go.
No wight ne myghte hir handes of it arace   685
Til she was slayn, right in the selve place.
    Now sith that maydens hadden swich despit
To been defouled with mannes foul delit,
Wel oghte a wyf rather hirselven slee
Than be defouled, as it thynketh me.   690
What shal I seyn of Hasdrubales wyf,
That at Cartage birafte hirself hir lyf?
For whan she saugh that Romayns wan the toun,
She took hir children alle, and skipte adoun
Into the fyr, and chees rather to dye   695
Than any Romayn dide hire vileynye.

663 *In despit:* against their will. 666 *God yeve hem meschaunce:* may God
damn them. 669 *Prively been stirt:* jumped secretly. 670 *Dreynte:*
drowned. 671 *Mecene:* Messene, city at war with Sparta in ancient
Greece; *leete enquere and seke:* ordered inquiry and search after. 672 *Of
Lacedomye:* from Lacedaemon (Sparta). 677 *Oppressed:* violated.
679 *Aristoclides:* a tyrant of Orchomenos in Arcadia. Chaucer takes the
story, like his other examples, from St. Jerome. 680 *Heet Stymphalides:*
called Stymphalis. 682 *Diana:* goddess of chastity; *right:* directly.
683 *Hente:* seized. 685 *Arace:* pull away. 687 *Despit:* indignation.
691 *Hasdrubales wyf:* See *Nun's Priest's Tale,* lines 543-8. 693 *Wan:*
(had) won. 694 *Skipte:* leapt quickly. 695 *Chees:* chose.

Hath nat Lucresse yslayn hirself, allas!
At Rome, whan that she oppressed was
Of Tarquyn, for hire thoughte it was a shame
To lyven whan that she had lost hir name?   700
The sevene maydens of Milesie also
Han slayn hemself, for verrey drede and wo,
Rather than folk of Gawle hem sholde oppresse.
Mo than a thousand stories, as I gesse,
Koude I now telle as touchynge this mateere.   705
Whan Habradate was slayn, his wyf so deere
Hirselven slow, and leet hir blood to glyde
In Habradates woundes depe and wyde,
And seyde, ' My body, at the leeste way,
Ther shal no wight defoulen, if I may.'   710
    What sholde I mo ensamples heerof sayn,
Sith that so manye han hemselven slayn
Wel rather than they wolde defouled be?
I wol conclude that it is bet for me
To sleen myself than been defouled thus.   715
I wol be trewe unto Arveragus,
Or rather sleen myself in som manere,
As dide Demociones doghter deere
By cause that she wolde nat defouled be.
O Cedasus, it is ful greet pitee   720
To reden how thy doghtren deyde, allas!
That slowe hemself for swich a manere cas.
As greet a pitee was it, or wel moore,
The Theban mayden that for Nichanore
Hirselven slow, right for swich manere wo.   725
Another Theban mayden dide right so;
For oon of Macidonye hadde hire oppressed,
She with hire deeth hir maydenhede redressed.

697 *Lucresse:* Lucretia was raped by Tarquinius Sextus, son of the last king of early Rome in the 6th century B.C. 701 *Milesie:* Miletus, Ionian city on coast of Asia Minor. 703 *Folk of Gawle:* Gauls or Galatians, Celtic people in Asia Minor who sacked Miletus 276 B.C. 704 *Mo:* more. 706 *Habradate:* Abradates, king of Susiana in the south-west Persian empire, was killed fighting for Cyrus the Great in the 6th century B.C., and his wife Panthea stabbed herself on his corpse. 710 *If I may:* if I can prevent it. 711 *Ensamples:* examples. 718 *Democion:* Demotion's daughter killed herself rather than marry anyone other than her fiancé Leosthenes, Athenian general who was killed 323 B.C. 720 *Cedasus:* Scedasus of Leuctra in Boeotia, whose two daughters were raped by Spartans in the 4th century B.C. 721 *Doghtren:* daughters. 724 *Nichanore:* Nicanor, an officer of Alexander the Great at the taking of Thebes 336 B.C.

What shal I seye of Nicerates wyf,
That for swich cas birafte hirself hir lyf?
How trewe eek was to Alcebiades   730
His love, that rather for to dyen chees
Than for to suffre his body unburyed be.
Lo, which a wyf was Alceste," quod she.
" What seith Omer of goode Penalopee?
Al Greece knoweth of hire chastitee.   735
Pardee, of Laodomya is writen thus,
That whan at Troie was slayn Protheselaus,
Ne lenger wolde she lyve after his day.
The same of noble Porcia telle I may;
Withoute Brutus koude she nat lyve,   740
To whom she hadde al hool hir herte yive.
The parfit wyfhod of Arthemesie
Honured is thurgh al the Barbarie.
O Teuta, queene! thy wyfly chastitee
To alle wyves may a mirour bee.   745
The same thyng I seye of Bilyea,
Of Rodogone, and eek Valeria."
    Thus pleyned Dorigen a day or tweye,
Purposynge evere that she wolde deye.
But nathelees, upon the thridde nyght,   750
Hoom cam Arveragus, this worthy knyght,
And asked hire why that she weep so soore;

729 *Nicerates wyf:* killed herself rather than fall into the hands of the
Thirty Tyrants of Athens, who had killed her husband.   731 *Alcebiades:*
Alcibiades, Athenian commander, was assassinated 404 B.C. Timandra,
his concubine, defied the order of the Thirty Tyrants not to bury his
body.   734   *Which:* what; *Alceste:* Alcestis, wife of Admetus, legendary
king of Pherae in Thessaly, died in her husband's place.   735 *Penalopee:*
Penelope, wife of Odysseus in Homer's *Odyssey*, faithfully resisted her
importunate suitors during her husband's absence.   737 *Pardee:*
indeed; *Laodomya:* Laodamia refused to survive the death of her hus-
band Protesilaus, legendary king of Phylace in Thessaly.   740 *Porcia:*
wife of M. Junius Brutus (78?-42 B.C.), said to have killed herself by
swallowing hot embers.   743 *Arthemesie:* Artemisia, widow of Mausolus,
king of Caria in Asia Minor, commemorated his death by erecting a
great sepulchre at Halicarnassus which became known as the Mausol-
eum.   744 *Barbarie:* barbarian territory.   745 *Teuta:* queen of Illyria
(roughly, modern Yugoslavia) in its struggle against Rome in the 3rd
century B.C.   747 *Bilyea:* Bilia, wife of Duillius, Roman consul who
won a naval battle against the Carthaginians at Mylae 260 B.C.   748
Rodogone: Rhodogune, daughter of Darius the Great of Persia (548-
485 B.C.), refused to marry a second time; *Valeria:* daughter of M.
Valerius Messalla Corvinus (64 B.C.-A.D. 8), refused to remarry after the
death of her husband Servius.

And she gan wepen ever lenger the moore.
" Allas," quod she, " that evére was I born!   755
Thus have I seyd," quod she, " thus have I sworn "—
And toold hym al as ye han herd bifore;
It nedeth nat reherce it yow namoore.
This hcusbonde, with glad chiere, in freendly wyse
Answerde and seyde as I shal yow devyse: 760
" Is thei oght elles, Dorigen, but this? "
    " Nay, nay," quod she, " God helpe me so as wys!
This is to muche, and it were Goddes wille."
    " Ye, wyf," quod he, " lat slepen that is stille.
It may be wel, paraventure, yet to day.   765
Ye shul youre trouthe holden, by my fay!
For God so wisly have mercy upon me,
I hadde wel levere ystiked for to be
For verray love which that I to yow have,
But if ye sholde youre trouthe kepe and save.   770
Trouthe is the hyeste thyng that man may kepe "—
But with that word he brast anon to wepe,
And seyde, " I yow forbede, up peyne of deeth,
That nevere, whil thee lasteth lyf ne breeth,
To no wight telle thou of this aventure,—   775
As I may best, I wol my wo endure,—
Ne make no contenance of hevynesse,
That folk of yow may demen harm or gesse."
    And forth he cleped a squier and a mayde:
" Gooth forth anon with Dorigen," he sayde,   780
" And bryngeth hire to swich a place anon."
They take hir leve, and on hir wey they gon,
But they ne wiste why she thider wente.
He nolde no wight tellen his entente.
    Paraventure an heep of yow, ywis,   785
Wol holden hym a lewed man in this
That he wol putte his wyf in jupartie.
Herkneth the tale er ye upon hire crie.
She may have bettre fortune than yow semeth;
And whan that ye han herd the tale, demeth.   790
    This squier, which that highte Aurelius,
On Dorigen that was so amorus,
Of aventure happed hire to meete

754 *Ever lenger the moore:* still more and more. 762 *As wys:* as surely (he will). 763 *And:* if. 764 *That:* what. 766 *Fay:* faith. 767 *God so wisely:* may God truly. 768 *Ystiked:* stabbed to death. 770 *But if:* if ... not. 772 *Brast anon to weepe:* suddenly burst into tears. 773 *Up:* upon. 778 *Demen harm:* think evil. 786 *Lewed:* wrong-headed. 790 *Dem eth:*judge.

Amydde the toun, right in the quykkest strete,
As she was bown to goon the wey forth right
Toward the gardyn ther as she had hight.   795
And he was to the gardyn-ward also;
For wel he spyed whan she wolde go
Out of hir hous to any maner place.
But thus they mette, of aventure or grace,   800
And he saleweth hire with glad entente,
And asked of hire whiderward she wente;
And she answerde, half as she were mad,
" Unto the gardyn, as myn housbonde bad,
My trouthe for to holde, allas! allas! "   805
    Aurelius gan wondren on this cas,
And in his herte hadde greet compassioun
Of hire and of hire lamentacioun,
And of Arveragus, the worthy knyght,
That bad hire holden al that she had hight,   810
So looth hym was his wyf sholde breke hir trouthe;
And in his herte he caughte of this greet routhe,
Considerynge the beste on every syde,
That fro his lust yet were hym levere abyde
Than doon so heigh a cherlyssh wrecchednesse   815
Agayns franchise and alle gentillesse;
For which in fewe wordes seyde he thus:
" Madame, seyth to youre lord Arveragus,
That sith I se his grete gentillesse
To yow, and eek I se wel youre distresse,   820
That him were levere han shame (and that were routhe)
Than ye to me sholde breke thus youre trouthe,
I have wel levere evere to suffre wo
Than I departe the love bitwix yow two.
I yow relesse, madame, into youre hond   825
Quyt every serement and every bond
That ye han maad to me as heerbiforn,
Sith thilke tyme which that ye were born.
My trouthe I plighte, I shal yow never repreve
Of no biheste, and heere I take my leve,   830
As of the treweste and the beste wyf
That evere yet I knew in al my lyf."
But every wyf be war of hire beheeste!

794 *Quykkest:* busiest.   795 *Bown:* ready, bound. 800 *Of aventure or
grace:* by chance or by the divine will.   814 *Fro his lust . . . abyde:* keep
off his desire. 816 *Franchise:* free and generous behaviour.   824 *De-
parte:* split, break. 826 *Quyt:* discharged; *serement:* oath. 829-30 'I
swear to you, I shall never reproach you over your promise.'

On Dorigen remembreth, atte leeste.
Thus kan a squier doon a gentil dede   835
As wel as kan a knyght, withouten drede.
   She thonketh hym upon hir knees al bare,
And hoom unto hir housbonde is she fare,
And tolde hym al, as ye han herd me sayd;
And be ye siker, he was so weel apayd   840
That it were inpossible me to wryte.
What sholde I lenger of this cas endyte?
   Arveragus and Dorigen his wyf
In sovereyn blisse leden forth hir lyf.
Nevere eft ne was ther angre hem bitwene.   845
He cherisseth hire as though she were a queene,
And she was to hym trewe for everemoore.
Of thise two folk ye gete of me namoore.
   Aurelius, that his cost hath al forlorn,
Curseth the tyme that evere he was born: 850
" Allas," quod he, " allas, that I behighte
Of pured gold a thousand pound of wighte
Unto this philosophre! How shal I do?
I se namoore but that I am fordo.
Myn heritage moot I nedes selle,   855
And been a beggere; heere may I nat dwelle,
And shamen al my kynrede in this place,
But I of hym may gete bettre grace.
But nathelees, I wole of hym assaye,
At certeyn dayes, yeer by yeer, to paye,   860
And thanke hym of his grete curteisye.
My trouthe wol I kepe, I wol nat lye."
   With herte soor he gooth unto his cofre,
And broghte gold unto this philosophre,
The value of fyve hundred pound, I gesse,   865
And hym bisecheth, of his gentillesse,
To graunte hym dayes of the remenaunt;
And seyde, " Maister, I dar wel make avaunt,
I failled nevere of my trouthe as yit.
For sikerly my dette shal be quyt   870
Towardes yow, howevere that I fare
To goon a-begged in my kirtle bare.

839 *Sayd:* say it (?). 840 *Apayd:* pleased. 842 *Of this cas endyte:*
relate about this matter. 845 *Eft:* afterwards. 849 *Cost:* expendi-
ture; *forlorn:* lost. 852 *Pured:* refined. 854 *Fordo:* undone, ruined.
858 *But:* unless. 859 *Of hym assaye:* try to approach him. 867 *Dayes
of the remenaunt:* time to pay the remainder. 872 'going begging in my
scanty tunic.'

But wolde ye vouche sauf, upon seuretee,
Two yeer or thre for to respiten me,
Thanne were I wel; for elles moot I selle   875
Myn heritage; ther is namoore to telle."
    This philosophre sobrely answerde,
And seyde thus, whan he thise wordes herde:
" Have I nat holden covenant unto thee? "
    " Yes, certes, wel and trewely," quod he.   880
    " Hastow nat had thy lady as thee liketh? "
    " No, no," quod he, and sorwefully he siketh.
    " What was the cause? tel me if thou kan."
    Aurelius his tale anon bigan,
And tolde hym al, as ye han herd bifoore;   885
It nedeth nat to yow reherce it moore.
    He seide, " Arveragus, of gentillesse,
Hadde levere dye in sorwe and in distresse
Than that his wyf were of hir trouthe fals."
The sorwe of Dorigen he tolde hym als;   890
How looth hire was to been a wikked wyf,
And that she levere had lost that day hir lyf,
And that hir trouthe she swoor thurgh innocence,
She nevere erst hadde herd speke of apparence.
" That made me han of hire so greet pitee;   895
And right as frely as he sente hire me,
As frely sente I hire to hym ageyn.
This al and som; ther is namoore to seyn."
    This philosophre answerde, " Leeve brother,
Everich of yow dide gentilly til oother.   900
Thou are a squier, and he is a knyght;
But God forbede, for his blisful myght,
But if a clerk koude doon a gentil dede
As wel as any of yow, it is no drede!
    Sire, I releesse thee thy thousand pound,   905
As thou right now were cropen out of the ground,
Ne nevere er now ne haddest knowen me.
For, sire, I wol nat taken a peny of thee
For al my craft, ne noght for my travaille.
Thou hast ypayed wel for my vitaille.   910
It is ynough, and farewel, have good day! "
And took his hors, and forth he goth his way.

873 *Wolde ye:* if you would; *seuretee:* security. 890 *Als:* also. 894
Apparence: magic, illusionism. 898 *This al and som:* this is the whole
story. 899 *Leeve:* dear. 904 *It is no drede:* no doubt. 906 *Cropen:*
crept. 909 *Craft:* skill; *travaille:* work.

Lordynges, this question, thanne, wol I aske now,
Which was the mooste fre, as thynketh yow?
Now telleth me, er that ye ferther wende.   915
I kan namoore; my tale is at an ende.

THE PARDONER'S PROLOGUE AND TALE

PROLOGUE

Radix malorum est Cupiditas. Ad Thimotheum, 6°.

" Lordynges," quod he, " in chirches whan I preche,
I peyne me to han an hauteyn speche,
And rynge it out as round as gooth a belle,
For I kan al by rote that I telle.
My theme is alwey oon, and evere was—   5
Radix malorum est Cupiditas.
    First I pronounce whennes that I come,
And thanne my bulles shewe I, alle and some.
Oure lige lordes seel on my patente,
That shewe I first, my body to warente,   10
That no man be so boold, ne preest ne clerk,
Me to destourbe of Cristes hooly werk,
And after that thanne telle I forth my tales;
Bulles of popes and of cardynales,
Of patriarkes and bishopes I shewe,   15
And in Latyn I speke a wordes fewe,
To saffron with my predicacioun,
And for to stire hem to devocioun.
Thanne shewe I forth my longe cristal stones,
Ycrammed ful of cloutes and of bones,—   20
Relikes been they, as wenen they echoon.
Thanne have I in latoun a sholder-boon
Which that was of an hooly Jewes sheep.
' Goode men,' I seye, ' taak of my wordes keep;

913 *Lordynges:* gentlemen. 914 *Fre:* generous-minded; *as thynketh
yow:* as it seems to you. 2 *Peyne me:* take pains: *hauteyn:* lofty.
5 *Theme:* text. 6 'The love of money is the root of (all) evils.' (*I Tim.*
vi. 10). 7 *Pronounce whennes that:* announce from where. 8 *Bulles:*
bulls, papal edicts; *alle and some:* one and all. 9 a bishop's seal on the
papal licence. 10 *My body to warente:* to protect my person. 11 *Clerk:*
cleric. 12 *Destourbe of:* hinder from. 17 'to flavour my preaching
with.' 19 *Cristal stones:* glass containers. 20 *Cloutes:* rags. 21 *As
wenen they echoon:* as they all imagine. 22 *Latoun:* brass-like metal.

If that this boon be wasshe in any welle, 25
If cow, or calf, or sheep, or oxe swelle
That any worm hath ete, or worm ystonge,
Taak water of that welle and wassh his tonge,
And it is hool anon; and forthermoore,
Of pokkes and of scabbe, and every soore 30
Shal every sheep be hool that of this welle
Drynketh a draughte. Taak kep eek what I telle:
If that the good-man that the beestes oweth
Wol every wyke, er that the cok hym croweth,
Fastynge, drynken of this welle a draughte, 35
As thilke hooly Jew oure eldres taughte,
His beestes and his stoor shal multiplie.
    And, sires, also it heeleth jalousie;
For though a man be falle in jalous rage,
Lat maken with this water his potage, 40
And nevere shal he moore his wyf mystriste,
Though he the soothe of hir defaute wiste,
Al had she taken preestes two or thre.
    Heere is a miteyn eek, that ye may se.
He that his hand wol putte in this mitayn, 45
He shal have multipliyng of his grayn,
Whan he hath sowen, be it whete or otes,
So that he offre pens, or elles grotes.
    Goode men and wommen, o thyng warne I yow:
If any wight be in this chirche now 50
That hath doon synne horrible, that he
Dar nat, for shame, of it yshryven be,
Or any womman, be she yong or old,
That hath ymaad hir housbonde cokewold,
Swich folk shal have no power ne no grace 55
To offren to my relikes in this place.
And whoso fyndeth hym out of swich blame,
He wol come up and offre in Goddes name,
And I assoille him by the auctoritee
Which that by bulle ygraunted was to me.' 60
    By this gaude have I wonne, yeer by yeer,
An hundred mark sith I was pardoner.

27 'that has eaten any worm (or snake) or been stung by one.'
33 *Oweth:* owns. 37 *Stoor:* stock. 40 *Potage:* soup. 44 *Miteyn:*
mitten. 48 *So:* provided; *grotes:* groats, fourpenny pieces. 57 *Out
of:* without. 59 *Assoille:* absolve. 61 *Gaude:* trick (i.e. stimulating
contributions by forbidding 'horrible sinners' to make an offering).
62 *An hundred mark:* about £66, equal perhaps to £2,000 in terms of
1962; quite a tidy annual *radix* of further *malorum*.

I stonde lyk a clerk in my pulpet,
And whan the lewed peple is doun yset,
I preche so as ye han herd bifoore, 65
And telle an hundred false japes moore.
Thanne peyne I me to strecche forth the nekke,
And est and west upon the peple I bekke,
As dooth a dowve sittynge on a berne.
Myne handes and my tonge goon so yerne 70
That it is joye to se my bisynesse.
Of avarice and of swich cursednesse
Is al my prechyng, for to make hem free
To yeven hir pens, and namely unto me.
For myn entente is nat but for to wynne, 75
And nothyng for correccioun of synne.
I rekke nevere, whan that they been beryed,
Though that hir soules goon a-blackeberyed!
For certes, many a predicacioun
Comth ofte tyme of yvel entencioun; 80
Som for plesance of folk and flaterye,
To been avaunced by ypocrisye,
And som for veyne glorie, and som for hate.
For whan I dar noon oother weyes debate,
Thanne wol I stynge hym with my tonge smerte 85
In prechyng, so that he shal nat asterte
To been defamed falsly, if that he
Hath trespased to my bretheren or to me.
For though I telle noght his propre name,
Men shal wel knowe that it is the same, 90
By signes, and by othere circumstances.
Thus quyte I folk that doon us displesances;
Thus spitte I out my venym under hewe
Of hoolynesse, to semen hooly and trewe.
    But shortly myn entent I wol devyse: 95
I preche of no thyng but for coveityse.
Therfore my theme is yet, and evere was,
Radix malorum est Cupiditas.
Thus kan I preche agayn that same vice
Which that I use, and that is avarice. 100

63 *Clerk:* proper ecclesiastic. 64 *Lewed peple:* lay folk, congregation;
yset: seated. 68 *Bekke:* nod. 69 *Berne:* barn. 70 *Yerne:* eagerly.
71 *Bisynesse:* activity (almost=stage 'business'). 74 *Namely:* specially.
78 *A-blakeberyed:* blackberrying, wandering. 86 *Asterte:* escape.
87 *To been:* from being. 95 *Shortly:* briefly; *devyse:* relate. 96
Coveityse: avarice.

But though myself be gilty in that synne,
Yet kan I maken oother folk to twynne
From avarice, and soore to repente.
But that is nat my principal entente;
I preche nothyng but for coveitise.   105
Of this mateere it oghte ynogh suffise.
    Thanne telle I hem ensamples many oon
Of olde stories longe tyme agoon.
For lewed peple loven tales olde;
Swiche thynges kan they wel reporte and holde.   110
What, trowe ye, that whiles I may preche,
And wynne gold and silver for I teche,
That I wol lyve in poverte wilfully?
Nay, nay, I thoghte it nevere, trewely!
For I wol preche and begge in sondry landes;   115
I wol nat do no labour with myne handes,
Ne make baskettes, and lyve therby,
By cause I wol nat beggen ydelly.
I wol noon of the apostles countrefete;
I wol have moneie, wolle, chese, and whete,   120
Al were it yeven of the povereste page,
Or of the povereste wydwe in a village,
Al sholde hir children sterve for famyne.
Nay, I wol drynke licour of the vyne,
And have a joly wenche in every toun.   125
But herkneth, lordynges, in conclusioun:
Youre likyng is that I shal telle a tale.
Now have I dronke a draughte of corny ale,
By God, I hope I shal yow telle a thyng
That shal by reson been at youre likyng.   130
For though myself be a ful vicious man,
A moral tale yet I yow telle kan,
Which I am wont to preche for to wynne.
Now hoold youre pees! my tale I wol bigynne."

102 *Twynne* (*from*): give up. 107 *Ensamples*: 'exempla', illustrative stories used by preachers. 110 *Reporte and holde:* tell over again and remember. 111 *Trowe ye:* do you suppose. 112 *For:* because. 113 'Voluntary poverty' would have been meritorious (as in the religious orders). 118 *Ydelly:* without good results. 119 *Countrefete:* imitate. The reference may be to the Apostle Paul who according to Langland's *Piers Plowman* 'panyers . . . made' (cf. the *baskettes* of line 117). 128 *Corny:* tasting strong of the malt.

TALE

In Flaundres whilom was a compaignye   135
Of yonge folk that haunteden folye,
As riot, hasard, stywes, and tavernes,
Where as with harpes, lutes, and gyternes,
They daunce and pleyen at dees bothe day and nyght,
And eten also and drynken over hir myght,   140
Thurgh which they doon the devel sacrifise
Withinne that develes temple, in cursed wise,
By superfluytee abhomynable.
Hir othes been so grete and so dampnable
That it is grisly for to heere hem swere.   145
Oure blissed Lordes body they totere,—
Hem thoughte that Jewes rente hym noght ynough;
And ech of hem at otheres synne lough.
And right anon thanne comen tombesteres
Fetys and smale, and yonge frutesteres,   150
Syngeres with harpes, baudes, wafereres,
Whiche been the verray develes officeres
To kyndle and blowe the fyr of lecherye,
That is annexed unto glotonye.
The hooly writ take I to my witnesse   155
That luxurie is in wyn and dronkenesse.
   Lo, how that dronken Looth, unkyndely,
Lay by his doghtres two, unwityngly;
So dronke he was, he nyste what he wroghte.
   Herodes, whoso wel the stories soghte,   160
Whan he of wyn was repleet at his feeste,
Right at his owene table he yaf his heeste
To sleen the Baptist John, ful giltelees.
   Senec seith a good word doutelees;
He seith he kan no difference fynde   165
Bitwix a man that is out of his mynde

137 *Riot:* riotous living; *hasard:* gambling; *stywes:* brothels. 138
Gyternes: citterns (early type of guitar). 139 *Dees:* dice. 143 *Super-
fluytee:* excess. 146 *Totere:* tear to shreds. 148 *Lough:* laughed.
149 *Tombesteres:* dancing-girls, acrobats. 150 *Fetys and smale:* neat
and slim; *frutesteres:* fruit-sellers. 151 *Baudes:* bawds; *wafereres:*
confectioners. 154 *Annexed:* attached, close. 156 *Luxurie:* lechery.
157 *Looth:* Lot (see *Gen.* xix. 30-36); *unkyndely:* unnaturally. 160
Herodes: Herod the Great (*c.* 73-4 B.C.). See *Matt.* xiv, *Mark* vi. *Whoso
wel the stories soghte:* as anyone knows who has consulted the histories.
162 *Heeste:* commandment. 164 *Senec:* L. Annæus Seneca (*c.* 4 B.C.-
A.D.65), Roman statesman, writer, and philosopher. See his *Epist.*
lxxxiii. 18.

And a man which that is dronkelewe,
But that woodnesse, yfallen in a shrewe,
Persevereth lenger than doth dronkenesse.
O glotònye, ful of cursednesse!   170
O cause first of oure confusioun!
O original of oure dampnacioun,
Til Crist hadde boght us with his blood agayn!
Lo, how deere, shortly for to sayn,
Aboght was thilke cursed vileynye!   175
Corrupt was al this world for glotonye.
    Adam oure fader, and his wyf also,
Fro Paradys to labour and to wo
Were dryven for that vice, it is no drede.
For whil that Adam fasted, as I rede,   180
He was in Paradys; and whan that he
Eet of the fruyt deffended on the tree,
Anon he was out cast to wo and peyne.
O glotonye, on thee wel oghte us pleyne!
O, wiste a man how manye maladyes   185
Folwen of excesse and of glotonyes,
He wolde been the moore mesurable
Of his diete, sittynge at his table.
Allas! the shorte throte, the tendre mouth,
Maketh that est and west and north and south,   190
In erthe, in eir, in water, men to swynke
To gete a glotoun deyntee mete and drynke!
Of this matiere, o Paul, wel kanstow trete:
" Mete unto wombe, and wombe eek unto mete,
Shal God destroyen bothe," as Paulus seith.   195
Allas! a foul thyng is it, by my feith,
To seye this word, and fouler is the dede,
Whan man so drynketh of the white and rede
That of his throte he maketh his pryvee,
Thurgh thilke cursed superfluitee.   200
    The apostel wepyng seith ful pitously,
" Ther walken manye of whiche yow toold have I—
I seye it now wepyng, with pitous voys—
That they been enemys of Cristes croys,
Of which the ende is deeth, wombe is hir god! "   205

167 *Dronkelewe:* drunk. 168 *Woodnesse:* madness; *shrewe:* rascal.
171 *Confusioun:* ruin. 173 *Boght . . . agayn:* redeemed. 182 *Eet:* ate;
deffended: forbidden. 187 *Mesurable:* moderate. 189 *The shorte throte:*
the brief delight of swallowing. 191 *Swynke:* labour. 192 *Gete a glotoun:*
provide for a glutton. 194-5 See *I Cor.* vi. 13. 198 *The white and rede:*
white and red wine. 199 *Pryvee:* privy. 201-5 See *Phil.* iii. 18-19.

O wombe! O bely! O stynkyng cod,
Fulfilled of dong and of corrupcioun!
At either ende of thee foul is the soun.
How greet labour and cost is thee to fynde!
Thise cookes, how they stampe, and streyne, and grynde,   210
And turnen substaunce into accident,
To fulfille al thy likerous talent!
Out of the harde bones knokke they
The mary, for they caste noght awey
That may go thurgh the golet softe and swoote.   215
Of spicerie of leef, and bark, and roote
Shal been his sauce ymaked by delit,
To make hym yet a newer appetit.
But, certes, he that haunteth swiche delices
Is deed, whil that he lyveth in tho vices.   220
   A lecherous thyng is wyn, and dronkenesse
Is ful of stryvyng and of wrecchednesse.
O dronke man, disfigured is thy face,
Sour is thy breeth, foul artow to embrace,
And thurgh thy dronke nose semeth the soun   225
As though thou seydest ay " Sampsoun, Sampsoun! "
And yet, God woot, Sampsoun drank nevere no wyn.
Thou fallest as it were a styked swyn;
Thy tonge is lost, and al thyn honeste cure;
For dronkenesse is verray sepulture   230
Of mannes wit and his discrecioun.
In whom that drynke hath dominacioun
He kan no conseil kepe, it is no drede.
Now kepe yow fro the white and fro the rede,
And namely fro the white wyn of Lepe,   235
That is to selle in Fysshstrete or in Chepe.
This wyn of Spaigne crepeth subtilly
In othere wynes, growynge faste by,

206 *Cod:* bag. 207 *Fulfilled:* filled full. 208 *Soun:* sound. 209 *Thee to fynde:* to provide for you. 210 *Stampe:* pound. 211 *Substaunce:* essential quality; *accident:* visible, material form. 212 *Likerous talent:* gluttonous appetite. 214 *Mary:* marrow. 215 *Softe and swoote:* easily and sweetly. 217 *By delit:* according to his pleasure. 219 *Delices:* sensual gratifications. 220 *Tho:* those. 222 *Stryvyng:* strife. 227 Cf. *Judges* xiii. 4, *Num.* vi. 2-5. 228 *Styked:* stuck, pierced. 229 *Honeste cure:* care for what is decent. 233 *Conseil:* secrets. 235 *Lepe:* town near Cadiz, Spain, known for its potent wines. 236 *Fysshstrete:* now Fish Hill Street, near London Bridge; *Chepe:* Cheapside, street in the City between St. Paul's Cathedral **and** the Poultry. 237-8 refers to underhand mixing of wines by vintners. *Growynge faste by:* growing close by (i.e. in Spain and Gascony, but also in the wily vintner's casks).

Of which ther ryseth swich fumositee
That whan a man hath dronken draughtes thre,   240
And weneth that he be at hoom in Chepe,
He is in Spaigne, right at the toune of Lepe,—
Nat at the Rochele, ne at Burdeux toun;
And thanne wol he seye " Sampsoun, Sampsoun! "
    But herkneth, lordynges, o word, I yow preye,   245
That alle the sovereyn actes, dar I seye,
Of victories in the Olde Testament,
Thurgh verray God, that is omnipotent,
Were doon in abstinence and in preyere.
Looketh the Bible, and ther ye may it leere.   250
    Looke, Attilla, the grete conquerour,
Deyde in his sleep, with shame and dishonour,
Bledynge ay at his nose in dronkenesse.
A capitayn sholde lyve in sobrenesse.
And over al this, avyseth yow right wel   255
What was comaunded unto Lamuel—
Nat Samuel, but Lamuel, seye I;
Redeth the Bible, and fynde it expresly
Of wyn-yevyng to hem that han justise.
Namoore of this, for it may wel suffise.   260
    And now that I have spoken of glotonye,
Now wol I yow deffenden hasardrye.
Hasard is verray mooder of lesynges,
And of deceite, and cursed forswerynges,
Blaspheme of Crist, manslaughtre, and wast also   265
Of catel and of tyme; and forthermo,
It is repreeve and contrarie of honour
For to ben holde a commune hasardour.
And ever the hyer he is of estaat,
The moore is he yholden desolaat.   270
If that a prynce useth hasardrye,
In alle governaunce and policye
He is, as by commune opinioun,
Yholde the lasse in reputacioun.
    Stilbon, that was a wys embassadour,   275

239 *Fumositee:* vapours rising from stomach.   243 *The Rochele* . . .
Burdeux: La Rochelle and Bordeaux, ports on French Atlantic coast.
251 *Attila:* (*c.* A.D. 406-53), ruler of the Huns.   256 *Lamuel:* Lemuel.
Cf. *Prov.* xxxi. 4-5. 259 *Justice:* administration of justice.   262
Deffenden hasardrye: forbid gambling. 263 *Lesynges:* lies. 266 *Catel:*
goods. 267 *Repreeve:* reproach. 270 *Desolaat:* abandoned. 272
Governaunce and policye: government and public affairs.   275 *Stilbon:*
mistake for Chilon of Lacedæmon (Sparta), one of the 'Seven Sages'
of Greece in the 7th-6th centuries B.C.

Was sent to Corynthe, in ful greet honour,
Fro Lacidomye, to make hire alliaunce.
And whan he cam, hym happede, par chaunce,
That alle the gretteste that were of that lond,
Pleyynge atte hasard he hem fond.   280
For which, as soone as it myghte be,
He stal hym hoom agayn to his contree,
And seyde, " Ther wol I nat lese my name,
Ne I wol nat take on me so greet defame,
Yow for to allie unto none hasardours.   285
Sendeth othere wise embassadours;
For, by my trouthe, me were levere dye
Than I yow sholde to hasardours allye.
For ye, that been so glorious in honours,
Shul nat allyen yow with hasardours   290
As by my wyl, ne as by my tretee."
This wise philosophre, thus seyde hee.
    Looke eek that to the kyng Demetrius,
The kyng of Parthes, as the book seith us,
Sente him a paire of dees of gold in scorn,   295
For he hadde used hasard ther-biforn;
For which he heeld his glorie or his renoun
At no value or reputacioun.
Lordes may fynden oother maner pley
Honest ynough to dryve the day awey.   300
    Now wol I speke of othes false and grete
A word or two, as olde bookes trete.
Gret sweryng is a thyng abhominable,
And fals sweryng is yet moore reprevable.
The heighe God forbad sweryng at al,   305
Witnesse on Mathew; but in special
Of sweryng seith the hooly Jeremye,
" Thou shalt swere sooth thyne othes, and nat lye,
And swere in doom, and eek in rightwisnesse ";
But ydel sweryng is a cursednesse.   310
Bihoold and se that in the firste table
Of heighe Goddes heestes honurable,
Hou that the seconde heeste of hym is this:
" Take nat my name in ydel or amys."

280 *Hasard:*   hazard, a dicing game.   282 *Stal hym:*   stole, crept.
291 *Tretee:*   agreement.   293 *Demetrius:*   Demetrius Nicator, king of
Syria in the 2nd century B.C., taken prisoner by the Parthians.   306 See
Matt. v. 34.   307-9 See *Jer.* iv. 2.   309 *Doom:*   justice.   311 *Firste
table:*   first tablet of the Ten Commandments.   313 the Second Com-
mandment according to the division in the Vulgate Bible, the Third in
the Authorised Version.

Lo, rather he forbedeth swich sweryng 315
Than homycide or many a cursed thyng;
I seye that, as by ordre, thus it stondeth;
This knoweth, that his heestes understondeth,
How that the seconde heeste of God is that.
And forther over, I wol thee telle al plat, 320
That vengeance shal nat parten from his hous
That of his othes is to outrageous.
"By Goddes precious herte," and "By his nayles,"
And "By the blood of Crist that is in Hayles,
Sevene is my chaunce, and thyn is cynk and treye!" 325
"By Goddes armes, if thou falsly pleye,
This daggere shal thurghout thyn herte go!"—
This fruyt cometh of the bicched bones two,
Forsweryng, ire, falsenesse, homycide.
Now, for the love of Crist, that for us dyde, 330
Lete youre othes, bothe grete and smale.
But, sires, now wol I telle forth my tale.

   Thise riotoures thre of whiche I telle,
Longe erst er prime rong of any belle,
Were set hem in a taverne for to drynke, 335
And as they sat, they herde a belle clynke
Biforn a cors, was caried to his grave.
That oon of hem gan callen to his knave:
"Go bet," quod he, "and axe redily
What cors is this that passeth heer forby; 340
And looke that thou reporte his name weel."
   "Sire," quod this boy, "it nedeth never-a-deel;
It was me toold er ye cam heer two houres.
He was, pardee, an old felawe of youres;
And sodeynly he was yslayn to-nyght, 345
Fordronke, as he sat on his bench upright.
There cam a privee theef men clepeth Deeth,
That in this contree al the peple sleeth,
And with his spere he smoot his herte atwo,
And wente his wey withouten wordes mo. 350

315 *Rather:* earlier. 318 *That:* the one who. 320 *Forther over:* furthermore; *plat:* flatly. 321-2 Cf. *Ecclus.* xxiii. 11. 324 *Hayles:* A phial said to contain some of Christ's blood was kept in Hayles Abbey, Gloucestershire. 325 *Cynk and treye:* five and three. The line refers to the specific game called hazard (cf. line 280). 328 *Bicched bones:* cursed dice. 331 *Lete:* leave. 333 *Ryotoures:* roisterers. 334 *Erst er:* before; *prime:* canonical hour beginning at 6 a.m. 9 a.m. was 'high prime.' 338 *Knave:* boy, servant. 339 *Go bet:* go quickly (lit. 'better'); *axe redily:* ask at once. 340 *Forby:* near by. 345 *To-nyght:* last night, the night just past. 347 *Privee:* secret.

He hath a thousand slayn this pestilence.
And, maister, er ye come in his presence,
Me thynketh that it were necessarie
For to be war of swich an adversarie.
Beth redy for to meete hym everemoore;   355
Thus taughte me my dame; I sey namoore."
" By seinte Marie! " seyde this taverner,
" The child seith sooth, for he hath slayn this yeer,
Henne over a mile, withinne a greet village,
Bothe man and womman, child, and hyne, and page;   360
I trowe his habitacioun be there.
To been avysed greet wysdom it were,
Er that he dide a man a dishonour."
    " Ye, Goddes armes! " quod this riotour,
" Is it swich peril with hym for to meete?   365
I shal hym seke by wey and eek by strete,
I make avow to Goddes digne bones!
Herkneth, felawes, we thre been al ones;
Lat ech of us holde up his hand til oother,
And ech of us bicomen otheres brother,   370
And we wol sleen this false traytour Deeth.
He shal be slayn, he that so manye sleeth,
By Goddes dignitee, er it be nyght! "
    Togidres han thise thre hir trouthes plight
To lyve and dyen ech of hem for oother,   375
As though he were his owene ybore brother.
And up they stirte, al dronken in this rage,
And forth they goon towardes that village
Of which the taverner hadde spoke biforn.
And many a grisly ooth thanne han they sworn,   380
And Cristes blessed body al torente—
Deeth shal be deed, if that they may hym hente!
    Whan they han goon nat fully half a mile,
Right as they wolde han troden over a stile,
An oold man and a povre with hem mette.   385
This olde man ful mekely hem grette,
And seyde thus, " Now, lordes, God yow see! "
    The proudeste of thise riotoures three

351 *This pestilence:* during this plague. 356 *Dame:* mother. 359
Henne: from here. 360 *Hyne:* labourer. 362 *Avysed:* forewarned.
367 *Digne:* worthy. 368 *Ones:* of one mind. 376 *Ybore:* born.
385 *An oold man:* This mysterious and impressive figure may be seen as a
messenger of Death, and seems to hold also certain overtones of the
Wandering Jew. 387 *God yow see:* a courteous form of greeting, though
not devoid of ironic implication.

Answerde agayn, " What, carl, with sory grace!
Why artow al forwrapped save thy face?   390
Why lyvestow so longe in so greet age? "
   This olde man gan looke in his visage,
And seyde thus: " For I ne kan nat fynde
A man, though that I walked into Ynde,
Neither in citee ne in no village,   395
That wolde chaunge his youthe for myn age;
And therfore moot I han myn age stille,
As longe tyme as it is Goddes wille.
Ne Deeth, allas! ne wol nat han my lyf.
Thus walke I, lyk a restelees kaityf,   400
And on the ground, which is my moodres gate,
I knokke with my staf, bothe erly and late,
And seye ' Leeve mooder, leet me in!
Lo how I vanysshe, flessh, and blood, and skyn!
Allas! whan shul my bones been at reste?   405
Mooder, with yow wolde I chaunge my cheste
That in my chambre longe tyme hath be,
Ye, for an heyre clowt to wrappe in me! '
But yet to me she wol nat do that grace,
For which ful pale and welked is my face.   410
   But, sires, to yow it is no curteisye
To speken to an old man vileynye,
But he trespasse in word, or elles in dede.
In Hooly Writ ye may yourself wel rede:
' Agayns an oold man, hoor upon his heed,   415
Ye sholde arise;' wherfore I yeve yow reed,
Ne dooth unto an oold man noon harm now,
Namoore than that ye wolde men did to yow
In age, if that ye so longe abyde.
And God be with yow, where ye go or ryde!   420
I moot go thider as I have to go."
   " Nay, olde cherl, by God, thou shalt nat so,"
Seyde this oother hasardour anon;
" Thou partest nat so lightly, by Seint John!
Thou spak right now of thilke traytour Deeth,   425
That in this contree alle oure freendes sleeth.

389 *Carl:* churl, peasant; *with sory grace:* an imprecation—'bad luck to
you'. 390 *Forwrapped:* wrapped up. 394 *Ynde:* India. 400 *Kaityf:*
captive, wretched man. 404 *Vanysshe:* waste away. 406 *Cheste:*
clothes-chest. 408 *Heyre clowt to wrappe in me:* haircloth to wrap me in,
i.e. as a shroud. 410 *Welked:* withered. 415-16 See *Levit.* xix. 32.
Agayns: in the presence of. 416 *Yeve yow reed:* give you advice.
420 *Wher:* whether; *go:* walk.

Have heer my trouthe, as thou art his espye,
Telle where he is, or thou shalt it abye,
By God, and by the hooly sacrement!
For soothly thou art oon of his assent   430
To sleen us yonge folk, thou false theef! "
   " Now, sires," quod he, " if that yow be so leef
To fynde Deeth, turne up this croked wey,
For in that grove I lafte hym, by my fey,
Under a tree, and there he wole abyde;   435
Noght for youre boost he wole him no thyng hyde.
Se ye that ook? Right there ye shal hym fynde.
God save yow, that boghte agayn mankynde,
And yow amende! " Thus seyde this olde man;
And everich of thise riotoures ran   440
Til he cam to that tree, and ther they founde
Of floryns fyne of gold ycoyned rounde
Wel ny an eighte busshels, as hem thoughte.
No lenger thanne after Deeth they soughte,
But ech of hem so glad was of that sighte,   445
For that the floryns been so faire and brighte,
That doun they sette hem by this precious hoord.
The worste of hem, he spak the firste word.
   " Bretheren," quod he, " taak kep what that I seye;
My wit is greet, though that I bourde and pleye.   450
This tresor hath Fortune unto us yiven,
In myrthe and joliftee oure lyf to lyven,
And lightly as it comth, so wol we spende.
Ey! Goddes precious dignitee! who wende
To-day that we sholde han so fair a grace?   455
But myghte this gold be caried fro this place
Hoom to myn hous, or elles unto youres—
For wel ye woot that al this gold is oures—
Thanne were we in heigh felicitee.
But trewely, by daye it may nat bee.   460
Men wolde seyn that we were theves stronge,
And for oure owene tresor doon us honge.
This tresor moste ycaried be by nyghte
As wisely and as slyly as it myghte.
Wherfore I rede that cut among us alle   465
Be drawe, and lat se wher the cut wol falle;

428 *Abye:* pay for. 430 *Assent:* opinion. 432 *Leef:* anxious.
436 *Boost:* threat. 442 *Floryns:* A florin had the value of 6s. 8d.
450 *Bourde:* joke. 454 *Wende:* would have imagined. 461 *Stronge:*
violent, dangerous. 462 *Doon us honge:* have us hanged. 464 *Slyly:*
craftily.

And he that hath the cut with herte blithe
Shal renne to the town, and that ful swithe,
And brynge us breed and wyn ful prively.
And two of us shul kepen subtilly 470
This tresor wel; and if he wol nat tarie,
Whan it is nyght, we wol this tresor carie,
By oon assent, where as us thynketh best."
That oon of hem the cut broghte in his fest,
And bad hem drawe, and looke where it wol falle; 475
And it fil on the yongeste of hem alle,
And forth toward the toun he wente anon.
And also soone as that he was gon,
That oon of hem spak thus unto that oother:
" Thow knowest wel thou art my sworen brother; 480
Thy profit wol I telle thee anon.
Thou woost wel that oure felawe is agon.
And heere is gold, and that ful greet plentee,
That shal departed been among us thre.
But nathelees, if I kan shape it so 485
That it departed were among us two,
Hadde I nat doon a freendes torn to thee? "
    That oother answered, " I noot hou that may be.
He woot wel that the gold is with us tweye;
What shal we doon? What shal we to hym seye? " 490
    " Shal it be conseil? " seyde the firste shrewe,
" And shal I tellen in a wordes fewe
What we shal doon, and brynge it wel aboute."
    " I graunte," quod that oother, " out of doute,
That, by my trouthe, I wol thee nat biwreye." 495
    " Now," quod the firste, " thou woost wel we be tweye,
And two of us shul strenger be than oon.
Looke whan that he is set, that right anoon
Arys as though thou woldest with hym pleye,
And I shal ryve hym thurgh the sydes tweye 500
Whil that thou strogelest with hym as in game,
And with thy daggere looke thou do the same;
And thanne shal al this gold departed be,
My deere freend, bitwixen me and thee.
Thanne may we bothe oure lustes all fulfille, 505
And pleye at dees right at oure owene wille."
And thus acorded been thise shrewes tweye
To sleen the thridde, as ye han herd me seye.

468 *Swithe:* quickly. 470 *Subtilly:* secretly. 484 *Departed:* divided.
491 *Shal it be conseil:* Can you keep your mouth shut? 498 *Set:* seated.

This yongeste, which that wente to the toun,
Ful ofte in herte he rolleth up and doun   510
The beautee of thise floryns newe and brighte.
" O Lord! " quod he, " if so were that I myghte
Have al this tresor to myself allone,
Ther is no man that lyveth under the trone
Of God that sholde lyve so murye as I! "   515
And atte laste the feend, oure enemy,
Putte in his thought that he sholde poyson beye,
With which he myghte sleen his felawes tweye;
For-why the feend foond hym in swich lyvynge
That he hadde leve him to sorwe brynge.   520
For this was outrely his fulle entente,
To sleen hem bothe, and nevere to repente.
And forth he gooth, no lenger wolde he tarie,
Into the toun, unto a pothecarie,
And preyde hym that he hym wolde selle   525
Som poyson, that he myghte his rattes quelle;
And eek ther was a polcat in his hawe,
That, as he seyde, his capouns hadde yslawe,
And fayn he wolde wreke hym, if he myghte,
On vermyn that destroyed hym by nyghte.   530
    The pothecarie answerde, " And thou shalt have
A thyng that, also God my soule save,
In al this world ther is no creature,
That eten or dronken hath of this confiture
Noght but the mountance of a corn of whete,   535
That he ne shal his lif anon forlete;
Ye, sterve he shal, and that in lasse while
Than thou wolt goon a paas nat but a mile,
This poysoun is so strong and violent."
    This cursed man hath in his hond yhent   540
This poysoun in a box, and sith he ran
Into the nexte strete unto a man,
And borwed of hym large botelles thre;
And in the two his poyson poured he;
The thridde he kepte clene for his drynke.   545
For al the nyght he shoop hym for to swynke
In cariynge of the gold out of that place.
And whan this riotour, with sory grace,

519 *Lyvynge:* way of life.   520 *Leve:* leave.   526 *Quelle:* kill.
527 *Hawe:* yard.   529 *Wreke:* avenge.   530 *Destroyed:* disturbed.
532 *Also:* as.   534 *Confiture:* concoction.   535 *Mountance:* amount;
corn: grain.   536 *Forlete:* lose.   537 *Sterve:* die.   538 *Goon a paas:*
walk at an easy pace.   546 *Shoop him:* planned.

Hadde filled with wyn his grete botels thre,
To his felawes agayn repaireth he.   550
   What nedeth it to sermone of it moore?
For right as they hadde cast his deeth bifoore,
Right so they han hym slayn, and that anon.
And when that this was doon, thus spak that oon:
" Now lat us sitte and drynke, and make us merie,   555
And afterward we wol his body berie."
And with that word it happed hym, par cas,
To take the botel ther the poyson was,
And drank, and yaf his felawe drynke also,
For which anon they storven bothe two,   560
   But certes, I suppose that Avycen
Wroot nevere in no canon, ne in no fen,
Mo wonder signes of empoisonyng
Than hadde thise wrecches two, er hir endyng.
Thus ended been thise homycides two.   565
And eek the false empoysonere also.
   O cursed synne of alle cursednesse!
O traytours homycide, O wikkednesse!
O glotonye, luxurie, and hasardrye!
Thou blasphemour of Crist with vileynye   570
And othes grete, of usage and of pride!
Allas! mankynde, how may it bitide
That to thy creatour, which that the wroghte,
And with his precious herte-blood thee boghte,
Thou art so fals and so unkynde, allas?   575
   Now, goode men, God foryeve yow youre trespas,
And ware yow fro the synne of avarice!
Myn holy pardoun may yow alle warice,
So that ye offre nobles or sterlynges,
Or elles silver broches, spoones, rynges.   580
Boweth youre heed under this hooly bulle!
Cometh up, ye wyves, offreth of youre wolle!
Youre names I entre heer in my rolle anon;
Into the blisse of hevene shul ye gon.
I yow assoille, by myn heigh power,   585
Yow that wol offre, as clene and eek as cleer
As ye were born.—And lo, sires, thus I preche.
And Jhesu Crist, that is oure soules leche,

557 *Par cas:* by chance. 560 *Storven:* died. 561 *Avycen:* Avicenna or
Ibn-Sina (980-1037), Moslem physician and philosopher, author of a
'Canon of Medicine.' 562 *Fen:* section (Arabic *fann*). 578 *Warice:*
preserve. 579 *So:* provided; *nobles:* gold coins valued at 6s. 8d.;
sterlynges: silver pennies. 588 *Leche:* physician.

So graunte yow his pardoun to receyve,
For that is best; I wol yow nat deceyve.   590
   But, sires, o word forgat I in my tale:
I have relikes and pardoun in my male,
As faire as any man in Engelond,
Whiche were me yeven by the popes hond.
If any of yow wole, of devocion,   595
Offren, and han myn absolucion,
Com forth anon, and kneleth heere adoun,
And mekely receyveth my pardoun;
Or elles taketh pardoun as ye wende,
Al newe and fressh at every miles ende,   600
So that ye offren, alwey newe and newe,
Nobles or pens, whiche that be goode and trewe.
It is an honour to everich that is heer
That ye mowe have a suffisant pardoneer
T'assoille yow, in contree as ye ryde,   605
For aventures whiche that may bityde.
Paraventure ther may fallen oon or two
Doun of his hors, and breke his nekke atwo.
Looke which a seuretee is it to yow alle
That I am in youre felaweshipe yfalle,   610
That may assoille yow, bothe moore and lasse,
Whan that the soule shal fro the body passe.
I rede that oure Hoost heere shal bigynne,
For he is moost envoluped in synne.
Com forth, sire Hoost, and offre first anon,   615
And thou shalt kisse the relikes everychon,
Ye, for a grote! Unbokele anon thy purs.''
   '' Nay, nay! '' quod he, '' thanne have I Cristes curs!
Lat be,'' quod he, '' it shal nat be, so theech!
Thou woldest make me kisse thyn olde breech,   620
And swere it were a relyk of a seint,
Though it were with thy fundement depeint!
But, by the croys which that Seint Eleyne fond,
I wolde I hadde thy coillons in myn hond
In stide of relikes or of seintuarie.   625
Lat kutte hem of, I wol thee helpe hem carie;

592 *Male:* wallet. 601 *Newe and newe:* afresh. 604 *Mowe:* are able
to; *suffisant:* competent. 609 *Which a seuretee:* what security. 611
Bothe moore and lasse: one and all, high and low. 619 *So theech:* so may I
prosper. 620 *Breech:* breeches. 622 *Depeint:* stained. 623 refers to
the 'finding of the true Cross' by the empress Helena (*c.* 247-*c.* 327 A.D.),
mother of Constantine the Great. 624 *Coillons:*   testicles. 625
Seintuarie: holy object.

They shul be shryned in an hogges tord! "
 This Pardoner answerde nat a word;
So wrooth he was, no word ne wolde he seye.
 " Now," quod oure Hoost, " I wol no lenger pleye   630
With thee, ne with noon oother angry man."
But right anon the worthy Knyght bigan,
Whan that he saugh that al the peple lough,
" Namoore of this, for it is right ynough!
Sire Pardoner, be glad and myrie of cheere;   635
And ye, sire Hoost, that been to me so deere,
I prey yow that ye kisse the Pardoner.
And Pardoner, I prey thee, drawe thee neer,
And, as we diden, lat us laughe and pleye."
Anon they kiste, and ryden forth hir weye.   640

Robert Henryson

fl. 1475—1500

THE TESTAMENT OF CRESSEID

Of the brilliant group of poets who wrote in Scotland in the late fifteenth and early sixteenth centuries, and are rather inadequately referred to as ' Scottish Chaucerians,' Henryson was the nearest in spirit and sympathies to Chaucer. His *Testament of Cresseid* is a sequel to Chaucer's *Troilus and Criseyde*, and was in fact printed as an epilogue to that poem in early editions of Chaucer's work. The ' sin-and-retribution ' theme, however, and the extraordinary pathos in the last encounter of Troilus and Cresseid, produce an original emphasis and effect in the Scottish poem.

I

Ane doolie sessoun to ane cairfull dyte
Suld correspond, and be equivalent.
Richt sa it wes quhen I began to wryte
This tragedie, the wedder richt fervent
Quhen Aries in middis of the Lent   5
Schouris of Haill can fra the North discend
That scantlie fra the cauld I micht defend.

627 *Tord:* turd. 634 *Right ynough:* quite enough. 640 *Ryden:* rode.
1 *Doolie sessoun:* gloomy season; *cairfull dyte:* sad piece of writing.
3 *Sa:* so. 4 *Fervent:* bitter. 5 *Aries:* the Ram, sign of the Zodiac (mid-March to mid-April); *middis of the Lent:* about the beginning of April. 6 *Can:* caused to. 7 *Scantlie:* scarcely.

II

Yit nevertheles within myne Oratur
I stude, quhen Titan had his bemis bricht
Withdrawin doun, and sylit under cure   10
And fair Venus the bewtie of the nicht
Uprais, and set unto the west full richt
Hir goldin face in oppositioun
Of God Phebus direct discending doun.

III

Throw out the glas hir bemis brast sa fair   15
That I micht se on everie syde me by
The Northin wind had purifyit the Air
And sched the mistie cloudis fra the sky,
The froist freisit, the blastis bitterly
Fra Pole Artik come quhisling loud and schill,   20
And causit me remufe aganis my will.

IV

For I traistit that Venus, luifis Quene,
To quhome sum tyme I hecht obedience,
My faidit hart of lufe scho wald mak grene,
And therupon with humbill reverence,   25
I thocht to pray hir hie Magnificence,
Bot for greit cald as than I lattit was,
And in my Chalmer to the fyre can pas.

V

Thocht lufe be hait, yit in ane man of age
It kendillis nocht sa sone as in youtheid,   30
Of quhome the blude is flowing in ane rage,
And in the auld the curage doif and deid,
Of quhilk the fyre outward is best remeid;
To help be Phisike quhair that nature faillit
I am expert, for baith I have assailit.   35

8 *Oratur:* private chapel. 9 *Titan:* the Sun. 10 *Sylit under cure:* hidden under cover. 11 *Venus:* the planet. 14 *Phebus:* Greek sun-god. 15 *Brast:* burst. 20 *Come:* came; *schill:* shrill. 22 *Traistit:* trusted. 23 *Hecht:* promised. 24 *Scho:* she. 27 *Than:* then; *lattit:* prevented. 28 *Chalmer:* chamber, room; *can:* did. 29 *Thocht:* though; *hait:* hot. 32 *Doif:* dull. 33 *Quhilk:* which. 34 *Be:* by. 35 *Assaillit:* tried.

VI

I mend the fyre and beikit me about,
Than tuik ane drink my spreitis to comfort,
And armit me weill fra the cauld thairout:
To cut the winter nicht and mak it schort
I tuik ane Quair, and left all uther sport,　　　　　　40
Writtin be worthie Chaucer glorious,
Of fair Cresseid, and worthie Troylus.

VII

And thair I fand, efter that Diomeid
Ressavit had that Lady bricht of hew,
How Troilus neir out of wit abraid,　　　　　　45
And weipit soir with visage paill of hew,
For quhilk wanhope his teiris can renew
Quhill Esperus rejoisit him agane,
Thus quhyle in Joy he levit, quhyle in pane.

VIII

Of hir behest he had greit comforting,　　　　　　50
Traisting to Troy that scho suld mak retour,
Quhilk he desyrit maist of eirdly thing
Forquhy scho was his only Paramour;
Bot quhen he saw passit baith day and hour
Of hir ganecome, than sorrow can oppres　　　　　　55
His wofull hart in cair and hevines.

IX

Of his distres me neidis nocht reheirs,
For worthie Chauceir in the samin buik
In gudelie termis and in Joly veirs
Compylit hes his cairis, quha will luik.　　　　　　60
To brek my sleip ane uther quair I tuik,
In quhilk I fand the fatall destenie
Of fair Cresseid, that endit wretchitlie.

36 *Mend:* sorted; *beikit:* warmed. 40 *Quair:* book. 45 *Abraid:* started. 47 *Wanhope:* despair. 48 *Quhill:* till; *Esperus:* Venus. 49 *Quhyle:* sometimes. 50 *Behest:* promise. 51 *Retour:* return. 52 *Eirdly:* earthly. 53 *Forquhy:* because. 55 *Ganecome:* return. 58 *Samin:* same. 60 *Quha:* for anyone who.

X

Quha wait gif all that Chauceir wrait was trew?
Nor I wait nocht gif this narratioun   65
Be authoreist, or fenyeit of the new
Be sum Poeit, throw his Inventioun,
Maid to report the Lamentatioun
And wofull end of this lustie Cresseid,
And quhat distres scho thoillit, and quhat deid.   70

XI

Quhen Diomeid had all his appetyte,
And mair, fulfillit of this fair Ladie,
Upon ane uther he set his haill delyte
And send to hir ane Lybell of repudie,
And hir excludit fra his companie.   75
Than desolait scho walkit up and doun,
And sum men sayis into the Court commoun.

XII

O fair Creisseid, the flour and A per se
Of Troy and Grece, how was thou fortunait!
To change in filth all thy Feminitie   80
And be with fleschlie lust sa maculait
And go amang the Greikis air and lait
Sa giglotlike, takand thy foull plesance!
I have pietie thou suld fall sic mischance.

XIII

Yit nevertheless quhat ever men deme or say   85
In scornefull langage of thy brukkilnes,
I sall excuse als far furth as I may
Thy womanheid, thy wisdome and fairnes:
The quhilk Fortoun hes put to sic distres
As hir pleisit, and nathing throw the gilt   90
Of the, throw wickit langage to be spilt.

64 *Quha wait gif:* who knows whether. 66 *Fenyeit:* feigned. 69 *Lustie:* pleasure-loving. 70 *Thoillit:* endured; *deid:* death. 73 *Haill:* whole. 74 *Send:* sent; *lybell of repudie:* bill of divorcement. 77 *Into the Court common:* onto the streets. 78 *A per se:* paragon. 79 *Fortunait:* doomed. 81 *Maculait:* spotted, stained. 82 *Air:* early. 83 *Giglotlike:* like a harlot. 84 *Fall:* have, get; *sic:* such. 86 *Brukkilnes:* unreliability, frailty. 87 *Excuse:* i.e. 'excuse you on account of'; *als:* as. 91 *The:* thee; *wickit:* slanderous; *spilt:* destroyed.

XIV

This fair Lady in this wyse destitute
Of all comfort and consolatioun,
Richt privelie but fellowschip on fute
Disagysit passit far out of the toun   95
Ane myle or twa, unto ane Mansioun
Beildit full gay, quhair hir father Calchas
Quhilk than amang the Greikis dwelland was.

XV

Quhen he hir saw, the caus he can Inquyre
Of hir cumming; scho said, siching full soir: 100
' Fra Diomeid had gottin his desyre
He wox werie, and wald of me no moir.'
Quod Calchas, ' douchter, weip thou not thairfoir;
Peraventure all cummis for the best;
Welcum to me, thou art full deir ane Gest.'   105

XVI

This auld Calchas, efter the Law was tho,
Wes keiper of the Tempill as ane Preist,
In quhilk Venus and hir Sone Cupido
War honourit, and his Chalmer was thame neist,
To quhilk Cresseid with baill aneuch in breist   110
Usit to pas, hir prayeris for to say;
Quhill at the last, upon ane Solempne day,

XVII

As custome was, the pepill far and neir
Befoir the none, unto the Tempill went
With Sacrifice devoit in thair maneir: 115
Bot still Cresseid, hevie in hir Intent,
Into the Kirk wald not hir self present,
For giving of the pepill ony deming
Of hir expuls fra Diomeid the King:

94 *Privelie:* secretly; *but:* without. 97 *Beildit:* decoratea. 101 *Fra:* once. 102 *Wox:* grew. 103 *Quod:* said; *thairfoir:* for that. 106 *Efter . . . tho:* as the law then was. 109 *Thame neist:* next to them. 110 *Baill aneuch:* plenty of unhappiness.

XVIII

Bot past into ane secreit Orature   120
Quhair scho micht weip hir wofull desteny,
Behind hir bak scho cloisit fast the dure
And on hir kneis bair fell doun in hy.
Upon Venus and Cupide angerly
Scho cryit out, and said on this same wyse,   125
'Allace that ever I maid you Sacrifice.

XIX

'Ye gave me anis ane devine responsaill
That I suld be the flour of luif in Troy,
Now am I maid ane unworthie outwaill,
And all in cair translatit is my Joy   130
Quha sall me gyde? quha sall me now convoy
Sen I fra Diomeid and Nobill Troylus
Am clene excludit, as abject odious?

XX

'O fals Cupide, is nane to wyte bot thow,
And thy Mother, of lufe the blind Goddes!   135
Ye causit me alwayis understand and trow
The seid of lufe was sawin in my face,
And ay grew grene throw your supplie and grace.
Bot now allace that seid with froist is slane
And I fra luifferis left and all forlane.'   140

XXI

Quhen this was said, doun in ane extasie
Ravischit in spreit intill ane dreame scho fell,
And be apperance hard quhair scho did ly
Cupide the King ringand ane silver bell,
Quhilk men micht heir fra hevin unto hell;   145
At quhais sound befoir Cupide appeiris
The seven Planetis discending fra thair Spheiris,

---

123 *Hy:* haste. 129 *Outwaill:* outcast. 132 *Sen:* since. 133 *Abject
odious:* hateful outcast. 134 *Wyte:* blame. 138 *Supplie:* help. 140
Forlane: forgotten, forsaken. 141 *Extasie:* swoon. 147 The classical
deities, coming down from the spheres of Ptolemaic astronomy.

XXII

Quhilk hes power of all thing generabill
To reull and steir be thair greit Influence
Wedder and wind, and coursis variabill:
And first of all Saturne gave his sentence,
Quhilk gave to Cupide litill reverence,
Bot as ane busteous Churle on his maneir
Come crabitlie with auster luik and cheir.

150

XXIII

His face fronsit, his lyre was lyke the Leid,
His teith chatterit, and cheverit with the Chin,
His Ene drowpit, how sonkin in his heid,
Out of his Nois the Meldrop fast can rin,
With lippis bla and cheikis leine and thin;
The Iceschoklis that fra his hair doun hang
Was wonder greit, and as ane speir als lang.

155

160

XXIV

Atouir his belt his lyart lokkis lay
Felterit unfair, ouirfret with Froistis hoir,
His garmound and his gyis full gay of gray,
His widderit weid fra him the wind out woir;
Ane busteous bow within his hand he boir,
Under his girdill ane flasche of felloun flanis
Fedderit with Ice, and heidit with hailstanis.

165

XXV

Than Juppiter richt fair and amiabill,
God of the Starnis in the Firmament,
And Nureis to all thing generabill,
Fra his Father Saturne far different,
With burelie face, and browis bricht and brent,
Upon his heid ane Garland wonder gay
Of flouris fair, as it had bene in May.

170

175

148 *Generabill:* living. 153 *Busteous:* rough, rude. 155 *Fronsit:* wrinkled; *lyre:* complexion; *lyke the Leid:* leaden. 156 *Cheverit:* shivered, shook. 157 *How:* hollow. 158 *Meldrop:* mucus. 159 *Bla:* livid. 162 *Atouir:* about, over; *lyart:* grizzled. 163 *Felterit unfair:* matted in an ugly fashion; *ouirfret:* laced. 164 *Gyis:* clothing. 165 *Out woir:* blew out. 166 *Busteous:* sturdy. 167 *Flasche of felloun flanis:* quiver of deadly arrows. 173 *Burelie:* handsome; *brent:* smooth.

XXVI

His voice was cleir, as Cristall were his Ene,
As goldin wyre sa glitterand was his hair;
His garmound and his gyis full gay of grene,
With golden listis gilt on everie gair;
Ane burelie brand about his middil bair;   180
In his richt hand he had ane groundin speir,
Of his Father the wraith fra us to weir.

XXVII

Nixt efter him come Mars the God of Ire,
Of strife, debait, and all dissensioun,
To chide and fecht, als feirs as ony fyre;   185
In hard Harnes, hewmound and Habirgeoun,
And on his hanche ane roustie fell Fachioun;
And in his hand he had ane roustie sword;
Wrything his face with mony angrie word,

XXVIII

Schaikand his sword, befoir Cupide he come   190
With reid visage, and grislie glowrand Ene,
And at his mouth ane bullar stude of fome
Lyke to ane Bair quhetting his Tuskis kene,
Richt Tuilyeour lyke, but temperance in tene;
Ane horne he blew, with mony bosteous brag,   195
Quhilk all this warld with weir hes maid to wag.

XXIX

Than fair Phebus, Lanterne and Lamp of licht,
Of man and beist, baith frute and flourisching,
Tender Nureis, and banischer of nicht,
And of the warld causing be his moving   200
And Influence, lyfe in all eirdlie thing,
Without comfort of quhome, of force to nocht
Must all ga die that in this warld is wrocht:

---

179 *Listis:* borders; *gair:* gore. 182 *Weir:* ward off. 186 *Hewmound
and Habirgeoun:* helmet and coat of mail. 187, 188 *Roustie:* bronze-
coloured (?), or perhaps simply rusty (and all the more nasty!); *fach-
ioun:* falchion, curved sword. 192 *Bullar:* bubbling. 193 *Bair:* boar.
194 *Tuilyeour lyke:* like a bully; *but temperance in tene:* immoderately
angry. 195 *Bosteous brag:* loud, fierce blast. 196 *Weir:* war.

XXX

As King Royall he raid upon his Chair
The quhilk Phaeton gydit sum tyme upricht;   205
The brichtnes of his face quhen it was bair
Nane micht behald for peirsing of his sicht.
This goldin Cart with fyrie bemis bricht
Four yokkit steidis full different of hew,
But bait or tyring, throw the Spheiris drew.   210

XXXI

The first was soyr, with Mane als reid as Rois,
Callit Eoye into the Orient;
The secund steid to Name hecht Ethios,
Quhitlie and paill, and sum deill ascendent;
The thrid Peros, richt hait and richt fervent;   215
The feird was blak, callit Philegoney
Quhilk rollis Phebus doun into the sey.

XXXII

Venus was thair present that goddes gay,
Hir Sonnis querrell for to defend and mak
Hir awin complaint, cled in ane nyce array,   220
The ane half grene, the uther half Sabill black;
Quhyte hair as gold kemmit and sched abak;
Bot in hir face semit greit variance,
Quhyles perfyte treuth, and quhyles Inconstance.

XXXIII

Under smyling scho was dissimulait,   225
Provocative, with blenkis Amorous,
And suddanely changit and alterait,
Angrie as ony Serpent vennemous
Richt pungitive, with wordis odious.
Thus variant scho was, quha list tak keip,   230
With ane Eye lauch, and with the uther weip:

---

205 Phaet(h)on, son of Phœbus, tried to drive his father's solar chariot.
210 *But bait:* without stopping. 211 *Soyr:* sorrel. 212 *Eoye:* Eous,
one of the sun-god's horses; *into:* in. 213 *Ethios:* Æthon. 214
Quhitlie: whitish. 215 *Peros:* Pyrois. 216 *Philegoney:* Phlegon.
222 *Quhyte:* fair; *kemmit and sched abak:* combed and parted back.
225 *Dissimulait:* deceitful. 226 *Blenkis:* glances. 229 *Pungitive:*
stinging. 230 *Quha list tak keip:* for anyone engaged in watching her.
231 *Lauch . . . weip:* laughed . . . wept.

XXXIV

In taikning that all fleschelie Paramour
Quhilk Venus hes in reull and governance,
Is sum tyme sweit, sum tyme bitter and sour,
Richt unstabill, and full of variance,   235
Mingit with cairfull Joy and fals plesance,
Now hait, now cauld, now blyith, now full of wo,
Now grene as leif, now widderit and ago.

XXXV

With buik in hand than come Mercurius
Richt Eloquent, and full of Rethorie,   240
With polite termis and delicious,
With pen and Ink to report al reddie,
Setting sangis and singand merilie:
His Hude was reid, heklit atouir his Croun,
Lyke to ane Poeit of the auld fassoun.   245

XXXVI

Boxis he bair with fyne Electuairis,
And sugerit Syropis for digestioun,
Spycis belangand to the Pothecairis,
With mony hailsum sweit Confectioun,
Doctour in Phisick cled in ane Skarlot goun,   250
And furrit weill, as sic ane aucht to be,
Honest and gude, and not ane word culd le.

XXXVII

Nixt efter him come Lady Cynthia
The last of all, and swiftest in hir Spheir,
Of colour blak, buskit with hornis twa,   255
And in the nicht scho listis best appeir;
Haw as the Leid, of colour nathing cleir:
For all hir licht scho borrowis at hir brother
Titan, for of hir self scho hes nane uther.

---

232 *Taikning:* token.   241 *Polite:* polished.   244 *Heklit:* folded like
a crest, or a turban.   246 *Electuairis:* medicines containing powders
mixed with syrups.   253 *Cynthia:*   moon-goddess.   255 *Buskit:*
adorned.   256 *Listis:* likes.   257 *Haw:* livid.

XXXVIII

Hir gyse was gray, and ful of spottis blak,   260
And on hir breist ane Churle paintit full evin,
Beirand ane bunche of Thornis on his bak,
Quhilk for his thift micht clim na nar the hevin.
Thus quhen thay gadderit war, thir Goddes sevin,
Mercurius thay cheisit with ane assent   265
To be foirspeikar in the Parliament.

XXXIX

Quha had bene thair, and liken for to heir
His facound toung, and termis exquisite,
Of Rethorick the prettick he micht leir,
In brief Sermone ane pregnant sentence wryte: 270
Befoir Cupide veiling his Cap alyte,
Speiris the caus of that vocatioun,
And he anone schew his Intentioun.

XL

' Lo! ' (quod Cupide), ' quha will blaspheme the name
Of his awin God, outher in word or deid,   275
To all Goddis he dois baith lak and schame,
And suld have bitter panis to his meid.
I say this by yone wretchit Cresseid
The quilk throw me was sum tyme flour of lufe,
Me and my Mother starklie can reprufe,   280

XLI

' Saying of hir greit Infelicitie
I was the caus, and my Mother Venus,
Ane blind Goddess hir cald that micht not se,
With sclander and defame Injurious;
Thus hir leving unclene and Lecherous   285
Scho wald returne on me and my Mother,
To quhome I schew my grace abone all uther.

261-3 The Man in the Moon was traditionally the man who was put to death for gathering sticks on the sabbath (see *Numbers* xv. 32-36). 263 *Na nar:* no nearer. 264 *Thir:* these. 266 *Foirspeikar:* spokesman. 267 *Liken for to heir:* in a position to hear. 268 *Facound:* eloquent. 269 *Prettick:* practice, tricks; *leir:* learn. 270 *Sermone:* discourse. 271 *Veiling . . . alyte:* lowering . . . a little. 272 *Speiris:* asks; *vocatioun:* summons to a meeting. 273 *Schew:* showed. 276 *Lak:* reproach. 277 *Meid:* reward. 280 *Starklie:* strongly. 287 *Abone:* above.

XLII

' And sen ye ar all sevin deificait,
Participant of devyne sapience,
This greit Injurie done to our hie estait   290
Me think with pane we suld mak recompence;
Was never to Goddes done sic violence.
Asweill for yow, as for myself I say,
Thairfo.r ga help to revenge I yow pray.'

XLIII

Mercurius to Cupide gave answeir   295
And said: ' Schir King my counsall is that ye
Refer yow to the hiest Planeit heir,
And to him tak the lawest of degre,
The pane of Cresseid for to modifie;
As god Saturne, with him tak Cynthia.'   300
' I am content ' (quod he), ' to tak thay twa.'

XLIV

Than thus proceidit Saturne and the Mone
Quhen thay the mater rypelie had degest,
For the dispyte to Cupide scho had done,
And to Venus oppin and manifest,   305
In all hir lyfe with pane to be opprest
And torment sair with seiknes Incurabill,
And to all lovers be abhominabill.

XLV

This duleful sentence Saturne tuik on hand
And passit doun quhair cairfull Cresseid lay,   310
And on hir heid he laid ane frostie wand;
Than lawfullie on this wyse can he say:
' Thy greit fairnes and all thy bewtie gay,
Thy wantoun blude, and eik thy goldin Hair,
Heir I exclude fra the for evermair.   315

XLVI

' I change thy mirth into Melancholy,
Quhilk is the Mother of all pensivenes;
Thy Moisture and thy heit in cald and dry;
Thyne Insolence, thy play and wantones
To greit diseis; thy Pomp and thy riches   320

299 *The pane . . . to modifie:* to assess the punishment. 301 *Thay:*
those. 318 The melancholy 'humour' in medieval physiology was cold
and dry, the sanguine humour hot and moist.

In mortall neid; and greit penuritie
Thou suffer sall, and as ane beggar die.'

XLVII

O cruell Saturne! fraward and angrie,
Hard is thy dome, and to malitious;
On fair Cresseid quhy hes thou na mercie,   325
Quhilk was sa sweit, gentill and amorous?
Withdraw thy sentence and be gracious
As thou was never; sa schawis thow thy deid,
Ane wraikfull sentence gevin on fair Cresseid.

XLVIII

Than Cynthia, quhen Saturne past away,   330
Out of hir sait discendit doun belyve,
And red ane bill on Cresseid quhair scho lay,
Contening this sentence diffinityve:
' Fra heit of bodie I the now depryve,
And to thy seiknes sal be na recure,   335
Bot in dolour thy dayis to Indure.

XLIX

' Thy Cristall Ene minglit with blude I mak,
Thy voice sa cleir unplesand hoir and hace,
Thy lustie lyre ouirspred with spottis blak,
And lumpis haw appeirand in thy face.   340
Quhair thou cummis, Ilk man sal fle the place.
This sall thou go begging fra hous to hous
With Cop and Clapper lyke ane Lazarous.'

L

This doolie dreame, this uglye visioun
Brocht to ane end, Cresseid fra it awoik,   345
And all that Court and convocatioun
Vanischit away, than rais scho up and tuik
Ane poleist glas, and hir schaddow culd luik:
And quhen scho saw hir face sa deformait
Gif scho in hart was wa aneuch God wait.   350

---

323 *Fraward:* harsh, inimical.   324 *Dome:* judgement.   329 *Wraikfull:*
vengeful.   331 *Belyve:*   right away.   332 *Bill:*   document.   335
Recure: recovery.   338 *Hoir and hace:*   rough and hoarse.   341 *Ilk:*
each.   342 *This:*   thus.   343 i.e. with the leper's begging-bowl and
warning clap-dish.   348 *Hir schaddow culd luik:*   looked at her reflection.
350 *Gif:* whether; *wait:* knows.

LI

Weiping full sair, ' Lo quhat it is ' (quod sche),
' With fraward langage for to mufe and steir
Our craibit Goddis, and sa is sene on me!
My blaspheming now have I bocht full deir.
All eirdlie Joy and mirth I set areir.   355
Allace this day, allace this wofull tyde,
Quhen I began with my Goddis for to Chyde.'

LII

Be this was said ane Chyld come fra the Hall
To warne Cresseid the Supper was reddy,
First knokkit at the dure, and syne culd call: 360
' Madame your Father biddis yow cum in hy.
He hes mervell sa lang on grouf ye ly,
And sayis your prayers bene to lang sum deill:
The goddis wait all your Intent full weill.'

LIII

Quod scho: ' Fair Chyld ga to my Father deir,   365
And pray him cum to speik with me anone.'
And sa he did, and said: ' douchter quhat cheir? '
' Allace ' (quod scho), ' Father my mirth is gone.'
' How sa ' (quod he); and scho can all expone
As I have tauld, the vengeance and the wraik   370
For hir trespas, Cupide on hir culd tak.

LIV

He luikit on hir uglye Lipper face,
The quhilk befor was quhyte as Lillie flour,
Wringand his handis oftymes he said allace
That he had levit to se that wofull hour,   375
For he knew weill that thair was na succour
To hir seiknes, and that dowblit his pane.
Thus was thair cair aneuch betuix thame twane.

352 *Fraward:* adverse. 358 *Be:* after; *chyld:* servant; *hall:* dining-
hall. 360 *Syne:* then. 362 *On grouf:* prostrate. 369 *Expone:* ex-
plain.

LV

Quhen thay togidder murnit had full lang,
Quod Cresseid: 'Father, I wald not be kend.   380
Thairfoir in secreit wyse ye let me gang
Into yone Hospitall at the tounis end.
And thidder sum meit for Cheritie me send
To leif upon, for all mirth in this eird
Is fra me gane, sic is my wickit weird.'   385

LVI

Than in ane Mantill and ane baver Hat,
With Cop and Clapper wonder prively,
He opnit ane secreit yet, and out thair at
Convoyit hir, that na man suld espy,
Into ane Village half ane myle thairby,   390
Delyverit hir in at the Spittaill hous,
And daylie sent hir part of his Almous.

LVII

Sum knew hir weill, and sum had na knawledge
Of hir becaus scho was sa deformait,
With bylis blak ouirspred in hir visage,   395
And hir fair colour faidit and alterait.
Yit thay presumit for her hie regrait
And still murning, scho was of Nobill kin:
With better will thairfoir they tuik hir in.

LVIII

The day passit, and Phebus went to rest,   400
The Cloudis blak ouirquhelmit all the sky.
God wait gif Cresseid was ane sorrowfull Gest,
Seing that uncouth fair and Harbery:
But meit or drink scho dressit hir to ly
In ane dark Corner of the Hous allone: 405
And on this wyse weiping, scho maid her mone:

380 *Kend:*   recognised.   385 *Weird:*   fate.   388 *Yet:*   gate.   391
Spittaill hous: hospital.   392 *Almous:*   alms.   395 *Bylis:*   eruptions.
397 *Regrait:*   complaining.   403 *Fair and Harbery:*   provision and
lodging.

THE COMPLAINT OF CRESSEID

LIX

' O sop of sorrow, sonkin into cair:
O Cative Creisseid, for now and ever mair,
Gane is thy Joy and all thy mirth in Eir,
Of all blyithnes now art thou blaiknit bair.   410
Thair is na Salve may saif the of thy sair,
Fell is thy Fortoun, wickit is thy weird:
Thy blys is baneist, and thy baill on breird:
Under the Eirth, God gif I gravin wer,
Quhair nane of Grece nor yit of Troy micht heird.   415

LX

' Quhair is thy Chalmer wantounlie besene?
With burely bed and bankouris browderit bene,
Spycis and Wyne to thy Collatioun,
The Cowpis all of gold and silver schene:
The sweit Meitis, servit in plaittis clene,   420
With Saipheron sals of ane gud sessoun:
Thy gay garmentis with mony gudely Goun,
Thy plesand Lawn pinnit with goldin prene:
All is areir, thy greit Royall Renoun.

LXI

' Quhair is thy garding with thir greissis gay?   425
And fresche Flowris, quhilk the Quene Floray
Had paint it plesandly in everie pane,
Quhair thou was wont full merilye in May,
To walk and tak the dew be it was day
And heir the Merle and Mavis mony ane,   430
With Ladyis fair in Carrolling to gane,
And se the Royall Rinkis in thair array,
In garmentis gay garnischit on everie grane.

410 *Blaiknit bair:* darkened and destitute. 413 *Baneist:* banished;
thy baill on breird: your misery springing up. 414 *Gravin:* buried.
415 *Heird:* hear it. 416 *Wantounlie besene:* luxuriously furnished.
417 *Bankouris browderit bene:* finely embroidered bench-coverings.
419 *Schene:* bright. 421 *Saipheron sals:* saffron sauce. 423 *Prene:*
pin. 424 *Areir:* gone. 427 *Pane:* bed. 429 *Be:* when. 430 *Merle
and Mavis:* blackbird and thrush. 432 *Rinkis:* knights. 433 *On
everie grane:* in every colour.

LXII

'Thy greit triumphand fame and hie honour,
Quhair thou was callit of Eirdlye wichtis Flour,   435
All is decayit, thy weird is welterit so.
Thy hie estait is turnit in darknes dour.
This Lipper Ludge tak for thy burelie Bour.
And for thy bed tak now ane bunche of stro,
For waillit Wyne, and Meitis thou had tho,   440
Tak mowlit Breid, Peirrie and Ceder sour:
Bot Cop and Clapper, now is all ago.

LXIII

'My cleir voice, and courtlie carrolling,
Quhair I was wont with Ladyis for to sing,
Is rawk as Ruik, full hiddeous hoir and hace,   445
My plesand port all utheris precelling:
Of lustines I was hald maist conding.
Now is deformit the Figour of my face,
To luik on it, na Leid now lyking hes:
Sowpit in syte, I say with sair siching,   450
Ludgeit amang the Lipper Leid, allace.

LXIV

'O Ladyis fair of Troy and Grece, attend
My miserie, quhilk nane may comprehend:
My frivoll Fortoun, my Infelicitie:
My greit mischief quhilk na man can amend.   455
Be war in tyme, approchis neir the end,
And in your mynd ane mirrour mak of me:
As I am now, peradventure that ye
For all your micht may cum to that same end,
Or ellis war, gif ony war may be.   460

LXV

'Nocht is your fairnes bot ane faiding Flour,
Nocht is your famous laud and hie honour
Bot wind Inflat in uther mennis eiris.
Your roising reid to rotting sall retour:
Exempill mak of me in your Memour,   465

---

436 *Welterit:* overturned. 438 *Lipper Ludge:* leper-house. 440
Waillit: choice; *tho:* then. 441 *Mowlit:* mouldy. 445 *Rawk:*
raucous. 446 *Precelling:* excelling. 447 *Lustines:* flourishing beauty;
conding: worthy. 449 *Leid:* person. 450 *Sowpit in syte:* soaked in
sorrow. 451 *Leid:* folk. 460 *War:* worse. 463 *Inflat:* puffed up.
464 *Roising:* rosy complexion.

Quhilk of sic thingis wofull witnes beiris,
All Welth in Eird, away as Wind it weiris.
Be war thairfoir, approchis neir the hour:
Fortoun is fikkill, quhen scho beginnis and steiris.'

LXVI

Thus chydand with hir drerie destenye,   470
Weiping, scho woik the nicht fra end to end.
Bot all in vane; hir dule, hir cairfull cry
Micht not remeid, nor yit hir murning mend.
Ane Lipper Lady rais and till hir wend,
And said: ' quhy spurnis thow aganis the Wall,   475
To sla thy self, and mend nathing at all?

LXVII

' Sen thy weiping dowbillis bot thy wo,
I counsall the mak vertew of ane neid,
To leir to clap thy Clapper to and fro,
And leir efter the Law of Lipper Leid.'   480
Thair was na buit, bot furth with thame scho yeid,
Fra place to place, quhill cauld and hounger sair
Compellit hir to be ane rank beggair.

LXVIII

That samin tyme of Troy the Garnisoun,
Quhilk had to Chiftane worthie Troylus,   485
Throw Jeopardie of Weir had strikken doun
Knichtis of Grece in number mervellous,
With greit tryumphe and Laude victorious
Agane to Troy richt Royallie they raid
The way quhair Cresseid with the Lipper baid.   490

LXIX

Seing that companie thai come, all with ane stevin
Thay gaif ane cry and schuik coppis gude speid.
Said ' worthie Lordis for goddis lufe of Hevin,
To us Lipper part of your Almous deid.'
Than to thair cry Nobill Troylus tuik heid,   495
Having pietie, neir by the place can pas
Quhair Cresseid sat, not witting quhat scho was.

469 *Steirs:* stirs. 470 *Chydand:* arguing, contending. 472 *Dule:* grief.
474 *Till:* to. 481 *Na buit:* nothing for it; *yeid:* went. 484 *Garnisoun:*
garrison. 490 *With the Lipper baid:* stayed with the leper folk. 491
Stevin: voice. 494 *Almous deid:* gift of charity.

LXX

Than upon him scho kest up baith hir Ene,
And with ane blenk it come into his thocht,
That he sumtime hir face befoir had sene.   500
Bot scho was in sic plye he knew hir nocht,
Yit than hir luik into his mynd it brocht
The sweit visage and amorous blenking
Of fair Cresseid sumtyme his awin darling.

LXXI

Na wonder was, suppois in mynd that he   505
Tuik hir Figure sa sone, and lo now quhy:
The Idole of ane thing in cace may be
Sa deip Imprentit in the fantasy
That it deludis the wittis outwardly,
And sa appeiris in forme and lyke estait,   510
Within the mynd as it was figurait.

LXXII

Ane spark of lufe than till his hart culd spring
And kendlit all his bodie in ane Fyre.
With hait Fevir ane sweit and trimbling
Him tuik, quhill he was reddie to expyre.   515
To beir his Scheild his Breist began to tyre.
Within ane quhyle he changit mony hew,
And nevertheless not ane ane uther knew.

LXXIII

For Knichtlie pietie and memoriall
Of fair Cresseid, ane Gyrdill can he tak,   520
Ane Purs of gold, and mony gay Jowall,
And in the Skirt of Cresseid doun can swak;
Than raid away, and not ane word he spak,
Pensive in hart, quhill he come to the Toun,
And for greit care oft syis almaist fell doun.   525

LXXIV

The Lipper folk to Cresseid than can draw,
To se the equall distributioun
Of the Almous, bot quhen the gold thay saw,
Ilk ane to uther prevelie can roun,

---

501 *Plye:* plight. 507 *Idole:* mental image. 522 *Can swak:* flung.
525 *Oft syis:* many times. 529 *Can roun:* whispered.

And said: ' Yone Lord hes mair affectioun, 530
How ever it be, unto yone Lazarous
Than to us all, we knaw be his Almous.'

LXXV

' Quhat Lord is yone ' (quod scho), ' have ye na feill,
Hes done to us so greit humanitie? '
' Yes ' (quod a Lipper man), ' I knaw him weill, 535
Schir Troylus it is, gentill and fre: '
Quhen Cresseid understude that it was he,
Stiffer than steill, thair stert ane bitter stound
Throwout hir hart, and fell doun to the ground.

LXXVI

Quhen scho ouircome, with siching sair and sad, 540
With mony cairfull cry and cald ochane:
' Now is my breist with stormie stoundis stad,
Wrappit in wo, ane wretch full will of wane.'
Than swounit scho oft or scho culd refrane,
And ever in hir swouning cryit scho thus: 545
' O fals Cresseid and trew Knicht Troylus.

LXXVII

' Thy lufe, thy lawtie, and thy gentilnes,
I countit small in my prosperitie,
Sa elevait I was in wantones,
And clam upon the fickill quheill sa hie: 550
All Faith and Lufe I promissit to the,
Was in the self fickill and frivolous:
O fals Cresseid, and trew Knicht Troilus.

LXXVIII

' For lufe of me thou keipt gude continence,
Honest and chaist in conversatioun. 555
Of all Wemen protectour and defence
Thou was, and helpit thair opinioun.
My mynd in fleschelie foull affectioun
Was Inclynit to Lustis Lecherous:
Fy fals Cresseid, O trew Knicht Troylus. 560

---

533 *Feill:* idea. 536 *Gentill and fre:* noble and generous. 538 *Stound:*
sharp pang. 540 *Ouircome:* came to. 541 *Cald ochane:* shivering
'alas'(Gael.). 542 *Stad:* beset. 543 *Will of wane:* at a loss to know
what to do. 544 *Or:* before. 547 *Lawtie:* loyalty. 550 *Fickill
quheill:* the wheel of Fortune. 557 *Opinioun:* reputation.

LXXIX

' Lovers be war and tak gude heid about
Quhome that ye lufe, for quhome ye suffer paine.
I lat yow wit, thair is richt few thairout
Quhome ye may traist to have trew lufe agane.
Preif quhen ye will, your labour is in vaine.   565
Thairfoir I reid ye tak thame as ye find,
For thay ar sad as Widdercok in Wind.

LXXX

' Becaus I knaw the greit unstabilnes
Brukkill as glas, into my self I say,
Traisting in uther als greit unfaithfulnes,   570
Als unconstant, and als untrew of fay:
Thocht sum be trew, I wait richt few ar thay,
Quha findis treuth lat him his Lady ruse:
Nane but my self as now I will accuse.'

LXXXI

Quhen this was said, with Paper scho sat doun,   575
And on this maneir maid hir Testament.
' Heir I beteiche my Corps and Carioun
With Wormis and with Taidis to be rent.
My Cop and Clapper and myne Ornament,
And all my gold the Lipper folk sall have   580
Quhen I am deid, to burie me in grave.

LXXXII

' This Royal Ring, set with this Rubie reid,
Quhilk Troylus in drowrie to me send,
To him agane I leif it quhen I am deid,
To mak my cairfull deid unto him kend: 585
Thus I conclude schortlie and mak ane end,
My Spreit I leif to Diane quhair scho dwellis,
To walk with hir in waist Woddis and Wellis.

LXXXIII

' O Diomeid, thou hes baith Broche and Belt
Quhilk Troylus gave me in takning   590

563 *Wit:* know; *thairout:* in the world. 565 *Preif:* try to prove it.
566 *Reid:* advise. 567 *Sad:* steadfast. 569 *Into:* within. 571 *Fay:*
faith. 573 *Ruse:* praise. 577 *Beteiche:* bequeath. 578 *Taidis:* toads.
583 *Drowrie:* pledge of love. 587 *Diane:* Diana as goddess of chastity.

Of his trew lufe,' and with that word scho swelt.
And sone ane Lipper man tuik of the Ring,
Syne buryit hir withouttin tarying:
To Troylus furthwith the Ring he bair,
And of Cresseid the deith he can declair. 595

LXXXIV

Quhen he had hard hir greit infirmitie,
Hir Legacie and Lamentatioun,
And how scho endit in sic povertie,
He swelt for wo, and fell doun in ane swoun,
For greit sorrow his hart to brist was boun: 600
Siching full sadlie, said: ' I can no moir,
Scho was untrew, and wo is me thairfoir.'

LXXXV

Sum said he maid ane Tomb of Merbell gray,
And wrait hir name and superscriptioun,
And laid it on hir grave quhair that scho lay, 605
In goldin Letteris, conteining this ressoun:
' Lo fair Ladyis, Cresseid, of Troyis toun,
Sumtyme countit the flour of Womanheid,
Under this stane lait Lipper lyis deid.'

LXXXVI

Now worthie Wemen, in this Ballet schort 610
Made for your worschip and Instructioun,
Of Cheritie, I monische and exhort,
Ming not your lufe with fals deceptioun.
Beir in your mynd this schort conclusioun
Of fair Cresseid, as I have said befoir. 615
Sen scho is deid, I speik of hir no moir.

591 *Swelt:* died. 599 *Swelt:* fainted. 600 *Boun:* ready. 606
Ressoun: statement. 610 *Ballet:* poem. 611 *Worschip:* honour.

Edmund Spenser

c. 1552—1599

COLIN CLOUT'S COME HOME AGAIN

Published 1595. A bitter-sweet pastoral allegory, in which
Sir Walter Raleigh visits Spenser in Ireland, and persuades
him to come back for a period to Elizabeth's court in London.
It is an exile's picture of court and courtiers: part eulogy, part
attack. Many of the persons in his lists of poets and court ladies
cannot be at all certainly identified.

TO THE RIGHT
worthy and noble Knight
Sir *Walter Raleigh*, Captaine of her Majestie's
Guard, Lord Wardein of the Stanneries*,
and Lieutenant of the County of
Cornwall.

*Sir, that you may see that I am not alwaies ydle as yee thinke, though not greatly
well occupied, nor altogither undutifull, though not precisely officious, I make you
present of this simple pastorall, unworthie of your higher conceipt for the meanesse
of the stile, but agreeing with the truth in circumstance and matter. The which I
humbly beseech you to accept in part of paiment of the infinite debt in which I
acknowledge my selfe bounden unto you, for your singular favours and sundrie good
turnes shewed to me at my late being in England, and with your good countenance
protect against the malice of evill mouthes, which are alwaies wide open to carpe at
and misconstrue my simple meaning. I pray continually for your happinesse. From
my house of Kilcolman the 27. of December. 1591.*

Yours ever humbly.
Ed. Sp.

The shepheards boy (best knowen by that name)
That after *Tityrus* first sung his lay,
Laies of sweet love, without rebuke or blame,
Sate (as his custome was) upon a day,
Charming his oaten pipe unto his peres,   5
The shepheard swaines that did about him play:
Who all the while with greedie listfull eares,
Did stand astonisht at his curious skill,
Like hartlesse deare, dismayd with thunders sound.
At last when as he piped had his fill,   10

---

* *Stanneries* (or Stannaries): tin-mining districts.
2 *Tityrus:* Chaucer (with undertones of Virgil).   5 *Charming:* playing.
7 *Listfull:* attentive.   9 *Hartlesse:* timid.

He rested him: and sitting then around,
One of those groomes (a jolly groome was he,
As ever piped on an oaten reed,
And lov'd this shepheard dearest in degree,
Hight *Hobbinol*) gan thus to him areed.   15
  Colin my liefe, my life, how great a losse
Had all the shepheards nation by thy lacke!
And I poore swaine of many greatest crosse:
That sith thy *Muse* first since thy turning backe
Was heard to sound as she was wont on hye,   20
Hast made us all so blessed and so blythe.
Whilest thou wast hence, all dead in dole did lie:
The woods were heard to waile full many a sythe,
And all their birds with silence to complaine:
The fields with faded flowers did seem to mourne,   25
And all their flocks from feeding to refraine:
The running waters wept for thy returne,
And all their fish with languour did lament:
But now both woods and fields, and floods revive,
Sith thou art come, their cause of meriment,   30
That us late dead, hast made againe alive:
But were it not too painfull to repeat
The passed fortunes, which to thee befell
In thy late voyage, we thee would entreat,
Now at thy leisure them to us to tell.   35
  To whom the shepheard gently answered thus,
Hobbin thou temptest me to that I covet:
For of good passed newly to discus,
By dubble usurie doth twise renew it.
And since I saw that Angels blessed eie,   40
Her worlds bright sun, her heavens fairest light,
My mind full of my thoughts satietie,
Doth feed on sweet contentment of that sight:
Since that same day in nought I take delight,
Ne feeling have in any earthly pleasure,   45
But in remembrance of that glorious bright,
My lifes sole blisse, my hearts eternall threasure.

12 *Groomes:* young shepherds.   15 *Hight:* called; *Hobbinol:* some-
times said to be Spenser's friend Gabriel Harvey (1545?-1630?), but
Harvey is not likely to have been living in Ireland; *gan:* began to, did;
areed: proclaim, talk.   16 *Colin:* Spenser is Colin Clout, the simple,
rustic shepherd-poet; *liefe:* dear.   18 *Crosse:* affliction, 'greatest'
because of his special friendship.   19 *Sith:* since.   22 *Dole:* sadness.
23 *Sythe:* time.   39 *Usurie:* interest.   40 *Angel:* Queen Elizabeth.
45 *Ne:* nor.   46 *Bright:* brilliant person.

Wake then my pipe, my sleepie *Muse* awake,
Till I have told her praises lasting long:
Hobbin desires, thou maist it not forsake,   50
Harke then ye jolly shepheards to my song.
   With that they all gan throng about him neare,
With hungrie eares to heare his harmonie:
The whiles their flocks devoyd of dangers feare,
Did round about them feed at libertie.   55
   One day (quoth he) I sat, (as was my trade)
Under the foote of *Mole* that mountaine hore,
Keeping my sheepe amongst the cooly shade,
Of the greene alders by the *Mullaes* shore:
There a straunge shepheard chaunst to find me out,   60
Whether allured with my pipes delight,
Whose pleasing sound yshrilled far about,
Or thither led by chaunce, I know not right:
Whom when I asked from what place he came,
And how he hight, himselfe he did ycleepe,   65
The shepheard of the Ocean by name,
And said he came far from the main-sea deepe.
He sitting me beside in that same shade,
Provoked me to plaie some pleasant fit,
And when he heard the musicke which I made,   70
He found himselfe full greatly pleasd at it:
Yet æmuling my pipe, he tooke in hond
My pipe before that æmuled of many,
And plaid theron; (for well that skill he cond)
Himselfe as skilfull in that art as any.   75
He pip'd, I sung; and when he sung, I piped,
By chaunge of turnes, each making other mery,
Neither envying other, nor envied,
So piped we, untill we both were weary.
   There interrupting him, a bonie swaine,   80
That *Cuddy* hight, him thus atweene bespake:
And should it not thy readie course restraine,
I would request thee *Colin*, for my sake,

---

57 *Mole:* used by Spenser for a range of mountains in Southern Ireland, including the Ballyhoura and Galty hills, stretching from Buttevant to Cahir; *hore:* grey. 59 *Mulla:* Spenser's name for the river Awbeg, a tributary of the Blackwater, rising in the Ballyhoura hills. 60 *A straunge shepheard:* Sir Walter Raleigh (*c.* 1552-1618). 65 *Hight:* was called; *ycleepe:* call. 66 reflecting Raleigh's fame as a voyager; cf. his poem to Queen Elizabeth entitled *The Ocean to Cynthia.* 69 *Fit:* piece of music. 72 *Æmuling:* emulating. 74 *Cond:* had learned. 80 *Bonie:* good-looking. 81 *Cuddy:* identification dubious.

To tell what thou didst sing, when he did plaie.
For well I weene it worth recounting was,   85
Whether it were some hymne, or morall laie,
Or carol made to praise thy loved lasse.
   Nor of my love, nor of my losse (quoth he).
I then did sing, as then occasion fell:
For love had me forlorne, forlorne of me,   90
That made me in that desart chose to dwell.
But of my river *Bregogs* love I soong,
Which to the shiny *Mulla* he did beare,
And yet doth beare, and ever will, so long
As water doth within his bancks appeare.   95
   Of fellowship (said then that bony Boy)
Record to us that lovely lay againe:
The staie whereof, shall nought these eares annoy,
Who all that *Colin* makes, do covet faine.
   Heare then (quoth he) the tenor of my tale,   100
In sort as I it to that shepheard told:
No leasing new, nor Grandams fable stale,
But auncient truth confirm'd with credence old.
   Old father *Mole*, (*Mole* hight that mountain gray
That walls the Northside of *Armulla* dale)   105
He had a daughter fresh as floure of May,
Which gave that name unto that pleasant vale;
Mulla the daughter of old *Mole*, so hight
The Nimph, which of that water course has charge,
That springing out of *Mole*, doth run downe right   110
To *Buttevant*, where spreading forth at large,
It giveth name unto that auncient Cittie,
Which *Kilnemullah* cleped is of old:
Whose ragged ruines breed great ruth and pittie,
To travailers, which it from far behold.   115
Full faine she lov'd, and was belov'd full faine,
Of her owne brother river, *Bregog* hight,
So hight because of this deceitfull traine,
Which he with *Mulla* wrought to win delight.
But her old sire more carefull of her good,   120

---

85 *Weene:* suppose. 90 *Forlorne:* deserted. 92 *Bregog:* river flowing
through Spenser's land at Kilcolman and joining the river Awbeg.
96 *Of fellowship:* for friendship's sake. 98 *Staie:* duration. 102 *Leas-
ing:* falsehood. 105 *Armulla:* Spenser's name for the valley of the
river Blackwater. 109 *Nimph:* nature-spirit. 111 *Buttevant:* town on
the Awbeg, a few miles from Kilcolman. 112-13 Spenser's etymology.
113 *Cleped:* called. 118 Bregog means 'deceitful'; *traine:* stratagem.

And meaning her much better to preferre,
Did thinke to match her with the neighbour flood,
Which *Allo* hight, Broad-water called farre:
And wrought so well with his continuall paine,
That he that river for his daughter wonne: 125
The dowre agreed, the day assigned plaine,
The place appointed where it should be doone.
Nath'lesse the Nymph her former liking held;
For love will not be drawne, but must be ledde,
And *Bregog* did so well her fancie weld,   130
That her good will he got her first to wedde.
But for her father sitting still on hie,
Did warily still watch which way she went,
And eke from far observ'd with jealous eie,
Which way his course the wanton *Bregog* bent,   135
Him to deceive for all his watchfull ward,
The wily lover did devise this slight:
First into many parts his streame he shar'd,
That whilest the one was watcht, the other might
Pass unespide to meete her by the way;   140
And then besides, those little streames so broken
He under ground so closely did convay,
That of their passage doth appeare no token,
Till they into the *Mullaes* water slide.
So secretly did he his love enjoy: 145
Yet not so secret, but it was descride,
And told her father by a shepheards boy.
Who wondrous wroth for that so foule despight,
In great avenge did roll downe from his hill
Huge mightie stones, the which encomber might   150
His passage, and his water-courses spill.
So of a River, which he was of old,
He none was made, but scattred all to nought,
And lost emong those rocks into him rold,
Did lose his name: so deare his love he bought.   155
    Which having said, him *Thestylis* bespake,
Now by my life this was a mery lay:

123 *Allo . . . Broad-water:* now the Blackwater. 130 *Weld:* control.
131 *Wedde:* pledge as his. 132 *For:* because. 134 *Eke:* also.
141-4 The Bregog sinks underground for two miles of its course and re-
appears just before it joins the Awbeg. Spenser, like James Joyce after
him, mythologises from genuine topography. The 'stones' of line 150
are boulders loosened by glacial action. 155 *Lose his name:* i.e. as a
river in the sense of a continuously visible stream. 156 *Thestylis:*
Spenser's friend Lodowick Bryskett (d.1611).

Worthie of *Colin* selfe, that did it make.
But read now eke of friendship I thee pray,
What dittie did that other shepheard sing?   160
For I do covet most the same to heare,
As men use most to covet forreine thing.
That shall I eke (quoth he) to you declare.
His song was all a lamentable lay,
Of great unkindnesse, and of usage hard,   165
Of *Cynthia* the Ladie of the sea,
Which from her presence faultlesse him debard.
And ever and anon with singults rife,
He cryed out, to make his undersong
Ah my loves queene, and goddesse of my life,   170
Who shall me pittie, when thou doest me wrong?
    Then gan a gentle bony lasse to speake,
That *Marin* hight, Right well he sure did plaine:
That could great *Cynthiaes* sore displeasure breake,
And move to take him to her grace againe.   175
But tell on further *Colin*, as befell
Twixt him and thee, that thee did hence dissuade.
    When thus our pipes we both had wearied well,
(Quoth he) and each an end of singing made,
He gan to cast great lyking to my lore,   180
And great dislyking to my lucklesse lot:
That banisht had my selfe, like wight forlore,
Into that waste, where I was quite forgot.
The which to leave, thenceforth he counseld mee,
Unmeet for man, in whom was ought regardfull,   185
And wend with him, his *Cynthia* to see:
Whose grace was great, and bounty most rewardfull.
Besides her peerlesse skill in making well
And all the ornaments of wondrous wit,
Such as all womankynd did far excell: 190
Such as the world admyr'd and praised it:
So what with hope of good, and hate of ill,
He me perswaded forth with him to fare:
Nought tooke I with me, but mine oaten quill:
Small needments else need shepheard to prepare.   195
So to the sea we came; the sea? that is
A world of waters heaped up on hie,

159 *Read:* tell. 166 *Cynthia:* Queen Elizabeth. 168 *Singults:* sobs.
173 *Marin:* unidentified; *plaine:* complain. 180 *Lore:* ability in
discourse. 182 *Forlore:* abandoned. 185 *Regardfull:* worthy of re-
gard. 188 *Making:* composing poetry.

Rolling like mountaines in wide wildernesse,
Horrible, hideous, roaring with hoarse crie.
  ˜And is the sea (quoth *Coridon*) so fearfull?   200
    Fearful much more (quoth he) than hart can fear:
Thousand wyld beasts with deep mouthes gaping direfull
Therin stil wait poore passengers to teare.
Who life doth loath, and longs death to behold,
Before he die, alreadie dead with feare,   205
And yet would live with heart halfe stonie cold,
Let him to sea, and he shall see it there.
And yet as ghastly dreadfull, as it seemes,
Bold men presuming life for gaine to sell,
Dare tempt that gulf, and in those wandring stremes   210
Seek waies unknowne, waies leading down to hell.
For as we stood there waiting on the strond,
Behold an huge great vessell to us came,
Dauncing upon the waters back to lond,
As if it scornd the daunger of the same,   215
Yet was it but a wooden frame and fraile,
Glewed togither with some subtile matter,
Yet had it armes and wings, and head and taile,
And life to move it selfe upon the water.
Strange thing, how bold and swift the monster was,   220
That neither car'd for wynd, nor haile, nor raine,
Nor swelling waves, but thorough them did passe
So proudly, that she made them roare againe.
The same aboord us gently did receave,
And without harme us farre away did beare,   225
So farre that land our mother us did leave,
And nought but sea and heaven to us appeare.
Then hartlesse quite and full of inward feare,
That shepheard I besought to me to tell,
Under what skie, or in what world we were,   230
In which I saw no living people dwell.
Who me recomforting all that he might,
Told me that that same was the Regiment,
Of a great shepheardesse, that *Cynthia* hight,
His liege his Ladie, and his lifes Regent.   235
If then (quoth I) a shepheardesse she bee,
Where be the flockes and heards which she doth keep?
And where may I the hills and pastures see,
On which she useth for to feed her sheepe?

200 *Coridon:* unidentified. 233 *Regiment:* dominion. Elizabeth, like
Britannia, 'rules the waves'. 235 *Liege:* superior, overlord.

These be the hills (quoth he) the surges hie,   240
On which faire *Cynthia* her heards doth feed:
Her heards be thousand fishes with their frie,
Which in the bosome of the billowes breed.
Of them the shepheard which hath charge in chief,
Is *Triton* blowing loud his wreathed horne: 245
At sound whereof, they all for their relief
Wend too and fro at evening and at morne.
And *Proteus* eke with him does drive his heard
Of stinking Seales and Porcpisces together,
With hoary head and deawy dropping beard,   250
Compelling them which way he list, and whether.
And I among the rest of many least,
Have in the Ocean charge to me assignd:
Where I will live or die at her beheast,
And serve and honour her with faithfull mind.   255
Besides an hundred Nymphs all heavenly borne,
And of immortall race, doo still attend
To wash faire *Cynthiaes* sheep, when they be shorne,
And fold them up, when they have made an end.
Those be the shepheards which my *Cynthia* serve,   260
At sea, beside a thousand moe at land:
For land and sea my *Cynthia* doth deserve
To have in her commandement at hand.
Thereat I wondred much, till wondring more
And more, at length we land far off descryde: 265
Which sight much gladed me; for much afore
I feard, least land we never should have eyde:
Thereto our ship her course directly bent,
As if the way she perfectly had knowne.
We *Lunday* passe; by that same name is ment   270
An Island, which the first to west was showne.
From thence another world of land we kend,
Floting amid the sea in jeopardie,
And round about with mightie white rocks hemd,
Against the seas encroching crueltie.   275
Those same the shepheard told me, were the fields
In which dame *Cynthia* her landheards fed,
Faire goodly fields, than which *Armulla* yields
None fairer, nor more fruitfull to be red.

245 *Triton:* Greek sea-god, here the Lord High Admiral. 248
Proteus: Neptune's herdsman in Greek mythology, here a chief naval
officer. 249 *Porcpisces:* porpoises. 251 *List:* pleases. 270-1 Lundy
Island, in the Bristol Channel. 272 *Kend:* caught sight of. 279 *Red:*
found.

The first to which we nigh approched, was   280
An high headland thrust far into the sea,
Like to an horne, wherof the name it has,
Yet seemed to be a goodly pleasant lea:
There did a loftie mount at first us greet,
Which did a stately heape of stones upreare,   285
That seemd amid the surges for to fleet,
Much greater than that frame, which us did beare:
There did our ship her fruitfull wombe unlade,
And put us all ashore on *Cynthias* land.
    What land is that thou meanst (then *Cuddy* sayd)   290
And is there other, than whereon we stand?
    Ah *Cuddy* (then quoth *Colin*) thous a fon,
That hast not seene least part of natures worke;
Much more there is unkend, than thou doest kon,
And much more that does from mens knowledge lurke.   295
For that same land much larger is than this,
And other men and beasts and birds doth feed:
There fruitfull corne, faire trees, fresh herbage is
And all things else that living creatures need.
Besides most goodly rivers there appeare,   300
No whit inferiour to thy *Funchins* praise,
Or unto *Allo* or to *Mulla* cleare:
Nought hast thou foolish boy seene in thy daies.
But if that land be there (quoth he) as here,
And is theyr heaven likewise there all one?   305
And if like heaven, be heavenly graces there,
Like as in this same world where we do wone?
    Both heaven and heavenly graces do much more
(Quoth he) abound in that same land, than this.
For there all happie peace and plenteous store   310
Conspire in one to make contented blisse:
No wayling there nor wretchednesse is heard,
No bloodie issues nor no leprosies,
No griesly famine, nor no raging sweard,
No nightly bodrags, nor no hue and cries: 315
The shepheards there abroad may safely lie,
On hills and downes, withouten dread or daunger:
No ravenous wolves the good mans hope destroy,
Nor outlawes fell affray the forest raunger.

282 i.e. Cornwall.   284 *Loftie mount:*   perhaps St. Michael's Mount
near Penzance.   286 *Fleet:* float.   292 *Fon:* fool.   301 *Funchin:* the
river Funshion, tributary of the Blackwater.   307 *Wone:* live.   314
Sweard: sword.   315 *Bodrags:* raids (Irish).   316 *Abroad:* in the open.
319 *Affray:* terrify.

There learned arts do florish in great honor,   320
And Poets wits are had in peerlesse price:
Religion hath lay powre to rest upon her,
Advancing vertue and suppressing vice.
For end, all good, all grace there freely growes,
Had people grace it gratefully to use: 325
For God his gifts there plenteously bestowes,
But gracelesse men them greatly do abuse.
    But say on further, then said *Corylas*,
The rest of thine adventures, that betyded.
    Foorth on our voyage we by land did passe,   330
(Quoth he) as that same shepheard still us guyded,
Untill that we to *Cynthiaes* presence came:
Whose glorie, greater than my simple thought,
I found much greater than the former fame;
Such greatnes I cannot compare to ought: 335
But if I her like ought on earth might read,
I would her lyken to a crowne of lillies,
Upon a virgin brydes adorned head,
With Roses dight and Goolds and Daffadillies;
Or like the circlet of a Turtle true,   340
In which all colours of the rainbow bee;
Or like faire *Phebes* garlond shining new,
In which all pure perfection one may see.
But vaine it is to thinke by paragone
Of earthly things, to judge of things divine: 345
Her power, her mercy, and her wisedome, none
Can deeme, but who the Godhead can define.
Why then do I base shepheard bold and blind,
Presume the things so sacred to prophane?
More fit it is t'adore with humble mind,   350
The image of the heavens in shape humane.
    With that *Alexis* broke his tale asunder,
Saying, By wondring at thy *Cynthiaes* praise,
Colin, thy selfe thou mak'st us more to wonder,
And her upraising, doest thy selfe upraise.   355
But let us heare what grace she shewed thee,
And how that shepheard strange, thy cause advanced?
    The shepheard of the Ocean (quoth he)
Unto that Goddesse grace me first enhanced,

322 *Rest upon:* support. 328 *Corylas:* unidentified. 336 *Read:* describe. 339 *Dight:* adorned; *goolds:* marigolds. 340-1 i.e. a dove's neck. 342 *Phebes garlond:* the glory of the moon, or perhaps a lunar rainbow. 344 *Paragone:* comparison. 352 *Alexis:* unidentified. 359 *Enhanced:* recommended.

And to mine oaten pipe enclin'd her eare, 360
That she thenceforth therein gan take delight,
And it desir'd at timely hours to heare,
All were my notes but rude and roughly dight.
For not by measure of her owne great mynd,
And wondrous worth she mott my simple song, 365
But joyd that country shepheard ought could fynd
Worth harkening to, emongst the learned throng.
   Why? (said *Alexis* then) what needeth shee
That is so great a shepheardesse her selfe,
And hath so many shepheards in her fee, 370
To heare thee sing, a simple silly Elfe?
Or be the shepheards which do serve her laesie,
That they list not their mery pipes applie?
Or be their pipes untunable and craesie,
That they cannot her honour worthylie? 375
   Ah nay (said *Colin*) neither so, nor so:
For better shepheards be not under skie,
Nor better hable, when they list to blow
Their pipes aloud, her name to glorifie.
There is good *Harpalus*, now woxen aged 380
In faithfull service of faire *Cynthia*:
And there is *Corydon* though meanly waged,
Yet hablest wit of most I know this day.
And there is sad *Alcyon* bent to mourne,
Though fit to frame an everlasting dittie, 385
Whose gentle spright for *Daphnes* death doth tourn
Sweet layes of love to endlesse plaints of pittie.
Ah pensive boy pursue that brave conceipt,
In thy sweet Eglantine of *Meriflure*,
Lift up thy notes unto their wonted height, 390
That may thy *Muse* and mates to mirth allure.
There eke is *Palin* worthie of great praise,
Albe he envie at my rustick quill:

363 *All were my notes:* although my notes were. 365 *Mott:* measured.
369 *Shepheardesse:* i.e. poetess. 380 ff. Harpalus, Corydon, Palin,
Alcon, Amyntas, and Aetion are poets whose identification is quite
uncertain. Alcyon (line 384) is Sir Arthur Gorges (*c.* 1557-1625),
Palemon (line 396) seems to be Thomas Churchyard (1520?-1604),
Alabaster is William Alabaster (1567-1640), Daniell (line 424) is
Samuel Daniel (*c.* 1563-1619), and Astrofell (line 449) is Sir Philip
Sidney (1554-86). 380 *Woxen:* grown. 386 *Spright:* spirit; *Daphne:*
his wife, Lady Douglas Howard, who died 1590. Cf. Spenser's *Daph-
naïda.* 388 *Conceipt:* conception. 389 In a pastoral poem by Gorges,
Eglantine stands for Elizabeth, and Meriflure (or Mirefleur) is the royal
tower in Greenwich Park. Presumably *Eglantine of Meriflure* is a lost
poem by Gorges. 393 *Albe:* although.

And there is pleasing *Alcon,* could he raise
His tunes from laies to matter of more skill.   395
And there is old *Palemon* free from spight,
Whose carefull pipe may make the hearer rew:
Yet he himselfe may rewed be more right,
That sung so long untill quite hoarse he grew.
And there is *Alabaster* throughly taught,   400
In all this skill, though knowen yet to few:
Yet were he knowne to *Cynthia* as he ought,
His Eliseïs would be redde anew.
Who lives that can match that heroick song,
Which he hath of that mightie Princesse made?   405
O dreaded Dread, do not thy selfe that wrong,
To let thy fame lie so in hidden shade:
But call it forth, O call him forth to thee,
To end thy glorie which he hath begun:
That when he finisht hath as it should be,   410
No braver Poeme can be under Sun.
Nor *Po* nor *Tyburs* swans so much renowned,
Nor all the brood of *Greece* so highly praised,
Can match that *Muse* when it with bayes is crowned,
And to the pitch of her perfection raised.   415
And there is a new shepheard late up sprong,
The which doth all afore him far surpasse:
Appearing well in that well tuned song,
Which late he sung unto a scornfull lasse.
Yet doth his trembling *Muse* but lowly flie,   420
As daring not too rashly mount on hight,
And doth her tender plumes as yet but trie,
In loves soft laies and looser thoughts delight.
Then rouze thy feathers quickly *Daniell,*
And to what course thou please thy selfe advance: 425
But most me seemes, thy accent will excell,
In Tragick plaints and passionate mischance.
And there that shepheard of the Ocean is,
That spends his wit in loves consuming smart:
Full sweetly tempred is that *Muse* of his   430
That can empierce a Princes mightie hart.
There also is (ah no, he is not now)
But since I said he is, he quite is gone,
Amyntas quite is gone and lies full low,
Having his *Amaryllis* left to mone.   435

397 *Carefull:* sad.   403 *Eliseïs:* an unfinished epic poem in honour of
Elizabeth.   412 *Po nor Tyburs swans:* the Roman poets.

Helpe, O ye shepheards helpe ye all in this,
Helpe *Amaryllis* this her losse to mourne:
Her losse is yours, your losse *Amyntas* is,
Amyntas floure of shepheards pride forlorne:
He whilest he lived was the noblest swaine,   440
That ever piped in an oaten quill:
Both did he other, which could pipe, maintaine,
And eke could pipe himselfe with passing skill.
And there though last not least is *Aetion*,
A gentler shepheard may no where be found: 445
Whose *Muse* full of high thoughts invention,
Doth like himselfe Heroically sound.
All these, and many others mo remaine,
Now after *Astrofell* is dead and gone:
But while as *Astrofell* did live and raine,   450
Amongst all these was none his Paragone.
All these do florish in their sundry kynd,
And do their *Cynthia* immortall make:
Yet found I lyking in her royall mynd,
Not for my skill, but for that shepheards sake.   455
    Then spake a lovely lasse, hight *Lucida*,
Shepheard, enough of shepheards thou hast told,
Which favour thee, and honour *Cynthia*:
But of so many Nymphs which she doth hold
In her retinew, thou hast nothing sayd;   460
That seems, with none of them thou favor foundest,
Or art ingratefull to each gentle mayd,
That none of all their due deserts resoundest.
    Ah far be it (quoth *Colin Clout*) fro me,
That I of gentle Mayds should ill deserve: 465
For that my selfe I do professe to be
Vassall to one, whom all my dayes I serve;
The beame of beautie sparkled from above,
The floure of vertue and pure chastitie,
The blossome of sweet joy and perfect love,   470
The pearle of peerlesse grace and modestie:
To her my thoughts I daily dedicate,
To her my heart I nightly martyrize:
To her my love I lowly do prostrate,
To her my life I wholly sacrifice: 475
My thought, my heart, my love, my life is shee,
And I hers ever onely, ever one:
One ever I all vowed hers to bee,
One ever I, and others never none.

451 *Paragone:* equal.   456 *Lucida:* unidentified.   459 *Nymphs:* ladies.

Then thus *Melissa* said; Thrice happie Mayd,   480
Whom thou doest so enforce to deifie:
That woods, and hills, and valleyes thou hast made
Her name to eccho unto heaven hie.
But say, who else vouchsafed thee of grace?
    They all (quoth he) me graced goodly well,   485
That all I praise, but in the highest place,
Urania, sister unto *Astrofell,*
In whose brave mynd, as in a golden cofer,
All heavenly gifts and riches locked are:
More rich than pearles of *Ynde,* or gold of *Opher,*   490
And in her sex more wonderfull and rare.
Ne lesse praise worthie I *Theana* read,
Whose goodly beames though they be over dight
With mourning stole of carefull wydowhead,
Yet through that darksome vale do glister bright;   495
She is the well of bountie and brave mynd,
Excelling most in glorie and great light:
She is the ornament of womankind,
And Courtes chief garlond with all vertues dight.
Therefore great *Cynthia* her in chiefest grace   500
Doth hold, and next unto her selfe advance,
Well worthie of so honourable place,
For her great worth and noble governance.
Ne lesse praise worthie is her sister deare,
Faire *Marian,* the *Muses* onely darling: 505
Whose beautie shyneth as the morning cleare,
With silver deaw upon the roses pearling.
Ne lesse praise worthie is *Mansilia,*
Best knowne by bearing up great *Cynthiaes* traine:
That same is she to whom *Daphnaida*   510
Upon her neeces death I did complaine.
She is the paterne of true womanhead,
And onely mirrhor of feminitie:
Worthie next after *Cynthia* to tread,
As she is next her in nobilitie.   515

480 *Melissa:* unidentified. 487 *Urania:* Mary Sidney, Countess of
Pembroke (1557-1621). 490 *Ophir* (cf. *1 Kings* ix. 28) has not been
identified: perhaps Southern Arabia. 492 *Theana:* probably Anne,
widow of Ambrose Dudley, Earl of Warwick, who died 1590. 493
Dight: covered. 499 *Dight:* adorned. 505 *Marian:* seems to be
Helena, Marchioness of Northampton (1549-1635); after the marquis's
death in 1571, she married Sir Thomas Gorges and became Sir Arthur
Gorges' aunt; Spenser dedicated his poem *Daphnaïda* to her.

Ne lesse praise worthie *Galathea* seemes,
Than best of all that honourable crew,
Faire *Galathea* with bright shining beames,
Inflaming feeble eyes that her do view.
She there then waited upon *Cynthia*,   520
Yet there is not her won, but here with us
About the borders of our rich *Coshma*,
Now made of *Maa* the Nymph delitious.
Ne lesse praisworthie faire *Neæra* is,
Neæra ours, not theirs, though there she be,   525
For of the famous Shure, the Nymph she is,
For high desert, advaunst to that degree.
She is the blosome of grace and curtesie,
Adorned with all honourable parts:
She is the braunch of true nobilitie,   530
Belov'd of high and low with faithfull harts.
Ne lesse praisworthie *Stella* do I read,
Though nought my praises of her needed arre,
Whom verse of noblest shepheard lately dead
Hath prais'd and rais'd above each other starre.   535
Ne lesse praisworthie are the sisters three,
The honor of the noble familie:
Of which I meanest boast my selfe to be,
And most that unto them I am so nie.
Phyllis, Charillis, and sweet *Amaryllis,*   540
Phyllis the faire, is eldest of the three:
The next to her, is bountifull *Charillis.*
But th'youngest is the highest in degree.
Phyllis the floure of rare perfection,
Faire spreading forth her leaves with fresh delight,   545
That with their beauties amorous reflexion,
Bereave of sence each rash beholders sight.
But sweet *Charillis* is the Paragone
Of peerless price, and ornament of praise,
Admyr'd of all, yet envied of none,   550
Through the myld temperance of her goodly raies.

---

516 *Galathea:* identification dubious.   521 *Won:* home.   522 *Coshma:*
barony in the middle valley of the Maigue.   523 *Maa:* river Maigue,
rising north of Kilcolman and flowing into the Shannon estuary.   524
Neæra: identification dubious.   526 *Shure:* river Suir, flowing into
Waterford estuary.   532 *Stella:* identification dubious; *read:* count.
534 Sidney's sonnet-sequence *Astrophel and Stella.* 540 Elizabeth, Anne,
and Alice Spencer, daughters of Sir John Spencer (d.1586) of Althorp,
Northamptonshire.

Thrice happie do I hold thee noble swaine.
The which art of so rich a spoile possest,
And it embracing deare without disdaine,
Hast sole possession in so chaste a brest: 555
Of all the shepheards daughters which there bee,
(And yet there be the fairest under skie,
Or that elsewhere I ever yet did see)
A fairer Nymph yet never saw mine eie:
She is the pride and primrose of the rest,   560
Made by the maker selfe to be admired:
And like a goodly beacon high addrest,
That is with sparks of heavenle beautie fired.
But *Amaryllis*, whether fortunate,
Or else unfortunate may I aread,   565
That freed is from *Cupids* yoke by fate,
Since which she doth new bands adventure dread.
Shepheard what ever thou hast heard to be
In this or that praysd diversly apart,
In her thou maist them all assembled see,   570
And seald up in the threasure of her hart.
Ne thee lesse worthie gentle *Flavia*,
For thy chaste life and vertue I esteeme:
Ne thee lesse worthie curteous *Candida*,
For thy true love and loyaltie I deeme.   575
Besides yet many mo that *Cynthia* serve,
Right noble Nymphs, and high to be commended:
But if I all should praise as they deserve,
This sun would faile me ere I halfe had ended.
Therefore in closure of a thankfull mynd,   580
I deeme it best to hold eternally,
Their bounteous deeds and noble favours shrynd,
Than by discourse them to indignifie.
    So having said, *Aglaura* him bespake:
Colin, well worthie were those goodly favours   585
Bestowd on thee, that so of them doest make,
And them requitest with thy thankfull labours.
But of great *Cynthiaes* goodnesse and high grace,
Finish the storie which thou hast begunne.
    More eath (quoth he) it is in such a case   590
How to begin, than know how to have donne.

552 *Thee:* perhaps her third husband, Robert Sackville, Earl of Dorset
(1561-1609), whom she married 1592. 566 Alice's husband, the Earl of
Derby, died 1594. 567 *New bands adventure:* risk another marriage. 572 ff.
Flavia and Candida are probably meant as types rather than as indivi-
duals. 584 *Aglaura:* unidentified. 586 *Make:* write poetry. 590 *Eath:* easy.

For everie gift and everie goodly meed,
Which she on me bestowd, demaunds a day;
And everie day, in which she did a deed,
Demaunds a yeare it duly to display.   595
Her words were like a streame of honny fleeting,
The which doth softly trickle from the hive:
Hable to melt the hearers heart unweeting,
And eke to make the dead againe alive.
Her deeds were like great clusters of ripe grapes,   600
Which load the braunches of the fruitfull vine:
Offring to fall into each mouth that gapes,
And fill the same with store of timely wine.
Her lookes were like beames of the morning Sun,
Forth looking through the windowes of the East: 605
When first the fleecie cattell have begun
Upon the perled grasse to make their feast.
Her thoughts are like the fume of Franckincence,
Which from a golden Censer forth doth rise:
And throwing forth sweet odours mounts fro thence   610
In rolling globes up to the vauted skies.
There she beholds with high aspiring thought,
The cradle of her owne creation:
Emongst the seats of Angels heavenly wrought,
Much like an Angell in all forme and fashion.   615
    Colin (said Cuddy then) thou hast forgot
Thy selfe, me seemes, too much, to mount so hie
Such loftie flight, base shepheard seemeth not,
From flocks and fields, to Angels and to skie.
    True (answered he) but her great excellence,   620
Lifts me above the measure of my might:
That being fild with furious insolence,
I feele my selfe like one yrapt in spright.
For when I thinke of her, as oft I ought,
Then want I words to speake it fitly forth: 625
And when I speake of her what I have thought,
I cannot thinke according to her worth.
Yet will I thinke of her, yet will I speake,
So long as life my limbs doth hold together,
And when as death these vitall bands shall breake,   630
Her name recorded I will leave for ever.
Her name in every tree I will endosse,
That as the trees do grow, her name may grow:

592 *Meed:* reward. 622 *Furious insolence:* exulting inspiration. 632
Endosse: inscribe.

And in the ground each where will it engrosse,
And fill with stones, that all men may it know.   635
The speaking woods and murmuring waters fall,
Her name Ile teach in knowen termes to frame:
And eke my lambs when for their dams they call,
Ile teach to call for *Cynthia* by name.
And long while after I am dead and rotten,   640
Amongst the shepheards daughters dancing rownd,
My layes made of her shall not be forgotten,
But sung by them with flowry gyrlonds crownd.
And ye, who so ye be, that shall survive:
When as ye heare her memory renewed,   645
Be witnesse of her bountie here alive,
Which she to *Colin* her poore shepheard shewed.
    Much was the whole assembly of those heards,
Moov'd at his speech, so feelingly he spake:
And stood awhile astonisht at his words,   650
Till *Thestylis* at last their silence brake,
Saying, Why *Colin*, since thou foundst such grace
With *Cynthia* and all her noble crew:
Why didst thou ever leave that happie place,
In which such wealth might unto thee accrew?   655
And back returnedst to this barrein soyle,
Where cold and care and penury do dwell:
Here to keep sheepe, with hunger and with toyle,
Most wretched he, that is and cannot tell.
    Happie indeed (said *Colin*) I him hold,   660
That may that blessed presence still enjoy,
Of fortune and of envy uncomptrold,
Which still are wont most happie states t'annoy:
But I by that which little while I prooved:
Some part of those enormities did see,   665
The which in Court continually hooved,
And followd those which happie seemd to bee.
Therefore I silly man, whose former dayes
Had in rude fields bene altogether spent,
Durst not adventure such unknowen wayes,   670
Nor trust the guile of fortunes blandishment,
But rather chose back to my sheep to tourne,
Whose utmost hardnesse I before had tryde,
Then having learnd repentance late, to mourne
Emongst those wretches which I there descryde.   675
    Shepheard (said *Thestylis*) it seemes of spight

634 *Engrosse:* clearly write.   666 *Hooved:* persisted.

Thou speakest thus gainst their felicitie,
Which thou enviest, rather than of right
That ought in them blameworthie thou doest spie.
  Cause have I none (quoth he) of cancred will   680
To quite them ill, that me demeand so well:
But selfe-regard of private good or ill,
Moves me of each, so as I found, to tell,
And eke to warne yong shepheards wandring wit,
Which through report of that lives painted blisse,   685
Abandon quiet home, to seeke for it,
And leave their lambes to losse, misled amisse.
For sooth to say, it is no sort of life,
For shepeard fit to lead in that same place,
Where each one seeks with malice and with strife,   690
To thrust downe other into foule disgrace,
Himselfe to raise: and he doth soonest rise
That best can handle his deceitfull wit,
In subtil shifts, and finest sleights devise,
Either by slaundring his well deemed name,   695
Through leasings lewd, and fained forgerie:
Or else by breeding him some blot of blame,
By creeping close into his secrecie;
To which him needs a guilefull hollow hart,
Masked with faire dissembling curtesie,   700
A filed toung furnisht with tearmes of art,
No art of schoole, but Courtiers schoolery.
For arts of schoole have there small countenance,
Counted but toyes to busie ydle braines,
And there professours find small maintenance,   705
But to be instruments of others gaines.
Ne is there place for any gentle wit,
Unlesse to please, it selfe it can applie:
But shouldred is, or out of doore quite shit,
As base, or blunt, unmeet for melodie.   710
For each mans worth is measured by his weed,
As harts by hornes, or asses by their eares:
Yet asses been not all whose eares exceed,
Nor yet all harts, that hornes the highest beares.
For highest lookes have not the highest mynd,   715
Nor haughtie words most full of highest thoughts:
But are like bladders blowen up with wynd,
That being prickt do vanish into noughts.

680 *Cancred:* malignant. 681 *Demeand:* treated. 696 *Lewd:* wicked.
701 *Filed:* polished. 709 *Shit:* shut. 711 *Weed:* dress.

Even such is all their vaunted vanitie,
Nought else but smoke, that fumeth soone away: 720
Such is their glorie that in simple eie
Seeme greatest, when their garments are most gay.
So they themselves for praise of fooles do sell,
And all their wealth for painting on a wall;
With price whereof, they buy a golden bell,   725
And purchase highest rowmes in bowre and hall:
Whiles single Truth and simple honestie
Do wander up and downe despys'd of all;
Their plaine attire such glorious gallantry
Disdaines so much, that none them in doth call.   730
  Ah *Colin* (then said *Hobbinol*) the blame
Which thou imputest, is too generall,
As if not any gentle wit of name,
Nor honest mynd might there be found at all.
For well I wot, sith I my selfe was there,   735
To wait on *Lobbin* (*Lobbin* well thou knewest)
Full many worthie ones then waiting were,
As ever else in Princes Court thou vewest.
Of which, among you many yet remaine,
Whose names I cannot readily now ghesse: 740
Those that poore Sutors papers do retaine,
And those that skill of medicine professe.
And those that do to *Cynthia* expound
The ledden of straunge languages in charge:
For *Cynthia* doth in sciences abound,   745
And gives to their professors stipends large.
Therefore unjustly thou doest wyte them all,
For that which thou mislikedst in a few.
  Blame is (quoth he) more blamelesse generall,
Than that which private errours doth pursew: 750
For well I wot, that there amongst them bee,
Full many persons of right worthie parts,
Both for report of spotlesse honestie,
And for profession of all learned arts,
Whose praise hereby no whit impaired is,   755
Though blame do light on those that faultie bee,
For all the rest do most-what fare amis,
And yet their owne misfaring will not see:
For either they be puffed up with pride,
Or fraught with envie that their galls do swell,   760

735 *Wot:* know.   736 *Lobbin:* perhaps Robert Dudley, Earl of Leicester (*c.* 1532-88).   744 *Ledden:* form of speaking.   747 *Wyte:* blame.

Or they their dayes to ydlenesse divide,
Or drownded lie in pleasures wastefull well,
In which like Moldwarps nousling still they lurke,
Unmyndfull of chiefe parts of manlinesse,
And do themselves for want of other worke, 765
Vaine votaries of laesie love professe,
Whose service high so basely they ensew,
That *Cupid* selfe of them ashamed is,
And mustring all his men in *Venus* vew,
Denies them quite for servitors of his. 770
    And is love then (said *Corylas*) once knowne
In Court, and his sweet lore professed there?
I weened sure he was our God alone:
And only woond in fields and forests here.
    Not so (quoth he) love most aboundeth there. 775
For all the walls and windows there are writ,
All full of love, and love, and love my deare,
And all their talke and studie is of it.
Ne any there doth brave or valiant seeme,
Unlesse that some gay Mistresse badge he beares: 780
Ne any one himselfe doth ought esteeme,
Unlesse he swim in love up to the eares.
But they of love and of his sacred lere,
(As it should be) all otherwise devise,
Than we poore shepheards are accustomed here, 785
And him do sue and serve all otherwise.
For with lewd speeches and licentious deeds,
His mightie mysteries they do prophane,
And use his ydle name to other needs,
But as a complement for courting vaine. 790
So him they do not serve as they professe,
But make him serve to them for sordid uses,
Ah my dread Lord, that doest liege hearts possesse,
Avenge thy selfe on them for their abuses.
But we poore shepheards, whether rightly so, 795
Or through our rudenesse into errour led,
Do make religion how we rashly go,
To serve that God, that is so greatly dred;
For him the greatest of the Gods we deeme,
Borne without Syre or couples, of one kynd, 800

763 *Moldwarps:* moles. 767 *Ensew:* pursue. 768 *Cupid:* boy-god of
love and son of the love-goddess Venus in Roman mythology, but here
equated rather with the more powerful Greek Eros. 783 *Lere:* lore.
797 *Make religion:* act with the greatest care. 800 *Couples of one kynd:*
sexual conjunction.

For *Venus* selfe doth soly couples seeme,
Both male and female, through commixture joynd,
So pure and spotlesse *Cupid* forth she brought,
And in the gardens of *Adonis* nurst:
Where growing, he his owne perfection wrought,   805
And shortly was of all the Gods the first.
Then got he bow and shafts of gold and lead,
In which so fell and puissant he grew,
That *Jove* himselfe his powre began to dread,
And taking up to heaven, him godded new.   810
From thence he shootes his arrowes every where
Into the world, at randon as he will,
On us fraile men, his wretched vassals here,
Like as himselfe us pleaseth, save or spill.
So we him worship, so we him adore   815
With humble hearts to heaven uplifted hie,
That to true loves he may us evermore
Preferre, and of their grace us dignifie:
Ne is there shepheard, ne yet shepheards swaine,
What ever feeds in forest or in field,   820
That dare with evil deed or leasing vaine
Blaspheme his powre, or termes unworthie yield.
    Shepheard it seemes that some celestiall rage
Of love (quoth *Cuddy*) is breath'd into thy brest,
That powreth forth these oracles so sage,   825
Of that high powre, wherewith thou art possest.
But never wist I till this present day
Albe of love I alwayes humbly deemed,
That he was such an one, as thou doest say,
And so religiously to be esteemed.   830
Well may it seeme by this thy deep insight,
That of that God the Priest thou shouldest bee:
So well thou wot'st the mysterie of his might,
As if his godhead thou didst present see.
    Of loves perfection perfectly to speake,   835
Or of his nature rightly to define,
Indeed (said *Colin*) passeth reasons reach,
And needs his priest t'expresse his powre divine.
For long before the world he was y'bore
And bred above in *Venus* bosome deare: 840

804 *Gardens of Adonis:* Cf. Spenser's *Faerie Queene*, III. vi. 29ff. Adonis
was the lover of Aphrodite, Greek love-goddess. 807 *Gold and lead:*
happy and unhappy love. 810 *Godded:* deified. 814 *Spill:* destroy.
818 *Preferre:* promote. 827 *Wist:* knew. 828 *Deemed:* thought.

For by his powre the world was made of yore,
And all that therein wondrous doth appeare.
For how should else things so far from attone
And so great enemies as of them bee,
Be ever drawne together into one,   845
And taught in such accordance to agree?
Through him the cold began to covet heat,
And water fire; the light to mount on hie,
And th'heavie downe to peize; the hungry t'eat
And voydnesse to seeke full satietie.   850
So being former foes, they wexed friends,
And gan by litle learne to love each other:
So being knit, they brought forth other kynds
Out of the fruitfull wombe of their great mother.
Then first gan heaven out of darknesse dread   855
For to appeare, and brought forth chearfull day:
Next gan the earth to shew her naked head,
Out of deep waters which her drownd alway.
And shortly after, everie living wight
Crept forth like wormes out of her slimie nature,   860
Soone as on them the Suns life giving light,
Had powred kindly heat and formall feature,
Thenceforth they gan each one his like to love,
And like himselfe desire for to beget,
And Lyon chose his mate, the Turtle Dove   865
Her deare, the Dolphin his owne Dolphinet:
But man that had the sparke of reasons might,
More than the rest to rule his passion,
Chose for his love the fairest in his sight,
Like as himselfe was fairest by creation.   870
For beautie is the bayt which with delight
Doth man allure, for to enlarge his kynd,
Beautie the burning lamp of heavens light,
Darting her beames into each feeble mynd:
Against whose powre, nor God nor man can fynd,   875
Defence, ne ward the daunger of the wound,
But being hurt, seeke to be medicynd
Of her that first did stir that mortall stownd.
Then do they cry and call to love apace,
With praiers lowd importuning the skie,   880
Whence he them heares, and when he list shew grace,
Does graunt them grace that otherwise would die.

843 *Attone:* agreement. 844 *As of them bee:* as they are amongst
themselves. 849 *Peize:* weigh, press. 866 *Dolphinet:* female dolphin.
878 *Stownd:* assault.

So love is Lord of all the world by right,
And rules the creatures by his powrfull saw:
All being made the vassalls of his might,   885
Through secret sence which therto doth them draw.
Thus ought all lovers of their lord to deeme:
And with chaste heart to honor him alway:
But who so else doth otherwise esteeme,
Are outlawes, and his lore do disobay.   890
For their desire is base, and doth not merit,
The name of love, but of disloyall lust:
Ne mongst true lovers they shall place inherit,
But as Exuls out of his court be thrust.
    So having said, *Melissa* spake at will,   895
Colin, thou now full deeply hast divynd:
Of love and beautie, and with wondrous skill,
Hast *Cupid* selfe depainted in his kynd.
To thee are all true lovers greatly bound,
That doest their cause so mightily defend: 900
But most, all wemen are thy debtors found,
That doest their bountie still so much commend.
    That ill (said *Hobbinol*) they him requite,
For having loved ever one most deare:
He is repayd with scorne and foule despite,   905
That yrkes each gentle heart which it doth heare.
    Indeed (said *Lucid*) I have often heard
Faire *Rosalind* of divers fowly blamed:
For being to that swaine too cruell hard,
That her bright glorie else hath much defamed.   910
But who can tell what cause had that faire Mayd
To use him so that used her so well:
Or who with blame can justly her upbrayd,
For loving not? for who can love compell?
And sooth to say, it is foolhardie thing,   915
Rashly to wyten creatures so divine,
For demigods they be and first did spring
From heaven, though graft in frailnesse feminine.
And well I wote, that oft I heard it spoken,
How one that fairest *Helene* did revile,   920
Through judgement of the Gods to been ywroken
Lost both his eyes and so remaynd long while,

884 *Saw:* decree. 896 *Divynd:* interpreted and explained. 908
Rosalind: unidentified; *of divers:* by many. 920 The Greek poet
Stesichorus (*c.* 640-*c.* 555 B.C.) traditionally attacked Helen of Troy in
one of his poems and was punished with temporary blindness. 921
Ywroken: avenged.

Till he recanted had his wicked rimes,
And made amends to her with treble praise:
Beware therefore, ye groomes, I read betimes,   925
How rashly blame of *Rosalind* ye raise.
    Ah shepheards (then said *Colin*) ye ne weet
How great a guilt upon your heads ye draw:
To make so bold a doome with words unmeet,
Of thing celestiall which ye never saw.   930
For she is not like as the other crew
Of shepheards daughters which emongst you bee,
But of divine regard and heavenly hew,
Excelling all that ever ye did see.
Not then to her that scorned thing so base,   935
But to my selfe the blame that lookt so hie:
So hie her thoughts as she her selfe have place,
And loath each lowly thing with loftie eie.
Yet so much grace let her vouchsafe to grant
To simple swaine, sith her I may not love: 940
Yet that I may her honour paravant,
And praise her worth, though far my wit above.
Such grace shall be some guerdon for the griefe,
And long affliction which I have endured:
Such grace sometimes shall give me some reliefe,   945
And ease of paine which cannot be recured.
And ye my fellow shepheards which do see
And heare the languours of my too long dying,
Unto the world for ever witnesse bee,
That hers I die, nought to the world denying,   950
This simple trophe of her great conquest.
    So having ended, he from ground did rise,
And after him uprose eke all the rest:
All loth to part, but that the glooming skies
Warnd them to draw their bleating flocks to rest.   955

925 *Read:* advise.   929 *Doome:* judgement.   941 *Paravant:* above all
others.   946 *Recured:* healed.

EPITHALAMION

Celebrates Spenser's second marriage, to Elizabeth Boyle, probably on 11th June, 1594.

Ye learned sisters which have oftentimes
Beene to me ayding, others to adorne:
Whom ye thought worthy of your gracefull rymes,
That even the greatest did not greatly scorne
To heare theyr names sung in your simple layes,   5
But joyed in theyr prayse;
And when ye list your owne mishaps to mourne,
Which death, or love, or fortunes wreck did rayse,
Your string could soone to sadder tenor turne,
And teach the woods and waters to lament   10
Your dolefull dreriment:
Now lay those sorrowfull complaints aside,
And having all your heads with girland crownd,
Helpe me mine owne loves prayses to resound,
Ne let the same of any be envide: 15
So Orpheus did for his owne bride,
So I unto my selfe alone will sing,
The woods shall to me answer and my Eccho ring.

Early before the worlds light giving lampe,
His golden beame upon the hils doth spred,   20
Having disperst the nights unchearefull dampe,
Doe ye awake, and with fresh lusty-hed,
Go to the bowre of my beloved love,
My truest turtle dove,
Bid her awake; for Hymen is awake,   25
And long since ready forth his maske to move,
With his bright Tead that flames with many a flake,
And many a bachelor to waite on him,
In theyr fresh garments trim.
Bid her awake therefore and soone her dight,   30
For lo the wished day is come at last,

1 *Ye learned sisters:* the Muses. 7 *List:* wished. 15 *Ne:* nor. 16
Orpheus . . . bride: the poet Orpheus and his wife Eurydice in Greek
mythology. 22 *Lusty-hed:* energy, vigour. 25 *Hymen:* Greek god of
marriage. 26 *Maske:* 'masque', procession. 27 *Tead:* torch. 30 *Her
dight:* get herself dressed and ready.

That shall for al the paynes and sorrowes past,
Pay to her usury of long delight:
And whylest she doth her dight,
Doe ye to her of joy and solace sing,   35
That all the woods may answer and your eccho ring.

Bring with you all the Nymphes that you can heare
Both of the rivers and the forrests greene:
And of the sea that neighbours to her neare,
Al with gay girlands goodly wel beseene.   40
And let them also with them bring in hand,
Another gay girland
For my fayre love of lillyes and of roses,
Bound truelove wize with a blew silke riband.
And let them make great store of bridale poses,   45
And let them eeke bring store of other flowers
To deck the bridale bowers.
And let the ground whereas her foot shall tread,
For feare the stones her tender foot should wrong
Be strewed with fragrant flowers all along,   50
And diapred lyke the discolored mead.
Which done, doe at her chamber dore awayt,
For she will waken strayt,
The whiles doe ye this song unto her sing,
The woods shall to you answer :   . your Eccho ring.   55

Ye Nymphs of Mulla which with carefull heed,
The silver scaly trouts doe tenu full well,
And greedy pikes which use therein to feed,
(Those trouts and pikes all others doo excell)
And ye likewise which keepe the rushy lake,   60
Where none doo fishes take,
Bynd up the locks the which hang scatterd light,
And in his waters which your mirror make,
Behold your faces as the christall bright,
That when you come whereas my love doth lie,   65
No blemish she may spie.
And eke ye lightfoot mayds which keepe the deere,
That on the hoary mountayne use to towre,

37 *Nymphes:* female nature-spirits in Greek mythology; *that you can
heare:* that can hear you. 40 *Goodly wel beseene:* beautifully well pro-
vided. 46 *Eeke:* also. 48 *Whereas:* where. 51 *Diapred:* variegated;
discolored mead: variously coloured meadow. 56 *Mulla:* river Awbeg
in southern Ireland; Kilcolman Castle, where Spenser lived, is near this
river.

And the wylde wolves which seeke them to devoure,
With your steele darts doo chace from comming neer   70
Be also present heere,
To helpe to decke her and to help to sing,
That all the woods may answer and your eccho ring.

Wake, now my love, awake; for it is time,
The Rosy Morne long since left Tithones bed,   75
All ready to her silver coche to clyme,
And Phœbus gins to shew his glorious hed.
Hark how the cheerefull birds do chaunt theyr laies
And carroll of loves praise.
The merry Larke hir mattins sings aloft,   80
The thrush replyes, the Mavis descant playes,
The Ouzell shrills, the Ruddock warbles soft,
So goodly all agree with sweet consent,
To this dayes merriment.
Ah my deere love why doe ye sleepe thus long,   85
When meeter were that ye should now awake,
T'awayt the comming of your joyous make,
And hearken to the birds lovelearned song,
The deawy leaves among.
For they of joy and pleasance to you sing,   90
That all the woods them answer and theyr eccho ring.

My love is now awake out of her dreame,
And her fayre eyes like stars that dimmed were
With darksome cloud, now shew theyr goodly beams
More bright than Hesperus his head doth rere.   95
Come now ye damzels, daughters of delight,
Helpe quickly her to dight,
But first come ye fayre houres which were begot
In Joves sweet paradice, of Day and Night,
Which doe the seasons of the yeare allot,   100
And al that ever in this world is fayre
Doe make and still repayre.
And ye three handmayds of the Cyprian Queene,
The which doe still adorne her beauties pride,

75 *Tithones bed:* Tithonus, in Greek mythology, was loved and carried
away by Eos the dawn-goddess. 77 *Phœbus:*   Greek sun-god.   81
Mavis: song-thrush; *descant:* melody improvised as an accompaniment.
82 *Ouzell:* blackbird; *ruddock:* robin. 83 *Consent:* (i) agreement,
(ii) harmony. 87 *Make:* mate. 95 *Hesperus:* the 'evening star' (the
planet Venus). 98 *Houres:* daughters of Jove, the supreme deity.
103 *Cyprian Queene:* Venus, goddess of love, born from the sea off
Cyprus.

Helpe to addorne my beautifullest bride: 105
And as ye her array, still throw betweene
Some graces to be seene,
And as ye use to Venus, to her sing,
The whiles the woods shal answer and your eccho ring.

Now is my love all ready forth to come,   110
Let all the virgins therefore well awayt,
And ye fresh boyes that tend upon her groome
Prepare your selves; for he is comming strayt.
Set all your things in seemely good aray
Fit for so joyfull day,   115
The joyfulst day that ever sunne did see.
Faire Sun, shew forth thy favourable ray,
And let thy lifull heat not fervent be
For feare of burning her sunshyny face,
Her beauty to disgrace.   120
O fayrest Phœbus, father of the Muse,
If ever I did honour thee aright,
Or sing the thing, that mote thy mind delight,
Doe not thy servants simple boone refuse,
But let this day let this one day be myne,   125
Let all the rest be thine.
Then I thy soverayne prayses loud wil sing,
That all the woods shal answer and theyr eccho ring.

Harke how the Minstrels gin to shrill aloud
Their merry Musick that resounds from far,   130
The pipe, the tabor, and the trembling Croud,
That well agree withouten breach or jar.
But most of all the Damzels doe delite,
When they their tymbrels smyte,
And thereunto doe daunce and carrol sweet,   135
That all the sences they doe ravish quite,
The whyles the boyes run up and downe the street,
Crying aloud with strong confused noyce,
As if it were one voyce.
Hymen io Hymen, Hymen they do shout,   140
That even to the heavens theyr shouting shrill
Doth reach, and all the firmament doth fill,
To which the people standing all about,

121 The sun-god was also god of poetry. 123 *Mote:* could. 131
Tabor: small drum; *croud:* fiddle. 134 *Tymbrels:* tambourines.
140 *Io:* exclamation of joy (Gk.).

As in approvance doe thereto applaud
And loud advaunce her laud,   145
And evermore they Hymen Hymen sing,
That al the woods them answer and theyr eccho ring.

Loe where she comes along with portly pace
Lyke Phœbe from her chamber of the East,
Arysing forth to run her mighty race,   150
Clad all in white, that seemes a virgin best.
So well it her beseemes that ye would weene
Some angell she had beene.
Her long loose yellow locks lyke golden wyre,
Sprinckled with perle, and perling flowres a tweene,   155
Doe lyke a golden mantle her attyre,
And being crowned with a girland greene,
Seeme lyke some mayden Queene.
Her modest eyes abashed to behold
So many gazers, as on her do stare,   160
Upon the lowly ground affixed are.
Ne dare lift up her countenance too bold,
But blush to heare her prayses sung so loud,
So farre from being proud.
Nathlesse doe ye still loud her prayses sing,   165
That all the woods may answer and your eccho ring.

Tell me ye merchants daughters did ye see
So fayre a creature in your towne before,
So sweet, so lovely, and so mild as she,
Adornd with beautyes grace and vertues store,   170
Her goodly eyes lyke Saphyres shining bright,
Her forehead yvory white,
Her cheekes lyke apples which the sun hath rudded,
Her lips lyke cherryes charming men to byte,
Her brest like to a bowle of creame uncrudded,   175
Her paps lyke lyllies budded,
Her snowie necke lyke to a marble towre,
And all her body like a pallace fayre,
Ascending uppe with many a stately stayre,
To honors seat and chastities sweet bowre.   180
Why stand ye still ye virgins in amaze,
Upon her so to gaze,
Whiles ye forget your former lay to sing,
To which the woods did answer and your eccho ring.

148 *Portly:* stately.   149 *Phœbe:* Greek moon-goddess.   175 *Un-
crudded:* uncurdled.

But if ye saw that which no eyes can see, 185
The inward beauty of her lively spright,
Garnisht with heavenly guifts of high degree,
Much more then would ye wonder at that sight,
And stand astonisht lyke to those which red
Medusaes mazeful hed. 190
There dwels sweet love and constant chastity,
Unspotted fayth and comely womanhood,
Regard of honour and mild modesty,
There vertue raynes as Queene in royal throne,
And giveth lawes alone, 195
The which the base affections doe obay,
And yeeld theyr services unto her will,
Ne thought of thing uncomely ever may
Thereto approch to tempt her mind to ill.
Had ye once seene these her celestial threasures, 200
And unrevealed pleasures,
Then would ye wonder and her prayses sing,
That al the woods should answer and your echo ring.

Open the temple gates unto my love,
Open them wide that she may enter in, 205
And all the postes adorne as doth behove,
And all the pillours deck with girlands trim,
For to recyve this Saynt with honour dew,
That commeth in to you.
With trembling steps and humble reverence, 210
She commeth in, before th'almighties vew,
Of her ye virgins learne obedience,
When so ye come into those holy places,
To humble your proud faces:
Bring her up to th'high altar, that she may 215
The sacred ceremonies there partake,
The which do endlesse matrimony make,
And let the roring Organs loudly play
The praises of the Lord in lively notes,
The whiles with hollow throates 220
The Choristers the joyous Antheme sing,
That al the woods may answere and their eccho ring.

Behold whiles she before the altar stands
Hearing the holy priest that to her speakes
And blesseth her with his two happy hands, 225

190 *Medusa's mazeful hed:* the petrifying gaze of Medusa, one of the
Gorgons in Greek mythology.

How the red roses flush up in her cheekes,
And the pure snow with goodly vermill stayne,
Like crimsin dyde in grayne,
That even th'Angels which continually,
About the sacred Altare doe remaine,   230
Forget their service and about her fly,
Ofte peeping in her face that seemes more fayre,
The more they on it stare.
But her sad eyes still fastened on the ground,
Are governed with goodly modesty,   235
That suffers not one looke to glaunce awry,
Which may let in a little thought unsownd.
Why blush ye love to give to me your hand,
The pledge of all our band?
Sing ye sweet Angels, Alleluya sing,   240
That all the woods may answere and your eccho ring.

Now al is done; bring home the bride againe,
Bring home the triumph of our victory,
Bring home with you the glory of her gaine,
With joyance bring her and with jollity.   245
Never had man more joyfull day than this,
Whom heaven would heape with blis.
Make feast therefore now all this live long day,
This day for ever to me holy is,
Poure out the wine without restraint or stay,   250
Poure not by cups, but by the belly full,
Poure out to all that wull,
And sprinkle all the postes and wals with wine,
That they may sweat, and drunken be withall.
Crowne ye God Bacchus with a coronall,   255
And Hymen also crowne with wreaths of vine,
And let the Graces daunce unto the rest;
For they can doo it best:
The whiles the maydens doe theyr carroll sing,
To which the woods shal answer and theyr eccho ring.   260

Ring ye the bels, ye yong men of the towne,
And leave your wonted labors for this day:
This day is holy; doe ye write it downe,
That ye for ever it remember may.
This day the sunne is in his chiefest hight,   265

227 *Vermill:* vermilion. 234 *Sad:* grave. 255 *Bacchus:* Greek god of
wine. 257 *Graces:* three sister goddesses in Greek mythology, givers of
beauty and charm.

With Barnaby the bright,
From whence declining daily by degrees,
He somewhat loseth of his heat and light,
When once the Crab behind his back he sees.
But for this time it ill ordained was,   270
To chose the longest day in all the yeare,
And shortest night, when longest fitter weare:
Yet never day so long, but late would passe.
Ring ye the bels, to make it weare away,
And bonefiers make all day,   275
And daunce about them, and about them sing:
That all the woods may answer, and your eccho ring.

Ah when will this long weary day have end,
And lende me leave to come unto my love?
How slowly do the houres theyr numbers spend!   280
How slowly does sad Time his feathers move!
Hast thee O fayrest Planet to thy home
Within the Westerne fome:
Thy tyred steedes long since have need of rest.
Long though it be, at last I see it gloome,   285
And the bright evening star with golden creast
Appeare out of the East.
Fayre childe of beauty, glorious lampe of love
That all the host of heaven in rankes doost lead,
And guydest lovers through the nightes dread,   290
How chearefully thou lookest from above,
And seemst to laugh atweene thy twinkling light
As joying in the sight
Of these glad many which for joy doe sing,
That all the woods them answer and their eccho ring.   295

Now ceasse ye damsels your delights forepast;
Enough is it, that all the day was youres:
Now day is doen, and night is nighing fast:
Now bring the Bryde into the brydall boures.
Now night is come, now soone her disaray,   300
And in her bed her lay;
Lay her in lillies and in violets,
And silken courteins over her display,
And odourd sheetes, and Arras coverlets.

266 *Barnaby the bright:* St. Barnabas' Day (11 June), the longest day of
the year under the old calendar.   269 *Crab:* zodiacal constellation
Cancer (mid-June to mid-July).   304 *Arras coverlets:* rich fabrics from
Arras in north France.

Behold how goodly my faire love does ly   305
In proud humility;
Like unto Maia, when as Jove her tooke,
In Tempe, lying on the flowry gras,
Twixt sleepe and wake, after she weary was,
With bathing in the Acidalian brooke.   310
Now it is night, ye damsels may be gon,
And leave my love alone,
And leave likewise your former lay to sing:
The woods no more shal answere, nor your echo ring.

Now welcome night, thou night so long expected,   315
That long daies labour doest at last defray,
And all my cares, which cruell love collected,
Hast sumd in one, and cancelled for aye:
Spread thy broad wing over my love and me,
That no man may us see,   320
And in thy sable mantle us enwrap,
From feare of perrill and foule horror free.
Let no false treason seeke us to entrap,
Nor any dread disquiet once annoy
The safety of our joy: 325
But let the night be calme and quietsome,
Without tempestuous storms or sad afray:
Lyke as when Jove with fayre Alcmena lay,
When he begot the great Tirynthian groome:
Or lyke as when he with thy selfe did lie,   330
And begot Majesty.
And let the mayds and yongmen cease to sing:
Ne let the woods them answer, nor theyr eccho ring.

Let no lamenting cryes, nor dolefull teares,
Be heard all night within nor yet without: 335
Ne let false whispers, breeding hidden feares,
Breake gentle sleepe with misconceived dout.
Let no deluding dreames, nor dreadful sights
Make sudden sad affrights;
Ne let housefyres, nor lightnings helpelesse harmes,   340

307 *Maia:* Greek goddess, mother of Hermes. 308 *Tempe:* valley in
Thessaly, Greece. 310 *Acidalian brooke:* fountain in Bœotia, Greece.
328 *Alcmena:* Jove lay with Alcmena for a night prolonged to the length
of three. 329 *Tirynthian groome:* Hercules, born at Tiryns in the
Peloponnese. 330-1 Spenserian mythology: suggestion of some
primordial act, like the begetting of the Hours. 340 *Helplesse:* in-
escapable.

Ne let the Pouke, nor other evill sprights,
Ne let mischivous witches with theyr charmes,
Ne let hob Goblins, names whose sence we see not,
Fray us with things that be not.
Let not the shriech Oule, nor the Storke be heard: 345
Nor the night Raven that still deadly yels,
Nor damned ghosts cald up with mighty spels,
Nor griesly vultures make us once affeard:
Ne let th'unpleasant Quyre of Frogs still croking
Make us to wish theyr choking. 350
Let none of these theyr drery accents sing;
Ne let the woods them answer, nor theyr eccho ring.

But let stil Silence trew night watches keepe,
That sacred peace may in assurance rayne,
And tymely sleep, when it is tyme to sleepe, 355
May poure his limbs forth on your pleasant playne,
The whiles an hundred little winged loves,
Like divers fethered doves,
Shall fly and flutter round about your bed,
And in the secret darke, that none reproves, 360
Their prety stealthes shal worke, and snares shal spread
To filch away sweet snatches of delight,
Conceald through covert night.
Ye sonnes of Venus, play your sports at will,
For greedy pleasure, carelesse of your toyes, 365
Thinks more upon her paradise of joyes,
Than what ye do, albe it good or ill.
All night therefore attend your merry play,
For it will soone be day:
Now none doth hinder you, that say or sing, 370
Ne will the woods now answer, nor your Eccho ring.

Who is the same, which at my window peepes?
Or whose is that faire face, that shines so bright,
Is it not Cinthia, she that never sleepes,
But walkes about high heaven al the night? 375
O fayrest goddesse, do thou not envy
My love with me to spy:
For thou likewise didst love, though now unthought,
And for a fleece of woll, which privily,

341 *Pouke:* Puck, goblin. 345 *Shriech Oule:* screech-owl. 365 *Toyes:*
love-play. 374 *Cinthia:* Cynthia, another name for Artemis or Diana,
the moon-goddess.

The Latmian shephard once unto thee brought,   380
His pleasures with thee wrought.
Therefore to us be favorable now;
And sith of wemens labours thou hast charge,
And generation goodly dost enlarge,
Encline thy will t'effect our wishfull vow,   285
And the chast wombe informe with timely seed,
That may our comfort breed:
Till which we cease our hopefull hap to sing,
Ne let the woods us answere, nor our Eccho ring.

And thou great Juno, which with awful might   390
The lawes of wedlock still dost patronize,
And the religion of the faith first plight
With sacred rites hast taught to solemnize:
And eeke for comfort often called art
Of women in their smart,   395
Eternally bind thou this lovely band,
And all thy blessings unto us impart.
And thou glad Genius, in whose gentle hand,
The bridale bowre and geniall bed remaine,
Without blemish or staine,   400
And the sweet pleasures of theyr loves delight
With secret ayde doest succour and supply,
Till they bring forth the fruitfull progeny,
Send us the timely fruit of this same night.
And thou fayre Hebe, and thou Hymen free,   405
Grant that it may so be.
Til which we cease your further prayse to sing,
Ne any woods shal answer, nor your Eccho ring.

And ye high heavens, the temple of the gods,
In which a thousand torches flaming bright   410
Doe burne, that to us wretched earthly clods,
In dreadful darknesse lend desired light;
And all ye powers which in the same remayne,
More than we men can fayne,
Poure out your blessing on us plentiously,   415
And happy influence upon us raine,
That we may raise a large posterity,

380 *Latmian shephard:* Endymion, loved by the moon, lived on Mt.
Latmos in Caria, Asia Minor. 386 *Informe:* imbue, give 'form' to.
390 *Juno:* Jove's wife was patroness of marriage and childbirth. 398
Genius: tutelary spirit presiding over every man's conception and birth
399 *Geniall:* nuptial. 405 *Hebe:* Greek goddess of youth and vigour

Which from the earth, which they may long possesse,
With lasting happinesse,
Up to your haughty pallaces may mount,   420
And for the guerdon of theyr glorious merit
May heavenly tabernacles there inherit,
Of blessed Saints for to increase the count.
So let us rest, sweet love, in hope of this,
And cease till then our tymely joyes to sing,   425
The woods no more us answer, nor our eccho ring.

Song made in lieu of many ornaments,
With which my love should duly have bene dect,
Which cutting off through hasty accidents,
Ye would not stay your dew time to expect,   430
But promist both to recompens,
Be unto her a goodly ornament,
And for short time an endlesse moniment.

Anonymous

SIR PATRICK SPENS

The King sits in Dunfermline town,
   Drinking the blude-red wine;
" O whare will I get a skeely skipper,
   To sail this new ship of mine! "

O up and spake an eldern knight,   5
   Sat at the King's right knee,—
" Sir Patrick Spens is the best sailor
   The ever sail'd the sea."

Our King has written a braid letter,
   And seal'd it with his hand,   10
And sent it to Sir Patrick Spens,
   Was walking on the strand.

" To Noroway, to Noroway,
   To Noroway o'er the faem;
The King's daughter of Noroway,   15
   'Tis thou maun bring her hame."

3 *Skeely:* skilful. 9 *Braid:* broad, of royal size. 14 *Faem:* foam.
16 *Maun:* must.

The first word that Sir Patrick read,
  Sae loud loud laughed he;
The neist word that Sir Patrick read,
  The tear blinded his e'e.   20

" O wha is this has done this deed,
  And tauld the King o' me,
To send us out, at this time of the year,
  To sail upon the sea?

" Be it wind, be it weet, be it hail, be it sleet,   25
  Our ship must sail the faem;
The King's daughter of Noroway,
  'Tis we must fetch her hame."

They hoysed their sails on Monenday morn,
  Wi' a' the speed they may;   30
They hae landed in Noroway,
  Upon a Wodensday.

They hadna been a week, a week,
  In Noroway, but twae,
When that the lords o' Noroway   35
  Began aloud to say,—

" Ye Scottishmen spend a' our King's goud,
  And a' our Queenis fee."
" Ye lie, ye lie, ye liars loud!
  Fu' loud I hear ye lie.   40

" For I brought as much white monie,
  As gane my men and me,
And I brought a half-fou o' gude red goud,
  Out o'er the sea wi' me.

" Make ready, make ready, my merrymen a'!   45
  Our gude ship sails the morn."
" Now, ever alake, my master dear,
  I fear a deadly storm!

19 *Neist:* next. 37 *Goud:* gold. 38 *Fee:* money. 42 *Gane:* suffice.
43 *Half-fou:* half bushel. 46 *The morn:* to-morrow.

" I saw the new moon, late yestreen,
    Wi' the auld moon in her arm;   50
And, if we gang to sea, master,
    I fear we'll come to harm."

They hadna sail'd a league, a league,
    A league but barely three,
When the lift grew dark, and the wind blew loud,   55
    And gurly grew the sea.

The ankers brak, and the top-masts lap,
    It was sic a deadly storm;
And the waves cam o'er the broken ship,
    Till a' her sides were torn.   60

" O where will I get a gude sailor,
    To take my helm in hand,
Till I get up to the tall top-mast,
    To see if I can spy land."

" O here am I, a sailor gude,   65
    To take the helm in hand,
Till you go up to the tall top-mast;
    But I fear you'll ne'er spy landl."

He hadna gane a step, a step,
    A step but barely ane,   70
When a bout flew out of our goodly ship,
    And the salt sea it came in.

" Gae, fetch a web o' the silken claith,
    Another o' the twine,
And wap them into our ship's side,   75
    And let na the sea come in."

They fetched a web o' the silken claith,
    Another o' the twine,
And they wapped them round that gude ship's side,
    But still the sea came in.   80

---

49 *Yestreen:* last night. 55 *Lift:* sky. 56 *Gurly:* threatening, stormy.
57 *Lap:* sprang. 71 *Bout:* bolt. 74 *O' the twine:* i.e. canvas, sail-
cloth. 75 *Wap:* bind, or technically, 'frap' (i.e. pass turns of a cable
round middle of hull to prevent ship from splitting in heavy seas).

O laith, laith, were our gude Scots lords
   To weet their cork-heel'd shoon!
But lang or a' the play was play'd,
   They wat their hats aboon.

And mony was the feather-bed,   85
   That flatter'd on the faem;
And mony was the gude lord's son,
   That never mair cam hame.

The ladyes wrang their fingers white,
   The maidens tore their hair,   90
A' for the sake of their true loves;
   For them they'll see nae mair.

O lang, lang, may the ladyes sit,
   Wi' their fans into their hand,
Before they see Sir Patrick Spens   95
   Come sailing to the strand!

And lang, lang, may the maidens sit,
   Wi' their goud kaims in their hair,
A' waiting for their ain dear loves!
   For them they'll see nae mair.   100

Half owre, half owre to Aberdour,
   'Tis fifty fathoms deep,
And there lies gude Sir Patrick Spens,
   Wi' the Scots lords at his feet.

THE GAY GOSHAWK

' O well's me o my gay goss-hawk,
   That he can speak and flee;
He'll carry a letter to my love,
   Bring back another to me.'

' O how can I your true-love ken,   5
   Or how can I her know?
Whan frae her mouth I never heard couth,
   Nor wi my eyes her saw.'

81 *Laith:* loath. 83 *Lang or:* long before. 86 *Flatter'd:* floated.
98 *Kaims:* combs. 101 *Aberdour:* it is not certain whether this is the
port in the Firth of Forth, or the one in northern Aberdeenshire.
The ballad may reflect some historical event, but this has not been
satisfactorily identified. 1 *Well's me o:* I am lucky with. 7 *Heard couth:*
received a message.

'O well sal ye my true-love ken,
  As soon as you her see;
For, of a' the flowrs in fair Englan,   10
  The fairest flowr is she.

'At even at my love's bowr-door
  There grows a bowing birk,
An sit ye down and sing thereon,   15
  As she gangs to the kirk.

'An four-and-twenty ladies fair
  Will wash and go to kirk,
But well shall ye my true-love ken,
  For she wears goud on her skirt.   20

'An four and twenty gay ladies
  Will to the mass repair,
But well sal ye my true-love ken,
  For she wears goud on her hair.'

O even at that lady's bowr-door   25
  There grows a bowin birk,
An he set down and sang thereon,
  As she ged to the kirk.

'O eet and drink, my marys a',
  The wine flows you among,   30
Till I gang to my shot-window,
  An hear yon bonny bird's song.

'Sing on, sing on, my bonny bird,
  The song ye sang the streen,
For I ken by your sweet singin   35
  You're frae my true-love sen.'

14 *Birk:* birch. 20 *Goud:* gold. 29 *Marys:* maids. 31 *Shot-window:* projecting window. 34 *The streen:* last night.

O first he sang a merry song,
   An then he sang a grave,
An then he peckd his feathers gray,
   To her the letter gave.   40

' Ha, there's a letter frae your love,
   He says he sent you three;
He canna wait your love langer,
   But for your sake he'll die.

' He bids you write a letter to him;   45
   He says he's sent you five;
He canna wait your love langer,
   Tho you're the fairest woman alive.'

' Ye bid him bake his bridal-bread,
   And brew his bridal-ale,   50
An I'll meet him in fair Scotlan
   Lang, lang or it be stale.'

She's doen her to her father dear,
   Fa'n low down on her knee:
' A boon, a boon, my father dear,   55
   I pray you, grant it me.'

' Ask on, ask on, my daughter,
   An granted it sal be;
Except ae squire in fair Scotlan,
   An him you sall never see.'   60

' The only boon, my father dear,
   That I do crave of the,
Is, gin I die in southin lands,
   In Scotland to bury me.

' An the firstin kirk that ye come till,   65
   Ye gar the bells be rung,
An the nextin kirk that ye come till,
   Ye gar the mess be sung.

' An the thirdin kirk that ye come till,
   You deal gold for my sake,
An the fourthin kirk that ye come till,   70
   You tarry there till night.'

52 *Lang or:* long before. 53 *Doen her:* gone. 63 *Gin:* if; *southin:*
southern. 65 *Till:* to. 66 *Gar:* make, cause.

She is doen her to her bigly bowr,
   As fast as she coud fare,
An she has tane a sleepy draught,   75
   That she had mixed wi care.

She's laid her down upon her bed,
   An soon she's fa'n asleep,
And soon oer every tender limb
   Cauld death began to creep.   80

Wh.. night was flown, an day was come,
   N.. ane that did her see
But thought she was as surely dead
   As ony lady could be.

Her father an her brothers dear   85
   Gard make to her a bier;
The tae half was o guid red gold,
   The tither o silver clear.

Her mither an her sisters fair
   Gard work for her a sark;   90
The tae half was o cambrick fine,
   The tither o needle wark.

The firstin kirk that they came till,
   They gard the bells be rung,
An the nextin kirk that they came till,   95
   They gard the mess be sung.

The thirdin kirk that they came till,
   They dealt gold for her sake,
An the fourthin kirk that they came till,
   Lo, there they met her make!   100

' Lay down, lay down the bigly bier,
   Lat me the dead look on; '
Wi cherry cheeks and ruby lips
   She lay an smil'd on him.

' O ae sheave o your bread, true-love,   105
   An ae glass o your wine,
For I hae fasted for your sake
   These fully days is nine.

73 *Bigly:* pleasant, fine. 87 *The tae:* the one. 88 *The tither:* the
other. 90 *Sark:* shirt, i.e. shroud. 100 *Make:* mate, lover.

'Gang hame, gang hame, my seven bold brothers,
  Gang hame and sound your horn;   110
An ye may boast in southin lans
  Your sister's playd you scorn.'

LITTLE MUSGRAVE AND LADY BARNARD

As it fell one holy-day,
    Hay downe
  As many be in the yeare,
When young men and maids together did goe,
  Their mattins and masse to heare,   5

Little Musgrave came to the church-dore;
  The preist was at private masse;
But he had more minde of the faire women
  Than he had of our lady's grace.

The one of them was clad in green,   10
  Another was clad in pall,
And then came in my lord Barnard's wife,
  The fairest amonst them all.

She cast an eye on Little Musgrave,
  As bright as the summer sun;   15
And then bethought this Little Musgrave,
  This lady's heart have I woonn.

Quoth she, I have loved thee, Little Musgrave,
  Full long and many a day;
'So have I loved you, fair lady,   20
  Yet never word durst I say.'

'I have a bower at Bucklesfordbery,
  Full daintyly it is deight;
If thou wilt wend thither, thou Little Musgrave,
  Thou's lig in mine armes all night.'   25

22 *Bucklesfordbery:* not identified; other versions of the ballad have
Bucklesfieldberry, Dalisberry, and Mulberry. 23 *Deight:* furnished.
25 *Thou's lig:* thou shalt lie.

Quoth he, I thank yee, faire lady,
  This kindness thou showest to me;
But whether it be to my weal or woe,
  This night I will lig with thee.

With that he heard, a little tynë page,   30
  By his ladye's coach as he ran:
'All though I am my ladye's foot-page
  Yet I am Lord Barnard's man.'

'My lord Barnard shall knowe of this,
  Whether I sink or swim;'   35
And ever where the bridges were broake
  He laid him downe to swimme.

'A sleepe or wake, thou Lord Barnard,
  As thou art a man of life,
For Little Musgrave is at Bucklesfordbery,   40
  A bed with thy own wedded wife.'

'If this be true, thou little tiny page,
  This thing thou tellest to me,
Then all the land in Bucklesfordbery
  I freely will give to thee.   45

'But if it be a ly, thou little tiny page,
  This thing thou tellest to me,
On the highest tree in Bucklesfordbery
  Then hanged shalt thou be.'

He called up his merry men all: 50
  'Come saddle me my steed;
This night must I go to Bucklesfordbery,
  For I never had greater need.'

And some of them whistld, and some of them sung,
  And some these words did say,   55
And ever when my lord Barnard's horn blew,
  'Away, Musgrave, away!'

'Methinks I hear the thresel-cock,
  Methinks I hear the jaye;
Methinks I hear my lord Barnard,   60
  And I would I were away.'

58 *Thresel-cock:* song-thrush.

' Lye still, lye still, thou Little Musgrave,
  And huggell me from the cold;
'T is nothing but a shephard's boy,
  A driving his sheep to the fold.   65

' Is not thy hawke upon a perch?
  Thy steed eats oats and hay;
And thou a fair lady in thine armes,
  And wouldst thou bee away? '

With that my lord Barnard came to the dore,   70
  And lit a stone upon;
He plucked out three silver keys,
  And he opend the dores each one.

He lifted up the coverlett,
  He lifted up the sheet: 75
' How now, how now, thou Littell Musgrave,
  Doest thou find my lady sweet? '

' I find her sweet,' quoth Little Musgrave,
  ' The more 't is to my paine;
I would gladly give three hundred pounds   80
  That I were on yonder plaine.'

' Arise, arise, thou Littell Musgrave,
  And put thy clothës on;
It shall nere be said in my country
  I have killed a naked man.   85

' I have two swords in one scabberd,
  Full deere they cost my purse;
And thou shalt have the best of them,
  And I will have the worse.'

The first stroke that Little Musgrave stroke,   90
  He hurt Lord Barnard sore;
The next stroke that Lord Barnard stroke,
  Little Musgrave nere struck more.

With that bespake this faire lady,
  In bed whereas she lay: 95
' Although thou'rt dead, thou Little Musgrave,
  Yet I for thee will pray.

63 *Huggell:* hug. 71 *Lit:* alighted

'And wish well to thy soule will I,
  So long as I have life;
So will I not for thee, Barnard,   100
  Although I am thy wedded wife.'

He cut her paps from off her brest;
  Great pitty it was to see
That some drops of this ladie's heart's blood
  Ran trickling downe her knee.   105

'Woe worth you, woe worth, my mery men all,
  You were nere borne for my good;
Why did you not offer to stay my hand,
  When you see me wax so wood?

'For I have slaine the bravest sir knight   110
  That ever rode on steed;
So have I done the fairest lady
  That ever did woman's deed.

'A grave, a grave,' Lord Barnard cryd,
  'To put these lovers in;   115
But lay my lady on the upper hand,
  For she came of the better kin.'

TAM LIN

O I forbid you, maidens a',
  That wear gowd on your hair,
To come or gae by Carterhaugh,
  For young Tam Lin is there.

There's nane that gaes by Carterhaugh   5
  But they leave him a wad;
Either their rings, or green mantles,
  Or else their maidenhead.

---

106 *Worth:* befall.   109 *Wax so wood:* became so enraged.   2 *Gowd:*
gold.   3 *Carterhaugh:* wooded peninsula at junction of Ettrick and
Yarrow rivers, Selkirkshire.   6 *Wad:* forfeit.

Janet has kilted her green kirtle
   A little aboon her knee,   10
And she has broded her yellow hair
   A little aboon her bree,
And she's awa' to Carterhaugh
   As fast as she can hie.

When she came to Carterhaugh   15
   Tam Lin was at the well,
And there she fand his steed standing,
   But away was himsel.

She had na pu'd a double rose,
   A rose but only twa,   20
Till up then started young Tam Lin,
   Says, ' Lady, thou's pu' nae mae.

' Why pu's thou the rose, Janet,
   And why breaks thou the wand?
Or why comes thou to Carterhaugh   25
   Withoutten my command? '

' Carterhaugh it is my ain,
   My daddie gave it me;
I'll come and gang by Carterhaugh
   And ask nae leave at thee.'   30

Janet has kilted her green kirtle
   A little aboon her knee,
And she has snooded her yellow hair
   A little aboon her bree,
And she is to her father's ha'   35
   As fast as she can hie.

Four and twenty ladies fair
   Were playing at the ba',
And out then cam the fair Janet,
   Ance the flower amang them a'.   40

Four and twenty ladies fair
   Were playing at the chess,
And out then cam the fair Janet,
   As green as onie gless.

12 *Bree:* brow. 22 *Thou's:* thou shalt.

Out then spak an auld grey knight,   45
  Lay o'er the castle wa',
And says, ' Alas, fair Janet, for thee,
  But we'll be blamed a'.'

' Haud your tongue, ye auld fac'd knight,
  Some ill death may ye die,   50
Father my bairn on whom I will,
  I'll father nane on thee.'

Out then spak her father dear,
  And he spak meek and mild,
' And ever alas, sweet Janet,' he says,   55
  ' I think thou gaes wi' child.'

' If that I gae wi' child, father,
  Mysel maun bear the blame;
There's ne'er a laird about your ha'
  Shall get the bairn's name.   60

' If my love were an earthly knight,
  As he's an elfin grey,
I wadna gie my ain true-love
  For nae lord that ye hae.

' The steed that my true-love rides on   65
  Is lighter than the wind;
Wi' siller he is shod before,
  Wi' burning gowd behind.'

Janet has kilted her green kirtle
  A little aboon her knee,   70
And she has snooded her yellow hair
  A little aboon her bree,
And she's awa to Carterhaugh
  As fast as she can hie.

When she cam to Carterhaugh   75
  Tam Lin was at the well,
And there she fand his steed standing,
  But away was himsel.

58 *Maun:* must.

She had na pu'd a double rose,
　A rose but only twa,
Till up then started young Tam Lin,
　Says, ' Lady, thou pu's nae mae. 　　　　　　80

' Why pu's thou the rose, Janet,
　Amang the groves sae green,
And a' to kill the bonie babe 　　　　　　　85
　That we gat us between? '

' O tell me, tell me, Tam Lin,' she says,
　' For's sake that died on tree,
If e'er ye was in holy chapel,
　Or Christendom did see? ' 　　　　　　　90

' Roxbrugh he was my grandfather,
　Took me with him to bide,
And ance it fell upon a day
　That wae did me betide.

' And ance it fell upon a day, 　　　　　　95
　A cauld day and a snell,
When we were frae the hunting come,
　That frae my horse I fell.
The queen o fairies she caught me.
　In yon green hill to dwell. 　　　　　　100

' And pleasant is the fairy-land;
　But an eerie tale to tell!—
Ay at the end of seven years
　We pay a tiend to hell.
I am sae fair and fu' o' flesh 　　　　　　105
　I'm fear'd it be mysel.

' But the night is Halloween, lady,
　The morn is Hallowday,
Then win me, win me an ye will,
　For weel I wat ye may. 　　　　　　　110

' Just at the mirk and midnight hour
　The fairy folk will ride,

90 i.e. 'Were you ever christened?' 96 *Snell:* sharp. 104 *Tiend:*
tithe. 108 *The morn:* tomorrow. 111 *Mirk:* dark, murky.

And they that wad their true-love win
  At Milescross they maun bide.'

'But how shall I thee ken, Tam Lin,   115
  Or how my true-love know,
Amang sae mony unco knights,
  The like I never saw?'

'O first let pass the black, lady,
  And syne let pass the brown,   120
But quickly run to the milk-white steed,
  Pu' ye his rider down.

'For I'll ride on the milk-white steed,
  And ay nearest the town;
Because I was an earthly knight   125
  They gie me that renown.

'My right hand will be glov'd, lady,
  My left hand will be bare,
Cockt up shall my bonnet be,
  And kaim'd down shall my hair,   130
And thae's the takens I gie thee,
  Nae doubt I will be there.

'They'll turn me in your arms, lady,
  Into an esk and adder,
But hold me fast and fear me not,   135
  I am your bairn's father.

'They'll turn me to a bear sae grim,
  And then a lion bold,
But hold me fast and fear me not,
  As ye shall love your child.   140

'Again they'll turn me in your arms
  To a red het gaud of airn,
But hold me fast and fear me not,
  I'll do to you nae harm.

'And last they'll turn me in your arms   145
  Into the burning gleed;

114 Symbolic name: crossroads have always attracted superstitions and legends. 117 *Unco:* strange. 120 *Syne:* then. 130 *Kaimd:* combed. 134 *Esk:* newt. 142 *Gaud of airn:* rod of iron. 146 *Gleed:* ember.

Then throw me into well water,
  O throw me in wi' speed.

'And then I'll be your ain true-love,
  I'll turn a naked knight;   150
Then cover me wi' your green mantle,
  And cover me out o' sight.'

Gloomy, gloomy was the night,
  And eerie was the way,
As fair Jenny in her green mantle   155
  To Milescross she did gae.

About the middle o' the night
  She heard the bridles ring,
This lady was as glad at that
  As any earthly thing.   160

First she let the black pass by,
  And syne she let the brown,
But quickly she ran to the milk-white steed
  And pu'd the rider down.

Sae weel she minded what he did say   165
  And young Tam Lin did win,
Syne cover'd him wi' her green mantle
  As blythe's a bird in spring.

Out then spak the queen o' fairies,
  Out of a bush o' broom: 170
'Them that has gotten young Tam Lin
  Has gotten a stately groom.'

Out then spak the queen o' fairies,
  And an angry queen was she:
'Shame betide her ill-far'd face   175
  And an ill death may she die,
For she's ta'en awa' the boniest knight
  In a' my companie.

'But had I kend, Tam Lin,' she says,
  'What now this night I see,   180
I wad hae ta'en out thy twa grey een
  And put in twa een o' tree.'

175 *Ill-far'd:* unbecoming, ugly. 182 *Tree:* wood.

Ben Jonson

1572—1637

TO PENSHURST

Thou art not, PENSHURST, built to envious show,
  Of touch, or marble; nor canst boast a row
Of polish'd pillars, or a roofe of gold:
  Thou hast no lantherne, whereof tales are told;
Or stayre, or courts; but stand'st an ancient pile,   5
  And these grudg'd at, art reverenc'd the while.
Thou joy'st in better markes, of soyle, of ayre,
  Of wood, of water: therein thou art faire.
Thou hast thy walkes for health, as well as sport:
  Thy *Mount*, to which the *Dryads* doe resort,   10
Where PAN, and BACCHUS their high feasts have made,
  Beneath the broad beech, and the chest-nut shade;
That taller tree, which of a nut was set,
  At his great birth, where all the *Muses* met.
There, in the writhed barke, are cut the names   15
  Of many a SYLVANE, taken with his flames.
And thence, the ruddy *Satyres* oft provoke
  The lighter *Faunes*, to reach thy *Ladies oke*.
Thy copp's, too, nam'd of GAMAGE, thou hast there,
  That never fails to serve thee season'd deere,   20
When thou would'st feast, or exercise thy friends.
  The lower land, that to the river bends,
Thy sheepe, thy bullocks, kine, and calves doe feed:
  The middle grounds thy mares, and horses breed.
Each banke doth yeeld thee coneyes; and the topps   25
  Fertile of wood, ASHORE, and SYDNEY's copp's,
To crowne thy open table, doth provide
  The purpled pheasant, with the speckled side:

1 *Penshurst:* Penshurst Place, home of the Sidney family, near Tunbridge Wells in Kent. 2 *Touch:* black granite or marble. 10 *Dryads:* female tree-spirits in Greek mythology. 11 *Pan:* Greek god of flocks and shepherds; *Bacchus:* another name for Dionysus, Greek god of wine and revelry. 14 *His:* i.e. Sir Philip Sidney's (1554-86). 16 *Sylvane:* countryman, rustic. 17 *Satyres:* half-human, half-animal attendants of Dionysus. 18 *Faunes:* satyr-like rural deities in Roman mythology. 19 *Copp's:* coppice; *Gamage:* Barbara Gamage married Sir Robert Sidney (1563-1626), younger brother of Sir Philip, in 1584. 25 *Coneyes:* rabbits. 26 *Ashore, etc.:* two woods in the grounds.

The painted partrich lyes in every field,
   And, for thy messe, is willing to be kill'd.   30
And if the high-swolne *Medway* faile thy dish,
   Thou hast thy ponds, that pay thee tribute fish,
Fat, aged carps, that runne into thy net.
And pikes, now weary their owne kinde to eat,
As loth, the second draught, or cast to stay,   35
   Officiously, at first, themselves betray.
Bright eeles, that emulate them, and leape on land,
   Before the fisher, or into his hand.
Then hath thy orchard fruit, thy garden flowers,
   Fresh as the ayre, and new as are the houres.   40
The earely cherry, with the later plum,
   Fig, grape, and quince, each in his time doth come:
The blushing apricot, and woolly peach
   Hang on thy walls, that every child may reach.
And though thy walls be of the countrey stone,   45
   They'are rear'd with no mans ruine, no mans grone,
There's none that dwell about them, wish them downe;
   But all come in, the farmer, and the clowne:
And no one empty-handed, to salute
   Thy lord, and lady, though they have no sute.   50
Some bring a capon, some a rurall cake,
   Some nuts, some apples; some that thinke they make
The better cheeses, bring 'hem; or else send
   By their ripe daughters, whom they would commend
This way to husbands; and whose baskets beare   55
   An embleme of themselves, in plum, or peare.
But what can this (more than expresse their love)
   Adde to thy free provisions, farre above
The neede of such? whose liberall boord doth flow,
   With all, that hospitalitie doth know!   60
Where comes no guest, but is allow'd to eate,
   Without his feare, and of thy lords owne meate:
Where the same beere, and bread, and selfe-same wine,
   That is his Lordships, shall be also mine,
And I not faine to sit (as some, this day,   65
   At great mens tables) and yet dine away.
Here no man tells my cups; nor, standing by,
   A waiter, doth my gluttony envy:
But gives me what I call, and lets me eate,
   He knowes, below, he shall finde plentie of meate,   70

31 *Medway:* river in Kent; its estuary meets that of the Thames.
35 *Draught:* take of fish (by net). 36 *Officiously:* obligingly. 48
Clowne: peasant. 67 *Tells:* counts.

Thy tables hoord not up for the next day,
  Nor, when I take my lodging, need I pray
For fire, or lights, or livorie: all is there;
  As if thou, then, wert mine, or I raign'd here:
There's nothing I can wish, for which I stay.   75
  That found King JAMES, when hunting late, this way,
With his brave sonne, the Prince, they saw thy fires
  Shine bright on every harth as the desires
Of thy *Penates* had beene set on flame,
  To entertayne them; or the countrey came,   80
With all their zeale, to warm their welcome here.
  What (great, I will not say, but) sodayne cheare
Did'st thou, then, make 'hem! and what praise was heap'd
  On thy good lady, then! who, therein, reap'd
The just reward of her high huswifery;   85
  To have her linnen, plate, and all things nigh,
When she was farre: and not a roome, but drest,
  As if it had expected such a guest!
These, PENSHURST, are thy praise, and yet not all.
  Thy lady's noble, fruitfull, chaste withall.   90
His children thy great lord may call his owne:
  A fortune, in this age, but rarely knowne.
They are, and have beene taught religion: Thence
  Their gentler spirits have suck'd innocence.
Each morne, and even, they are taught to pray,   95
  With the whole household, and may, every day,
Reade, in their vertuous parents noble parts,
  The mysteries of manners, armes, and arts.
Now, PENSHURST, they that will proportion thee
  With other edifices, when they see   100
Those proud, ambitious heaps, and nothing else,
  May say, their lords have built, but thy lord dwells.

---

73 *Livorie:* provision, allowance. 76 *James:* James I (1566-1625).
79 *Penates:* guardian spirits of the household in Roman mythology.
91 *Thy great lord:* Sir Robert Sidney became Baron Sidney of Penshurst
in 1603.

John Donne

1572—1631

THE STORM

This poem, with its companion-piece *The Calm*, refers to the
damaging of the fleet with which Raleigh and Essex had meant
to destroy the new Spanish Armada in 1597, and to their subse-
quent equally unsuccessful 'Islands Voyage' to the Azores in
search of the Spaniards' American treasure-ships. Donne, who
took part in the expedition, describes both storm and doldrums
with atmospheric realism.

To Mr. Christopher Brooke

Thou which art I, ('tis nothing to be soe)
Thou which art still thy selfe, by these shalt know
Part of our passage; And, a hand, or eye
By *Hilliard* drawne, is worth an history,
By a worse painter made; and (without pride)   5
When by thy judgment they are dignifi'd,
My lines are such: 'Tis the preheminence
Of friendship onely to'impute excellence.
England to whom we'owe, what we be, and have,
Sad that her sonnes did seeke a forraine grave   10
(For, Fates, or Fortunes drifts none can soothsay,
Honour and misery have one face and way)
From out her pregnant intrailes sigh'd a winde
Which at th'ayres middle marble roome did finde
Such strong resistance, that it selfe it threw   15
Downeward againe; and so when it did view
How in the port, our fleet deare time did leese,
Withering like prisoners, which lye but for fees,
Mildly it kist our sailes, and, fresh and sweet,
As to a stomack sterv'd, whose insides meete,   20

1 *Thou:* Christopher Brooke, an intimate friend of Donne's and co-
student of law. He wrote verse, became a bencher at Lincoln's Inn, and
died 1628. 4 *Hilliard:* Nicholas Hilliard (1537-1619), distinguished
miniature painter. 14 *Th'ayre's middle marble roome:* the cold white
'middle region' of the atmosphere in medieval cosmology. 17 *Leese:*
lose. 18 *Fees:* fees due to the jailer.

Meate comes, it came; and swole our sailes, when wee
So joyd, as *Sara*'her swelling joy'd to see.
But 'twas but so kinde, as our countrimen,
Which bring friends one dayes way, and leave them then.
Then like two mighty Kings, which dwelling farre   25
Asunder, meet against a third to warre,
The South and West winds joyn'd, and, as they blew,
Waves like a rowling trench before them threw.
Sooner than you read this line, did the gale,
Like shot, not fear'd till felt, our sailes assaile;   30
And what at first was call'd a gust, the same
Hath now a stormes, anon a tempests name.
Jonas, I pitty thee, and curse those men,
Who when the storm rag'd most, did wake thee then;
Sleepe is paines easiest salve, and doth fullfill   35
All offices of death, except to kill.
But when I wakt, I saw, that I saw not;
I, and the Sunne, which should teach mee'had forgot
East, West, Day, Night, and I could onely say,
If 'the world had lasted, now it had beene day.   40
Thousands our noyses were, yet wee 'mongst all
Could none by his right name, but thunder call:
Lightning was all our light, and it rain'd more
Than if the Sunne had drunke the sea before.
Some coffin'd in their cabbins lye,'equally   45
Griev'd that they are not dead, and yet must dye;
And as sin-burd'ned soules from graves will creepe,
At the last day, some forth their cabbins peepe:
And tremblingly'aske what newes, and doe heare so,
Like jealous husbands, what they would not know.   50
Some sitting on the hatches, would seeme there,
With hideous gazing to feare away feare.
Then note they the ships sicknesses, the Mast
Shak'd with this ague, and the Hold and Wast
With a salt dropsie clog'd, and all our tacklings   55
Snapping, like too-high-stretched treble strings.
And from our totterd sailes, ragges drop downe so,
As from one hang'd in chaines, a yeare agoe.
Even our Ordinance plac'd for our defence,
Strive to breake loose, and scape away from thence.   60

22 *Sara:* see *Gen.* xxi. 1-7. 33-34 *Ionas, etc.:* see *Jonah* i. 4-6. 54
Wast: waist, mid section of upper deck. 57 *Totterd:* shaken, buffeted.
59 *Ordinance:* ordnance, here used as a plural.

Pumping hath tir'd our men, and what's the gaine?
Seas into seas throwne, we suck in againe;
Hearing hath deaf'd our saylers; and if they
Knew how to heare, there's none knowes what to say.
Compar'd to these stormes, death is but a qualme,   65
Hell somewhat lightsome, and the'Bermuda calme.
Darknesse, lights elder brother, his birth-right
Claims o'r this world, and to heaven hath chas'd light.
All things are one, and that one none can be,
Since all formes, uniforme deformity   70
Doth cover, so that wee, except God say
Another *Fiat*, shall have no more day.
So violent, yet long these furies bee,
That though thine absence sterve me,'I wish not thee.

THE CALM

Our storme is past, and that storms tyrannous rage,
A stupid calme, but nothing it, doth swage.
The fable is inverted, and farre more
A blocke afflicts, now, than a storke before.
Stormes chafe, and soone weare out themselves, or us;   5
In calmes, Heaven laughs to see us languish thus.
As steady'as I can wish, that my thoughts were,
Smooth as thy mistresse glasse, or what shines there,
The sea is now. And, as the Iles which wee
Seeke, when wee can move, our ships rooted bee.   10
As water did in stormes, now pitch runs out:
As lead, when a fir'd Church becomes one spout.
And all our beauty, and our trimme, decayes,
Like courts removing, or like ended playes.
The fighting place now seamens ragges supply;   15
And all the tackling is a frippery.
No use of lanthornes; and in one place lay
Feathers and dust, to day and yesterday.

66 *The' Bermuda:* the seas and reefs about Bermuda in the West Atlantic.
67-68 See *Gen.* i. 1-4.   72 *Fiat:* 'let there be [light]' (Lat. *fiat lux*).
2 *Swage:* assuage.   3-4 In Æsop's fable, the frogs asked Zeus for a king
but complained when he gave them a log; when he replaced the log by
a snake (in later versions a stork) they were even worse off.   16 *Frippery:*
old-clothes shop.   17 *Lanthornes:* The lanterns hanging at the stern to
guide the following ships were useless.

Earths hollownesses, which the worlds lungs are,
Have no more winde than the upper valt of aire. 20
We can nor lost friends, nor sought foes recover,
But meteorlike, save that wee move not, hover.
Onely the Calenture together drawes
Deare friends, which meet dead in great fishes jawes:
And on the hatches as on Altars lyes 25
Each one, his owne Priest, and owne Sacrifice.
Who live, that miracle do multiply
Where walkers in hot Ovens, doe not dye.
If in despite of these, wee swimme, that hath
No more refreshing, than our brimstone Bath, 30
But from the sea, into the ship we turne,
Like parboyl'd wretches, on the coales to burne.
Like *Bajazet* encag'd, the shepheards scoffe,
Or like slacke sinew'd *Sampson*, his haire off,
Languish our ships. Now, as a Miriade 35
Of Ants, durst th'Emperours lov'd snake invade,
The crawling Gallies, Sea-gaoles, finny chips,
Might brave our Pinnaces, now bed-ridde ships.
Whether a rotten state, and hope of gaine,
Or to disuse mee from the queasie paine 40
Of being belov'd, and loving, or the thirst
Of honour, or faire death, out pusht mee first,
I lose my end: for here as well as I
A desperate may live, and a coward die.
Stagge, dogge, and all which from or towards flies, 45
Is paid with life, or prey, or doing dyes.
Fate grudges us all, and doth subtly lay
A scourge, 'gainst which wee all forget to pray,
He that at sea prayes for more winde, as well
Under the poles may begge cold, heat in hell. 50
What are wee then? How little more alas
Is man now, than before he was? he was

---

21 *Lost friends:* Raleigh and his ships lost the main fleet off Spain and
had to rejoin it at the Azores. 23 *Calenture:* tropical fever in which a
delirious sailor imagines the sea is a green field and tries to jump into it.
32 *Parboyl'd:* half-boiled. 33 *Bajazet(h):* captive Turkish emperor in
Christopher Marlowe's play *Tamburlaine the Great*; Tamburlaine, the
Scythian shepherd and conqueror, mocks him and draws him about in a
cage. 34 *Sampson:* see *Judges* xvi. 18-21. 35-36 The Roman emperor
Tiberius had a pet snake which according to Suetonius was devoured by
ants: a warning against mob violence. 37 *Finny chips:* the light-
weight galleys with their moving fringe of oars. 47-48 We 'forget to
pray' against the cessation of wind because at sea wind is a more natural
expectation than stillness.

Nothing; for us, wee are for nothing fit;
Chance, or our selves still disproportion it.
Wee have no power, no will, no sense; I lye,   55
I should not then thus feele this miserie.

ELEGY XVI

ON HIS MISTRESS

By our first strange and fatall interview,
By all desires which thereof did ensue,
By our long starving hopes, by that remorse
Which my words masculine perswasive force
Begot in thee, and by the memory   5
Of hurts, which spies and rivals threatned me,
I calmly beg: But by thy parents wrath,
By all paines, which want and divorcement hath,
I conjure thee, and all the oathes which I
And thou have sworne to seale joynt constancy,   10
Here I unsweare, and oversweare them thus,
Thou shalt not love by wayes so dangerous.
Temper, ô faire Love, loves impetuous rage,
Be my true Mistris still, not my faign'd Page;
I'll goe, and, by thy kinde leave, leave behinde   15
Thee, onely worthy to nurse in my minde,
Thirst to come backe; ô if thou die before,
My soule from other lands to thee shall soare.
Thy (else Almighty) beautie cannot move
Rage from the Seas, nor thy love teach them love,   20
Nor tame wilde Boreas harshnesse; Thou hast reade
How roughly hee in peeces shivered
Faire Orithea, whom he swore he lov'd.
Fall ill or good, 'tis madnesse to have prov'd
Dangers unurg'd; Feed on this flattery,   25
That absent Lovers one in th'other be.
Dissemble nothing, not a boy, nor change
Thy bodies habite, nor mindes; bee not strange
To thy selfe only; All will spie in thy face
A blushing womanly discovering grace;   30

21-23 In Greek mythology, Oreithyia, daughter of Erechtheus, was
carried off by Boreas, the north wind.   30 *Discovering:* revealing.

Richly cloath'd Apes, are call'd Apes, and as soone
Ecclips'd as bright we call the Moone the Moone.
Men of France, changeable Camelions,
Spittles of diseases, shops of fashions,
Loves fuellers, and the rightest company   35
Of Players, which upon the worlds stage be,
Will quickly knowe thee, and alas!
Th'indifferent Italian, as we passe
His warme land, well content to thinke thee Page,
Will hunt thee with such lust, and hideous rage,   40
As *Lots* faire guests were vext. But none of these
Nor spungy hydroptique Dutch shall thee displease,
If thou stay here. O stay here, for, for thee
England is onely a worthy Gallerie,
To walke in expectation, till from thence   45
Our greatest King call thee to his presence.
When I am gone, dreame me some happinesse,
Nor let thy lookes our long hid love confesse,
Nor praise, nor dispraise me; Blesse nor curse
Openly loves force, nor in bed fright thy Nurse   50
With midnights startings, crying out, oh, oh
Nurse, ô my love is slaine, I saw him goe
O'r the white Alpes alone; I saw him I,
Assail'd, fight, taken, stabb'd, bleed, fall, and die.
Augure me better chance, except dread *Jove*   55
Thinke it enough for me to'have had thy love.

SATIRE III

Donne expresses, with his customary tension and energy, not only
his own religious doubts as he stands half-way between Catholicism
and Anglicanism in the last decade of the sixteenth century, but
a crisis in the conscience of many at that time. Must men not
serve Truth, rather than either Unity or Authority?

Kinde pitty chokes my spleene; brave scorn forbids
Those teares to issue which swell my eye-lids;
I must not laugh, nor weepe sinnes, and be wise,
Can railing then cure these worne maladies?

34 *Spittles:* hospitals. 35 *Fuellers:* inflamers, inciters. 37 *Knowe . . .
knowe:* recognise . . . assault. 38 *Indifferent:* erotically impartial.
40-41 See *Gen.* xix. 4-5. 42 *Hydroptique:* dropsical, bloated. 44
Gallerie: entrance corridor. 55 *Jove:* supreme Roman deity.

Is not our Mistresse faire Religion,   5
As worthy of all our Soules devotion,
As vertue was to the first blinded age?
Are not heavens joyes as valiant to asswage
Lusts, as earths honour was to them? Alas,
As wee do them in meanes, shall they surpasse   10
Us in the end, and shall thy fathers spirit
Meete blinde Philosophers in heaven, whose merit
Of strict life may be imputed faith, and heare
Thee, whom hee taught so easie wayes and neare
To follow, damn'd? O if thou dar'st, feare this;   15
This feare great courage, and high valour is.
Dar'st thou ayd mutinous Dutch, and dar'st thou lay
Thee in ships woodden Sepulchers, a prey
To leaders rage, to stormes, to shot, to dearth?
Dar'st thou dive seas, and dungeons of the earth?   20
Hast thou couragious fire to thaw the ice
Of frozen North discoveries? and thrise
Colder than Salamanders, like divine
Children in th'oven, fires of Spaine, and the line,
Whose countries limbecks to our bodies bee,   25
Canst thou for gaine beare? and must every hee
Which cryes not, Goddesse, to thy Mistresse, draw,
Or eate thy poysonous words? courage of straw!
O desperate coward, wilt thou seeme bold, and
To thy foes and his (who made thee to stand   30
Sentinell in his worlds garrison) thus yeeld,
And for forbidden warres, leave th'appointed field?
Know thy foes: The foule Devill (whom thou
Strivest to please,) for hate, not love, would allow
Thee faine, his whole Realme to be quit; and as   35
The worlds all parts wither away and passe,
So the worlds selfe, thy other lov'd foe, is
In her decrepit wayne, and thou loving this,
Dost love a withered and worne strumpet; last,
Flesh (it selfes death) and joyes which flesh can taste, 40

7 *Blinded:* pre-Christian, lacking revelation. Cf. also line 12. 17 *Ayd mutinous Dutch:* fight for the Dutch against their Spanish overlords. 23 *Salamanders:* were supposed to live in fire. 24 *Children in th' oven:* see *Daniel* iii. 19-27; *fires of Spaine:* the Inquisition; *the line:* the equator. 25 *Limbecks:* alembics, used in distilling. 32 *For forbidden warres:* i.e. courting dangers to the point of self-destruction. 33-35 'You don't need to run to meet the Devil—he is only too glad to be quit of your importuning, by putting his kingdom into your hands.' 40 *It selfes:* its own.

Thou lovest; and thy faire goodly soule, which doth
Give this flesh power to taste joy, thou dost loath.
Seeke true religion. O where? Mirreus
Thinking her unhous'd here, and fled from us,
Seekes her at Rome; there, because hee doth know   45
That shee was there a thousand yeares agoe,
He loves her ragges so, as wee here obey
The statecloth where the Prince sate yesterday.
Crantz to such brave Loves will not be inthrall'd,
But loves her onely, who at Geneva is call'd   50
Religion, plaine, simple, sullen, yong,
Contemptuous, yet unhansome; As among
Lecherous humors, there is one that judges
No wenches wholsome, but course country drudges.
Graius stayes still at home here, and because   55
Some Preachers, vile ambitious bauds, and lawes
Still new like fashions, bid him thinke that shee
Which dwels with us, is onely perfect, hee
Imbraceth her, whom his Godfathers will
Tender to him, being tender, as Wards still   60
Take such wives as their Guardians offer, or
Pay valewes. Carelesse Phrygius doth abhorre
All, because all cannot be good, as one
Knowing some women whores, dares marry none.
Graccus loves all as one, and thinkes that so   65
As women do in divers countries goe
In divers habits, yet are still one kinde,
So doth, so is Religion; and this blind-
nesse too much light breeds; but unmoved thou
Of force must one, and forc'd but one allow;   70
And the right; aske thy father which is shee,
Let him aske his; though truth and falshood bee
Neare twins, yet truth a little elder is;
Be busie to seeke her, beleeve mee this,
Hee's not of none, nor worst, that seekes the best.   75
To adore, or scorne an image, or protest,
May all be bad; doubt wisely; in strange way
To stand inquiring right, is not to stray;
To sleepe, or runne wrong, is. On a huge hill,
Cragged, and steep, Truth stands, and hee that will   80

57 *Still:* for ever. 60-62 A recusant, whether Catholic or Puritan,
could be fined for failing to attend the Church of England services.
68-69 *This blindnesse, etc.:* One can be too tolerant, too 'enlightened.'

Reach her, about must, and about must goe;
And what the hills suddennes resists, winne so;
Yet strive so, that before age, deaths twilight,
Thy Soule rest, for none can worke in that night.
To will, implyes delay, therefore now doe: 85
Hard deeds, the bodies paines; hard knowledge too
The mindes indeavours reach, and mysteries
Are like the Sunne, dazling, yet plaine to all eyes.
Keepe the truth which thou hast found; men do not stand
In so ill case here, that God hath with his hand   90
Sign'd Kings blanck-charters to kill whom they hate,
Nor are they Vicars, but hangmen to Fate.
Foole and wretch, wilt thou let thy Soule be tyed
To mans lawes, by which she shall not be tryed
At the last day? Oh, will it then boot thee   95
To say a Philip, or a Gregory,
A Harry, or a Martin taught thee this?
Is not this excuse for mere contraries,
Equally strong? cannot both sides say so?
That thou mayest rightly obey power, her bounds know;   100
Those past, her nature, and name is chang'd; to be
Then humble to her is idolatrie.
As streames are, Power is; those blest flowers that dwell
At the rough streames calme head, thrive and do well,
But having left their roots, and themselves given   105
To the streames tyrannous rage, alas, are driven
Through mills, and rockes, and woods, and at last, almost
Consum'd in going, in the sea are lost:
So perish Soules, which more chuse mens unjust
Power from God claym'd, than God himselfe to trust.   110

John Milton

1608—1674

PARADISE REGAINED

This version of the tempting of Jesus is based on Luke's Gospel.
Although the austereness and apparent negativism of Milton's
rejections in this poem will always exasperate the humanist,

95 *Boot:* help, avail. 96 *Philip* . . . *Gregory:* Philip II of Spain . . .
Pope Gregory XIII or XIV. 97 *Harry* . . . *Martin:* Henry VIII of
England . . . Martin Luther.

Paradise Regained is a permanently valid reminder (permanent, because it need not be interpreted in Luke's or Milton's terms) that man shall not live by bread alone, and that great ends may prove recalcitrant even to great means.

THE FIRST BOOK

I who ere while the happy Garden sung,
By one maɲs disobedience lost, now sing
Recoverd Paradise to all mankind,
By one mans firm obedience fully tri'd
Through all temptation, and the Tempter foild   5
In all his wiles, defeated and repulst,
And *Eden* rais'd in the wast Wilderness.
   Thou Spirit who ledst this glorious Eremite
Into the Desert, his Victorious Field
Against the Spiritual Foe, and broughtst him thence   10
By proof th' undoubted Son of God, inspire,
As thou art wont, my prompted Song else mute,
And bear through highth or depth of natures bounds
With prosperous wing full summd to tell of deeds
Above Heroic, though in secret done,   15
And unrecorded left through many an Age,
Worthy t' have not remaind so long unsung.
   Now had the great Proclaimer with a voice
More awful than the sound of Trumpet, cri'd
Repentance, and Heav'ns Kingdom nigh at hand   20
To all Baptiz'd: to his great Baptism flockd
With aw the Regions round, and with them came
From *Nazareth* the Son of *Joseph* deemd
To the flood *Jordan*, came as then obscure,
Unmarkt, unknown; but him the Baptist soon   25
Descri'd, divinely warnd, and witness bore
As to his worthier, and would have resign'd
To him his Heav'nly Office, nor was long
His witness unconfirmd: on him baptiz'd
Heav'n op'nd, and in likeness of a Dove   30
The Spirit descended, while the Fathers voice
From Heav'n pronounc'd him his beloved Son.

1-3 *Paradise Lost* was published 1667, *Paradise Regained* 1671. 2 *One man:* Adam. 4 *One man:* Jesus. 8 *Thou Spirit:* the Spirit of God; *Eremite:* desert-dweller, anchorite. 14 *Full summd:* mature. 18 *Proclaimer:* John the Baptist. 23 *Nazareth:* town in Galilee, Palestine. 24 *Jordan:* main river of Palestine.
   A.L.P.

F

That heard the Adversary, who roving still
About the World, at that assembly fam'd
Would not be last, and with the voice divine   35
Nigh Thunder-strook, th' exalted man, to whom
Such high attest was giv'n, a while survey'd
With wonder, then with envy fraught and rage
Flies to his place, nor rests, but in mid air
To Councel summons all his mighty Peers,   40
Within thick Clouds and dark ten-fold involv'd,
A gloomy Consistory; and them amidst
With looks agast and sad he thus bespake.
    O ancient Powers of Air and this wide World,
For much more willingly I mention Air,   45
This our old Conquest, than remember Hell
Our hated habitation; well ye know
How many Ages, as the years of men,
This Universe we have possest, and rul'd
In manner at our will th' affairs of Earth,   50
Since *Adam* and his facil consort *Eve*
Lost Paradise deceiv'd by me, though since
With dread attending when that fatal wound
Shall be inflicted by the Seed of *Eve*
Upon my head, long the decrees of Heav'n   55
Delay, for longest time to him is short;
And now too soon for us the circling hours
This dreaded time have compast, wherein we
Must bide the stroak of that long threat'nd wound,
At least if so we can, and by the head   60
Brok'n be not intended all our power
To be infring'd, our freedom and our being
In this fair Empire won of Earth and Air;
For this ill news I bring, the Womans seed
Destind to this, is late of Woman born: 65
His birth to our just fear gave no small cause,
But his growth now to youths full flowr, displaying
All vertue, grace and wisdom to atchieve
Things highest, greatest, multiplies my fear.
Before him a great Prophet, to proclaim   70
His coming, is sent Harbinger, who all
Invites, and in the Consecrated stream
Pretends to wash off sin, and fit them so
Purifi'd to receive him pure, or rather

33 *Adversary:* Satan; *still:* as always.   50 *In manner:* as if.   51 *Facil:*
suggestible.   53 *Attending:* waiting; *that fatal wound:* See *Gen.* iii. 15.
62 *Infring'd:* shattered.

To do him honour as thir King; all come,   75
And he himself among them was baptiz'd,
Not thence to be more pure, but to receive
The testimony of Heaven, that who he is
Thenceforth the Nations may not doubt; I saw
The Prophet do him reverence, on him rising   80
Out of the water, Heav'n above the Clouds
Unfold her Crystal Dores, thence on his head
A perfet Dove descend, what e're it meant,
And out of Heav'n the Sovran voice I heard,
This is my Son belov'd, in him am pleas'd.   85
His Mother then is mortal, but his Sire,
Hee who obtains the Monarchy of Heav'n,
And what will he not do to advance his Son?
His first-begot we know, and sore have felt,
When his fierce thunder drove us to the deep;   90
Who this is we must learn, for man he seems
In all his lineaments, though in his face
The glimpses of his Fathers glory shine.
Ye see our danger on the utmost edge
Of hazard, which admits no long debate,   95
But must with something sudden be oppos'd,
Not force, but well coucht fraud, well woven snares,
Ere in the head of Nations he appear
Thir King, thir Leader, and Supream on Earth.
I, when no other durst, sole undertook   100
The dismal expedition to find out
And ruin *Adam*, and th' exploit performd
Successfully; a calmer voyage now
Will waft me; and the way found prosperous once
Induces best to hope of like success.   105
    He ended, and his words impression left
Of much amazement to th' infernal Crew,
Distracted and surpriz'd with deep dismay
At these sad tidings; but no time was then
For long indulgence to thir fears or grief: 110
Unanimous they all commit the care
And management of this main enterprize
To him thir great Dictator, whose attempt
At first against mankind so well had thriv'd
In *Adams* overthrow, and led thir march   115

87 *Obtains:* holds. 90 See *Paradise Lost,* Book VI. 97 *Well coucht:*
hidden as in an ambush. 100-2 See *Paradise Lost,* Book II; *dismal:*
dreadful. 103 *Calmer:* i.e. because he no longer has to fight his way up
from Hell through Chaos.

From Hells deep-vaulted Den to dwell in light,
Regents and Potentates, and Kings, yea gods
Of many a pleasant Realm and Province wide.
So to the Coast of *Jordan* he directs
His easie steps, girded with snaky wiles,   120
Where he might likeliest find this new-declar'd,
This Man of men, attested Son of God,
Temptation and all guile on him to try;
So to subvert whom he suspected rais'd
To end his Raign on Earth so long enjoy'd: 125
But contrary unweeting he fulfilld
The purpos'd Counsel pre-ordaind and fixt
Of the most High, who in full frequence bright
Of Angels, thus to *Gabriel* smiling spake.
  Gabriel this day by proof thou shalt behold,   130
Thou and all Angels conversant on Earth
With man or mens affairs, how I begin
To verifie that solemn message late,
On which I sent thee to the Virgin pure
In *Galilee*, that she should bear a Son   135
Great in Renown, and calld the Son of God;
Then toldst her doubting how these things could be
To her a Virgin, that on her should come
The Holy Ghost, and the power of the highest
Ore-shadow her: this man born and now up-grown,   140
To shew him worthy of his birth divine
And high prediction, henceforth I expose
To Satan; let him tempt and now assay
His utmost suttlety, because he boasts
And vaunts of his great cunning to the throng   145
Of his Apostasie; he might have learnt
Less over-weening, since he faild in *Job*,
Whose constant perseverance overcame
Whate're his cruel malice could invent.
He now shall know I can produce a man   150
Of femal Seed, far abler to resist
All his sollicitations, and at length
All his vast force, and drive him back to Hell,
Winning by Conquest what the first man lost
By fallacy surpriz'd. But first I mean   155

126 *Unweeting:* unconsciously. 128 *Frequence:* assembly. 129 *Gabriel:*
one of the chief angels; he announced the coming of Jesus to his mother
Mary. See *Luke* i. 26-38. 135 *Galilee:* province of north Palestine.
145-6 *Throng Of his Apostasie:* crowd of his co-rebels. 147 *Since he faild
in Job:* Cf. *Job* i and xlii. 155 *Fallacy:* deceptive arguments.

To exercise him in the Wilderness,
There he shall first lay down the rudiments
Of his great warfare, ere I send him forth
To conquer Sin and Death the two grand foes,
By Humiliation and strong Sufferance: 160
His weakness shall orecome Satanic strength
And all the World, and mass of sinful flesh;
That all the Angels and Ætherial Powers,
They now, and men hereafter may discern,
From what consummat vertue I have chose   165
This perfet Man, by merit calld my Son,
To earn Salvation for the Sons of men.
  So spake th' Eternal Father, and all Heaven
Admiring stood a space, then into Hymns
Burst forth, and in Celestial measures mov'd,   170
Circling the Throne and Singing, while the hand
Sung with the voice, and this the argument.
  Victory and Triumph to the Son of God
Now entring his great duel, not of arms,
But to vanquish by wisdom hellish wiles.   175
The Father knows the Son; therefore secure
Ventures his filial Vertue, though untri'd,
Against whate're may tempt, whate're seduce,
Allure, or terrifie, or undermine.
Be frustrate all ye stratagems of Hell,   180
And devilish machinations come to naught.
  So they in Heav'n thir Odes and Vigils tun'd:
Mean while the Son of God, who yet some days
Lodg'd in *Bethabara* where *John* baptiz'd,
Musing and much revolving in his brest,   185
How best the mighty work he might begin
Of Saviour to mankind, and which way first
Publish his God-like office now mature,
One day forth walkd alone, the Spirit leading
And his deep thoughts, the better to converse   190
With solitude, till farr from track of men,
Thought following thought, and step by step led on,
He enterd now the bordering Desert wild,
And with dark shades and rocks environd round,
His holy Meditations thus persu'd.   195
  O what a multitude of thoughts at once
Awak'nd in me swarm, while I consider
What from within I feel my self, and hear

176 *Secure:* with no anxiety.   180 *Frustrate:* frustrated.   182 *Vigils:*
hymns.   184 *Bethabara:* the ford of Jordan, and the town beside it.

What from without comes oft'n to my ears,
Ill sorting with my present state compar'd. 200
When I was yet a child, no childish play
To me was pleasing, all my mind was set
Serious to learn and know, and thence to do
What might be publick good; my self I thought
Born to that end, born to promote all truth, 205
All righteous things: therefore above my years,
The Law of God I red, and found it sweet,
Made it my whole delight, and in it grew
To such perfection, that ere yet my age
Had measur'd twice six years, at our great Feast 210
I went into the Temple, there to hear
The Teachers of our Law, and to propose
What might improve my knowledge or thir own;
And was admir'd by all, yet this not all
To which my Spirit aspir'd, victorious deeds 215
Flam'd in my heart, heroic acts, one while
To rescue *Israel* from the *Roman* yoke,
Then to subdue and quell ore all the earth
Brute violence and proud Tyrannick pow'r,
Till truth were freed, and equity restor'd: 220
Yet held it more humane, more heav'nly first
By winning words to conquer willing hearts,
And make perswasion do the work of fear;
At least to try, and teach the erring Soul
Not wilfully mis-doing, but unware 225
Misled; the stubborn onely to subdue.
These growing thoughts my Mother soon perceiving
By words at times cast forth inly rejoyc'd,
And said to me apart, high are thy thoughts
O Son, but nourish them and let them soar 230
To what highth sacred vertue and true worth
Can raise them, though above example high;
By matchless Deeds express thy matchless Sire.
For know, thou art no Son of mortal man,
Though men esteem thee low of Parentage, 235
Thy Father is th' Eternal King, who rules
All Heav'n and Earth, Angels and Sons of men,
A messenger from God fore-told thy birth
Conceiv'd in me a Virgin, he fore-told
Thou shouldst be great and sit on *Davids* Throne, 240
And of thy Kingdom there should be no end.

210 *Great Feast:* the Jewish Passover. 214 *Admir'd:* marvelled at.
240 *David:* great king of Israel.

At thy Nativity a glorious Quire ·
Of Angels in the fields of *Bethlehem* sung
To Shepherds watching at thir folds by night,
And told them the Messiah now was born,   245
Where they might see him, and to thee they came;
Directed to the Manger where thou laist,
For in the Inn was left no better room:
A Starr, not seen before in Heav'n appearing
Guided the Wise Men thither from the East,   250
To honour thee with Incense, Myrrh, and Gold,
By whose bright course led on they found the place,
Affirming it thy Starr new grav'n in Heaven,
By which they knew thee King of *Israel* born.
Just *Simeon* and Prophetic *Anna*, warnd   255
By Vision, found thee in the Temple, and spake
Before the Altar and the vested Priest,
Like things of thee to all that present stood.
This having heard, strait I again revolv'd
The Law and Prophets, searching what was writ   260
Concerning the Messiah, to our Scribes
Known partly, and soon found of whom they spake
I am; this chiefly, that my way must lie
Through many a hard assay eev'n to the death,
Ere I the promised Kingdom can attain,   265
Or work Redemption for mankind, whose sins
Full weight must be transferrd upon my head.
Yet neither thus disheart'nd or dismay'd,
The time prefixt I waited, when behold
The Baptist, (of whose birth I oft had heard,   270
Not knew by sight) now come, who was to come
Before Messiah and his way prepare.
I as all others to his Baptism came,
Which I believ'd was from above; but hee
Strait knew me, and with loudest voice proclaimd   275
Mee him (for it was shewn him so from Heaven)
Mee him whose Harbinger he was; and first
Refus'd on mee his Baptism to conferr,
As much his greater, and was hardly won;
But as I rose out of the laving stream,   280
Heav'n op'nd her eternal doors, from whence
The Spirit descended on me like a Dove,
And last the sum of all, my Father's voice,

243 *Bethlehem:* town near Jerusalem, home of David and birthplace of
Jesus. 255 See *Luke* ii. 25-38. 262 *Of whom:* i.e. 'that he of whom'.
264 *Assay:* test.

Audibly heard from Heav'n, pronounc'd me his,
Mee his beloved Son, in whom alone   285
He was well pleas'd; by which I knew the time
Now full, that I no more should live obscure,
But op'nly begin, as best becomes
The Autority which I deriv'd from Heaven.
And now by some strong motion I am led   290
Into this Wilderness, to what intent
I learn not yet, perhaps I need not know;
For what concerns my knowledge God reveals.
    So spake our Morning Starr then in his rise,
And looking round on every side beheld   295
A pathless Desert, dusk with horrid shades;
The way he came not having markt, return
Was difficult, by human steps untrod;
And he still on was led, but with such thoughts
Accompanied of things past and to come   300
Lodg'd in his brest, as well might recommend
Such Solitude before choicest Society.
Full forty days he passd, whether on hill
Sometimes, anon in shady vale, each night
Under the covert of some ancient Oak,   305
Or Cedar, to defend him from the dew,
Or harbourd in one Cave, is not reveald;
Nor tasted human food, nor hunger felt
Till those days ended, hungerd then at last
Among wild Beasts: they at his sight grew mild,   310
Nor sleeping him nor waking harmd, his walk
The fiery Serpent fled, and noxious Worm,
The Lion and fierce Tiger glar'd aloof.
But now an aged man in Rural weeds,
Following, as seemd, the quest of some stray Ewe,   315
Or witherd sticks to gather; which might serve
Against a Winters day when winds blow keen,
To warm him wet returnd from field at Eve,
He saw approach, who first with curious eye
Perus'd him, then with words thus utterd spake.   320
    Sir, what ill chance hath brought thee to this place
So farr from path or road of men, who pass
In Troop or Caravan, for single none
Durst ever, who returnd, and dropd not here
His Carcass, pin'd with hunger and with droughth?   325
I ask the rather, and the more admire,
For that to me thou seem'st the man, whom late
296 *Horrid:* shaggy. 312 *Worm:* snake.

Our new baptizing Prophet at the Ford
Of *Jordan* honourd so, and calld thee Son
Of God; I saw and heard, for wee sometimes   330
Who dwell this wild, constraind by want, come forth
To Town or Village nigh (nighest is farr)
Where aught we hear, and curious are to hear,
What happ'ns new; Fame also finds us out.
    To whom the Son of God. Who brought m? hither   335
Will bring me hence, no other Guide I seek.
    By Miracle he may, reply'd the Swain,
What other way I see not, for we here
Live on tough roots and stubs, to thirst inur'd
More than the Camel, and to drink go farr,   340
Men to much misery and hardship born;
But if thou be the Son of God, Command
That out of these hard stones be made thee bread;
So shalt thou save thy self and us relieve
With Food, whereof we wretched seldom taste.   345
    He ended, and the Son of God reply'd.
Think'st thou such force in Bread? is it not writt'n
(For I discern thee other than thou seem'st)
Man lives not by Bread onely, but each Word
Proceeding from the mouth of God; who fed   350
Our Fathers here with Manna; in the Mount
Moses was forty days, nor eat nor drank,
And forty days *Elijah* without food
Wanderd this barren waste, the same I now:
Why dost thou then suggest to me distrust,   355
Knowing who I am, as I know who thou art?
    Whom thus answerd th' Arch-Fiend now undisguis'd.
'Tis true, I am that Spirit unfortunate,
Who leagu'd with millions more in rash revolt
Kept not my happy Station, but was driv'n   360
With them from bliss to the bottomless deep,
Yet to that hideous place not so confin'd
By rigour unconniving, but that oft
Leaving my dolorous Prison I enjoy
Large liberty to round this Globe of Earth,   365
Or range in th' Air, nor from the Heav'n of Heav'ns
Hath he excluded my resort sometimes.

333 *Aught:* anything. 334 *What:* of what; *fame:* rumour. 347 *Is it
not written, etc.:* See *Deut.* viii. 3. 351 *The Mount:* Mt. Sinai, where
Moses received the Ten Commandments. 353-4 See *1 Kings* xix. 4-8.
363 *Unconniving:* unremitting.

I came among the Sons of God, when he
Gave up into my hands *Uzzean Job*
To prove him, and illustrat his high worth;   370
And when to all his Angels he propos'd
To draw the proud King *Ahab* into fraud
That he might fall in *Ramoth*, they demurring,
I undertook that office, and the tongues
Of all his flattering Prophets glibbd with lyes   375
To his destruction, as I had in charge.
For what he bids I do; though I have lost
Much lustre of my native brightness, lost
To be belov'd of God, I have not lost
To love, at least contemplat and admire   380
What I see excellent in good, or fair,
Or vertuous, I should so have lost all sense.
What can be then less in me than desire
To see thee and approach thee, whom I know
Declar'd the Son of God, to hear attent   385
Thy wisdom, and behold thy God-like deeds?
Men generally think me much a foe
To all mankind: why should I? they to me
Never did wrong or violence, by them
I lost not what I lost, rather by them   390
I gaind what I have gaind, and with them dwell
Copartner in these Regions of the World,
If not disposer; lend them oft my aid,
Oft my advice by presages and signs,
And answers, oracles, portents and dreams,   395
Whereby they may direct thir future life.
Envy they say excites me, thus to gain
Companions of my misery and wo.
At first it may be; but long since with wo
Nearer acquainted, now I feel by proof,   400
That fellowship in pain divides not smart,
Nor light'ns aught each mans peculiar load.
Small consolation then, were Man adjoind:
This wounds me most (what can it less) that Man,
Man fall'n shall be restor'd, I never more.   405
    To whom our Saviour sternly thus reply'd.
Deservedly thou griev'st, compos'd of lyes
From the beginning, and in lies wilt end;
Who boast'st release from Hell, and leave to come
Into the Heav'n of Heavens; thou com'st indeed,   410

368-70 See *Job* i.   370 *Illustrat:* glorify.   371-6 See *1 Kings* xxii. 19-22.
372 *Fraud:* deluded evildoing.   385 *Attent:* attentively.

As a poor miserable captive thrall
Comes to the place where he before had sat
Among the Prime in Splendour, now depos'd,
Ejected, emptied, gaz'd, unpitied, shunnd,
A spectacle of ruin or of scorn   415
To all the Host of Heaven; the happy place
Imparts to thee no happiness, no joy,
Rather inflames thy torment, representing
Lost bliss, to thee no more communicable,
So never more in Hell than when in Heaven.   420
But thou art serviceable to Heav'ns King.
Wilt thou impute to obedience what thy fear
Extorts, or pleasure to do ill excites?
What but thy malice mov'd thee to misdeem
Of righteous *Job*, then cruelly to afflict him   425
With all inflictions, but his patience won?
The other service was thy chosen task,
To be a lyer in four hunderd mouths;
For lying is thy sustenance, thy food.
Yet thou pretend'st to truth; all Oracles   430
By thee are giv'n, and what confest more true
Among the Nations? that hath been thy craft,
By mixing somewhat true to vent more lyes.
But what have been thy answers, what but dark
Ambiguous and with double sense deluding,   435
Which they who askd have seldom understood,
And not well understood as good not known?
Who ever by consulting at thy shrine
Returnd the wiser, or the more instruct
To flye or follow what concernd him most,   440
And run not sooner to his fatal snare?
For God hath justly giv'n the Nations up
To thy Delusions; justly, since they fell
Idolatrous, but when his purpose is
Among them to declare his Providence   445
To thee not known, whence hast thou then thy truth,
But from him or his Angels President
In every Province, who themselves disdaining
To approach thy Temples, give thee in command
What to the smallest tittle thou shalt say   450
To thy Adorers; thou with trembling fear,

413 *Prime:* foremost. 428 referring to the 400 false prophets of Ahab
(line 375). 430-1 referring to the belief that the fallen angels survived
as pagan deities and oracles. 439 *Instruct:* instructed. 447 *President:*
presiding.

Or like a Fawning Parasite obey'st;
Then to thy self ascrib'st the truth fore-told.
But this thy glory shall be soon retrencht;
No more shalt thou by oracling abuse   455
The Gentiles; henceforth Oracles are ceast,
And thou no more with Pomp and Sacrifice
Shalt be enquir'd at *Delphos* or elsewhere,
At least in vain, for they shall find thee mute.
God hath now sent his living Oracle   460
Into the World, to teach his final will,
And sends his Spirit of Truth henceforth to dwell
In pious Hearts, an inward Oracle
To all truth requisite for men to know.
    So spake our Saviour; but the suttle Fiend,   465
Though inly stung with anger and disdain,
Dissembl'd, and this Answer smooth returnd.
    Sharply thou hast insisted on rebuke,
And urg'd me hard with doings, which not will
But misery hath wrested from me; where   470
Easily canst thou find one miserable,
And not inforc't oft-times to part from truth,
If it may stand him more in stead to lye,
Say and unsay, feign, flatter, or abjure?
But thou art plac't above me, thou art Lord;   475
From thee I can and must submiss endure
Check or reproof, and glad to scape so quit.
Hard are the ways of Truth, and rough to walk,
Smooth on the tongue discourst, pleasing to th' ear,
And tuneable as Silvan Pipe or Song;   480
What wonder then if I delight to hear
Her dictates from thy mouth? most men admire
Vertue, who follow not her lore: permit me
To hear thee when I come (since no man comes)
And talk at least, though I despair to attain.   485
Thy Father, who is holy, wise and pure,
Suffers the Hypocrit or Atheous Priest
To tread his Sacred Courts, and minister
About his Altar, handling holy things,
Praying or vowing, and voutsaf'd his voice   490
To *Balaam* Reprobate, a Prophet yet

458 *Delphos:* Delphi, in central Greece, shrine of the oracle of Apollo.
470-4 Here the father of lies is very strikingly 'mixing somewhat true.'
476 *Submiss:* submissively. 487 *Atheous:* atheistic. 490-2 See *Num.*
xxiii. Balaam may have been accursed ('reprobate'), yet God spoke
through his voice.

Inspir'd; disdain not such access to me.
To whom our Saviour with unalterd brow.
Thy coming hither, though I know thy scope,
I bid not or forbid; do as thou find'st   495
Permission from above; thou canst not more.
   He added not; and Satan bowing low
His gray dissimulation, disappeard
Into thin Air diffus'd: for now began
Night with her sullen wing to double-shade   500
The Desert, Fowls in thir clay nests were coucht ;
And now wild Beasts came forth the woods to roam.

THE SECOND BOOK

   Mean while the new-baptiz'd, who yet remaind
At *Jordan* with the Baptist, and had seen
Him whom they heard so late expresly calld
Jesus Messiah Son of God declar'd,
And on that high Autority had believ'd,   5
And with him talkt, and with him lodg'd, I mean
Andrew and *Simon,* famous after known
With others though in Holy Writ not nam'd,
Now missing him thir joy so lately found,
So lately found, and so abruptly gone,   10
Began to doubt, and doubted many days,
And as the days increas'd, increas'd thir doubt:
Sometimes they thought he might be onely shewn,
And for a time caught up to God, as once
Moses was in the Mount, and missing long;   15
And the great *Thisbite* who on fiery wheels
Rode up to Heaven, yet once again to come.
Therefore as those young Prophets then with care
Sought lost *Elijah,* so in each place these
Nigh to *Bethabara;* in *Jerico*   20
The City of Palms, *Ænon,* and *Salem* Old,
Machærus and each Town or City walld
On this side the broad lake *Genezaret,*

494 *Scope:* aim. 4 *Messiah:* God's Anointed, the long-promised
deliverer of the Jewish people. 7 Andrew and his brother Simon Peter,
two of the apostles. 15 See I. 351-2. 16 *The great Thisbite:* Elijah.
See *II Kings* ii. 11. 17 *Once again to come:* as John the Baptist. 18-19
See *II Kings* ii. 15-17. 20 *Jeric(h)o:* very ancient city in the Jordan
valley, north-east of Jerusalem. 21 *Ænon . . . Salem:* places somewhere
on west bank of Jordan (cf. *John* iii. 23). 22 *Machærus:* stronghold
east of Dead Sea. 23 *Genezaret:* Sea of Galilee.

Or in *Perea,* but returnd in vain.
Then on the bank of *Jordan,* by a Creek: 25
Where winds with Reeds, and Osiers whisp'ring play
Plain Fishermen, no greater men them call,
.Close in a Cottage low together got
Thir unexpected loss and plaints out breath'd.
Alas, from what high hope to what relapse   30
Unlookt for are we fall'n; our eyes beheld
Messiah certainly now come, so long
Expected of our Fathers; we have heard
His words, his wisdom full of grace and truth,
Now, now, for sure, deliverance is at hand,   35
The Kingdom shall to *Israel* be restor'd:
Thus we rejoyc'd, but soon our joy is turnd
Into perplexity and new amaze:
For whither is he gone, what accident
Hath rapt him from us? will he now retire   40
After appearance, and again prolong
Our expectation? God of *Israel,*
Send thy Messiah forth, the time is come;
Behold the Kings of th' Earth how they oppress
Thy chosen, to what highth thir pow'r unjust   45
They have exalted, and behind them cast
All fear of thee, arise and vindicate
Thy Glory, free thy people from thir yoke:
But let us wait; thus farr he hath performd,
Sent his Anointed, and to us reveald him,   50
By his great Prophet, pointed at and shown,
In publick, and with him we have converst;
Let us be glad of this, and all our fears
Lay on his Providence; he will not fail
Nor will withdraw him now, nor will recall,   55
Mock us with his blest sight, then snatch him hence,
Soon we shall see our hope, our joy return.
      Thus they out of thir plaints new hope resume
To find whom at the first they found unsought:
But to his Mother *Mary,* when she saw   60
Others returnd from Baptism, not her Son,
Nor left at *Jordan,* tidings of him none;
Within her brest, though calm; her brest though pure,
Motherly cares and fears got head, and rais'd
Some troubl'd thoughts, which she in sighs thus clad.   65
      O what avails me now that honour high
To have conceiv'd of God, or that salute
24 *Perea:* region east of Jordan.   60 *To:* for.

Hale highly favourd, among women blest;
While I to sorrows am no less advanc't,
And fears as eminent, above the lot   70
Of other women, by the birth I bore,
In such a season born when scarce a Shed
Could be obtaind to shelter him or me
From the bleak air; a Stable was our warmth,
A Manger his, yet soon enforc't to flye   75
Thence into *Egypt*, till the Murd'rous King
Were dead, who sought his life, and missing filld
With Infant blood the streets of *Bethlehem*;
From *Egypt* home returnd, in *Nazareth*
Hath been our dwelling many years, his life   80
Privat, unactive, calm, contemplative,
Little suspicious to any King; but now
Full grown to Man, acknowledg'd, as I hear,
By *John* the Baptist, and in publick shown,
Son ownd from Heaven by his Father's voice;   85
I lookd for some great change; to Honour? no,
But trouble, as old *Simeon* plain fore-told,
That to the fall and rising he should be
Of many in *Israel*, and to a sign
Spok'n against, that through my very Soul   90
A sword shall pierce, this is my favourd lot,
My Exaltation to Afflictions high;
Afflicted I may be, it seems, and blest;
I will not argue that, nor will repine.
But where delays he now? some great intent   95
Conceals him: when twelve years he scarce had seen,
I lost him, but so found, as well I saw
He could not lose himself; but went about
His Father's business; what he meant I mus'd,
Since understand; much more his absence now   100
Thus long to some great purpose he obscures.
But I to wait with patience am inur'd;
My heart hath been a store-house long of things
And sayings laid up, portending strange events.
    Thus *Mary* pondering oft, and oft to mind   105
Recalling what remarkably had past
Since first her Salutation heard, with thoughts
Meekly compos'd awaited the fulfilling:
The while her Son tracing the Desert wild,

68 Cf. *Luke* i. 28.   76 *The Murd'rous King:* Herod the Great, King of Judea (*c.* 73-4 B.C.), who ordered the Massacre of the Innocents in Bethlehem.   87-91 Cf. *Luke* ii. 34-35.   101 *Obscures:* conceals.

Sole but with holiest Meditations fed,   110
Into himself descended, and at once
All his great work to come before him set;
How to begin, how to accomplish best
His end of being on Earth, and mission high:
For Satan with slye preface to return   115
Had left him vacant, and with speed was gon
Up to the middle Region of thick Air,
Where all his Potentates in Council sate;
There without sign of boast, or sign of joy,
Sollicitous and blank he thus began.   120
    Princes, Heav'ns ancient Sons, Æthereal Thrones,
Demonian Spirits now, from th' Element
Each of his reign allotted, rightlier calld,
Powers of Fire, Air, Water, and Earth beneath,
So may we hold our place and these mild seats   125
Without new trouble; such an Enemy
Is risen to invade us, who no less
Threat'ns than our expulsion down to Hell;
I, as I undertook, and with the vote
Consenting in full frequence was impowr'd,   130
Have found him, viewd him, tasted him, but find
Farr other labour to be undergon
Than when I dealt with *Adam* first of Men,
Though *Adam* by his Wives allurement fell,
However to this Man inferior farr,   135
If he be Man by Mothers side at least,
With more than human gifts from Heav'n adornd,
Perfections absolute, Graces divine,
And amplitude of mind to greatest Deeds.
Therefore I am returnd, lest confidence   140
Of my success with *Eve* in Paradise
Deceive ye to perswasion over-sure
Of like succeeding here; I summon all
Rather to be in readiness, with hand
Or counsel to assist; lest I who erst   145
Thought none my equal, now be over-matcht.
    So spake th' old Serpent doubting, and from all
With clamour was assur'd thir utmost aid
At his command; when from amidst them rose

116 *Vacant:* unoccupied. 117 This cold stormy middle region or belt
was traditionally the haunt of demonic and malignant spirits. 120
Sollicitous and blank: anxious and nonplussed. 121 *Thrones:* one of the
chief orders of angels. 122 *Demonian spirits now:* devils malignly
associated with the four elements (fire, air, water, earth).

Belial the dissolutest Spirit that fell, 150
The sensuallest, and after *Asmodai*
The fleshliest Incubus, and thus advis'd.
　Set women in his eye and in his walk,
Among daughters of men the fairest found;
Many are in each Region passing fair 155
As the noon Skie; more like to Goddesses
Than Mortal Creatures, graceful and discreet,
Expert in amorous Arts, enchanting tongues
Perswasive, Virgin majesty with mild
And sweet allayd, yet terrible to approach, 160
Skilld to retire, and in retiring draw
Hearts after them tangl'd in Amorous Nets.
Such object hath the power to soft'n and tame
Severest temper, smooth the rugged'st brow,
Enerve, and with voluptuous hope dissolve, 165
Draw out with credulous desire, and lead
At will the manliest, resolutest brest,
As the Magnetic hardest Iron draws.
Women, when nothing else, beguil'd the heart
Of wisest *Solomon*, and made him build, 170
And made him bow to the Gods of his Wives.
　To whom quick answer Satan thus returnd.
Belial, in much uneven scale thou weigh'st
All others by thy self; because of old
Thou thy self doat'st on womankind, admiring 175
Thir shape, thir colour, and attractive grace,
None are, thou think'st, but tak'n with such toys.
Before the Flood thou with thy lusty Crew,
False-titl'd Sons of God, roaming the Earth
Cast wanton eyes on the daughters of men, 180
And coupl'd with them, and begot a race.
Have we not seen, or by relation heard,
In Courts and Regal Chambers how thou lurk'st,
In Wood or Grove by mossie Fountain side,
In Valley or Green Meadow to way-lay 185
Some beauty rare, *Calisto, Clymene,*
Daphne, or *Semele, Antiopa,*
Or *Amymone, Syrinx,* many more

150 *Belial:* one of the chief rebel angels (cf. *Paradise Lost*, I. 490 ff.).
151 *Asmodai:* a lustful angel in the apocryphal *Book of Tobit.* 152
Incubus: evil spirit descending on a sleeping person like a nightmare.
160 *Allayd:* tempered. 164 *Temper:* disposition. 165 *Enerve:*
enervate. 168 *Magnetic:* magnet. 169-71 See *I Kings* xi. 1-8.
178-81 Cf. *Gen.* vi. 1-2. 186-8 nymphs of Greek mythology, loved and
pursued by the Greek gods.

Too long, then lay'st thy scapes on names ador'd,
Apollo, Neptune, Jupiter, or *Pan,*   190
Satyr, or Fawn, or Silvan? But these haunts
Delight not all; among the Sons of Men, ,
How many have with a smile made small account
Of beauty and her lures, easily scornd
All her assaults, on worthier things intent?   195
Remember that *Pellean* Conquerour,
A youth, how all the Beauties of the East
He slightly viewd, and slightly over-passd;
How hee sirnam'd of *Africa* dismissd
In his prime youth the fair *Iberian* maid.   200
For *Solomon* he liv'd at ease, and full
Of honour, wealth, high fare, aimd not beyond
Higher design than to enjoy his State;
Thence to the bait of Women lay expos'd;
But hee whom we attempt is wiser far   205
Than *Solomon,* of more exalted mind,
Made and set wholly on th' accomplishment
Of greatest things; what woman will you find,
Though of this Age the wonder and the fame,
On whom his leisure will voutsafe an eye   210
Of fond desire? or should she confident,
As sitting Queen ador'd on Beauties Throne,
Descend with all her winning charms begirt
To enamour, as the Zone of *Venus* once
Wrought that effect on *Jove,* so Fables tell;   . 215
How would one look from his Majestick brow
Seated as on the top of Vertues hill,
Discount'nance her despis'd, and put to rout
All her array; her femal pride deject,
Or turn to reverent awe? for Beauty stands   220
In th' admiration onely of weak minds
Led captive; cease to admire, and all her Plumes
Fall flat and shrink into a trivial toy,
At every sudden slighting quite abasht:
Therefore with manlier objects we must try   225
His constancy, with such as have more shew

189 *Too long:* i.e. to recount them all; *scapes:* escapades. 190 *Apollo:*
sun-god; *Neptune:* sea-god; *Jupiter:* father of the gods; *Pan:* nature-
god. 191 *Satyr . . . Fawn . . . Silvan:* minor rural deities associated with
woods and forests. 196 *Pellean Conquerour:* Alexander the Great (356-
323 B.C.), born at Pella, Macedonia. 199 *Hee sirnam'd of Africa:*
Scipio Africanus (236/5-c. 183 B.C.), said by Livy to have been courteous
towards one of his Spanish prisoners. 214-15 Juno won over Jove
when she wore the girdle of Venus.

Of worth, of honour, glory, and popular praise;
Rocks whereon greatest men have oftest wreckt;
Of that which onely seems to satisfie
Lawful desires of Nature, not beyond;   230
And now I know he hungers where no food
Is to be found, in the wide Wilderness;
The rest commit to mee, I shall let pass
No advantage, and his strength as oft assay.

    He ceas'd, and heard thir grant in loud acclaim;   235
Then forthwith to him takes a chosen band
Of Spirits likest to himself in guile
To be at hand, and at his beck appear,
If cause were to unfold some active Scene
Of various Persons each to know his part;   240
Then to the Desert takes with these his flight;
Where still from shade to shade the Son of God
After forty days fasting had remaind,
Now hungring first, and to himself thus said.

    Where will this end? four times ten days I have past   245
Wandring this woody maze, and human food
Nor tasted, nor had appetite: that Fast
To Vertue I impute not, or count part
Of what I suffer here; if Nature need not,
Or God support Nature without repast   250
Though needing, what praise is it to endure?
But now I feel I hunger, which declares,
Nature hath need of what she asks; yet God
Can satisfie that need some other way,
Though hunger still remain: so it remain   255
Without this bodies wasting, I content me,
And from the sting of Famin fear no harm,
Nor mind it, fed with better thoughts that feed
Mee hungring more to do my Fathers will.

    It was the hour of night, when thus the Son   260
Commun'd in silent walk, then laid him down
Under the hospitable covert nigh
Of Trees thick interwoven; there he slept,
And dreamd, as appetite is wont to dream,
Of meats and drinks, Natures refreshment sweet;   265
Him thought, he by the Brook of *Cherith* stood
And saw the Ravens with thir horny beaks
Food to *Elijah* bringing Ev'n and Morn,

240 *Persons:* actors. 255 *So:* if. 264 *Appetite:* hunger, a hungry
man. 266 *Him thought:* it seemed to him. 266-76 See *I Kings* xvii.
1-6, and xix. 1-8.

Though ravenous, taught to abstain from what they brought:
He saw the Prophet also how he fled   270
Into the Desert, and how there he slept
Under a Juniper; then how awak't,
He found his Supper on the coals prepar'd,
And by the Angel was bid rise and eat,
And eat the second time after repose,   275
The strength whereof suffic'd him forty days;
Sometimes that with *Elijah* he partook,
Or as a guest with *Daniel* at his pulse.
Thus wore out night, and now the Harald Lark
Left his ground-nest, high towring to descry   280
The morns approach, and greet her with his Song:
As lightly from his grassy Couch up rose
Our Saviour, and found all was but a dream ;
Fasting he went to sleep, and fasting wak'd.
Up to a hill anon his steps he reard,   285
From whose high top to ken the prospect round,
If Cottage were in view, Sheep-cote or Herd;
But Cottage, Herd or Sheep-cote none he saw,
Onely in a bottom saw a pleasant Grove,
With chaunt of tuneful Birds resounding loud;   290
Thither he bent his way, determind there
To rest at noon, and enterd soon the shade
High rooft and walks beneath, and alleys brown
That op'nd in the midst a woody Scene,
Natures own work it seemd (Nature taught Art)   295
And to a Superstitious eye the haunt
Of Wood-Gods and Wood-Nymphs; he viewd it round,
When suddenly a man before him stood,
Not rustic as before, but seemlier clad,
As one in City, or Court, or Palace bred,   300
And with fair speech these words to him addressd.
    With granted leave officious I return,
But much more wonder that the Son of God
In this wild solitude so long should bide
Of all things destitute, and well I know,   ·   305
Not without hunger. Others of some note,
As story tells, have trod this Wilderness;
The Fugitive Bond-woman with her Son

277 *That:* i.e. 'him thought that' (line 266). 278 See *Dan.* i. 8-19; *pulse:*
simple meal of peas, beans, lentils, etc. 289 *Bottom:* low valley. 293
Brown: dark. 295 *Nature taught Art:* nature improved, perhaps by Satan
himself. 302 *Officious:* ministering. 308 Hagar and Ishmael (see *Gen.*
xxi. 9-19). Milton seems to confuse Ishmael with his son Nebaioth.

Out cast *Nebaioth*, yet found he relief
By a providing Angel; all the race   310
Of *Israel* here had famisht, had not God
Raind from Heav'n Manna, and that Prophet bold
Native of *Thebez* wandring here was fed
Twice by a voice inviting him to eat.
Of thee these forty days none hath regard,   315
Forty and more deserted here indeed.
    To whom thus Jesus; what conclud'st thou hence?
They all had need, I as thou seest have none.
    How hast thou hunger then? Satan reply'd,
Tell me if Food were now before thee set,   320
Wouldst thou not eat? Thereafter as I like
The giver, answerd Jesus. Why should that
Cause thy refusal, said the suttle Fiend,
Hast thou not right to all Created things,
Owe not all Creatures by just right to thee   325
Duty and Service, nor to stay till bid,
But tender all thir power? nor mention I
Meats by the Law unclean, or offerd first
To Idols, those young *Daniel* could refuse;
Nor profferd by an Enemy, though who   330
Would scruple that, with want opprest? behold
Nature asham'd, or better to express,
Troubl'd that thou shouldst hunger, hath purveyd
From all the Elements her choicest store
To treat thee as beseems, and as her Lord   335
With honour, onely deign to sit and eat.
    He spake no dream, for as his words had end,
Our Saviour lifting up his eyes beheld
In ample space under the broadest shade
A Table richly spred, in regal mode,   340
With dishes pil'd, and meats of noblest sort
And savour, Beasts of chase, or Fowl of game,
In pastry built, or from the spit, or boild,
Gris-amber-steamd; all Fish from Sea or Shore,
Freshet, or purling Brook, of shell or fin,   345
And exquisitest name, for which was draind
Pontus and *Lucrine* Bay, and *Afric* Coast.
Alas how simple, to these Cates compar'd,

310-12 See *Exod.* xvi. 35. 312-14 Elijah (see lines 16-17). Thebez,
a town in Ephraim, is taken by Milton as Elijah's birthplace (usually said
to be Thisbe, in Gilead). 344 *Gris-amber:* ambergris, used as a sauce.
347 *Pontus:* the Black Sea; *Lucrine Bay:* lagoon near Naples, famed for
its oysters. 348 *Cates:* delicacies.

Was that crude Apple that diverted *Eve!*
And at a stately side-board by the wine   350
That fragrant smell diffus'd, in order stood
Tall stripling youths rich clad, of fairer hew
Than *Ganymed* or *Hylas*; distant more
Under the Trees now trippd, now solemn stood
Nymphs of *Diana*'s train, and *Naiades*   355
With fruits and flowers from *Amalthea*'s horn,
And Ladies of th' *Hesperides*, that seemd
Fairer than feignd of old, or fabl'd since
Of Fairy Damsels met in Forest wide
By Knights of *Logres*, or of *Lyones*,   360
Lancelot or *Pelleas*, or *Pellenore*,
And all the while Harmonious Airs were heard
Of chiming strings, or charming pipes, and winds
Of gentlest gale *Arabian* odors fannd
From thir soft wings, and *Flora*'s earliest smells.   365
Such was the Splendour, and the Tempter now
His invitation earnestly renewd.
    What doubts the Son of God to sit and eat?
These are not Fruits forbidd'n, no interdict
Defends the touching of these viands pure,   370
Their taste no knowledge works, at least of evil,
But life preserves, destroys life's enemy,
Hunger, with sweet restorative delight.
All these are Spirits of Air, and Woods, and Springs,
Thy gentle Ministers, who come to pay   375
Thee homage, and acknowledge thee thir Lord:
What doubt'st thou Son of God? sit down and eat.
    To whom thus Jesus temperatly reply'd.
Said'st thou not that to all things I had right?
And who withholds my pow'r that right to use?   380
Shall I receive by gift what of my own,
When and where likes me best, I can command?
I can at will, doubt not, as soon as thou,

349 *Diverted:* perverted. 353 *Ganymed(e):* cupbearer of Zeus; *Hylas:* young companion of Hercules. 355 *Diana:* goddess of the hunt; *Naiades:* river-nymphs. 356 *Amalthea's horn:* the cornucopia or horn of plenty. Amalthea nursed Zeus with goat's milk. 357 *Ladies of th' Hesperides:* goddesses of the idyllic far-western gardens of Greek mythology. 360 *Logres:* Loegria, name in Arthurian legend of middle and eastern England; *Lyones(se):* in Arthurian legend, the land (now submerged) between Cornwall and the Scilly Isles. 361 knights of Arthurian legend. 363 *Charming:* singing, musical. 364 *Gale:* breeze. 365 *Flora:* Roman flower-goddess. 370 *Defends:* prohibits. 382 *Likes:* pleases.

Command a Table in this Wilderness,
And call swift flights of Angels ministrant   385
Arrayd in Glory on my cup to attend:
Why shouldst thou then obtrude this diligence,
In vain, where no acceptance it can find,
And with my hunger what hast thou to do?
Thy pompous Delicacies I contemn,   390
And count thy specious gifts no gifts but guiles.
    To whom thus answerd Satan malecontent.
That I have also power to give thou seest;
If of that pow'r I bring thee voluntary
What I might have bestowd on whom I pleas'd,   395
And rather opportunely in this place
Chose to impart to thy apparent need,
Why shouldst thou not accept it? but I see
What I can do or offer is suspect;
Of these things others quickly will dispose   400
Whose pains have earned the far-fet spoil. With that
Both Table and Provision vanishd quite
With sound of Harpies wings, and Talons heard;
Onely th' importune Tempter still remaind,
And with these words his temptation persu'd.   405
    By hunger, that each other Creature tames,
Thou art not to be harmd, therefore not mov'd;
Thy temperance invincible besides,
For no allurement yields to appetite,
And all thy heart is set on high designs,   410
High actions: but wherewith to be atchiev'd?
Great acts require great means of enterprise,
Thou art unknown, unfriended, low of birth,
A Carpenter thy Father known, thy self
Bred up in poverty and streights at home;   415
Lost in a Desert here and hunger-bit:
Which way or from what hope dost thou aspire
To greatness? whence Autority deriv'st,
What Followers, what Retinue canst thou gain,
Or at thy heels the dizzy Multitude,   420
Longer than thou canst feed them on thy cost?
Money brings Honour, Friends, Conquest, and Realms;
What rais'd *Antipater* the *Edomite*,
And his Son *Herod* plac'd on *Judahs* Throne;

394 *Voluntary:* voluntarily. 401 *Far-fet:* far-fetched. 403 *Harpies:* fabulous rapacious monsters, part woman, part vulture. 404 *Importune:* importunate. 423 *Antipater:* (d.43 B.C.), nobleman from Edom who became governor of Judea and father of Herod the Great.

(Thy throne) but gold that got him puissant friends?   425
Therefore, if at great things thou wouldst arrive,
Get Riches first, get Wealth, and Treasure heap,
Not difficult, if thou heark'n to me,
Riches are mine, Fortune is in my hand;
They whom I favour thrive in wealth amain,   430
While Virtue, Valour, Wisdom sit in want.
    To whom thus Jesus patiently reply'd.
Yet Wealth without these three is impotent,
To gain dominion or to keep it gaind.
Witness those ancient Empires of the Earth,   435
In highth of all thir flowing wealth dissolv'd:
But men endu'd with these have oft attaind
In lowest poverty to highest deeds;
Gideon and *Jephtha*, and the Shepherd lad,
Whose off-spring on the Throne of *Judah* sat   440
So many Ages, and shall yet regain
That seat, and reign in *Israel* without end.
Among the Heathen, (for throughout the World
To me is not unknown what hath been done
Worthy of Memorial) canst thou not remember   445
Quintius, Fabricius, Curius, Regulus ?
For I esteem those names of men so poor
Who could do mighty things, and could contemn
Riches though offerd from the hand of Kings.
And what in mee seems wanting, but that I   450
May also in this poverty as soon
Accomplish what they did, perhaps and more?
Extoll not Riches then, the toil of Fools,
The wise mans cumbrance if not snare, more apt
To slack'n Virtue, and abate her edge,   455
Than prompt her to do aught may merit praise.
What if with like aversion I reject
Riches and Realms; yet not for that a Crown,
Gold'n in shew, is but a wreath of thorns,
Brings dangers, troubles, cares, and sleepless nights   460

439 *Gideon and Jephtha:* Jewish national leaders (see *Judges* vi. 11-16 and
xi. 1-11); *the Shepherd lad:* David. 446 *Quintius:* L. Quinctius Cin-
cinnatus, Roman general and statesman (5th cent. B.C.); *Fabricius:* C.
Fabricius Luscinus (early 3rd cent. B.C.), Roman consul; *Curius:*
Manius Curius Dentatus (early 3rd cent. B.C.), Roman consul; *Regulus:*
M. Atilius Regulus (3rd cent. B.C.), Roman consul. These were men
renowned for their integrity and simplicity of mind. 457 ff. Jesus is
rejecting worldly rule not because it is burdensome or dishonourable,
but because its authority is not inward enough to touch and change
'the inner man, the nobler part'. 458 *For that:* because.

To him who wears the Regal Diadem,
When on his shoulders each mans burden lies;
For therein stands the office of a King,
His Honour, Vertue, Merit and chief Praise,
That for the Publick all this weight he bears.   465
Yet he who reigns within himself, and rules
Passions, Desires, and Fears, is more a King;
Which every wise and vertuous man attains:
And who attains not, ill aspires to rule
Cities of men, or head-strong Multitudes,,   470
Subject himself to Anarchy within,
Or lawless passions in him which he serves.
But to guide Nations in the way of truth
By saving Doctrin, and from errour lead
To know, and knowing worship God aright,   475
Is yet more Kingly, this attracts the Soul,
Governs the inner man, the nobler part;
That other ore the body onely reigns,
And oft by force, which to a generous mind
So reigning can be no sincere delight.   480
Besides to give a Kingdom hath been thought
Greater and nobler done, and to lay down
Far more magnanimous, than to assume.
Riches are needless then, both for themselves,
And for thy reason why they should be sought,   485
To gain a Scepter, oftest better misst.

THE THIRD BOOK

So spake the Son of God, and Satan stood
A while as mute confounded what to say,
What to reply, confuted and convinc't
Of his weak arguing, and fallacious drift;
At length collecting all his Serpent wiles,   5
With soothing words renewd, him thus accosts.
    I see thou know'st what is of use to know,
What best to say canst say, to do canst do;
Thy actions to thy words accord, thy words
To thy large heart give utterance due, thy heart   10
Conteins of good, wise, just, the perfet shape.
Should Kings and Nations from thy mouth consult,
Thy Counsel would be as the Oracle

3 *Convinc't:* convicted.   11 *Shape:* mould.

Urim and *Thummim*, those oraculous gems
On *Aarons* brest: or tongue of Seers old   15
Infallible; or wert thou sought to deeds
That might require th' array of warr, thy skill
Of conduct would be such, that all the World
Could not sustain thy Prowess, or subsist
In battel, though against thy few in arms.   20
These God-like Vertues wherefore dost thou hide?
Affecting privat life, or more obscure
In savage Wilderness, wherefore deprive
All Earth her wonder at thy acts, thy self
The fame and glory, glory the reward   25
That sole excites to high attempts the flame
Of most erected Spirits, most temperd pure
Ætherial, who all pleasures else despise,
All treasures and all gain esteem as dross,
And dignities and powers all but the highest?   30
Thy years are ripe, and over-ripe, the Son
Of *Macedonian Philip* had ere these
Won *Asia* and the Throne of *Cyrus* held
At his dispose, young *Scipio* had brought down
The *Carthaginian* pride, young *Pompey* quelld   35
The *Pontic* King and in triumph had rode.
Yet years, and to ripe years judgment mature,
Quench not the thirst of glory, but augment.
Great *Julius*, whom now all the World admires,
The more he grew in years, the more inflam'd   40
With glory, wept that he had liv'd so long
Inglorious: but thou yet art not too late.
    To whom our Saviour calmly thus reply'd.
Thou neither dost perswade me to seek wealth
For Empires sake, nor Empire to affect   45
For glories sake by all thy argument.
For what is glory but the blaze of fame,
· The peoples praise, if always praise unmixt?

14 *Urim and Thummim:* adornments used in divination. See *Exod.*
xxviii. 29-30. 18 *Conduct:*   leadership. 22 *Affecting:*   preferring.
31-34 Alexander the Great defeated Persia at the battle of Arbela at the
age of twenty-five. 33 *Cyrus:* (*c.* 600-529 B.C.), founder of Persian
empire. 34-35 Scipio defeated the Carthaginians in Spain at the age
of twenty-seven. 35-36 Pompey (106-48 B.C.) was not 'young' when he
conquered Mithridates, the Pontic king (66 B.C.), but he had distin-
guished himself early elsewhere. 37 *To:* added to. 39-42 Julius
Caesar (102?-44 B.C.) is said to have wept, comparing his achievements
beside those of Alexander.

And what the people but a herd confus'd,
A miscellaneous rabble, who extoll   50
Things vulgar, and well weighd, scarce worth the praise,
They praise and they admire they know not what;
And know not whom, but as one leads the other;
And what delight to be by such extolld,
To live upon their tongues and be their talk,   55
Of whom to be disprais'd were no small praise?
His lot who dares be singularly good.
Th' intelligent among them and the wise
Are few, and glory scarce of few is rais'd.
This is true glory and renown, when God   60
Looking on th' Earth, with approbation marks
The just man, and divulges him through Heaven
To all his Angels, who with true applause
Recount his praises; thus he did to *Job*,
When to extend his fame through Heav'n and Earth,   65
As thou to thy reproach mayst well remember,
He askd thee, hast thou seen my servant *Job* ?
Famous he was in Heaven, on Earth less known;
Where glory is false glory, attributed
To things not glorious, men not worthy of fame.   70
They err who count it glorious to subdue
By Conquest farr and wide, to over-run
Large Countries, and in field great Battels win,
Great Cities by assault: what do these Worthies,
But rob and spoil, burn, slaughter, and enslave   75
Peaceable Nations, neighbouring, or remote,
Made Captive, yet deserving freedom more
Than those thir Conquerours, who leave behind
Nothing but ruin wheresoe're they rove,
And all the flourishing works of peace destroy,   80
Then swell with pride, and must be titl'd Gods,
Great Benefactors of mankind, Deliverers,
Worshipt with Temple, Priest and Sacrifice;
One is the Son of *Jove*, of *Mars* the other,
Till Conquerour Death discover them scarce men,   85
Rowling in brutish vices, and deformd,
Violent or shameful death thir due reward.
But if there be in glory aught of good,
It may by means far different be attaind

49 ff. This passage reflects Milton's post-Restoration bitterness and
disappointment rather than the views of Jesus, as is shown by the
inappropriate word 'calmly' in line 43. 62 *Divulges:* proclaims.
67 Cf. *Job* i. 8.

Without ambition, warr, or violence;   90
By deeds of peace, by wisdom eminent,
By patience, temperance; I mention still
Him whom thy wrongs with Saintly patience born,
Made famous in a Land and times obscure;
Who names not now with honour patient *Job* ?   95
Poor *Socrates* (who next more memorable?)
By what he taught and sufferd for so doing,
For truths sake suffering death unjust, lives now
Equal in fame to proudest Conquerours.
Yet if for fame and glory aught be done,   100
Aught sufferd; if young *African* for fame
His wasted Country freed from *Punic* rage,
The deed becomes unprais'd, the man at least,
And loses, though but verbal, his reward.
Shall I seek glory then, as vain men seek   105
Oft not deserv'd? I seek not mine, but his
Who sent me, and thereby witness whence I am.
    To whom the Tempter murmuring thus reply'd.
Think not so slight of glory; therein least,
Resembling thy great Father: hee seeks glory,   110
And for his glory all things made, all things
Orders and governs, nor content in Heaven
By all his Angels glorifi'd, requires
Glory from men, from all men good or bad,
Wise or unwise, no difference, no exemption;   115
Above all Sacrifice, or hallowd gift
Glory he requires, and glory he receives
Promiscuous from all Nations, Jew, or Greek,
Or Barbarous, nor exception hath declar'd;
From us his foes pronounc't glory he exacts.   120
    To whom our Saviour fervently reply'd.
And reason; since his Word all things produc'd,
Though chiefly not for glory as prime end,
But to shew forth his goodness, and impart
His good communicable to every soul   125
Freely; of whom what could he less expect
Than glory and benediction, that is thanks,
The slightest, easiest, readiest recompence
From them who could return him nothing else,

96 *Socrates:* great Greek philosopher (469-399 B.C.), condemned to death
on false charges of blasphemy and the propagation of wrong doctrines
among the youth of Athens.   101-4 Scipio Africanus saved Italy from
invasion in the Second Punic War, but Rome showed little gratitude.

And not returning that would likeliest render   130
Contempt instead, dishonour, obloquy?
Hard recompence, unsutable return
For so much good, so much beneficence.
But why should man seek glory? who of his own
Hath nothing, and to whom nothing belongs   135
But condemnation, ignominy, and shame?
Who for so many benefits receiv'd
Turnd recreant to God, ingrate and false,
And so of all true good himself despoild,
Yet, sacrilegious, to himself would take   140
That which to God alone of right belongs;
Yet so much bounty is in God, such grace,
That who advance his glory, not thir own,
Them he himself to glory will advance.
    So spake the Son of God; and here again   145
Satan had not to answer, but stood strook
With guilt of his own sin, for he himself
Insatiable of glory had lost all,
Yet of another Plea bethought him soon.
    Of glory as thou wilt, said he, so deem,   150
Worth or not worth the seeking, let it pass:
But to a Kingdom thou art born, ordaind
To sit upon thy Father *Davids* Throne;
By Mothers side thy Father, though thy right
Be now in powerful hands, that will not part   155
Easily from possession won with arms;
Judæa now and all the promisd land
Reduc't a Province under *Roman* yoke,
Obeys *Tiberius*; nor is always rul'd
With temperat sway; oft have they violated   160
The Temple, oft the Law with foul affronts,
Abominations rather, as did once
Antiochus: and think'st thou to regain
Thy right by sitting still or thus retiring?
So did not *Machabeus*: he indeed   165
Retir'd unto the Desert, but with arms;
And ore a mighty King so oft prevaild,

138 *Recreant . . . ingrate:* unfaithful . . . ungrateful. 159 *Tiberius:*
(42 B.C.-A.D. 37), Roman emperor who appointed Pontius Pilate in
A.D. 26 as procurator of Judea. 163 *Antiochus:* Antiochus Epiphanes,
king of Syria from 175 to 164 B.C., tried to destroy the Jewish religion.
His invasion and desecrations provoked the rising of the Maccabees.
165 *Machabeus:* Judas Maccabæus (d.161 B.C.), Jewish warrior and
national leader against the Syrians. His family established a new
dynasty.

That by strong hand his Family obtaind,
Though Priests, the Crown, and *Davids* Throne usurpd,
With *Modin* and her Suburbs once content.   170
If Kingdom move thee not, let move thee Zeal,
And Duty; Zeal and Duty are not slow;
But on Occasions forelock watchful wait.
They themselves rather are occasion best,
Zeal of thy Fathers house, Duty to free   175
Thy Country from her Heathen servitude;
So shalt thou best fulfill, best verifie
The Prophets old, who sung thy endless raign,
The happier raign the sooner it begins,
Raign then; what canst thou better do the while?   180
     To whom our Saviour answer thus returnd.
All things are best fulfilld in thir due time,
And time there is for all things, Truth hath said:
If of my raign Prophetic Writ hath told
That it shall never end, so when begin   185
The Father in his purpose hath decreed,
He in whose hand all times and seasons roul.
What if he hath decreed that I shall first
Be try'd in humble state, and things adverse,
By tribulations, injuries, insults,   190
Contempts, and scorns, and snares, and violence,
Suffering, abstaining, quietly expecting
Without distrust or doubt, that he may know
What I can suffer, how obey? who best
Can suffer, best can do; best reign, who first   195
Well hath obeyd; just tryal ere I merit
My exaltation without change or end.
But what concerns it thee when I begin
My everlasting Kingdom, why art thou
Sollicitous, what moves thy inquisition?   200
Know'st thou not that my rising is thy fall,
And my promotion will be thy destruction?
     To whom the Tempter inly rackt reply'd.
Let that come when it comes; all hope is lost
Of my reception into grace; what worse?   205
For where no hope is left, is left no fear;
If there be worse, the expectation more
Of worse torments me than the feeling can.
I would be at the worst; worst is my Port,
My harbour and my ultimate repose,   210

170 *Modin:* obscure Judean birthplace of Judas Maccabæus. 171
Kingdom: kingship.

The end I would attain, my final good.
My error was my error, and my crime
My crime; whatever for it self condemnd,
And will alike be punisht; whether thou
Raign or raign not; though to that gentle brow   215
Willingly I could flye, and hope thy raign,
From that placid aspect and meek regard,
Rather than aggravate my evil state,
Would stand between me and thy Fathers ire,
(Whose ire I dread more than the fire of Hell)   220
A shelter and a kind of shading cool
Interposition, as a summers cloud.
If I then to the worst that can be hast,
Why move thy feet so slow to what is best,
Happiest both to thy self and all the World,   225
That thou who worthiest art should'st be thir King?
Perhaps thou linger'st in deep thoughts detaind
Of the enterprise so hazardous and high;
No wonder, for though in thee be united
What of perfection can in man be found,   230
Or human nature can receive, consider
Thy life hath yet been privat, most part spent
At home, scarce viewd the *Gallilean* Towns,
And once a year *Jerusalem*, few days
Short sojourn; and what thence could'st thou observe?   235
The World thou hast not seen, much less her glory,
Empires, and Monarchs, and thir radiant Courts,
Best school of best experience, quickest insight
In all things that to greatest actions lead.
The wisest, unexperienc't, will be ever   240
Timorous and loth, with novice modesty,
(As he who seeking Asses found a Kingdom)
Irresolute, unhardy, unadventrous:
But I will bring thee where thou soon shalt quit
Those rudiments, and see before thine eyes   245
The Monarchies of th' Earth, thir pomp and state,
Sufficient introduction to inform
Thee, of thy self so apt, in regal Arts,
And regal Mysteries; that thou may'st know
How best thir opposition to withstand.   250
    With that (such power was giv'n him then) he took

213-14 'Whatever my crime is, its condemnation and punishment are
automatic and unremitting.' 242 Saul. See *I Sam.* ix-x.

The Son of God up to a Mountain high.
It was a Mountain at whose verdant feet
A spacious plain out strecht in circuit wide
Lay pleasant; from his side two rivers flowd,   255
Th' one winding, th' other strait, and left between
Fair Champain with less rivers interveind,
Then meeting joind thir tribute to the Sea:
Fertil of corn the glebe, of oil and wine,
With herds the pastures throngd, with flocks the hills,   260
Huge Cities and high towr'd, that well might seem
The seats of mightiest Monarchs, and so large
The Prospect was, that here and there was room
For barren desert fountainless and dry.
To this high mountain top the Tempter brought   265
Our Saviour, and new train of words began.
    Well have we speeded, and ore hill and dale,
Forest and field, and flood, Temples and Towers
Cut shorter many a league; here thou behold'st
Assyria and her Empires ancient bounds,   270
Araxes and the *Caspian* lake, thence on
As farr as *Indus* East, *Euphrates* West,
And oft beyond; to South the *Persian* Bay,
And inaccessible th' *Arabian* drouth:
Here *Ninevee*, of length within her wall   275
Several days journey, built by *Ninus* old,
Of that first gold'n Monarchy the seat,
And seat of *Salmanassar*, whose success
Israel in long captivity still mourns;
There *Babylon* the wonder of all tongues,   280
As ancient, but rebuilt by him who twice
Judah and all thy Father *Davids* house
Led captive, and *Jerusalem* laid waste,

---

252 *A Mountain:* This may be seen as Mt. Niphates, high range in
eastern Turkey, with the 'two rivers' of line 255 the Tigris and the
Euphrates.   257 *Champain:*   flat, open country.   271 *Araxes:*   now
Aras, the Armenian river flowing east into the Caspian Sea.   272 *Indus:*
great river of north-west India; *Euphrates:* great river of Asia Minor,
flowing into the Persian Gulf.   275 *Ninevee:* capital city of ancient
Assyria, on east bank of river Tigris, opposite Mosul.   276 *Ninus:*
legendary founder of Nineveh.   278 *Salmanassar:*   name of several
kings of Assyria. Israel was attacked by Shalmaneser IV, but his general,
Sargon, who usurped the throne 722 B.C., was the real conqueror of
Samaria.   280 *Babylon:* ancient capital of Babylonia, on river Euph-
rates about 60 miles north of Baghdad.   281 *Him:* Nebuchadnezzar,
Babylonian king who attacked Israel 605 and 597 B.C.

Till *Cyrus* set them free; *Persepolis*
His City there thou seest, and *Bactra* there;   285
Ecbatana her structure vast there shews,
And *Hecatompylos* her hunderd gates,
There *Susa* by *Choaspes*, amber stream,
The drink of none but Kings; of later fame
Built by *Emathian*, or by *Parthian* hands,   290
The great *Seleucia*, *Nisibis*, and there
Artaxata, *Teredon*, *Ctesiphon*,
Turning with easie eye thou may'st behold.
All these the *Parthian*, now some Ages past,
By great *Arsaces* led, who founded first   295
That Empire, under his dominion holds
From the luxurious Kings of *Antioch* won.
And just in time thou com'st to have a view
Of his great power; for now the *Parthian* King
In *Ctesiphon* hath gatherd all his Host   300
Against the *Scythian*, whose incursions wild
Have wasted *Sogdiana*; to her aid
He marches now in hast; see, though from farr,
His thousands, in what martial equipage
They issue forth, Steel Bows, and Shafts thir arms   305
Of equal dread in flight, or in persuit;
All Horsemen, in which fight they most excell;
See how in warlike muster they appear,
In Rhombs and wedges, and half-moons, and wings.
He lookd and saw what numbers numberless   310

284 Cyrus 'set them free' by taking Babylon 538 B.C. and allowing the
captive Jews to return to Israel; *Persepolis*: ancient Persian capital, in
southern Persia. 285 *Bactra*: now Balkh in Afghanistan, was the
capital of the Persian province of Bactria. 286 *Ecbatan(a)*: now
Hamadan, ancient capital of Media, captured by Cyrus 549 B.C. 287
Hecatompylos: city 'of a hundred gates', in Parthia. 288 *Susa by Choaspes*:
chief city of ancient south-west Persia. The river Choaspes, flowing into
the Persian gulf, was thought to have such pure water that Cyrus would
drink no other. 290 *Emathian*: Macedonian. 291 *Seleucia*: great city
on west bank of Tigris, south-east of Baghdad, built by Seleucus,
Alexander the Great's general, who founded the Seleucid dynasty;
Nisibis: city on the Tigris, in northern Mesopotamia. 292 *Artaxata*:
ancient capital of Armenia, on the Araxes; *Teredon*: ancient city near
mouth of Tigris and Euphrates; *Ctesiphon*: ancient Parthian capital, on
the Tigris near Seleucia. 295-7 Arsaces broke the Seleucid power *c.*
250 B.C. and founded the Parthian dynasty. Antioch, now Antakieh,
was a city in Syria, founded by Seleucus 300 B.C. 301 *The Scythian*:
people living east and north of Caspian Sea. 302 *Sogdiana*: remote
Parthian province, south-east of Aral Sea. 309 *Rhombs*: infantry
formation in shape of diamond.

The City gates out powr'd, light armed Troops
In coats of Mail and military pride;
In Mail thir horses clad, yet fleet and strong,
Prauncing thir riders bore, the flower and choice
Of many Provinces from bound to bound;   315
From *Arachosia*, from *Candaor* East,
And *Margiana* to th' *Hyrcanian* cliffs
Of *Caucasus*, and dark *Iberian* dales,
From *Atropatia* and the neighbouring plains
Of *Adiabene*, *Media*, and the South   320
Of *Susiana* to *Balsara's* hav'n.
He saw them in thir forms of battel rang'd,
How quick they wheeld, and flying behind them shot
Sharp sleet of arrowie showers against the face
Of thir persuers, and overcame by flight;   325
The field all iron cast a gleaming brown,
Nor wanted clouds of foot, nor on each horn,
Cuirassiers all in steel for standing fight;
Chariots or Elephants endorst with Towers
Of Archers, nor of labouring Pioners   330
A multitude with Spades and Axes armd
To lay hills plain, fell woods, or valleys fill,
Or where plain was raise hill, or over-lay
With bridges rivers proud, as with a yoke;
Mules after these, Camels and Dromedaries,   335
And Waggons fraught with Utensils of warr.
Such forces met not, nor so wide a camp,
When *Agrican* with all his Northern powers
Besieg'd *Albracca*, as Romances tell;
The City of *Gallaphrone*, from thence to win   340
The fairest of her Sex *Angelica*
His daughter, sought by many Prowest Knights,
Both *Paynim*, and the Peers of *Charlemane*.

---

316 *Arachosia:* eastern province of Parthia, west of river Indus; *Candaor:* Kandahar, in Afghanistan. 317 *Margiana:* province south-east of Caspian Sea; *Hyrcanian cliffs:* probably Milton means the Caspian shore near the Caucasus. 318 *Iberian dales:* between Caspian and Black Sea. 319 *Atropatia:* north Media. 320 *Adiabene:* flat district around Nineveh. 321 *Susiana:* southern province, on Persian Gulf; *Balsara:* Basra, port on Tigris-Euphrates confluence, identified in Milton's time with Teredon (line 292). 323 *Flying behind them shot:* i.e. 'Parthian shots.' 329 *Endorst:* covered on the back, howdahed. 330 *Pioners:* army pioneers. 338-43 Agrican is king of Tartary, Gallaphrone is king of Cathay, and Albracca is Gallaphrone's stronghold, in Boiardo's romance *Orlando Innamorato;* many of Charlemagne's knights were also involved in the fighting. 342 *Prowest:* bravest. 343 *Paynim:* pagan.

Such and so numerous was thir Chivalrie;
At sight whereof the Fiend yet more presum'd,   345
And to our Saviour thus his words renewd.
   That thou may'st know I seek not to engage
Thy Vertue, and not every way secure
On no slight grounds thy safety; hear, and mark
To what end I have brought thee hither and shewn   350
All this fair sight; thy Kingdom though foretold
By Prophet or by Angel, unless thou
Endeavour, as thy Father *David* did,
Thou never shalt obtain; prediction still
In all things, and all men, supposes means;   355
Without means us'd, what it predicts revokes.
But say thou wert possest of *Davids* Throne
By free consent of all, none opposite,
Samaritan or *Jew*; how could'st thou hope
Long to enjoy it quiet and secure,   360
Between two such enclosing enemies
Roman and *Parthian?* therefore one of these
Thou must make sure thy own, the *Parthian* first
By my advice, as nearer and of late
Found able by invasion to annoy   365
Thy country, and captive lead away her Kings
Antigonus, and old *Hyrcanus* bound,
Maugre the *Roman*: it shall be my task
To render thee the *Parthian* at dispose;
Chuse which thou wilt by conquest or by league   370
By him thou shalt regain, without him not,
That which alone can truly reinstall thee
In *Davids* royal seat, his true Successour,
Deliverance of thy brethren, those ten Tribes
Whose off-spring in his Territory yet serve   375
In *Habor*, and among the *Medes* disperst,
Ten Sons of *Jacob*, two of *Joseph* lost
Thus long from *Israel*; serving as of old
Thir Fathers in the land of *Egypt* serv'd,
This offer sets before thee to deliver.   380

344 *Chivalrie:* army.   367 *Antigonus:* became king of Judea 40 B.C.
with Parthian help (the opposite of Milton's suggestion), was executed
by Herod the Great 37 B.C.; *Hyrcanus:* uncle of Antigonus, was High
Priest, and although taken captive by the Parthians he too was eventually
killed by Herod, 30 B.C.   368 *Maugre:* despite.   374-8 referring to the
Assyrian conquest (lines 278-9) of the ten northern tribes of Israel (in-
cluding Ephraim and Manasseh, named after the sons of Joseph) and
their forced dispersal in Media and beside the Habor (a tributary of the
Euphrates).

These if from servitude thou shalt restore
To thir inheritance, then, nor till then,
Thou on the Throne of *David* in full glory,
From *Egypt* to *Euphrates* and beyond
Shalt raign, and *Rome* or *Cæsar* not need fear.   385
  To whom our Saviour answerd thus unmov'd.
Much ostentation vain of fleshly arm,
And fragile arms, much instrument of warr
Long in preparing, soon to nothing brought,
Before mine eyes thou hast set; and in my ear   390
Vented much policy, and projects deep
Of enemies, of aids, battels and leagues,
Plausible to the World, to mee worth naught.
Means I must use thou say'st, prediction else
Will unpredict and fail me of the Throne: 395
My time I told thee, (and that time for thee
Were better fardest off) is not yet come;
When that comes think not thou to find me slack
On my part aught endeavouring, or to need
Thy politic maxims, or that cumbersome   400
Luggage of warr there shewn me, argument
Of human weakness rather than of strength.
My brethren, as thou call'st them; those Ten Tribes
I must deliver, if I mean to raign
Davids true heir, and his full Scepter sway   405
To just extent over all *Israels* Sons;
But whence to thee this zeal, where was it then
For *Israel*, or for *David*, or his Throne,
When thou stood'st up his Tempter to the pride
Of numbring *Israel*, which cost the lives   410
Of threescore and ten thousand *Israelites*
By three days Pestilence? such was thy zeal
To *Israel* then, the same that now to me.
As for those captive Tribes, themselves were they
Who wrought thir own captivity, fell off   415
From God to worship Calves, the Deities
Of *Egypt*, *Baal* next and *Ashtaroth*,
And all th' Idolatries of Heathen round,
Besides thir other worse than heathenish crimes;
Nor in the land of thir captivity   420

384 Cf. *Gen*. xv. 18.   393 *Plausible to:* normally applauded in. 409-12
See *I Chron*. xxi. 1-14.   414-17 See *I Kings* xii. 25-32 (idolatry of
Jeroboam) and xvi. 29-33 (idolatry of Ahab).   417 *Baal:* general
name for chief god among Phœnicians and Canaanite peoples; *Ash-
taroth:* Ashtoreth, Phœnician goddess of fertility.

Humbl'd themselves, or penitent besought
The God of thir fore-fathers; but so dy'd
Impenitent, and left a race behind
Like to themselves, distinguishable scarce
From Gentils, but by Circumcision vain,   425
And God with Idols in thir worship joind.
Should I of these the liberty regard,
Who freed, as to thir ancient Patrimony,
Unhumbl'd, unrepentant, unreformd,
Headlong would follow; and to thir Gods perhaps   430
Of *Bethel* and of *Dan?* no, let them serve
Thir enemies, who serve Idols with God.
Yet hee at length, time to himself best known,
Remembring *Abraham* by some wond'rous call
May bring them back repentant and sincere,   435
And at thir passing cleave the *Assyrian* flood,
While to thir native land with joy they hast,
As the Red Sea and *Jordan* once he cleft,
When to the promisd land thir Fathers passd;
To his due time and providence I leave them.   440
     So spake *Israels* true King, and to the Fiend
Made answer meet, that made void all his wiles.
So fares it when with truth falshood contends.

THE FOURTH BOOK

     Perplext and troubl'd at his bad success
The Tempter stood, nor had what to reply,
Discoverd in his fraud, thrown from his hope,
So oft, and the perswasive Rhetoric
That sleekd his tongue, and won so much on *Eve,*   5
So little here, nay lost; but *Eve* was *Eve,*
This farr his over-match, who self deceiv'd
And rash, before-hand had no better weigh'd
The strength he was to cope with, or his own:
But as a man who had been matchless held   10
In cunning, over-reacht where least he thought,
To salve his credit, and for very spite
Still will be tempting him who foils him still,
And never cease, though to his shame the more;
Or as a swarm of flies in vintage time,   15

431 *Bethel . . . Dan:* northern cities where Jeroboam had set up his idols.
1 *Success:* result.

About the wine-press where sweet moust is powrd,
Beat off, returns as oft with humming sound;
Or surging waves against a solid rock,
Though all to shivers dasht, the assault renew,
Vain battry, and in froth or bubbles end: 20
So Satan, whom repulse upon repulse
Met ever; and to shameful silence brought,
Yet gives not ore though desperat of success,
And his vain importunity persues.
He brought our Saviour to the Western side   25
Of that high mountain, whence he might behold
Another plain, long but in bredth not wide;
Washt by the Southern Sea, and on the North
To equal length backt with a ridge of hills
That screend the fruits of th' earth and seats of men   30
From cold *Septentrion* blasts, thence in the midst
Divided by a river, of whose banks
On each side an Imperial City stood,
With Towers and Temples proudly elevate
On seven small Hills, with Palaces adornd,   35
Porches and Theatres, Baths, Aqueducts,
Statues and Trophees, and Triumphal Arcs,
Gardens and Groves presented to his eyes,
Above the highth of Mountains interpos'd.
By what strange Parallax or Optic skill   40
Of vision multipli'd through air, or glass
Of Telescope, were curious to enquire:
And now the Tempter thus his silence broke.
    The City which thou seest no other deem
Than great and glorious *Rome*, Queen of the Earth   45
So farr renownd, and with the spoils enricht
Of Nations; there the Capitol thou seest
Above the rest lifting his stately head
On the *Tarpeian* rock, her Cittadel
Impregnable, and there Mount *Palatine*   50
Th' Imperial Palace, compass huge, and high
The Structure, skill of noblest Architects,
With gilded battlements, conspicuous farr,
Turrets and Terrases, and glittering Spires.
Many a fair Edifice besides, more like   55

16 *Moust:* must, unfermented grape-juice. 27 *Another plain:* Latium,
in central Italy. 28 *Southern Sea:* Mediterranean. 29 *Ridge of hills:*
Apennines. 31 *Septentrion blasts:* north winds. 32 *A river:* Tiber.
33 *Imperial City:* Rome. 37 *Arcs:* arches. 40 *Strange Parallax:* trick
involving apparent displacement of objects from normal angle of vision·

Houses of gods (so well I have dispos'd
My Aerie Microscope) thou may'st behold
Outside and inside both, pillars and roofs
Carv'd work, the hand of fam'd Artificers
In Cedar, Marble, Ivory or Gold.   60
Thence to the gates cast round thine eye, and see
What conflux issuing forth, or entring in,
Pretors, Proconsuls to thir Provinces
Hasting or on return, in robes of State;
Lictors and rods the ensigns of thir power,   65
Legions and Cohorts, turmes of horse and wings:
Or Embassies from Regions farr remote
In various habits on the *Appian* ro d,
Or on th' *Æmilian*, some from fa   st South,
Syene, and where the shadow both way falls,   70
Meroe Nilotic Ile, and more to West,
The Realm of *Bocchus* to the Black-moor Sea;
From the *Asian* Kings and *Parthian* among these,
From *India* and the gold'n *Chersoness*,
And utmost I..dian Ile *Taprobane*,   75
Dusk faces with white silk'n Turbants wreath'd:
From *Gallia*, *Gades*, and the *Brittish* West,
Germans and *Scythians*, and *Sarmatians* North
Beyond *Danubius* to the *Tauric* Pool.
All Nations now to *Rome* obedience pay,   80
To *Romes* great Emperour, whose wide domain
In ample Territory, wealth and power,
Civility of Manners, Arts, and Arms,
And long Renown thou justly may'st preferr
Before the *Parthian*; these two Thrones except,   85

63 *Pretors:* praetors, magistrates whose work involved governmental
activity in the provinces; *proconsuls:* acting consuls. 65 *Lictors:*
attendants of chief officials, carrying bundles of rods (fasces) as a symbol
of authority. 66 *Turmes:* troops; *wings:* cavalry flanks. 68 *Appian
road:* the Appian Way from Rome to Brindisi. 69 *Th' Æmilian:* the
Æmilian Way, a part of the great Flaminian Way, led north from Rome
in the direction of Piacenza and Milan. 70 *Syene:* Aswan, Upper
Egypt. 71 *Meroe:* region in south Nubia, surrounded by branches of
the Nile. Pliny speaks of shadows disappearing there twice a year, and
adds that near Mount Maleus in India shadows fall to the south in
summer and to the north in winter. 72 *Bocchus:* king (2nd cent. B.C.)
of Gaetulia in North Africa (now, approximately, Algeria); *Black-
moor Sea:* south-west Mediterranean. 74 *Gold'n Chersoness:* the
Chersonesus Aurea, probably the Malay Peninsula. 75 *Taprobane:* Ceylon.
77 *Gallia, Gades:* France, Cadiz. 78 *Sarmatians:* people, perhaps of
Iranian stock, inhabiting region of Poland and west Russia. 79
Tauric Pool: Sea of Azov. 83 *Civility:* civilised quality.

The rest are barbarous, and scarce worth the sight,
Shar'd among petty Kings too farr remov'd;
These having shewn thee, I have shewn thee all
The Kingdoms of the World, and all thir glory.
This Emperour hath no Son, and now is old,   90
Old, and lascivious, and from *Rome* retir'd
To *Capreæ* an Iland small but strong
On the *Campanian* shore, with purpose there
His horrid lusts in privat to enjoy,
Committing to a wicked Favourite   95
All publick cares, and yet of him suspicious,
Hated of all, and hating; with what ease
Indu'd with Regal Vertues as thou art,
Appearing, and beginning noble deeds,
Might'st thou expell this monster from his Throne   100
Now made a stye, and in his place ascending
A victor people free from servil yoke?
And with my help thou may'st; to me the power
Is given, and by that right I give it thee.
Aim therefore at no less than all the World,   105
Aim at the highest, without the highest attaind
Will be for thee no sitting, or not long
On *Davids* Throne, be propheci'd what will.
    To whom the Son of God unmov'd reply'd.
Nor doth this grandeur and majestic show   110
Of luxury, though calld magnificence,
More than of arms before, allure mine eye,
Much less my mind; though thou should'st add to tell
Thir sumptuous gluttonies, and gorgeous feasts
On *Cittron* tables or *Atlantic* stone;   115
(For I have also heard, perhaps have red)
Thir wines of *Setia*, *Cales*, and *Falerne*,
Chios and *Creet*, and how they quaff in Gold,
Crystal and Myrrhine cups imbost with Gems
And studs of Pearl, to me should'st tell who thirst   120
And hunger still: then Embassies thou shew'st
From Nations farr and nigh; what honour that,

---

90 *This Emperour:* Tiberius (42 B.C.-A.D. 37). 92 *Capreæ:* Capri, in
the Bay of Naples off the ancient province of Campania. 95 *Favourite:*
L. Ælius Sejanus (*c.* 20 B.C.-A.D. 31). 115 *Cittron:* fragrant wood of a
North African tree used by Romans in making fine furniture; *Atlantic
stone:* marble from Atlas Mountains. 117 *Setia:* city in Latium, near
Rome; *Cales ... Falerne:* cities in Campania, near Mt. Vesuvius. 118
Chios and Creet: Greek islands famed for their wines. 119 *Myrrhine:*
made of highly-prized *murra*, perhaps a translucent stone, perhaps glass.

But tedious wast of time to sit and hear
So many hollow complements and lies,
Outlandish flatteries? then proceed'st to talk   125
Of the Emperour, how easily subdu'd,
How gloriously; I shall, thou say'st, expell
A brutish monster: what if I withall
Expell a Devil who first made him such?
Let his tormenter Conscience find him out,   130
For him I was not sent, nor yet to free
That people victor once, now vile and base,
Deservedly made vassal, who once just,
Frugal, and mild, and temperat, conquerd well,
But govern ill the Nations under yoke,   135
Peeling thir Provinces, exhausted all
By lust and rapine; first ambitious grown
Of triumph that insulting vanity;
Then cruel, by thir sports to blood enur'd
Of fighting beasts, and men to beasts expos'd,   140
Luxurious by thir wealth, and greedier still,
And from the daily Scene effeminate.
What wise and valiant man would seek to free
These thus degenerat, by themselves enslav'd,
Or could of inward slaves make outward free?   145
Know therefore when my season comes to sit
On *Davids* Throne, it shall be like a tree
Spreading and over-shadowing all the Earth,
Or as a stone that shall to pieces dash
All Monarchies besides throughout the World,   150
And of my Kingdom there shall be no end:
Means there shall be to this, but what the means,
Is not for thee to know, nor mee to tell.
   To whom the Tempter impudent repli'd.
I see all offers made by me how slight   155
Thou valu'st, because offerd, and reject'st:
Nothing will please the difficult and nice,
Or nothing more than still to contradict:
On th' other side know also thou, that I
On what I offer set as high esteem,   160
Nor what I part with mean to give for naught;
All these which in a moment thou behold'st,
The Kingdoms of the World to thee I give;
For giv'n to me, I give to whom I please,
No trifle; yet with this reserve, not else,   165

   136 *Peeling:* pillaging, mulcting.   142 *Scene:* theatre stage.   157
Nice: fastidious.

On this condition, if thou wilt fall down,
And worship me as thy superior Lord,
Easily done, and hold them all of me;
For what can less so great a gift deserve?
 Whom thus our Saviour answerd with disdain. 170
I never lik'd thy talk, thy offers less,
Now both abhorr, since thou hast dar'd to utter
Th' abominable terms, impious condition;
But I endure the time, till which expir'd,
Thou hast permission on me. It is writt'n 175
The first of all Commandments, Thou shalt worship
The Lord thy God, and onely him shalt serve;
And dar'st thou to the Son of God propound
To worship thee accurst, now more accurst
For this attempt bolder than that on *Eve*, 180
And more blaspheamous? which expect to rue.
The Kingdoms of the World to thee were giv'n,
Permitted rather, and by thee usurpt,
Other donation none thou canst produce:
If giv'n, by whom but by the King of Kings, 185
God over all supream? if giv'n to thee,
By thee how fairly is the Giver now
Repaid? But gratitude in thee is lost
Long since. Wert thou so void of fear or shame,
As offer them to mee the Son of God, 190
To mee my own, on such abhorred pact,
That I fall down and worship thee as God?
Get thee behind me; plain thou now appear'st
That Evil one, Satan for ever damnd.
 To whom the Fiend with fear abasht reply'd. 195
Be not so sore offended, Son of God;
Though Sons of God both Angels are and Men,
If I to try whether in higher sort
Than these thou bear'st that title, have propos'd
What both from Men and Angels I receive, 200
Tetrarchs of fire, air, flood, and on the earth
Nations besides from all the quarterd winds,
God of this World invok't and World beneath;
Who then thou art, whose coming is foretold
To mee so fatal, mee it most concerns. 205
The tryal hath indamag'd thee no way,
Rather more honour left and more esteem;

184 *Donation:* privilege authorised by superior power. 201 *Tetrarch:* ruler of a quarter province (of the four elements). Satan's authority is confirmed by both demons and men. Cf. II. 122-4.

Mee naught advantag'd, missing what I aimd.
Therefore let pass, as they are transitory,
The Kingdoms of this World; I shall no more   210
Advise thee, gain them as thou canst, or not.
And thou thy self seem'st otherwise inclin'd
Than to a worldly Crown, addicted more
To contemplation and profound dispute,
As by that early action may be judg'd,   215
When slipping from thy Mothers eye thou went'st
Alone into the Temple; there wast found
Among the gravest Rabbi's disputant
On points and questions fitting *Moses* Chair,
Teaching not taught; the childhood shews the man,   220
As morning shews the day. Be famous then
By wisdom; as thy Empire must extend,
So let extend thy mind ore all the World,
In knowledge, all things in it comprehend,
All knowledge is not coucht in *Moses* Law,   225
The *Pentateuch* or what the Prophets wrote,
The Gentiles also know, and write, and teach
To admiration, led by Natures light;
And with the Gentiles much thou must converse,
Ruling them by perswasion as thou mean'st;   230
Without thir learning how wilt thou with them,
Or they with thee hold conversation meet?
How wilt thou reason with them, how refute
Thir Idolisms, Traditions, Paradoxes?
Error by his own arms is best evinc't.   235
Look once more ere we leave this specular Mount
Westward, much nearer by Southwest, behold
Where on the *Ægean* shore a City stands
Built nobly, pure the air, and light the soil,
Athens the eye of *Greece*, Mother of Arts   240
And Eloquence, native to famous wits
Or hospitable, in her sweet recess,
City or Suburban, studious walks and shades;
See there the Olive Grove of *Academe*,
Plato's retirement, where the *Attic* Bird   245
Trills her thick-warbl'd notes the summer long,

219 *Fitting Moses Chair:* concerning the interpretation of the Mosaic
Law.   226 *Pentateuch:* first five books of the Old Testament.   234
Idolisms: prejudiced beliefs.   235 *Evinc't:* conquered.   236 *Specular
Mount:* high observation-point.   241 *Wits:* as we should say, 'brains'.
244 *Academe:*   the Academy where Plato (*c.* 427-348 B.C.) taught.
245 *Attic Bird:* nightingale.

There flowrie hill *Hymettus* with the sound
Of Bees industrious murmur oft invites
To studious musing; there *Ilissus* rouls
His whispering stream; within the walls then view   250
The schools of ancient Sages; his who bred
Great *Alexander* to subdue the World,
Lyceum there, and painted *Stoa* next:
There thou shalt hear and learn the secret power
Of harmony in tones and numbers hit   255
By voice or hand, and various-measur'd verse,
Æolian charms and *Dorian Lyric* Odes,
And his who gave them breath, but higher sung,
Blind *Melesigenes* thence *Homer* calld,
Whose Poem *Phœbus* challeng'd for his own.   260
Thence what the lofty grave Tragœdians taught
In *Chorus* or *Iambic*, teachers best
Of moral prudence, with delight receiv'd
In brief sententious precepts, while they treat
Of fate, and chance, and change in human life;   265
High actions, and high passions best describing:
Thence to the famous Orators repair,
Those ancient, whose resistless eloquence
Wielded at will that fierce Democratie,
Shook th' Arsenal and fulmind over *Greece*,   270
To *Macedon*, and *Artaxerxes* Throne;
To sage Philosophy next lend thine ear,
From Heav'n descended to the low-rooft house
Of *Socrates*, see there his Tenement,
Whom well inspir'd the Oracle pronounc'd   275
Wisest of men; from whose mouth issu'd forth
Mellifluous streams that waterd all the schools
Of Academics old and new, with those
Sirnam'd *Peripatetics*, and the Sect

247 *Hill Hymettus:* range south-east of Athens, famed for its bees.
249 *Ilissus:* river flowing through Athens. 251-3 Aristotle (384-22
B.C.), the philosopher who tutored Alexander the Great, taught in the
Lyceum, a park outside Athens (not 'within the walls'). 253 *Stoa:*
colonnade, decorated with wall-paintings, in the Athens market-place,
where Zeno the Stoic philosopher (*fl. c.* 300 B.C.) taught. 257 *Æolian
charms:* songs by poets from the north-west coast of Asia Minor and its
islands (e.g. Sappho); *Dorian . . . Odes:* odes in the Dorian dialect (e.g.
by Pindar). 259 *Melesigenes:* Homer, in one tradition, was born by
the river Meles, near Smyrna in Asia Minor. 260 *Phœbus:* Apollo, god
of poetry. 270 *Fulmin'd:* thundered. 271 *Artaxerxes Throne:* Persia.
279 *Peripatetics:* followers of Aristotle.

Epicurean, and the *Stoic* severe;   280
These here revolve, or, as thou lik'st, at home,
Till time mature thee to a Kingdoms waight;
These rules will render thee a King compleat
Within thy self, much more with Empire joind.
  To whom our Saviour sagely thus repli'd.   285
Think not but that I know these things, or think
I know them not; nor therefore am I short
Of knowing what I ought: he who receives
Light from above, from the fountain of light,
No other doctrin needs, though granted true;   290
But these are false, or little else but dreams,
Conjectures, fancies, built on nothing firm.
The first and wisest of them all professd
To know this onely, that he nothing knew;
The next to fabling fell and smooth conceits;   295
A third sort doubted all things, though plain sense;
Others in vertue plac'd felicity,
But vertue joind with riches and long life;
In corporal pleasure hee, and careless ease;
The Stoic last in Philosophic pride,   300
By him calld vertue; and his vertuous man,
Wise, perfet in himself, and all possessing
Equal to God, oft shames not to preferr,
As fearing God nor man, contemning all
Wealth, pleasure, pain or torment, death and life,   305
Which when he lists, he leaves, or boasts he can,
For all his tedious talk is but vain boast,
Or suttle shifts conviction to evade.
Alas what can they teach, and not mislead;
Ignorant of themselves, of God much more,   310
And how the World began, and how man fell
Degraded by himself, on Grace depending?
Much of the Soul they talk, but all awrie,
And in themselves seek vertue, and to themselves
All glory arrogate, to God give none,   315
Rather accuse him under usual names,
Fortune and Fate, as one regardless quite
Of mortal things. Who therefore seeks in these
True wisdom, finds her not, or by delusion

---

280 *Epicurean:* following the philosopher Epicurus (341-270 B.C.).
293 *The first:* Socrates. 295 *The next:* Plato; *conceits:* images, figures.
296 *A third sort:* the school of Sceptics, founded by Pyrrho (c. 360-270
B.C.). 297 *Others:* the Peripatetics. 299 *Hee:* Epicurus. 308 *Conviction:* defeat in argument.

Farr worse, her false resemblance onely meets,   320
An empty cloud. However many books
Wise men have said are wearisom; who reads
Incessantly, and to his reading brings not
A spirit and judgment equal or superior,
(And what he brings, what needs he elsewhere seek)   325
Uncertain and unsettl'd still remains,
Deep verst in books and shallow in himself,
Crude or intoxicate, collecting toys,
And trifles for choice matters, worth a spunge;
As Childern gathering pibles on the shore.   330
Or if I would delight my privat hours
With Music or with Poem, where so soon
As in our native Language can I find
That solace? All our Law and Story strew'd
With Hymns, or Psalms with artful terms inscrib'd,   335
Our Hebrew Songs and Harps in *Babylon*,
That pleas'd so well our Victors ear, declare
That rather *Greece* from us these Arts deriv'd;
Ill imitated, while they loudest sing
The vices of thir Deities, and thir own   340
In Fable, Hymn, or Song, so personating
Thir Gods ridiculous, and themselves past shame.
Remove thir swelling Epithetes thick laid
As varnish on a Harlots cheek, the rest,
Thin sown with aught of profit or delight,   345
Will farr be found unworthy to compare
With *Sions* songs, to all true tasts excelling,
Where God is prais'd aright, and Godlike men,
The Holiest of Holies, and his Saints;
Such are from God inspir'd, not such from thee;   350
Unless where moral vertue is exprest
By light of Nature not in all quite lost.
Thir Orators thou then extoll'st, as those
The top of Eloquence, Statists indeed,
And lovers of thir Country, as may seem;   355
But herein to our Prophets farr beneath,
As men divinely taught, and better teaching
The solid rules of Civil Government

328 *Crude:* unable to digest. 334 *Story:* history. 335 *With artful terms
inscrib'd:* marked with classifications showing well-developed art (i.e.
generic terms such as 'psalms', 'songs', and 'prayers', and other terms
indicating method of performance). 336 Sée *Psalm* cxxxvii. 341 *Per-
sonating:* impersonating. 347 *Sions songs:* Hebrew poetry and music.
354 *Statists:* statesmen.

In thir majestic unaffected stile
Than all the Oratory of *Greece* and *Rome*.   360
In them is plainest taught, and easiest learnt,
What makes a Nation happy, and keeps it so,
What ruins Kingdoms, and lays Cities flat;
These onely with our Law best form a King.

So spake the Son of God; but Satan now   365
Quite at a loss, for all his darts were spent,
Thus to our Saviour with stern brow reply'd.

Since neither wealth, nor honour, arms nor arts,
Kingdom nor Empire pleases thee, nor aught
By mee propos'd in life contemplative,   370
Or active, tended on by glory, or fame,
What dost thou in this World? the Wilderness
For thee is fittest place, I found thee there,
And thither will return thee, yet remember
What I foretell thee, soon thou shalt have cause   375
To wish thou never hadst rejected thus
Nicely or cautiously my offerd aid,
Which would have set thee in short time with ease
On *Davids* Throne; or Throne of all the World,
Now at full age, fulness of time, thy season,   380
When Prophesies of thee are best fulfilld.
Now contrary, if I read aught in Heaven,
Or Heav'n write aught of Fate, by what the Starrs
Voluminous, or single characters,
In thir conjunction met, give me to spell,   385
Sorrows, and labours, opposition, hate,
Attends thee, scorns, reproaches, injuries,
Violence and stripes, and lastly cruel death,
A Kingdom they portend thee, but what Kingdom,
Real or Allegoric I discern not,   390
Nor when, eternal sure, as without end,
Without beginning; for no date prefixt
Directs me in the Starry Rubric set.

So saying he took (for still he knew his power
Not yet expir'd) and to the Wilderness   395
Brought back the Son of God, and left him there,
Feigning to disappear. Darkness now rose,
As.day-light sunk, and brought in lowring night
Her shadowy off-spring unsubstantial both,

377 *Nicely:* critically. 385 *Conjunction:* apparent proximity of two
heavenly bodies, an astrologically unfavourable sign; *spell:* read,
interpret. 393 *Rubric:* descriptive heading, pattern of prognostica-
tion.

Privation meer of light and absent day.   400
Our Saviour meek and with untroubl'd mind
After his aerie jaunt, though hurried sore,
Hungry and cold betook him to his rest,
Wherever, under some concourse of shades
Whose branching arms thick intertwin'd might shield   405
From dews and damps of night his shelterd head,
But shelterd slept in vain, for at his head
The Tempter watchd, and soon with ugly dreams
Disturbed his sleep; and either Tropic now
'Gan thunder, and both ends of Heav'n, the Clouds   410
From many a horrid rift abortive pourd
Fierce rain with lightning mixt, water with fire
In ruine reconcil'd: nor slept the winds
Within thir stony caves, but rushd abroad
From the four hinges of the World, and fell   415
On the vext Wilderness, whose tallest Pines,
Though rooted deep as high, and sturdiest Oaks
Bow'd thir Stiff necks, load'n with stormy blasts,
Or torn up sheer: ill wast thou shrouded then,
O patient Son of God, yet onely stoodst   420
Unshak'n; nor yet staid the terror there,
Infernal Ghosts, and Hellish Furies, round
Environd thee, some howld, some yelld, some shriekd,
Some bent at thee thir fiery darts, while thou
Sat'st unappalld in calm and sinless peace.   425
Thus passd the night so foul, till morning fair
Came forth with Pilgrim steps in amice gray;
Who with her radiant finger stilld the roar
Of thunder, chas'd the clouds, and laid the winds,
And grisly Spectres, which the Fiend had rais'd   430
To tempt the Son of God with terrors dire.
And now the Sun with more effectual beams
Had cheard the face of Earth, and dry'd the wet
From drooping plant, or dropping tree; the birds
Who all things now behold more fresh and green,   435
After a night of storm so ruinous,
Cleard up their choicest notes in bush and spray
To gratulate the sweet return of morn;

402 *Jaunt:* tiring journey. 409 *Either Tropic:* both northern and south-
ern regions of the sky. 413 *In ruine:* as they fell together. 414 *Stony
caves:* Cf. the cave of the winds described in Virgil's *Aeneid*, I, 52-63.
420 *Onely:* as no one else could. 427 *Amice:* monastic cape or hood
lined with (or made of) grey fur. 436 *So ruinous:* falling so fiercely.
438 *Gratulate:* welcome, give thanks for.

Nor yet amidst this joy and brightest morn
Was absent, after all his mischief done,   440
The Prince of darkness, glad would also seem
Of this fair change, and to our Saviour came,
Yet with no new device, they all were spent,
Rather by this his last affront resolv'd,
Desperat of better course, to vent his rage,   445
And mad despite to be so oft repelld.
Him walking on a Sunny hill he found,
Backt on the North and West by a thick wood,
Out of the wood he starts in wonted shape;
And in a careless mood thus to him said.   450
    Fair morning yet betides thee Son of God,
After a dismal night; I heard the rack
As Earth and Skie would mingle; but my self
Was distant; and these flaws, though mortals fear them
As dangerous to the pillard frame of Heaven,   455
Or to the Earths dark basis underneath,
Are to the main as inconsiderable,
And harmless, if not wholsom, as a sneeze
To mans less universe, and soon are gone;
Yet as being oft times noxious where they light   460
On man, beast, plant, wastful and turbulent,
Like turbulencies in the affairs of men,
Over whose heads they rore, and seem to point,
They oft fore-signifie and threat'n ill:
This Tempest at this Desert most was bent;   465
Of men at thee, for onely thou here dwell'st.
Did I not tell thee, if thou didst reject
The perfet season offerd with my aid
To win thy destind seat, but wilt prolong
All to the push of Fate, persue thy way   470
Of gaining *Davids* Throne no man knows when,
For both the when and how is no where told,
Thou shalt be what thou art ordaind, no doubt;
For Angels have proclaimd it, but concealing
The time and means: each act is rightliest done,   475
Not when it must, but when it may be best.
If thou observe not this, be sure to find,
What I foretold thee, many a hard assay
Of dangers, and adversities and pains,
Ere thou of *Israels* Scepter get fast hold;   .   480

449 *Wonted:* normal, undisguised. 452 *Rack:* ruinous crash. 454
Flaws: cracks, tumults. 457 *Main:* cosmos. 459 *Mans less universe:*
the human body.

Whereof this ominous night that clos'd thee round,
So many terrors, voices, prodigies
May warn thee, as a sure fore-going sign.
    So talkd he, while the Son of God went on
And staid not, but in brief him answerd thus.   485
    Mee worse than wet thou find'st not; other harm
Those terrors which thou speak'st of, did me none;
I never feard they could, though noising loud
And threatning nigh; what they can do as signs
Betok'ning, or ill boding, I contemn   490
As false portents, not sent from God, but thee;
Who knowing I shall raign past thy preventing,
Obtrud'st thy offerd aid, that I accepting
At least might seem to hold all power of thee,
Ambitious spirit, and wouldst be thought my God,   495
And storm'st refus'd, thinking to terrifie
Mee to thy will; desist, thou art discernd
And toil'st in vain, nor me in vain molest.
    To whom the Fiend now swoln with rage reply'd:
Then hear, O Son of *David*, Virgin-born;   500
For Son of God to me is yet in doubt,
Of the Messiah I have heard foretold
By all the Prophets; of thy birth at length
Announc't by *Gabriel* with the first I knew,
And of the Angelic Song in *Bethlehem* field,   505
On thy birth-night, that sung thee Saviour born.
From that time seldom have I ceast to eye
Thy infancy, thy childhood, and thy youth,
Thy manhood last, though yet in privat bred;
Till at the Ford of *Jordan* whither all   510
Flockd to the Baptist, I among the rest,
Though not to be Baptiz'd, by voice from Heav'n
Heard thee pronounc't the Son of God belov'd.
Thenceforth I thought thee worth my nearer view
And narrower Scrutiny, that I might learn   515
In what degree or meaning thou art calld
The Son of God, which bears no single sense;
The Son of God I also am, or was,
And if I was, I am; relation stands;
All men are Sons of God; yet thee I thought   520
In some respect far higher so declar'd.
Therefore I watchd thy footsteps from that hour,
And followd thee still on to this wast wild;
Where by all best conjectures I collect

505-6 See *Luke* ii. 8-14.   524 *Collect:* gather.

Thou art to be my fatal enemy.   525
Good reason then, if I before-hand seek
To understand my Adversary, who
And what he is; his wisdom, power, intent,
By parl, or composition, truce, or league
To win him, or win from him what I can.   530
And opportunity I here have had
To try thee, sift thee, and confess have found thee
Proof against all temptation as a rock
Of Adamant, and as a Center, firm
To th' utmost of meer man both wise and good,   535
Not more; for Honours, Riches, Kingdoms, Glory
Have been before contemnd, and may agen:
Therefore to know what more thou art than man,
Worth naming Son of God by voice from Heav'n,
Another method I must now begin.   540
    So saying he caught him up, and without wing
Of *Hippogrif* bore through the Air sublime
Over the Wilderness and ore the Plain;
Till underneath them fair *Jerusalem*,
The holy City lifted high her Towers,   545
And higher yet the glorious Temple reard
Her pile, farr off appearing like a Mount
Of Alablaster, topt with gold'n Spires:
There on the highest Pinnacle he set
The Son of God; and added thus in scorn: 550
    There stand, if thou wilt stand; to stand upright
Will ask thee skill; I to thy Fathers house
Have brought thee, and highest plac't, highest is best,
Now shew thy Progeny; if not to stand,
Cast thy self down; safely if Son of God: 555
For it is written, He will give command
Concerning thee to his Angels, in thir hands
They shall up lift thee, lest at any time
Thou chance to dash thy foot against a stone.
    To whom thus Jesus: also it is writt'n,   560
Tempt not the Lord thy God, he said and stood.
But Satan smitt'n with amazement fell
As when Earth's Son *Antæus* (to compare

---

529 *Parl . . . composition:* negotiation . . . agreement.   534 *Center:*
point of equilibrium.   542 *Hippogrif(f):* fabulous creature with forepart
of griffin (eagle head and wings) and hindquarters of horse; *sublime:*
high up.   554 *Shew thy Progeny:* prove your parentage.   563 *Antæus:*
giant in Greek mythology, crushed by Hercules.

Small things with greatest) in *Irassa* strove
With *Joves Alcides*, and oft foild still rose,   565
Receiving from his mother Earth new strength,
Fresh from his fall, and fiercer grapple joind,
Throttl'd at length in th' Air, expir'd and fell;
So after many a foil the Tempter proud,
Renewing fresh assaults, amidst his pride   570
Fell whence he stood to see his Victor fall.
And as that *Theban* Monster that propos'd
Her riddle, and him, who solv'd it not, devour'd;
That once found out and solv'd, for grief and spite
Cast her self headlong from th' *Ismenian* steep,   575
So strook with dread and anguish fell the Fiend,
And to his crew, that sat consulting, brought
Joyless triumphals of his hop't success,
Ruin, and desperation, and dismay,
Who durst so proudly tempt the Son of God.   580
So Satan fell, and strait a fiery Globe
Of Angels on full sail of wing flew nigh,
Who on their plumy Vans receiv'd him soft
From his uneasie station, and upbore
As on a floating couch through the blithe Air,   585
Then in a flowry valley set him down
On a green bank, and set before him spred
A table of Celestial Food, Divine,
Ambrosial, Fruits fetcht from the Tree of Life,
And from the Fount of Life Ambrosial drink,   590
That soon refreshd him wearied, and repaird
What hunger, if aught hunger had impaird,
Or thirst, and as he fed, Angelic Quires
Sung Heav'nly Anthems of his victory
Over temptation, and the Tempter proud.   595
True Image of the Father, whether thron'd
In the bosom of bliss, and light of light
Conceiving, or remote from Heaven, enshrin'd
In fleshly Tabernacle, and human form,
Wandring the Wilderness, whatever place,   600
Habit, or state, or motion, still expressing

564 *Irassa:* town in Libya. 565 *Joves Alcides:* Hercules, son of Jove.
572 *Theban Monster:* the Sphinx on the acropolis at Thebes in Bœotia.
574 *Once found out:* The Sphinx's riddle was answered correctly by
Œdipus. 575 *Th' Ismenian steep:* the hill above the river Ismenus.
578 *Triumphals:* tokens of victory. 581 *Globe:* compact troop or crowd.
583 *Vans:* wings. 589 *Ambrosial:* heavenly, delectable. 597-8 *Light
of light conceiving:* 'receiving and reflecting the life-giving illumination
emanating from his Father'.

The Son of God, with Godlike force indu'd
Against th' Attempter of thy Fathers Throne,
And Thief of Paradise; him long of old
Thou didst debell, and down from Heaven cast   605
With all his Army, now thou hast aveng'd
Supplanted *Adam*, and by vanquishing
Temptation, hast regaind lost Paradise,
And frustrated the conquest fraudulent:
Hee never more henceforth will dare set foot   610
In Paradise to tempt; his snares are broke:
For though that seat of earthly bliss be faild,
A fairer Paradise is founded now
For *Adam* and his chosen Sons, whom thou
A Saviour art come down to re-install,   615
Where they shall dwell secure, when time shall be
Of Tempter and Temptation without fear.
But thou, Infernal Serpent, shalt not long
Rule in the Clouds; like an Autumnal Starr
Or Lightning thou shalt fall from Heav'n trod down   620
Under his feet: for proof, ere this thou feel'st
Thy wound, yet not thy last and deadliest wound
By this repulse receiv'd, and hold'st in Hell
No triumph; in all her gates *Abaddon* rues
Thy bold attempt; hereafter learn with awe   625
To dread the Son of God: hee all unarmd
Shall chase thee with the terror of his voice
From thy Demoniac holds, possession foul,
Thee and thy Legions, yelling they shall flye,
And beg to hide them in a herd of Swine,   630
Lest he command them down into the deep
Bound, and to torment sent before thir time.
Hail Son of the most High, heir of both Worlds,
Queller of Satan, on thy glorious work
Now enter, and begin to save mankind.   635
   Thus they the Son of God our Saviour meek
Sung Victor, and from Heav'nly Feast refresht
Brought on his way with joy; hee unobserv'd
Home to his Mothers house privat returnd.

---

605 *Debell:* conquer. 612 *Faild:* gone. 619 *Autumnal Starr:* meteor
(commonly seen in autumn). 624 *Abaddon:* Hell. 629-32 Cf. *Matt.*
viii. 28-32.

Sir John Suckling

1609—1642

A BALLAD UPON A WEDDING

The wedding, which Suckling describes in the subtly adopted
guise of a warm and ingenuous countryman come to town,
was between Roger Boyle (Baron Broghill) and Lady Margaret
Howard, and took place in 1641.

I tell thee *Dick* where I have been,
Where I the rarest things have seen;
  Oh things without compare!
Such sights again cannot be found
In any place on English ground,   5
  Be it at Wake, or Fair.

At *Charing-Crosse*, hard by the way
Where we (thou know'st) do sell our Hay,
  There is a house with stairs;
And there did I see coming down   10
Such folk as are not in our town,
  Vorty at least, in Pairs.

Amongst the rest, one Pest'lent fine,
(His beard no bigger though than thine)
  Walkt on before the rest: 15
Our Landlord looks like nothing to him:
The King (God bless him) 'twould undo him,
  Should he go still so drest.

At Course-a-Park, without all doubt,
He should have just been taken out   20
  By all the Maids i' th' Town:
Though lusty *Roger* there had been,
Or little *George* upon the Green,
  Or *Vincent* of the Crown.

1 *Dick:* perhaps the poet Richard Lovelace (1618-58).   7-8 *The way,
etc.:* Haymarket, in London.   12 *Vorty:* the countryman's 'forty'.   13
Pest'lent: confoundedly (slang).   19 *Course-a-Park:* country game like
Barley-break or Kiss-in-the-ring.

But wot you what? the youth was going   25
To make an end of all his wooing;
    The Parson for him staid;
Yet by his leave (for all his haste)
He did not so much wish all past,
    (Perchance) as did the maid.   30

The maid (and thereby hangs a tale)
For such a maid no Whitsun-ale
    Could ever yet produce:
No Grape that's kindly ripe, could be
So sound, so plump, so soft as she,   35
    Nor half so full of Juice.

Her finger was so small, the Ring
Would not stay on, which they did bring,
    It was too wide a Peck;
And to say truth (for out it must)   40
It lookt like a great Collar (just)
    About our young Colts neck.

Her feet beneath her Petticoat,
Like little mice stole in and out,
    As if they fear'd the light: 45
But oh! she dances such a way
No Sun upon an Easter day
    Is half so fine a sight.

He would have kist her once or twice,
But she would not, she was so nice,   50
    She would not do't in sight,
And then she lookt as who should say,
I will do what I list to day;
    And you shall do't at night.

Her Cheeks so rare a white was on,   55
No Dazy makes comparison,
    (Who sees them is undone)
For streaks of red were mingled there,
Such as are on a Katherine Pear,
    (The side that's next the Sun).   60

32 *Whitsun-ale:* parish festival at Whitsun. 39 *Peck:* great deal
50 *Nice:* shy, modest. 59 *Katherine Pear:* small, early variety of pear·

Her lips were red, and one was thin,
Compar'd to that was next her chin;
   (Some Bee had stung it newly).
But (*Dick*) her eyes so guard her face;
I durst no more upon them gaze,   65
   Than on the Sun in *July*.

Her mouth so small when she does speak,
Thou'dst swear her teeth her words did break,
   That they might passage get,
But she so handled still the matter,   70
They came as good as ours, or better,
   And are not spent a whit.

If wishing should be any sin,
The Parson himself had guilty bin;
   (She lookt that day so purely),   75
And did the youth so oft the feat
At night, as some did in conceit,
   It would have spoil'd him, surely.

Passion o' me! How I run on!
There's that that would be thought upon,   80
   (I trow) besides the Bride:
The bus'nesse of the Kitchin's great,
For it is fit that men should eat;
   Nor was it there deni'd.

Just in the nick the Cook knockt thrice,   85
And all the waiters in a trice
   His summons did obey,
Each serving man with dish in hand,
Marcht boldly up, like our Train'd Band,
   Presented, and away.   90

When all the meat was on the Table,
What man of knife, or teeth, was able
   To stay to be intreated?
And this the very reason was,
Before the Parson could say Grace,
   The Company was seated.   95

Now hats fly off, and youths carouse;
Healths first go round, and then the house,
  The Bride's came thick and thick;
And when 'twas nam'd anothers health,   100
Perhaps he made it hers by stealth.
  (And who could help it, *Dick*?)

O' th' sudden up they rise and dance;
Then sit again and sigh, and glance:
  Then dance again and kisse: 105
Thus sev'ral waies the time did passe,
Till ev'ry Woman wisht her place,
  And ev'ry Man wisht his.

By this time all were stoln aside
To counsel and undresse the Bride;   110
  But that he must not know:
But yet 'twas thought he guess'd her mind,
And did not mean to stay behind
  Above an hour or so.

When in he came (*Dick*) there she lay   115
Like new-faln snow melting away
  ('Twas time I trow to part)
Kisses were now the only stay,
Which soon she gave, as who would say,
  God b'w'ye with all my heart.   120

But just as heav'ns would have to cross it,
In came the Bridemaids with the Posset:
  The Bridegroom eat in spight;
For had he left the Women to't
It would have cost two hours to do't,   125
  Which were too much that night.

At length the candles out, and now
All that they had not done, they do:
  What that is, who can tell?
But I believe it was no more   130
Than thou and I have done before
  With *Bridget*, and with *Nell*.

122 *Posset:* hot drink.

Richard Crashaw

1612—1649

HYMN TO ST. TERESA*

Love thou art absolute sole Lord
Of life and death.—To prove the word,
Wee'l now appeale to none of all
Those thy old Souldiers, Great and tall
Ripe men of Martyrdome, that could reach downe,   5
With strong armes, their Triumphant crowne:
Such as could with lustie breath,
Speake loud into the face of death,
Their great Lord's glorious name; To none
Of those whose spatious bosomes spread a throne   10
For love at large to fill: spare Blood and sweat,
And see him take a privat seat,
Making his mansion in the mild
And milky soule of a soft child.
Scarce hath she learnt to lisp the name,   15
Of Martyr; yet she thinkes it shame
Life should so long play with that breath,
Which spent can buy so brave a death.
She never undertooke to know,
What death with love should have to doe;   20
Nor hath she e're yet understood
Why to shew love, she should shed blood,
Yet though she can not tell you why,
She can *love*, and she can *dye*.
Scarce hath she blood enough, to make   25
A guilty sword blush for her sake;
Yet hath she a heart dare hope to prove,
How much lesse strong is Death than Love.
Be Love but there, let poore six yeares
Be pos'd with the maturest feares   30
Man trembles at, you streight shall find
Love knows no nonage, nor the Mind.

---

* St. Teresa of Avila (1515-82), Spanish nun, mystic, and reformer of
the Carmelite order. Crashaw's poem is based on incidents recorded in
her autobiography. 32 *Nonage:* immaturity, minority.

'Tis *Love*, not years nor Limbs, that can
Make the *Martyr* or the *Man*.
Love toucht her *Heart*, and lo it beates   35
High, and burnes with such brave Heates,
Such *Thirsts* to dye, as dares drink up,
A thousand cold *Deaths* in one cup.
Good reason; for she breathes all *fire*,
Her weake brest heaves with strong desire,   40
Of what she may with fruitlesse wishes
Seeke for amongst her Mothers Kisses.

Since 'tis not to be had at home,
Shee'l travell for *A Martyrdome*.
No *Home* for hers confesses she,   45
But where she may a Martyr be.
Shee'l to the *Moores* and trade with them,
For this unvalued *Diadem*,
Shee'l offer them her dearest Breath,
With *Christ*'s name in't, in change for death.   50
Shee'l bargain with them, and will give
Them God, and teach them how to live
In him; Or if they this deny,
For him, she'l teach them how to dye.
So shall she leave amongst them sown,   55
Her *Lord*'s blood, or at least her *own*.
Farewell then all the world! Adiew,
Teresa is no more for you:
Farewell all pleasures, sports, and joys,
(Never till now esteemed *Toyes*)   60
Farewell what ever deare may bee,
Mother's armes or Father's Knee.
Farewell house and farewell home!
She's for the *Moores*, and *Martyrdome*.

Sweet not so fast! Lo thy faire *Spouse*,   65
Whom thou seekst with so swift vowes
Calls thee back, and bidds thee come,
T'embrace a milder Martyrdome.
Blest powers forbid thy tender life,
Should bleed upon a barbarous Knife;   70
Or some base hand have power to race
Thy Brest's soft cabinet, and uncase
A soule kept there so sweet. O no;
Wise Heaven will never have it so.

Thou art *Loves* Victim; and must dye   75
A death more mysticall and *high*.
Into *Loves* armes thou shalt let fall
A still surviving funerall.
His is the *Dart* must make the *Death*
Whose stroake shall taste thy hallow'd *breath*;   80
A Dart thrice dipt in that rich *flame*,
Which writes thy spouses radiant *Name*,
Upon the roofe of Heav'n, where ay
It shines, and with a sovereigne Ray
Beates bright upon the burning faces   85
Of soules, which in that Name's sweet graces
Find everlasting smiles; so rare,
So spirituall, pure, and faire,
Must be th' immortall instrument,
Upon whose choice point shall be sent,   90
A life so lov'd; And that there be
Fit executioners for thee,
The fair'st and first borne sons of fire,
Blest *Seraphims*, shall leave their Quire,
And turne *Love's Souldiers*, upon thee,   95
To exercise their *Archerie*.
O how oft shalt thou complaine
Of a sweet and subtile *paine!*
Of intollerable *joyes!*
Of a *death*, in which who *dyes*   100
Loves his *death*, and dyes againe,
And would for ever so be slaine!
And lives, and dyes; and knowes not why
To live; But that he thus may never leave to dye.
How kindly will thy gentle *Heart*   105
Kisse the sweetly-killing *Dart!*
And close in his embraces keepe,
Those *delicious wounds* that *weepe*
Balsome to heale themselves with. Thus
When these thy *Deathes*, so numerous,   110
Shall all at last dye into one,
And melt thy soules sweet *mansion*;
Like a soft lump of Incense, hasted
By too hot a fire, and wasted
Into perfuming clouds, so fast   115
Shalt thou exhale to Heav'n at last,
In a resolving sigh, and then,
O what? Aske not the tongues of men.

Angells cannot tell. Suffice,
Thy self shall feele thine own full joyes,   120
And hold them fast for ever. There,
So soon as thou shalt first *appeare,*
The Moon of maiden stars, thy white
Mistresse, attended by such bright
Soules as thy shining-self, shall come,   125
And in her first rankes make thee roome.
Where 'mongst her snowy family
Immortall welcomes waite for thee.
O what delight, when reveal'd life shall stand,
And teach thy lips heav'n with his hand,   130
On which thou now maist to thy wishes,
Heape up thy *consecrated kisses!*
What joyes shall seize thy soule, when she
Bending her blessed eyes on thee
(Those second smiles of Heav'n) shall dart   135
Her mild rayes through thy melting Heart!
Angells thy old friends, there shall greet thee,
Glad at their owne home now to meet thee.
All thy good works which went before,
And waited for thee at the doore,   140
Shall owne thee there; and all in one
Weave a *Constellation*
Of crownes with which the King thy spouse,
Shall build up thy triumphant browes.
All thy old woes shall now smile on thee,   145
And thy Paines sit bright upon thee.
All thy sorrows here shall shine,
And thy suff'rings be divine;
Teares shall take comfort, and turn *Gems,*
And *wrongs* repent to *Diadems.*   150
Ev'n thy *Deaths* shall live; and new
Dresse the soule, that erst they slew.
Thy Wounds shall blush to such bright scars,
As keep account of the *Lamb*'s wars.
Those *rare workes* where thou shalt leave writ,   155
Loves noble *Historie,* with wit
Taught thee by none but him, while here
They feed our *soules,* shall cloath thine there.
Each heav'nly word, by whose hid flame
Our hard hearts shall strike fire, the same   160
Shall flourish on thy browes, and be
Both *fire* to us, and *flame* to thee;

Whose light shall live bright, in thy Face
By *glorie*, in our Hearts by *grace*.
Thou shalt looke round about, and see   165
Thousands of crown'd soules throng to bee
Themselves thy *crowne*; sonnes of thy vowes,
The virgin-births, with which thy soveraigne spouse
Made fruitfull thy faire soul. Goe now
And with them all about thee, bow   170
To him, Put on (hee'l say) put on
(*My Rosie Love*) That thy rich Zone,
Sparkling with the sacred flames,
Of thousand soules, whose happy names
Heav'n keeps upon thy score (Thy bright   175
Life brought them first to kisse the light
That kindled them to stars) and so
Thou with the *Lamb*, thy Lord, shalt goe;
And where soe're he sets his white
Steps, walk with *Him* those waies of light,   180
Which who in death would live to see,
Must learne in life to dye like Thee.

Andrew Marvell

1621—1678

AN HORATIAN ODE
UPON CROMWELL'S RETURN FROM IRELAND

Probably written between Cromwell's return from Ireland in
May, 1650 and his departure for the Scottish campaign in July.
The fine political detachment which critics have praised in this
poem is achieved at the cost of a rather chilling conception of
history; yet such is Marvell's art that even the ruthless ' man of
destiny ' theme, and the brutality of the falcon image (lines 91-96),
are mitigated by his suggesting that the conqueror is ' still in the
Republick's hand.'

The forward Youth that would appear
Must now forsake his *Muses* dear,
    Nor in the Shadows sing
    His Numbers languishing.

172 *Zone:* belt, girdle. 1 *Forward:* eager, ambitious; *appear:* become
known to the public.

'Tis time to leave the Books in dust,   5
And oyl th' unused Armours rust,
  Removing from the Wall
  The Corslet of the Hall.
So restless *Cromwel* could not cease
In the inglorious Arts of Peace,   10
But through adventrous War
  Urged his active Star.
And, like the three fork'd Lightning, first
Breaking the Clouds where it was nurst,
  Did thorough his own Side   15
  His fiery way divide.
For 'tis all one to Courage high
The Emulous or Enemy;
  And with such to inclose
  Is more than to oppose.   20
Then burning through the Air he went,
And Pallaces and Temples rent:
  And *Cæsars* head at last
  Did through his Laurels blast.
'Tis Madness to resist or blame   25
The force of angry Heavens flame:
  And, if we would speak true,
  Much to the Man is due
Who, from his private Gardens, where
He liv'd reserved and austere,   30
  As if his highest plot
  To plant the Bergamot,
Could by industrious Valour climbe
To ruine the great Work of Time,
  And cast the Kingdome old   35
  Into another Mold.
Though Justice against Fate complain,
And plead the antient Rights in vain:
  But those do hold or break
  As Men are strong or weak.   40
Nature that hateth emptiness,
Allows of penetration less:

9 *Cromwel(l):* Oliver Cromwell (1599-1658), Lord Protector of the Commonwealth from 1653 till his death. 15 *His own Side:* the Parliamentary party. 19-20 Such a man may find his own party stifling, whereas contact with the enemy may be bracing. 23 *Cæsar:* King Charles I (1600-49). 24 *Laurels:* thought, in classical times, to be a preservative against lightning. 32 *Bergamot:* a fine variety of pear, recently introduced. 42 *Penetration:* imagined simultaneous occupation of same space by two bodies.

And therefore must make room
Where greater Spirits come.
What Field of all the Civil Wars,   45
Where his were not the deepest Scars?
   And *Hampton* shows what part
   He had of wiser Art.
Where, twining subtile fears with hope,
He wove a Net of such a scope,   50
   That *Charles* himself might chase
   To *Caresbrooks* narrow case.
That thence the *Royal Actor* born
The *Tragick Scaffold* might adorn:
   While round the armed Bands   55
   Did clap their bloody hands.
He nothing common did or mean
Upon that memorable Scene:
   But with his keener Eye
   The Axes edge did try: 60
Nor call'd the *Gods* with vulgar spight
To vindicate his helpless Right,
   But bow'd his comely Head,
   Down as upon a Bed.
This was that memorable Hour   65
Which first assur'd the forced Pow'r.
   So when they did design
   The *Capitols* first Line,
A bleeding Head where they begun,
Did fright the Architects to run;   70
   And yet in that the *State*
   Foresaw its happy Fate.
And now the *Irish* are asham'd
To see themselves in one Year tam'd;
   So much one Man can do,   75
   That does both act and know.
They can affirm his Praises best,
And have, though overcome, confest

47-52 Charles fled from Hampton Court to Carisbrooke Castle on the Isle of Wight Nov. 1647. It is probably untrue that Cromwell encouraged or connived at this for his own ambitions, though it helped eventually to destroy the king. 51 'That Charles might seem to be a free agent in effecting his escape.' 52 *Narrow case:* (i) 'encasing' prison or trap, (ii) difficult plight. 58 *Scene:* the main meaning is 'stage'. 66 *Forced:* gained by force. 67-72 The Capitol at Rome was said to be named after a human head ('caput') uncovered among its foundations and interpreted as a good omen.

How good he is, how just,
And fit for highest Trust: 80
Nor yet grown stiffer with Command,
But still in the *Republick*'s hand:
    How fit he is to sway
    That can so well obey.
He to the *Commons Feet* presents   85
A *Kingdome*, for his first years rents:
And, what he may, forbears
His Fame to make it theirs:
And has his Sword and Spoyls ungirt,
To lay them at the *Publick*'s skirt.   90
    So when the Falcon high
    Falls heavy from the Sky,
She, having kill'd, no more does search,
But on the next green Bow to pearch;
    Where, when he first does lure,   95
    The Falckner has her sure.
What may not then our *Isle* presume
While Victory his Crest does plume!
    What may not others fear
    If thus he crown each Year!   100
A *Cæsar* he ere long to *Gaul*,
To *Italy* an *Hannibal*,
    And to all States not free
    Shall *Clymacterick* be.
The *Pict* no shelter now shall find   105
Within his party-colour'd Mind;
    But from this Valour sad
    Shrink underneath the Plad:
Happy if in the tufted brake
The *English Hunter* him mistake;   110
    Nor lay his Hounds in near
    The *Caledonian* Deer.
But thou the Wars and Fortunes Son
March indefatigably on:
    And for the last effect   115
    Still keep thy Sword erect;

90 *Publick:* republic, commonwealth.   101-2 alluding to Julius Cæsar's
invasion of France 58 B.C. and the Carthaginian Hannibal's invasion of
Italy 218 B.C.   104 *Clymacterick:* crucial, historically critical.   105-6
Pict: punning on the supposed derivation from Latin *pingere* ('to paint');
party-colour'd: variegated, untrustworthy: a frequent English charge
against the Scots at this period.   107 *Sad:* firm, unmoved.
A.L.P.

                                                              H

Besides the force it has to fright
The Spirits of the shady Night,
  The same *Arts* that did *gain*
  A *Pow'r* must it *maintain*.   120

THE GARDEN

I

How vainly men themselves amaze
To win the Palm, the Oke, or Bayes;
And their uncessant Labours see
Crown'd from some single Herb or Tree,
Whose short and narrow verged Shade   5
Does prudently their Toyles upbraid;
While all Flow'rs and all Trees do close
To weave the Garlands of repose.

II

Fair quiet, have I found thee here,
And Innocence thy Sister dear!   10
Mistaken long, I sought you then
In busie Companies of Men.
Your sacred Plants, if here below,
Only among the Plants will grow.
Society is all but rude,   15
To this delicious Solitude.

III

No white nor red was ever seen
So am'rous as this lovely green.
Fond Lovers, cruel as their Flame,
Cut in these Trees their Mistress name.   20
Little, Alas, they know, or heed,
How far these Beauties Hers exceed!
Fair Trees! where s'eer your barkes I wound,
No Name shall but your own be found.

IV

When we have run our Passions heat,   25
Love hither makes his best retreat.
The *Gods*, that mortal Beauty chase,

117-18 the sword with its hilt being held up like an exorcising cross.
1 *Amaze:* bewilder. 2 *Palm* . . . *Oke* . . . *Bayes:* symbolic awards;
general, civic, and poetic. 15 'All society is merely barbarous.'

Still in a Tree did end their race.
Apollo hunted *Daphne* so,
Only that She might Laurel grow.   30
And *Pan* did after *Syrinx* speed,
Not as a Nymph, but for a Reed.

V

What wond'rous Life in this I lead!
Ripe Apples drop about my head;
The Luscious Clusters of the Vine
Upon my Mouth do crush their Wine;   35
The Nectaren, and curious Peach,
Into my hands themselves do reach;
Stumbling on Melons, as I pass,
Insnar'd with Flow'rs, I fall on Grass.   40

VI

Mean while the Mind, from pleasure less,
Withdraws into its happiness:
The Mind, that Ocean where each kind
Does streight its own resemblance find;
Yet it creates, transcending these,
Far other Worlds, and other Seas;   45
Annihilating all that's made
To a green Thought in a green Shade.

VII

Here at the Fountains sliding foot,
Or at some Fruit-trees mossy root,
Casting the Bodies Vest aside,   50
My Soul into the boughs does glide:
There like a Bird it sits, and sings,
Then whets, and combs its silver Wings;
And, till prepar'd for longer flight,
Waves in its Plumes the various Light.   55

VIII

Such was that happy Garden-state,
While Man there walk'd without a Mate:

29-30 Daphne, in Greek mythology, escaped the pursuing Apollo by
being turned into a laurel tree.   31-32 Syrinx similarly escaped from
Pan by being changed into a reed.   37 *Curious:* fine, choice.   43-44 It
was commonly believed that species on land had their counterparts in
the sea. *Streight:* directly, immediately.   54 *Whets:* preens.   56
Various: changing.   57 i.e., in Eden

After a Place so pure, and sweet,
What other Help could yet be meet!   60
But 'twas beyond a Mortal's share
To wander solitary there:
Two Paradises 'twere in one
To live in Paradise alone.

IX

How well the skilful Gardner drew   65
Of flow'rs and herbes this Dial new;
Where from above the milder Sun
Does through a fragrant Zodiack run;
And, as it works, th' industrious Bee
Computes its time as well as we.   70
How could such sweet and wholsome Hours
Be reckon'd but with herbs and flow'rs!

THE CHARACTER OF HOLLAND

A literary shot fired during the First Dutch War (1652-54), probably after the English naval victory off Portland Bill in February, 1653.

Holland, that scarce deserves the name of *Land*,
As but th' Off-scouring of the *Brittish Sand*;
And so much Earth as was contributed
By *English Pilots* when they heav'd the Lead;
Or what by th' Oceans slow alluvion fell,   5
Of shipwrackt Cockle and the Muscle-shell;
This indigested vomit of the Sea
Fell to the *Dutch* by just Propriety.
   Glad then, as Miners that have found the Oar,
They with mad labour fish'd the *Land* to *Shoar*;   10
And div'd as desperately for each piece
Of Earth, as if't had been of *Ambergreece*;
Collecting anxiously small Loads of Clay,
Less than what building Swallows bear away;
Or than those Pills which sordid Beetles roul,   15
Tranfusing into them their Dunghil Soul.
   How did they rivet, with Gigantick Piles,
Thorough the Center their new-catched Miles;

66 *Dial:* floral sundial.   5 *Alluvion:* marine deposit.

And to the stake a strugling Country bound,
Where barking Waves still bait the forced Ground;   20
Building their *watry Babel* far more high
To reach the *Sea* than those to scale the *Sky.*
   Yet still his claim the Injur'd Ocean laid,
And oft at Leap-frog ore their Steeples plaid:
As if on purpose it on Land had come   25
To shew them what's their *Mare Liberum.*
A daily deluge over them does boyl;
The Earth and Water play at *Level-coyl;*
The Fish oft-times the Burger dispossest,
And sat not as a Meat but as a Guest;   30
And oft the *Tritons* and the *Sea-Nymphs* saw
Whole sholes of *Dutch* serv'd up for *Cabillau;*
Or as they over the new Level rang'd
For pickled *Herring,* pickled *Heeren* chang'd.
Nature, it seem'd, asham'd of her mistake,   35
Would throw their Land away at *Duck* and *Drake.*
   Therefore *Necessity,* that first made *Kings,*
Something like *Government* among them brings.
For as with *Pygmees* who best kills the *Crane,*
Among the *hungry* he that treasures *Grain,*   40
Among the *blind* the one-ey'd blinkard reigns,
So rules among the *drowned* he that *draines.*
Not who first see the *rising Sun* commands,
But who could first discern the *rising Lands.*
Who best could know to pump an Earth so leak   45
Him they their *Lord* and *Country's Father* speak.
To make a *Bank* was a great *Plot of State;*
Invent a *Shov'l* and be a *Magistrate.*
Hence some small *Dyke-grave* unperceiv'd invades
The *Pow'r,* and grows as 'twere a *King of Spades.*   50
But for less envy some *joynt States* endures,
Who look like a *Commission of the Sewers.*
For these *Half-anders,* half wet, and half dry,
Nor bear *strict service,* nor *pure Liberty.*

19-20 The image is taken from bear-baiting. 21 *Babel:* See *Gen.* xi.
4-9. 26 *Mare Liberum:* 'the free sea' (Lat.), a doctrine argued by the
sea-conscious Dutch. 28 *Level-coyl:* from 'lever le cul' (Fr.), rough
game involving unseating of one person by another. 31 *Tritons:* mer-
men of Greek mythology. 32 *Cabillau:* (Dutch *kabeljauw*), codfish.
34 *Heeren:* men (Dutch). 36 *Duck and Drake:* game of skimming
stones across surface of water. 39 See Homer's *Iliad,* III. 1-7. 45 *Leak:*
leaky. 49 *Dyke-grave:* officer in charge of sea-walls in Holland. 53
Half-anders: though claiming to be Holl-anders.

'Tis probable *Religion* after this   55
Came next in order; which they could not miss.
How could the *Dutch* but be converted, when
Th' *Apostles* were so many Fishermen?
Besides the Waters of themselves did rise,
And, as their Land, so them did re-baptize.   60
Though *Herring* for their *God* few voices mist,
And *Poor-John* to have been th' *Evangelist.*
Faith, that could never Twins conceive before,
Never so fertile, spawn'd upon this shore:
More pregnant than their *Marg'ret,* that laid down   65
For *Hans-in-Kelder* of a whole *Hans-Town.*
    Sure when *Religion* did it self imbark,
And from the *East* would *Westward* steer its Ark,
It struck, and splitting on this unknown ground,
Each one thence pillag'd the first piece he found: 70
Hence *Amsterdam, Turk-Christian-Pagan-Jew,*
Staple of Sects and Mint of Schisme grew;
That *Bank of Conscience,* where not one so strange
Opinion but finds Credit, and Exchange.
In vain for *Catholicks* our selves we bear;   75
The *universal Church* is onely there.
Nor can Civility there want for *Tillage,*
Where wisely for their *Court* they chose a *Village.*
How fit a Title clothes their *Governours,*
Themselves the *Hogs* as all their Subjects *Bores*!   80
    Let it suffice to give their Country Fame
That it had one *Civilis* call'd by Name,
Some Fifteen hundred and more years ago;
But surely never any that was so.
    See but their *Mairmaids* with their *Tails of Fish,*   85
Reeking at *Church* over the *Chafing-Dish.*
A vestal Turf enshrin'd in Earthen Ware
Fumes through the loop-holes of a wooden Square.
Each to the *Temple* with these *Altars* tend,
But still does place it at her *Western End*:   90

61 *Herring:* the same pun as at line 34. 62 *Poor-John:* dried salted
hake. 65 *Marg'ret:* Countess Margaret, daughter of Florent IV,
reputedly gave birth to 365 children in 1278. 66 *Hans-in-Kelder:*
'Hans-in-the-cellar' (Dutch), child in the womb; *Hans-Town:* town of
the Hanseatic League. 72 *Staple:* trading centre. 78 *A Village:* The
Hague. 80 *Hogs:* pun on *Hoog-mogenden,* 'high and mighty', title of the
States-General; *Bores:* pun on *Boers.* 82 *Civilis:* (1st cent. A.D.), leader
of the Batavi against the Romans. 86 *Chafing-Dish:* charcoal stove
used in Dutch churches. 87 *Vestal:* (i) sacred, (ii) burning, (iii)
brought by the young women.

While the fat steam of *Female Sacrifice*
Fills the *Priests Nostrils* and puts out his *Eyes*.
  Or what a Spectacle the *Skipper gross*,
A *Water-Hercules Butter-Coloss*,
Tunn'd up with all their sev'ral *Towns of Beer*;   95
When Stagg'ring upon some Land, *Snick and Sneer*,
They try, like Statuaries, if they can,
Cut out each others *Athos* to a Man:
And carve in their large Bodies, where they please,
The Armes of the *United Provinces*.   100
  But when such Amity at home is show'd;
What then are their confederacies abroad?
Let this one court'sie witness all the rest;
When their whole Navy they together prest,
Not Christian Captives to redeem from Bands: 105
Or intercept the Western golden Sands:
No, but all ancient Rights and Leagues must vail,
Rather than to the *English* strike their sail;
To whom their weather-beaten *Province* ows
It self, when as some greater Vessel tows   110
A Cock-boat tost with the same wind and fate;
We buoy'd so often up their *sinking State*.
  Was this *Jus Belli & Pacis*; could this be
Cause why their *Burgomaster of the Sea*
Ram'd with Gun-powder, flaming with Brand wine,   115
Should raging hold his Linstock to the Mine?
While, with feign'd *Treaties*, they invade by stealth
Our sore new circumcised *Common wealth*.
  Yet of his vain Attempt no more he sees
Than of *Case-Butter* shot and *Bullet-Cheese*.   120
And the torn Navy stagger'd with him home,
While the Sea laught it self into a foam,

94 'A huge strong greasy amphibious Dutchman.' 95 *Towns of Beer:*
alluding to Dutch place-names beginning Beer- or Bier-. 96 *Snick and
Sneer:* thrust and slash with a knife (from Dutch *steken and snijen*). 97-98
The Greek sculptor Deinocrates wanted to carve a figure out of Mt.
Athos. 107 *Vail:* allow to drop. The reference in these lines is to the
incident in the English Channel in 1652, when Dutch ships refused to
'vail' (lower their flags) to the English fleet. 111 *Cock-boat:* small
ship's boat. 113 *Jus Belli & Pacis:* 'the law of war and peace' (Lat.);
referring to a treatise on international law by the Dutch jurist and poet
Hugo Grotius (1583-1645). 114 *Burgomaster of the Sea:* the Dutch
admiral Martin Tromp (1597-1653). 115 *Brand wine:* (Dutch
brandewijn, 'burnt wine'), brandy. 116 *Linstock:* forked staff for hold-
ing match. 118 See *Gen.* xxxiv. 120 Case-shot consisted of small
projectiles within a canister, fired from a cannon; here, no more
effective than butter-balls.

'Tis true since that (as fortune kindly sports,)
A wholesome Danger drove us to our Ports.
While half their banish'd keels the Tempest tost,   125
Half bound at home in Prison to the frost:
That ours mean time at leizure might careen,
In a calm Winter, under Skies Serene.
As the obsequious Air and Waters rest,
Till the dear *Halcyon* hatch out all its nest.   130
The *Common wealth* doth by its losses grow;
And, like its own Seas, only Ebbs to flow.
Besides that very Agitation laves,
And purges out the corruptible waves.
    And now again our armed *Bucentore*   135
Doth yearly their *Sea-Nuptials* restore.
And now the *Hydra of seaven Provinces*
Is strangled by our *Infant Hercules.*
Their Tortoise wants its vainly stretched neck;
Their Navy all our Conquest or our Wreck: 140
Or, what is left, their *Carthage* overcome
Would render fain unto our better *Rome.*
Unless our *Senate,* lest their Youth disuse,
The War, (but who would) Peace if begg'd refuse.
    For now of nothing may our *State* despair,   145
Darling of Heaven, and of Men the Care;
Provided that they be what they have been,
Watchful abroad, and honest still within.
For while our *Neptune* doth a *Trident* shake,
Steel'd with those piercing Heads, *Dean, Monck* and *Blake,*   150
And while *Jove* governs in the highest Sphere,
Vainly in *Hell* let *Pluto* domineer.

---

123 *Since that:* i.e. later in 1652, during an engagement off Dungeness
in which Tromp was victorious; *kindly:* by its nature.   130 *Halcyon:*
kingfisher, anciently supposed to breed during the winter solstice in a
nest on a calm sea.   134 Some of the British naval officers were dis-
charged for inefficiency.   135-6 *Bucentore . . . Sea-Nuptials:* alludes to
the Venetian state barge (It. *bucintoro*) from which the Doge performed
the annual ceremony of 'wedding the sea'.   137-8 Hercules in Greek
mythology strangled snakes in his childhood, and later killed the Hydra,
a many-headed reptile. The *seaven Provinces* make up Holland, and the
reference is probably to the English victory at Portland in February,
1653.   149 *Neptune:*   Roman sea-god, represented carrying a three-
pronged spear.   150 The three 'heads' of the trident are the admirals
Richard Deane (1610-53), George Monck, Duke of Albemarle (1608-
70), and Robert Blake (1599-1657).   151 *Jove:* Roman supreme deity.
152 *Pluto:* Greek god of the underworld.

John Dryden

1631—1700

ABSALOM AND ACHITOPHEL

In the political allegory of this satire Dryden attacks the Whig
leader Shaftesbury's attempt to oust the Catholic Duke of York,
Charles II's brother and heir, in favour of the Protestant Duke
of Monmouth, his illegitimate son. The poem was published
(November, 1681) while Shaftesbury was awaiting trial for high
treason, and was evidently meant to prejudice the issue against
him. The indictment was thrown out, but Shaftesbury fled to
Holland in 1682.

—Si Propiùs stes
*Te Capiet Magis—**
[HORACE, Ars Poetica 361-2]

TO THE READER

'Tis not my intention to make an Apology for my Poem: *Some will think it needs
no Excuse, and others will receive none. The Design, I am sure, is honest: but
he who draws his Pen for one Party, must expect to make Enemies of the other.
For,* Wit *and* Fool, *are Consequents of* Whig *and* Tory: *And every man is a
Knave or an Ass to the contrary side. There's a Treasury of Merits in the
Phanatick Church, as well as in the* Papist; *and a Pennyworth to be had of
Saintship, Honesty, and Poetry, for the Leud, the Factious, and the Blockheads:
But the longest Chapter in* Deuteronomy, *has not Curses enow for an Anti-
Bromingham†. My Comfort is, their manifest Prejudice to my Cause, will
render their Judgment of less Authority against me. Yet if a Poem have a
Genius, it will force its own reception in the World. For there's a sweetness in
good Verse, which Tickles even while it Hurts: And, no man can be heartily
angry with him, who pleases him against his will. The Commendation of
Adversaries, is the greatest Triumph of a Writer; because it never comes unless
Extorted. But I can be satisfied on more easy termes: If I happen to please the
more Moderate sort, I shall be sure of an honest Party; and, in all probability,
of the best Judges; for, the least Concern'd, are commonly the least Corrupt:
And, I confess, I have laid in for those, by rebating the Satyre, (where Justice
would allow it) from carrying too sharp an Edge. They, who can Criticize
so weakly, as to imagine I have done my Worst, may be Convinc'd, at their own
Cost, that I can write Severely, with more ease, than I can Gently. I have but
laught at some mens Follies, when I coud have declaim'd against their Vices; and,
other mens Vertues I have commended, as freely as I have tax'd their Crimes. And
now, if you are a Malitious Reader, I expect you should return upon me, that I*

* The motto, at once serious and ironic reads: 'If you stand closer, you
will get more of an effect.'   † Anti-Bromingham: Tory.

233

affect to be thought more Impartial than I am. But, *if men are not to be judg'd by their Professions, God forgive you* Common-wealths-men, *for professing so plausibly for the Government.* You cannot be so Unconscionable, *as to charge me for not Subscribing of my Name; for that woud reflect too grosly upon your own Party, who never dare, though they have the advantage of a Jury to secure them. If you like not my* Poem, *the fault may, possibly, be in my Writing:* (though 'tis hard *for an Author to judge against himself;*) But, *more probably, 'tis in your Morals, which cannot bear the truth of it. The Violent, on both sides, will condemn the Character of* Absalom, *as either too favourably, or too hardly drawn. But, they are not the Violent, whom I desire to please. The fault, on the right hand, is to Extenuate, Palliate, and Indulge; and, to confess freely, I have endeavour'd to commit it. Besides the respect which I owe his Birth, I have a greater for his Heroique Vertues; and,* David *himself, coud not be more tender of the Young-man's Life, than I woud be of his Reputation. But, since the most excellent Natures are always the most easy; and, as being such, are the soonest perverted by ill Counsels, especially when baited with Fame and Glory, 'tis no more a wonder that he withstood not the temptations of* Achitophel, *than it was for* Adam, *not to have resisted the two Devils: the Serpent, and the Woman. The conclusion of the Story, I purposely forbore to prosecute; because, I coud not obtain from my self, to shew* Absalom Unfortunate. *The Frame of it, was cut out, but for a Picture to the Wast; and, if the Draught be so far true, 'tis as much as I design'd.*

Were I the Inventour, *who am only the Historian, I shoud certainly conclude the Piece, with the Reconcilement of* Absalom *to* David. *And, who knows but this may come to pass? Things were not brought to an Extremity where I left the Story: There seems, yet, to be room left for a Composure; hereafter, there may only be for Pity. I have not, so much as an uncharitable Wish against* Achitophel; *but, am content to be Accus'd of a good natur'd Errour; and, to hope with* Origen††, *that the Devil himself may, at last, be sav'd. For which reason, in this* Poem, *he is neither brought to set his house in Order, nor to dispose of his Person afterwards, as he in Wisedom shall think fit. God is infinitely merciful; and his Vicegerent is only not so, because he is not Infinite.*

The true end of Satyre, *is the amendment of Vices by correction. And he who writes Honestly, is no more an Enemy to the Offender, than the Physician to the Patient, when he prescribes harsh Remedies to an inveterate Disease: for those, are only in order to prevent the Chyrurgeon's work of an* Ense rescindendum†††, *which I wish not to my very Enemies. To conclude all, If the Body Politique have any Analogy to the Natural, in my weak judgment, an Act of* Oblivion *were as necessary in a Hot, Distemper'd State, as an* Opiate *woud be in a Raging Fever.*

In pious times, e'r Priest-craft did begin,
Before *Polygamy* was made a Sin;
When Man, on many, multiply'd his kind,
E'r one to one was, cursedly, confin'd:
When Nature prompted and no Law deny'd   5
Promiscuous Use of Concubine and Bride;

†† *Origen:* the early Christian scholar (*c.* 185–*c.* 254).   ††† *Chyrurgeon:* surgeon; *ense rescindendum:* 'to be cut away by the sword' (Lat.).

Then, *Israel*'s Monarch, after Heaven's own heart,
His vigorous warmth did, variously, impart
To Wives and Slaves: And, wide as his Command,
Scatter'd his Maker's Image through the Land.   10
Michal, of Royal Blood, the Crown did wear,
A Soyl ungrateful to the Tiller's care:
Not so the rest; for several Mothers bore
To God-like *David*, several sons before.
But since like Slaves his Bed they did ascend,   15
No True Succession could their Seed attend.
Of all this Numerous Progeny was none
So Beautiful, so Brave as *Absolon*:
Whether, inspir'd by some diviner Lust,
His Father got him with a greater Gust;   20
Or that his Conscious Destiny made way
By manly Beauty to Imperial Sway.
Early in Foreign Fields he won Renown,
With Kings and States ally'd to *Israel*'s Crown:
In Peace the thoughts of War he coud remove,   25
And seem'd as he were only born for Love.
What e'r he did was done with so much ease,
In him alone, 'twas Natural to please;
His motions all accompanied with grace;
And *Paradise* was open'd in his face.   30
With secret Joy, indulgent *David* view'd
His Youthful Image in his Son renew'd;
To all his wishes Nothing he deny'd,
And made the Charming *Annabel* his Bride.
What faults he had (for who from faults is free?)   35
His Father coud not, or he woud not see.
Some warm excesses, which the Law forbore,
Were constru'd Youth that purg'd by boyling o'r:
And *Amnon*'s Murther, by a specious Name,
Was call'd a Just Revenge for injur'd Fame.   40
Thus Prais'd, and Lov'd, the Noble Youth remain'd,
While *David*, undisturb'd, in *Sion* raign'd.
But Life can never be sincerely blest:
Heav'n punishes the bad, and proves the best.

7 *Israel's Monarch:* David; here standing for Charles II (1630-85)'
(*I Sam.* xiii. 13-14.)   11 *Michal:* Catherine of Braganza (1638-1705),
whom Charles II married 1662. (*II Sam.* vi. 23.)   16 *Attend:* expect.
18 *Absolon:*   James Scott (1649-85), illegitimate son of Charles II,
created Duke of Monmouth 1663. (*II Sam.* iii. 3.)   20 *Gust:* gusto.
34   *Annabel:* Anne, Countess of Buccleuch (1651-1732).   39 *Amnon's
Murther:* possibly a reference to an attack made on Sir John Coventry
1670. (*II Sam.* xxiii.)   42 *Sion:* London.   44 *Proves:* tests.

The *Jews*, a Headstrong, Moody, Murm'ring race   45
As ever try'd th' extent and stretch of grace;
God's pamper'd People, whom, debauch'd with ease,
No King could govern, nor no God could please;
(Gods they had try'd of every shape and size
That God-smiths could produce, or Priests devise:)   50
These *Adam*-wits, too fortunately free,
Began to dream they wanted liberty;
And when no rule, no president was found
Of men, by Laws less circumscrib'd and bound;
They led their wild desires to Woods and Caves;   55
And thought that all but Savages were Slaves.
They who when *Saul* was dead, without a blow,
Made foolish *Ishbosheth* the Crown forgo;
Who banisht *David* did from *Hebron* bring,
And, with a General Shout, proclaim'd him King: 60
Those very *Jews*, who, at their very best
Their Humour more than Loyalty exprest,
Now wondred why, so long, they had obey'd
An Idol-Monarch which their hands had made:
Thought they might ruine him they could create;   65
Or melt him to that Golden Calf, a State.
But these were randome Bolts: No form'd Design,
Nor Interest made the Factious Croud to joyn:
The sober part of *Israel*, free from stain,
Well knew the value of a peaceful raign;   70
And, looking backward with a wise afright,
Saw Seames of wounds, dishonest to the sight:
In contemplation of whose ugly Scars,
They Curst the memory of Civil Wars.
The moderate sort of Men, thus qualify'd,   75
Inclin'd the Ballance to the better side;
And *David*'s mildness manag'd it so well,
The bad found no occasion to Rebell.
But, when to Sin our byast Nature leans,
The careful Devil is still at hand with means;   80
And providently Pimps for ill desires:
The Good Old Cause reviv'd, a Plot requires.

45 *The Jews:* the English.   53 *President:* precedent.   57-58 *Saul* . . .
Ishbosheth: Oliver Cromwell (1599-1658) and his son Richard (1626-
1712). (*II Sam.* iii-iv.)   59 *Hebron:*   Scotland, where Charles was
crowned 1651, ten years before his coronation in England. (*II Sam.* v.
1-5).   62 *Humour:* caprice.   66 *State:* i.e. republic.   72 *Seames:* sut-
ures; *dishonest:* shameful, indecent.   80 *Still:* always.   81 *Providently:*
opportunistically.   82 *The Good Old Cause:* the Commonwealth.

Plots, true or false, are necessary things,
To raise up Common-wealths, and ruin Kings.

Th' inhabitants of old *Jerusalem*   85
Were *Jebusites*: the Town so call'd from them;
And their's the Native right——
But when the chosen People grew more strong,
The rightful cause at length became the wrong;
And every loss the men of *Jebus* bore,   90
They still were thought God's enemies the more.
Thus, worn and weaken'd, well or ill content,
Submit they must to *David*'s Government:
Impoverisht, and depriv'd of all Command,
Their Taxes doubled as they lost their Land,   95
And, what was harder yet to flesh and blood,
Their Gods disgrac'd, and burnt like common Wood.
This set the Heathen Priesthood in a flame,
For Priests of all Religions are the same:
Of whatsoe'er descent their Godhead be,   100
Stock, Stone, or other homely Pedigree,
In his defence his Servants are as bold
As if he had been born of beaten Gold.
The *Jewish Rabbins* though their Enemies,
In this conclude them honest men and wise: 105
For 'twas their duty, all the Learned think,
T'espouse his Cause by whom they eat and drink.
From hence began that Plot, the Nation's Curse,
Bad in itself, but represented worse,
Rais'd in extremes, and in extremes decry'd,   110
With Oaths affirm'd, with dying Vows deny'd,
Not weigh'd, or winnow'd by the Multitude,
But swallow'd in the Mass, unchew'd and crude.
Some Truth there was, but dash'd and brew'd with Lyes;
To please the Fools, and puzzle all the Wise.   115
Succeeding Times did equal Folly call,
Believing nothing, or believing all.
Th' *Egyptian* Rites the *Jebusites* embrac'd,
Where Gods were recommended by their Tast.
Such sav'ry Deities must needs be good,   120
As serv'd at once for Worship and for Food.

85 *Jerusalem:* London. 86 *Jebusites:* Roman Catholics. (*Joshua* xv.
63.) 108 *That Plot, etc.:* the Popish Plot of 1678, by which it was said
that Charles was to be killed, James enthroned, and Protestantism sup-
pressed. 118 *Egyptian:* French. 120-1 referring to transubstantiation.

By force they could not Introduce these Gods;
For Ten to One, in former days was odds.
So Fraud was us'd, (the Sacrificers Trade,)
Fools are more hard to Conquer than Perswade.   125
Their busie Teachers mingled with the *Jews*,
And rak'd, for Converts, even the Court and Stews:
Which *Hebrew* Priests the more unkindly took,
Because the Fleece accompanies the Flock.
Some thought they God's Anointed meant to slay   130
By Guns, invented since full many a day:
Our Authour swears it not; but who can know
How far the Devil and *Jebusites* may go?
This Plot, which fail'd for want of common Sense,
Had yet a deep and dangerous Consequence: 135
For, as when raging Fevers boyl the Blood,
The standing Lake soon floats into a Flood;
And ev'ry hostile Humour, which before
Slept quiet in its Channels, bubbles o'r:
So, several Factions from this first Ferment,   140
Work up to Foam, and threat the Government.
Some by their Friends, more by themselves thought wise,
Oppos'd the Pow'r, to which they could not rise.
Some had in Courts been Great, and thrown from thence,
Like Fiends, were hardened in Impenitence.   145
Some by their Monarch's fatal mercy grown,
From Pardon'd Rebels, Kinsmen to the Throne,
Were raised in Pow'r and Publick Office high:
Strong Bands, if Bands ungrateful men coud tye.

Of these the false *Achitophel* was first: 150
A Name to all succeeding Ages Curst.
For close Designs, and crooked Counsels fit;
Sagacious, Bold, and Turbulent of wit:
Restless, unfixt in Principles and Place;
In Pow'r unpleased, impatient of Disgrace.   155
A fiery Soul, which working out its way, ⎫
Fretted the Pigmy Body to decay: ⎬
And o'r inform'd the Tenement of Clay. ⎭
A daring Pilot in extremity;
Pleas'd with the Danger, when the Waves went high   160

---

129 *Fleece:* income (from tithes). 138 *Humour:* body fluid. 150
Achitophel: Anthony Ashley Cooper, Earl of Shaftesbury (1621-83).
(*II Sam.* xv-xvii.) 154 *Place:* office. 157 *Fretted:* eroded. 158 *O'r*
informed: was too powerful for, pressed against the bounds of.

He sought the Storms; but for a Calm unfit,
Would Steer too nigh the Sands, to boast his Wit.
Great Wits are sure to Madness near ally'd,
And thin Partitions do their Bounds divide:
Else, why should he, with Wealth and Honour blest,   165
Refuse his Age the needful hours of Rest?
Punish a Body which he coud not please,
Bankrupt of Life, yet Prodigal of Ease?
And all to leave, what with his Toyl he won,
To that unfeather'd, two-legg'd thing, a Son: 170
Got, while his Soul did hudled Notions try;
And born a shapeless Lump, like Anarchy.
In Friendship false, implacable in Hate:
Resolv'd to Ruine or to Rule the State.
To Compass this the Triple Bond he broke; }   175
The Pillars of the Publick Safety shook: }
And fitted *Israel* for a Foreign Yoke. }
Then, seiz'd with Fear, yet still affecting Fame,
Usurp'd a Patriot's All-attoning Name.
So easie still it proves in Factious Times,   180
With publick Zeal to cancel private Crimes:
How safe is Treason, and how sacred ill,
Where none can sin against the Peoples Will:
Where Crouds can wink; and no offence be known,
Since in anothers guilt they find their own.   185
Yet, Fame deserv'd, no Enemy can grudge;
The Statesman we abhor, but praise the Judge.
In *Israels* courts ne'er sat an *Abbethdin*
With more discerning Eyes or Hands more clean:
Unbrib'd, unsought, the Wretched to redress;   190
Swift of Dispatch, and easie of Access.
Oh, had he been content to serve the Crown,
With Vertues only proper to the Gown;
Or, had the rankness of the Soyl been freed
From Cockle, that opprest the Noble Seed;   195
David, for him his tuneful Harp had strung,
And Heav'n had wanted one Immortal Song.
But wild Ambition loves to slide, not stand;
And Fortunes Ice prefers to Vertues Land:

175 *Triple Bond:* the Triple Alliance of 1668 between England, Holland, and Sweden, which had in any case already been secretly broken by Charles in his negotiations with France.   188 *Abbethdin:* judge. Shaftesbury was Lord Chancellor.   196-7 'David would have written a secular poem in praise of Achitophel, in place of one of his divine psalms.'

Achitophel, grown weary to possess   200
A lawful Fame, and lazie Happiness,
Disdain'd the Golden Fruit to gather free,
And lent the Croud his Arm to shake the Tree.
Now, manifest of Crimes, contriv'd long since,
He stood at bold Defiance with his Prince: 205
Held up the Buckler of the Peoples Cause,
Against the Crown; and sculk'd behind the Laws.
The wish'd occasion of the Plot he takes;
Some Circumstances finds, but more he makes.
By buzzing Emissaries, fills the ears   210
Of list'ning Crouds, with Jealosies and Fears
Of Arbitrary Counsels brought to light,
And proves the King himself a *Jebusite.*
Weak Arguments! which yet he knew full well,
Were strong with People easie to Rebell.   215
For, govern'd by the *Moon,* the giddy *Jews*
Tread the same Track when she the Prime renews:
And once in twenty Years, their Scribes record,
By natural Instinct they change their Lord.
Achitophel still wants a Chief, and none   220
Was found so fit as Warlike *Absolon:*
Not, that he wish'd his Greatness to create,
(For Polititians neither love nor hate:)
But, for he knew, his Title not allow'd,
Would keep him still depending on the Croud: 225
That Kingly pow'r, thus ebbing out, might be
Drawn to the Dregs of a Democracie.
Him he attempts, with studied Arts to please,
And sheds his Venome, in such words as these.

Auspicious Prince! at whose Nativity   230
Some Royal Planet rul'd the Southern Sky;
Thy longing Countries Darling and Desire;
Their cloudy Pillar, and their guardian Fire:
Their second *Moses,* whose extended Wand
Divides the Seas, and shows the promis'd Land: 235
Whose dawning Day, in every distant Age,
Has exercis'd the Sacred Prophets rage:
The Peoples Pray'r, the glad Diviners Theam,
The Young mens Vision and the Old mens Dream!
Thee, *Saviour,* Thee, the Nations Vows confess;   240
And, never satisfy'd with seeing, bless:

200 *To possess:* of possessing. 217 *Prime:* beginning of a 19-year
cycle. 233-5 See *Exod.* xiii-xiv. 237 *Rage:* fervour.

Swift, unbespoken Pomps, thy steps proclaim,
And stammering Babes are taught to lisp thy Name.
How long wilt thou the general Joy detain;
Starve, and defraud the People of thy Raign?   245
Content ingloriously to pass thy days
Like one of Vertues Fools that Feeds on Praise;
Till thy fresh Glories, which now shine so bright,
Grow Stale and Tarnish with our dayly sight.
Believe me, Royal Youth, thy Fruit must be,   250
Or gather'd Ripe, or rot upon the Tree.
Heav'n, has to all allotted, soon or late,
Some lucky Revolution of their Fate:
Whose Motions, if we watch and guide with Skill,
(For human Good depends on human Will,)   255
Our Fortune rolls as from a smooth Descent,
And, from the first impression, takes the Bent:
But, if unseiz'd, she glides away like wind;
And leaves repenting Folly far behind.
Now, now she meets you, with a glorious prize,   260
And spreads her Locks before her as she flies.
Had thus Old *David*, from whose Loyns you spring,
Not dar'd, when Fortune call'd him, to be King,
At *Gath* an Exile he might still remain,
And Heavens Anoynting Oyl had been in vain.   265
Let his successful Youth your hopes engage,
But shun th' example of Declining Age.
Behold him setting in his Western Skies,
The Shadows length'ning as the Vapours rise.
He is not now, as when on *Jordan's* Sand ⎫   270
The Joyful People throng'd to see him Land, ⎬
Cov'ring the *Beach*, and black'ning all the *Strand*: ⎭
But, like the Prince of Angels from his height,
Comes tumbling downward with diminish'd light:
Betray'd by one poor Plot to publick Scorn,   275
(Our only blessing since his Curst Return:)
Those heaps of People which one Sheaf did bind,
Blown off and scatter'd by a puff of Wind.
What strength can he to your Designs oppose,
Naked of Friends, and round beset with Foes?   280
If *Pharaoh's* doubtful succour he shoud use,

251 *Or . . . or:* either . . . or.   261 The goddess Fortuna was so re-
presented, in order that those she approached might seize the oppor-
tunity she offered.   264 *Gath:* Brussels. (*I Sam.* xxvii. 1-4.)   270
Jordan's Sand: Dover beach. (*II Sam.* xix. 15.)   281 *Pharaoh:* **Louis
XIV** of France (1638-1715).

A Foreign Aid woud more incense the *Jews*:
Proud *Egypt* woud dissembled Friendship bring;
Foment the War, but not support the King:
Nor woud the Royal Party e'r unite   285
With *Pharaoh*'s arms, t' assist the *Jebusite*;
Or if they shoud, their Interest soon would break,
And with such odious Aid make *David* weak.
All sorts of men by my successful Arts,
Abhorring Kings, estrange their alter'd Hearts   290
From *David*'s Rule: And 'tis the general Cry,
Religion, Common-wealth, and Liberty.
If you as Champion of the Publique Good,
Add to their Arms a Chief of Royal Blood;
What may not *Israel* hope, and what Applause   295
Might such a General gain by such a Cause?
Not barren Praise alone, that Gaudy Flow'r,
Fair only to the sight, but solid Pow'r:
And Nobler is a limited Command,
Giv'n by the Love of all your Native Land,   300
Than a Successive Title, Long, and Dark,
Drawn from the Mouldy Rolls of *Noah*'s ark.

What cannot Praise effect in Mighty Minds,
When Flattery Sooths, and when Ambition Blinds!
Desire of Pow'r, on Earth a Vitious Weed,   305
Yet, sprung from High, is of Cœlestial Seed:
In God 'tis Glory: And when Men Aspire,
'Tis but a Spark too much of Heavenly Fire.
Th' Ambitious Youth, too Covetous of Fame,
Too full of Angels Metal in his Frame,   310
Unwarily was led from Vertues ways,
Made Drunk with Honour, and Debauch'd with Praise.
Half loath, and half consenting to the Ill,
(For Loyal Blood within him strugled still,)
He thus reply'd—And what Pretence have I   315
To take up Arms for Publick Liberty?
My Father Governs with unquestion'd Right;
The Faiths Defender, and Mankinds Delight:
Good, Gracious, Just, observant of the Laws;
And Heav'n by Wonders has espous'd his Cause.   320
Whom has he Wrong'd in all his Peaceful Raign?
Who sues for Justice to his Throne in Vain?

310 *Angels Metal:* pun on the obsolete gold coin *angel,* and on *metal/
mettle.* 320 See Dryden's poem *Annus Mirabilis: The Year of Wonders,
1666.*

What Millions has he pardon'd of his Foes,
Whom Just Revenge did to his Wrath expose?
Mild, Easie, Humble, Studious of our Good;   325
Enclin'd to Mercy, and averse from Blood.
If Mildness Ill with Stubborn *Israel* Suit,
His Crime is God's beloved Attribute.
What could he gain, his People to Betray,
Or change his Right, for Arbitrary Sway?   330
Let Haughty *Pharaoh* Curse with such a Raign
His Fruitful *Nile*, and Yoak a Servile Train.
If *Davids* Rule *Jerusalem* Displease,
The *Dog-Star* heats their Brains to this Disease.
Why then shoud I, Encouraging the Bad,   335
Turn Rebel, and run Popularly Mad?
Were he a Tyrant who, by Lawless Might,
Opprest the *Jews*, and rais'd the *Jebusite*,
Well might I Mourn; but Nature's holy Bands
Would Curb my Spirits, and Restrain my Hands;   340
The People might assert their Liberty;
But what was Right in them, were Crime in me.
His Favour leaves me nothing to require;
Prevents my Wishes, and out-runs Desire.
What more can I expect while *David* lives,   345
All but his Kingly Diadem he gives;
And that: But there he paus'd; then Sighing, said,
Is Justly destin'd for a Worthier head.
For when my Father from his Toyls shall Rest,
And late Augment the Number of the Blest: 350
His Lawful Issue shall the Throne ascend,
Or the *Collat'ral* Line, where that shall end.
His Brother, though Opprest with Vulgar Spight,
Yet Dauntless and Secure of Native Right,
Of every Royal Vertue stands possest;   355
Still Dear to all the Bravest, and the Best.
His Courage Foes, his Friends his Truth Proclaim;
His Loyalty the King, the World his Fame.
His Mercy ev'n th' Offending Croud will find,
For sure he comes of a Forgiving Kind.   360
Why shoud I then Repine at Heavens Decree,
Which gives me no Pretence to Royalty?
Yet oh that Fate Propitiously Inclin'd,
Had rais'd my Birth, or had debas'd my Mind;

334 *Dog-Star:* Sirius, thought to be a cause of hate and disturbance in late summer. 344 *Prevents:* anticipates. 353 *His Brother:* James, Duke of York (1633-1701).

To my large Soul, not all her Treasure lent,   365
And then Betray'd it to a mean Descent.
I find, I find my mounting Spirits Bold,
And *Davids* part disdains my Mothers Mold.
Why am I Scanted by a Niggard Birth?
My Soul Disclaims the Kindred of her Earth: 370
And made for Empire, Whispers me within;
Desire of Greatness is a God-like Sin.

   Him Staggering so when Hells dire Agent found,
While fainting Vertue scarce maintain'd her Ground,
He pours fresh Forces in, and thus Replies: 375

   Th' eternal God Supreamly Good and Wise,
Imparts not these Prodigious Gifts in vain;
What Wonders are Reserv'd to bless your Raign?
Against your will your Arguments have shown,
Such Vertue's only giv'n to guide a Throne.   380
Not that your Father's Mildness I contemn;
But manly Force becomes the Diadem.
'Tis true, he grants the People all they crave;
And more perhaps than Subjects ought to have:
For Lavish Grants suppose a Monarch tame   385
And more his Goodness than his Wit proclaim.
But when shoud People strive their Bonds to break,
If not when Kings are Negligent or Weak?
Let him give on till he can give no more,
The thrifty Sanhedrin shall keep him poor: 390
And every Sheckle which he can receive,
Shall cost a Limb of his Prerogative.
To ply him with new Plots shall be my care,
Or plunge him deep in some Expensive War;
Which when his Treasure can no more supply,   395
He must, with the Remains of Kingship, buy.
His faithful Friends, our Jealosies and Fears
Call *Jebusites*; and *Pharaohs* Pensioners:
Whom, when our Fury from his Aid has torn,
He shall be naked left to publick Scorn.   400
The next Successor, whom I fear and hate,
My Arts have made Obnoxious to the State;
Turn'd all his Vertues to his Overthrow,
And gain'd our Elders to pronounce a Foe.
His Right, for Sums of necessary Gold,   405
Shall first be Pawn'd, and afterwards be Sold:
390 *Sanhedrin:* Parliament.

Till time shall Ever-wanting *David* draw,
To pass your doubtful Title into Law:
If not; the People have a Right Supreme
To make their Kings; for Kings are made for them.　410
All Empire is no more than Pow'r in Trust,
Which when resum'd, can be no longer Just.
Succession, for the general Good design'd,
In its own wrong a Nation cannot bind:
If altering that, the People can relieve,　415
Better one suffer, than a Nation grieve.
The *Jews* well know their pow'r: e'r *Saul* they chose,
God was their King, and God they durst Depose.
Urge now your Piety, your Filial Name,
A Father's Right, and Fear of future Fame;　420
The Publick Good, that Universal Call,
To which even Heav'n submitted, answers all.
Nor let his Love enchant your generous Mind;
'Tis Natures trick to propagate her Kind.
Our fond Begetters, who woud never die,　425
Love but themselves in their Posterity.
Or let his Kindness by th' Effects be try'd,
Or let him lay his vain Pretence aside.
God said he lov'd your Father; coud he bring
A better Proof, than to anoynt him King?　430
It surely shew'd he lov'd the Shepherd well,
Who gave so fair a Flock as *Israel*.
Woud *David* have you thought his Darling Son?
What means he then, to Alienate the Crown?
The name of Godly he may blush to bear:　435
'Tis after Gods own heart to Cheat his Heir.
He to his Brother gives Supreme Command;
To you a Legacie of Barren Land:
Perhaps th' old Harp, on which he thrums his Layes:
Or some dull *Hebrew* Ballad in your Praise.　440
Then the next Heir, a Prince, Severe and Wise,
Already looks on you with Jealous Eyes,
Sees through the thin Disguises of your Arts,
And markes your Progress in the Peoples Hearts.
Though now his mighty Soul its Grief contains;　445
He meditates Revenge who least Complains.
And like a Lyon, Slumb'ring in the way,
Or Sleep dissembling, while he waits his Prey,
His fearless Foes within his Distance draws,
Constrains his Roaring, and Contracts his Paws:　450

412 *Resum'd:* reassumed as a possession.

Till at the last, his time for Fury found,
He shoots with sudden Vengeance from the Ground:
The Prostrate Vulgar, passes o'r and Spares;
But with a Lordly Rage, his Hunters teares.
Your Case no tame Expedients will afford;   455
Resolve on Death, or Conquest by the Sword,
Which for no less a Stake than Life, you Draw,
And Sel.-defence is Natures Eldest Law.
Leave the warm People no Considering time;
For then Rebellion may be thought a Crime.   460
Prevail your self of what Occasion gives,
But try your Title while your Father lives;
And that your Arms may have a fair Pretence,
Proclaim, you take them in the King's Defence:
Whose Sacred Life each minute woud Expose,   465
To Plots, from seeming Friends, and secret Foes.
And who can sound the depth of *David*'s Soul?
Perhaps his fear, his kindness may Controul.
He fears his Brother, though he loves his Son,
For plighted Vows too late to be undone.   470
If so, by Force he wishes to be gain'd,
Like Womens Leachery, to seem Constrain'd:
Doubt not, but when he most affects the Frown,
Commit a pleasing Rape upon the Crown.
Secure his Person to secure your Cause;   475
They who possess the Prince, possess the Laws.

     He said, And this Advice above the rest,
With *Absalom*'s Mild Nature suited best;
Unblam'd of Life (Ambition set aside,)
Not stain'd with Cruelty, nor puft with Pride,   480
How happy had he been, if Destiny
Had higher plac'd his Birth, or not so high!
His Kingly Vertues might have claim'd a Throne,
And blest all other Countries but his own:
But charming Greatness, since so few refuse;   485
'Tis Juster to Lament him, than Accuse.
Strong were his hopes a Rival to remove,
With Blandishments to gain the publick Love;
To Head the Faction while their Zeal was hot,
And Popularly Prosecute the Plot.   490
To farther this, *Achitophel* Unites
The Malecontents of all the *Israelites*:
Whose differing Parties he could wisely Joyn,

459 *Warm:* heated, stirred.   461 *Prevail:* avail.

For several Ends, to serve the same Design.
The Best, and of the Princes some were such,   495
Who thought the pow'r of Monarchy too much:
Mistaken Men, and Patriots in their Hearts;
Not Wicked, but seduc'd by Impious Arts.
By these the Springs of Property were bent,
And wound so high, they Crack'd the Government.   500
The next for Interest sought t' embroil the State,
To sell their Duty at a dearer rate;
And make their *Jewish* Markets of the Throne,
Pretending Publick Good, to serve their own.
Others thought Kings an useless heavy Load,   505
Who Cost too much, and did too little Good.
These were for laying Honest *David* by
On Principles of pure good Husbandry.
With them joyn'd all th' Haranguers of the Throng,
That thought to get Preferment by the Tongue.   510
Who follow next, a double Danger bring,
Not only hating *David*, but the King,
The *Solymæan* Rout; well Vers'd of old,
In Godly Faction, and in Treason bold;
Cowring and Quaking at a Conqu'ror's Sword,   515
But Lofty to a Lawful Prince Restor'd;
Saw with Disdain an *Ethnick* Plot begun,
And Scorned by *Jebusites* to be Out-done.
Hot *Levites* Headed these; who pul'd before
From th' *Ark*, which in the Judges days they bore,   520
Resum'd their Cant, and with a Zealous Cry,
Pursu'd their old belov'd Theocracy.
Where Sanhedrin and Priest enslav'd the Nation
And justify'd their Spoils by Inspiration:
For who so fit for Reign as *Aaron*'s Race,   525
If once Dominion they could found in Grace?
These led the Pack; though not of surest scent,
Yet deepest mouth'd against the Government.
A numerous Host of dreaming Saints succeed;
Of the true old Enthusiastick Breed: 530
'Gainst Form and Order they their Pow'r employ;
Nothing to Build, and all things to Destroy.

499-500 'They tried to correct too meticulously the disposal and balance
of power, and so strained the mechanism of government.' 513 *Solymæan
Rout:* London mob. Solyma is Jerusalem. 517 *Ethnick:* Gentile, i.e.
Catholic. 519 *Levites:* Dissenting clergymen ousted from their benefices
by the Act of Uniformity 1662. (*II Chron.* xi. 14-15.) 525 *Aaron's Race:*
the clergy.

But far more numerous was the Herd of such,
Who think too little, and who talk too much.
These, out of meer instinct, they knew not why,   535
Ador'd their Fathers God, and Property:
And, by the same blind Benefit of Fate,
The Devil and the *Jebusite* did hate:
Born tc be sav'd, even in their own despight;
Because they could not help believing right.   540
Such were the Tools; but a whole Hydra more
Remains, of sprouting heads too long to score.

Some of their Chiefs were Princes of the Land;
In the first Rank of these did *Zimri* stand:
A man so various, that he seem'd to be   545
Not one, but all Mankind's Epitome.
Stiff in Opinions, always in the wrong;
Was Every thing by starts, and Nothing long:
But, in the course of one revolving Moon,
Was Chymist, Fidler, States-man, and Buffoon;   550
Then all for Women, Painting, Rhiming, Drinking,
Besides ten thousand Freaks that dy'd in thinking.
Blest Madman, who coud every hour employ,
With something New to wish, or to enjoy!
Railing and praising were his usual Theams;   555
And both (to shew his Judgment) in Extreams:
So over Violent, or over Civil,
That every Man, with him, was God or Devil.
In squand'ring Wealth was his peculiar Art:
Nothing went unrewarded, but Desert.   560
Begger'd by Fools, whom still he found too late:
He had his Jest, and they had his Estate.
He laugh'd himself from Court; then sought Relief
By forming Parties, but coud ne'r be Chief:
For, spight of him, the weight of Business fell   565
On *Absalom* and wise *Achitophel*:
Thus, wicked but in Will, of Means bereft,
He left not Faction, but of that was left.

Titles and Names 'twere tedious to Reherse
Of Lords, below the Dignity of Verse.   570
Wits, Warriors, Commonwealths-men were the best:
Kind Husbands and meer Nobles all the rest.

541 *Hydra:* many-headed monster in Greek mythology. 544 *Zimri:*
George Villiers, Duke of Buckingham (1628-87). (*I Kings* xvi. 8-20,
II Kings ix. 31.)

And, therefore in the name of Dulness, be
The well-hung *Balaam* and cold *Caleb* free;
And Canting *Nadab* let Oblivion damn,   575
Who made new Porridge for the Paschal Lamb.
Let Friendships holy Band some Names assure,
Some their own Worth, and some let Scorn secure.
Nor shall the Rascal Rabble here have Place,
Whom Kings no Titles gave, and God no Grace: 580
Not Bull-fac'd *Jonas*, who coud Statutes draw
To mean Rebellion, and make Treason Law.
But he, though bad, is follow'd by a worse,
The Wretch, who Heav'ns Anoynted dar'd to Curse.
Shimei, whose Youth did early Promise bring   585
Of Zeal to God, and Hatred to his King;
Did wisely from Expensive Sins refrain,
And never broke the Sabbath, but for Gain:
Nor ever was he known an Oath to vent,
Or Curse, unless against the Government.   590
Thus, heaping Wealth, by the most ready way
Among the *Jews*, which was to Cheat and Pray;
The City, to reward his pious Hate
Against his Master, chose him Magistrate:
His Hand a Vare of Justice did uphold;   595
His Neck was loaded with a Chain of Gold.
During his Office, Treason was no Crime.
The Sons of *Belial* had a Glorious Time:
For *Shimei*, though not prodigal of pelf,
Yet lov'd his wicked Neighbour as himself: 600
When two or three were gather'd to declaim ⎫
Against the Monarch of *Jerusalem*,   ⎬
Shimei was always in the midst of them.   ⎭
And, if they Curst the King when he was by,
Woud rather Curse, than break good Company.   605
If any durst his Factious Friends accuse,
He pact a Jury of dissenting *Jews*:

574 *Well-hung:* (i) glib, (ii) lascivious; *Balaam:* perhaps Theophilus
Hastings, Earl of Huntingdon (1650-1701) (*Num.* xxiii. 11, *II Peter* ii.
15-16); *Caleb:* probably Arthur Capel, Earl of Essex (1632-83). 575
Nadab: William, Lord Howard of Escrick (1626-94), a Dissenter who
was imprisoned for libelling the king. (*Exod.* vi. 23, *Lev.* x. 1.) 576
Howard reputedly took the sacrament in prison, using 'lamb's wool'
(hot ale mixed with spice and apple-pulp) for wine. 581 *Jonas:* Sir
William Jones (1631-82), the Attorney-General who conducted the
Popish Plot prosecutions. 585 *Shimei:* Slingsby Bethel (1617-97), a
London sheriff. (*II Sam.* xvi. 5-13.) 595 *Vare:* staff of office. 598
Sons of Belial: rebels and rioters. (*Deut.* xiii. 13, *II Sam.* xx. 1-2.)

Whose fellow-feeling, in the godly Cause,
Would free the suff'ring Saint from Human Laws.
For Laws are only made to Punish those　　　　　　610
Who serve the King, and to protect his Foes.
If any leisure time he had from Pow'r,
(Because 'tis Sin to misimploy an hour;)
His bus'ness was, by Writing, to Persuade
That kings were Useless, and a Clog to Trade:　　615
And, that his noble Stile he might refine,
No *Rechabite* more shund the fumes of Wine.
Chaste were his Cellars, and his Shrieval Board
The Grossness of a City Feast abhor'd:
His Cooks, with long disuse, their Trade forgot;　620
Cool was his Kitchen, though his Brains were hot.
Such Frugal Vertue Malice may accuse;
But sure 'twas necessary to the *Jews*:
For Towns once burnt, such Magistrates require
As dare not tempt Gods Providence by Fire.　　625
With Spiritual Food he fed his Servants well,
But free from Flesh, that made the *Jews* rebell:
And *Moses*'s Laws he held in more account,
For forty days of Fasting in the Mount.

To speak the rest, who better are forgot,　　　　630
Would tyre a well-breath'd Witness of the Plot:
Yet, *Corah*, thou shalt from Oblivion pass;
Erect thy self thou Monumental Brass:
High as the Serpent of thy Metal made,
While Nations stand secure beneath thy shade.　　635
What though his Birth were base, yet Comets rise
From Earthy Vapours, ere they shine in Skies.
Prodigious Actions may as well be done
By Weavers issue, as by Princes son.
This Arch-Attestor for the Publick Good,　　　　640
By that one Deed enobles all his Bloud.
Who ever ask'd the Witnesses high race,
Whose Oath with Martyrdom did *Stephen* grace?
Ours was a *Levite*, and as times went then,
His tribe were God-almighties Gentlemen.　　　　645
Sunk were his Eyes, his Voice was harsh and loud,
Sure signs he neither Cholerick was, nor Proud:

617 *Rechabite:* abstainer. (*Jer.* xxxv.) 618 *Shrieval:* sheriff's. 632
Corah: Titus Oates (1649-1705) provided evidence of the Popish Plot
before the Privy Council 1678. (*Num.* xvi.) 633-4 Cf. *Num.* xxi. 6-9.
642-3 See *Acts* vi. 9-15.

His long Chin prov'd his Wit; his Saint-like Grace
A Church Vermilion, and a *Moses*'s Face.
His Memory, miraculously great,   650
Coud Plots, exceeding mans belief, repeat;
Which, therefore cannot be accounted Lies,
For Human Wit coud never such devise.
Some future Truths are mingled in his Book;
But, where the Witness fail'd, the Prophet spoke: 655
Some things like Visionary flights appear;
The Spirit caught him up, the Lord knows where:
And gave him his *Rabinical* degree
Unknown to Foreign University.
His Judgment yet his Mem'ry did excel,   660
Which piec'd his wondrous Evidence so well:
And suited to the temper of the Times;
Then groaning under *Jebusitick* Crimes.
Let *Israels* foes suspect his Heav'nly call,
And rashly judge his Writ Apocryphal;   665
Our Laws for such affronts have Forfeits made:
He takes his Life, who takes away his Trade.
Were I myself in Witness *Corahs* place,
The Wretch who did me such a dire disgrace
Should whet my memory, though once forgot,   670
To make him an Appendix of my Plot.
His Zeal to Heav'n, made him his Prince despise,
And load his Person with indignities:
But Zeal peculiar privilege affords,
Indulging latitude to deeds and words: 675
And *Corah* might for *Agags* murther call,
In terms as coarse as *Samuel* us'd to *Saul*.
What others in his Evidence did joyn,
(The best that coud be had for love or coyn,)
In *Corahs* own predicament will fall: 680
For *Witness* is a Common Name to all.

   Surrounded thus with Friends of every sort,
Deluded *Absalom* forsakes the Court:
Impatient of high hopes, urg'd with renown,
And Fir'd with near possession of a Crown.   685

649 *Moses*'s *Face:* alludes to the illuminated face of Moses coming down
from Mt. Sinai. (*Exod.* xxxiv. 29). 658 At Salamanca, he claimed.
676 *Agag:* may be Sir Edmund Godfrey (1621-78), a London magis-
trate, or more probably William Howard, Viscount Stafford (1614-80).
(*I Sam.* xv. 32-33.)

Th' admiring Croud are dazled with surprize,
And on his goodly person feed their eyes:
His joy conceal'd, he sets himself to show;
On each side bowing popularly low:
His looks, his gestures, and his words he frames,   690
And with familiar ease repeats their Names.
Thus, form'd by Nature, furnished out with Arts,
He glides unfelt into their secret hearts:
Then with a kind compassionating look,
And sighs, bespeaking pity ere he spoke,   695
Few words he said, but easie those and fit,
More slow than Hybla drops, and far more sweet.

    I mourn, my Country-men, your lost Estate,
Though far unable to prevent your Fate:
Behold a Banish'd man, for your dear cause   700
Expos'd a prey to Arbitrary Laws!
Yet oh! that I alone coud be undone,
Cut off from Empire, and no more a Son!
Now all your Liberties a spoil are made;   ⎫
Egypt and Tyrus intercept your Trade,   ⎬   705
And Jebusites your Sacred Rites invade.   ⎭
My Father, whom with reverence yet I name,
Charm'd into Ease, is careless of his Fame:
And, brib'd with petty sums of Foreign Gold,
Is grown in Bathsheba's Embraces old: 710
Exalts his Enemies, his Friends destroys,
And all his pow'r against himself employs.
He gives, and let him give my right away:
But why should he his own and yours betray?
He only, he can make the Nation bleed,   715
And he alone from my revenge is freed.
Take then my tears (with that he wip'd his Eyes)
'Tis all the Aid my present pow'r supplies:
No Court-Informer can these Arms accuse;
These Arms may Sons against their Fathers use;   720
And, 'tis my wish, the next Successor's raign
May make no other Israelite complain.

    Youth, Beauty, Graceful Action seldom fail:
But Common Interest always will prevail:

697 *Hybla:* town in Sicily, famed for honey.   700 Monmouth was in
exile at Brussels, 1679.   705 *Tyrus:* Holland.   710 *Bathsheba:* Louise-
Renée de Kéroualle (1649-1734), created Duchess of Portsmouth, 1673.
(*II Sam.* xi.)

And pity never Ceases to be shown 725
To him, who makes the Peoples wrongs his own.
The Croud, (that still believe their Kings oppress,)
With lifted hands their young *Messiah* bless:
Who now begins his Progress to ordain,
With Chariots, Horsemen, and a num'rous train; 730
From East to West his Glories he displays:
And, like the Sun, the Promis'd Land survays.
Fame runs before him as the Morning-Star,
And shouts of Joy salute him from afar:
Each house receives him as a Guardian God; 735
And Consecrates the Place of his abode:
But hospitable Treats did most commend
Wise *Issachar*, his wealthy Western Friend.
This moving Court, that caught the Peoples Eyes,
And seem'd but Pomp, did other Ends disguise: 740
Achitophel had form'd it, with intent
To sound the depths, and fathom where it went,
The Peoples hearts, distinguish Friends from Foes;
And try their strength, before they came to Blows.
Yet all was colour'd with a smooth pretence 745
Of specious love, and duty to their Prince.
Religion, and Redress of Grievances,
Two names, that always cheat and always please,
Are often urg'd; and good King *Davids* life
Endanger'd by a Brother and a Wife. 750
Thus, in a Pageant Show, a Plot is made;
And Peace it self is War in Masquerade.
Oh foolish *Israel*! never warn'd by Ill:
Still the same Bait, and circumvented still!
Did ever men forsake their present ease, 755
In midst of health imagine a Disease;
Take pains Contingent mischiefs to foresee,
Make Heirs for Monarchs, and for God decree?
What shall we think! can People give away
Both for themselves and Sons, their Native sway? 760
Then they are left Defenceless, to the Sword
Of each unbounded Arbitrary Lord:
And Laws are vain, by which we Right enjoy,
If Kings unquestion'd can those Laws destroy.
Yet if the Croud be Judge of Fit and Just, 765
And Kings are only Officers in Trust,

738 *Issachar:* Thomas Thynne (1648-82), wealthy friend of Monmouth.
(*Gen.* xlix. 14-15.)

Then this resuming Cov'nant was declar'd
When Kings were made, or is for ever barr'd:
If those who gave the Scepter, coud not tye
By their own Deed their own Posterity,   770
How then coud *Adam* bind his future Race?
How coud his Forfeit on Mankind take place?
Or how coud heavenly Justice damn us all,
Who ne'r consented to our Fathers Fall?
Then Kings are Slaves to those whom they command,   775
And Tenants to their Peoples pleasure stand.
Add, that the Pow'r for Property allow'd,
Is mischievously seated in the Croud:
For who can be secure of private Right,
If Sovereign Sway may be dissolv'd by Might?   780
Nor is the Peoples Judgment always true:
The Most may err as grosly as the Few;
And faultless Kings run down, by Common Cry,
For Vice, Oppression, and for Tyranny.
What Standard is there in a fickle rout,   785
Which, flowing to the Mark, runs faster out?
Nor only Crouds, but Sanhedrins may be
Infected with this publick Lunacy:
And Share the madness of Rebellious Times,
To Murther Monarchs for Imagin'd crimes.   790
If they may Give and Take when e'r they please,
Not Kings alone, (the Godheads Images,)
But Government it self at length must fall
To Natures state, where all have Right to all.
Yet, grant our Lords the People Kings can make,   795
What prudent men a setled Throne woud shake?
For whatsoe'r their Sufferings were before,
That Change they Covet makes them suffer more.
All other Errors but disturb a State;
But Innovation is the Blow of Fate.   800
If ancient Fabricks nod, and threat to fall,
To Patch the Flaws, and Buttress up the Wall,
Thus far 'tis Duty; but here fix the Mark:
For all beyond it is to touch our Ark.
To change Foundations, cast the Frame anew,   805

767 *Resuming:* renewed through regular succession (i.e. the covenant
between king and people must not be broken arbitrarily by altering the
succession: that the king should choose his successor is fundamental).
777 'the political power allowed to property-owners.' 786 *Mark:*
high-water-mark. 800 *Innovation:* revolution. 804 *Touch our Ark:*
disturb what we hold most sacred. (*I Chron.* xiii. 9-10.)

Is work for Rebels who base Ends pursue:
At once Divine and Human Laws controul,
And mend the Parts by ruine of the Whole.
The Tamp'ring World is subject to this Curse,
To Physick their Disease into a Worse.   810

   Now what Relief can Righteous *David* bring?
How Fatal 'tis to be too good a King!
Friends he has few, so high the madness grows;
Who dare be such, must be the Peoples Foes:
Yet some there were, ev'n in the worst of days;   815
Some let me name, and Naming is to praise.

   In this short File *Barzillai* first appears;
Barzillai crown'd with Honour and with Years:
Long since, the rising Rebels he withstood
In Regions Waste, beyond the *Jordans* Flood: 820
Unfortunately Brave to buoy the State;
But sinking underneath his Master's Fate:
In Exile with his God-like Prince he Mourn'd,
For him he Suffer'd, and with him Return'd.
The Court he practis'd, not the Courtiers Art: 825
Large was his Wealth, but larger was his Heart:
Which, well the Noblest Objects knew to chuse,
The Fighting Warriour, and Recording Muse.
His Bed coud once a Fruitful Issue boast:
Now more than half a Father's Name is lost.   830
His Eldest Hope, with every Grace adorn'd,
By me (so Heav'n will have it) always Mourn'd
And always honour'd, snatch'd in manhoods prime
By' unequal Fates, and Providences crime:
Yet not before the Goal of Honour won,   835
All Parts fulfill'd of Subject and of Son; }
Swift was the Race, but short the Time to run. }
Oh Narrow Circle, but of Pow'r Divine,
Scanted in Space, but perfect in thy Line!
By Sea, by Land, thy Matchless Worth was known;   840
Arms thy Delight, and War was all thy Own:
Thy force, Infus'd, the fainting *Tyrians* prop'd;
And haughty *Pharaoh* found his Fortune stop'd.
Oh Ancient Honour, Oh unconquer'd Hand,
Whom Foes unpunish'd never coud withstand!   845

817 *Barzillai:* James Butler, Duke of Ormonde (1610-88). (*II Sam.* xix.
31-39.) 819-20 Ormonde was Lord Lieutenant of Ireland. *Jordans
Flood:* the Irish Channel. 831 Thomas, Earl of Ossory (1634-80).

But *Israel* was unworthy of thy Name:
Short is the date of all Immoderate Fame.
It looks as Heav'n our Ruine had design'd,
And durst not trust thy Fortune and thy Mind.
Now, free from Earth, thy disencumbred Soul   850
Mounts up, and leaves behind the Clouds and Starry Pole:
From thence thy kindred Legions mayst thou bring,
To aid the Guardian Angel of thy King.
Here stop my Muse, here cease thy painful flight;
No pinions can pursue Immortal height: 855
Tell good *Barzillai* thou canst sing no more,
And tell thy Soul she shoud have fled before;
Or fled she with his life, and left this Verse
To hang on her departed Patron's Herse?
Now take thy steepy flight from Heav'n, and see   860
If thou canst find on Earth another *He*;
Another he would be too hard to find:
See then whom thou canst see not far behind.
Zadock the Priest, whom, shunning Pow'r and Place,
His lowly mind advanc'd to *David*'s Grace: 865
With him the *Sagan of Jerusalem,*
Of hospitable Soul and noble Stem;
Him of the Western dome, whose weighty sense
Flows in fit words and heavenly eloquence.
The Prophets Sons by such Example led,   870
To Learning and to Loyalty were bred:
For *Colleges* on bounteous Kings depend,
And never Rebel was to Arts a Friend.
To these succeed the Pillars of the Laws,
Who best coud plead, and best can judge a Cause.   875
Next them a train of Loyal Peers ascend:
Sharp judging *Adriel* the Muses Friend,
Himself a Muse—In Sanhedrins debate
True to his Prince, but not a Slave of State.
Whom *David*'s love with Honours did adorn,   880
That from his disobedient Son were torn.
Jotham of piercing Wit and pregnant Thought,
Endew'd by nature, and by learning taught

859 *Herse:* framework over a bier, hung with decorations and epitaphs.
864 *Zadock:* William Sancroft (1617-93), Archbishop of Canterbury.
(*II Sam.* viii. 17.) 866 *Sagan of Jerusalem:* Henry Compton (1632-1713),
Bishop of London. A *sagan* is a Jewish high priest's deputy. 868 John
Dolben (1625-86), Dean of Westminster. 870 the boys of West-
minster School. 877 *Adriel:* John Sheffield, Earl of Mulgrave (1648-
1721). 882 *Jotham:* George Savile, Marquis of Halifax (1633-95).
(*Judges* ix. 1-21.)

To move Assemblies, who but only try'd
The worse a while, then chose the better side;   885
Nor chose alone, but turn'd the Balance too;
So much the weight of one brave man can do.
Hushai the friend of *David* in distress,
In publick storms of manly stedfastness;
By Foreign Treaties he inform'd his Youth;   890
And joyn'd Experience to his Native Truth.
His frugal care supply'd the wanting Throne,
Frugal for that, but bounteous of his own:
'Tis easie Conduct when Exchequers flow,
But hard the task to manage well the low: 895
For Sovereign Power is too deprest or high,
When Kings are forc'd to sell, or Crouds to buy.
Indulge one labour more, my weary Muse,
For *Amiel*, who can *Amiel*'s praise refuse?
Of ancient race by birth, but nobler yet   900
In his own worth, and without Title great:
The Sanhedrin long time as Chief he rul'd,
Their Reason guided, and their Passion cool'd:
So dextrous was he in the Crown's defence,
So form'd to speak a Loyal Nations Sense,   905
That as their Band was *Israels* Tribes in small,
So fit was he to represent them all.
Now rasher Charioteers the Seat ascend,
Whose loose Carriers his steady Skill commend:
They, like th' unequal Ruler of the Day,   910
Misguide the Seasons, and mistake the Way;
While he withdrawn at their mad Labour smiles,
And safe enjoys the Sabbath of his Toyls.

These were the chief; a small but faithful Band ⎫
Of Worthies, in the Breach who dar'd to stand, ⎬   915
And tempt th' united Fury of the Land. ⎭
With grief they view'd such powerful Engines bent
To batter down the lawful Government:
A numerous Faction with pretended frights,
In Sanhedrins to plume the Regal Rights;   920
The true Successor from the Court remov'd;

888 *Hushai:* Laurence Hyde, Earl of Rochester (1642-1711). (*II Sam.*
xvi. 16-19.) 899 *Amiel:* Edward Seymour (1633-1708), Speaker of the
House of Commons. (*I Chron.* xxvi. 4-8.) 909 *Carriers:* careering.
910 *Th'unequal Ruler of the Day:* Phaethon, son of Phœbus in Greek
mythology, tried unsuccessfully to control the chariot of the sun. 920
Plume: pluck, strip.
A.L.P.   I

The plot, by hireling Witnesses improv'd:
These Ills they saw, and, as their Duty bound,
They shew'd the King the danger of the Wound:
That no Concessions from the Throne woud please;   925
But Lenitives fomented the Disease;
That *Absalom*, ambitious of the Crown,
Was made the Lure to draw the People down;
That false *Achitophel's* pernitious Hate
Had turn'd the Plot to ruine Church and State: 930
The Council violent, the Rabble worse
That *Shimei* taught *Jerusalem* to Curse.

    With all these loads of Injuries opprest,
And long revolving, in his careful Brest
Th' event of things; at last his patience tir'd,   935
Thus from his Royal Throne, by Heav'n inspir'd,
The God-like *David* spoke; with awful fear
His Train their Maker in their Master hear.

    Thus long have I, by Native Mercy sway'd,
My Wrongs dissembl'd, my Revenge delay'd: 940
So willing to forgive th' Offending Age;
So much the Father did the King asswage.
But now so far my Clemency they slight,
Th' Offenders question my Forgiving Right.
That one was made for many, they contend;   945
But 'tis to Rule, for that's a Monarch's End.
They call my tenderness of Blood, my Fear,
Though Manly tempers can the longest bear.
Yet, since they will divert my Native course,
'Tis time to shew I am not Good by Force.   950
Those heap'd Affronts that haughty Subjects bring,
Are burthens for a Camel, not a King:
Kings are the publick Pillars of the State,
Born to sustain and prop the Nations weight:
If my young *Sampson* will pretend a Call   955
To shake the Column, let him share the Fall:
But oh that yet he woud repent and live!
How easie 'tis for Parents to forgive!
With how few Tears a Pardon might be won
From Nature, pleading for a Darling son!   960
Poor pitied Youth, by my Paternal care,

926 *Lenitives:* soothing medicines.   935 *Event:* outcome.   947 *Tenderness of:* reluctance to shed.   955-6 See *Judges* xv. 25-31.

Rais'd up to all the Height his Frame coud bear:
Had God ordain'd his Fate for Empire born,
He woud have giv'n his Soul another turn:
Gull'd with a Patriot's name, whose Modern sense   965
Is one that woud by Law supplant his Prince:
The Peoples Brave, the Politicians Tool;
Never was Patriot yet, but was a Fool.
Whence comes it that Religion and the Laws
Should more be *Absaloms* than *Davids* Cause?   970
His old Instructor, ere he lost his Place,
Was never thought indu'd with so much Grace.
Good Heav'ns, how Faction can a Patriot Paint!
My Rebel ever proves my Peoples Saint:
Woud *They* impose an Heir upon the Throne?   975
Let Sanhedrins be taught to give their Own.
A King's at least a part of Government;
And mine as requisite as their Consent:
Without my leave a future King to choose,
Infers a Right the present to Depose: 980
True, they petition me t' approve their Choice:
But *Esaus* Hands suit ill with *Jacobs* Voice.
My Pious Subjects for my Safety pray,
Which to Secure, they take my Pow'r away.
From Plots and Treasons Heav'n preserve my Years,   985
But save me most from my Petitioners.
Unsatiate as the barren Womb or Grave;
God cannot Grant so much as they can Crave.
What then is left but with a Jealous Eye
To guard the Small remains of Royalty?   990
The Law shall still direct my peaceful Sway,
And the same Law teach Rebels to obey:
Votes shall no more Establish'd Pow'r controul,
Such Votes as make a Part exceed the Whole:
No groundless Clamours shall my Friends remove,   995
Nor Crouds have pow'r to Punish ere they Prove;
For Gods, and God-like Kings their Care express,
Still to defend their Servants in distress.   ·
Oh that my Pow'r to Saving were confin'd: ⎫
Why am I forc'd, like Heav'n, against my mind,   ⎬   1000
To make Examples of another Kind?   ⎭
Must I at length the Sword of Justice draw?
Oh curst Effects of necessary Law!
How ill my Fear they by my Mercy scan,

967 *Brave:* champion.   982 See *Gen.* xxvii. 21-23.

Beware the Fury of a Patient Man.   1005
Law they require, let Law then show her Face;
They could not be content to look on Grace,
Her hinder parts, but with a daring Eye
To tempt the terror of her Front, and Dye.
By their own Arts 'tis Righteously decreed,   1010
Those dire Artificers of Death shall bleed.
Against themselves their Witnesses will Swear,
Till, Viper-like, their Mother Plot they tear,
And suck for Nutriment that bloudy gore
Which was their Principle of Life before.   1015
Their *Belial* with their *Belzebub* will fight;
Thus on my Foes, my Foes shall do me Right.
Nor doubt th' event; for Factious crouds engage
In their first Onset, all their Brutal Rage;
Then, let 'em take an unresisted Course;   1020
Retire and Traverse, and Delude their Force:
But when they stand all Breathless, urge the fight,
And rise upon 'em with redoubled might:
For Lawful Pow'r is still Superiour found,
When long driv'n back, at length it stands the ground.   1025

He said. Th' Almighty, nodding, gave consent;
And peals of Thunder shook the Firmament.
Henceforth a Series of new time began,
The mighty Years in long Procession ran:
Once more the God-like *David* was Restor'd,   1030
And willing Nations knew their Lawful Lord.

MAC FLECKNOE
OR A SATIRE UPON THE
TRUE-BLUE-PROTESTANT POET, T. S.

Published 1682, but written apparently in 1678, and circulated
in manuscript. Dryden had both literary and political bones to
pick with Thomas Shadwell, though no specific occasion for the
sharp attack of this poem is known. Richard Flecknoe was
chosen probably as a mere type of the haplessly unwitty poetaster,
though he was also an unsuccessful francophil playwright with a
chip on his shoulder about the debasement of the English stage,
and Dryden as an established (and at this period pro-English)

1006-8 Cf. *Exod.* xxxiii. 20-23.   1016 *Belial . . . Belzebub:* names of
important 'false gods' in Palestine.

dramatist did not find it hard to be irritated by him. He had
already been satirised by Andrew Marvell in his poem *Fleckno,
an English Priest at Rome.*

All human things are subject to decay,
And, when Fate summons, Monarchs must obey:
This *Flecknoe* found, who, like *Augustus,* young
Was call'd to Empire, and had govern'd long:
In Prose and Verse was own'd, without dispute   5
Through all the Realms of *Non-sense,* absolute.
This aged Prince now flourishing in Peace,
And blest with issue of a large increase,
Worn out with business, did at length debate
To settle the Succession of the State: 10
And pond'ring which of all his Sons was fit
To Reign, and wage immortal War with Wit,
Cry'd, 'tis resolv'd; for Nature pleads that He
Should onely rule, who most resembles me:
Sh[adwell] alone my perfect image bears,   15
Mature in dullness from his tender years;
Sh[adwell] alone, of all my Sons, is he
Who stands confirm'd in full stupidity.
The rest to some faint meaning make pretence,
But *Sh[adwell]* never deviates into sense.   20
Some Beams of Wit on other souls may fall,
Strike through and make a lucid intervall;
But *Sh[adwell]*'s genuine night admits no ray,
His rising Fogs prevail upon the Day:
Besides, his goodly Fabrick fills the eye,   25
And seems design'd for thoughtless Majesty:
Thoughtless as Monarch Oakes, that shade the plain,
And, spread in solemn state, supinely reign.
Heywood and *Shirley* were but Types of thee,
Thou last great Prophet of Tautology: 30
Even I, a dunce of more renown than they,
Was sent before but to prepare thy way:

3 *Flecknoe:* Richard Flecknoe (d.1678?), dramatist, poet, and travel-
writer. His rough picaresque poem *The Diarium,* and his letters on foreign
travel, are worth reading. He wrote, ironically enough, a poetic eulogy
of Dryden in 1670. *Augustus:* the first Roman Emperor (63 B.C.-A.D. 14).
15 *Sh[adwell]:* Thomas Shadwell (1642?-92), dramatist and poet.
Despite Dryden's abuse, his plays are far from dull. Since Flecknoe was
Irish, Shadwell as his 'son' was called MacFlecknoe. 29 *Heywood and
Shirley:* Thomas Heywood (*c.* 1574-1641) and James Shirley (1596-
1666), dramatists.

And coarsely clad in *Norwich* Drugget came
To teach the Nations in thy greater name.
My warbling Lute, the Lute I whilom strung   35
When to King *John* of *Portugal* I sung,
Was but the prelude to that glorious day,
When thou on silver *Thames* did'st cut thy way,
With well tim'd Oars before the Royal Barge,
Swell'd with the Pride of thy Celestial charge;   40
And big with Hymn, Commander of an Host,
The like was ne'er in *Epsom* Blankets tost.
Methinks I see the new *Arion* Sail,
The Lute still trembling underneath thy nail.
At they well sharpned thumb from Shore to Shore   45
The Treble squeaks for fear, the Bases roar:
Echoes from *Pissing-Ally*, *Sh[adwell]* call,
And *Sh[adwell]* they resound from *A[ston]* *Hall*.
About thy boat the little Fishes throng,
As at the Morning Toast, that Floats along.   50
Sometimes as Prince of thy Harmonious band
Thou wield'st thy Papers in thy threshing hand.
St. *André*'s feet ne'er kept more equal time,
Not ev'n the feet of thy own *Psyche*'s rhime:
Though they in number as in sense excell,   55
So just, so like tautology they fell,
That, pale with envy, *Singleton* forswore   ⎫
The Lute and Sword which he in Triumph bore,   ⎬
And vow'd he ne'er would act *Villerius* more.   ⎭
Here stopt the good old *Syre*; and wept for joy   60
In silent raptures of the hopefull boy.
All Arguments, but most his Plays, perswade,
That for anointed dullness he was made.

---

33 *Norwich Drugget:* coarse woollen material.   36 Flecknoe had travel-
led in Portugal.   42 *Epsom Blankets:* a double reference to Shadwell's
play *Epsom-Wells* (1673) and to the character of Sir Samuel Hearty who
is tossed in a blanket in his play *The Virtuoso* (1676).   43 *Arion:* half-
mythical Greek poet, saved from drowning by a dolphin.   47 *Pissing-
Alley:* Two alleys in London had this name. Probably the one now
absorbed into the west end of Cannon Street, in the City, is meant.   48
Aston Hall: No such place in London has been identified. It may con-
ceal an ironical reference to Shadwell's friend Colonel Edmund As(h)ton,
a minor poet attacked elsewhere as 'dull Aston'.   53-54 *St. André . . .
Psyche:* St. André was a French dancer in Shadwell's opera *Psyche*
(1675).   57 *Singleton:* John Singleton (d.1686), musician and singer.
59 *Villerius:* character in Davenant's opera *The Siege of Rhodes* (1656).

Close to the Walls which fair *Augusta* bind,
(The fair *Augusta* much to fears inclin'd)   65
An ancient fabrick, raised t' inform the sight,
There stood of yore, and *Barbican* it hight:
A watch Tower once; but now, so Fate ordains,
Of all the Pile an empty name remains.
From its old Ruins Brothel-houses rise,   70
Scenes of lewd loves, and of polluted joys,
Where their vast Courts the Mother-Strumpets keep,
And, undisturb'd by Watch, in silence sleep.
Near these a Nursery erects its head,
Where Queens are form'd, and future Hero's bred;   75
Where unfledg'd Actors learn to laugh and cry,
Where infant Punks their tender voices try,
And little *Maximins* the Gods defy.
Great *Fletcher* never treads in Buskins here,
Nor greater *Johnson* dares in Socks appear.   80
But gentle *Simkin* just reception finds
Amidst this Monument of vanisht minds;
Pure Clinches, the suburbian Muse affords;
And *Panton* waging harmless war with words.
Here *Flecknoe*, as a place to Fame well known,   85
Ambitiously design'd his *Sh[adwell]*'s throne.
For ancient *Decker* prophesi'd long since,
That in this Pile should Reign a mighty Prince,
Born for a scourge of Wit, and flayle of Sense,
To whom true dullness should some *Psyches* owe,   90
But Worlds of *Misers* from his pen should flow;
Humorists and *Hypocrites* it should produce,
Whole *Raymond* Families, and Tribes of *Bruce*.

Now Empress *Fame* had publisht the renown
Of *Sh[adwell]*'s Coronation through the Town.   95
Rows'd by report of Fame, the Nations meet,
From near *Bun-Hill*, and distant *Watling-street*.

64 *Augusta:* a Roman title for London.   67 *Barbican:* formerly stood
in front of Aldersgate, London;   *hight:*   was called.   74 *Nursery:* a
'nursery theatre' established 1664.   78 *Maximin:* character in Dryden's
heroic play *Tyrannick Love* (1670).   79 *Fletcher:* John Fletcher (1579-
1625), dramatist.   80 *Johnson:* Ben Jonson (1572-1637), dramatist
and poet.   81 *Simkin:* character in popular farces.   83 *Clinches:* word-
play.   84 *Panton:* character in farce (?).   87 *Decker:* Thomas Dekker
(*c.* 1572-1632), dramatist.   91-92 *The Miser, The Humorists,* and *The
Hypocrite* are titles of plays by Shadwell.   93 *Raymond . . . Bruce:* charac-
ters in Shadwell's plays.   97 *Bun-Hill:* in Finsbury, London;   *Watling-
street:* the Roman highway that passed through London.

No *Persian* Carpets spread th' imperial way,
But scatter'd Limbs of mangled Poets lay;
From dusty shops neglected Authors come,   100
Martyrs of Pies, and Reliques of the Bum.
Much *Heywood*, *Shirley*, *Ogleby* there lay,
But loads of *Sh*[*adwell*] almost choakt the way.
Bilk't *Stationers* for Yeomen stood prepar'd,
And *H*[*erringman*] was Captain of the Guard.   105
The hoary Prince in Majesty appear'd,
High on a Throne of his own Labours rear'd.
At his right hand our young *Ascanius* sate
Rome's other hope, and Pillar of the State.
His Brows thick fogs, instead of glories, grace,   110
And lambent dullness plaid around his face.
As *Hannibal* did to the Altars come,
Swore by his *Syre* a mortal Foe to *Rome*;
So *Sh*[*adwell*] swore, nor should his Vow bee vain,
That he till Death true dullness would maintain;   115
And in his father's Right, and Realms defence,
Ne'er to have Peace with Wit, nor truce with Sense.
The King himself the sacred Unction made,
As King by Office, and as Priest by Trade:
In his sinister hand, instead of Ball,   120
He plac'd a mighty Mug of potent Ale;
Love's Kingdom to his right he did convey,
At once his Sceptre and his rule of Sway;
Whose righteous Lore the Prince had practis'd young,
And from whose Loyns recorded *Psyche* sprung.   125
His temples last with Poppies were o'erspread,
That nodding seem'd to consecrate his head:
Just at that point of time, if Fame not lye,
On his left hand twelve reverend *Owls* did fly.
So *Romulus*, 'tis sung, by *Tyber's Brook*,   130
Presage of Sway from twice six Vultures took.
Th' admiring throng loud acclamations make,
And Omens of his future Empire take.
The *Syre* then shook the honours of his head,
And from his brows damps of oblivion shed   135

＊

101 *Martyrs of Pies:* Cf. Swift's *On the Death of Dr. Swift*, lines 259-60.
Pies were laid on such remaindered paper.   102 *Ogleby:* John Ogilby
(1600-76), Scottish author, printer, cartographer, and translator.   105
H[*erringman*]:   Henry Herringman had published both Dryden and
Shadwell.   108 *Ascanius:* son of Æneas in Virgil's *Æneid*.   122 *Love's
Kingdom:* pastoral play by Flecknoe.

Full on the filial dullness: long he stood,
Repelling from his Breast the raging God; }
At length burst out in this prophetick mood: }

Heavens bless my Son, from *Ireland* let him reign
To far *Barbadoes* on the Western main;   140
Of his Dominion may no end be known,
And greater than his Father's be his Throne.
Beyond loves Kingdom let him stretch his Pen;
He paused, and all the people cry'd *Amen.*
Then thus, continued he, my Son, advance   145
Still in new Impudence, new Ignorance.
Success let others teach, learn thou from me
Pangs without birth, and fruitless Industry.
Let *Virtuoso's* in five years be Writ;
Yet not one thought accuse thy toyl of Wit.   150
Let gentle *George* in triumph tread the Stage,
Make *Dorimant* betray, and *Loveit* rage;
Let *Cully, Cockwood, Fopling,* charm the Pit,
And in their folly shew the Writers wit.
Yet still thy fools shall stand in thy defence,   155
And justifie their Author's want of sense.
Let 'em be all by thy own model made
Of dullness, and desire no foreign aid:
That they to future ages may be known,
Not Copies drawn, but Issue of thy own.   160
Nay let thy men of wit too be the same,
All full of thee, and differing but in name;
But let no alien S[e]dl[e]y interpose
To lard with wit thy hungry *Epsom* prose.
And when false flowers of *Rhetorick* thou would'st cull, 165
Trust Nature, do not labour to be dull;
But write thy best, and top; and in each line
Sir *Formal's* oratory will be thine.
Sir *Formal,* though unsought, attends thy quill,
And does thy *Northern Dedications* fill.   170
Nor let false friends seduce thy mind to fame,
By arrogating *Johnson's* Hostile name.

149 *Virtuoso's:* refers to Shadwell's play *The Virtuoso.* 151 *Gentle George:* Sir George Etherege (*c.* 1634/5-91?), dramatist. 152-3 *Dorimant . . . Fopling:* characters in Etherege's plays. 163 *S[e]dl[e]y:* Sir Charles Sedley (1639?-1701), dramatist and poet who wrote a prologue to Shadwell's *Epsom-Wells.* 168 *Sir Formal:* character in *The Virtuoso.* 170 *Northern Dedications:* Many of Shadwell's plays were dedicated to the Duke or Duchess of Newcastle. 172 Shadwell was a vehement admirer of Ben Jonson.

Let Father *Flecknoe* fire thy mind with praise,
And Uncle *Ogleby* thy envy raise.
Thou art my blood, where *Johnson* has no part: 175
What share have we in Nature or in Art?
Where did his wit on learning fix a brand,
And rail at Arts he did not understand?
Where made he love in Prince *Nicander*'s vein,
Or swept the dust in *Psyche*'s humble strain?   180
Where sold he Bargains, Whip-stich, kiss my Arse,
Promis'd a Play and dwindled to a Farce?
When did his Muse from *Fletcher* scenes purloin,
As thou whole *Eth'ridg* dost transfuse to thine?
But so transfus'd as Oyl on Wat'rs flow,   185
His always floats above, thine sinks below.
This is thy Province, this thy wondrous way,
New Humours to invent for each new Play:
This is that boasted Byas of thy mind,
By which one way, to dullness, 'tis inclined.   190
Which makes thy writings lean on one side still,
And in all changes that way bends thy will.
Nor let thy mountain belly make pretence
Of likeness; thine's a tympany of sense.
A Tun of Man in thy large Bulk is writ,   195
But sure thou 'rt but a Kilderkin of wit.
Like mine thy gentle numbers feebly creep,
Thy Tragick Muse gives smiles, thy Comick sleep.
With whate'er gall thou sett'st thy self to write,
Thy inoffensive Satyrs never bite.   200
In thy fellonious heart, though Venom lies,
It does but touch thy *Irish* pen, and dyes.
Thy Genius calls thee not to purchase fame
In keen Iambicks, but mild Anagram:
Leave writing Plays, and chuse for thy command   205
Some peacefull Province in Acrostick Land.
There thou maist Wings display, and Altars raise,
And torture one poor word Ten thousand ways.
Or if thou would'st thy diff'rent talents suit,
Set thy own Songs, and sing them to thy lute.   210

179 *Nicander:* character in *Psyche.* 181 *Sold . . . bargains:* engaged in
bawdy backchat; *whip-stitch:* exclamation implying sudden movement.
193-4 Jonson, like Shadwell, was far from slim. 194 *Tympany of sense:*
empty, senseless swelling. 196 *Kilderkin:* quarter part of a tun. 204
Iambics: used for satire in Greek poetry. 207 *Wings . . . Altars:* refers to
the specially shaped poems which were a fashion in the 17th century.

He said, but his last words were scarcely heard, ⎫
For *Bruce* and *Longvil* had a *Trap* prepar'd, ⎬
And down they sent the yet declaiming Bard. ⎭
Sinking he left his Drugget robe behind,
Borne upwards by a subterranean wind. 215
The Mantle fell to the young Prophet's part,
With double portion of his Father's Art.

John Wilmot, Earl of Rochester

1647—1680

A SATIRE AGAINST MANKIND

This vigorous and bitter poem, which won the admiration of
Voltaire, Goethe, and Tennyson, is more than the cry of a
disillusioned man of the world: it expresses, with the fierceness
such a disillusionment may well give, the impact of deist,
materialist, and sceptical ideas on the brittle society of the
Restoration.

    Were I (who to my cost already am
One of those strange prodigious Creatures *Man*)
A Spirit free, to choose for my own share,
What Case of Flesh, and Blood, I pleas'd to weare,
I'd be a *Dog*, a *Monkey*, or a *Bear*, 5
Or any thing but that vain *Animal*,
Who is so proud of being rational.
The senses are too gross, and he'll contrive
A Sixth, to contradict the other Five;
And before certain instinct, will preferr 10
Reason, which Fifty times for one does err:
Reason, an *Ignis fatuus*, in the *Mind*,
Which leaving light of Nature, sense behind;
Pathless and dang'rous wandring ways it takes,
Through errors, Fenny-*Boggs*, and Thorny *Brakes*; 15
Whilst the misguided follower, climbs with pain,
Mountains of Whimseys, heap'd in his own *Brain*:
Stumbling from thought to thought, falls head-long down,
Into doubts boundless Sea, where like to drown,
Books bear him up awhile, and makes him try, 20

212-13 parodying an incident in Shadwell's *The Virtuoso*. 12 *Ignis
fatuus:* will-o'-the-wisp.

To swim with Bladders of *Philosophy*;
In hopes still t'oretake the'escaping light,
The *Vapour* dances in his dazled sight,
Till spent, it leaves him to eternal Night.
Then Old Age, and experience, hand in hand,   25
Lead him to death, and make him understand,
After a search so painful, and so long,
That all his Life he has been in the wrong;
Hudled in dirt, the reas'ning *Engine* lyes,
Who was so proud, so witty, and so wise.   30
Pride drew him in, as *Cheats*, their *Bubbles*, catch,
And makes him venture, to be made a *Wretch*.
His wisdom did his happiness destroy,
Aiming to know what *World* he shou'd enjoy;
And *Wit*, was his vain frivolous pretence,   35
Of pleasing others, at his own expence.
For *Witts* are treated just like common *Whores*,
First they're enjoy'd, and then kickt out of *Doores*:
The pleasure past, a threatning doubt remains,
That frights th'enjoyer, with succeeding pains: 40
Women and *Men* of *Wit*, are dang'rous Tools,
And ever fatal to admiring *Fools*.
Pleasure allures, and when the *Fopps* escape,
'Tis not that they're belov'd, but fortunate.
And therefore what they fear, at least they hate.   45
    But now methinks some formal Band, and Beard,
Takes me to task, come on Sir I'm prepar'd.
    Then by your favour, any thing that's writ
Against this gibeing jingling knack call'd Wit,
Likes me abundantly, but you take care,   50
Upon this point, not to be too severe.
Perhaps my Muse, were fitter for this part,
For I profess, I can be very smart
On Wit, which I abhor with all my heart:
I long to lash it in some sharp Essay,   55
But your grand indiscretion bids me stay,
And turns my Tide of Ink another way.
What rage ferments in your degen'rate mind,
To make you rail at Reason, and Mankind?
Blest glorious Man! to whom alone kind Heav'n,   60
An everlasting Soul has freely giv'n;
Whom his great Maker took such care to make,
That from himself he did the Image take;

46 *Band:* clergyman (wearing a 'Geneva band').

And this fair frame, in shining Reason *drest,*
To dignifie his Nature, *above* Beast: 65
Reason, *by whose aspiring influence,*
We take a flight beyond material sense,
Dive into Mysteries, then soaring pierce
The flaming limits of the Universe,
Search Heav'n and Hell, find out what's acted there,   70
And give the World true grounds of hope and fear.
　　Hold mighty Man, I cry, all this we know,
From the Pathetique Pen of *Ingello*;
From *P[atrick's] Pilgrim, S[ibbs'] soliloquies,*
And 'tis this very reason I despise.   75
This supernatural gift, that makes a *Myte,*
Think he is the Image of the Infinite:
Comparing his short life, void of all rest,
To the *Eternal,* and the ever blest;
This busie, puzling, stirrer up of doubt,   80
That frames deep *Mysteries,* then finds 'em out;
Filling with Frantick Crowds of thinking *Fools,*
Those Reverend *Bedlams, Colledges,* and *Schools,*
Borne on whose Wings, each heavy *Sot* can pierce
The limits of the boundless Universe: 85
So charming Oyntments, make an Old *Witch* flie,
And bear a Crippled Carcass through the Skie.
'Tis this exalted Pow'r, whose bus'ness lies,
In *Nonsense,* and impossibilities.
This made a Whimsical *Philosopher,*   90
Before the spacious *World,* his *Tub* prefer,
And we have modern *Cloysterd Coxcombs,* who
Retire to think, cause they have naught to do.
But thoughts, are giv'n for Actions government,
Where Action ceases, thoughts impertinent: 95
Our *Sphere* of Action, is lifes happiness,
And he who thinks Beyond, thinks like an *Ass.*
Thus, whilst 'gainst false reas'ning I inveigh,
I own right *Reason,* which I wou'd obey:
That *Reason* that distinguishes by sense,   100
And gives us *Rules,* of good, and ill from thence:
That bounds desires, with a reforming Will,
To keep 'em more in vigour, not to kill.

73 *Ingello:* Nathaniel Ingelo (1621?-83), Doctor of Divinity, musician,
and author of an allegorical religious romance *Bentivolio and Urania.*
74 *P[atrick's] Pilgrim: The Parable of the Pilgrim,* a religious allegory by
Simon Patrick, Bishop of Ely (1626-1707). *S[ibbs']:* Richard Sibbes
(1577-1635), Puritan clergyman, lecturer, and author.

Your *Reason* hinders, mine helps t'enjoy,
Renewing Appetites, yours wou'd destroy.   105
My Reason is my *Friend*, yours is a *Cheat*,
Hunger call's out, my Reason bids me eat;
Perversely yours, your Appetite does mock,
This asks for Food, that answers what's a Clock?
This plain distinction Sir your doubt secures,   110
'Tis not true Reason I despise but yours.
Thus I think Reason righted, but for *Man*,
I'le nere recant, defend him if you can.
For all his Pride, and his Philosophy,
'Tis evident, *Beasts* are in their degree,   115
As wise at least, and better far than he.
Those *Creatures*, are the wisest who attain,
By surest means, the ends at which they aim.
If therefore *Jowler*, finds, and Kills his *Hares*,
Better than *M[eres]*, supplyes Committee Chairs;   120
Though one's a *States-man*, th'other but a *Hound*,
Jowler, in Justice, wou'd be wiser found.
You see how far *Mans* wisedom here extends,
Look next, if humane Nature makes amends;
Whose Principles, most gen'rous are, and just,   125
And to whose *Moralls*, you wou'd sooner trust.
Be Judge your self, I'le bring it to the test,
Which is the basest *Creature, Man,* or *Beast*?
Birds, feed on *Birds, Beasts,* on each other prey,
But Savage *Man* alone, does *Man,* betray: 130
Prest by necessity, they Kill for Food,
Man undoes *Man,* to do himself no good.
With Teeth, and Claws by Nature arm'd they hunt,
Natures allowances, to supply their want.
But *Man*, with smiles, embraces, Friendships, praise, 135
Unhumanely his Fellows life betrays;
With voluntary pains, works his distress,
Not through necessity, but wantonness.
For hunger, or for Love, they fight, or tear,
Whilst wretched *Man,* is still in Arms for fear;   140
For fear he armes, and is of Armes afraid,
By fear, to fear, successively betray'd,
Base fear, the source whence his best passions came,
His boasted Honor, and his dear bought Fame.
That lust of Pow'r, to which he's such a *Slave*,   145
And for the which alone he dares be brave:

120 *M[eres]*: Sir Thomas Meres or Meeres (1635-1715), M.P. for
Lincoln under Charles II.

To which his various Projects are design'd,
Which makes him gen'rous, affable, and kind:
For which he takes such pains to be thought wise,
And screws his actions, in a forc'd disguise: 150
Leading a tedious life in Misery,
Under laborious, mean *Hypocrisie.*
Look to the bottom, of his vast design,
Wherein *Mans* Wisdom, Pow'r, and Glory joyn:
The good he acts, the ill he does endure,   155
'Tis all for fear, to make himself secure.
Meerly for safety, after Fame we thirst,
For all Men, wou'd be *Cowards* if they durst.
And honesty's against all common sense,
Men must be *Knaves,* 'tis in their own defence.   160
Mankind's dishonest, if you think it fair,
Amongst known *Cheats,* to play upon the square,
You'le be undone——
Nor can weak truth, your reputation save,
The *Knaves,* will all agree to call you *Knave.*   165
Wrong'd shall he live, insulted o're, opprest,
Who dares be less a *Villain,* than the rest.
Thus Sir you see what human Nature craves,
Most Men are *Cowards,* all Men shou'd be *Knaves:*
The diff'rence lyes (as far as I can see)   170
Not in the thing it self, but the degree;
And all the subject matter of debate,
Is only who's a *Knave,* of the first *Rate?*
    All this with indignation have I hurl'd,
At the pretending part of the proud World,   175
Who swolne with selfish vanity, devise
False freedomes, holy Cheats, and formal Lyes
Over their fellow *Slaves* to tyrannize.
    But if in *Court,* so just a Man there be,
(In *Court,* a just Man, yet unknown to me)   180
Who does his needful flattery direct,
Not to oppress, and ruine, but protect;
Since flattery, which way so ever laid,
Is still a Tax on that unhappy Trade;
If so upright a *States-Man,* you can find,   185
Whose passions bend to his unbyass'd Mind;
Who does his Arts, and *Policies* apply,
To raise his *Country,* not his *Family;*
Nor while his Pride, own'd Avarice withstands,
Receives sly Bribes, from *Friends* corrupted hands;   190
Is there a *Church-Man* who on *God* relyes?

Whose Life, his Faith, and Doctrine Justifies?
Not one blown up, with vain Prelatique Pride,
Who for reproof of Sins, does *Man* deride:
Whose envious heart with sawcy Eloquence,   195
Dares chide at *Kings*, and raile at Men of sense,
Who from his Pulpit, vents more peevish Lyes,
More bitter railings, scandals, Calumnies,
Than at a Gossipping, are thrown about,
When the good *Wives*, get drunk, and then fall out: 200
None of that sensual *Tribe*, whose Tallents lye,
In Avarice, *Pride*, *Sloth*, and *Gluttony*,
Who hunt good Livings, but abhor good Lives,
Whose Lust exalted, to that height arrives,
They act *Adultery* with their own *Wives*,   205
And e're a score of Years compleated be,
Can from the lofty *Pulpit* proudly see,
Half a large *Parish*, their own *Progeny*:
Nor doating B—— who wou'd be ador'd,
For domineering at the *Councel Board*;   210
A greater *Fop*, in business at Fourscore,
Fonder of serious *Toyes*, affected more,
Than the gay glitt'ring *Fool*, at Twenty proves,
With all his noise, his tawdrey Cloths, and Loves:
But a meek humble Man, of modest sense,   215
Who Preaching peace, does practice continence;
Whose pious life's a proof he does believe,
Misterious truths, which no *Man* can conceive:—
If upon *Earth* there dwell such *God-like Men*,
I'le here recant my *Paradox* to them,   220
Adore those *Shrines* of *Virtue*, *Homage* pay,
And with the *Rabble World*, their *Laws* obey.
If such there are, yet grant me this at least,
Man differs more from *Man*, than *Man* from *Beast*.

---

199 *Gossipping:* gathering of female relatives at a birth.   209 *B——:*
perhaps Thomas Barlow, Bishop of Lincoln (1607-91).

Matthew Prior

1664—1721

JINNY THE JUST

Jinny was Prior's housekeeper and mistress, and in addition to looking after him in London she accompanied him to the Netherlands and France during the decade 1690-99. He last refers to her in a letter in 1706. This affectionate poem, both warm-hearted and entertaining, is sufficient epitaph for her.

Releas'd from the Noise of the Butcher and Baker,
Who, my old friends be thanked, did seldom forsake Her,
And from the soft Duns of my Landlord the Quaker,

From chiding the footmen and watching the lasses,
From Nel that burn't milk too, and Tom that brake glasses   5
(Sad mischeifs through which a good housekeeper passes!),

From some real Care but more fancied vexation,
From a life partly-colour'd half reason half passion,
Here lyes after all the best Wench in the Nation.

From the Rhine to the Po, from the Thames to the Rhone   10
Joanna or Janneton, Jinny or Joan
Twas all one to Her by what name She was known.

For the Idiom of words very little She heeded,
Provided the Matter She drove at Succeeded,
She took and gave languages just as she needed: 15

So for Kitching and markett, for bargain and Sale
She paid English or Dutch or French down on the Nail,
But in telling a Story She Sometimes did fail;

Then begging excuse as she happen'd to stammer,
With respect to her betters but none to her Grammer,   20
Her blush helpt Her out and her jargon became Her.

3 *Duns:* demands for payment.

273

Her habit and mein she Endeavour'd to frame
To the different Gout of the place where she came,
Her outside still chang'd, but her Inside the Same:

At the Hague in her Slippers and hair as the mode is,   25
At Paris all falbalow'd fine as a Goddess,
And at censuring London in Smock sleeves and Bodice,

She order'd affairs that few people could tell
In what part about Her that mixture did dwell
Of Vrough or Mistresse or Mademoiselle.   30

For Her Sirname and race let the Heraults e'n answer,
Her own proper worth was enough to advance Her,
And He who lik'd Her little valu'd her Grandsire.

But from what House soever her lineage may come
I wish my own Jinny but out of her tomb,   35
Though all her relations were there in her Room.

Of such terrible beauty She never could boast
As with absolute sway o'er all hearts rules the roast
When J[acob] bawls out to the Chair for a toast;

But of good household features her Person was made,   40
Nor by faction cry'd up nor of censure afraid,
And her beauty was rather for use than Parade;

Her blood so well mixt and flesh so well pasted
That though her Youth faded her comliness lasted,
The blue was worn off but the plum was well tasted.   45

Less smooth than her Skin and Less White than her breast
Was this polisht stone beneath which she lyes prest:
Stop, reader and sigh while thou think'st on the rest.

With a just trim of virtue her Soul was endued,
Not affectedly pious nor Secretly Lewd   50
She cutt even between the Coquette, and the Prude,

And Her will with her duty so equally stood
That Seldom oppos'd she was commonly good
And did pretty well, doing just what She wou'd.

23 *Gout:* taste, manners. 26 *Falbalow'd:* flounced. 39 *J[acob].*
probably the publisher Jacob Tonson (1656-1736), who was secretary
of the Kit-Cat Club, to which Prior belonged.

Declining all power She found means to persuade, 55
Was then most regarded, when most she obey'd,
The Mistresse in truth when She seem'd but the Maid.

Such care of her own proper actions she took
That on other folks lives She had no time to look,
So Censure and Praise were struck out of her book. 60

Her thought still confin'd to its own little sphere
She minded not who did excell or did err
But just as the Matter related to Her.

Then too when her private tribunal was rear'd
Her mercy so mixt with her judgement appear'd 65
That her foes were condemnd and her friends always clear'd.

Her religion so well with her learning did suit
That in practice sincere, and in controverse mute
She show'd She knew better to live than dispute.

Some parts of the Bible by heart she recited 70
And much in historical Chapters delighted
But in points about faith she was something short sighted;

So Notions and modes she referr'd to the Scholes
And in matters of Conscience adher'd to two rules,
To advise with no biggots and jeast with no fools; 75

And Scrupling but little, enough She believ'd,
By Charity ample small sins she retriev'd,
And when She had New Cloaths she always receiv'd.

Thus still whilst her Morning unseen fled away
In ordering the Linnin and making the Tea 80
That She Scarce could have time for the Psalms of the Day;

And while after Dinner the Night came so soon
That half she propos'd very seldom was done,
With twenty God bless Me's how this day is gon;

While she read and accounted and pay'd and abated, 85
Eat and drank, play'd and work't, laught and cry'd, lov'd and
   hated
As answer'd the End of her being created:
85 *Abated:* deducted.

In the midst of her Age came a cruell desease
Which neither her broths nor recepts could appease,
So down dropt her Clay, may her Soul be at Peace.   90

Retire from this Sepulchre all the prophane,
Ye that love for debauch or that marry for gain,
Retire least Ye trouble the Manes of J[ane].

But Thou that know'st love above Interest or lust,
Strew the Myrtle and rose on this once belov'd dust,   95
And shed one pious tear upon Jinny the Just.

Tread Soft on her grave, and do right to her honour,
Let neither rude hand nor Ill tongue light upon her,
Do all the Small favours that now can be don her.

And when what Thou lik't Shall return to her Clay,   100
For so I'm persuaded She must do one day,
What ever fantastic J[ohn] Asgil may Say,

When as I have don now thou shalt sett up a Stone
For Something however distinguisht or known,
May Some pious friend the misfortune bemoan   105
And make thy Concern by reflexion his own.

Jonathan Swift

1667—1745

A DESCRIPTION OF A CITY SHOWER

OCTOBER, 1710

Careful Observers may foretel the Hour
(By sure Prognosticks) when to dread a Show'r:
While Rain depends, the pensive Cat gives o'er
Her Frolicks, and pursues her Tail no more.
Returning Home at Night, you'll find the Sink   5
Strike your offended Sense with double Stink.

89 *Recepts:* recipes, prescriptions. 93 *Manes:* shades, spirits. 102
John Asgill (1659-1738), Irish lawyer and M.P., published a treatise
which aimed to prove that 'Man may be translated from hence into
that Eternal Life, without passing through Death'. 3 *Depends:* impends.

If you be wise, then go not far to Dine,
You'll spend in Coach-hire more than save in Wine.
A coming Show'r your shooting Corns presage,
Old Aches throb, your hollow Tooth will rage.   10
Saunt'ring in Coffee-house is *Dulman* seen;
He damns the Climate, and complains of *Spleen.*

  Mean while the South rising with dabbled Wings,
A Sable Cloud athwart the Welkin flings,
That swill'd more Liquor than it could contain,   15
And like a Drunkard gives it up again.
Brisk *Susan* whips her Linnen from the Rope,
While the first drizzling Show'r is born aslope:
Such is that Sprinkling, which some careless Quean
Flirts on you from her Mop, but not so clean.   20
You fly, invoke the Gods; then turning, stop
To rail; she singing, still whirls on her Mop.
Nor yet the Dust had shun'd the unequal Strife,
But aided by the Wind, fought still for Life;
And wafted with its Foe by vi'lent Gust,   25
'Twas doubtful which was Rain, and which was Dust.
Ah! where must needy Poet seek for Aid,
When Dust and Rain at once his Coat invade?
His only Coat, where Dust confus'd with Rain,
Roughen the Nap, and leave a mingled Stain.   30

  Now in contiguous Drops the Flood comes down,
Threat'ning with Deluge this *devoted* Town.
To Shops in Crowds the daggled Females fly,
Pretend to cheapen Goods, but nothing buy.
The Templer spruce, while ev'ry Spout's abroach,   35
Stays till 'tis fair, yet *seems* to call a Coach.
The tuck'd-up Sempstress walks with hasty Strides,
While Streams run down her oil'd Umbrella's Sides.
Here various Kinds by various Fortunes led,
Commence Acquaintance underneath a Shed.   40
Triumphant Tories, and desponding Whigs,
Forget their Feuds, and join to save their Wigs.
Box'd in a Chair the Beau impatient sits,
While Spouts run clatt'ring o'er the Roof by Fits;

10 *Aches:* a dissyllable, pronounced *aitches.* 12 *Spleen:* depression,
moroseness, irritability. 14 *Welkin:* sky. 19 *Quean:* woman. 32
Devoted: (i) industrious, (ii) doomed. 33 *Daggled:* wet and mud-
splashed. 34 *Cheapen:* price. 35 *Templer:* barrister, from the Inner
or Middle Temple in London.

And ever and anon with frightful Din   45
The Leather sounds; he trembles from within.
So, when *Troy* Chair-men bore the Wooden Steed,
Pregnant with *Greeks*, impatient to be freed,
(Those Bully *Greeks*, who, as the Moderns do,
Instead of paying Chair-Men, run them thro')   50
Laoco'on struck the Out-side with his Spear,
And each imprison'd Hero quak'd for Fear.

Now from all Parts the swelling Kennels flow,
And bear their Trophies with them as they go:
Filths of all Hues and Odours seem to tell   55
What Streets they sail'd from, by the Sight and Smell.
They, as each Torrent drives with rapid Force,
From *Smithfield*, or St. *Pulchre*'s shape their Course,
And in huge Confluent join at *Snow-Hill* Ridge,
Fall from the *Conduit* prone to *Holborn Bridge*.   60
Sweepings from Butchers' Stalls, Dung, Guts, and Blood,   ⎫
Drown'd Puppies, stinking Sprats, all drench'd in Mud,   ⎬
Dead Cats and Turnip-Tops come tumbling down the Flood. ⎭

49 *Bully:* grand, admirable. 50 *Chair-men:* men who carried sedan-
chairs. 51 *Laocoon:* priest who warned Trojans against accepting the
wooden horse. 53 *Kennels:* drains, gutters. 58 *Smithfield:* open space
in the city of London, famed for its markets, fairs, and executions; *St.
Pulchre's:* St. Sepulchre's Church. 59 *Snowhill:* street near St.
Sepulchre's, joining Holborn Conduit. 60 *Conduit:* The torrent of
garbage falls from the Holborn Conduit into the river Fleet. The
Conduit was taken down in 1746. (The modern Holborn Viaduct was
built in 1869.) 61-63 These three last lines were intended against that
licentious Manner of modern Poets, in making three Rhimes together,
which they call *Triplets;* and the last of the three, was two or some
Times more Syllables longer, called an *Alexandrian.* These *Triplets* and
Alexandrians were brought in by Dryden and other Poets in the Reign of
Charles II. They were the mere Effect of Haste, Idleness, and Want of
Money; and have been wholely avoided by the best Poets, since these
Verses were written. (S.)

VERSES ON THE DEATH OF DR. SWIFT

OCCASIONED
BY READING A MAXIM IN ROCHEFOUCAULT

*Dans l'adversité de nos meilleurs amis nous trouvons
quelque chose, qui ne nous deplaist pas.*

In the Adversity of our best Friends, we find
something that doth not displease us.

As *Rochefoucault* his Maxims drew
From Nature, I believe 'em true:
They argue no corrupted Mind
In him; the Fault is in Mankind.

This Maxim more than all the rest   5
Is thought too base for human Breast;
' In all Distresses of our Friends
' We first consult our private Ends,
' While Nature kindly bent to ease us,
' Points out some Circumstance to please us.'   10

If this perhaps your Patience move,
Let Reason and Experience prove.

We all behold with envious Eyes,
Our *Equal* rais'd above our *Size*;
Who would not at a crowded Show,   15
Stand high himself, keep others low?
I love my Friend as well as you,
But would not have him stop my View;
Then let me have the higher Post:
I ask but for an Inch at most.   20

If in a Battle you should find,
One, whom you love of all Mankind,
Had some heroick Action done,
A Champion kill'd, or Trophy won;
Rather than thus be over-topt,   25
Would you not wish his Lawrels cropt?

1 *Rochefoucault:* François, Duc de La Rochefoucauld (1613-80),
French moralist; his *Maximes* were published 1665.

Dear honest *Ned* is in the Gout,
Lies rackt with Pain, and you without:
How patiently you hear him groan!
How glad the Case is not your own!   30

What Poet would not grieve to see,
His Brethern write as well as he?
But rather than they should excel,
He'd wish his Rivals all in Hell.

Her End when Emulation misses,   35
She turns to Envy, Stings and Hisses:
The strongest Friendship yields to Pride,
Unless the Odds be on our Side.

Vain human Kind! Fantastick Race!
Thy various Follies, who can trace?   40
Self-love, Ambition, Envy, Pride,
Their Empire in our Hearts divide:
Give others Riches, Power, and Station,
'Tis all on me an Usurpation.
I have no Title to aspire;   45
Yet, when you sink, I seem the higher;
In POPE, I cannot read a Line,
But with a Sigh, I wish it mine:
When he can in one Couplet fix
More Sense than I can do in Six: 50
It gives me such a jealous Fit,
I cry, Pox take him, and his Wit.

Why must I be outdone by GAY,
In my own hum'rous biting Way?

ARBUTHNOT is no more my Friend,   55
Who dares to Irony pretend;
Which I was born to introduce,
Refin'd it first, and shew'd its Use.

ST. JOHN, as well as PULTNEY knows,
That I had some Repute for Prose;   60

47 *Pope:* Alexander Pope (1688-1744), poet.   53 *Gay:* John Gay
(1685-1732), poet and dramatist.   55 *Arbuthnot:* John Arbuthnot
(1667-1735), physician, pamphleteer, friend of Swift and Pope.   59 *St.
John:* Henry St. John, Viscount Bolingbroke (1678-1751); *Pultney:*
William Pulteney, Earl of Bath (1684-1764).

And till they drove me out of Date,
Could maul a Minister of State:
If they have mortify'd my Pride,
And made me throw my Pen aside;
If with such Talents Heav'n hath blest 'em   65
Have I not Reason to detest 'em?

  To all my Foes, dear Fortune, send
Thy Gifts, but never to my Friend:
I tamely can endure the first,
But, this with Envy makes me burst.   70

  Thus much may serve by way of Proem,
Proceed we therefore to our Poem.

  The Time is not remote, when I
Must by the Course of Nature dye:
When I foresee my special Friends,   75
Will try to find their private Ends:
Tho' it is hardly understood,
Which way my Death can do them good;
Yet, thus methinks, I hear 'em speak;
See, how the Dean begins to break: 80
Poor Gentleman, he droops apace,
You plainly find it in his Face:
That old Vertigo in his Head,
Will never leave him, till he's dead:
Besides, his Memory decays,   85
He recollects not what he says;
He cannot call his Friends to Mind;
Forgets the Place where last he din'd:
Plyes you with Stories o'er and o'er,
He told them fifty Times before.   90
How does he fancy we can sit,
To hear his out-of-fashion'd Wit?
But he takes up with younger Fokes,
Who for his Wine will bear his Jokes:
Faith, he must make his Stories shorter,   95
Or change his Comrades once a Quarter:
In half the Time, he talks them round;
There must another Sett be found.

  For Poetry, he's past his Prime,
He takes an Hour to find a Rhime: 100
71 *Proem:* preface.

His Fire is out, his Wit decay'd,
His Fancy sunk, his Muse a Jade.
I'd have him throw away his Pen;
But there's no talking to some Men.

  And, then their Tenderness appears,   105
By adding largely to my Years:
' He's older than he would be reckon'd,
' And well remembers *Charles* the Second.

  ' He hardly drinks a Pint of Wine;
' And that, I doubt, is no good Sign.   110
' His Stomach too begins to fail:
' Last Year we thought him strong and hale;
' But now, he's quite another Thing;
' I wish he may hold out till Spring.'

  Then hug themselves, and reason thus;   115
' It is not yet so bad with us.'

  In such a Case they talk in Tropes,
And, by their Fears express their Hopes:
Some great Misfortune to portend,
No Enemy can match a Friend;   120
With all the Kindness they profess,
The Merit of a lucky Guess,
(When daily Howd'y's come of Course,
And Servants answer; *Worse and Worse*)
Would please 'em better than to tell,   125
That, GOD be prais'd, the Dean is well.
Then he who prophecy'd the best,
Approves his Foresight to the rest:
' You know, I always fear'd the worst,
' And often told you so at first: '   130
He'd rather chuse that I should dye,
Than his Prediction prove a Lye.
Not one foretels I shall recover;
But, all agree, to give me over.

  Yet should some Neighbour feel a Pain,   135
Just in the Parts, where I complain;
How many a Message would he send?
What hearty Prayers that I should mend?

117 *Tropes:* figures of rhetoric.

Enquire what Regimen I kept?
What gave me Ease, and how I slept?   140
And more lament, when I was dead,
Than all the Sniv'llers round my Bed.

My good Companions, never fear,
For though you may mistake a Year;
Though your Prognosticks run too fast,   145
They must be verify'd at last.

' Behold the fatal Day arrive!
' How is the Dean? He's just alive.
' Now the departing Prayer is read:
' He hardly breathes. The Dean is dead.   150
' Before the Passing-Bell begun,
' The News thro' half the Town has run.
' O, may we all for Death prepare!
' What has he left? And who's his Heir?
' I know no more than what the News is,   155
' 'Tis all bequeath'd to Publick Uses.
' To publick Use! a perfect Whim!
' What had the Publick done for him!
' Meer Envy, Avarice, and Pride!
' He gave it all:—But first he dy'd.   160
' And had the Dean, in all the Nation,
' No worthy Friend, no poor Relation?
' So ready to do Strangers good,
' Forgetting his own Flesh and Blood? '

Now *Grub-street* Wits are all employ'd;   165
With Elegies the Town is cloy'd:
Some Paragraph in ev'ry Paper,
To *curse* the *Dean*, or *bless* the *Drapier*.

The Doctors tender of their Fame,
Wisely on me lay all the Blame: 170
' We must confess his Case was nice;
' But he would never take Advice:

165 *Grub-street:* now Milton Street, E.C.2.   168 The Author imagines,
that the Scriblers of the prevailing Party, which he always opposed,
will libel him after his Death; but that others will remember him with
Gratitude, who consider the Service he had done to *Ireland*, under the
Name of M. B. Drapier, by utterly defeating the destructive Project
of *Wood*'s Half-pence, in five Letters to the People of *Ireland*, at that
Time read universally, and convincing every Reader. (S.)

'Had he been rul'd, for ought appears,
'He might have liv'd these Twenty Years:
'For when we open'd him, we found   175
'That all his vital Parts were sound.'

From *Dublin* soon to *London* spread,
'Tis told at Court, the Dean is dead.

Kind Lady *Suffolk* in the Spleen,
Runs laughing up to tell the [Queen].   180
The [Queen], so Gracious, Mild, and Good,
Cries, ' Is he gone? 'Tis time he should.
' He's dead you say; then let him rot;
' I'm glad the M[eda]ls were forgot.
' I promis'd them I own; but when?   185
' I only was the [Princess] then;
' But now as Consort of [a King],
' You know 'tis quite a different Thing.'

Now *Chartres* at Sir *R[obert]*'s Levee,
Tells, with a Sneer, the Tidings heavy: 190

178 The Dean supposeth himself to dye in *Ireland*, where he was born.
(S.)   179 Mrs. *Howard*, afterwards Countess of *Suffolk*, then of the Bed-
chamber to the Queen, professed much Friendship for the Dean. The
Queen then Princess, sent a dozen times to the Dean (then in *London*)
with her commands to attend her; which at last he did, by Advice of all
his Friends. She often sent for him afterwards, and always treated him
very Graciously. He taxed her with a Present worth Ten Pounds, which
she promised before he should return to *Ireland*, but on his taking Leave,
the Medals were not ready. (S.)   184 The Medals were to be sent to
the Dean in four Months, but she forgot them, or thought them too dear.
The Dean, being in *Ireland*, sent Mrs. *Howard* a piece of *Indian* Plad made
in that Kingdom; which the Queen seeing took from her, and wore it
herself, and sent to the Dean for as much as would cloath herself and
children, desiring he would send the Charge of it. He did the former.
It cost thirty five Pounds, but he said he would have nothing except the
Medals: He went next summer to *England*, was treated as usual, and she
being then Queen, the Dean was promised a Settlement in *England*, but
return'd as he went, and instead of Favour or Medals, hath been ever
since under her Majestie's Displeasure. (S.)   189 *Chartres* is a most in-
famous, vile Scoundrel, grown from a Foot-Boy, or worse, to a pro-
digious Fortune both in *England* and *Scotland*: He had a way of in-
sinuating himself into all Ministers, under every Change, either as a
Pimp, Flatterer, or Informer. He was tryed at Seventy for a Rape, and
came off by sacrificing a great Part of his Fortune (he is since dead, but
this Poem still preserves the scene and Time it was writ in). (S.)
Chartres: Francis Charteris (1675-1732); *Sir Robert:* Sir Robert Walpole
(1676-1745).

'Why, is he dead without his Shoes?'
(Cries *Bob*) ' I'm Sorry for the News;
' Oh, were the Wretch but living still,
' And in his Place my good Friend *Will*;
' Or, had a Mitre on his Head   195
' Provided *Bolingbroke* were dead.'

Now *Curl* his Shop from Rubbish drains;
Three genuine Tomes of *Swift's* Remains.
And then to make them pass the glibber,
Revis'd by *Tibbalds, Moore*, and *Cibber*.   200
He'll treat me as he does my Betters.
Publish my Will, my Life, my Letters.

192 Sir *Robert Walpole*, Chief Minister of State, treated the Dean in
1726, with great Distinction, invited him to Dinner at *Chelsea*, with the
Dean's Friends chosen on Purpose; appointed an Hour to talk with him
of *Ireland*, to which *Kingdom* and *People* the Dean found him no great
Friend; for he defended *Wood's* Project of Half-pence, &c. for which the
Dean would see him no more; and upon his next Year's Return to
England, Sir *Robert*, on an accidental Meeting, made him a civil Compli-
ment; but, the Dean never made him another Visit. (S.)   194 Mr.
William Pultney, from being Sir Robert's intimate Friend, detesting his
Administration, opposed his Measures, and joined with my *Lord
Bolingbroke*, to represent his Conduct in an excellent Paper, called the
Craftsman, which is still continued. (S.)   196 *Henry St. John*, Lord
Viscount *Bolingbroke*, Secretary of State to *Queen Anne* of blessed Memory.
He is reckoned the most Universal Genius in *Europe; Walpole* dreading
his Abilities, treated him most injuriously, working with King *George I*
who forgot his Promise of restoring the said Lord, upon the restless
Importunity of the said *Walpole*. (S.)   197 *Curl* hath been the most
infamous Bookseller of any Age or Country: His Character in Part may
be found in Mr. Pope's Dunciad. He published three Volumes all
charged on the Dean, who never writ three Pages of them: He hath used
many of the Dean's Friends in almost as vile a Manner. (S.)   *Curl:*
Edmund Curll (1675-1747).   200 Three stupid Verse Writers in *London;*
the last to the Shame of the Court, and the highest Disgrace to Wit and
Learning, was made Laureat. *Moore*, commonly called *Jemmy Moore*,
Son of *Arthur Moore*, whose Father was Jaylor of *Monaghan* in *Ireland*.
See the Character of *Jemmy Moore*, and *Tibbalds, Theobald*, in the
Dunciad. (S.)   *Tibbalds:* Lewis Theobald (1688-1744), editor, dramatist
and poet;   *Moore:* James Moore Smythe (1702-34), minor poet and
dramatist;   *Cibber:* Colley Cibber (1671-1757), dramatist and actor.
202 *Curl* is notoriously infamous for publishing the Lives, Letters, and
last Wills and Testaments of the Nobility and Ministers of State, as well
as of all the Rogues, who are hanged at *Tyburn*. He hath been in Custody
of the House of Lords, for publishing or forging the Letters of many
Peers; which made the Lords enter a Resolution in their Journal Book,
that no Life or Writings of any Lord should be published without the
Consent of the next Heir at Law, or Licence from their House. (S.)

Revive the Libels born to dye;
Which POPE must bear, as well as I.

Here shift the Scene, to represent   205
How those I love, my Death lament.
Poor POPE will grieve a Month; and GAY
A Week; and ARBUTHNOT a Day.

St. JOHN himself will scarce forbear,
To bite his Pen, and drop a Tear.   210
The rest will give a Shrug and cry,
I'm sorry; but we all must dye.
Indifference clad in Wisdom's Guise,
All Fortitude of Mind supplies:
For how can stony Bowels melt,   215
In those who never Pity felt;
When *We* are lash'd, *They* kiss the Rod;
Resigning to the Will of God.

The Fools, my Juniors by a Year,
Are tortur'd with Suspence and Fear.   220
Who wisely thought my Age a Screen,
When Death approach'd, to stand between:
The Screen remov'd, their Hearts are trembling,
They mourn for me without dissembling.

My female Friends, whose tender Hearts   225
Have better learn'd to act their Parts,
Receive the News in *doleful Dumps*,
' The Dean is dead, (*and what is Trumps?*)
' Then Lord have Mercy on his Soul.
' (Ladies I'll venture for the *Vole*.)   230
' Six Deans they say must bear the Pall.
' (I wish I knew what *King* to call.)
' Madam, your Husband will attend
' The Funeral of so good a Friend.
' No Madam, 'tis a shocking Sight,   235
' And he's engag'd To-morrow Night!
' My Lady *Club* wou'd take it ill
' If he should fail her at *Quadrill*.
' He lov'd the Dean. (*I lead a Heart*.)
' But dearest Friends, they say, must part.   240

230 *Vole:* term in quadrille, for winning all tricks. 238 *Quadrill:*
quadrille, fashionable 18th-century card game.

'His Time was come, he ran his Race;
'We hope he's in a better Place.'

    Why do we grieve that Friends should dye?
No Loss more easy to supply.
One Year is past; a different Scene;   245
No further mention of the Dean;
Who now, alas, no more is mist,
Than if he never did exist.
Where's now this Fav'rite of *Apollo*?
Departed; *and his Works must follow:*   250
Must undergo the common Fate;
His Kind of Wit is out of Date.
Some Country Squire to *Lintot* goes,
Enquires for SWIFT in Verse and Prose:
Says *Lintot*, ' I have heard the Name: 255
' He dy'd a Year ago.' The same.
He searcheth all his Shop in vain;
' Sir, you may find them in *Duck-lane*:
' I sent them with a Load of Books,
' Last *Monday* to the Pastry-cooks.   260
' To fancy they could live a Year!
' I find you're but a Stranger here.
' The Dean was famous in his Time;
' And had a Kind of Knack at Rhyme:
' His way of Writing now is past;   265
' The Town hath got a better Taste:
' I keep no antiquated Stuff;
' But, spick and span I have enough.
' Pray, do but give me leave to shew 'em,
' Here's *Colley Cibber*'s Birth-day Poem.   270
' This Ode you never yet have seen,
' By [*Stephen Duck*], upon the Queen.
' Then, here's a Letter finely penn'd
' Against the *Craftsman* and his Friend;
' It clearly shews that all Reflection   275
' On Ministers, is Disaffection.

---

249 *Apollo:* classical god of the sun, poetry, and music. 253 *Bernard Lintot*, a Bookseller in *London*. Vide Mr. Pope's Dunciad. (S.) *Lintot:* Barnaby Bernard Lintot (1675-1736). 258 A Place in *London* where old Books are sold. (S.) 272 *Stephen Duck:* self-educated countryman poet (1705-56). 274 *The Craftsman:* a journal in which Bolingbroke and Pulteney attacked Walpole.

'Next, here's Sir *Robert*'s Vindication,
'And Mr. *Henly*'s last Oration:
'The Hawkers have not got 'em yet,
'Your Honour please to buy a Set?   280

'Here's *Woolston*'s Tracts, the twelfth Edition;
''Tis read by ev'ry Politician:
'The Country Members, when in Town,
'To all their Boroughs send them down:
'You never met a Thing so smart;   285
'The Courtiers have them all by Heart:
'Those Maids of Honour (who can read)
'Are taught to use them for their Creed.
'The Rev'rend Author's good Intention,
'Hath been rewarded with a Pension: 290
'He doth an Honour to his Gown,
'By bravely running *Priest-craft* down:
'He shews, as sure as GOD's in *Gloc'ster*,
'That [JESUS] was a Grand Impostor:
'That all his Miracles were Cheats,   295
'Perform'd as Juglers do their Feats:
'The Church had never such a Writer:
'A Shame, he hath not got a Mitre!'

Suppose me dead; and then suppose
A Club assembled at the *Rose*;   300
Where from Discourse of this and that,
I grow the Subject of their Chat:
And, while they toss my Name about,
With Favour some, and some without;

277 *Walpole* hath a Set of Party Scriblers, who do nothing else but write in his Defence. (S.)   278 *Henly* is a Clergyman, who wanting both Merit and Luck to get Preferment, or even to keep his Curacy in the Established Church, formed a new Conventicle, which he calls an Oratory. There, at set Times, he delivereth strange Speeches compiled by himself and his Associates, who share the Profit with him: Every Hearer pays a Shilling each Day for Admittance. He is an absolute Dunce, but generally reputed crazy. (S.)   *Henly:* John Henley (1692-1756), eccentric preacher.   281 *Wolston* was a Clergyman, but for want of Bread, hath in several Treatises, in the most Blasphemous Manner, attempted to turn Our Saviour and his Miracles into Ridicule. He is much caressed by many great Courtiers, and by all the Infidels, and his Books read generally by the Court Ladies. (S.)   *Wolston:* Thomas Woolston (1670-1733), free-thinking clergyman.   300 *Rose:* the Rose Tavern, in Russell Street, Covent Garden; demolished 1776.

One quite indiff'rent in the Cause,   305
My Character impartial draws:

' The Dean, if we believe Report,
' Was never ill receiv'd at Court:
' As for his Works in Verse and Prose,
' I own my self no Judge of those: 310
' Nor, can I tell what Criticks thought 'em;
' But, this I know, all People bought 'em;
' As with a moral View design'd
' To cure the Vices of Mankind:
' His Vein, ironically grave,   315
' Expos'd the Fool, and lash'd the Knave:
' To steal a Hint was never known,
' But what he writ was all his own.

' He never thought an Honour done him,
' Because a Duke was proud to own him: 320
' Would rather slip aside, and chuse
' To talk with Wits in dirty Shoes:
' Despis'd the Fools with Stars and Garters,
' So often seen caressing *Chartres*:
' He never courted Men in Station,   325
' *Nor Persons had in Admiration;*
' Of no Man's Greatness was afraid,
' Because he sought for no Man's Aid.
' Though trusted long in great Affairs,
' He gave himself no haughty Airs: 330
' Without regarding private Ends,
' Spent all his Credit for his Friends:
' And only chose the Wise and Good;
' No Flatt'rer's; no Allies in Blood;
' But succour'd Virtue in Distress,   335
' And seldom fail'd of good Success;
' As Numbers in their Hearts must own,
' Who, but for him, had been unknown.

' With Princes kept a due Decorum,
' But never stood in Awe before 'em: 340
' He follow'd *David*'s Lesson just,
' *In Princes never put thy Trust.*
' And, would you make him truly sower;
' Provoke him with a *Slave in Power*:

341 *David's Lesson:* See *Psalm* cxlvi. 3.
A.L.P.   K

'The I[rish] S[enate], if you nam'd,   345
'With what Impatience he declaim'd!
'Fair LIBERTY was all his Cry;
'For her he stood prepar'd to die;
'For her he boldly stood alone;
'For her he oft expos'd his own.   350
'Two Kingdoms, just as Faction led,
'Had set a Price upon his Head;
'But, not a Traytor could be found,
'To sell him for Six Hundred Pound.

'Had he but spar'd his Tongue and Pen,   355
'He might have rose like other Men:
'But, Power was never in his Thought;
'And, Wealth he valu'd not a Groat:
'Ingratitude he often found,
'And pity'd those who meant the Wound: 360
'But, kept the Tenor of his Mind,
'To merit well of human Kind:
'Nor made a Sacrifice of those
'Who still were true, to please his Foes.
'He labour'd many a fruitless Hour   365
'To reconcile his Friends in Power;
'Saw Mischief by a Faction brewing,
'While they pursu'd each others Ruin.
'But, finding vain was all his Care,
'He left the Court in meer Despair.   370

351 In the Year 1713, the late Queen was prevailed with by an Address
of the House of Lords in *England*, to publish a Proclamation, promising
Three Hundred Pounds to discover the Author of a Pamphlet called,
The Publick Spirit of the Whigs; and in *Ireland*, in the Year 1724, my Lord
Carteret, at his first coming into the Government, was prevailed on to
issue a Proclamation for promising the like Reward of Three Hundred
Pounds, to any Person who could discover the Author of a Pamphlet
called, the *Drapier's Fourth Letter* &c. writ against that destructive Project
of coining Half-pence for *Ireland;* but in neither Kingdom was the Dean
discovered. (S.)   365 Queen Anne's Ministers fell to Variance from
the first Year after their Ministry began: *Harcourt* the Chancellor, and
Lord *Bolingbroke* the Secretary, were discontented with the Treasurer
Oxford, for his too much Mildness to the Whig Party; this Quarrel grew
higher every Day till the Queen's Death. The Dean who was the only
Person that endeavoured to reconcile them, found it impossible; and
thereupon retired to the Country about ten Weeks before that fatal
Event: Upon which he returned to his Deanry in *Dublin*, where for
many Years he was worried by the new People in Power, and had
Hundreds of Libels writ against him in *England*. (S.)

'And, oh! how short are human Schemes!
'Here ended all our golden Dreams.
'What St. JOHN's Skill in State Affairs,
'What ORMOND's *Valour*, OXFORD's Cares,
'To save their sinking Country lent,   375
'Was all destroy'd by one Event.
'Too soon that precious Life was ended,
'On which alone our Weal depended.
'When up a dangerous Faction starts,
'With Wrath and Vengeance in their Hearts;   380
'*By solemn League and Cov'nant bound,*
'To ruin, slaughter, and confound;
'To turn Religion to a Fable,
'And make the Government a *Babel*:
'Pervert the Laws, disgrace the Gown,   385
'Corrupt the [Senate], rob the [Crown];
'To sacrifice old [England's] Glory,
'And make her infamous in Story.
'When such a Tempest shook the Land,
'How could unguarded Virtue stand?   390

'With Horror, Grief, Despair the Dean
'Beheld the dire destructive Scene:
'His friends in Exile, or the Tower,
'Himself within the Frown of Power;
'Pursu'd by base envenom'd Pens,   395
'Far to the Land of Sl[ave]s and Fens;
'A servile Race in Folly nurs'd,
'Who truckle most, when treated worst.

374 *Ormond:* James Butler, Duke of Ormonde (1665-1745); *Oxford:*
Robert Harley, Earl of Oxford (1661-1724).   377 In the Height of the
Quarrel between the Ministers, the Queen died. (S.)   379 Upon
Queen Anne's Death the Whig Faction was restored to Power, which
they exercised with the utmost Rage and Revenge; impeached and
banished the Chief Leaders of the Church Party, and stripped all their
Adherents of what Employments they had, after which, *England* was
never known to make so mean a Figure in *Europe:* The greatest pre-
ferments in the Church in both Kingdoms were given to the most
ignorant Men; Fanaticks were publicly caress'd; *Ireland* utterly ruin'd
and enslav'd; only great Ministers heaping up Millions: And so affairs
continue till this present 3d. day of May 1732, and are likely to go on in
the same Manner. (S.)   394 Upon the Queen's Death, the Dean re-
turned to live in *Dublin*, at his Deanry-House; Numberless Libels were
writ against him in *England*, as a Jacobite; he was insulted in the Street,
and at Nights he was forced to be attended by his Servants armed. (S.)
396 The Land of Slaves and Fens, is *Ireland*. (S.)

‘ By Innocence and Resolution,
‘ He bore continual Persecution;   400
‘ While Numbers to Preferment rose;
‘ Whose Merits were, to be his Foes.
‘ When, *ev’n his own familiar Friends*
‘ Intent upon their private Ends;
‘ Like Renegadoes now he feels,   405
‘ *Against him lifting up their Heels.*

‘ The Dean did by his Pen defeat
‘ An infamous destructive Cheat.
‘ Taught Fools their Int’rest how to know;
‘ And gave them Arms to ward the Blow.   410
‘ Envy hath own’d it was his doing,
‘ To save that helpless Land from Ruin,
‘ While they who at the Steerage stood,
‘ And reapt the Profit, sought his Blood.

‘ To save them from their evil Fate,   415
‘ In him was held a Crime of State.
‘ A wicked Monster on the Bench,
‘ Whose Fury Blood could never quench;
‘ As vile and profligate a Villain,
‘ As modern *Scroggs*, or old *Tressilian*;   420
‘ Who long all Justice had discarded,
‘ *Nor fear’d he GOD, nor Man regarded*;

408 One *Wood*, a Hardware-man from *England*, had a Patent for coining
Copper Half-pence for Ireland, the Sum of 108,000 l. which in the Con-
sequence, must leave that Kingdom without Gold or Silver (See
Drapier’s Letters). (S.) *An infamous, etc.*: William Wood (1671-1730),
English businessman and iron manufacturer. 417 One *Whitshed* was
then Chief Justice: He had some years before prosecuted a Printer for a
Pamphlet writ by the Dean, to persuade the People of *Ireland* to wear
their own Manufactures. *Whitshed* sent the Jury down eleven Times, and
kept them nine Hours, until they were forced to bring in a special Ver-
dict. He sat as Judge afterwards on the Trial of the Printer of the
Drapier’s Fourth Letter; but the Jury, against all he could say or swear,
threw out the Bill: All the Kingdom took the *Drapier’s* Part, except the
Courtiers, or those who expected Places. The *Drapier* was celebrated in
many Poems and Pamphlets: His sign was set up in most of the Streets
of *Dublin* (where many of them still continue) and in several Country
Towns. (S.) *A wicked, etc.*: William Whitshed (1679-1727). 420
Scroggs was Chief Justice under King *Charles* the Second: His Judgement
always varied in State Tryals, according to Directions from Court.
Tressilian was a wicked Judge, hanged above three hundred years ago.
(S.) *Scroggs:* Sir William Scroggs (1623?-83); *Tressilian:* Sir Robert
Tresilian (d.1388).

' Vow'd on the Dean his Rage to vent,
' And make him of his Zeal repent;
' But Heav'n his Innocence defends,   425
' The grateful People stand his Friends:
' Not Strains of Law, nor Judge's Frown,
' Nor Topicks brought to please the C[rown],
' Nor Witness hir'd, nor Jury pick'd,
' Prevail to bring him in convict.   430

' In Exile with a steady Heart,
' He spent his Life's declining Part;
' Where Folly, Pride, and Faction sway,
' Remote from St. JOHN, POPE, and GAY.

' His Friendship there to few confin'd,   435
' Were always of the midling Kind:
' No Fools of Rank, a mungril Breed,
' Who fain would pass for [Lords] indeed:
' Where Titles give no Right or Power,
' And P[eerage] is a wither'd Flower,   440
' He would have held it a Disgrace,
' If such a Wretch had known his Face.
' On Rural Squires, that Kingdom's Bane,
' He vented oft his Wrath in vain:
' [Biennial] Squires, to Market brought;   445
' Who sell their Souls and [Votes] for Naught;
' The [Country stript] go joyful back,
' To [rob] the Church, their Tenants rack,
' Go snacks with [Thieves and Rapparees],
' And, keep the Peace, to pick up Fees: 450

431 In *Ireland*, which he had Reason to call a Place of Exile; to which Country nothing could have driven him, but the Queen's Death, who had determined to fix him in *England*, in Spight of the Duchess of *Somerset*, &c. (S.) 434 *Henry St. John*, Lord Viscount *Bolingbroke*, mentioned before. (S.) 435 In *Ireland* the Dean was not acquainted with one single Lord Spiritual or Temporal. He only conversed with private Gentlemen of the Clergy or Laity, and but a small Number of either. (S.) 439 The Peers of *Ireland* lost great Part of their Jurisdiction by one single Act, and tamely submitted to the infamous Mark of Slavery without the least Resentment or Remonstrance. (S.) 445 The Parliament (as they call it) in *Ireland* meet but once in two Years, and after giving five times more than they can afford, return home to reimburse themselves by all Country Jobs and Oppressions, of which some few only are here mentioned. (S.) 449 The Highway-men in *Ireland* are, since the Late Wars there, usually called Rapparees, which was a Name given to those *Irish* soldiers who in small Parties used, at that Time, to plunder the Protestants. (S.)

' In every Job to have a Share,
' A Jayl or [Barrack] to repair;
' And turn the [Tax] for publick Roads
' Commodious to their own Abodes.

 ' Perhaps I may allow, the Dean   455
' Had too much Satyr in his Vein;
' And seem'd determin'd not to starve it,
' Because no Age could more deserve it.
' Yet, Malice never was his Aim;
' He lash'd the Vice but spar'd the Name.   460
' No Individual could resent,
' Where Thousands equally were meant.
' His Satyr points at no Defect,
' But what all Mortals may correct;
' For he abhorr'd that senseless Tribe,   465
' Who call it Humour when they jibe:
' He spar'd a Hump or crooked Nose,
' Whose Owners set not up for Beaux.
' True genuine Dulness mov'd his Pity,
' Unless it offer'd to be witty.   470
' Those, who their Ignorance confess'd,
' He ne'er offended with a Jest;
' But laugh'd to hear an Idiot quote,
' A Verse from *Horace*, learn'd by Rote.

 ' He knew an hundred pleasant Stories,   475
' With all the Turns of *Whigs* and *Tories*:
' Was chearful to his dying Day,
' And Friends would let him have his Way.

 ' He gave the little Wealth he had,
' To build a House for Fools and Mad: 480
' And shew'd by one satyric Touch,
' No Nation wanted it so much:
' That Kingdom he hath left his Debtor,
' I wish it soon may have a Better.'

---

452 The Army in *Ireland* is lodged in Barracks, the building and re-
pairing whereof, and other Charges, have cost a prodigious Sum to that
unhappy Kingdom. (S.) 478 *And:* perhaps meaning 'if'. 483
Meaning *Ireland*, where he now lives, and probably may die. (S.)

Alexander Pope

1688—1744

THE RAPE OF THE LOCK

AN HEROI-COMICAL POEM

Nolueram, Belinda, tuos violare capillos,
Sed juvat hoc precibus me tribuisse tuis.
MARTIAL

To Mrs. ARABELLA FERMOR*

MADAM,

IT will be in vain to deny that I have some Regard for this Piece, since I Dedicate it to You. Yet You may bear me Witness, it was intended only to divert a few young Ladies, who have good Sense and good Humour enough, to laugh not only at their Sex's little unguarded Follies, but at their own. But as it was communicated with the Air of a Secret, it soon found its Way into the World. An imperfect Copy having been offer'd to a Bookseller, You had the Good-Nature for my Sake to consent to the Publication of one more correct: This I was forc'd to before I had executed half my Design, for the *Machinery* was entirely wanting to compleat it.

The *Machinery*, Madam, is a Term invented by the Criticks, to signify that Part which the Deities, Angels, or Dæmons are made to act in a Poem: For the ancient Poets are in one respect like many modern Ladies; Let an Action be never so trivial in itself, they always make it appear of the utmost Importance. These Machines I determin'd to raise on a very new and odd Foundation, the *Rosicrucian*† Doctrine of Spirits.

I know how disagreeable it is to make use of hard Words before a Lady; but 'tis so much the Concern of a Poet to have his Works understood, and particularly by your Sex, that You must give me leave to explain two or three difficult Terms.

The *Rosicrucians* are a people I must bring You acquainted with. The best Account I know of them is in a French Book call'd *Le Comte de Gabalis*††, which both in its Title and Size is so like a *Novel*, that many of the Fair Sex have read it for one by Mistake. According to these Gentlemen, the four Elements are inhabited by Spirits, which they call *Sylphs, Gnomes, Nymphs,* and *Salamanders.* The *Gnomes*, or Dæmons of Earth, delight in Mischief; but the *Sylphs,* whose Habitation is in the Air,

---

* (*c.* 1688/90-1738); married Francis Perkins 1714/15; probably known personally to Pope.   † *Rosicrucian:* 'secret' mystical doctrine related to alchemy and foreshadowing theosophy.   †† *Le Comte de Gabalis:* by the Abbé de Montfaucon de Villars (1670; English translation 1680).

are the best-condition'd Creatures imaginable. For they say, any
Mortals may enjoy the most intimate Familiarities with these gentle
Spirits, upon a Condition very easy to all true *Adepts*, an inviolate
Preservation of Chastity.

As to the following Canto's, all the Passages of them are as Fabulous,
as the Vision at the Beginning, or the Transformation at the End;
(except the Loss of your Hair, which I always mention with Reverence).
The Human Persons are as Fictitious as the Airy ones; and the Character
of *Belinda*, as it is now manag'd, resembles You in nothing but in Beauty.

If this Poem had as many Graces as there are in Your Person, or in
Your Mind, yet I could never hope it should pass thro' the World half
so Uncensur'd as You have done. But let its Fortune be what it will,
mine is happy enough, to have given me this Occasion of assuring You
that I am, with the truest Esteem, MADAM,

Your Most Obedient, Humble Servant,

A. POPE.

CANTO I

What dire Offence from am'rous Causes springs,
What mighty Contests rise from trivial Things,
I sing—This verse to CARYLL, Muse! is due:
This, ev'n *Belinda* may vouchsafe to view:
Slight is the Subject, but not so the Praise, 5
If She inspire, and He approve my Lays.
  Say what strange Motive, Goddess! cou'd compel
A well-bred *Lord* t' assault a gentle *Belle*?
O say what stranger Cause, yet unexplor'd,
Cou'd make a gentle *Belle* reject a *Lord*? 10
In Tasks so bold, can Little Men engage,
And in soft Bosoms dwells such mighty Rage?
  Sol thro' white Curtains shot a tim'rous Ray,
And op'd those Eyes that must eclipse the Day;
Now Lap-dogs give themselves the rowzing Shake, 15
And sleepless Lovers, just at Twelve, awake:

1-3 Pope imitates the epic opening: this establishes at once the tone of
his 'heroi-comical poem'. 3 *Caryll:* John Caryll (1666?-1736), a close
friend of Pope. 5 *Slight is the Subject:* Lord Petre (see line 8) cut off a
lock of Arabella Fermor's hair in 1711, and Caryll asked Pope to write a
poem which might 'make a jest of it' and dissolve the coolness that had
arisen between the two families. Pope's first brief version of the poem
was published 1712, and the present complete version 1714. The
Catholic families of Fermors, Carylls, and Petres were interconnected.
8 *A well-bred Lord:* Robert, Lord Petre (1690-1713); married Catherine
Warmsley 1712; not known personally to Pope.

Thrice rung the Bell, the Slipper knock'd the Ground,
And the press'd Watch return'd a silver Sound.
Belinda still her downy Pillow prest,
Her guardian SYLPH prolong'd the balmy Rest: 20
'Twas He had summon'd to her silent Bed
The Morning-Dream that hover'd o'er her Head;
A Youth more glitt'ring than a *Birth-night Beau*,
(That ev'n in Slumber caus'd her Cheek to glow)
Seem'd to her Ear his winning Lips to lay,   25
And thus in Whispers said, or seem'd to say.
    Fairest of Mortals, thou distinguish'd Care
Of thousand bright Inhabitants of Air!
If e'er one Vision touch'd thy infant Thought,
Of all the Nurse and all the Priest have taught;   30
Of airy Elves by Moonlight Shadows seen,
The silver Token, and the circled Green,
Or Virgins visited by Angel-Pow'rs,
With Golden Crowns and Wreaths of heav'nly Flowers;
Hear and believe! thy own Importance know,   35
Nor bound thy narrow Views to Things below.
Some secret Truths from Learned Pride conceal'd,
To Maids alone and Children are reveal'd:
What tho' no Credit doubting Wits may give?
The Fair and Innocent shall still believe.   40
Know then, unnumber'd Spirits round thee fly,
The light *Militia* of the lower Sky:
These, tho' unseen, are ever on the Wing,
Hang o'er the *Box*, and hover round the *Ring*.
Think what an Equipage thou hast in Air,   45
And view with scorn *Two Pages* and a *Chair*.
As now your own, our Beings were of old,
And once inclos'd in Woman's beauteous Mold;
Thence, by a soft Transition, we repair
From earthly Vehicles to these of Air.   50
Think not, when Woman's transient Breath is fled,
That all her Vanities at once are dead:
Succeeding Vanities she still regards,
And tho' she plays no more, o'erlooks the Cards.

17 *The Slipper, etc.:* i.e. to fetch her maid, who presumably failed to answer either this summons or the bell.   18 *The press'd Watch:* a watch which chimed when pressed.   23 *Birth-night Beau:* guest at royal birthday celebrations.   44 *The Ring:* fashionable drive for coaches in Hyde Park.   45 *Equipage:* coach, horses, and footmen.   46 *Chair:* sedan chair.

Her Joy in gilded Chariots, when alive,   55
And Love of *Ombre*, after Death survive.
For when the Fair in all their Pride expire,
To their first Elements their Souls retire:
The Sprights of fiery Termagants in Flame
Mount up, and take a *Salamander*'s name.   60
Soft yielding Minds to Water glide away,
And sip with *Nymphs*, their Elemental Tea.
The graver Prude sinks downward to a *Gnome*,
In search of Mischief still on Earth to roam.
The light Coquettes in *Sylphs* aloft repair,   65
And sport and flutter in the Fields of Air.
    Know farther yet; Whoever fair and chaste
Rejects Mankind, is by some *Sylph* embrac'd:
For Spirits, freed from mortal Laws, with ease
Assume what Sexes and what Shapes they please.   70
What guards the Purity of melting Maids,
In Courtly Balls, and Midnight Masquerades,
Safe from the treach'rous Friend, the daring Spark,
The Glance by Day, the Whisper in the Dark;
When kind Occasion prompts their warm Desires,   75
When Musick softens, and when Dancing fires?
'Tis but their *Sylph*, the wise Celestials know,
Tho' *Honour* is the Word with Men below.
    Some Nymphs there are, too conscious of their Face,
For Life predestin'd to the *Gnomes*' Embrace.   80
These swell their Prospects and exalt their Pride,
When Offers are disdain'd, and Love deny'd.
Then gay Ideas crowd the vacant Brain;
While Peers and Dukes, and all their sweeping Train,
And Garters, Stars, and Coronets appear,   85
And in soft sounds, *Your Grace* salutes their Ear.
'Tis these that early taint the Female Soul,
Instruct the Eyes of young *Coquettes* to roll,
Teach Infant-Cheeks a bidden Blush to know,
And little Hearts to flutter at a *Beau*.   90
    Oft when the World imagine Women stray,
The *Sylphs* thro' mystic Mazes guide their Way,
Thro' all the giddy Circle they pursue,
And old Impertinence expel by new.

56 *Ombre:* elaborate card game of Spanish origin, then at the height of
its popularity. 58 *First Elements:* dominant characteristics. 59
Termagants: scolding, bad-tempered women. 60 Salamanders were
supposed to live in fire. 89 *Bidden:* rising to the bait of interested
inquiry. 94 *Impertinence:* trifling.

What tender Maid but must a Victim fall   95
To one Man's Treat, but for another's Ball?
When *Florio* speaks, what Virgin could withstand,
If gentle *Damon* did not squeeze her Hand?
With varying Vanities, from ev'ry Part,
They shift the moving Toyshop of their Heart;   100
Where Wigs with Wigs, with Sword-knots Sword-knots strive,
Beaux banish Beaux, and Coaches Coaches drive.
This erring Mortals Levity may call;
Oh blind to Truth! the *Sylphs* contrive it all.

Of these am I, who thy Protection claim,   105
A watchful Spright, and *Ariel* is my Name.
Late, as I rang'd the Crystal Wilds of Air,
In the clear Mirror of thy ruling *Star*
I saw, alas! some dread Event impend,
Ere to the Main this Morning Sun descend,   110
But Heav'n reveals not what, or how, or where:
Warn'd by thy *Sylph*, oh Pious Maid beware!
This to disclose is all thy Guardian can.
Beware of all, but most beware of Man!

He said; when *Shock*, who thought she slept too long,   115
Leap'd up, and wak'd his Mistress with his Tongue.
'Twas then, *Belinda*, if Report say true,
Thy Eyes first open'd on a *Billet-doux*;
Wounds, Charms, and *Ardors*, were no sooner read,
But all the Vision vanish'd from thy Head.   120

And now, unveil'd, the *Toilet* stands display'd,
Each Silver Vase in mystic Order laid.
First, rob'd in White, the Nymph intent adores
With Head uncover'd, the *Cosmetic* Pow'rs.
A heav'nly Image in the Glass appears,   125
To that she bends, to that her Eyes she rears;
Th' inferior Priestess, at her Altar's side,
Trembling, begins the sacred Rites of Pride.
Unnumber'd Treasures ope at once, and here
The various Off'rings of the World appear;   130
From each she nicely culls with curious Toil,
And decks the Goddess with the glitt'ring Spoil.
This Casket *India's* glowing Gems unlocks,

96 *Treat:* party (with food and drink). 101 *Sword-knots:* ribbons
fixed on sword-hilts. 105 *Thy Protection claim:* claim to be your pro-
tector. 115 *Shock:* the shaggy-haired shough, popular (when trimmed)
as a lap-dog. 116 Belinda opens her eyes for the second time. 118 i.e.
'opened on their first love-letter.' The 'report' of line 117 was of course
untrue.

And all *Arabia* breathes from yonder Box.
The Tortoise here and Elephant unite,   135
Transform'd to *Combs*, the speckled and the white.
Here Files of Pins extend their shining Rows,
Puffs, Powders, Patches, Bibles, Billet-doux.
Now awful Beauty puts on all its Arms;
The Fair each moment rises in her Charms,   140
Repairs her Smiles, awakens ev'ry Grace,
And calls forth all the Wonders of her Face;
Sees by Degrees a purer Blush arise,
And keener Lightnings quicken in her Eyes.
The busy *Sylphs* surround their darling Care;   145
These set the Head, and those divide the Hair,
Some fold the Sleeve, whilst others plait the Gown;
And *Betty*'s prais'd for Labours not her own.

CANTO II

Not with more Glories, in th' Etherial Plain,
The Sun first rises o'er the purpled Main,
Than issuing forth, the Rival of his Beams
Launch'd on the Bosom of the Silver *Thames*.
Fair Nymphs, and well-drest Youths around her shone,   5
But ev'ry Eye was fix'd on her alone.
On her white Breast a sparkling *Cross* she wore,
Which *Jews* might kiss, and Infidels adore.
Her lively Looks a sprightly Mind disclose,
Quick as her Eyes, and as unfix'd as those: 10
Favours to none, to all she Smiles extends,
Oft she rejects, but never once offends.
Bright as the Sun, her Eyes the Gazers strike,
And, like the Sun, they shine on all alike.
Yet graceful Ease, and Sweetness void of Pride,   15
Might hide her Faults, if *Belles* had Faults to hide:
If to her share some Female Errors fall,
Look on her Face, and you'll forget 'em all.
    This Nymph, to the Destruction of Mankind,
Nourish'd two Locks, which graceful hung behind   20
In equal Curls, and well conspir'd to deck
With shining Ringlets the smooth Iv'ry Neck.
Love in these Labyrinths his Slaves detains,
And mighty Hearts are held in slender Chains.

144 Belinda uses belladonna drops, or applies eye-shadow.

With hairy Sprindges we the Birds betray,   25
Slight Lines of Hair surprize the Finny Prey,
Fair Tresses Man's Imperial Race insnare,
And Beauty draws us with a single Hair.
  Th' Advent'rous *Baron* the bright Locks admir'd,
He saw, he wish'd, and to the Prize aspir'd: 30
Resolv'd to win, he meditates the way,
By Force to ravish, or by Fraud betray;
For when Success a Lover's Toil attends,
Few ask, if Fraud or Force attain'd his Ends.
  For this, ere *Phœbus* rose, he had implor'd   35
Propitious Heav'n, and ev'ry Pow'r ador'd,
But chiefly *Love*—to *Love* an Altar built,
Of twelve vast *French* Romances, neatly gilt.
There lay three Garters, half a Pair of Gloves;
And all the Trophies of his former Loves.   40
With tender *Billet-doux* he lights the Pyre,
And breathes three am'rous Sighs to raise the Fire.
Then prostrate falls, and begs with ardent Eyes
Soon to obtain, and long possess the Prize:
The Pow'rs gave Ear, and granted half his Pray'r,   45
The rest, the Winds dispers'd in empty Air.
  But now secure the painted Vessel glides,
The Sun-beams trembling on the floating Tydes:
While melting Musick steals upon the Sky,
And soften'd Sounds along the Waters die.   50
Smooth flow the Waves, the Zephyrs gently play,
Belinda smil'd, and all the World was gay.
All but the *Sylph*—With careful thoughts opprest,
Th' impending Woe sate heavy on his Breast.
He summons strait his Denizens of Air;   55
The lucid Squadrons round the Sails repair:
Soft o'er the Shrouds Aërial Whispers breathe,
That seem'd but *Zephyrs* to the Train beneath.
Some to the Sun their Insect-Wings unfold,
Waft on the Breeze, or sink in Clouds of Gold;   60
Transparent Forms, too fine for mortal Sight,
Their fluid Bodies half dissolv'd in Light,
Loose to the Wind their airy Garments flew,
Thin glitt'ring Textures of the filmy Dew,

25 *Sprindges:* snares. 29 *Baron:* Lord Petre. 35 *Phœbus:* Greek sun-
god. 39-40 This fetishism might suggest a roué; the Baron, only
twenty-one, is presumably one of the 'daring Sparks' of line 73; but he
took no offence at the poem. 53 *Careful:* anxious. 56 *Lucid:* trans-
lucent. 57 *Shrouds:* rigging.

Dipt in the richest Tincture of the Skies,   65
Where Light disports in ever-mingling Dyes,
While ev'ry Beam new transient Colours flings,
Colours that change whene'er they wave their Wings.
Amid the Circle, on the gilded Mast,
Superior by the Head, was *Ariel* plac'd;   70
His Purple Pinions op'ning to the Sun,
He rais'd his Azure Wand, and thus begun.
　　Ye *Sylphs* and *Sylphids*, to your Chief give Ear!
Fays, Fairies, Genii, Elves, and *Dæmons,* hear!
Ye know the Spheres and various Tasks assign'd,   75
By Laws Eternal, to th' Aërial Kind.
Some in the Fields of purest *Æther* play,
And bask and whiten in the Blaze of Day.
Some guide the Course of wand'ring Orbs on high,
Or roll the Planets thro' the boundless Sky.   80
Some less refin'd, beneath the Moon's pale Light
Pursue the Stars that shoot athwart the Night,
Or suck the Mists in grosser Air Below,
Or dip their Pinions in the painted Bow,
Or brew fierce Tempests on the wintry Main,   85
Or o'er the Glebe distil the kindly Rain.
Others on Earth o'er human Race preside,
Watch all their Ways, and all their Actions guide:
Of these the Chief the Care of Nations own,
And guard with Arms Divine the *British Throne.*   90
　　Our humbler Province is to tend the Fair,
Not a less pleasing, tho' less glorious Care:
To save the Powder from too rude a Gale,
Nor let th' imprison'd Essences exhale;
To draw fresh Colours from the vernal Flow'rs;   95
To steal from Rainbows e'er they drop in Show'rs
A brighter Wash; to curl their waving Hairs,
Assist their Blushes, and inspire their Airs;
Nay oft, in Dreams, Invention we bestow,
To change a *Flounce,* or add a *Furbelow.*   100
　　This Day, black Omens threat the brightest Fair
That e'er deserv'd a watchful Spirit's Care;
Some dire Disaster, or by Force, or Slight;
But what, or where, the Fates have wrapt in Night.
Whether the Nymph shall break *Diana*'s law,   105
Or some frail *China* Jar receive a Flaw;

73 *Sylphids:* female sylphs (in *Le Comte de Gabalis*).   93 *Gale:* breeze.
100 *Furbelow:* pleated border on gown or petticoat.   103 *Or . . . or:*
either . . . or.   105 *Diana's law:* chastity.

Or stain her Honour, or her new Brocade;
Forget her Pray'rs, or miss a Masquerade;
Or lose her Heart, or Necklace, at a Ball;
Or whether Heav'n has doom'd that *Shock* must fall.   110
Haste then ye Spirits! to your Charge repair:
The flutt'ring Fan be *Zephyretta*'s Care;
The Drops to thee, *Brillante*, we consign;
And, *Momentilla*, let the Watch be thine;
Do thou, *Crispissa*, tend her fav'rite Lock;   115
Ariel himself shall be the Guard of Shock.
   To Fifty chosen *Sylphs*, of special Note,
We trust th' important Charge, the *Petticoat*:
Oft have we known that sev'n-fold Fence to fail,
Tho' stiff with Hoops, and arm'd with Ribs of Whale;   120
Form a strong Line about the Silver Bound,
And guard the wide Circumference around.
   Whatever Spirit, careless of his Charge,
His Post neglects, or leaves the Fair at large,
Shall feel sharp Vengeance soon o'ertake his Sins,   125
Be stopp'd in *Vials*, or transfix'd with Pins;
Or plung'd in Lakes of bitter *Washes* lie,
Or wedg'd whole Ages in a *Bodkin*'s eye:
Gums and *Pomatums* shall his Flight restrain,
While clogg'd he beats his silken Wings in vain;   130
Or Alom-*Styptics* with contracting Pow'r
Shrink his thin Essence like a rivell'd Flow'r:
Or, as *Ixion* fix'd, the Wretch shall feel
The giddy Motion of the whirling Mill,
In Fumes of burning Chocolate shall glow,   135
And tremble at the Sea that froths below!
   He spoke; the Spirits from the Sails descend;
Some, Orb in Orb, around the Nymph extend;
Some thrid the mazy Ringlets of her Hair;
Some hang upon the Pendants of her Ear;   140
With beating Hearts the dire Event they wait,
Anxious, and trembling for the Birth of Fate.

---

113 *Drops:* diamond ear-pendants.   127 *Bitter Washes:* liquid cos-
metic preparations.   128 *Bodkin:*   blunt-pointed needle.   129 *Pom-
atums:* pomades, scented ointments.   132 *Rivell'd:* shrivelled, wrinkled.
133 *Ixion:* in Greek mythology, was tortured on a revolving wheel.
134 *Mill:* chocolate-mill, for grinding the roasted cacao-seeds.   139
Thrid: thread.

CANTO III

Close by those Meads for ever crown'd with Flow'rs,
Where *Thames* with Pride surveys his rising Tow'rs,
There stands a Structure of Majestic Frame,
Which from the neighb'ring *Hampton* takes its Name.
Here *Britain*'s Statesmen oft the Fall foredoom   5
Of Foreign Tyrants, and of Nymphs at home;
Here Thou, great ANNA! whom three Realms obey,
Dost sometimes Counsel take—and sometimes *Tea.*
   Hither the Heroes and the Nymphs resort,
To taste awhile the Pleasures of a Court;   10
In various Talk th' instructive hours they past,
Who gave the *Ball,* or paid the *Visit* last:
One speaks the Glory of the *British Queen,*
And one describes a charming *Indian Screen;*
A third interprets Motions, Looks, and Eyes;   15
At ev'ry Word a Reputation dies.
Snuff, or the *Fan,* supply each Pause of Chat,
With singing, laughing, ogling, *and all that.*
   Mean while, declining from the Noon of Day,
The Sun obliquely shoots his burning Ray;   20
The hungry Judges soon the Sentence sign,
And Wretches hang that Jury-men may Dine;
The Merchant from th' *Exchange* returns in Peace,
And the long Labours of the *Toilet* cease.
Belinda now, whom Thirst of Fame invites,   25
Burns to encounter two advent'rous Knights,
At *Ombre* singly to decide their Doom;
And swells her Breast with Conquests yet to come.
Straight the three Bands prepare in Arms to join,
Each Band the number of the Sacred Nine.   30
Soon as she spreads her Hand, th' Aëriel Guard
Descend, and sit on each important Card:
First *Ariel* perch'd upon a *Matadore,*
Then each, according to the Rank they bore;
For *Sylphs,* yet mindful of their ancient Race,   35
Are, as when Women, wondrous fond of Place.

3-4 Hampton Court Palace, 15 miles south-west of London.   7 *Anna:*
Queen Anne (1665-1714);   *three Realms:*   England, Wales, Scotland.
25-28 Belinda acts as the principal player or 'ombre'.   30 Each player
has nine cards.   33 *Matadore:* chief trump card (Ace of Spades, Ace of
Clubs, deuce of black trump suit, seven of red).

Behold, four *Kings* in Majesty rever'd,
With hoary Whiskers and a forky Beard;
And four fair *Queens* whose hands sustain a Flow'r,
Th' expressive Emblem of their softer Pow'r;   40
Four *Knaves* in Garbs succinct, a trusty Band,
Caps on their Heads, and Halberds in their Hand;
And Particolour'd Troops, a shining Train,
Draw forth to Combat on the velvet Plain.
  The skilful Nymph reviews her Force with Care: 45
Let Spades be Trumps! she said, and Trumps they were.
  Now move to War her sable *Matadores*,
In Show like Leaders of the swarthy *Moors.*
Spadillio first, unconquerable Lord!
Led off two captive Trumps, and swept the Board.   50
As many more *Manillio* forc'd to yield,
And march'd a Victor from the verdant Field.
Him *Basto* follow'd, but his Fate more hard
Gain'd but one Trump and one *Plebeian* Card.
With his broad Sabre next, a Chief in Years,   55
The hoary Majesty of *Spades* appears,
Puts forth one manly leg, to sight reveal'd,
The rest his many-colour'd Robe conceal'd.
The Rebel-*Knave*, who dares his Prince engage,
Proves the just Victim of his royal Rage.   60
Ev'n mighty *Pam*, that Kings and Queens o'erthrew,
And mow'd down Armies in the fights of *Lu*,
Sad Chance of War! now destitute of Aid,
Falls undistinguish'd by the victor *Spade!*
  Thus far both Armies to *Belinda* yield;   65
Now to the *Baron* Fate inclines the Field.
His warlike *Amazon* her Host invades,
Th' imperial Consort of the Crown of *Spades.*
The *Club*'s black Tyrant first her Victim dy'd,
Spite of his haughty Mien, and barb'rous Pride: 70
What boots the regal Circle on his Head,
His giant Limbs, in State unwieldy spread;

---

38 *Whiskers:* moustache. 41 *Succinct:* short. 42 *Halberds:* weapons like combined spear and battle-axe. 49 *Spadillio:* spadille, the highest trump: the Ace of Spades. 51 *Manillio:* manille, the second highest trump: the deuce of trumps when trumps are black (as here), the seven when they are red. 53 *Basto:* the third trump: the Ace of Clubs. 61 *Pam:* In the game of five-card loo, the Jack of Clubs was called Pam and was the highest card. 62 *Lu:* round game played with three or five cards.

That long behind he trails his pompous Robe,
And of all Monarchs only grasps the Globe?
The *Baron* now his *Diamonds* pours apace; 75
Th' embroider'd *King* who shows but half his Face,
And his refulgent *Queen*, with Pow'rs combin'd,
Of broken Troops an easy Conquest find.
Clubs, Diamonds, Hearts, in wild Disorder seen,
With Throngs promiscuous strow the level Green. 80
Thus when dispers'd a routed Army runs,
Of *Asia*'s Troops, and *Africk*'s sable Sons,
With like Confusion different Nations fly,
Of various Habit, and of various Dye,
The pierc'd Battalions dis-united fall, 85
In Heaps on Heaps; one Fate o'erwhelms them all.
The *Knave* of *Diamonds* tries his wily Arts,
And wins (oh shameful Chance!) the *Queen* of *Hearts*.
At this, the Blood the Virgin's Cheek forsook,
A livid Paleness spreads o'er all her Look; 90
She sees, and trembles at th' approaching Ill,
Just in the Jaws of Ruin, and *Codille*.
And now, (as oft in some distemper'd State)
On one nice *Trick* depends the gen'ral Fate.
An *Ace* of *Hearts* steps forth: The *King* unseen 95
Lurk'd in her Hand, and mourn'd his captive *Queen*:
He springs to Vengeance with an eager pace,
And falls like Thunder on the prostrate *Ace*.
The Nymph exulting fills with Shouts the Sky;
The Walls, the Woods, and long Canals reply. 100
Oh thoughtless Mortals! ever blind to Fate,
Too soon dejected, and too soon elate!
Sudden, these Honours shall be snatch'd away,
And curs'd for ever this Victorious Day.

For lo! the Board with Cups and Spoons is crown'd, 105
The Berries crackle, and the Mill turns round;
On shining Altars of *Japan* they raise
The silver Lamp; the fiery Spirits blaze:
From silver Spouts the grateful Liquors glide,
While *China*'s Earth receives the smoking Tyde: 110
At once they gratify their Scent and Taste,
And frequent Cups prolong the rich Repast.

92 *Codille:* defeat of the main player by an opponent. Belinda, though
left with the King of Hearts, fears she may not be able to follow the
Baron's suit. 95-98 When red was not trump, a red King took pre-
cedence over a red Ace. 106 The coffee beans are roasted and ground.
107 *Shining Altars of Japan:* lacquered tables. 109 *Grateful:* pleasant.

Strait hover round the Fair her Airy Band;
Some, as she sipp'd, the fuming Liquor fann'd,
Some o'er her Lap their careful Plumes display'd,   115
Trembling, and conscious of the rich Brocade.
Coffee, (which makes the Politician wise,
And see thro' all things with his half-shut Eyes)
Sent up in Vapours to the *Baron*'s Brain
New Stratagems, the radiant Lock to gain.   120
Ah cease rash Youth! desist ere 'tis too late,
Fear the just Gods, and think of *Scylla*'s Fate!
Chang'd to a Bird, and sent to flit in Air,
She dearly pays for *Nisus*' injur'd Hair!
But when to Mischief Mortals bend their Will,   125
How soon they find fit Instruments of Ill!
Just then, *Clarissa* drew with tempting Grace
A two-edg'd Weapon from her shining Case:
So Ladies in Romance assist their Knight,
Present the Spear, and arm him for the Fight.   130
He takes the Gift with rev'rence, and extends
The little Engine on his Fingers' Ends;
This just behind *Belinda*'s Neck he spread,
As o'er the fragrant Steams she bends her Head.
Swift to the Lock a thousand Sprights repair,   135
A thousand Wings, by turns, blow back the Hair;
And thrice they twitch'd the Diamond in her Ear;
Thrice she look'd back, and thrice the Foe drew near.
Just in that instant, anxious *Ariel* sought
The close Recesses of the Virgin's Thought;   140
As on the Nosegay in her Breast reclin'd,
He watch'd th' Ideas rising in her Mind,
Sudden he view'd, in spite of all her Art,
An Earthly Lover lurking at her Heart.
Amaz'd, confus'd, he found his Pow'r expir'd,   145
Resign'd to Fate, and with a Sigh retir'd.
The Peer now spreads the glitt'ring *Forfex* wide,
T' inclose the Lock; now joins it, to divide.
Ev'n then, before the fatal Engine clos'd,
A wretched *Sylph* too fondly interpos'd;   150
Fate urg'd the Sheers, and cut the *Sylph* in twain,
(But Airy Substance soon unites again)

122-4 Scylla, in Greek mythology, plucked a hair from the head of her
father, King Nisus, and was turned into a sea-bird, eternally pursued by
her father in the form of a sea-eagle.   127 *Clarissa:*   not identified.
128 *Case:* tweezer-case, étui.   147 *Forfex:* scissors.

The meeting Points the sacred Hair dissever
From the fair Head, for ever and for ever!
Then flash'd the living Lightning from her Eyes,   155
And Screams of Horror rend th' affrighted Skies.
Not louder Shrieks to pitying Heav'n are cast,
When Husbands or when Lapdogs breathe their last;
Or when rich *China* Vessels fall'n from high,
In glitt'ring Dust and painted Fragments lie!   160
    Let Wreaths of Triumph now my Temples twine,
(The Victor cry'd) the glorious Prize is mine!
While Fish in Streams, or Birds delight in Air,
Or in a Coach and Six the *British* Fair,
As long as *Atalantis* shall be read,   165
Or the small Pillow grace a Lady's Bed,
While *Visits* shall be paid on solemn Days,
When num'rous Wax-lights in bright Order blaze,
While Nymphs take Treats, or Assignations give,
So long my Honour, Name, and Praise shall live!   170
    What Time wou'd spare, from Steel receives its date,
And Monuments, like Men, submit to Fate!
Steel cou'd the Labour of the Gods destroy,
And strike to Dust th' imperial Tow'rs of *Troy*;
Steel cou'd the Works of mortal Pride confound,   175
And hew triumphal Arches to the Ground.
What Wonder then, fair Nymph! thy Hairs shou'd feel
The conqu'ring Force of unresisted Steel?

CANTO IV

But anxious Cares the pensive Nymph oppress'd,
And secret Passions labour'd in her Breast.
Not youthful Kings in Battle seiz'd alive,
Not scornful Virgins who their Charms survive,
Not ardent Lovers robb'd of all their Bliss,   5
Not ancient Ladies when refus'd a Kiss,
Not Tyrants fierce that unrepenting die,
Not *Cynthia* when her *Manteau's* pinn'd awry,
E'er felt such Rage, Resentment, and Despair,
As thou, sad Virgin! for thy ravish'd Hair.   10

165 *Atalantis:* Mrs. Mary Manley's *Secret Memoirs and Manners of several Persons of Quality, of Both Sexes. From the New Atalantis, an Island in the Mediterranean* (1709 f.). 173 Troy was supposed to have been built by the gods Apollo and Poseidon. 8 *Manteau:* loose upper garment.

For, that sad moment, when the *Sylphs* withdrew,
And *Ariel* weeping from *Belinda* flew,
Umbriel, a dusky melancholy Spright,
As ever sully'd the fair face of Light,
Down to the Central Earth, his proper Scene, 15
Repair'd to search the gloomy Cave of *Spleen*.
   Swift on his sooty Pinions flits the *Gnome*,
And in a Vapour reach'd the dismal Dome.
No cheerful Breeze this sullen Region knows,
The dreaded *East* is all the Wind that blows. 20
Here in a Grotto, shelter'd close from Air,
And screen'd in Shades from Day's detested Glare,
She sighs for ever on her pensive Bed,
Pain at her side, and *Megrim* at her Head.
   Two Handmaids wait the Throne: alike in Place, 25
But diff'ring far in Figure and in Face.
Here stood *Ill-nature* like an *ancient Maid*,
Her wrinkled Form in *Black* and *White* array'd;
With store of Pray'rs, for Mornings, Nights, and Noons,
Her Hand is fill'd; her Bosom with Lampoons. 30
   There *Affectation* with a sickly Mien
Shows in her Cheek the Roses of Eighteen,
Practis'd to Lisp, and hang the Head aside,
Faints into Airs, and languishes with Pride;
On the rich Quilt sinks with becoming Woe, 35
Wrapt in a Gown, for Sickness, and for Show.
The Fair-ones feel such Maladies as these,
When each new Night-dress gives a new Disease.
   A constant *Vapour* o'er the Palace flies;
Strange Phantoms rising as the Mists arise; 40
Dreadful, as Hermit's Dreams in haunted Shades,
Or bright, as Visions of expiring Maids.
Now glaring Fiends, and Snakes on rolling Spires,
Pale Spectres, gaping Tombs, and purple Fires:
Now Lakes of liquid Gold, *Elysian* Scenes, 45
And crystal Domes, and Angels in Machines.
   Unnumber'd Throngs on every side are seen,
Of Bodies chang'd to various Forms by *Spleen*.
Here living *Tea-pots* stand, one Arm held out,
One bent; the Handle this, and that the Spout: 50

18 *Vapour:* The fashionable malady of 'spleen', a morose irritability of
temper, was also called 'the vapours'. 24 *Megrim:* nervous headache.
25 *Wait:* attend. 35-38 The art of negligee was never more studied
than when ladies received visits in bed. 43 *Spires:* coils.

A Pipkin there like *Homer's Tripod* walks;
Here sighs a Jar, and there a Goose-pye talks;
Men prove with Child, as pow'rful Fancy works,
And Maids turn'd Bottels, call aloud for Corks.
    Safe past the *Gnome* thro' this fantastick Band,   55
A Branch of healing *Spleenwort* in his Hand.
Then thus address'd the Pow'r—Hail, wayward Queen!
Who rule the Sex to Fifty from Fifteen:
Parent of Vapours and of female Wit,
Who give th' *hysteric,* or *poetic* Fit,   60
On various Tempers act by various ways,
Make some take Physick, others scribble Plays;
Who cause the Proud their Visits to delay,
And send the Godly in a Pett, to pray.
A Nymph there is, that all thy Pow'r disdains,   65
And thousands more in equal Mirth maintains.
But oh! if e'er thy *Gnome* could spoil a Grace,
Or raise a Pimple on a beauteous Face,
Like Citron-Waters Matrons' Cheeks inflame,
Or change Complexions at a losing Game;   70
If e'er with airy Horns I planted Heads,
Or rumpled Petticoats, or tumbled Beds,
Or caus'd Suspicion when no Soul was rude,
Or discompos'd the Head-dress of a Prude,
Or e'er to costive Lap-dog gave Disease,   75
Which not the Tears of brightest Eyes could ease:
Hear me, and touch *Belinda* with Chagrin;
That single Act gives half the World the Spleen.
    The Goddess with a discontented Air
Seems to reject him, tho' she grants his Pray'r.   80
A wond'rous Bag with both her Hands she binds,
Like that where once *Ulysses* held the Winds;
There she collects the Force of Female Lungs,
Sighs, Sobs, and Passions, and the War of Tongues.
A Vial next she fills with fainting Fears,   85
Soft Sorrows, melting Griefs, and flowing Tears.
The *Gnome* rejoicing bears her Gifts away,
Spreads his black Wings, and slowly mounts to **Day.**

---

51 *Pipkin:* small earthen cooking-pot; *Homer's Tripod:* See *Iliad* XVIII.
372 ff. 52 Alludes to a real fact, a Lady of distinction imagin'd
herself in this condition. (P.) 56 *Spleenwort:* hart's-tongue fern,
recommended to the splenetic. 69 *Citron-Waters:* drink made of brandy
flavoured with the peel of citrons or lemons. 71 *Airy Horns:* the imag-
inary horns of the deceived husband. 82 See *Odyssey* X. 19 ff.

Sunk in *Thalestris'* Arms the Nymph he found,
Her Eyes dejected and her Hair unbound.   90
Full o'er their Heads the swelling Bag he rent,
And all the Furies issu'd at the Vent.
Belinda burns with more than mortal Ire,
And fierce *Thalestris* fans the rising Fire.
O wretched Maid! she spread her Hands, and cry'd,   95
(While *Hampton's* Ecchos, wretched Maid! reply'd)
Was it for this you took such constant Care
The *Bodkin, Comb,* and *Essence* to prepare?
For this your Locks in Paper Durance bound,
For this with tort'ring Irons wreath'd around?   100
For this with Fillets strain'd your tender Head,
And bravely bore the double Loads of Lead?
Gods! shall the Ravisher display your Hair,
While the Fops envy, and the Ladies stare!
Honour forbid! at whose unrivall'd Shrine   105
Ease, Pleasure, Virtue, All, our Sex resign.
Methinks already I your Tears survey,
Already hear the horrid things they say,
Already see you a degraded Toast,
And all your Honour in a Whisper lost!   110
How shall I, then, your helpless Fame defend?
'Twill then be Infamy to seem your Friend!
And shall this Prize, th' inestimable Prize,
Expos'd thro' Crystal to the gazing Eyes,
And heighten'd by the Diamond's circling Rays,   115
On that Rapacious Hand for ever blaze?
Sooner shall Grass in *Hyde-park Circus* grow,
And Wits take Lodgings in the Sound of *Bow*;
Sooner let Earth, Air, Sea, to *Chaos* fall,
Men, Monkies, Lap-dogs, Parrots, perish all!   120
    She said; then raging to *Sir Plume* repairs,
And bids her *Beau* demand the precious Hairs:
(*Sir Plume,* of amber *Snuff-box* justly vain,
And the nice Conduct of a *clouded Cane*)

89 *Thalestris:* either Mrs. Elizabeth Morley, sister of Sir George Browne
(see line 121), or (more probably) Sir George Browne's wife (née
Gertrude Morley). 98 *Bodkin:* long hair-pin. 99-102 refers to curl-
papers fixed by strips of soft lead. 113-16 She envisages the hair set in a
ring on the Baron's hand. 118 Those living within the sound of the
bells of Bow Church in Cheapside might be 'true Cockneys', but the City
was not the centre of wit and fashion. 121 *Sir Plume:* Sir George
Browne (d. 1730), cousin of Arabella Fermor's mother; he was much
angered by the naughty accuracy of the portrait. 124 *Clouded:*
veined, curiously marked.

With earnest Eyes, and round unthinking Face,   125
He first the Snuff-box open'd, then the Case,
And thus broke out—My Lord, why, what the devil?
Z—ds! damn the Lock! 'fore Gad, you must be civil!
Plague on't! 'tis past a Jest—nay prithee, pox!
Give her the Hair—he spoke, and rapp'd his Box.   130
    It grieves me much (reply'd the Peer again)
Who speaks so well should ever speak in vain.
But by this Lock, this sacred Lock I swear,
(Which never more shall join its parted Hair;
Which never more its Honours shall renew,   135
Clipp'd from the lovely Head where late it grew)
That while my Nostrils draw the vital Air,
This Hand, which won it, shall for ever wear.
He spoke, and speaking, in proud Triumph spread
The long-contended Honours of her Head.   140
    But *Umbriel*, hateful *Gnome!* forbears not so;
He breaks the Vial whence the Sorrows flow.
Then see! the *Nymph* in beauteous Grief appears,
Her Eyes half-languishing, half-drown'd in Tears;
On her heav'd Bosom hung her drooping Head,   145
Which, with a Sigh, she rais'd; and thus she said.
    For ever curs'd be this detested Day,
Which snatch'd my best, my fav'rite Curl away!
Happy! ah ten times happy had I been,
If *Hampton-Court* these Eyes had never seen!   150
Yet am not I the first mistaken Maid,
By Love of *Courts* to num'rous Ills betray'd.
Oh had I rather un-admir'd remain'd
In some lone Isle, or distant *Northern* Land;
Where the gilt *Chariot* never marks the Way,   155
Where none learn *Ombre*, none e'er taste *Bohea!*
There kept my Charms conceal'd from mortal Eye,
Like Roses that in Deserts bloom and die.
What mov'd my Mind with youthful Lords to roam?
Oh had I stay'd, and said my Pray'rs at home!   160
'Twas this, the Morning *Omens* seem'd to tell;
Thrice from my trembling hand the *Patch-box* fell;
The tott'ring *China* shook without a Wind,
Nay, *Poll* sat mute, and *Shock* was most unkind!
A *Sylph* too warn'd me of the Threats of Fate,   165
In mystic Visions, now believ'd too late!
See the poor Remnants of these slighted Hairs!

135 *Honours:* glory, beauty.   156 *Bohea:* black China tea.

My hands shall rend what ev'n thy Rapine spares:
These, in two sable Ringlets taught to break,
Once gave new Beauties to the snowie Neck; 170
The Sister-Lock now sits uncouth, alone,
And in its Fellow's Fate foresees its own;
Uncurl'd it hangs, the fatal Sheers demands,
And tempts once more, thy sacrilegious Hands.
Oh hadst thou, Cruel! been content to seize 175
Hairs less in sight, or any Hairs but these!

CANTO V

She said: the pitying Audience melt in Tears,
But *Fate* and *Jove* had stopp'd the *Baron*'s Ears.
In vain *Thalestris* with Reproach assails,
For who can move when fair *Belinda* fails?
Not half so fix'd the *Trojan* cou'd remain, 5
While *Anna* begg'd and *Dido* rag'd in vain.
Then grave *Clarissa* graceful wav'd her Fan;
Silence ensu'd, and thus the Nymph began.
　　Say why are Beauties prais'd and honour'd most,
The wise Man's Passion, and the vain Man's Toast? 10
Why deck'd with all that Land and Sea afford,
Why Angels call'd, and Angel-like ador'd?
Why round our Coaches crowd the white-glov'd Beaux,
Why bows the Side-box from its inmost Rows;
How vain are all these Glories, all our Pains, 15
Unless good Sense preserve what Beauty gains:
That Men may say, when we the Front-box grace:
Behold the first in Virtue, as in Face!
Oh! if to dance all Night, and dress all Day,
Charm'd the Small-pox, or chas'd Old-age away; 20
Who would not scorn what Huswife's Cares produce,
Or who would learn one earthly thing of Use?
To patch, nay ogle, might become a Saint,
Nor could it sure be such a Sin to paint.
But since, alas! frail Beauty must decay, 25
Curl'd or uncurl'd, since Locks will turn to grey;
Since painted, or not painted, all shall fade,
And she who scorns a Man, must die a Maid;
What then remains, but well our Pow'r to use,
And keep Good-humour still whate'er we lose? 30

2, 5-6 'Destiny and divine influence' kept Æneas deaf to the entreaties
of Dido and Anna (*Æneid* IV).

And trust me, Dear! Good-humour can prevail,
When Airs, and Flights, and Screams, and Scolding fail.
Beauties in vain their pretty Eyes may roll;
Charms strike the Sight, but Merit wins the Soul.
   So spoke the Dame, but no Applause ensu'd;   35
Belinda frown'd, Thalestris call'd her Prude.
To Arms, to Arms! the fierce Virago cries,
And swift as Lightning to the Combat flies.
All side in Parties, and begin th' Attack;
Fans clap, Silks rustle, and tough Whalebones crack;   40
Heroes' and Heroines' Shouts confus'dly rise,
And bass, and treble Voices strike the Skies.
No common Weapons in their Hands are found,
Like Gods they fight, nor dread a mortal Wound.
   So when bold Homer makes the Gods engage,   45
And heav'nly Breasts with human Passions rage;
'Gainst Pallas, Mars; Latona, Hermes Arms;
And all Olympus rings with loud Alarms:
Jove's Thunder roars, Heav'n trembles all around,
Blue Neptune storms, the bellowing Deeps resound: 50
Earth shakes her nodding Tow'rs, the Ground gives way,
And the pale Ghosts start at the Flash of Day!
   Triumphant Umbriel on a Sconce's height
Clapp'd his glad Wings, and sate to view the Fight:
Propp'd on their Bodkin Spears, the Sprights survey   55
The growing Combat, or assist the Fray.
   While thro' the Press enrag'd Thalestris flies,
And scatters Death around from both her Eyes,
A Beau and Witling perish'd in the Throng,
One died in Metaphor, and one in Song.   60
O cruel Nymph! a living Death I bear,
Cry'd Dapperwit, and sunk beside his Chair.
A mournful Glance Sir Fopling upwards cast,
Those Eyes are made so killing—was his last.
Thus on Mæander's flow'ry Margin lies   65
Th' expiring Swan, and as he sings he dies.
   When bold Sir Plume had drawn Clarissa down,
Chloe stepp'd in, and kill'd him with a Frown;

37 Virago: female warrior, amazon. 45-52 Cf. Iliad XX. 54 ff. 53
Sconce: hanging candlestick. 55 Bodkin: hair-pin (seen as a weapon).
62 Dapperwit: character in Wycherley's play Love in a Wood (1672).
63 Sir Fopling: main character in Etherege's play The Man of Mode
(1676). 64 The words are from a song in Buononcini's opera Camilla,
which was very popular from its first English performance 1706. 65
Mæander: river in Asia Minor.

She smil'd to see the doughty Hero slain,
But at her Smile, the Beau reviv'd again.   70
  Now *Jove* suspends his golden Scales in Air,
Weighs the Men's Wits against the Lady's Hair;
The doubtful Beam long nods from side to side;
At length the Wits mount up, the Hairs subside.
  See fierce *Belinda* on the *Baron* flies,   75
With more than usual Lightning in her Eyes:
Nor fear'd the Chief th' unequal Fight to try,
Who sought no more than on his Foe to die.
But this bold Lord with manly Strength endu'd,
She with one Finger and a Thumb subdu'd: 80
Just where the Breath of Life his Nostrils drew,
A Charge of *Snuff* the wily Virgin threw;
The *Gnomes* direct, to ev'ry Atom just,
The pungent Grains of titillating Dust.
Sudden, with starting Tears each Eye o'erflows,   85
And the high Dome re-ecchoes to his Nose.
  Now meet thy Fate, incens'd *Belinda* cry'd,
And drew a deadly *Bodkin* from her Side.
(The same, his ancient Personage to deck,
Her great great Grandsire wore about his Neck   90
In three *Seal-rings*; which after, melted down,
Form'd a vast *Buckle* for his Widow's Gown:
Her infant Grandame's *Whistle* next it grew,
The *Bells* she jingled, and the *Whistle* blew;
Then in a *Bodkin* grac'd her Mother's Hairs,   95
Which long she wore, and now *Belinda* wears.)
  Boast not my Fall (he cry'd) insulting Foe!
Thou by some other shalt be laid as low.
Nor think, to die dejects my lofty Mind:
All that I dread, is leaving you behind!   100
Rather than so, ah let me still survive,
And burn in *Cupid*'s Flames—but burn alive.
  Restore the Lock! she cries; and all around
Restore the Lock! the vaulted Roofs rebound.
Not fierce *Othello* in so loud a Strain   105
Roar'd for the Handkerchief that caus'd his Pain.
But see how oft Ambitious Aims are cross'd,
And Chiefs contend 'till all the Prize is lost!
The Lock, obtain'd with Guilt, and kept with Pain,
In ev'ry place is sought, but sought in vain: 110
With such a Prize no Mortal must be blest,
So Heav'n decrees! with Heav'n who can contest?

Some thought it mounted to the Lunar Sphere,
Since all things lost on Earth are treasur'd there.
There Heroes' Wits are kept in pond'rous Vases,   115
And Beaux' in *Snuff-boxes* and *Tweezer-cases.*
There broken Vows and death-bed Alms are found,
And Lovers' Hearts with Ends of Riband bound;
The Courtier's Promises, and Sick Man's Pray'rs,
The Smiles of Harlots, and the Tears of Heirs,   120
Cages of Gnats, and Chains to yoak a Flea;
Dry'd Butterflies, and Tomes of Casuistry.
     But trust the Muse—she saw it upward rise,
Tho' mark'd by none but quick, poetic Eyes:
(So *Rome*'s great Founder to the Heav'ns withdrew,   125
To *Proculus* alone confess'd in view)
A sudden Star, it shot thro' liquid Air,
And drew behind a radiant *Trail of Hair.*
Not *Berenice*'s Locks first rose so bright,
The Heav'ns bespangling with dishevell'd Light.   130
The *Sylphs* behold it kindling as it flies,
And pleas'd pursue its Progress thro' the Skies.
     This the *Beau-monde* shall from the *Mall* survey,
And hail with Musick its propitious Ray.
This the blest Lover shall for *Venus* take,   135
And send up Vows from *Rosamonda*'s Lake.
This *Partridge* soon shall view in cloudless Skies,
When next he looks thro' *Galileo*'s Eyes;
And hence th' egregious Wizard shall foredoom
The Fate of *Louis*, and the Fall of *Rome*.   140
     Then cease, bright Nymph! to mourn thy ravish'd Hair
Which adds new Glory to the shining Sphere!
Not all the Tresses that fair Head can boast
Shall draw such Envy as the Lock you lost.

125-6 Romulus, according to legend, vanished in a thunderstorm·
Proculus, a senator, told the story of his death to the Roman people.
127 *Liquid:* clear.   128 *Trail of Hair:* a play on the etymology of
'comet'.   129 *Berenice:* wife and sister of Ptolemy III of Egypt (reigned
246-221 B.C.); she dedicated to the gods a lock of her hair, which dis-
appeared and was said to be transformed into the constellation Coma
Berenices (Berenice's Hair).   133 *The Mall:* enclosed avenue in St.
James's Park, a fashionable promenade.   134 *Musick:* Serenades and
dances were frequent in the Park.   135 *Venus:* the planet, and the god-
dess of love.   136 *Rosamonda's Lake:* pond in St. James's Park, resort of
lovers.   137 *Partridge:* John Partridge (1644-1715), well-known and
much-mocked astrologer.   138 *Thro' Galileo's Eyes:* i.e. using a tele-
scope.   140 *Louis:* Louis XIV of France (1638-1715); *Rome:* the
Papacy.

For, after all the Murders of your Eye,   145
When, after Millions slain, your self shall die:
When those fair Suns shall sett, as sett they must,
And all those Tresses shall be laid in Dust;
This Lock, the Muse shall consecrate to Fame,
And 'midst the Stars inscribe *Belinda's* Name.   150

MORAL ESSAYS

EPISTLE IV

To RICHARD BOYLE, Earl of BURLINGTON*

The four *Moral Essays* (the title is Warburton's, not Pope's) are
verse epistles in which some question of general import is
discussed satirically against a background of contemporary
personalities and theories. The epistle to Burlington (1731) is
concerned with taste, illustrated mainly by reference to gardening
and architecture, and argues for sense, proportion, and use, in
opposition to the more flamboyant æsthetics of those in whom a
little taste, like a little learning, is a dangerous thing.

Of the Use of RICHES.

'Tis strange, the Miser should his Cares employ,
To gain those Riches he can ne'er enjoy:
Is it less strange, the Prodigal should waste
His wealth, to purchase what he ne'er can taste?
Not for himself he sees, or hears, or eats;   5
Artists must chuse his Pictures, Music, Meats:
He buys for Topham, Drawings and Designs,
For Pembroke Statues, dirty Gods, and Coins;
Rare monkish Manuscripts for Hearne alone,
And Books for Mead, and Butterflies for Sloane.   10
Think we all these are for himself? no more
Than his fine Wife, alas! or finer Whore.
    For what has Virro painted, built, and planted?
Only to show, how many Tastes he wanted.

* Richard Boyle (1695-1753) was a diligent propagator and designer of
neo-classical   architecture.   6 *Artists:*   art   experts.   7 *Topham:*
Richard Topham (d.1735), collector.   8 *Pembroke:* Thomas Herbert,
Earl of Pembroke (1656-1733), collector.   9 *Hearne:* Thomas Hearne
(1678-1735), medievalist.   10 *Mead:*   Richard Mead (1673-1754),
physician; *Sloane:* Sir Hans Sloane (1660-1753), physician.

What brought Sir Visto's ill got wealth to waste?   15
Some Dæmon whisper'd, " Visto! have a Taste."
Heav'n visits with a Taste the wealthy fool,
And needs no Rod but Ripley with a Rule.
See! sportive fate, to punish awkward pride,
Bids Bubo build, and sends him such a Guide: 20
A standing sermon, at each year's expense,
That never Coxcomb reach'd Magnificence!
  You show us, Rome was glorious, not profuse,
And pompous buildings once were things of Use.
Yet shall (my Lord) your just, your noble rules   25
Fill half the land with Imitating Fools;
Who random drawings from your sheets shall take,
And of one beauty many blunders make;
Load some vain Church with old Theatric state,
Turn Arcs of triumph to a Garden-gate;   30
Reverse your Ornaments, and hang them all
On some patch'd dog-hole ek'd with ends of wall;
Then clap four slices of Pilaster on't,
That, lac'd with bits of rustic, makes a Front;
Or call the winds thro' long Arcades to roar,   35
Proud to catch cold at a Venetian door;
Conscious they act a true Palladian part,
And if they starve, they starve by rules of art.
  Oft have you hinted to your brother Peer,
A certain truth, which many buy too dear: 40
Something there is more needful than Expense,
And something previous ev'n to Taste—'tis Sense:
Good Sense, which only is the gift of Heav'n,
And tho' no Science, fairly worth the seven:
A Light, which in yourself you must perceive;   45
Jones and Le Nôtre have it not to give.
  To build, to plant, whatever you intend,
To rear the Column, or the Arch to bend,
To swell the Terras, or to sink the Grot;
In all, let Nature never be forgot.   50

18 *Ripley:* Thomas Ripley (d.1758), architect. 20 *Bubo:* George
Bubb Dodington, Baron Melcombe (1691-1762), politician; his mansion
at Eastbury in Dorset was designed by Vanbrugh. 23 The Earl of
Burlington was then publishing the Designs of Inigo Jones, and the
Antiquities of Rome by Palladio. (P.) 36 A door or window so called,
from being much practised at Venice, by Palladio and others. (P.)
44 *Seven:* the medieval *trivium* (grammar, rhetoric, logic) and *quadrivium*
(arithmetic, geometry, astronomy, music). 46 *Jones:* Inigo Jones
(1573-1652), architect, the 'English Palladio'; *Le Nôtre:* André Le
Nôtre (1613-1700), French landscape gardener.

But treat the Goddess like a modest fair,
Nor over-dress, nor leave her wholly bare;
Let not each beauty ev'rywhere be spy'd,
Where half the skill is decently to hide.
He gains all points, who pleasingly confounds,   55
Surprizes, varies, and conceals the Bounds.
  Consult the Genius of the Place in all;
That tells the Waters or to rise, or fall,
Or helps th' ambitious Hill the Heav'ns to scale,
Or scoops in circling theatres the Vale;   60
Calls in the Country, catches op'ning glades,
Joins willing woods, and varies shades from shades;
Now breaks, or now directs, th' intending Lines;
Paints as you plant, and, as you work, designs.
  Still follow Sense, of ev'ry Art the Soul,   65
Parts answ'ring parts shall slide into a whole,
Spontaneous beauties all around advance,
Start ev'n from Difficulty, strike from Chance;
Nature shall join you; Time shall make it grow
A Work to wonder at—perhaps a STOWE.   70
  Without it, proud Versailles! thy glory falls;
And Nero's Terraces desert their walls:
The vast Parterres a thousand hands shall make,
Lo! COBHAM comes, and floats them with a Lake:
Or cut wide views thro' Mountains to the Plain,   75
You'll wish your hill or shelter'd seat again.
Ev'n in an ornament its place remark,
Nor in an Hermitage set Dr. Clarke.
  Behold Villario's ten years' toil compleat;
His Quincunx darkens, his Espaliers meet;   80
The Wood supports the Plain, the parts unite,
And strength of Shade contends with strength of Light;
A waving Glow the bloomy beds display,
Blushing in bright diversities of day,
With silver-quiv'ring rills mæander'd o'er—   85
Enjoy them, you! Villario can no more;
Tir'd of the scene Parterres and Fountains yield,
He finds at last he better likes a Field.

70 *Stowe:* country house and gardens in Buckinghamshire. 73
Parterres: areas of flower-beds. 74 *Cobham:* Richard Temple, Viscount
Cobham (1675-1749). Stowe was his family seat. 78 *Clarke:* Samuel
Clarke (1675-1729), philosopher and unorthodox theologian whose
bust was placed in the Hermitage in Richmond Park. 80 *Quincunx:*
arrangement of five trees, four planted to form a square or rectangle and
one in the centre; *espaliers:* trees trained on lattice-work.

Thro' his young Woods how pleas'd Sabinus stray'd,
Or sat delighted in the thick'ning shade,   90
With annual joy the redd'ning shoots to greet,
Or see the stretching branches long to meet!
His Son's fine Taste an op'ner Vista loves,
Foe to the Dryads of his Father's groves;
One boundless Green, or flourish'd Carpet views,   95
With all the mournful family of Yews;
The thriving plants ignoble broomsticks made,
Now sweep those Alleys they were born to shade.
      At Timon's Villa let us pass a day,
Where all cry out, " What sums are thrown away! "   100
So proud, so grand; of that stupendous air,
Soft and Agreeable come never there.
Greatness, with Timon, dwells in such a draught
As brings all Brobdignag before your thought.
To compass this, his building is a Town,   105
His pond an Ocean, his parterre a Down:
Who but must laugh, the Master when he sees,
A puny insect, shiv'ring at a breeze!
Lo, what huge heaps of littleness around!
The whole, a labour'd Quarry above ground.   110
Two Cupids squirt before: a Lake behind
Improves the keenness of the Northern wind.
His Gardens next your admiration call,
On ev'ry side you look, behold the Wall!
No pleasing Intricacies intervene,   115
No artful wildness to perplex the scene;
Grove nods at grove, each Alley has a brother,
And half the platform just reflects the other.
The suff'ring eye inverted Nature sees,
Trees cut to Statues, Statues thick as trees;   120

---

94 *Dryads:* female tree-spirits in Greek mythology.   95 The two
extremes in parterres, which are equally faulty; a *boundless Green*, large
and naked as a field, or a *flourished Carpet*, where the greatness and
nobleness of the piece is lessened by being divided into too many parts,
with scroll'd works and beds, of which the examples are frequent. (P.)
96 *mournful family of Yews:* touches upon the ill taste of those who are so
fond of Evergreens (particularly Yews, which are the most tonsile) as to
destroy the nobler Forest-trees, to make way for such little ornaments as
Pyramids of dark-green continually repeated, not unlike a Funeral
Procession. (P.)   99 *At Timon's Villa:* This description is intended to
compromise the principles of a false Taste of Magnificence, and to
exemplify what was said before, that nothing but Good Sense can attain
it. (P.)   104 *Brobdi(n)gnag:* land of giants in Swift's *Gulliver's Travels.*

With here a Fountain, never to be play'd;
And there a Summer-house, that knows no shade,
Here Amphitrite sails thro' myrtle bow'rs;
There Gladiators fight, or die, in flow'rs;
Un-water'd see the drooping sea-horse mourn,   125
And swallows roost in Nilus' dusty Urn.
  My Lord advances with majestic mien,
Smit with the mighty pleasure, to be seen:
But soft—by regular approach—not yet—
First thro' the length of yon hot Terras sweat,   130
And when up ten steep slopes you've dragg'd your thighs,
Just at his Study-door he'll bless your eyes.
  His Study! with what Authors is it stor'd?
In Books, not Authors, curious is my Lord;
To all their dated Backs he turns you round: 135
These Aldus printed, those Du Sueil has bound.
Lo some are Vellum, and the rest as good
For all his Lordship knows, but they are Wood.
For Locke or Milton 'tis in vain to look,
These shelves admit not any modern book.   140
  And now the Chapel's silver bell you hear,
That summons you to all the Pride of Pray'r:
Light quirks of Musick, broken and uneven,
Make the soul dance upon a Jig to Heaven.
On painted Ceilings you devoutly stare,   145
Where sprawl the Saints of Verrio or Laguerre,
On gilded clouds in fair expansion lye,
And bring all Paradise before your eye.

123 *Amphitrite:*   a sea-maiden in Greek mythology.   126 *Nilus:*
personified god of the Nile.   133 *His Study &c.:*   The false Taste in
Books; a satire on the vanity in collecting them, more frequent in men
of Fortune than the study to understand them. Many delight chiefly in
the elegance of the print, or of the binding; some have carried it so far, as
to cause the upper shelves to be filled with painted books of wood;
others pique themselves so much upon books in a language they do not
understand, as to exclude the most useful in one they do. (P.)   136
Aldus: Aldo Manuzio (1450-1515), Italian printer; *Du Sueil:* Augustin
Du Seuil (1673-1746), French book-binder.   139 *Locke:* John Locke
(1623-1704), philosopher.   142 The false Taste in *Music*, improper to
the subjects, as of light airs in churches, often practised by the organists,
&c. (P.)   145 And in *Painting* (from which even Italy is not free) of
naked figures in Churches, &c. which has obliged some Popes to put
draperies on some of those of the best masters. (P.)   146 *Verrio:* An-
tonio Verrio (1639-1707), Italian painter; *Laguerre:* Louis Laguerre
(1663-1721), French painter.
A.L.P.   L

To rest, the Cushion and soft Dean invite,
Who never mentions Hell to ears polite.   150
  But hark! the chiming Clocks to dinner call;
A hundred footsteps scrape the marble Hall:
The rich Buffet well-colour'd Serpents grace,
And gaping Tritons spew to wash your face.
Is this a dinner? this a Genial room?   155
No, 'tis a Temple, and a Hecatomb.
A solemn Sacrifice, perform'd in state,
You drink by measure, and to minutes eat.
So quick retires each flying course, you'd swear
Sancho's dread Doctor and his Wand were there.   160
Between each Act the trembling salvers ring,
From soup to sweet-wine, and God bless the King.
In plenty starving, tantaliz'd in state,
And complaisantly help'd to all I hate,
Treated, caress'd, and tir'd, I take my leave,   165
Sick of his civil Pride from Morn to Eve;
I curse such lavish cost, and little skill,
And swear no Day was ever past so ill.
  Yet hence the Poor are cloth'd, the Hungry fed;
Health to himself, and to his Infants bread   170
The Lab'rer bears: What his hard Heart denies,
His charitable Vanity supplies.
  Another age shall see the golden Ear
Embrown the Slope, and nod on the Parterre,
Deep Harvests bury all his pride has plann'd,   175
And laughing Ceres re-assume the land.
  Who then shall grace, or who improve the Soil?
Who plants like BATHURST, or who builds like BOYLE.

150 This is a fact; a reverend Dean preaching at Court, threatened the
sinner with punishment in "a place which he thought it not decent to
name in so polite an assembly". (P.) 153 Taxes the incongruity
of *Ornaments* (tho' sometimes practised by the ancients) where an open
mouth ejects the water into a fountain, or where the shocking images of
serpents, &c. are introduced in Grotto's or Buffets. (P.) *Buffet:* side-
board. 154 *Triton:* minor sea-god. 155 *Genial:* festive. 155-6 The
proud Festivals of some men are here set forth to ridicule, where pride
destroys the ease, and formal regularity all the pleasurable enjoyment
of the entertainment. (P.) 160 *Sancho's dread Doctor:* See Don Quixote,
Ch. xlvii. (P.) 169 *Yet hence the Poor, &c.:* The *Moral* of the whole,
where Providence is justified in giving Wealth to those who squander it
in this manner. A bad Taste employs more hands, and diffuses Expence
more than a good one. (P.) 176 *Ceres:* Roman corn-goddess. 178
Bathurst: Allen, Lord Bathurst (1685-1775), Tory politician interested
in landscape gardening; *Boyle:* dedicatee of the poem.

'Tis Use alone that sanctifies Expense,
And Splendour borrows all her rays from Sense.   180
   His Father's Acres who enjoys in peace,
Or makes his Neighbours glad, if he increase:
Whose chearful Tenants bless their yearly toil,
Yet to their Lord owe more than to the soil;
Whose ample Lawns are not asham'd to feed   185
The milky heifer and deserving steed;
Whose rising Forests, not for pride or show,
But future Buildings, future Navies, grow:
Let his plantations stretch from down to down,
First shade a Country, and then raise a Town.   190
   You too proceed! make falling Arts your care,
Erect new wonders, and the old repair;
Jones and Palladio to themselves restore,
And be whate'er Vitruvius was before:
'Till Kings call forth th' Ideas of your mind,   195
Proud to accomplish what such hands designed,
Bid Harbours open, public Ways extend,
Bid Temples, worthier of the God, ascend;
Bid the broad Arch the dang'rous Flood contain,
The Mole projected break the roaring Main;   200
Back to his bounds their subject Sea command,
And roll obedient Rivers thro' the Land:
These Honours, Peace to happy Britain brings,
These are Imperial Works, and worthy Kings.

190 *Country:* tract of country.   193 *Palladio:* Andrea Palladio (1518-
80), Italian architect.   194 *Vitruvius:* M. Vitruvius Pollio (fl. *c.* 40 B.C.),
Roman author of *De Architectura*.   195-7 *'Till Kings . . . Bid Harbours
open, &c.:* The poet after having touched upon the proper objects of
Magnificence and Expense, in the private works of great men, comes to
those great and public works which become a prince. This Poem was
published in the year 1732, when some of the new-built Churches, by
the act of Queen Anne, were ready to fall, being founded in boggy land
. . . others were vilely executed, thro' fraudulent cabals between under-
takers, officers, &c. Dagenham-breach had done very great mischiefs;
many of the Highways throughout England were hardly passable; and
most of those which were repaired by Turnpikes were made jobs for
private lucre, and infamously executed, even to the entrances of London
itself: The proposal of building a Bridge at Westminster had been
petition'd against and rejected; but in two years after the publication of
this poem, an Act for building a Bridge pass'd thro' both houses. (P.)

AN EPISTLE TO DR. ARBUTHNOT*

Published January, 1735, a month before Arbuthnot's death. This poem, written in Pope's most assured and sprightly style, deals with (in his own words) 'my Motives of writing, the objections to them & my answers ' and in a wider sense attempts his ' vindication from slanders of all sorts '—a very Popean vindication, however, proceeding in the belief that attack is the best part of defence.

Neque sermonibus Vulgi *dederis te, nec in* Præmiis *humanis spem posueris rerum tuarum: suis te oportet illecebris* ipsa Virtus *trahat ad verum decus. Quid de te alii loquantur, ipsi videant, sed loquentur tamen.*

TULLY

[*De Re Publica*, Lib. VI, cap. xxiii]

Shut, shut the door, good *John*! fatigu'd, I said,
Tye up the knocker, say I'm sick, I'm dead.
The Dog-star rages! nay 'tis past a doubt,
All *Bedlam*, or *Parnassus*, is let out:
Fire in each eye, and Papers in each hand,　　　　　　　　5
They rave, recite, and madden round the land.
　　What Walls can guard me, or what Shades can hide?
They pierce my Thickets, thro' my Grot they glide;
By land, by water, they renew the charge;
They stop the Chariot, and they board the Barge.　　　　10
No place is sacred, not the Church is free;
Ev'n *Sunday* shines no *Sabbath-day* to me:
Then from the *Mint* walks forth the Man of Ryme,
Happy! to catch me, just at Dinner-time.
　　Is there a Parson, much bemus'd in Beer,　　　　　　15
A maudlin Poetess, a ryming Peer,
A Clerk, foredoom'd his Father's soul to cross,
Who pens a Stanza, when he shou'd *engross*?
Is there, who lock'd from Ink and Paper, scrawls
With desp'rate Charcoal round his darken'd walls?　　　20
All fly to TWIT'NAM, and in humble strain
Apply to me, to keep them mad or vain.

* John Arbuthnot (1667-1735), physician, scholar, and writer.　1 *John:* John Serle, Pope's servant.　3 *Dog-star:* Sirius traditionally inflamed men's minds in late summer.　4 *Bedlam, or Parnassus:* the madhouse, or the muses' hill.　8 refers to Pope's elaborate garden at Twickenham. 13 *The Mint:* retreat for bankrupts and debtors in Southwark.　18 *Engross:* write legal documents.

Arthur, whose giddy Son neglects the Laws,
Imputes to me and my damn'd works the cause:
Poor *Cornus* sees his frantic Wife elope, 25
And curses Wit, and Poetry, and *Pope*.
Friend to my Life! (which did not you prolong,
The World had wanted many an idle Song)
What *Drop* or *Nostrum* can this Plague remove?
Or which must end me, a Fool's Wrath or Love? 30
A dire Dilemma! either way I'm sped,
If Foes, they write, if Friends, they read me dead.
Seiz'd and ty'd down to judge, how wretched I!
Who can't be silent, and who will not lye,
To laugh, were want of Goodness and of Grace, 35
And to be grave, exceeds all Pow'r of face.
I sit with sad Civility, I read
With honest anguish, and an aking head;
And drop at last, but in unwilling ears,
This saving counsel, " Keep your Piece nine years." 40
" Nine years! " cries he, who high in *Drury-lane*
Lull'd by soft Zephyrs thro' the broken Pane,
Rymes ere he wakes, and prints before *Term* ends,
Oblig'd by hunger, and Request of friends:
" The Piece you think is incorrect? why take it, 45
I'm all submission, what you'd have it, make it."
Three things another's modest wishes bound,
My Friendship, and a Prologue, and ten Pound.
Pitholeon sends to me: " You know his Grace,
I want a Patron; ask him for a Place." 50
Pitholeon libell'd me,—" but here's a Letter
Informs you, Sir, 'twas when he knew no better.
Dare you refuse him? *Curll* invites to dine,
He'll write a *Journal*, or he'll turn *Divine*."
Bless me! a Packet.—" 'Tis a stranger sues, 55
A Virgin Tragedy, an Orphan Muse."
If I dislike it, " Furies, death and rage! "
If I approve, " Commend it to the Stage."

23 *Arthur . . . Son:* Arthur Moore (1666?-1730), politician, and James Moore Smythe (1702-34), poet and dramatist. There was a quarrel of several years standing between Pope and Smythe. 25 *Cornus:* a cuckold; identification uncertain. 29 *Drop:* refers to the patent 'drop' of a quack doctor, Joshua Ward, which was being sold in 1743; *nostrum:* patent medicine. 40 See Horace, *Ars Poetica*, 386-9. 43 *Term:* More books were published during the law terms. 49 *Pitholeon:* The name taken from a foolish poet at *Rhodes*, who pretended much to *Greek*. (P.) Identification uncertain. 53 *Curl:* Edmund Curll (1675-1747), rascally bookseller.

There (thank my Stars) my whole Commission ends,
The Play'rs and I are, luckily, no friends.   60
Fir'd that the House reject him, " 'Sdeath I'll print it
And shame the fools—— Your Int'rest, Sir, with *Lintot*! "
Lintot, dull rogue! will think your price too much:
" Not Sir, if you revise it, and retouch."
All my demurs but double his Attacks;   65
At last he whispers, " Do, and we go snacks."
Glad of a quarrel, straight I clap the door,
Sir, let me see your works and you no more.
　　'Tis sung, when *Midas*' Ears began to spring,
(*Midas*, a sacred Person and a King)   70
His very Minister who spy'd them first,
(Some say his Queen) was forc'd to speak, or burst.
And is not mine, my Friend, a sorer case,
When ev'ry Coxcomb perks them in my face?
　　" Good friend forbear! you deal in dang'rous things,   75
I'd never name Queens, Ministers, or Kings;
Keep close to Ears, and those let Asses prick;
'Tis nothing "— Nothing? if they bite and kick?
Out with it, DUNCIAD! let the secret pass,
That Secret to each Fool, that he's an Ass: 80
The truth once told (and wherefore shou'd we lye?)
The Queen of *Midas* slept, and so may I.
　　You think this cruel? take it for a rule,
No creature smarts so little as a Fool.
Let Peals of Laughter, *Codrus*! round thee break,   85
Thou unconcern'd canst hear the mighty Crack.
Pit, Box, and Gall'ry in convulsions hurl'd,
Thou stand'st unshook amidst a bursting World.
Who shames a Scribler? break one cobweb thro',
He spins the slight, self-pleasing thread anew;   90
Destroy his Fib, or Sophistry; in vain,
The Creature's at his dirty work again;
Thron'd in the Centre of his thin designs;
Proud of a vast Extent of flimzy lines!
Whom have I hurt? has Poet yet, or Peer,   95
Lost the arch'd eye-brow, or *Parnassian* sneer?

---

63 *Lintot:*　Barnaby Bernard Lintot (1675-1736), bookseller.　66 *Go snacks:*　share, divide profits.　69 *Midas' Ears:*　in Greek mythology, Midas's ears were changed into those of an ass.　79 *Dunciad:*　Pope's poem (1728-43).　85 *Codrus:*　stock name (probably fictitious) for persistent poetaster.

And has not *Colly* still his Lord, and Whore?
His Butchers *Henley*, his Free-masons *Moor*?
Does not one Table *Bavius* still admit?
Still to one Bishop *Philips* seem a wit?   100
Still *Sappho*— " Hold! for God's sake—you'll offend:
No Names!—be calm!—learn Prudence of a Friend!
I too cou'd write, and I am twice as tall;
But Foes like these!"— One Flatt'rer's worse than all;
Of all mad Creatures, if the Learn'd are right,   105
It is the Slaver kills, and not the Bite.
A Fool quite angry is quite innocent:
Alas! 'tis ten times worse when they *repent*.
   One dedicates, in high Heroic prose,
And ridicules beyond a hundred foes: 110
One from all *Grubstreet* will my fame defend,
And more abusive, calls himself my friend.
This prints my *Letters*, that expects a Bribe,
And others roar aloud, " Subscribe, subscribe."
   There are, who to my Person pay their court: 115
I cough like *Horace*, and tho' lean, am short,
Ammon's great Son one shoulder had too high,
Such *Ovid's* nose, and " Sir! you have an *Eye*—"
Go on, obliging Creatures, make me see
All that disgrac'd my Betters, met in me: 120
Say for my comfort, languishing in bed,
" Just so immortal *Maro* held his head: "
And when I dye, be sure to let me know
Great *Homer* dy'd three thousand years ago.
   Why did I write? what sin to me unknown   125
Dipt me in Ink, my Parents', or my own?
As yet a Child, nor yet a Fool to Fame,
I lisp'd in Numbers, for the Numbers came.
I left no Calling for this idle trade,
No Duty broke, no Father disobey'd.   130
The Muse but serv'd to ease some Friend, not Wife,
To help me thro' this long Disease, my Life,

97 *Colly:* Colley Cibber (1671-1757), actor and dramatist. 98 *Henley:* John Henley (1692-1756), open-air preacher who gave a 'Butchers Lecture' in 1729; *Moor:* James Moore Smythe. 99 *Bavius:* poetaster satirized by Virgil. 100 The poet Ambrose Philips (1675?-1749) was secretary to Hugh Boulter who later became Primate of Ireland. 101 *Sapho:* Sappho (7th cent. B.C.), Greek poetess. 114 Publishers often sought subscribers, so as to guarantee part of the cost of a book before publication. 116 *Horace:* (65-8 B.C.), Latin poet. 117 *Ammon's great Son:* Alexander the Great (356-323 B.C.). 118 *Ovid:* (43 B.C.-*c.* A.D. 17), Latin poet. 122 *Maro:* Virgil.

To second, ARBUTHNOT! thy Art and Care,
And teach, the Being you preserv'd, to bear.
  But why then publish? *Granville* the polite,   135
And knowing *Walsh,* wou'd tell me I could write;
Well-natur'd *Garth* inflam'd with early praise,
And *Congreve* lov'd, and *Swift* endur'd my Lays;
The courtly *Talbot, Somers, Sheffield* read,
Ev'n mitred *Rochester* wou'd nod the head,   140
And *St. John*'s self (great *Dryden*'s friends before)
With open arms receiv'd one Poet more.
Happy my Studies, when by these approv'd!
Happier their Author, when by these belov'd!
From these the world will judge of Men and Books,   145
Not from the *Burnets, Oldmixons,* and *Cooks.*
  Soft were my Numbers, who cou'd take offence
While pure Description held the place of Sense?
Like gentle *Fanny*'s was my flow'ry Theme,
A painted Mistress, or a purling Stream.   150
Yet then did *Gildon* draw his venal quill;
I wish'd the man a dinner, and sat still.
Yet then did *Dennis* rave in furious fret;
I never answer'd, I was not in debt.
If want provok'd, or madness made them print,   155
I wag'd no war with *Bedlam* or the *Mint.*
  Did some more sober Critic come abroad:
If wrong, I smil'd; if right, I kiss'd the rod.
Pains, reading, study, are their just pretence,
And all they want is spirit, taste, and sense.   160
Comma's and points they set exactly right,

---

135 *Granville:* George Granville, Baron Lansdowne (1667-1735),
statesman and poet. 136 *Walsh:* William Walsh (1663-1708), poet
and critic. 137 *Garth:* Sir Samuel Garth (1661-1719), physician and
poet. 138 *Congreve:* William Congreve (1670-1729), dramatist; *Swift:*
Jonathan Swift (1667-1745), satirist, pamphleteer, and poet. 139
Talbot: Charles Talbot, Duke of Shrewsbury (1660-1718), statesman;
Somers: John, Baron Somers (1651-1716), statesman; *Sheffield:* John
Sheffield, Duke of Buckingham (1648-1721), statesman and poet. 140
Rochester: Francis Atterbury, Bishop of Rochester (1662-1732). 141 *St.
John:* Henry St. John, Viscount Bolingbroke (1678-1751), statesman;
Dryden: John Dryden (1631-1700), poet, dramatist, and critic. 146
Burnets, etc.: Thomas Burnet (1694-1753), John Oldmixon (1673-1742),
and Thomas Cooke (1703-56) were miscellaneous writers who had
quarrelled with Pope. 147 *Numbers:* rhythms, verses. 149 *Fanny:*
John, Baron Hervey of Ickworth (1696-1743), statesman and poet.
151 *Gildon:* Charles Gildon (1665-1724), miscellaneous writer and
attacker of Pope. 153 *Dennis:* John Dennis (1657-1734), critic and
dramatist who quarrelled with Pope.

And 'twere a sin to rob them of their Mite.
Yet ne'er one sprig of Laurel grac'd these ribalds,
From slashing *Bentley* down to pidling *Tibalds.*
Each Wight who reads not, and but scans and spells,   165
Each Word-catcher that lives on syllables,
Ev'n such small Critics some regard may claim,
Preserv'd in *Milton*'s or in *Shakespeare*'s name.
Pretty! in Amber to observe the forms
Of hairs, or straws, or dirt, or grubs, or worms;   170
The things, we know, are neither rich nor rare,
But wonder how the Devil they got there?
  Were others angry? I excus'd them too;
Well might they rage, I gave them but their due.
A man's true merit 'tis not hard to find,   175
But each man's secret standard in his mind,
That Casting-weight Pride adds to Emptiness,
This, who can gratify? for who can *guess?*
The Bard whom pilfer'd Pastorals renown,
Who turns a *Persian* tale for half a crown,   180
Just writes to make his barrenness appear,
And strains from hard-bound brains eight lines a year:
He, who still wanting tho' he lives on theft,
Steals much, spends little, yet has nothing left:
And he, who now to sense, now nonsense leaning,   185
Means not, but blunders round about a meaning:
And he, whose Fustian's so sublimely bad,
It is not Poetry, but Prose run mad:
All these, my modest Satire bade *translate,*
And own'd, that nine such Poets made a *Tate.*   190
How did they fume, and stamp, and roar, and chafe!
And swear, not ADDISON himself was safe.
  Peace to all such! but were there One whose fires
True Genius kindles, and fair Fame inspires;
Blest with each Talent and each Art to please,   195
And born to write, converse, and live with ease:
Shou'd such a man, too fond to rule alone,
Bear, like the *Turk*, no brother near the throne,
View him with scornful, yet with jealous eyes,

164 *Bentley* . . . *Tibalds:* Richard Bentley (1662-1742) and Lewis
Theobald (1688-1744) were painstaking editorial scholars who attacked
Pope's laxness in translating Homer and editing Shakespeare. 179-80
Ambrose Philips. 187 *Fustian:* bombastic, worthless writing. 190
Tate: Nahum Tate (1652-1715), poet who rewrote *King Lear* and made
a continuation of *Absalom and Achitophel.* 192 *Addison:* Joseph Addison
(1672-1719), essayist, dramatist, and poet.

And hate for Arts that caus'd himself to rise;   200
Damn with faint praise, assent with civil leer,
And without sneering, teach the rest to sneer;
Willing to wound, and yet afraid to strike,
Just hint a fault, and hesitate dislike;
Alike reserv'd to blame, or to commend,   205
A tim'rous foe, and a suspicious friend;
Dreading ev'n fools, by Flatterers besieg'd,
And so obliging, that he ne'er oblig'd;
Like *Cato*, give his little Senate laws,
And sit attentive to his own applause;   210
While Wits and Templers ev'ry sentence raise,
And wonder with a foolish face of praise:——
Who but must laugh, if such a man there be?
Who woud not weep, if ATTICUS were he?
What tho' my Name stood rubric on the walls,   215
Or plaister'd posts, with Claps, in capitals?
Or smoaking forth, a hundred Hawkers' load,
On Wings of Winds came flying all abroad?
I sought no homage from the Race that write;
I kept, like *Asian* Monarchs, from their sight: 220
Poems I heeded (now be-rym'd so long)
No more than thou, great GEORGE! a Birth-day Song.
I ne'er with Wits or Witlings pass'd my days,
To spread about the Itch of Verse and Praise;
Nor like a Puppy daggled thro' the Town,   225
To fetch and carry Sing-song up and down;
Nor at Rehearsals sweat and mouth'd, and cry'd,
With Handkerchief and Orange at my side:
But sick of Fops, and Poetry, and Prate,
To *Bufo* left the whole *Castalian* State.   230
  Proud, as *Apollo* on his forked hill,
Sate full-blown *Bufo*, puff'd by ev'ry quill;
Fed with soft Dedication all day long,
Horace and he went hand in hand in song.
His Library, (where busts of Poets dead   235
And a true *Pindar* stood without a head)

209 *Cato:*   refers to Addison's drama. *Cato* (1713).   211 *Templers:*
lawyers from the Temple.   214 *Atticus:* Addison.   215 *Rubric:* painted
in red.   216 *Claps:* posters.   222 *George:* George II (1683-1760).   225
Daggled: splashed through the mud.   230 *Bufo:* composite portrait
of a dim-witted patron; *Castalian:* poetic; inspired by the Castalian
spring on Mount Parnassus.   231 *Apollo:* Greek god of the sun and
poetry; *forked hill:* Apollo was associated with one of the twin peaks of
Mount Parnassus.   236 *Pindar:* (*c.* 522-443 B.C.), Greek poet. There
was a craze in Pope's day for mutilated ('genuine antique') statues.

Receiv'd of Wits an undistinguish'd race,
Who first his Judgment ask'd, and then a Place:
Much they extoll'd his Pictures, much his Seat,
And flatter'd ev'ry day, and some days eat: 240
Till grown more frugal in his riper days,
He paid some Bards with Port, and some with Praise;
To some a dry Rehearsal was assign'd,
And others (harder still) he paid in kind.
Dryden alone (what wonder?) came not nigh,   245
Dryden alone escap'd this judging eye:
But still the Great have kindness in reserve,
He help'd to bury whom he help'd to starve.
    May some choice Patron bless each gray goose quill!
May ev'ry Bavius have his Bufo still!   250
So, when a Statesman wants a Day's defence,
Or Envy holds a whole Week's war with Sense,
Or simple Pride for Flatt'ry makes demands,
May Dunce by Dunce be whistled off my hands!
Blest be the Great! for those they take away,   255
And those they left me—For they left me GAY;
Left me to see neglected Genius bloom,
Neglected dye! and tell it on his Tomb:
Of all thy blameless Life the sole Return
My Verse, and QUEENSB'RY weeping o'er thy Urn!   260
    Oh let me live my own, and dye so too!
(To live and dye is all I have to do:)
Maintain a Poet's Dignity and Ease,
And see what friends, and read what books I please;
Above a Patron, tho' I condescend   265
Sometimes to call a Minister my Friend.
I was not born for Courts or great Affairs;
I pay my Debts, believe, and say my Pray'rs;
Can sleep without a Poem in my head;
Nor know, if Dennis be alive or dead.   270
    Why am I ask'd, what next shall see the light?
Heav'ns! was I born for nothing but to write?
Has Life no Joys for me? or (to be grave)
Have I no Friend to serve, no soul to save?
" I found him close with Swift "—" Indeed? no doubt"   275
(Cries prating Balbus) " something will come out."

256 Gay: John Gay (1685-1732), poet and dramatist.   260 Queensb'ry:
Charles Douglas, Duke of Queensbury (1698-1778), patron of Gay.
262 Cf. Sir John Denham's Of Prudence, line 94.   276 Balbus: Thomas
Hay, Earl of Kinnoull (1710-87), statesman.

'Tis all in vain, deny it as I will.
" No, such a Genius never can lye still; "
And then for mine obligingly mistakes
The first Lampoon Sir *Will* or *Bubo* makes.   280
Poor guiltless I! and can I chuse but smile,
When ev'ry Coxcomb knows me by my *Style*?
    Curst be the Verse, how well soe'er it flow,
That tends to make one worthy Man my foe,
Give Virtue scandal, Innocence a fear,   285
Or from the soft-eyed Virgin steal a tear!
But he, who hurts a harmless neighbour's peace,
Insults fall'n Worth, or Beauty in distress,
Who loves a Lye, lame slander helps about,
Who writes a Libel, or who copies out: 290
That Fop, whose pride affects a Patron's name,
Yet absent, wounds an Author's honest fame:
Who can your Merit selfishly approve,
And show the Sense of it without the Love;
Who has the Vanity to call you Friend,   295
Yet wants the Honour injur'd to defend;
Who tells whate'er you think, whate'er you say,
And, if he lye not, must at least betray:
Who to the *Dean*, and *silver Bell* can swear,
And sees at *Cannons* what was never there: 300
Who reads, but with a Lust to misapply,
Make Satire a Lampoon, and Fiction, Lye.
A Lash like mine no honest man shall dread,
But all such babling blockheads in his stead.
    Let *Sporus* tremble— " What? that Thing of silk,   305
Sporus, that mere white Curd of Ass's milk?
Satire or Sense, alas! can *Sporus* feel?
Who breaks a Butterfly upon a Wheel? "
    Yet let me slap this Bug with gilded wings,
This painted Child of Dirt that stinks and stings;   310
Whose Buzz the Witty and the Fair annoys,
Yet Wit ne'er tastes, and Beauty ne'er enjoys:
So well-bred Spaniels civilly delight
In mumbling of the Game they dare not bite.
Eternal Smiles his Emptiness betray,   315

280 *Sir Will:* Sir William Yonge (d.1755), politician; *Bubo:* George
Bubb Dodington, Baron Melcombe (1691-1762), politician. 299-300
Meaning the man who would have persuaded the Duke of Chandos
that Mr. P. meant him in those circumstances ridiculed in the Epistle on
Taste [*Moral Essays* IV, 141-50]. (P.); *Cannons:* seat of the Duke of
Chandos. 305 *Sporus:* Lord Hervey.

As shallow streams run dimpling all the way:
Whether in florid Impotence he speaks,
And, as the Prompter breathes, the Puppet squeaks;
Or at the Ear of *Eve*, familiar Toad,
Half Froth, half Venom, spits himself abroad,   320
In Puns, or Politicks, or Tales, or Lyes,
Or Spite, or Smut, or Rymes, or Blasphemies:
His Wit all see-saw: between *that* and *this*, ⎫
Now high, now low, now Master up, now Miss, ⎬
And he himself one vile Antithesis. ⎭   325
Amphibious Thing! that acting either Part,
The trifling Head, or the corrupted Heart,
Fop at the Toilet, Flatt'rer at the Board,
Now trips a Lady, and now struts a Lord.
Eve's Tempter thus the Rabbins have exprest,   330
A Cherub's face, a Reptile all the rest;
Beauty that shocks you, Parts that none will trust,
Wit that can creep, and Pride that licks the dust.
    Not Fortune's Worshipper, nor Fashion's Fool,
Not Lucre's Madman, nor Ambition's Tool,   335
Not proud, nor servile;—be one Poet's praise
That, if he pleas'd, he pleas'd by manly ways;
That Flatt'ry, ev'n to Kings, he held a shame:
And thought a Lye in Verse or Prose the same;
That not in Fancy's Maze he wander'd long,   340
But stoop'd to Truth, and moraliz'd his song:
That not for Fame, but Virtue's better end,
He stood the furious Foe, the timid Friend,
The damning Critic, half-approving Wit,
The Coxcomb hit, or fearing to be hit;   345
Laugh'd at the loss of Friends he never had,
The dull, the proud, the wicked, and the mad;
The distant Threats of Vengeance on his head,
The Blow unfelt, the Tear he never shed;
The Tale reviv'd, the Lye so oft o'erthrown;   350
Th' imputed Trash, and Dulness not his own;
The Morals blacken'd when the Writings scape,
The libell'd Person, and the pictur'd Shape;
Abuse on all he lov'd, or lov'd him, spread,
A Friend in Exile, or a Father, dead;   355
The Whisper, that to Greatness still too near,

319 See Milton's *Paradise Lost*, IV. 800. *Eve* is Queen Caroline (1683-
1737). 330 *Rabbins:* early Jewish doctors of the law. 341 *Stoop'd:*
swooped down (like a falcon). 353 *The pictur'd Shape:* Pope's enemies
caricatured his deformity.

Perhaps, yet vibrates on his Sov'reign's ear:—
Welcome for thee, fair Virtue! all the past;
For thee, fair Virtue! welcome ev'n the *last*!
  " But why insult the Poor, affront the Great? "   360
A Knave's a Knave, to me, in ev'ry State:
Alike my scorn, if he succeed or fail,
Sporus at Court, or *Japhet* in a Jayl,
A hireling Scribler, or a hireling Peer,
Knight of the Post corrupt, or of the Shire,   365
If on a Pillory, or near a Throne,
He gain his Prince's Ear, or lose his own.
  Yet soft by Nature, more a Dupe than Wit,
Sapho can tell you how this Man was bit:
This dreaded Sat'rist *Dennis* will confess   370
Foe to his Pride, but Friend to his Distress:
So humble, he has knock'd at *Tibbald's* door,
Has drunk with *Cibber*, nay has rym'd for *Moor*.
Full ten years slander'd, did he once reply?
Three thousand Suns went down on *Welsted's* Lye.   375
To please a *Mistress*, One aspers'd his life;
He lash'd him not, but let her be his *Wife*.
Let *Budgel* charge low *Grubstreet* on his quill,
And write whate'er he pleas'd, except his *Will*;
Let the two *Curls* of Town and Court, abuse   380
His Father, Mother, Body, Soul, and Muse.
Yet why? that Father held it for a rule

363 *Japhet:* Japhet Crook (1662-1734), forger. 365 *Knight of the post:* a hired perjurer at the law courts. 369 *Sapho:* Lady Mary Wortley Montague (1689-1762); *bit:* caught. 374 *Ten years:* It was so long after many libels before the Author of the *Dunciad* published that poem, till when, he never writ a word in answer to the many scurrilities and falsehoods concerning him. (P.). 375 *Welsted's Lye:* This man had the impudence to tell in print, that Mr. P. had occasioned a *Lady's death*, and to name a person he never heard of. He also publish'd that he libell'd the Duke of Chandos; with whom (it was added) that he had lived in familiarity, and received from him a present of *five hundred pounds:* the falsehood of both which is known to his Grace. Mr. P. never received any present, farther than the subscription for *Homer*, from him, or from *Any great Man* whatsoever. (P.). *Welsted:* Leonard Welsted (1688-1747), poet and clerk. 376 *One:* not identified. 378 *Let Budgel:* Budgel, in a weekly pamphlet called the *Bee*, bestowed much abuse on him, in the imagination that he writ some things about the *Last Will* of Dr. *Tindal*, in the *Grub-street Journal;* a Paper wherein he never had the least hand, direction, or supervisal, nor the least knowledge of its Author. (P.). *Budgel:* Eustace Budgell (1686-1737), miscellaneous writer. 380 Edmund Curll and Lord Hervey.

It was a Sin to call our Neighbour Fool,
That harmless Mother thought no Wife a Whore,—
Hear this, and spare his family, *James Moor*!   385
Unspotted Names! and memorable long,
If there be Force in Virtue, or in Song.
    Of gentle Blood (part shed in Honour's Cause,
While yet in *Britain* Honour had Applause)
Each Parent sprung— " What Fortune, pray? "— Their own,
And better got than *Bestia*'s from the Throne.   391
Born to no Pride, inheriting no Strife,
Nor marrying Discord in a Noble Wife,
Stranger to Civil and Religious Rage,
The good Man walk'd innoxious thro' his Age.   395
No Courts he saw, no Suits wou'd ever try,
Nor dar'd an Oath, nor hazarded a Lye.
Un-learn'd, he knew no Schoolman's subtle Art,
No Language, but the Language of the Heart.
By Nature honest, by Experience wise,   400
Healthy by Temp'rance and by Exercise:
His Life, tho' long, to sickness past unknown,
His Death was instant, and without a groan.
Oh grant me thus to live, and thus to dye!
Who sprung from Kings shall know less joy than I.   405
    O Friend! may each Domestick Bliss be thine!
Be no unpleasing Melancholy mine:
Me, let the tender Office long engage,
To rock the Cradle of reposing Age,
With lenient Arts extend a Mother's breath,   410
Make Languor smile, and smooth the bed of Death,
Explore the Thought, explain the asking Eye,
And keep a while one Parent from the Sky!
On Cares like these if Length of days attend,
May Heav'n, to bless those days, preserve my Friend,   415
Preserve him social, chearful, and serene,
And just as rich as when he serv'd a QUEEN!
Whether that Blessing be deny'd, or giv'n,
Thus far was right, the rest belongs to Heav'n.

---

391 *Bestia:*   perhaps the Duke of Marlborough (1650-1722).   417
Arbuthnot was the Queen's physician.

James Thomson

1700—1748

WINTER

The text of the first edition (1726). The poem was greatly
expanded when it was later incorporated in *The Seasons*.

Rapidus Sol
Nondum Hyemem contingit Equis. Jam præterit æstas.
VIRGIL

Glacialis HYEMS *canos hirsuta Capillos.*
OVID

See! WINTER comes, to rule the varied Year,
Sullen, and sad; with all his rising Train,
Vapours, and *Clouds*, and *Storms*: Be these my Theme,
These, that exalt the Soul to solemn Thought,
And heavenly musing. Welcome kindred Glooms!   5
Wish'd, wint'ry, Horrors, hail!—With frequent Foot,
Pleas'd, have I, in my cheerful Morn of Life,
When, nurs'd by careless *Solitude*, I liv'd,
And sung of Nature with unceasing Joy,
Pleas'd, have I wander'd thro' your rough Domains;   10
Trod the pure, virgin, Snows, myself as pure:
Heard the Winds roar, and the big Torrent burst:
Or seen the deep, fermenting, Tempest brew'd,
In the red, evening, Sky.—Thus pass'd the Time,
Till, thro' the opening Chambers of the South,   15
Look'd out the joyous *Spring*, look'd out, and smil'd.

Thee too, Inspirer of the toiling Swain!
Fair AUTUMN, yellow rob'd! I'll sing of thee,
Of thy last, temper'd, Days, and sunny Calms;
When all the golden *Hours* are on the Wing,   20
Attending thy Retreat, and round thy Wain,
Slow-rolling, onward to the Southern Sky.

Behold! the well-pois'd *Hornet*, hovering, hangs,
With quivering Pinions, in the genial Blaze;

21 *Wain:* chariot.   24 *Genial:* warm.
336

Flys off, in airy Circles: then returns,   25
And hums, and dances to the beating Ray.
Nor shall the Man, that, musing, walks alone,
And, heedless, strays within his radiant Lists,
Go unchastis'd away.—Sometimes, a Fleece
Of Clouds, wide-scattering, with a lucid Veil,   3o
Soft, shadow o'er th' unruffled Face of Heaven;
And, thro' their dewy Sluices, shed the Sun,
With temper'd Influence down. Then is the Time,
For those, whom *Wisdom*, and whom *Nature* charm,
To steal themselves from the degenerate Croud,   35
And soar above this *little* Scene of Things:
To tread low-thoughted *Vice* beneath their Feet:
To lay their Passions in a gentle Calm,
And woo lone *Quiet*, in her silent *Walks*.

Now, solitary, and in pensive Guise,   40
Oft, let me wander o'er the russet Mead,
Or thro' the pining Grove; where scarce is heard
One dying Strain, to chear the *Woodman*'s Toil:
Sad *Philomel*, perchance, pours forth her Plaint,
Far, thro' the withering Copse. Mean while, the Leaves,   45
That, late, the Forest clad with lively Green,
Nipt by the drizzly Night, and Sallow-hu'd,
Fall, wavering, thro' the Air; or shower amain,
Urg'd by the Breeze, that sobs amid the Boughs.
Then listening *Hares* forsake the rusling Woods,   50
And, starting at the frequent Noise, escape
To the rough Stubble, and the rushy Fen.
Then *Woodcocks*, o'er the fluctuating Main,
That glimmers to the Glimpses of the Moon,
Stretch their long Voyage to the woodland Glade   55
Where, wheeling with uncertain Flight, they mock
The nimble *Fowler*'s Aim.—Now *Nature* droops;
Languish the living Herbs, with pale Decay:
And all the *various Family* of Flowers
Their sunny Robes resign. The falling Fruits,   6o
Thro' the still Night, forsake the Parent-Bough,
That, in the first, grey, Glances of the Dawn,
Looks wild, and wonders at the wintry Waste.

The *Year*, yet pleasing, but declining fast,
Soft, o'er the secret Soul, in gentle Gales,   65

30 *Lucid:*   translucent. 44 *Philomel:*   the   nightingale. 65 *Gales:*
breezes.

A Philosophic Melancholly breathes,
And bears the swelling Thought aloft to Heaven.
Then forming *Fancy* rouses to conceive,
What never mingled with the Vulgar's Dream:
Then wake the tender *Pang*, the pitying *Tear*,   70
The *Sigh* for suffering Worth, the *Wish* prefer'd
For Humankind, the *Joy* to see them bless'd,
And all the *Social Off-spring* of the Heart!

Oh! bear me then to high, embowering, Shades;
To twilight Groves, and visionary Vales;   75
To weeping Grottos, and to hoary Caves;
Where Angel-Forms are seen, and Voices heard,
Sigh'd in low Whispers, that abstract the Soul,
From outward Sense, far into Worlds remote.

Now, when the Western Sun withdraws the Day,   80
And humid *Evening*, gliding o'er the Sky,
In her chill Progress, checks the straggling Beams,
And robs them of their gather'd, vapoury, Prey,
Where Marshes stagnate, and where Rivers wind,
Cluster the rolling *Fogs*, and swim along   85
The dusky-mantled Lawn: then slow descend,
Once more to mingle with their *Watry Friends*.

The vivid Stars shine out, in radiant Files;
And boundless *Ether* glows, till the fair Moon
Shows her broad Visage, in the crimson'd East;   90
Now, stooping, seems to kiss the passing Cloud:
Now, o'er the pure *Cerulean*, rides sublime.
Wide the pale Deluge floats, with silver Waves,
O'er the sky'd Mountain, to the low-laid Vale;
From the white Rocks, with dim Reflexion, gleams,   95
And faintly glitters thro' the waving Shades.

All Night, abundant Dews, unnoted, fall,
And, at Return of Morning, silver o'er
The Face of Mother-Earth; from every Branch
Depending, tremble the translucent Gems,   100
And, quivering, seem to fall away, yet cling,
And sparkle in the Sun, whose rising Eye,
With Fogs bedim'd, portends a beauteous Day.

100 *Depending:* hanging.

Now, giddy Youth, whom headlong Passions fire,
Rouse the wild Game, and stain the guiltless Grove,   105
With Violence, and Death; yet call it Sport,
To scatter Ruin thro' the Realms of *Love*,
And *Peace*, that thinks no ill: But These, the *Muse*,
Whose Charity, unlimited, extends
As Wide as *Nature* works, disdains to sing,   110
Returning to her nobler Theme in view—

For see! where *Winter* comes, himself, confest,
Striding the gloomy Blast. First Rains obscure
Drive thro' the mingling Skies, with Tempest foul;
Beat on the Mountain's Brow, and shake the Woods,   115
That, sounding, wave below. The dreary Plain
Lies overwhelm'd, and lost. The bellying Clouds
Combine, and deepening into Night, shut up
The Day's fair Face. The Wanderers of Heaven,
Each to his Home, retire; save those that love   120
To take their Pastime in the troubled Air,
And, skimming, flutter round the dimply Flood.
The Cattle, from th' untasted Fields, return,
And ask, with Meaning low, their wonted Stalls;
Or ruminate in the contiguous Shade: 125
Thither, the household, feathery, People croud,
The crested Cock, with all his female Train,
Pensive, and wet. Mean while, the Cottage-Swain
Hangs o'er the enlivening Blaze, and, taleful, there,
Recounts his simple Frolic: Much he talks,   130
And much he laughs, nor recks the Storm that blows
Without, and rattles on his humble Roof.

At last, the muddy Deluge pours along,
Resistless, roaring; dreadful down it comes
From the chapt Mountain, and the mossy Wild,   135
Tumbling thro' Rocks abrupt, and sounding far:
Then o'er the sanded Valley, floating, spreads,
Calm, sluggish, silent; till again constrain'd,
Betwixt two meeting Hills, it bursts a Way,
Where Rocks, and Woods o'erhang the turbid Stream.   140
There gathering triple Force, rapid, and deep,
It boils, and wheels, and foams, and thunders thro'.

Nature! great Parent! whose directing Hand
Rolls round the Seasons of the changeful Year,
How mighty! how majestick are thy Works!   145

With what a pleasing Dread they swell the Soul,
That sees, astonish'd! and, astonish'd sings!
You too, ye *Winds*! that now begin to blow,
With boisterous Sweep, I raise my Voice to you.
Where are your Stores, ye viewless *Beings*! say?   150
Where your aerial Magazines reserv'd,
Against the Day of Tempest perilous?
In what untravel'd Country of the Air,
Hush'd in still Silence, sleep you, when 'tis calm?

Late, in the louring Sky, red, fiery, Streaks   155
Begin to flush about; the reeling Clouds
Stagger with dizzy Aim, as doubting yet
Which Master to obey: while rising, slow
Sad, in the Leaden-colour'd East, the Moon
Wears a bleak Circle round her sully'd Orb.   160
Then issues forth the Storm, with loud Control,
And the thin Fabrick of the pillar'd Air
O'erturns, at once. Prone, on th' uncertain Main,
Descends th' Etherial Force, and plows its Waves,
With dreadful Rift: from the mid-Deep, appears,   165
Surge after Surge, the rising, wat'ry, War.
Whitening, the angry Billows rowl immense,
And roar their Terrors, through the shuddering Soul
Of feeble Man, amidst their Fury caught,
And, dash'd upon his Fate: Then, o'er the Cliff,   170
Where dwells the *Sea-Mew*, unconfin'd, they fly,
And, hurrying, swallow up the steril Shore.

The Mountain growls; and all its sturdy *Sons*
Stoop to the Bottom of the Rocks they shade:
Lone, on its Midnight-Side, and all aghast,   175
The dark, way-faring, *Stranger*, breathless, toils,
And climbs against the Blast—
Low, waves the rooted Forest, vex'd, and sheds
What of its leafy Honours yet remains.
Thus, struggling thro' the dissipated Grove,   180
The whirling Tempest raves along the Plain;
And, on the Cottage thacht, or lordly Dome,
Keen-fastening, shakes 'em to the solid Base.
Sleep, frighted, flies; the hollow Chimney howls,
The Windows rattle, and the Hinges creak.   185

Then, too, they say, thro' all the burthen'd Air,
180 *Dissipated:* scattered.

Long Groans are heard, shrill Sounds, and distant Sighs,
That, murmur'd by the *Demon* of the Night,
Warn the devoted *Wretch* of Woe, and Death!
Wild Uproar lords it wide: the Clouds commixt,   190
With Stars, swift-gliding, sweep along the Sky.
All Nature reels.—But hark! The *Almighty* speaks:
Instant, the chidden Storm begins to pant,
And dies, at once, into a noiseless Calm.

As yet, 'tis Midnight's Reign; the weary Clouds,   195
Slow-meeting, mingle into solid Gloom:
Now, while the drousy World lies lost in Sleep,
Let me associate with the low-brow'd *Night*,
And *Contemplation*, her sedate Compeer;
Let me shake off th' intrusive Cares of Day,   200
And lay the medling Senses all aside.

And now, ye lying *Vanities* of Life!
You ever-tempting, ever-cheating Train!
Where are you now? and what is your Amount?
Vexation, Disappointment, and Remorse.   205
Sad, sickening, Thought! and yet, deluded Man,
A Scene of wild, disjointed, Visions past,
And broken Slumbers, rises, still resolv'd,
With new-flush'd Hopes, to run your giddy Round.

Father of Light, and Life! Thou *Good Supreme*!   210
O! teach me what is Good! teach me thy self!
Save me from Folly, Vanity and Vice,
From every low Pursuit! and feed my Soul,
With Knowledge, conscious Peace, and Vertue pure,
Sacred, substantial, never-fading Bliss!   215

Lo! from the livid East, or piercing North,
Thick Clouds ascend, in whose capacious Womb,
A vapoury Deluge lies, to Snow congeal'd:
Heavy, they roll their fleecy World along;
And the Sky saddens with th' impending Storm.   220
Thro' the hush'd Air, the whitening Shower descends,
At first, thin-wavering; till, at last, the Flakes
Fall broad, and wide, and fast, dimming the Day,
With a continual Flow. See! sudden, hoar'd,
The Woods beneath the stainless Burden bow,   225
Blackning, along the mazy Stream it melts;
Earth's universal Face, deep-hid, and chill,

Is all one, dazzling, Waste. The Labourer-Ox
Stands cover'd o'er with Snow, and then demands
The Fruit of all his Toil. The Fowls of Heaven,   230
Tam'd by the cruel Season, croud around
The winnowing Store, and claim the little Boon,
That *Providence* allows. The foodless Wilds
Pour foith their brown *Inhabitants*; the Hare,
Tho' tin orous of Heart, and hard beset   235
By Death, in various Forms, dark Snares, and Dogs,
And more unpitying Men, the Garden seeks,
Urg'd on by *fearless* Want. The bleating Kind
Eye the bleak Heavens, and next, the glistening Earth,
With Looks of dumb Despair; then sad, dispers'd,   240
Dig, for the wither'd Herb, thro' Heaps of Snow.

Now, *Shepherds*, to your helpless Charge be kind;
Baffle the raging Year, and fill their Penns
With Food, at will: lodge them below the Blast,
And watch them strict; for from the bellowing East,   245
In this dire Season, oft the Whirlwind's Wing
Sweeps up the Burthen of whole wintry Plains,
In one fierce Blast, and o'er th' unhappy Flocks,
Lodged in the Hollow of two neighbouring Hills,
The billowy Tempest whelms; till, upwards urg'd,   250
The Valley to a shining Mountain swells,
That curls its Wreaths amid the freezing Sky.

Now, all amid the Rigours of the Year,
In the wild Depth of Winter, while without
The ceaseless Winds blow keen, be my Retreat   255
A rural, shelter'd, solitary, Scene;
Where ruddy Fire, and beaming Tapers join
To chase the chearless Gloom: there let me sit,
And hold high Converse with the mighty Dead,
Sages of ancient Time, as Gods rever'd,   260
As Gods beneficent, who blest Mankind,
With Arts, and Arms, and humaniz'd a World.
Rous'd at th' inspiring Thought—I throw aside
The long-liv'd Volume, and, deep-musing, hail
The sacred *Shades*, that, slowly-rising, pass   265
Before my wondering Eyes—First, *Socrates*,
Truth's early Champion, Martyr for his God:
Solon, the next, who built his Commonweal,

266 *Socrates:* Greek philosopher (469-399 B.C.). 268 *Solon:* Greek
statesman (*c.* 640-*c.* 558 B.C.).

On Equity's firm Base: *Lycurgus*, then,
Severely good, and him of rugged *Rome*,   270
Numa, who soften'd *her* rapacious *Sons*.
Cimon, sweet-soul'd, and *Aristides* just.
Unconquer'd *Cato*, virtuous in Extreme;
With that attemper'd Heroe, mild and firm,
Who wept the Brother, while the Tyrant bled.   275
Scipio, the humane Warriour, gently brave,
Fair Learning's Friend; who early sought the Shade,
To dwell, with *Innocence*, and *Truth*, retir'd.
And, equal to the best, the *Theban*, *He*
Who, *single*, rais'd his Country into Fame.   280
Thousands behind, the Boast of *Greece* and *Rome*,
Whom *Vertue* owns, the Tribute of a Verse
Demand, but who can count the Stars of Heaven?
Who sing their Influence on this lower World?
But see who yonder comes! nor comes alone,   285
With *sober* State, and of *majestic* Mien,
The Sister-Muses in his Train—'Tis He!
Maro! the best of Poets, and of Men!
Great *Homer* too appears, of *daring* Wing!
Parent of Song! and *equal*, by his Side,   290
The *British Muse*, join'd Hand in Hand, they walk,
Darkling, nor miss their Way to Fame's Ascent.

Society divine! Immortal Minds!
Still visit thus my Nights, for *you* reserv'd,
And mount my soaring Soul to Deeds like yours.   295
Silence! thou lonely *Power!* the Door be thine:
See, on the hallow'd Hour, that none intrude,
Save *Lycidas*, the Friend, with Sense refin'd,
Learning digested well, exalted Faith,
Unstudy'd Wit, and Humour ever gay.   300

Clear Frost succeeds, and thro' the blew Serene,
For Sight too fine, th' Ætherial Nitre flies,
To bake the Glebe, and bind the slip'ry Flood.
This of the wintry Season is the Prime;

269 *Lycurgus*: legendary Greek statesman and lawgiver. 271 *Numa*:
legendary Roman king, successor of Romulus. 272 *Cimon*: Greek
commander (*c*. 507-449 B.C.); *Aristides*: Greek statesman (*c*. 530-
468 B.C.). 273 *Cato*: Roman statesman and moralist (234-149 B.C.).
274 *That attemper'd Heroe*: Timoleon, Greek democrat, statesman, and
general (*c*. 411-*c*. 337 B.C.). 276 *Scipio*: Roman commander and patron
of letters (*c*. 185-129 B.C.). 279 *The Theban*: Epaminondas (*c*. 420-
362 B.C.), military commander. 288 *Maro*: Virgil.

Pure are the Days, and lustrous are the Nights,   305
Brighten'd with starry Worlds, till then unseen.
Mean while, the Orient, darkly red, breathes forth
An Icy Gale, that, in its mid Career,
Arrests the bickering Stream. The nightly Sky,
And all her glowing Constellations pour   310
Their rigid Influence down: It freezes on
Till Morn, late-rising, o'er the drooping World,
Lifts her pale Eye, unjoyous: then appears
The various Labour of the silent Night,
The pendant Isicle, the Frost-Work fair,   315
Where thousand Figures rise, the crusted Snow,
Tho' white, made whiter, by the fining North.
On blithsome Frolic bent, the youthful Swains,
While every Work of Man is laid at Rest,
Rush o'er the watry Plains, and, shuddering, view   320
The fearful Deeps below: or with the Gun,
And faithful Spaniel, range the ravag'd Fields,
And, adding to the Ruins of the Year,
Distress the Feathery, or the Footed *Game*.

But hark! the nightly Winds, with hollow Voice,   325
Blow, blustering, from the South—the Frost subdu'd,
Gradual, resolves into a weeping Thaw.
Spotted, the Mountains shine: loose Sleet descends,
And floods the Country round: the Rivers swell,
Impatient for the Day.—Those sullen Seas,   330
That wash th' ungenial Pole, will rest no more,
Beneath the Shackles of the mighty North;
But, rousing all their Waves, resistless heave,—
And hark!—the length'ning Roar, continuous, runs
Athwart the rifted Main; at once, it bursts,   335
And piles a thousand Mountains to the Clouds!
Ill fares the Bark, the Wretches' last Resort,
That, lost amid the floating Fragments, moors
Beneath the Shelter of an Icy Isle;
While Night o'erwhelms the Sea, and Horror looks   340
More horrible. Can human Hearts endure
Th' assembled *Mischiefs*, that besiege them round:
Unlist'ning *Hunger*, fainting *Weariness*,
The *Roar* of Winds, and Waves, the *Crush* of Ice,
Now, ceasing, now, renew'd, with louder Rage,   345
And bellowing round the Main: Nations remote,
Shook from their Midnight-Slumbers, deem they hear
317 *Fining*: refining.

Portentous Thunder, in the troubled Sky.
More to embroil the Deep, Leviathan,
And his unweildy Train, in horrid Sport,   350
Tempest the loosen'd Brine; while, thro' the Gloom,
Far, from the dire, unhospitable Shore,
The Lyon's Rage, the Wolf's sad Howl is heard,
And all the fell Society of Night.
Yet, *Providence*, that ever-waking *Eye*   355
Looks down, with Pity, on the fruitless Toil
Of Mortals, lost to Hope, and *lights* them safe,
Thro' all this dreary Labyrinth of Fate.

'Tis done!—Dread WINTER has subdued the Year,
And reigns, tremenduous, o'er the desart Plains!   360
How dead the Vegetable Kingdom lies!
How dumb the Tuneful! *Horror* wide extends
His solitary Empire.—Now, fond *Man*!
Behold thy pictur'd life: Pass some few Years,
Thy flow'ring SPRING, Thy short-liv'd SUMMER's Strength,   365
Thy sober AUTUMN, fading into Age,
And pale, concluding, WINTER shuts thy Scene,
And shrouds *Thee* in the Grave—where now, are fled
Those Dreams of Greatness? those unsolid Hopes
Of Happiness? those Longings after Fame?   370
Those restless Cares? those busy, bustling Days?
Those Nights of secret Guilt? those veering Thoughts,
Flutt'ring 'twixt Good, and Ill, that shar'd thy Life?
All, now, are vanish'd! *Vertue*, sole, survives,
Immortal, Mankind's never-failing Friend,   375
His Guide to Happiness on high—and see!
'Tis come, the Glorious *Morn*! the second Birth
Of Heaven, and Earth!—awakening *Nature* hears
Th' Almighty Trumpet's Voice, and starts to Life,
Renew'd, unfading. Now, th' Eternal *Scheme*,   380
That Dark Perplexity, that Mystic Maze,
Which Sight cou'd never trace, nor Heart conceive,
To *Reason*'s Eye, refin'd, clears up apace.
Angels, and Men, astonish'd, pause—and dread
To travel thro' the Depths of Providence,   385
Untry'd, unbounded. Ye vain *Learned*! see,
And, prostrate in the Dust, adore that *Power*,
And *Goodness*, oft arraign'd. See now the Cause,
Why conscious *Worth*, oppress'd, in secret long
Mourn'd, unregarded: Why the *Good Man*'s Share   390
In Life, was Gall, and Bitterness of Soul:

Why the lone *Widow*, and her *Orphans*, pin'd,
In starving Solitude; while *Luxury*,
In Palaces, lay prompting her low Thought,
To form unreal Wants: why Heaven-born *Faith*,   395
And *Charity*, prime Grace! wore the *red* Marks
Of *Persecution's* Scourge: Why licens'd *Pain*,
That cruel *Spoiler*, that embosom'd *Foe*,
Imbitter'd all our Bliss. Ye Good *Distrest*!
Ye noble *Few*! that, here, unbending, stand   400
Beneath Life's Pressures—yet a little while,
And all your Woes are past. *Time* swiftly fleets,
And wish'd *Eternity*, approaching, brings
Life undecaying, Love without Allay,
Pure flowing Joy, and Happiness sincere.   405

Thomas Gray

1716—1771

ELEGY WRITTEN IN A COUNTRY CHURCH-YARD

The Curfew tolls the kr ell of parting day,
The lowing herd wind slowly o'er the lea,
The plowman homeward plods his weary way,
And leaves the world to darkness and to me.

Now fades the glimmering landscape on the sight,   5
And all the air a solemn stillness holds,
Save where the beetle wheels his droning flight,
And drowsy tinklings lull the distant folds;

Save that from yonder ivy-mantled tow'r
The mopeing owl does to the moon complain   10
Of such, as wand'ring near her secret bow'r,
Molest her ancient solitary reign.

Beneath those rugged elms, that yew-tree's shade,
Where heaves the turf in many a mould'ring heap,
Each in his narrow cell for ever laid,   15
The rude Forefathers of the hamlet sleep.

16 *Rude:* rough, uneducated.

The breezy call of incense-breathing Morn,
The swallow twitt'ring from the straw-built shed,
The cock's shrill clarion, or the echoing horn,
No more shall rouse them from their lowly bed.   20

For them no more the blazing hearth shall burn,
Or busy housewife ply her evening care:
No children run to lisp their sire's return,
Or climb his knees the envied kiss to share.

Oft did the harvest to their sickle yield,   25
Their furrow oft the stubborn glebe has broke;
How jocund did they drive their team afield!
How bow'd the woods beneath their sturdy stroke!

Let not Ambition mock their useful toil,
Their homely joys, and destiny obscure;   30
Nor Grandeur hear with a disdainful smile,
The short and simple annals of the poor.

The boast of heraldry, the pomp of pow'r,
And all that beauty, all that wealth e'er gave,
Awaits alike th' inevitable hour.   35
The paths of glory lead but to the grave.

Nor you, ye Proud, impute to These the fault,
If Mem'ry o'er their Tomb no Trophies raise,
Where thro' the long-drawn isle and fretted vault
The pealing anthem swells the note of praise.   40

Can storied urn or animated bust
Back to its mansion call the fleeting breath?
Can Honour's voice provoke the silent dust,
Or Flatt'ry sooth the dull cold ear of Death?

Perhaps in this neglected spot is laid   45
Some heart once pregnant with celestial fire;
Hands, that the rod of empire might have sway'd,
Or wak'd to extasy the living lyre.

But Knowledge to their eyes her ample page
Rich with the spoils of time did ne'er unroll;   50
Chill Penury repress'd their noble rage,
And froze the genial current of the soul.

26 *Glebe:* soil.   41 *Storied:* (i) inscribed, (ii) celebrated, famous;
animated: lifelike.   52 *Genial:* (i) pertaining to genius, (ii) warm.

Full many a gem of purest ray serene,
The dark unfathom'd caves of ocean bear:
Full many a flower is born to blush unseen,   55
And waste its sweetness on the desert air.

Some village-Hampden, that with dauntless breast
The little Tyrant of his fields withstood;
Some mute inglorious Milton here may rest,
Some Cromwell guiltless of his country's blood.   60

Th'applause of list'ning senates to command,
The threats of pain and ruin to despise,
To scatter plenty o'er a smiling land,
And read their hist'ry in a nation's eyes,

Their lot forbad: nor circumscrib'd alone   65
Their growing virtues, but their crimes confin'd;
Forbad to wade through slaughter to a throne,
And shut the gates of mercy on mankind,

The struggling pangs of conscious truth to hide,
To quench the blushes of ingenuous shame,   70
Or heap the shrine of Luxury and Pride
With incense kindled at the Muse's flame.

Far from the madding crowd's ignoble strife,
Their sober wishes never learn'd to stray;
Along the cool sequester'd vale of life   75
They kept the noiseless tenor of their way.

Yet ev'n these bones from insult to protect
Some frail memorial still erected nigh,
With uncouth rhimes and shapeless sculpture deck'd,
Implores the passing tribute of a sigh.   80

Their name, their years, spelt by th' unlettered muse,
The place of fame and elegy supply:
And many a holy text around she strews,
That teach the rustic moralist to die.

For who to dumb Forgetfulness a prey,   85
This pleasing anxious being e'er resign'd,
Left the warm precincts of the chearful day,
Nor cast one longing ling'ring look behind?

57 *Hampden:* John Hampden (1594-1643) resisted Charles I's revival of
a ship-money tax.

On some fond breast the parting soul relies,
Some pious drops the closing eye requires; 90
Ev'n from the tomb the voice of Nature cries,
Ev'n in our Ashes live their wonted Fires.

For thee, who mindful of th' unhonour'd Dead
Dost in these lines their artless tale relate;
If chance, by lonely contemplation led, 95
Some kindred Spirit shall inquire thy fate,

Haply some hoary-headed Swain may say,
" Oft have we seen him at the peep of dawn
Brushing with hasty steps the dews away
To meet the sun upon the upland lawn. 100

" There at the foot of yonder nodding beech
That wreathes its old fantastic roots so high,
His listless length at noontide would he stretch,
And pore upon the brook that babbles by.

" Hard by yon wood, now smiling as in scorn, 105
Mutt'ring his wayward fancies he would rove,
Now drooping, woeful wan, like one forlorn,
Or craz'd with care, or cross'd in hopeless love.

" One morn I miss'd him on the custom'd hill,
Along the heath and near his fav'rite tree; 110
Another came; nor yet beside the rill,
Nor up the lawn, nor at the wood was he;

" The next with dirges due in sad array
Slow thro' the church-way path we saw him borne.
Approach and read (for thou can'st read) the lay, 115
Grav'd on the stone beneath yon aged thorn."

THE EPITAPH

Here rests his head upon the lap of Earth
A Youth to Fortune and to Fame unknown.
Fair Science frown'd not on his humble birth,
And Melancholy mark'd him for her own. 120

Large was his bounty, and his soul sincere,
Heav'n did a recompence as largely send:

He gave to Mis'ry all he had, a tear,
He gained from Heav'n ('twas all he wish'd) a friend.

No farther seek his merits to disclose,   125
Or draw his frailties from their dread abode,
(There they alike in trembling hope repose,)
The bosom of his Father and his God.

William Cowper

1731—1800

THE DIVERTING HISTORY
OF
JOHN GILPIN,
SHOWING HOW HE WENT FARTHER THAN HE
INTENDED, AND CAME SAFE HOME AGAIN

Published anonymously November 1782 in *The Public Advertiser*.
The poem became very popular and was reprinted as a chapbook.
Cowper himself saw the reason for its success: ' In a world like
this, abounding with subjects for satire, and with satirical wits to
mark them, a laugh that hurts nobody has at least the grace of
novelty to recommend it.' Various inconclusive attempts have
been made to identify the original of John Gilpin.

John Gilpin was a citizen
  Of credit and renown,
A train-band captain eke was he
  Of famous London town.

John Gilpin's spouse said to her dear—   5
  Though wedded we have been
These twice ten tedious years, yet we
  No holiday have seen.

To-morrow is our wedding-day,
  And we will then repair   10
Unto the Bell at Edmonton
  All in a chaise and pair.

3 *Train-band:* trained company of citizen soldiers.   11 *Edmonton:* in
east Middlesex, between Enfield and Tottenham.

My sister, and my sister's child,
  Myself, and children three,
Will fill the chaise; so you must ride   15
  On horseback after we.

He soon replied—I do admire
  Of womankind but one,
And you are she, my dearest dear,
  Therefore it shall be done.   20

I am a linen-draper bold,
  As all the world doth know,
And my good friend the calender
  Will lend his horse to go.

Quoth Mrs. Gilpin—That's well said;   25
  And, for that wine is dear,
We will be furnish'd with our own,
  Which is both bright and clear.

John Gilpin kiss'd his loving wife;
  O'erjoy'd was he to find   30
That, though on pleasure she was bent,
  She had a frugal mind.

The morning came, the chaise was brought,
  But yet was not allow'd
To drive up to the door, lest all   35
  Should say that she was proud.

So three doors off the chaise was stay'd,
  Where they did all get in;
Six precious souls, and all agog
  To dash through thick and thin!   40

Smack went the whip, round went the wheels,
  Were never folk so glad,
The stones did rattle underneath,
  As if Cheapside were mad.

John Gilpin at his horse's side   45
  Seiz'd fast the flowing mane,
And up he got, in haste to ride,
  But soon came down again;

23 *Calender:* one who presses or glazes cloth.   44 *Cheapside:* street in London, between St. Paul's Cathedral and the Poultry.

For saddle-tree scarce reach'd had he,
　　His journey to begin,
When, turning round his head, he saw
　　Three customers come in.　　　　　　　　50

So down he came; for loss of time,
　　Although it griev'd him sore,
Yet loss of pence, full well he knew,
　　Would trouble him much more.　　　　　　55

'Twas long before the customers
　　Were suited to their mind,
When Betty screaming came down stairs—
　　" The wine is left behind! "　　　　　　　60

Good lack! quoth he—yet bring it me,
　　My leathern belt likewise,
In which I bear my trusty sword
　　When I do exercise.

Now mistress Gilpin (careful soul!)　　　　　65
　　Had two stone bottles found,
To hold the liquor that she lov'd,
　　And keep it safe and sound.

Each bottle had a curling ear,
　　Through which the belt he drew,　　　　　70
And hung a bottle on each side,
　　To make his balance true.

Then, over all, that he might be
　　Equipp'd from top to toe,
His long red cloak, well brush'd and neat,　　75
　　He manfully did throw.

Now see him mounted once again
　　Upon his nimble steed,
Full slowly pacing o'er the stones,
　　With caution and good heed!　　　　　　　80

But, finding soon a smoother road
　　Beneath his well-shod feet,
The snorting beast began to trot,
　　Which gall'd him in his seat.

49 *Saddle-tree:* frame of saddle.

So, Fair and softly, John he cried,   85
  But John he cried in vain;
That trot became a gallop soon,
  In spite of curb and rein.

So stooping down, as needs he must
  Who cannot sit upright,
He grasp'd the mane with both his hands,   90
  And eke with all his might.

His horse, who never in that sort
  Had handled been before,
What thing upon his back had got   95
  Did wonder more and more.

Away went Gilpin, neck or nought;
  Away went hat and wig!—
He little dreamt, when he set out,
  Of running such a rig!   100

The wind did blow, the cloak did fly,
  Like streamer long and gay,
Till, loop and button failing both,
  At last it flew away.

Then might all people well discern   105
  The bottles he had slung;
A bottle swinging at each side,
  As hath been said or sung.

The dogs did bark, the children scream'd,
  Up flew the windows all;   110
And ev'ry soul cried out—Well done!
  As loud as he could bawl.

Away went Gilpin—who but he?
  His fame soon spread around—
He carries weight! he rides a race!   115
  'Tis for a thousand pound!

And still, as fast as he drew near,
  'Twas wonderful to view
How in a trice the turnpike-men
  Their gates wide open threw.   120

92 *Eke:* also.
A.L.P.   M

And now, as he went bowing down
  His reeking head full low,
The bottles twain behind his back
  Were shatter'd at a blow.

Down ran the wine into the road,   125
  Most piteous to be seen,
Which made his horse's flanks to smoke
  As they had basted been.

But still he seem'd to carry weight,
  With leathern girdle brac'd;   130
For all might see the bottle-necks
  Still dangling at his waist.

Thus all through merry Islington
  These gambols he did play,
And till he came unto the Wash   135
  Of Edmonton so gay.

And there he threw the wash about
  On both sides of the way,
Just like unto a trundling mop,
  Or a wild goose at play.   140

At Edmonton his loving wife
  From the balcony spied
Her tender husband, wond'ring much
  To see how he did ride.

Stop, stop, John Gilpin!—Here's the house—   145
  They all at once did cry;
The dinner waits, and we are tir'd:
  Said Gilpin—So am I!

But yet his horse was not a whit
  Inclin'd to tarry there;   150
For why?—his owner had a house
  Full ten miles off, at Ware.

133 *Islington:* then a village on the northern fringe of London, on the
way to Edmonton. 152 *Ware:* near Hertford, about 13 miles north of
Edmonton and about 25 miles from London.

So like an arrow swift he flew,
  Shot by an archer strong;
So did he fly—which brings me to   155
  The middle of my song.

Away went Gilpin, out of breath,
  And sore against his will,
Till at his friend the calender's
  His horse at last stood still.   160

The calender, amaz'd to see
  His neighbour in such trim,
Laid down his pipe, flew to the gate,
  And thus accosted him:—

What news? what news? your tidings tell;   165
  Tell me you must and shall—
Say why bare-headed you are come,
  Or why you come at all?

Now Gilpin had a pleasant wit,
  And lov'd a timely joke;   170
And thus unto the calender
  In merry guise he spoke:—

I came because your horse would come;
  And, if I well forebode,
My hat and wig will soon be here—   175
  They are upon the road.

The calender, right glad to find
  His friend in merry pin,
Return'd him not a single word,
  But to the house went in;   180

Whence straight he came with hat and wig;
  A wig that flow'd behind,
A hat not much the worse for wear,
  Each comely in its kind.

He held them up, and, in his turn,   185
  Thus show'd his ready wit—
My head is twice as big as your's,
  They therefore needs must fit.

178 *In merry pin:* in merry frame of mind.

But let me scrape the dirt away
    That hangs upon your face;   190
And stop and eat, for well you may
    Be in a hungry case.

Said John—It is my wedding-day,
    And all the world would stare,
If wife should dine at Edmonton   195
    And I should dine at Ware!

So, turning to his horse, he said—
    I am in haste to dine;
'Twas for your pleasure you came here,
    You shall go back for mine.   200

Ah, luckless speech, and bootless boast!
    For which he paid full dear;
For, while he spake, a braying ass
    Did sing most loud and clear;

Whereat his horse did snort, as he   205
    Had heard a lion roar,
And gallop'd off with all his might,
    As he had done before.

Away went Gilpin, and away
    Went Gilpin's hat and wig!   210
He lost them sooner than at first—
    For why?—they were too big!

Now, mistress Gilpin, when she saw
    Her husband posting down
Into the country far away,   215
    She pull'd out half a crown;

And thus unto the youth she said
    That drove them to the Bell—
This shall be yours when you bring back
    My husband safe and well.   220

The youth did ride, and soon did meet
    John coming back amain;
Whom in a trice he tried to stop,
    By catching at his rein;

214 *Posting:* hurrying.

But, not performing what he meant, 225
  And gladly would have done,
The frighted steed he frighted more,
  And made him faster run.

Away went Gilpin, and away
  Went post-boy at his heels!— 230
The post-boy's horse right glad to miss
  The lumb'ring of the wheels.

Six gentlemen upon the road,
  Thus seeing Gilpin fly,
With post-boy scamp'ring in the rear, 235
  They rais'd the hue and cry:

Stop thief! stop thief!—a highwayman!
  Not one of them was mute;
And all and each that pass'd that way
  Did join in the pursuit. 240

And now the turnpike gates again
  Flew open in short space;
The toll-men thinking, as before,
  That Gilpin rode a race.

And so he did—and won it too!— 245
  For he got first to town;
Nor stopp'd till where he had got up
  He did again get down.

Now let us sing—Long live the king,
  And Gilpin long live he;
And, when he next doth ride abroad, 250
  May I be there to see!

Robert Fergusson

1750—1774

AULD REIKIE

Auld Reikie, wale o' ilka town
That *Scotland* kens beneath the moon;
Whare couthy chiels at e'ening meet
Their bizzing *craigs* and *mou's* to weet;
And blythly gar auld care gae bye   5
Wi' blinkit and wi' bleering eye:
O'er lang frae thee the Muse has been
Sae frisky on the *Simmer's* green,
Whan flowers and gowans wont to glent
In bonny blinks upo' the bent;   10
But now the *leaves* of yellow dye,
Peel'd frae the *branches*, quickly fly;
And now frae nouther bush nor brier
The spreckl'd *mavis* greets your ear;
Nor bonny blackbird *skims* and *roves*   15
To seek his love in yonder groves.

Then *Reikie*, welcome! Thou canst charm
Unfleggit by the year's alarm;
Not Boreas, that sae snelly blows,
Dare here pap in his angry nose: 20
Thanks to our *dads*, whase biggin stands
A shelter to surrounding lands.

Now morn, with bonny purpie smiles,
Kisses the air-cock o' St. Giles;
Rakin their ein, the servant lasses   25
Early begin their lies and clashes;

---

1 *Auld Reikie:* 'Old Smoky': Edinburgh's nickname, earned by the
smoke from its high tenements; *wale:* choice, best; *ilka:* every. 3
Couthy chiels: friendly fellows. 4 *Bizzing craigs:* parched throats.
5 *Gar:* make. 9 *Gowans:* daisies; *glent:* gleam. 10 *Bent:* coarse
grass. 14 *Mavis:* song-thrush. 18 *Unfleggit:* undeterred. 19 *Boreas:*
Greek god of the north wind; *snelly:* keenly. 21 *Biggin:* building.
23 *Purpie:* purple, rosy. 24 *St. Giles:* the Church of St. Giles in the
High Street. 25 *Rakin:* rubbing open. 26 *Clashes:* chatter.

358

Ilk tells her friend of saddest distress,
That still she brooks frae scouling mistress;
And wi' her joe in turnpike stair
She'd rather snuff the stinking air,   30
As be subjected to her tongue,
When justly censur'd in the wrong.

On stair wi' *tub*, or *pat* in hand,
The barefoot *housemaids* loe to stand,
That antrin fock may ken how *snell*   35
Auld Reikie will at *morning smell*:
Then, with an *inundation big* as
The *burn* that 'neath the *Nor' Loch brig* is,
They kindly shower EDINA's roses,
To *quicken* and *regale* our *noses*.   40
Now some for this, wi' satire's leesh,
Ha'e gi'en auld Edinburgh a creesh:
But without souring nocht is sweet;
The morning smells that hail our street,
Prepare, and gently lead the way   45
To simmer canty, braw and gay:
Edina's sons mair eithly share
Her spices and her dainties rare,
Than he that's never yet been call'd
Aff frae his pladie or his fauld.   50

Now stair-head critics, senseless fools,
Censure their *aim*, and *pride* their rules,
In Luckenbooths, wi' glouring eye,
Their neighbours sma'est faults descry:
If ony loun should dander there,   55
Of aukward gate, and foreign air,
They trace his steps, till they can tell
His *pedigree* as weel's himsell.

Whan Phœbus blinks wi' warmer ray,
And schools at noon-day get the play,   60

29 *Joe:* boy-friend; *turnpike stair:* spiral staircase in tenement.   33 *Pat:*
chamber-pot.   35 *Antrin fock:* chance passers-by.   38 *Nor' Loch brig:*
the North Bridge, begun 1763 after the Nor' Loch (which covered what
is now Princes Street Gardens) had been drained.   41 *Leesh:* lash.
42 *Creesh:* whipping.   46 *Canty:* cheerful.   47 *Eithly:* easily.   50
Fauld: fold.   53 *Luckenbooths:* closed ('locked') shops in the High
Street, i.e. not open booths or stalls.   55 *Loun:* lad; *dander:* wander.
59 *Phœbus:* Greek sun-god.

Then bus'ness, weighty bus'ness, comes;
The trader glours; he doubts, he hums:
The lawyers eke to cross repair,
Their wigs to shaw, and toss an air;
While busy agent closely plies,   65
And a' his kittle cases tries.

   Now night, that's cunzied chief for fun,
Is wi' her usual rites begun;
Thro' ilka gate the torches blaze,
And globes send out their blinking rays.   70
The usefu' cadie plies in street,
To bide the profits o' his feet;
For by thir lads Auld Reikie's fock
Ken but a *sample* o' the stock
O' thieves, that nightly wad oppress,   75
And make baith goods and gear the less.
Near him the lazy chairman stands,
And wats na how to turn his hands,
Till some daft birky, ranting fu',
Has matters somewhere else to do;   80
The chairman willing gi'es his light
To deeds o' darkness and o' night:

   It's never sax-pence for a lift
That gars thir lads wi' fu'ness rift;
For they wi' better gear are paid,   85
And *whores* and *culls* support their trade.

   Near some lamp-post, wi' dowy face,
Wi' heavy ein, and sour grimace,
Stands she that beauty lang had kend,
Whoredom her trade, and vice her end.   90
But see whare now she wuns her bread
By that which nature ne'er decreed;
And sings sad music to the lugs,
'Mang bourachs o' damned whores and rogues.
Whane'er we reputation loss,   95
Fair chastity's transparent gloss!

66 *Kittle:*   tricky. 67 *Cunzied:*   recognized, counted. 71 *Cadie:*
messenger. 73 *Thir:* these. 77 *Chairman:* bearer of sedan-chair.
79 *Birky:* cheeky fellow; *ranting fu':* roaring drunk. 84 *Rift:* belch.
86 *Culls:* fools, dupes. 87 *Dowy:* sad. 93 *Lugs:* ears. 94 *Bourachs:*
groups, gatherings.

Redemption seenil kens the name,
But a's black misery and shame.

Frae joyous tavern, reeling drunk
Wi' fiery phizz, and ein half sunk,   100
Behad the bruiser, fae to a'
That in the reek o' gardies fa':
Close by his side, a feckless race
O' macaronies shew their face,
And think they're free frae skaith or harm,   105
While pith befriends their leader's arm:
Yet fearfu' aften o' their maught,
They quat the glory o' the faught
To this same warrior wha led
Thae heroes to bright honour's bed;   110
And aft the hack o' honour shines
In bruiser's face wi' broken lines:
Of them sad tales he tells anon,
Whan ramble and whan fighting's done;
And, like Hectorian, ne'er impairs   115
The brag and glory o' his sairs.

When feet in dirty gutters plash,
And fock to wale their fitstaps fash;
At night the macaroni drunk,
In pools or gutters aftimes sunk: 120
Hegh! what a fright he now appears,
Whan he his corpse dejected rears!
Look at that head, and think if there
The pomet slaister'd up his hair!
The cheeks observe, where now cou'd shine   125
The scancing glories o' carmine?
Ah, legs! in vain the silk-worm there
Display'd to view her eidant care;
For stink, instead of perfumes, grow,
And clarty odours fragrant flow.   130

97 *Seenil:* seldom. 100 *Phizz:* face. 102 *Reek o' gardies:* arm's reach.
104 *Macaronies:* fops, dandies. 105 *Skaith:* injury. 107 *Maught:*
strength. 108 *Quat:* quit. 110 *Thae:* those. 115 *Hectorian:* un-
identified, but no doubt connected with the name Hector and its later
connotation of 'braggart'; *impairs:* underplays, lessens. 116 *Sairs:*
wounds, bruises. 118 *Wale:* pick; *fash:* take care. 124 *Pomet:*
pomatum; *slaister'd up:* sleekly plastered. 126 *Scancing:* shining.
128 *Eidant:* diligent. 130 *Clarty:* filthy.

Now some to porter, some to punch,
Some to their wife, and some their wench,
Retire, while noisy ten-hours' drum
Gars a' your trades gae dandring home.
Now mony a club, jocose and free,　　　　　　　135
Gie a' to merriment and glee:
Wi' sang and glass, they fley the pow'r
O' care that wad harrass the hour:
For wine and Bacchus still bear down
Our thrawart fortune's wildest frown:　　　　　140
It maks you stark, and bauld, and brave,
Ev'n whan descending to the grave.

Now some, in *Pandemonium*'s shade,
Resume the gormandizing trade;
Whare eager *looks*, and glancing *ein*,　　　　　145
Forespeak a *heart* and *stamack* keen.
Gang on, my lads; it's lang sin syne
We kent auld *Epicurus*' line;
Save you, the *board* wad cease to rise,
Bedight wi' *daintiths* to the skies;　　　　　　150
And salamanders cease to swill
The *comforts* o' a *burning* gill.

But chief, O *Cape*! we crave thy aid,
To get our cares and poortith laid:
Sincerity, and genius true,　　　　　　　　　155
Of knights have ever been the due:
Mirth, music, porter deepest dy'd,
Are never here to worth deny'd;
And health, o' happiness the queen,
Blinks bonny, wi' her smile serene.　　　　　160

Tho' joy maist part Auld Reikie owns,
Eftsoons she kens sad sorrow's frowns;
What groupe is yon sae dismal, grim,
Wi' horrid aspect, cleeding dim?

133 *Ten-hours' drum:* warning drum at 10 p.m.　137 *Fley:* frighten
away.　139 *Bacchus:* Greek god of wine.　140 *Thrawart:* adverse.
141 *Stark:* strong.　143 *Pandemonium:* social club in Edinburgh.　148
Epicurus: (*c.* 340-270 B.C.), Greek hedonist philosopher.　150 *Daintiths:*
delicacies.　151 *Salamanders:* perhaps a nickname of members of the
Pandemonium or some other club.　153 *Cape:* social club in Edinburgh.
154 *Poortith:* poverty.　156 *Knights:* Cape Club members were given
knightly names. Fergusson was Sir Precenter.　164 *Cleeding:* clothing.

Says Death, they're mine, a dowy crew, 165
To me they'll quickly pay their last adieu.

How come mankind, whan lacking woe,
In *Saulie*'s face their hearts to show,
As if they were a clock to tell
That grief in them had rung her bell? 170
Then, what is man? why a' this phraze?
Life's spunk decay'd nae mair can blaze.
Let sober grief alone declare
Our fond anxiety and care:
Nor let the undertakers be 175
The only waefu' friends we see.

Come on, my Muse, and then rehearse
The gloomiest theme in a' your verse:
In morning, whan ane keeks about,
Fu' blyth and free frae ail, nae doubt 180
He lippens not to be misled
Amang the regions of the dead:
But straight a painted corp he sees,
Lang streekit 'neath its canopies.
Soon, soon will this his mirth controul, 185
And send d——n to his soul:
Or whan the dead-deal, (awful shape!)
Makes frighted mankind girn and gape,
Reflection then his reason sours,
For the niest dead-deal may be ours. 190
Whan Sybil led the Trojan down
To haggard *Pluto*'s dreary town,
Shapes war nor thae, I freely ween
Cou'd never meet the soldier's ein.

If kail sae green, or herbs, delight, 195
Edina's street attracts the sight;
Not Covent-garden, clad sae braw,
Mair fouth o' herbs can eithly shaw:
For mony a yeard is here sair sought,
That kail and cabbage may be bought; 200

168 *Saulie:* hired mourner. 171 *Phraze:* fuss. 179 *Keeks:* peers.
181 *Lippens:* trusts. 184 *Streekit:* laid out. 187 *Dead-deal:* board for
measuring and lifting corpse. 188 *Girn:* make faces. 190 *Niest:* next.
191-2 the visit of Æneas to the Underworld (Virgil, *Æneid*, VI). 193
War: worse. 195 *Kail:* colewort. 197 *Covent-garden:* vegetable
market in London. 198 *Fouth:* plenty.

And healthfu' sallad to regale,
Whan pamper'd wi' a heavy meal.
Glour up the street in simmer morn,
The birks sae green, and sweet brier-thorn,
Wi' spraingit flow'rs that scent the gale,   205
Ca' far away the morning smell,
Wi' which our ladies flow'r-pat's fill'd,
And every noxious vapour kill'd.
O nature! canty, blyth and free,
Whare is there keeking-glass like thee?   210
Is there on earth that can compare
Wi' Mary's shape, and Mary's air,
Save the empurpl'd speck, that grows
In the saft faulds of yonder rose?
How bonny seems the virgin breast,   215
Whan by the lillies here carest,
And leaves the mind in doubt to tell
Which maist in sweets and hue excel?

Gillespie's snuff should prime the nose
Of her that to the market goes,   220
If they wad like to shun the smells
That buoy up frae markest cells;
Whare wames o' painches' sav'ry scent
To nostrils gie great discontent.
Now wha in *Albion* could expect   225
O' cleanliness sic great neglect?
Nae Hottentot that daily lairs
'Mang tripe, or ither clarty wares,
Hath ever yet conceiv'd, or seen
Beyond the line, sic scenes unclean.   230

On Sunday here, an alter'd scene
O' men and manners meets our ein:
Ane wad maist trow some people chose
To change their faces wi' their clo'es,
And fain wad gar ilk neighbour think   235
They thirst for goodness, as for drink:
But there's an unco dearth o' grace,
That has nae mansion but the face,

204 *Birks:* birches.   205 *Spraingit:* streaked, variegated; *gale:* breeze.
206 *Ca':*   drive.   207 *Flow'r-pat:*   chamber-pot.   210 *Keeking-glass:*
mirror.   219 *Gillespie:*   Edinburgh tobacconist.   222 *Buoy:*   mount,
swell;   *markest:* darkest.   223 *Wames:* stomachs; *painches:* tripe.
225 *Albion:*   Britain.   227 *Lairs:* lies.   230 *Line:*   equator.   237
Unco: strange, great.

And never can obtain a part
In benmost corner of the heart. 240
Why should religion make us sad,
If good frae Virtue's to be had?
Na, rather gleefu' turn your face;
Forsake hypocrisy, grimace;
And never have it understood 245
You fleg mankind frae being good.

In afternoon, a' brawlie buskit,
The joes and lasses loe to frisk it:
Some tak a great delight to place
The modest *bon-grace* o'er the face; 250
Tho' you may see, if so inclin'd,
The turning o' the leg behind.
Now Comely-garden, and the Park,
Refresh them, after forenoon's wark;
Newhaven, Leith, or Canon-mills, 255
Supply them in their Sunday's gills:
Whare writers aften spend their pence,
To stock their heads wi' drink and sense.

While dandring cits delight to stray
To Castlehill, or public way, 260
Whare they nae other purpose mean,
Than that fool cause o' being seen;
Let me to *Arthur's Seat* pursue,
Whare bonny pastures meet the view;
And mony a wild-lorn scene accrues, 265
Befitting *Willie Shakespeare's* muse:
If fancy there would join the thrang,
The desart rocks and hills amang,
To echoes we should lilt and play,
And gie to *Mirth* the lee-lang day. 270

Or shou'd some canker'd biting show'r
The day and a' her sweets deflow'r,

240 *Benmost:* innermost. 246 *Fleg:* frighten. 247 *Brawlie buskit:* dressed in their best. 250 *Bon-grace:* shady bonnet. 253 *Comely-garden:* public gardens near Holyrood Palace; *the Park:* the Meadows, public park in the south side of the city. 255 *Newhaven:* fishing port north of Edinburgh, west of Leith; *Canon-mills:* village (now district) on north side of Edinburgh. 259 *Cits:* citizens. 260 *Castlehill:* street leading to the Castle. 263 *Arthur's Seat:* conical hill to south-east of Edinburgh. 270 *Lee-lang:* whole.

To Holyrood-house let me stray,
And gie to musing a' the day;
Lamenting what auld *Scotland* knew 275
Bien days for ever frae her view:
O HAMILTON, for shame! the muse
Would pay to thee her couthy vows,
Gin ye wad tent the humble strain,
And gie's our dignity again: 280
For O, waes me! the Thistle springs
In *domicile* of ancient kings,
Without a patriot to regret
Our *palace* and our ancient *state*.

Blest place! whare *debtors* daily run, 285
To rid themselves frae jail and dun;
Here, tho' sequester'd frae the din
That rings *Auld Reikie*'s wa's within,
Yet they may tread the sunny braes,
And brook Apollo's cheery rays; 290
Glour frae *St. Anthon*'s grassy hight,
O'er vales in simmer claise bedight,
Nor ever hing their head, I ween,
Wi' jealous fear o' being seen.
May I, whanever *duns* come nigh, 295
And shake my garret wi' their cry,
Scour here wi' haste, protection get,
To screen mysell frae them and debt;
To breathe the bliss of open sky,
And *Simon Fraser*'s bolts defy. 300

Now gin a lown should hae his claise
In thread-bare autumn o' their days,
St. *Mary*, broker's guardian saint,
Will satisfy ilk ail and want;
For mony a hungry writer there 305
Dives down at night, wi cleeding bare,
And quickly rises to the view
A gentleman, perfyte and new.

273 *Holyrood-house:* the chief royal Scottish palace, then in a state of
neglect and decay. 276 *Bien:* good, prosperous. 277 *Hamilton:* the
Duke of Hamilton was the hereditary keeper of the Palace. 279 *Tent:*
attend to, take heed of. 286 *Dun:* creditor. 290 *Brook:* enjoy. 291
St. Anthon: St. Anthony's Chapel stood on the slopes of Arthur's Seat.
292 *Claise:* clothes. 300 *Simon Fraser:* Keeper of the Tolbooth. 301
Gin: if. 303 St. Mary's Wynd was a street of dealers in old clothes.

Ye rich fock, look na wi' disdain
Upo' this ancient brokage lane!   310
For naked poets are supply'd
With what you to their wants deny'd.

Peace to thy shade, thou wale o' men,
DRUMMOND! relief to poortith's pain:
To thee the greatest bliss we owe,   315
And tribute's tear shall grateful flow:
The sick are cur'd, the hungry fed,
And dreams of comfort 'tend their bed:
As lang as *Forth* weets *Lothian*'s shore,
As lang's on *Fife* her billows roar,   320
Sae lang shall ilk whase country's dear,
To thy remembrance gie a tear.
By thee *Auld Reikie* thrave and grew
Delightfu' to her childer's view:
Nae mair shall *Glasgow* striplings threep   325
Their city's beauty and its shape,
While our new city spreads around
Her bonny wings on fairy ground.

But Provosts now that ne'er afford
The smaest dignity to *lord*,   330
Ne'er care tho' every scheme gae wild
That DRUMMOND's sacred hand has cull'd:
The spacious *Brig* neglected lies,
Tho' plagu'd wi' pamphlets, dunn'd wi' cries;
They heed not tho' destruction come   335
To gulp us in her gaunting womb.
O shame! that safety canna claim
Protection from a provost's name,
But hidden danger lies behind
To torture and to fleg the mind;   340
I may as weel bid *Arthur's Seat*
To *Berwick-Law* make gleg retreat,
As think that either will or art
Shall get the gate to win their heart;

314 *Drummond:* George Drummond (1687-1766), Lord Provost of
Edinburgh, responsible for much of the building of the New Town.
324 *Childer's:* children's. 325 *Threep:* repeat, assert, boast. 333
Brig: The new North Bridge had collapsed 1769. 334 *Dunn'd:* im-
portuned. 336 *Gaunting:* gaping. 342 *Berwick-Law:* North Berwick
Law, hill in East Lothian; *gleg:* quick. 344 *Gate:* way.

For POLITICS are a' their mark,   345
Bribes latent, and corruption dark:
If they can eithly turn the pence,
Wi' city's good they will dispense;
Nor care tho' a' her sons were lair'd
Ten fathom i' the auld kirk-yard.   350

To sing yet meikle does remain,
Undecent for a modest strain;
And since the poet's daily bread is
The favour of the Muse or ladies,
He downa like to gie offence   355
To delicacy's bonny sense;
Therefore the stews remain unsung,
And bawds in silence drop their tongue.

REIKIE, farewel! I ne'er cou'd part
Wi' thee but wi' a dowy heart;   360
Aft frae the *Fifan* coast I've seen,
Thee tow'ring on thy summit green;
So glowr the saints when first is given
A fav'rite keek o' glore and heaven;
On earth nae mair they bend their ein,   365
But quick assume angelic mein;
So I on *Fife* wad glowr no more,
But gallop'd to EDINA's shore.

George Crabbe

1754—1832

THE BOROUGH

Crabbe was brought up in Aldeburgh on the Suffolk coast, and
the 24 ' Letters ' of his book *The Borough* (1810) depict all aspects
of life in a lonely, squalid, poverty-stricken fishing-village. Both
nature and man are painted with a grim fidelity that makes a
salutary counterweight to the ' light that never was, on sea or

349 *Lair'd:* buried.   351 *Meikle:* much.   355 *Downa:* wouldn't.
357 *Stews:* brothels.

land.' ' Crabbe's the man,' said Byron; and in the narrow range
of what he does well, he is certainly unsurpassed.

Letter i

GENERAL DESCRIPTION

" Describe the Borough "—though our idle Tribe
May love Description, can we so describe,
That you shall fairly Streets and Buildings trace,
And all that gives distinction to a place?
This cannot be; yet, mov'd by your request,   5
A part I paint—let Fancy form the rest.

Cities and Towns, the various haunts of men,
Require the pencil; they defy the pen:
Could he, who sang so well the Grecian Fleet,
So well have sung of Alley, Lane, or Street?   10
Can measur'd lines these various Buildings show,
The Town-Hall Turning, or the Prospect Row?
Can I the seats of Wealth and Want explore,
And lengthen out my Lays from door to door?

Then let thy Fancy aid me—I repair   15
From this tall Mansion of our last-year's Mayor,
Till we the Out-skirts of the Borough reach,
And these half-buried Buildings next the Beach;
Where hang at open doors, the Net and Cork,
While squalid Sea-Dames mend the meshy work;   20
Till comes the hour, when fishing through the tide,
The weary Husband throws his Freight aside;
A living mass, which now demands the Wife,
Th' alternate labours of their humble Life.

Can Scenes like these withdraw thee from thy Wood,   25
Thy upland Forest or thy Valley's Flood?
Seek then thy Garden's shrubby bound, and look,
As it steals by, upon the bordering Brook;
That winding streamlet, limpid, lingering, slow,
Where the Reeds whisper when the Zephyrs blow: 30
Where in the midst, upon her throne of green,
Sits the large Lily as the Water's Queen;

1 *Describe the Borough*: Both the resident of the Borough and his inland
correspondent are, Crabbe says elsewhere, 'imaginary personages', but
each reflects the poet's own experience.   9 *Could he, who etc.*:   i.e.
Homer.

And makes the Current, forc'd awhile to stay,
Murmur and bubble as it shoots away;
Draw then the strongest contrast to that stream,   35
And our broad River will before thee seem.

   With ceaseless motion comes and goes the Tide,
Flowing, it fills the Channel vast and wide;
Then back to Sea, with strong majestic sweep
It rolls, in ebb yet terrible and deep: 40
Here Sampire-Banks and Salt-wort bound the Flood,
There Stakes and Sea-weeds withering on the Mud;
And higher up, a ridge of all things base,
Which some strong tide has roll'd upon the place.

   Thy gentle River boasts its pigmy Boat,   45
Urg'd on by pains, half grounded, half afloat;
While at her stern, an Angler takes his stand,
And marks the Fish he purposes to land;
From that clear space, where in the cheerful ray
Of the warm Sun the scaly People play.   50

   Far other Craft our prouder River shows,
Hoys, Pinks, and Sloops; Brigs, Brigantines, and Snows:
Nor Angler we on our wide stream descry,
But one poor Dredger where his Oysters lie:
He, cold and wet, and driving with the Tide,   55
Beats his weak arms against his tarry side,
Then drains the remnant of diluted gin,
To aid the warmth that languishes within;
Renewing oft his poor attempts to beat
His tingling fingers into gathering heat.   60

   He shall again be seen when Evening comes,
And social Parties crowd their favourite rooms;
Where, on the Table Pipes and Papers lie,
The steaming Bowl or foaming Tankard by;
'Tis then, with all these comforts spread around,   65
They hear the painful Dredger's welcome sound;
And few themselves the savoury boon deny,
The food that feeds, the living luxury.

41 *Sampire-Banks:* The jointed Glasswort. *Salicornia* is here meant, not
the true Sampire, the *Crithmum maritimum.* (C.) 52 *Hoys:* sloop-
rigged coastal vessels; *pinks:* flat-bottomed lug-sailed fishing boats;
snows: smallish three-masted sailing vessels. 66 *Painful:* laborious.

Yon is our Quay! those smaller Hoys from Town,
Its various Wares, for Country-use, bring down;   70
Those laden Waggons, in return, impart
The Country-produce to the City-mart:
Hark! to the Clamour in that miry Road,
Bounded and narrow'd by yon Vessel's Load;
The lumbering Wealth she empties round the place,   75
Package and Parcel, Hogshead, Chest and Case:
While the loud Seamen and the angry Hind,
Mingling in Business, bellow to the Wind.

Near these a Crew amphibious in the Docks,
Rear, for the Sea, those Castles on the Stocks: 80
See! the long Keel, which soon the Waves must hide,
See! the strong Ribs which form the roomy Side,
Bolts yielding slowly to the sturdiest stroke,
And Planks which curve and crackle in the smoke.
Around the whole rise cloudy Wreathes, and far   85
Bear the warm pungence of o'er-boiling Tar.

Dabbling on shore half-naked Sea-Boys crowd,
Swim round a Ship, or swing upon the Shroud;
Or in a Boat purloin'd, with Paddles play,
And grow familiar with the Watery Way: 90
Young though they be, they feel whose Sons they are,
They know what British Seamen do and dare;
Proud of that Fame, they raise and they enjoy
The rustic wonder of the Village-Boy.

Before you bid these busy Scenes adieu,   95
Behold the Wealth that lies in public view,
Those far-extended heaps of Coal and Coke,
Where fresh-fill'd Lime-kilns breathe their stifling Smoke.
This shall pass off, and you behold instead,
The Night-fire gleaming on its chalky bed;   100
When from the Light-house brighter beams will rise,
To show the Shipman where the Shallow lies.

Thy Walks are ever pleasant; every Scene
Is rich in beauty, lively, or serene—
Rich—is that varied View with Woods around,   105
Seen from the Seat, within the Shrubb'ry bound;

77 *Hind:* countryman.   88 *Shroud:* rigging.   105 *That varied View, etc.:*
the grounds of Belvoir Castle, Leicestershire, as seen from the parsonage
at Muston where Crabbe at one time held a living.

Where shines the distant Lake, and where appear
From Ruins bolting, unmolested Deer;
Lively—the Village-Green, the Inn, the Place,
Where t he good Widow schools her Infant-race;   110
Shops, whence are heard, the Hammer and the Saw,
And Village pleasures unreprov'd by Law.
Then how serene! when in your favourite Room,
Gales from your Jasmines soothe the Evening Gloom;
When from your upland Paddock you look down,   115
And just perceive the Smoke which hides the Town;
When weary Peasants at the close of Day
Walk to their Cots, and part upon the way;
When Cattle slowly cross the shallow Brook,
And Shepherds pen their Folds, and rest upon their Crook.   120

We prune our Hedges, prime our slender Trees,
And not hing looks untutor'd and at ease,
On the wide Heath, or in the flow'ry Vale,
We scent the Vapours of the sea-born Gale;
Broad-beaten Paths lead on from Stile to Stile,   125
And Sewers from Streets, the Road-side Banks defile;
Our guarded Fields a sense of danger show,
Where Garden-crops with Corn and Clover grow;
Fences are form'd of Wreck and plac'd around,
(With tenters tipp'd) a strong repulsive bound;   130
Wide and deep Ditches by the Gardens run,
And there in ambush lie the Trap and Gun;
Or yon broad Board, which guards each tempting Prize,
" Like a tall Bully, lifts its head and lies."

There stands a Cottage with an open door,   135
Its Garden undefended blooms before;
Her Wheel is still, and overturn'd her Stool,
While the lone Widow seeks the neighb'ring Pool;
This gives us hope, all views of Town to shun—
No! here are tokens of the Sailor-Son;   140
That old blue Jacket, and that Shirt of Check,
And silken Kerchief for the Seaman's neck;
Sea-spoils and Shells from many a distant Shore,
And furry Robe from frozen *Labrador*.

114 *Gales:* gentle breezes. 118 *Cots:* cottages. 121 *Prime:* trim.
130 *Tenters:* framework for stretching cloth. 134 refers to the Monu-
ment erected in Fish St. Hill to commemorate the Great Fire of London;
its inscription blamed the 'Popish faction' as the incendiaries. (See
Pope's *Moral Essays* III, 340). 138 *Pool:* harbour basin at river mouth.

Our busy Streets and Sylvan-walks between, 145
Fen, Marshes, Bog and Heath all intervene;
There are deep Pits, with watery Bases, found,
And curious Plants enrich the shady Ground,
There are the feathery Grass, the flowery Rush,
The *Gale's* rich balm, and *Sun-dew's* crimson blush, 150
Whose velvet Leaf with radiant beauty drest,
Forms a gay Pillow for the *Plover's* breast.

Not distant far, an House commodious made,
(Lonely yet public stands) for Sunday-trade;
Thither for this day free, gay Parties go,
Their Tea-house Walk, their tipling Rendezvous; 155
Their humble Couples sit in Corner-bowers,
Or gaily ramble for th' allotted hours;
Sailors and Lasses from the Town attend,
The Servant-Lover, the Apprentice-Friend; 160
With all the idle social Tribes who seek,
And find, their humble Pleasures, once a Week.

Turn to the Watery World!—but who to thee
(A wonder yet unview'd) shall paint—the Sea?
Various and vast, sublime in all its forms, 165
When lull'd by Zephyrs, or when rous'd by Storms,
Its colours changing, when from Clouds and Sun
Shades after shades upon the surface run;
Embrown'd and horrid now, and now serene,
In limpid blue, and evanescent green; 170
And oft the foggy Banks on Ocean lie,
Lift the far Sail, and cheat th' experienc'd Eye.

Be it the Summer-Noon: a sandy space
The ebbing Tide has left upon its place;
Then just the hot and stony Beach above, 175
Light twinkling Streams in bright confusion move;
(For heated thus, the warmer Air ascends,
And with the cooler in its fall contends)—
Then the broad bosom of the Ocean keeps
An equal motion; swelling as it sleeps, 180
Then slowly sinking; curling to the Strand,
Faint, lazy Waves o'ercreep the ridgy Sand,

150 *Gale:* bog-myrtle; *sun-dew:* a bog plant. 171-2 Of the effect of
these mists, known by the name of Fog-banks, wonderful and indeed
incredible relations are given; but their property of appearing to elevate
ships at sea, and to bring them in view, is, I believe, generally acknow-
ledged. (C.)

Or tap the tarry Boat with gentle blow,
And back return in silence, smooth and slow.
Ships in the Calm seem anchor'd; for they glide   185
On the still Sea, urg'd solely by the Tide:
Art thou not present, this calm Scene before,
Where all beside is pebbly length of Shore,
And far as eye can reach, it can discern no more?

Yet sometimes comes a ruffling Cloud to make   190
The quiet surface of the Ocean shake;
As an awaken'd Giant with a frown,
Might show his wrath, and then to sleep sink down.

View now the Winter-Storm! above, one Cloud,
Black and unbroken, all the Skies o'ershroud;   195
Th' unwieldy Porpoise through the day before,
Had roll'd in view of boding men on shore;
And sometimes hid and sometimes shew'd his form,
Dark as the cloud, and furious as the storm.

All where the eye delights, yet dreads to roam,   200
The breaking Billows cast the flying Foam
Upon the Billows rising—all the Deep
Is restless change; the Waves so swell'd and steep,
Breaking and sinking, and the sunken swells,
Nor one, one moment, in its station dwells: 205
But nearer Land you may the Billows trace,
As if contending in their watery chace;
May watch the mightiest till the Shoal they reach,
Then break and hurry to their utmost stretch;
Curl'd as they come, they strike with furious force,   210
And then re-flowing, take their grating course,
Raking the rounded Flints, which ages past
Roll'd by their rage, and shall to ages last.

Far off the Petrel, in the troubled way
Swims with her Brood, or flutters in the Spray;   215
She rises often, often drops again,
And sports at ease on the tempestuous Main.

High o'er the restless Deep, above the reach
Of Gunner's hope, vast flights of Wild-ducks stretch;
Far as the eye can glance on either side,   220
In a broad space and level line they glide:
All in their wedge-like figures from the North,
Day after day, flight after flight go forth.

In-shore their passage Tribes of Sea-gulls urge,
And drop for Prey within the sweeping Surge;   225
Oft in the rough opposing Blast they fly
Far back, then turn and all their force apply,
While to the Storm they give their weak complaining cry;
Or clap the sleek white Pinion to the breast,
And in the restless Ocean dip for Rest.   230

Darkness begins to reign; the louder Wind
Appals the weak and awes the firmer mind;
But frights not him, whom Evening and the Spray
In part conceal—yon Prowler on his way:
Lo! he has something seen; he runs apace,   235
As if he fear'd Companion in the chace;
He sees his Prize, and now he turns again,
Slowly and sorrowing—" Was your search in vain? "
Gruffly he answers, " 'Tis a sorry sight!
A Seaman's Body: there'll be more to-night! "   240

Hark! to those sounds, they're from Distress at Sea!
How quick they come! What terrors may there be!
Yes, 'tis a driven Vessel: I discern
Lights, signs of terror, gleaming from the Stern;
Others behold them too, and from the Town,   245
In various parties Seamen hurry down;
Their Wives pursue, and Damsels urg'd by dread,
Lest Men so dear be into danger led;
Their head the gown has hooded, and their call
In this sad night, is piercing like the squall;   250
They feel their kinds of power, and when they meet,
Chide, fondle, weep, dare, threaten or intreat.

See one poor Girl, all terror and alarm,
Has fondly seiz'd upon her Lover's arm;
" Thou shalt not venture; " and he answers " No!   255
I will not "—still she cries, " Thou shalt not go."

No need of this; not here the stoutest Boat,
Can through such Breakers, o'er such Billows float;
Yet may they view these Lights upon the Beach,
Which yield them Hope, whom Help can never reach.   260

From parted Clouds the Moon her radiance throws
On the wild Waves and all the Danger shows;

But shows them beaming in her shining vest,
Terrific splendour! gloom in glory drest!
This for a moment, and then Clouds again,   265
Hide every beam, and fear and darkness reign.

But Fear we now these Sounds? do Lights appear?
I see them not! the Storm alone I hear:
And lo! the Sailors homeward take their way;
Man must endure—let us submit and pray.   270

Such are our Winter-views: but Night comes on,
Now Business sleeps, and daily Cares are gone;
Now Parties form; and some their Friends assist,
To waste the idle hours at sober Whist;
The Tavern's pleasure, or the Concert's charm,   275
Unnumber'd moments of their sting disarm;
Play-bills and open Doors a Crowd invite,
To pass off one dread portion of the Night;
And Show and Song and Luxury combin'd,
Lift off from Man this burthen of Mankind.   280

Others advent'rous walk abroad and meet
Returning Parties pacing through the Street;
When various Voices in the dying Day,
Hum in our Walks, and greet us in our Way;
When Tavern-Lights flit on from Room to Room,   285
And guide the tippling Sailor staggering home:
There as we pass the jingling Bells betray,
How Business rises with the closing Day:
Now walking silent, by the River's side,
The Ear perceives the rimpling of the Tide;   290
Or measur'd cadence of the Lads who tow
Some enter'd Hoy, to fix her in her row;
Or hollow sound, which from the Parish-Bell,
To some departed Spirit bids farewell!

Thus shall you something of our BOROUGH know,   295
Far as a Verse, with Fancy's aid, can show;
Of Sea or River, of a Quay or Street,
The best Description must be incomplete;
But when an happier Theme succeeds, and when
Men are our subjects and the deeds of Men;   300
Then may we find the muse in happier style,
And we may sometimes sigh and sometimes smile.

290 *Rimpling:* rippling murmur.

William Blake

1757—1827

AUGURIES OF INNOCENCE

To see a World in a Grain of Sand
And a Heaven in a Wild Flower,
Hold Infinity in the palm of your hand
And Eternity in an hour.

A Robin Red breast in a Cage   5
Puts all Heaven in a Rage.
A dove house fill'd with doves & Pigeons
Shudders Hell thro' all its regions.
A dog starv'd at his Master's Gate
Predicts the ruin of the State.   10
A Horse misus'd upon the Road
Calls to Heaven for Human blood.
Each outcry of the hunted Hare
A fibre from the Brain does tear.
A Skylark wounded in the wing,   15
A Cherubim does cease to sing.
The Game Cock clip'd & arm'd for fight
Does the Rising Sun affright.
Every Wolf's & Lion's howl
Raises from Hell a Human Soul.   20
The wild deer, wand'ring here & there,
Keeps the Human Soul from Care.
The Lamb misus'd breeds Public strife
And yet forgives the Butcher's Knife.
The Bat that flits at close of Eve   25
Has left the Brain that won't Believe.
The Owl that calls upon the Night
Speaks the Unbeliever's fright.
He who shall hurt the little Wren
Shall never be belov'd by Men.   30
He who the Ox to wrath has mov'd
Shall never be by Woman lov'd.
The wanton Boy that kills the Fly
Shall feel the Spider's enmity.

377

He who torments the Chafer's sprite   35
Weaves a Bower in endless Night.
The Catterpiller on the Leaf
Repeats to thee thy Mother's grief.
Kill not the Moth nor Butterfly,
For the Last Judgment draweth nigh.   40
He who shall train the Horse to war
Shall never pass the Polar Bar.
The Beggar's Dog & Widow's Cat,
Feed them & thou wilt grow fat.
The Gnat that sings his Summer's song   45
Poison gets from Slander's tongue.
The poison of the Snake & Newt
Is the sweat of Envy's Foot.
The Poison of the Honey Bee
Is the Artist's Jealousy.   50
The Prince's Robes & Beggar's Rags
Are Toadstools on the Miser's Bags.
A truth that's told with bad intent
Beats all the Lies you can invent.
It is right it should be so;   55
Man was made for Joy and Woe,
And when this we rightly know,
Thro' the World we safely go.
Joy & Woe are woven fine,
A Clothing for the Soul divine;   60
Under every grief & pine
Runs a joy with silken twine.
The Babe is more than swadling Bands;
Throughout all these Human Lands
Tools were made, & Born were hands,   65
Every Farmer Understands.
Every Tear from Every Eye
Becomes a Babe in Eternity;
This is caught by Females bright
And return'd to its own delight.   70
The Bleat, the Bark, Bellow & Roar
Are Waves that Beat on Heaven's Shore.
The Babe that weeps the Rod beneath
Writes Revenge in realms of Death.
The Beggar's Rags, fluttering in Air,   75
Does to Rags the Heavens tear.

35 *Chafer:* cockchafer beetle.   42 'Shall never break through the
material universe, i.e. reach heaven.'

The Soldier, arm'd with Sword & Gun,
Palsied strikes the Summer's Sun.
The poor Man's Farthing is worth more
Than all the Gold on Afric's Shore.   80
One Mite wrung from the Lab'rer's hands
Shall buy & sell the Miser's Lands:
Or, if protected from on high,
Does that whole Nation sell & buy.
He who mocks the Infant's Faith   85
Shall be mock'd in Age & Death.
He who shall teach the Child to Doubt
The rotting Grave shall ne'er get out.
He who respects the Infant's faith
Triumphs over Hell & Death.   90
The Child's Toys & the Old Man's Reasons
Are the Fruits of the Two seasons.
The Questioner, who sits so sly,
Shall never know how to Reply.
He who replies to words of Doubt   95
Doth put the Light of Knowledge out.
The Strongest Poison ever known
Came from Cæsar's Laurel Crown.
Nought can deform the Human Race
Like to the Armour's iron brace.   100
When Gold & Gems adorn the Plow
To peaceful Arts shall Envy Bow.
A Riddle or the Cricket's Cry
Is to Doubt a fit Reply.
The Emmet's Inch & Eagle's Mile   105
Make Lame Philosophy to smile.
He who Doubts from what he sees
Will ne'er Believe, do what you Please.
If the Sun & Moon should doubt,
They'd immediately Go out.   110
To be in a Passion you Good may do,
But no Good if a Passion is in you.
The Whore & Gambler, by the State
Licenc'd, build that Nation's Fate.
The Harlot's cry from Street to Street   115
Shall weave Old England's winding Sheet.
The Winner's Shout, the Loser's Curse,
Dance before dead England's Hearse.
Every Night & every Morn

105 *Emmet:* ant.

Some to Misery are Born.   120
Every Morn & every Night
Some are Born to sweet delight.
Some are Born to sweet delight,
Some are Born to Endless Night.
We are led to Believe a Lie   125
When we see not Thro' the Eye
Which was Born in a Night to perish in a Night
When the Soul Slept in Beams of Light.
God Appears & God is Light
To those poor Souls who dwell in Night,   130
But does a Human Form Display
To those who Dwell in Realms of day.

Robert Burns

1759—1796

TAM O' SHANTER

A TALE

Of Brownyis and of Bogillis full is this buke.
GAWIN DOUGLAS

When chapman billies leave the street,
And drouthy neebors, neebors meet;
As market-days are wearing late,
An' folk begin to tak the gate;
While we sit bousing at the nappy,   5
An' getting fou and unco happy,
We think na on the lang Scots miles,
The mosses, waters, slaps, and styles,
That lie between us and our hame,
Whare sits our sulky, sullen dame,   10
Gathering her brows like gathering storm,
Nursing her wrath to keep it warm.

1 *Chapman billies:* pedlar fellows. 2 *Drouthy:* thirsty. 4 *Gate:* road.
5 *Nappy:* strong ale. 6 *Fou:* drunk; *unco:* very. 7 *Lang Scots miles:*
one Scots mile was in fact equal to 1.125 statute miles. 8 *Mosses:* bogs;
slaps: gaps in hedge or fence.

This truth fand honest *Tam o' Shanter*,
As he frae Ayr ae night did canter,
(Auld Ayr, wham ne'er a town surpasses,   15
For honest men and bonie lasses).

O *Tam*! had'st thou but been sae wise,
As ta'en thy ain wife *Kate's* advice!
She tauld thee weel thou was a skellum,
A blethering, blustering, drunken blellum;   20
That frae November till October,
Ae market day thou was nae sober;
That ilka melder, wi' the miller,
Thou sat as lang as thou had siller;
That ev'ry naig was ca'd a shoe on,   25
The smith and thee gat roaring fou on;
That at the Lord's house, ev'n on Sunday,
Thou drank wi' Kirkton Jean till Monday.
She prophesied that, late or soon,
Thou would be found, deep drown'd in Doon;   30
Or catch'd wi' warlocks in the mirk,
By *Alloway's* auld haunted kirk.

Ah, gentle dames! it gars me greet,
To think how monie counsels sweet,
How monie lengthen'd, sage advices,   35
The husband frae the wife despises!

13 *Fand:* found; *Tam o' Shanter:* probably based on Douglas Graham (1739-1811), tenant of the farm of Shanter near Maidens on the Carrick coast, and owner of a boat called *Tam o' Shanter.* 18 *Ta'en:* to have taken. 19 *Skellum:* rascal, scamp. 20 *Blethering:* ramblingly loquacious; *blellum:* windbag. 23 *Ilka melder:* at every grinding of the oats. 24 *Siller:* money. 25 *Ev'ry naig, etc.:* every nag that was shod. 28 *Kirkton Jean:* traditionally Jean Kennedy who kept an inn at Kirkoswald, two miles from Shanter. Burns plays with the name of her inn (which she kept with her sister), the 'Leddies' House', in line 27. Any village with a parish church was called a 'Kirkton'. 31 *Warlocks:* wizards; *mirk:* dark. 32 Alloway Kirk . . . is an old ruin in Ayrshire, hard by the road from Ayr to Maybole, on the banks of the river Doon, and very near the old bridge of that name. (B.) This church is also famous for being the place wherein the witches and warlocks used to hold their infernal meetings, or sabbaths, and prepare their magical unctions: here too they used to amuse themselves with dancing to the pipes of the muckle-horned Deel. Diverse stories of these horrid rites are still current; one of which my worthy friend Mr. Burns has here favoured me with in verse. (Francis Grose, *Antiquities of Scotland,* 1791.) 33 *Gars me greet:* makes me weep.

But to our tale: Ae market-night,
Tam had got planted unco right;
Fast by an ingle, bleezing finely,
Wi' reaming swats, that drank divinely;   40
And at his elbow, Souter *Johnny*,
His ancient, trusty, drouthy cronie;
Tam lo'ed him like a vera brither;
They had been fou for weeks thegither.
The night drave on wi' sangs and clatter;   45
And ay the ale was growing better:
The landlady and *Tam* grew gracious,
Wi' favours, secret, sweet, and precious:
The Souter tauld his queerest stories;
The landlord's laugh was ready chorus: 50
The storm without might rair and rustle,
Tam did na mind the storm a whistle.

Care, mad to see a man sae happy,
E'en drown'd himsel amang the nappy,
As bees flee hame wi' lades o' treasure,   55
The minutes wing'd their way wi' pleasure:
Kings may be blest, but *Tam* was glorious,
O'er a' the ills o' life victorious!

But pleasures are like poppies spread,
You seize the flow'r, its bloom is shed;   60
Or like the snow falls in the river,
A moment white—then melts for ever;
Or like the borealis race,
That flit ere you can point their place;
Or like the rainbow's lovely form   65
Evanishing amid the storm.—
Nae man can tether time or tide,
The hour approaches *Tam* maun ride;
That hour, o' night's black arch the key-stane,
That dreary hour he mounts his beast in;   70
And sic a night he taks the road in,
As ne'er poor sinner was abroad in.

The wind blew as 'twad blawn its last;
The rattling show'rs rose on the blast;

40 *Reaming swats:* frothy new ale. 41 *Souter Johnny:* traditionally
John Davidson, shoemaker ('souter') at Glenfoot, near Shanter. 45
Clatter: noisy talk. 51 *Rair:* roar. 55 *Lades:* loads. 61 *Falls:* that
falls. 68 *Maun:* must. 73 *As 'twad:* as if it would have.

The speedy gleams the darkness swallow'd; 75
Loud, deep, and lang, the thunder bellow'd;
That night, a child might understand,
The Deil had business on his hand.

Weel mounted on his grey meare, *Meg*,
A better never lifted leg, 80
Tam skelpit on thro' dub and mire,
Despising wind, and rain, and fire;
Whiles holding fast his guid blue bonnet;
Whiles crooning o'er an auld Scots sonnet;
Whiles glow'ring round wi' prudent cares, 85
Lest bogles catch him unawares:
Kirk-Alloway was drawing nigh,
Whare ghaists and houlets nightly cry.—

By this time he was cross the ford,
Whare in the snaw, the chapman smoor'd; 90
And past the birks and meikle stane,
Whare drunken *Charlie* brak's neck-bane;
And thro' the whins, and by the cairn,
Whare hunters fand the murder'd bairn;
And near the thorn, aboon the well, 95
Whare *Mungo's* mither hang'd hersel.—
Before him *Doon* pours all his floods;
The doubling storm roars thro' the woods;
The lightnings flash from pole to pole;
Near and more near the thunders roll: 100
When glimmering thro' the groaning trees,
Kirk-Alloway seem'd in a bleeze;
Thro' ilka bore the beams were glancing;
And loud resounded mirth and dancing.—

Inspiring bold *John Barleycorn*! 105
What dangers thou canst make us scorn!
Wi' tippenny, we fear nae evil;
Wi' usquebae, we'll face the Devil!—

81 *Skelpit:* spanked, dashed; *dub:* puddle. 83 *Whiles:* at times. 84
Sonnet: song. 85 *Glow'ring:* gazing and frowning. 88 *Houlets:* owls.
90 *Smoor'd:* smothered. 91 *Birks:* birches; *meikle:* big. 92 *Brak's:*
broke his. 96 *Mungo:* another name of Kentigern, 6th-century saint
who worked among the Britons of Strathclyde. There is a 'Mungo's
Well' between the Doon and Alloway Kirk, but the suicide of Mungo's
mother (Thenew) is an atmospheric addition. 103 *Bore:* chink.
105 *John Barleycorn:* malt liquor, whisky. 107 *Tippenny:* small beer at
twopence a pint. 108 *Usquebae:* whisky.

The swats sae ream'd in *Tammie's* noddle,
Fair play, he car'd na deils a boddle.   110
But *Maggie* stood, right sair astonish'd,
Till, by the heel and hand admonish'd,
She ventur'd forward on the light;
And, vow! *Tam* saw an unco sight!
Warlocks and witches in a dance;   115
Nae cotillion brent new frae *France*,
But hornpipes, jigs, strathspeys, and reels,
Put life and mettle in their heels.
A winnock-bunker in the east,
There sat auld Nick, in shape o' beast;   120
A towzie tyke, black, grim, and large,
To gie them music was his charge:
He screw'd the pipes and gart them skirl,
Till roof and rafters a' did dirl.—
Coffins stood round, like open presses,   125
That shaw'd the dead in their last dresses;
And by some devilish cantraip slight
Each in its cauld hand held a light.—
By which heroic *Tam* was able
To note upon the haly table,   130
A murderer's banes in gibbet airns;
Twa span-lang, wee, unchristen'd bairns;
A thief, new-cutted frae a rape,   .
Wi' his last gasp his gab did gape;
Five tomahawks, wi' bluid red-rusted;   135
Five scymitars, wi' murder crusted;
A garter, which a babe had strangled;
A knife, a father's throat had mangled,
Whom his ain son o' life bereft,
The grey hairs yet stack to the heft;   140
Wi' mair o' horrible and awefu',
Which ev'n to name wad be unlawfu'.

As *Tammie* glowr'd, amaz'd, and curious,
The mirth and fun grew fast and furious:
The piper loud and louder blew,   145
The dancers quick and quicker flew,

110 *Na:* not; *boddle:* 2d. Scots (⅓d. sterling). 114 *Unco:* marvel-
lous. 116 *Cotillion:* lively French dance; *brent new:* brand-new. 117
Strathspeys: Highland dances, slower than reels. 119 *Winnock-bunker:*
window-seat. 121 *Towzie tyke:* 'shaggy dog', raffish dishevelled old
blackguard. 123 *Gart them skirl:* made them shrill out. 124 *Dirl:*
ring, vibrate. 127 *Cantraip slight:* weird trick. 131 *Airns:* irons.
133 *Rape:* rope. 134 *Gab:* mouth. 140 *Stack:* stuck; *heft:* haft.

They reel'd, they set, they cross'd, they cleekit,
Till ilka carlin swat and reekit,
And coost her duddies to the wark,
And linket at it in her sark!   150

Now *Tam*, O *Tam*! had thae been queans,
A' plump and strapping in their teens,
Their sarks, instead o' creeshie flannen,
Been snaw-white seventeen hunder linen!
Thir breeks o' mine, my only pair,   155
That ance were plush, o' guid blue hair,
I wad hae gi'en them aff my hurdies,
For ae blink o' the bonie burdies!
But wither'd beldams, auld and droll,
Rigwoodie hags wad spean a foal,   160
Louping and flinging on a crummock,
I wonder did na turn thy stomach.

But *Tam* kend what was what fu' brawlie,
There was ae winsome wench and wawlie,
That night enlisted in the core,   165
(Lang after kend on *Carrick* shore;
For monie a beast to dead she shot,
An' perish'd monie a bonie boat,
An' shook baith meikle corn and bear,
And kept the country-side in fear).   170
Her cutty sark, o' Paisley harn,
That while a lassie she had worn,
In longitude tho' sorely scanty,
It was her best, and she was vauntie.—
Ah! little kend thy reverend grannie,   175
That sark she coft for her wee Nannie,
Wi' twa pund Scots ('twas a' her riches),
Wad ever grac'd a dance of witches!

147 *Cleekit:* hooked arms together. 148 *Carlin:* old woman, witch;
swat and reekit: sweated and steamed. 149 *Coost her duddies:* threw off
her bits of clothes. 150 *Linket at it:* tripped through the dance; *sark:*
shift, smock. 151 *Thae:* those; *queans:* young girls. 153 *Creeshie
flannen:* greasy flannel. 154 *Seventeen hunder:* woven on a fine frame of
1,700 divisions. 155 *Thir:* these. 157 *Hurdies:* hips. 158 *Burdies:*
lasses. 159 *Beldams:* crones. 160 *Rigwoodie:* bony, uncouth; *wad
spean:* such as would wean (i.e. through revulsion). 161 *Louping:*
leaping; *crummock:* staff with crooked head. 163 *Brawlie:* well. 164
Wawlie: fine, jolly. 165 *Core:* company. 167 *Dead:* death. 169
Meikle: much; *bear:* barley. 171 *Cutty:* short; *harn:* coarse flaxen
cloth. 174 *Vauntie:* proud. 176 *Coft:* bought. 177 *Twa pund Scots:*
3s. 4d. sterling.
A.L.P.   N

But here my Muse her wing maun cour;
Sic flights are far beyond her pow'r;   180
To sing how Nannie lap and flang
(A souple jade she was, and strang),
And how *Tam* stood, like ane bewitch'd,
And thought his very een enrich'd;
Ev'n Satan glowr'd, and fidg'd fu' fain,   185
And hotch'd and blew wi' might and main:
Till first ae caper, syne anither,
Tam tint his reason a' thegither,
And roars out, " Weel done, Cutty-sark! "
And in an instant all was dark: 190
And scarcely had he Maggie rallied,
When out the hellish legion sallied.

As bees bizz out wi' angry fyke,
When plundering herds assail their byke;
As open pussie's mortal foes,   195
When, pop! she starts before their nose;
As eager runs the market-crowd,
When " Catch the thief! " resounds aloud;
So Maggie runs, the witches follow,
Wi' monie an eldritch skriech and hollow.   200

Ah, *Tam*! Ah, *Tam*! thou'll get thy fairin!
In hell they'll roast thee like a herrin!
In vain thy *Kate* awaits thy comin!
Kate soon will be a woefu' woman!
Now, do thy speedy utmost, Meg,   205
And win the key-stane o' the brig;
There at them thou thy tail may toss,
A running stream they dare na cross.
But ere the key-stane she could make,
The fient a tail she had to shake!   210
For Nannie, far before the rest,
Hard upon noble Maggie prest,

179 *Cour:* lower, bend. 181 *Lap an' flang:* leaped and kicked. 185
Fidg'd fu' fain: twitched about with desire. 186 *Hotched:* shook,
jerked. 187 *Syne:* then. 188 *Tint:* lost. 193 *Fyke:* fuss, vexation.
194 *Herds:* shepherd-boys; *byke:* nest of wild bees. 195 *Pussie:* the
hare. 200 *Eldritch:* unearthly, bloodcurdling. 201 *Fairin:* deserts.
206 It is a well known fact that witches, or any evil spirits, have no
power to follow a poor wight any farther than the middle of the next
running stream.—It may be proper likewise to mention to the benighted
traveller, that when he falls in with *bogles*, whatever danger may be in his
going forward, there is much more hazard in turning back. (B.) 210
Fient: devil.

And flew at Tam wi' furious ettle;
But little wist she Maggie's mettle—
Ae spring brought off her master hale,   215
But left behind her ain grey tail:
The carlin claught her by the rump,
And left poor Maggie scarce a stump.

Now, wha this tale o' truth shall read,
Ilk man and mother's son, take heed: 220
Whene'er to drink you are inclin'd,
Or cutty sarks run in your mind,
Think, ye may buy the joys o'er dear,
Remember Tam o' Shanter's meare.

THE TWA DOGS

A TALE

'Twas in that place o' Scotland's Isle,
That bears the name o' *Auld King Coil*,
Upon a bonie day in June,
When wearin' thro' the afternoon,
Twa Dogs, that were na thrang at hame,   5
Forgathered ance upon a time.
    The first I'll name, they ca'd him *Cæsar*,
Was keepit for his Honor's pleasure;
His hair, his size, his mouth, his lugs,
Shew'd he was nane o' Scotland's dogs,   10
But whalpit some place far abroad,
Whare sailors gang to fish for Cod.
    His lockèd, letter'd, braw brass collar
Shew'd him the *gentleman* an' *scholar*;
But tho' he was o' high degree,   15
The fient a pride, na pride had he,
But wad hae spent an hour caressin,
Ev'n wi' a tinkler-gipsey's *messin*:

213 *Ettle:* purpose, effort. 215 *Hale:* whole. 217 *Claught:* clutched.
2 *Coil:* legendary king, supposed to have given his name to the district
of Kyle in central Ayrshire. 5 *Thrang:* busy. 6 *Forgathered:* met by
chance. 9 *Lugs:* ears. 11 *Whalpit:* whelped. 12 *Gang:* go. 13
Letter'd: inscribed; *braw:* handsome. 16 *Fient a:* devil a (bit of).
18 *Messin:* small, insignificant dog.

At kirk or market, mill or smiddie,
Nae tawted *tyke*, tho' e'er sae duddie,   20
But he wad stan't, as glad to see him,
An' stroan't on stanes an' hillocks wi' him.
    The tither was a *ploughman's collie*,
A rhyming, ranting, raving billie,
Wha for his friend an' comrade had him,   25
And in his freaks had *Luath* ca'd him,
After some dog in *Highland sang*,
Was made lang syne, Lord knows how lang.
    He was a gash an' faithfu' tyke,
As ever lap a sheugh or dyke.   30
His honest, sonsie, baws'nt face
Ay gat him friends in ilka place;
His breast was white, his touzie back
Weel clad wi' coat o' glossy black;
His gawcie tail, wi' upward curl,   35
Hung owre his hurdies wi' a swirl.
    Nae doubt but they were fain o' ither,
And unco pack an' thick thegither;
Wi' social nose whyles snuff'd an' snowkit;
Whyles mice an' moudieworts they howkit;   40
Whyles scour'd awa' in lang excursion,
An' worry'd ither in diversion;
Till tir'd at last wi' monie a farce,
They sat them down upon their arse,
An' there began a lang digression   45
About the *lords o' the creation*.

CÆSAR

I've aften wonder'd, honest *Luath*,
What sort o' life poor dogs like you have;
An' when the *gentry's* life I saw,
What way *poor bodies* liv'd ava.   50

19 *Smiddie:* smithy. 20 *Tawted tyke:* matted cur; *duddie:* ragged, shaggy. 21 *Wad stan't:* would have stopped. 22 *Stroan't:* pissed. 24 *Ranting . . . billie:* high-spirited fellow. 27 Cuchullin's dog in Ossian's *Fingal* (B.). Burns himself had a dog called Luath which was killed in 1784; the poem is, in this connection, an elegy. *The Twa Dogs* was completed in 1786 and printed in the Kilmarnock edition, where it comes first. 28 *Lang syne:* long ago. 29 *Gash:* sagacious, shrewd. 30 *Lap a sheugh or dyke:* jumped a ditch or wall. 31 *Sonsie, baws'nt:* good-natured, white-streaked. 32 *Ilka:* every. 33 *Touzie:* shaggy, unkempt. 35 *Gawcie:* big and handsome. 36 *Hurdies:* buttocks. 37 *Fain o' ither:* fond of each other. 38 *Unco pack:* extremely intimate. 39 *Whyles:* at times; *snowkit:* smelled, sniffed. 40 *Moudieworts:* moles; *howkit:* dug up. 50 *Ava:* at all.

Our *Laird* gets in his rackèd rents,
His coals, his kain, an' a' his stents:
He rises when he likes himsel;
His flunkies answer at the bell;
He ca's his coach; he ca's his horse;   55
He draws a bonie, silken purse
As lang's my tail, whare thro' the steeks,
The yellow letter'd *Geordie* keeks.
   Frae morn to e'en it's nought but toiling,
At baking, roasting, frying, boiling;   60
An' tho' the gentry first are stechin,
Yet ev'n the *ha' folk* fill their pechan
Wi' sauce, ragouts, an' sic like trashtrie,
That's little short o' downright wastrie.
Our *Whipper-in*, wee blastit wonner,   65
Poor worthless elf, it eats a dinner,
Better than onie *Tenant-man*
His Honour has in a' the lan':
An' what poor *Cot-folk* pit their painch in,
I own it's past my comprehension.   70

LUATH

   Trowth, *Cæsar*, whyles they're fash't eneugh;
A *Cotter* howkin in a sheugh,
Wi' dirty stanes biggin' a dyke,
Baring a quarry, an' sic like,
Himsel, a wife, he thus sustains,   75
A smytrie o' wee duddie weans,
An' nought but his han'-darg to keep
Them right an' tight in thack an' rape.
   An' when they meet wi' sair disasters,
Like loss o' health or want o' masters,   80
Ye maist wad think, a wee touch langer,
An' they maun starve o' cauld and hunger:
But how it comes, I never kend yet,
They're maistly wonderfu' contented;

51 *Racked:* extortionate. 52 *Kain:* rent in kind; *stents:* dues. 57
Steeks: stitches. 58 *Geordie:* George III guinea; *keeks:* peeps. 61
Stechin: stuffing themselves. 62 *Ha' folk:* servants; *pechan:* stomach.
65 *Whipper-in:* huntsman's assistant; *wonner:* wonder. 69 *Cot-folk:*
cottagers; *pit their painch in:* put in their paunch. 71 *Fash't:* bothered.
73 *Biggin:* building. 76 *Smytrie:* swarm; *weans:* children. 77 *Han'
darg:* hand labour. 78 *Thack an' rape:* thatch and rope, cover for
haystacks; 'a roof over their heads.' 81 *Maist:* almost. 82 *Maun:*
must.

An' buirdly chiels, an' clever hizzies,　　　　　85
Are bred in sic a way as this is.

CÆSAR

But then to see how ye're negleckit,
How huff'd, an' cuff'd, an' disrespeckit!
Lord, man, our gentry care as little
For *delvers, ditchers*, an' sic cattle;　　　　　90
They gang as saucy by poor folk,
As I wad by a stinking brock.
　I've notic'd, on our Laird's *court-day*,
An' monie a time my heart's been wae,
Poor *tenant bodies*, scant o' cash,　　　　　95
How they maun thole a *factor's* snash:
He'll stamp an' threaten, curse an' swear,
He'll *apprehend* them, *poind* their gear;
While they maun stan', wi' aspect humble,
An' hear it a', an' fear an' tremble!　　　　　100
　I see how folk live that hae riches;
But surely poor-folk maun be wretches!

LUATH

They're no sae wretched's ane wad think;
Tho' constantly on poortith's brink:
They're sae accustom'd wi' the sight,　　　　　105
The view o't gies them little fright.
　Then chance and fortune are sae guided,
They're ay in less or mair provided;
An' tho' fatigu'd wi' close employment,
A blink o' rest's a sweet enjoyment.　　　　　110
　The dearest comfort o' their lives,
Their grushie weans an' faithfu' wives;
The *prattling things* are just their pride,

---

85 *Buirdly chiels:* well-set-up lads; *hizzies:* young women. 88 *Huff'd:*
bullied. 92 *Brock:* badger. 93 *Court-day:* rent-day. 94 *Wae:* sad.
96-100 'My father's generous Master died; the farm proved a ruinous
bargain; and, to clench the curse, we fell into the hands of a Factor who
sat for the picture I have drawn of one in my Tale of two dogs.' (Burns,
letter to Dr. Moore, 1787). 96 *Thole:* endure; *snash:* abuse. 98
Poind: impound; *gear:* possessions. 99 *Staun':* stand. 104 *Poortith:*
poverty. 110 *Blink:* moment. 112 *Grushie:* thriving.

That sweetens a' their fire-side.

An' whyles twalpennie worth o' *nappy*   115
Can mak the bodies unco happy;
They lay aside their private cares,
To mind the Kirk and State affairs;
They'll talk o' *patronage* an' *priests*,
Wi' kindling fury i' their breasts,   120
Or tell what new taxation's comin,
An' ferlie at the folk in *Lon'on*.

As bleak-fac'd Hallowmass returns,
They get the jovial, ranting *Kirns*,
When *rural life*, of ev'ry station,   125
Unite in common recreation;
Love blinks, Wit slaps, an' social Mirth
Forgets there's Care upo' the earth.

That merry day the year begins,
They bar the door on frosty win's;   130
The nappy reeks wi' mantling ream,
An' sheds a heart-inspiring steam;
The luntin pipe, an' sneeshin mill,
Are handed round wi' right guid will;
The cantie auld folks, crackin crouse,   135
The young anes ranting thro' the house,—
My heart has been sae fain to see them,
That I for joy hae barkit wi' them.

Still it's owre true that ye hae said,
Sic game is now owre aften play'd;   140
There's monie a creditable stock
Or decent, honest fawsont folk,
Are riven out baith root an' branch,
Some rascal's pridefu' greed to quench,
Wha thinks to knit himsel the faster   145
In favor wi' some gentle Master,
Wha aiblins thrang a *parliamentin'*,
For Britain's guid his saul indentin'—

---

115 *Twalpennie . . . nappy:* 12 pence Scots (=1d. sterling) was the cost
of a quart of ale. 122 *Ferlie:* marvel. 123 *Hallowmass:* first week of
November. 124 *Kirns:* harvest-homes. 127 *Blinks:* throws glances.
131 *Reeks:* smokes; *ream:* cream, froth. 133 *Luntin:* smoking;
sneeshin mill: snuff-box. 135 *Cantie:* cheerful; *crackin crouse:* chatting
away merrily. 136 *Ranting:* romping. 137 *Fain:* glad. 140 *Owre:*
too. 142 *Fawsont:* well-doing. 147 *Aiblins:* maybe. 148 *Indentin':*
indenturing, committing.

CÆSAR

Haith, lad, ye little ken about it;
For Britain's guid! guid faith! I doubt it.   150
Say rather, gaun as *Premiers* lead him:
An' saying *aye* or *no's* they bid him:
At operas an' plays parading,
Mortgaging, gambling, masquerading:
Or maybe, in a frolic daft,   155
To *Hague* or *Calais* taks a waft,
To mak a tour, an' tak a whirl,
To learn *bon ton,* an' see the worl'.
    There, at *Vienna* or *Versailles,*
He rives his father's auld entails;   160
O by *Madrid* he takes the rout,
To thrum guitars, an' fecht wi' nowt;
Or down *Italian vista* startles,
Whore-hunting amang groves o' myrtles:
Then bowses drumlie *German-water,*   165
To mak himsel look fair an' fatter,
An' clear the consequential sorrows,
Love-gifts of Carnival signoras.
    For Britain's guid! for her destruction!
Wi' dissipation, feud an' faction!   170

LUATH

Hech man! dear sirs! is that the gate
They waste sae monie a braw estate!
Are we sae foughten an' harass'd
For gear to gang that gate at last?
O would they stay aback frae courts,   175
An' please themsels wi' countra sports,
It wad for ev'ry ane be better,
The Laird, the Tenant, an' the Cotter!
For thae frank, rantin, ramblin billies,
Fient haet o' them's ill-hearted fellows;   180

---

149 *Haith:* faith! (mild oath of surprise). 151 *Gaun:* going. 158 *Bon
ton:* good manners (Fr.). 160 *Rives:* breaks up, 'bursts'; *entails:*
strictly settled father-to-son inheritance of estate. 161 *Taks the rout:*
roams. 162 *Fecht wi' nowt:* fight with cattle. 163 *Vista:* avenue,
glade; *startles:* dashes. 165 *Drumlie German-water:* muddy water from
a German spa. 171 *Gate:* way. 173 *Foughten:* troubled. 174 *Gear:*
wealth, property. 179 *Thae:* those. 180 *Fient haet:* devil a one.

Except for breakin' o' their timmer,
Or speakin lightly o' their Limmer,
Or shootin of a hare or moor-cock,
The ne'er-a-bit they're ill to poor folk.
But will ye tell me, master *Cæsar*,   185
Sure great folk's life's a life o' pleasure?
Nae cauld nor hunger e'er can steer them,
The vera thought o't need na fear them.

CÆSAR

Lord, man, were ye but whyles whare I am,
The *gentles* ye wad ne'er envy 'em.   190
It's true they need na starve or sweat,
Thro' Winter's cauld, or Simmer's heat;
They've nae sair wark to craze their banes,
An' fill auld age wi' grips an' granes:
But human bodies are sic fools,   195
For a' their colleges an' schools,
That when nae real ills perplex them,
They mak enow themsels to vex them;
An' aye the less they hae to sturt them,
In like proportion, less will hurt them.   200
A countra fellow at the pleugh,
His *acre's* till'd, he's right eneugh;
A countra girl at her wheel,
Her *dizzen's* done, she's unco weel;
But Gentlemen, an' Ladies warst,   205
Wi' ev'ndown want o' wark are curst.
They loiter, lounging, lank, an' lazy;
Tho' deil-haet ails them, yet uneasy;
Their days insipid, dull, an' tasteless;
Their nights unquiet, lang, an' restless;   210
An' ev'n their sports, their balls an' races,
Their galloping through public places,
There's sic parade, sic pomp an' art,
The joy can scarcely reach the heart.
The Men cast out in *party-matches*,   215
Then sowther a' in deep debauches;

181 *Timmer:* timber. 182 *Limmer:* mistress. 187 *Steer:* touch. 193
Sair: heavy. 194 *Grips an' granes:* pains and groans. 199 *Sturt:* vex.
204 *Dizzen:* dozen 'cuts' of yarn, the amount she would spin in a day.
206 *Ev'ndown:* absolute. 208 *Deil-haet:* not a thing. 215 *Cast out:*
quarrel; *party-matches:* party contests. 216 *Sowther:* solder.

Ae night, they're mad wi' drink an' whoring,
Niest day their life is past enduring.
The Ladies arm-in-arm in clusters,
As great an' gracious a' as sisters;   220
But hear their *absent thoughts* o' ither,
They're a' run deils an' jads thegither.
Whyles, owre the wee bit cup an' platie,
They sip the scandal potion pretty;
Or lee-lang nights, wi' crabbit leuks,   225
Pore owre the devil's pictur'd beuks;
Stake on a chance a farmer's stackyard,
An' cheat like onie unhang'd blackguard.
    There's some exception, man an' woman;
But this is Gentry's life in common.   230

    By this, the sun was out o' sight,
An' darker gloamin brought the night:
The bum-clock humm'd wi' lazy drone,
The kye stood rowtin i' the loan;
When up they gat an' shook their lugs,   235
Rejoic'd they were na *men*, but *dogs*;
An' each took aff his several way,
Resolv'd to meet some ither day.

THE INVENTORY

Addressed to the surveyor of taxes in Ayr, Burns's friend and
patron Robert Aiken, who in 1786 required an account of the
poet's 'servants, carriages, carriage horses, riding horses, wives,
children' and general plenishing.

Sir, as your mandate did request,
I send you here a faithfu' list,
My servants, horses, carts and graith,
To which I'm free to tak my aith.

217 *Ae:* one. 218 *Niest:* next. 222 *Run deils:* perfect devils. 225
Lee-lang nights: all night long. 226 *Devil's pictur'd beuks:* playing-cards.
233 *Bum-clock:* humming beetle. 234 *Kye:* cows; *rowtin:* lowing;
loan: path between fields. 3 *Graith:* accoutrements. 4 *Aith:* oath.

    Imprimis, then, for carriage cattle,   5
I hae four brutes o' gallant mettle,
As ever drew before a pettle.
My *Lan'-afore*'s a guid, auld *has been*,
An' wight an' wilfu' a' his days been.
My *Lan'-ahin*'s a guid brown Filly,   10
That aft has borne me hame frae Killie,
An' your auld borough monie a time,
In days when riding was nae crime—
(But ance when in my wooing pride
I like a blockhead boost to ride,   15
The wilfu' creature sae I pat to,—
Lord pardon a' my sins, an' that too!
I play'd my fillie sic a shavie,
She's a' bedevil'd wi' the spavie).
My *Fur-ahin*'s a wordy beast,   20
As e'er in tug or tow was trac'd.—
The fourth's a Highland Donald hastie,
A damn'd red-wud Kilburnie blastie;
Forby, a cowte, o' cowtes the wale,
As ever ran afore a tail: 25
If he be spar'd to be a beast,
He'll draw me fifteen pund at least.

    Wheel-carriages I ha'e but few,
Three carts, an' twa are feckly new;
An auld wheelbarrow—mair for token,   30
Ae leg an' baith the trams are broken:
I made a poker o' the spin'le,
An' my auld mither brunt the trin'le.

    For men, I've three mischievous boys,
Run-deils for fechtin an' for noise: 35

---

5 *Imprimis:* in the first place.   7 *Pettle:* plough-staff (for clearing ploughshare of roots, weeds, etc.).   8 *Lan'-afore:* front left (of the four horses drawing the plough).   9 *Wight an' wilfu':* strong and willing. 10 *Lan'-ahin:* back left-hand horse; *weel-gaun:* well-going, smoothly working.   11 *Killie:* Kilmarnock, Ayrshire.   12 *Auld borough:* Ayr, a royal burgh since 1202.   15 *Boost to:* felt I had to.   16 *Pat to:* drove, oppressed.   18 *Shavie:* trick.   19 *Spavie:* spavin.   20 *Fur-ahin:* back right-hand horse; *wordy:* worthy.   21 *Tug or tow:* rawhide or rope (from which plough-traces were made).   22 *Highland Donald:* Highland pony or sheltie.   23 *Red-wud Kilburnie blastie:* mad, wild, ill-tempered creature from Kilbirnie, Ayrshire.   24 *Forby:* besides; *cowte:* colt; *wale:* pick.   27 *Pund:* pounds (sterling).   29 *Feckly:* mainly, as good as.   31 *Ae:* one; *trams:* shafts.   32 *Spin'le:* axle; *trin'le:* wheel.   33 *Brunt:* burnt.   35 *Run-deils:* perfect devils; *fechtin:* fighting.

A gaudsman ane, a thrasher t' other,
Wee Davoc hauds the nowte in fother.
I rule them as I ought, discreetly,
An' aften labour them completely;
An' ay on Sundays duly, nightly,   40
I on the *Questions* tairge them tightly;
Till, faith! wee Davoc's grown sae gleg,
Tho' scarcely langer than your leg,
He'll screed you aff *Effectual Calling*,
As fast as onie in the dwalling.   45

    I've nane in female servan' station,
(Lord keep me ay frae a' temptation!):
I hae nae wife, and that my bliss is,
An' ye hae laid nae tax on misses;
An' then, if kirk folks dinna clutch me,   50
I ken the deevils darena touch me.
Wi' weans I'm mair than weel contented,
Heav'n sent me ane mair than I wanted.
My sonsie, smirking, dear-bought Bess,
She stares the daddie in her face,   55
Enough of ought ye like but grace;
But her, my bonie sweet wee lady,
I've paid enough for her already,
An' gin ye tax her or her mither,
B' the Lord ye'se get them a' thegither!   60

    But pray, remember, Mr. Aiken,
Nae kind of licence out I'm takin':

36 *Gaudsman:* man or boy who accompanied the ploughman and guided
the horses; *thrasher:* thresher.   37 *Wee Davoc:* David Hutchieson, whose
father had been ploughman at Lochlea Farm, near Tarbolton, Ayrshire,
where Burns lived 1777-84. Burns looked after the boy when his father
died. *Hauds the nowte in fother:* keeps the cattle supplied with fodder.
39 *Labour them completely:* make them work at full stretch.   41 *Questions:*
the Shorter Catechism;   *tairge them tightly:* narrowly cross-examine
them.   42 *Gleg:* sharp.   44 *Screed . . . aff:* recite rapidly, reel off;
Effectual Calling: 'is the work of God's Spirit, whereby, convincing us of
our sin and misery, enlightening our minds in the knowledge of Christ,
and renewing our wills, he doth persuade and enable us to embrace
Jesus Christ, freely offered to us in the Gospel.'   49 *Misses:* mistresses.
52 *Weans:* children.   54 *Sonsie:* plump and good-natured; *smirking:*
pleasantly smiling;   *Bess:* his daughter by Elizabeth Paton, a servant at
Lochlea. Burns wrote his warm *Welcome to a Bastart Wean* when she was
born in 1785.   55-56 'She takes after her father in everything except
(his lack of) good behaviour.'   59 *Gin:* if.   60 *Ye'se:* you'll; *a'*
thegither; altogether.

Frae this time forth, I do declare
I'se ne'er ride horse nor hizzie mair;
Thro' dirt and dub for life I'll paidle,   65
Ere I sae dear pay for a saddle;
I've sturdy stumps, the Lord be thankit!
And a' my gates on foot I'll shank it.
The Kirk an' you may tak' you that,
It puts but little in your pat: 70
Sae dinna put me in your beuk,
Nor for my ten white shillings leuk.

    This list, wi' my ain han' I've wrote it,
The day and date as under notit;
Then know all ye whom it concerns,   75
Subscripsi huic,   ROBERT BURNS
                                        Mossgiel, February
                                           22d, 1786

EPISTLE TO JAMES SMITH

James Smith, son of a merchant, and the ' Wag in Mauchline '
of Burns's amusing epitaph, would be about 21 when the poet
wrote this piece, probably early in 1786. It appeared a few
months later in the Kilmarnock edition, which the poem shows
to have been revolving as an uncertain project in Burns's mind
at the time.

> *Friendship, mysterious cement of the soul!*
> *Sweet'ner of Life, and solder of Society!*
> *I owe thee much—*
>
>   BLAIR

Dear Smith, the sleest, paukie thief,
That e'er attempted stealth or rief,
Ye surely hae some warlock-breef
        Owre human hearts;
For ne'er a bosom yet was prief   5
        Against your arts.

64 *Hizzie:* 'hussy', girl. 65 *Dub:* puddles; *paidle:* tramp. 67
Stumps: legs. 68 *Gates:* ways; *shank it:* walk. 70 *Pat:* pot. 71
Dinna: don't. 76 *Subscripsi huic:* 'I have signed this' (Lat.). 1 *Slee'st:*
slyest; *pawkie:* shrewd, knowing, and humorous. 2 *Rief:* plunder.
3 *Warlock-breef:* wizard's spell. 5 *Prief:* proof.

For me, I swear by sun an' moon,
And ev'ry star that blinks aboon,
Ye've cost me twenty pair o' shoon,
  Just gaun to see you;   10
And ev'ry ither pair that's done,
  Mair taen I'm wi' you.

That auld, capricious carlin, *Nature*,
To mak amends for scrimpit stature,
She's turn'd you off, a human creature 15
  On her *first* plan;
And in her freaks, on ev'ry feature,
  She's wrote, *the Man*.

Just now I've taen the fit o' rhyme,
My barmie noddle's working prime, 20
My fancy yerkit up sublime
  Wi' hasty summon:
Hae ye a leisure-moment's time
  To hear what's comin?

Some rhyme a neebor's name to lash; 25
Some rhyme (vain thought!) for needfu' cash;
Some rhyme to court the countra clash,
  An' raise a din;
For me, an *aim* I never fash;
  I rhyme for *fun*. 30

The star that rules my luckless lot,
Has fated me the russet coat,
An' damn'd my fortune to the groat;
  But, in requit,
Has blest me with a *random shot* 35
  O' countra wit.

This while my notion's taen a sklent,
To try my fate in guid, black *prent*;
But still the mair I'm that way bent,
  Something cries, " Hoolie! 40
I red you, honest man, tak tent!
  Ye'll shaw your folly.

---

8 *Aboon:* above. 10 *Gaun:* going. 12 *Taen:* taken. 13 *Carlin:* old woman, hag. 14 *Scrimpit:* niggardly. 20 *Barmie noddle:* frothing head, fermenting wit. 21 *Yerkit up:* fermented, worked up. 27 *Countra clash:* local gossip. 29 *Fash:* bother about. 32 *Russet coat:* typifying rustic poverty. 37 *My notion's taen a sklent:* my fancy has taken a new slant. 40 *Hoolie:* easy does it! 41 *Red:* advise; *tak tent:* be careful!

" There's ither poets, much your betters,
Far seen in *Greek*, deep men o' *letters*,
Hae thought they had ensur'd their debtors,   45
     A' future ages;
Now moths deform, in shapeless tatters,
     Their unknown pages."

Then farewel hopes o' laurel-boughs,
To garland my poetic brows!
Henceforth I'll rove where busy ploughs   50
     Are whistling thrang;
An' teach the lanely heights an' howes
     My rustic sang.

I'll wander on wi' tentless heed   55
How never-halting moments speed,
Till fate shall snap the brittle thread;
     Then, all unknown,
I'll lay me with th' *inglorious dead*,
     Forgot and gone!   60

But why o' Death begin a tale?
Just now we're living sound an' hale;
Then top and maintop croud the sail,
     Heave *Care* o'er-side!
And large, before Enjoyment's gale,   65
     Let's tak the tide.

This life, sae far's I understand,
Is a' enchanted fairy-land,
Where Pleasure is the Magic-Wand,
     That, wielded right,   70
Maks Hours like Minutes, hand in hand,
     Dance by fu' light.

The *magic-wand* then let us wield;
For, ance that five-an'-forty's speel'd,
See crazy, weary, joyless Eild,   75
     Wi' wrinkl'd face,
Comes hostin, hirplin owre the field,
     Wi' creepin pace.

52 *Thrang:* busily. 53 *Howes:* valleys. 55 *Tentless:* careless. 74
Speel'd: climbed. 75 *Eild:* old age. 77 *Hostin, hirplin:* coughing and
hobbling.

When ance *life's day* draws near the gloamin,
Then fareweel vacant, careless roamin;   80
An' fareweel cheerfu' tankards foamin,
      An' social noise;
An' fareweel dear, deluding *woman*,
      The joy of joys!

O *Life*! how pleasant in thy morning,   85
Young Fancy's rays the hills adorning!
Cold-pausing Caution's lesson scorning,
      We frisk away,
Like school-boys, at th' expected warning,
      To joy an' play.   90

We wander there, we wander here,
We eye the *rose* upon the brier,
Unmindful that the *thorn* is near,
      Among the leaves;
And tho' the puny wound appear,   95
      Short while it grieves.

Some, lucky, find a flow'ry spot,
For which they never toil'd nor swat;
They drink the sweet and eat the fat,
      But care or pain;   100
And haply, eye the barren hut
      With high disdain.

With steady aim, some Fortune chase;
Keen hope does ev'ry sinew brace;
Thro' fair, thro' foul, they urge the race,   105
      And seize the prey:
Then canie, in some cozie place,
      They close the *day*.

And others, like your humble servan',
Poor wights! nae rules nor roads observin   110
To right or left, eternal swervin,
      They zig-zag on;
Till curst with age, obscure an' starvin,
      They aften groan.

98 *Swat:* sweated.   100 *But:* without.   107 *Canie:* quietly and safely comfortable.

Alas! what bitter toil an' straining— 115
But truce with peevish, poor complaining!
If Fortune's fickle *Luna* waning?
    E'en let her gang!
Beneath what light she had remaining,
    Let's sing our sang. 120

My pen I here fling to the door,
And kneel, " Ye *Pow'rs!* " and warm implore,
" Tho' I should wander *Terra* o'er,
    In all her climes,
Grant me but this, I ask no more, 125
    Ay rowth o' rhymes.

" Gie dreeping roasts to countra Lairds,
Till icicles hing frae their beards;
Gie fine braw claes to fine Life-guards,
    And Maids of Honour; 130
And yill an' whisky gie to Cairds,
    Until they sconner.

" A Title, *Dempster* merits it;
A Garter gie to *Willie Pitt*;
Gie wealth to some be-ledger'd Cit, 135
    In cent. per cent.
But gie me real, sterling Wit,
    And I'm content.

" While ye are pleas'd to keep me hale,
I'll sit down o'er my scanty meal, 140
Be't *water-brose* or *muslin-kail*,
    Wi' cheerfu' face,
As lang's the Muses dinna fail
    To say the grace."

---

118 *Gang:* go. 126 *Rowth:* abundance. 129 *Claes:* clothes. 131
Yill: ale; *cairds:* tinkers. 132 *Sconner:* sicken. 133 *Dempster:* George
Dempster (1732-1818), Scottish patriot, M.P. for Forfar and Fife
Burghs, exerted himself to improve Scottish agriculture and fisheries.
134 *Pitt:* William Pitt the Younger (1759-1806), English statesman.
135 *Cit:* 'citizen', shopkeeper, businessman. 141 *Water-brose:* oatmeal
stirred into boiling water; *muslin-kail:* thin broth of water, barley, and
greens.

An anxious e'e I never throws   145
Behint my lug, or by my nose;
I jouk beneath Misfortune's blows
        As weel's I may;
Sworn foe to Sorrow, Care, and Prose,
        I rhyme away.   150

O ye douce folk, that live by rule,
Grave, tideless-blooded, calm an' cool,
Compar'd wi' you—O fool! fool! fool!
        How much unlike!
Your hearts are just a standing pool,   155
        Your lives, a dyke!

Nae hare-brain'd, sentimental traces
In your unletter'd, nameless faces!
In *arioso* trills and graces
        Ye never stray;   160
But *gravissimo*, solemn basses
        Ye hum away.

Ye are sae *grave*, nae doubt ye're *wise*,
Nae ferly tho' ye do despise
The hairum-scairum, ram-stam boys,   165
        The rattling squad:
I see ye upward cast your eyes—
        Ye ken the road!—

Whilst I—but I shall haud me there,
Wi' you I'll scarce gang *onie where*—   170
Then, *Jamie*, I shall say nae mair,
        But quat my sang,
Content wi' *You* to mak a pair,
        Whare'er I gang.

146 *Lug:* ear; *by:* beyond. 147 *Jouk:* duck. 151 *Douce:* sedate and
respectable. 155 *Dyke:* wall. 159 *Arioso:* song-like (Ital.). 161
Gravissimo: very slowly and heavily (Ital.). 164 *Ferly:* wonder. 165
Ram-stam: roughly impetuous and reckless. 166 *Rattling:* boisterously
lively. 169 *Haud:* hold. 172 *Quat:* quit.

James Hogg

1770—1835

KILMENY

The 'Thirteenth Bard's Song' from *The Queen's Wake* (1813), in which seventeen minstrels compete before Mary Queen of Scots in retelling 'legends of our native land.' The visionary romance of Kilmeny brought out the best in Hogg's enthusiastic soul, and if it falls short of perfection we can trace this to the poet's belief that the 'strains that touch the heart' are 'bold, rapid, wild, and void of art.'

Bonny Kilmeny gaed up the glen;
But it wasna to meet Duneira's men,
Nor the rosy monk of the isle to see,
For Kilmeny was pure as pure could be.
It was only to hear the Yorlin sing,   5
And pu' the cress-flower round the spring;
The scarlet hypp and the hindberrye,
And the nut that hang frae the hazel tree;
For Kilmeny was pure as pure could be.
But lang may her minny look o'er the wa',   10
And lang may she seek i' the green-wood shaw;
Lang the laird of Duneira blame,
And lang, lang greet or Kilmeny come hame!

When many a day had come and fled,
When grief grew calm, and hope was dead,   15
When mess for Kilmeny's soul had been sung,
When the bedes-man had prayed, and the dead bell rung,
Late, late in a gloamin when all was still,
When the fringe was red on the westlin hill,
The wood was sere, the moon i' the wane,   20
The reek o' the cot hung over the plain,
Like a little wee cloud in the world its lane;

5 *Yorlin:* yellowhammer. 7 *Hindberrye:* wild raspberry. 10 *Minny:* mother. 11 *Shaw:* grove. 13 *Or:* before. 17 *Bedes-man:* one who prays for the souls of others. 22 *Its lane:* by itself.

403

When the ingle lowed with an eiry leme,
Late, late in the gloamin Kilmeny came hame!

" Kilmeny, Kilmeny, where have you been?   25
Lang hae we sought baith holt and den;
By linn, by ford, and green-wood tree,
Yet you are halesome and fair to see.
Where gat you that joup o' the lily scheen?
That bonny snood of the birk sae green?   30
And these roses, the fairest that ever were seen?
Kilmeny, Kilmeny, where have you been? "

Kilmeny looked up with a lovely grace,
But nae smile was seen on Kilmeny's face;
As still was her look, and as still was her ee,   35
As the stillness that lay on the emerant lea,
Or the mist that sleeps on a waveless sea.
For Kilmeny had been she knew not where,
And Kilmeny had seen what she could not declare;
Kilmeny had been where the cock never crew,   40
Where the rain never fell, and the wind never blew;
But it seemed as the harp of the sky had rung,
And the airs of heaven played round her tongue,
When she spake of the lovely forms she had seen,
And a land where sin had never been;   45
A land of love, and a land of light,
Withouten sun, or moon, or night;
Where the river swa'd a living stream,
And the light a pure celestial beam:
The land of vision it would seem,   50
A still, an everlasting dream.

In yon green-wood there is a waik,
And in that waik there is a wene,
And in that wene there is a maike,
That neither has flesh, blood, nor bane;   55
And down in yon green-wood he walks his lane.

In that green wene Kilmeny lay,
Her bosom happed wi' the flowerets gay;

23 *Ingle:* hearth; *lowed:* glowed; *leme:* gleam. 27 *Linn:* waterfall.
29 *Joup:* short gown. 48 *Swa'd:* rolled. 52 *Waik:* The word means
'watch'; Hogg is apparently repeating a phrase from the ballad
Erlinton ('But in my bower there is a wake') without understanding its
meaning. 53 *Wene:* dwelling-place. 54 *Maike:* mate, fellow. 56
His lane: alone. 58 *Happed:* covered.

But the air was soft and the silence deep,
And bonny Kilmeny fell sound asleep.   60
She kend nae mair, nor opened her ee,
Till waked by the hymns of a far countrye.
She 'wakened on a couch of the silk sae slim,
All striped wi' the bars of the rainbow's rim;
And lovely beings round were rife,   65
Who erst had travelled mortal life;
And aye they smiled, and 'gan to speer,
" What spirit has brought this mortal here? "

" Lang have I journeyed the world wide,"
A meek and reverend fere replied;   70
" Baith night and day I have watched the fair,
Eident a thousand years and mair.
Yes, I have watched o'er ilk degree,
Wherever blooms femenitye;
But sinless virgin, free of stain   75
In mind and body, fand I nane.
Never, since the banquet of time,
Found I a virgin in her prime,
Till late this bonny maiden I saw
As spotless as the morning snaw: 80
Full twenty years she has lived as free
As the spirits that sojourn this countrye:
I have brought her away frae the snares of men,
That sin or death she never may ken."

They clasped her waist and her hands sae fair,   85
They kissed her cheek, and they kemed her hair,
And round came many a blooming fere,
Saying, " Bonny Kilmeny, ye're welcome here!
Women are freed of the littand scorn:
O, blessed be the day Kilmeny was born!   90
Now shall the land of the spirits see,
Now shall it ken what a woman may be!
Many a lang year in sorrow and pain,
Many a lang year through the world we've gane,
Commissioned to watch fair womankind,   95
For it's they who nurice the immortal mind.
We have watched their steps as the dawning shone,
And deep in the green-wood walks alone;

67 *Speer:*   ask.   70 *Fere:*   friend, fellow.   72 *Eident:*   vigilant.
89 *Littand scorn:*   blameworthy tainting.

By lily bower and silken bed,
The viewless tears have o'er them shed;   100
Have soothed their ardent minds to sleep,
Or left the couch of love to weep.
We have seen! we have seen! but the time must come,
And the angels will weep at the day of doom!

" O, would the fairest of mortal kind   105
Aye keep the holy truths in mind,
That kindred spirits their motions see,
Who watch their ways with anxious ee,
And grieve for the guilt of humanitye!
O, sweet to Heaven the maiden's prayer,   110
And the sigh that heaves a bosom sae fair!
And dear to Heaven the words of truth,
And the praise of virtue frae beauty's mouth!
And dear to the viewless forms of air,
The minds that kyth as the body fair!   115

" O, bonny Kilmeny! free frae stain,
If ever you seek the world again,
That world of sin, of sorrow and fear,
O, tell of the joys that are waiting here;
And tell of the signs you shall shortly see;   120
Of the times that are now, and the times that shall be."

They lifted Kilmeny, they led her away,
And she walked in the light of a sunless day:
The sky was a dome of crystal bright,
The fountain of vision, and fountain of light: 125
The emerald fields were of dazzling glow,
And the flowers of everlasting blow.
Then deep in the stream her body they laid,
That her youth and her beauty never might fade;
And they smiled on heaven, when they saw her lie   130
In the stream of life that wandered bye.
And she heard a song, she heard it sung,
She kend not where; but sae sweetly it rung,
It fell on her ear like a dream of the morn:
" O! blest be the day Kilmeny was born!   135
Now shall the land of the spirits see,
Now shall it ken what a woman may be!
The sun that shines on the world sae bright,
A borrowed gleid frae the fountain of light;

115 *Kyth:* appear.   139 *Gleid:* spark, ember.

And the moon that sleeks the sky sae dun,   140
Like a gouden bow, or a beamless sun,
Shall wear away, and be seen nae mair,
And the angels shall miss them travelling the air.
But lang, lang after baith night and day,
When the sun and the world have elyed away;   145
When the sinner has gane to his waesome doom,
Kilmeny shall smile in eternal bloom! "

They bore her away, she wist not how,
For she felt not arm nor rest below;
But so swift they wained her through the light,   150
'Twas like the motion of sound or sight;
They seemed to split the gales of air,
And yet nor gale nor breeze was there.
Unnumbered groves below them grew,
They came, they past, and backward flew,   155
Like floods of blossoms gliding on,
In moment seen, in moment gone.
O, never vales to mortal view
Appeared like those o'er which they flew!
That land to human spirits given,   160
The lowermost vales of the storied heaven;
From thence they can view the world below,
And heaven's blue gates with sapphires glow,
More glory yet unmeet to know.

They bore her far to a mountain green,   165
To see what mortal never had seen;
And they seated her high on a purple sward,
And bade her heed what she saw and heard,
And note the changes the spirits wrought,
For now she lived in the land of thought.   170
She looked, and she saw nor sun nor skies,
But a crystal dome of a thousand dies:
She looked, and she saw nae land aright,
But an endless whirl of glory and light:
And radiant beings went and came   175
Far swifter than wind, or the linked flame.
She hid her een frae the dazzling view;
She looked again, and the scene was new.

She saw a sun on a summer skye,
And clouds of amber sailing bye;   180

145 *Elyed:* vanished. 150 *Wained:* carried.

A lovely land beneath her lay,
And that land had glens and mountains gray;
And that land had valleys and hoary piles,
And marled seas, and a thousand isles;
Its fields were speckled, its forests green,   185
And its lakes were all of the dazzling sheen,
Like magic mirrors, where slumbering lay
The sun and the sky and the cloudlet gray;
Which heaved and trembled, and gently swung,
On every shore they seemed to be hung;   190
For there they were seen on their downward plain
A thousand times and a thousand again;
In winding lake and placid firth,
Little peaceful heavens in the bosom of earth.

Kilmeny sighed and seemed to grieve,   195
For she found her heart to that land did cleave;
She saw the corn wave on the vale,
She saw the deer run down the dale;
She saw the plaid and the broad claymore,
And the brows that the badge of freedom bore;   200
And she thought she had seen the land before.

She saw a lady sit on a throne,
The fairest that ever the sun shone on!
A lion licked her hand of milk,
And she held him in a leish of silk;   205
And a leifu' maiden stood at her knee,
With a silver wand and melting ee;
Her sovereign shield till love stole in,
And poisoned all the fount within.

Then a gruff untoward bedes-man came,   210
And hundit the lion on his dame;
And the guardian maid wi' the dauntless ee,
She dropped a tear, and left her knee;
And she saw till the queen frae the lion fled,
Till the bonniest flower of the world lay dead;   215
A coffin was set on a distant plain,
And she saw the red blood fall like rain:

202-55 These visions may be strained into an uneasy historical allegory,
beginning with the opposition of John Knox's Protestantism to Mary
Queen of Scots, and involving the politico-religious strife of the 17th
century, the transformation of the Lion of Scotland into the British Lion
after the Union of the Crowns, and the attempt to check the career of
Napoleon in Hogg's own time.   206 *Leifu'*: gentle.

Then bonny Kilmeny's heart grew sair,
And she turned away, and could look nae mair.

Then the gruff grim carle girned amain,   220
And they trampled him down, but he rose again;
And he baited the lion to deeds of weir,
Till he lapped the blood to the kingdom dear;
And weening his head was danger-preef,
When crowned with the rose and clover leaf,   225
He gowled at the carle, and chased him away
To feed wi' the deer on the mountain gray.
He gowled at the carle, and he gecked at Heaven,
But his mark was set, and his arles given.
Kilmeny a while her een withdrew;   230
She looked again, and the scene was new.

She saw below her fair unfurled
One half of all the glowing world,
Where oceans rolled, and rivers ran,
To bound the aims of sinful man.   235
She saw a people, fierce and fell,
Burst frae their bounds like fiends of hell;
There lilies grew, and the eagle flew,
And she herked on her ravening crew,
Till the cities and towers were wrapt in a blaze,   240
And the thunder it roared o'er the lands and the seas.
The widows they wailed, and the red blood ran,
And she threatened an end to the race of man;
She never lened, nor stood in awe,
Till claught by the lion's deadly paw.   245
Oh! then the eagle swinked for life,
And brainzelled up a mortal strife;
But flew she north, or flew she south,
She met wi' the growl of the lion's mouth.

With a mooted wing and waefu' maen,   250
The eagle sought her eiry again;
But lang may she cower in her bloody nest,
And lang, lang sleek her wounded breast,
Before she sey another flight,
To play wi' the norland lion's might.   255

220 *Girned:* snarled. 226 *Gowled:* yelled. 228 *Gecked:* scoffed.
229 *Arles:* deserts, reward. 239 *Herked:* urged. 244 *Lened:* bowed.
245 *Claught:* clutched. 247 *Brainzelled:* stirred. 250 *Mooted:*
moulted, damaged. 254 *Sey:* attempt.

But to sing the sights Kilmeny saw,
So far surpassing nature's law,
The singer's voice wad sink away,
And the string of his harp wad cease to play.
But she saw till the sorrows of man were bye,   260
And all was love and harmony;
Till the stars of heaven fell calmly away,
Like the flakes of snaw on a winter day.

Then Kilmeny begged again to see
The friends she had left in her own countrye,   265
To tell of the place where she had been,
And the glories that lay in the land unseen;
To warn the living maidens fair,
The loved of Heaven, the spirits' care,
That all whose minds unmeled remain   270
Shall bloom in beauty when time is gane.

With distant music, soft and deep,
They lulled Kilmeny sound asleep;
And when she awakened, she lay her lane,
All happed with flowers in the green-wood wene.   275
When seven lang years had come and fled;
When grief was calm, and hope was dead;
When scarce was remembered Kilmeny's name,
Late, late in a gloamin Kilmeny came hame!
And O, her beauty was fair to see,   280
But still and steadfast was her ee!
Such beauty bard may never declare,
For there was no pride nor passion there;
And the soft desire of maiden's een
In that mild face could never be seen.   285
Her seymar was the lily flower,
And her cheek the moss-rose in the shower;
And her voice like the distant melodye,
That floats along the twilight sea.
But she loved to raike the lanely glen,   290
And keeped afar frae the haunts of men;
Her holy hymns unheard to sing,
To suck the flowers, and drink the spring.
But wherever her peaceful form appeared,
The wild beasts of the hill were cheered;   295

270 *Unmeled:* pure. 286 *Seymar:* loose dress or tunic. 290 *Raike:* rove through.

The wolf played blythly round the field,
The lordly byson lowed and kneeled;
The dun deer wooed with manner bland,
And cowered aneath her lily hand.
And when at even the woodlands rung, 300
When hymns of other worlds she sung
In ecstasy of sweet devotion,
O, then the glen was all in motion!
The wild beasts of the forest came,
Broke from their bughts and faulds the tame, 305
And goved around, charmed and amazed;
Even the dull cattle crooned and gazed,
And murmured and looked with anxious pain
For something the mystery to explain.
The buzzard came with the throstle-cock; 310
The corby left her houf in the rock;
The blackbird alang wi' the eagle flew;
The hind came tripping o'er the dew;
The wolf and the kid their raike began,
And the tod, and the lamb, and the leveret ran; 315
The hawk and the hern attour them hung,
And the merl and the mavis forhooyed their young;
And all in a peaceful ring were hurled:
It was like an eve in a sinless world!

When a month and a day had come and gane, 320
Kilmeny sought the green-wood wene;
There laid her down on the leaves sae green,
And Kilmeny on earth was never mair seen.
But O, the words that fell from her mouth,
Were words of wonder, and words of truth! 325
But all the land were in fear and dread,
For they kendna whether she was living or dead.
It wasna her hame, and she couldna remain;
She left this world of sorrow and pain,
And returned to the land of thought again. 330

305 *Bughts:* folds, pens. 306 *Goved:* stared. 311 *Corby:* raven;
houf: home. 315 *Tod:* fox. 316 *Attour:* above. 317 *Merl:* black-
bird; *forhooyed:* abandoned.

William Wordsworth

1770—1850

LINES

WRITTEN A FEW MILES ABOVE TINTERN ABBEY, ON
REVISITING THE BANKS OF THE WYE DURING A TOUR,
JULY 13, 1798

Five years have past; five summers, with the length
Of five long winters! and again I hear
These waters, rolling from their mountain-springs
With a soft inland murmur.—Once again
Do I behold these steep and lofty cliffs, 5
That on a wild secluded scene impress
Thoughts of more deep seclusion; and connect
The landscape with the quiet of the sky.
The day is come when I again repose
Here, under this dark sycamore, and view 10
These plots of cottage-ground, these orchard-tufts,
Which at this season, with their unripe fruits,
Are clad in one green hue, and lose themselves
'Mid groves and copses. Once again I see
These hedge-rows, hardly hedge-rows, little lines 15
Of sportive wood run wild: these pastoral farms,
Green to the very door; and wreaths of smoke
Sent up, in silence, from among the trees!
With some uncertain notice, as might seem
Of vagrant dwellers in the houseless woods, 20
Or of some Hermit's cave, where by his fire
The Hermit sits alone.

        These beauteous forms,
Through a long absence, have not been to me
As is a landscape to a blind man's eye:
But oft, in lonely rooms, and 'mid the din 25
Of towns and cities, I have owed to them
In hours of weariness, sensations sweet,
Felt in the blood, and felt along the heart;
And passing even into my purer mind,
With tranquil restoration:—feelings too 30
Of unremembered pleasure: such, perhaps,

4 Tintern Abbey is situated in the last stretch of the Wye valley, be-
tween Monmouth and the Severn estuary.

As have no slight or trivial influence
On that best portion of a good man's life,
His little, nameless, unremembered, acts
Of kindness and of love. Nor less, I trust, 35
To them I may have owed another gift,
Of aspect more sublime; that blessed mood
In which the burthen of the mystery,
In which the heavy and the weary weight
Of all this unintelligible world, 40
Is lightened:—that serene and blessed mood,
In which the affections gently lead us on,—
Until, the breath of this corporeal frame
And even the motion of our human blood
Almost suspended, we are laid asleep 45
In body, and become a living soul:
While with an eye made quiet by the power
Of harmony, and the deep power of joy,
We see into the life of things.

                              If this
Be but a vain belief, yet, oh! how oft— 50
In darkness and amid the many shapes
Of joyless daylight; when the fretful stir
Unprofitable, and the fever of the world,
Have hung upon the beatings of my heart—
How oft, in spirit, have I turned to thee, 55
O sylvan Wye! thou wanderer thro' the woods,
How often has my spirit turned to thee!

    And now, with gleams of half-extinguished thought,
With many recognitions dim and faint,
And somewhat of a sad perplexity, 60
The picture of the mind revives again:
While here I stand, not only with the sense
Of present pleasure, but with pleasing thoughts
That in this moment there is life and food
For future years. And so I dare to hope, 65
Though changed, no doubt, from what I was when first
I came among these hills; when like a roe
I bounded o'er the mountains, by the sides
Of the deep rivers, and the lonely streams,
Wherever nature led: more like a man 70
Flying from something that he dreads than one
Who sought the thing he loved. For nature then
(The coarser pleasures of my boyish days,

And their glad animal movements all gone by)
To me was all in all.—I cannot paint
What then I was. The sounding cataract   75
Haunted me like a passion: the tall rock,
The mountain, and the deep and gloomy wood,
Their colours and their forms, were then to me
An appetite; a feeling and a love,   80
That had no need of a remoter charm,
By thought supplied, nor any interest
Unborrowed from the eye.—That time is past,
And all its aching joys are now no more,
And all its dizzy raptures. Not for this   85
Faint I, nor mourn nor murmur; other gifts
Have followed; for such loss, I would believe,
Abundant recompense. For I have learned
To look on nature, not as in the hour
Of thoughtless youth; but hearing oftentimes   90
The still, sad music of humanity,
Nor harsh nor grating, though of ample power
To chasten and subdue. And I have felt
A presence that disturbs me with the joy
Of elevated thoughts; a sense sublime   95
Of something far more deeply interfused,
Whose dwelling is the light of setting suns,
And the round ocean, and the living air,
And the blue sky, and in the mind of man:
A motion and a spirit, that impels   100
All thinking things, all objects of all thought,
And rolls through all things. Therefore am I still
A lover of the meadows and the woods,
And mountains; and of all that we behold
From this green earth; of all the mighty world   105
Of eye, and ear,—both what they half create,
And what perceive; well pleased to recognise
In nature and the language of the sense
The anchor of my purest thoughts, the nurse,
The guide, the guardian of my heart, and soul   110
Of all my moral being.

                    Nor perchance,
If I were not thus taught, should I the more
Suffer my genial spirits to decay:
For thou art with me here upon the banks
Of this fair river; thou my dearest Friend,   115
My dear, dear Friend; and in thy voice I catch

The language of my former heart, and read
My former pleasures in the shooting lights
Of thy wild eyes. Oh! yet a little while
May I behold in thee what I was once,   120
My dear, dear Sister! and this prayer I make,
Knowing that Nature never did betray
The heart that loved her; 'tis her privilege,
Through all the years of this our life, to lead
From joy to joy: for she can so inform   125
The mind that is within us, so impress
With quietness and beauty, and so feed
With lofty thoughts, that neither evil tongues,
Rash judgments, nor the sneers of selfish men,
Nor greetings where no kindness is, nor all   130
The dreary intercourse of daily life,
Shall e'er prevail against us, or disturb
Our cheerful faith, that all which we behold
Is full of blessings. Therefore let the moon
Shine on thee in thy solitary walk;   135
And let the misty mountain-winds be free
To blow against thee: and, in after years,
When these wild ecstasies shall be matured
Into a sober pleasure; when thy mind
Shall be a mansion for all lovely forms,   140
Thy memory be as a dwelling-place
For all sweet sounds and harmonies; oh! then,
If solitude, or fear, or pain, or grief,
Should be thy portion, with what healing thoughts
Of tender joy wilt thou remember me,   145
And these my exhortations! Nor, perchance—
If I should be where I no more can hear
Thy voice, nor catch from thy wild eyes these gleams
Of past existence—wilt thou then forget
That on the banks of this delightful stream   150
We stood together; and that I, so long
A worshipper of Nature, hither came
Unwearied in that service: rather say
With warmer love—oh! with far deeper zeal
Of holier love. Nor wilt thou then forget,   155
That after many wanderings, many years
Of absence, these steep woods and lofty cliffs,
And this green pastoral landscape, were to me
More dear, both for themselves and for thy sake!

121 *Sister:* Dorothy Wordsworth (1771-1855).

THE OLD CUMBERLAND BEGGAR

For all its quietness and lack of bravura, this poem (written in
1797) springs from some of Wordsworth's strongest and deepest
feelings. Old, feeble, destitute, useless to society, the beggar is
still ' a silent monitor,' even to those only slightly less poor than
himself, of the thread by which all life hangs, and of that Lear-like
shock that realizes no man can sink ' so low as to be scorned
without a sin.'

Wordsworth has the following note on the poem: " The class
of Beggars, to which the Old Man here described belongs, will
probably soon be extinct. It consisted of poor, and, mostly, old
and infirm persons, who confined themselves to a stated round in
their neighbourhood, and had certain fixed days, on which, at
different houses, they regularly received alms, sometimes in money,
but mostly in provisions."

I saw an aged Beggar in my walk;
And he was seated, by the highway side,
On a low structure of rude masonry
Built at the foot of a huge hill, that they
Who lead their horses down the steep rough road   5
May thence remount at ease. The aged Man
Had placed his staff across the broad smooth stone
That overlays the pile; and, from a bag
All white with flour, the dole of village dames,
He drew his scraps and fragments, one by one;   10
And scanned them with a fixed and serious look
Of idle computation. In the sun,
Upon the second step of that small pile,
Surrounded by those wild unpeopled hills,
He sat, and ate his food in solitude: 15
And ever, scattered from his palsied hand,
That, still attempting to prevent the waste,
Was baffled still, the crumbs in little showers
Fell on the ground; and the small mountain birds,
Not venturing yet to peck their destined meal,   20
Approached within the length of half his staff.

Him from my childhood have I known; and then
He was so old, he seems not older now;

He travels on, a solitary Man,
So helpless in appearance, that for him 25
The sauntering Horseman throws not with a slack
And careless hand his alms upon the ground,
But stops,—that he may safely lodge the coin
Within the old Man's hat; nor quits him so,
But still, when he has given his horse the rein, 30
Watches the aged Beggar with a look
Sidelong, and half-reverted. She who tends
The toll-gate, when in summer at her door
She turns her wheel, if on the road she sees
The aged Beggar coming, quits her work, 35
And lifts the latch for him that he may pass.
The post-boy, when his rattling wheels o'ertake
The aged Beggar in the woody lane,
Shouts to him from behind; and, if thus warned
The old man does not change his course, the boy 40
Turns with less noisy wheels to the road-side,
And passes gently by, without a curse
Upon his lips or anger at his heart.

He travels on, a solitary Man;
His age has no companion. On the ground 45
His eyes are turned, and, as he moves along,
They move along the ground; and, evermore,
Instead of common and habitual sight
Of fields with rural works, of hill and dale,
And the blue sky, one little span of earth 50
Is all his prospect. Thus, from day to day,
Bow-bent, his eyes for ever on the ground,
He plies his weary journey; seeing still,
And seldom knowing that he sees, some straw,
Some scattered leaf, or marks which, in one track, 55
The nails of cart or chariot-wheel have left
Impressed on the white road,—in the same line,
At distance still the same. Poor Traveller!
His staff trails with him; scarcely do his feet
Disturb the summer dust; he is so still 60
In look and motion, that the cottage curs,
Ere he has passed the door, will turn away,
Weary of barking at him. Boys and girls,
The vacant and the busy, maids and youths,
And urchins newly breeched—all pass him by: 65
Him even the slow-paced waggon leaves behind.
But deem not this Man useless.—Statesmen! ye

A.L.P. o

Who are so restless in your wisdom, ye
Who have a broom still ready in your hands
To rid the world of nuisances; ye proud,   70
Heart-swoln, while in your pride ye contemplate
Your talents, power, or wisdom, deem him not
A burthen of the earth! 'Tis Nature's law
That none, the meanest of created things,
Of forms created the most vile and brute,   75
The dullest or most noxious, should exist
Divorced from good—a spirit and pulse of good,
A life and soul, to every mode of being
Inseparably*linked. Then be assured
That least of all can aught—that ever owned   80
The heaven-regarding eye and front sublime
Which man is born to—sink, howe'er depressed,
So low as to be scorned without a sin;
Without offence to God cast out of view;
Like the dry remnant of a garden-flower   85
Whose seeds are shed, or as an implement
Worn out and worthless. While from door to door,
This old Man creeps, the villagers in him
Behold a record which together binds
Past deeds and offices of charity   90
Else unremembered, and so keeps alive
The kindly mood in hearts which lapse of years,
And that half-wisdom half-experience gives,
Make slow to feel, and by sure steps resign
To selfishness and cold oblivious cares.   95
Among the farms and solitary huts,
Hamlets and thinly-scattered villages,
Where'er the aged Beggar takes his rounds,
The mild necessity of use compels
To acts of love; and habit does the work   100
Of reason; yet prepares that after-joy
Which reason cherishes. And thus the soul,
By that sweet taste of pleasure unpursued,
Doth find herself insensibly disposed
To virtue and true goodness. Some there are,   105
By their good works exalted, lofty minds,
And meditative, authors of delight
And happiness, which to the end of time
Will live, and spread, and kindle: even such minds,
In childhood, from this solitary Being,   110
Or from like wanderer, haply have received
(A thing more precious far than all that books

Or the solicitudes of love can do!)
That first mild touch of sympathy and thought,
In which they found their kindred with a world   115
Where want and sorrow were. The easy man
Who sits at his own door, —and, like the pear
That overhangs his head from the green wall,
Feeds in the sunshine; the robust and young,
The prosperous and unthinking, they who live   120
Sheltered, and flourish in a little grove
Of their own kindred;—all behold in him
A silent monitor, which on their minds
Must needs impress a transitory thought
Of self-congratulation, to the heart   125
Of each recalling his peculiar boons,
His charters and exemptions; and, perchance,
Though he to no one give the fortitude
And circumspection needful to preserve
His present blessings, and to husband up   130
The respite of the season, he, at least,
And 'tis no vulgar service, makes them felt.

     Yet further.——Many, I believe, there are
Who live a life of virtuous decency,
Men who can hear the Decalogue and feel   135
No self-reproach; who of the moral law
Established in the land where they abide
Are strict observers; and not negligent
In acts of love to those with whom they dwell,
Their kindred, and the children of their blood.   140
Praise be to such, and to their slumbers peace!
—But of the poor man ask, the abject poor;
Go, and demand of him, if there be here
In this cold abstinence from evil deeds,
And these inevitable charities,   145
Wherewith to satisfy the human soul?
No—man is dear to man; the poorest poor
Long for some moments in a weary life
When they can know and feel that they have been,
Themselves, the fathers and the dealers-out   150
Of some small blessings; have been kind to such
As needed kindness, for this single cause,
That we have all of us one human heart.
—Such pleasure is to one kind Being known,
My neighbour, when with punctual care, each week,   155

135 *Decalogue:* the Ten Commandments.

Duly as Friday comes, though pressed herself
By her own wants, she from her store of meal
Takes one unsparing handful for the scrip
Of this old Mendicant, and, from her door
Returning with exhilarated heart,   160
Sits by her fire, and builds her hope in heaven.

Then let him pass, a blessing on his head!
And while in that vast solitude to which
The tide of things has borne him, he appears
To breathe and live but for himself alone,   165
Unblamed, uninjured, let him bear about
The good which the benignant law of Heaven
Has hung around him: and, while life is his,
Still let him prompt the unlettered villagers
To tender offices and pensive thoughts.   170
—Then let him pass, a blessing on his head!
And, long as he can wander, let him breathe
The freshness of the valleys; let his blood
Struggle with frosty air and winter snows;
And let the chartered wind that sweeps the heath   175
Beat his grey locks against his withered face.
Reverence the hope whose vital anxiousness
Gives the last human interest to his heart.
May never HOUSE, misnamed of INDUSTRY,
Make him a captive!—for that pent-up din,   180
Those life-consuming sounds that clog the air,
Be his the natural silence of old age!
Let him be free of mountain solitudes;
And have around him, whether heard or not,
The pleasant melody of woodland birds.   185
Few are his pleasures: if his eyes have now
Been doomed so long to settle upon earth
That not without some effort they behold
The countenance of the horizontal sun,
Rising or setting, let the light at least   190
Find a free entrance to their languid orbs,
And let him, *where* and *when* he will, sit down
Beneath the trees, or on a grassy bank
Of highway side, and with the little birds
Share his chance-gathered meal; and, finally,   195
As in the eye of Nature he has lived,
So in the eye of Nature let him die!

158 *Scrip:* bag, satchel.   175 *Chartered:* privileged, free.   179 *House of
industry:* workhouse.

TO A HIGHLAND GIRL

(At Inversneyde, upon Loch Lomond)

Sweet Highland Girl, a very shower
Of beauty is thy earthly dower!
Twice seven consenting years have shed
Their utmost bounty on thy head:
And these grey rocks; that household lawn; 5
Those trees, a veil just half withdrawn;
This fall of water that doth make
A murmur near the silent lake;
This little bay; a quiet road
That holds in shelter thy Abode— 10
In truth together do ye seem
Like something fashioned in a dream;
Such Forms as from their covert peep
When earthly cares are laid asleep!
But, O fair Creature! in the light 15
Of common day, so heavenly bright,
I bless Thee, Vision as thou art,
I bless thee with a human heart;
God shield thee to thy latest years!
Thee, neither know I, nor thy peers; 20
And yet my eyes are filled with tears.

With earnest feeling I shall pray
For thee when I am far away:
For never saw I mien, or face,
In which more plainly I could trace 25
Benignity and home-bred sense
Ripening in perfect innocence.
Here scattered, like a random seed,
Remote from men, Thou dost not need
The embarrassed look of shy distress, 30
And maidenly shamefacedness:
Thou wear'st upon thy forehead clear
The freedom of a Mountaineer:
A face with gladness overspread!
Soft smiles, by human kindness bred! 35
And seemliness complete, that sways
Thy courtesies, about thee plays;

With no restraint, but such as springs
From quick and eager visitings
Of thoughts that lie beyond the reach   40
Of thy few words of English speech:
A bondage sweetly brooked, a strife
That gives thy gestures grace and life!
So have I, not unmoved in mind,
Seen birds of tempest-loving kind—   45
Thus beating up against the wind.

    What hand but would a garland cull
For thee who art so beautiful?
O happy pleasure! here to dwell
Beside thee in some heathy dell;   50
Adopt your homely ways, and dress,
A Shepherd, thou a Sherpherdess!
But I could frame a wish for thee
More like a grave reality:
Thou art to me but as a wave   55
Of the wild sea; and I would have
Some claim upon thee, if I could,
Though but of common neighbourhood.
What joy to hear thee, and to see!
Thy elder Brother I would be,   60
Thy Father—anything to thee!

    Now thanks to Heaven! that of its grace
Hath led me to this lonely place.
Joy have I had; and going hence
I bear away my recompense.   65
In spots like these it is we prize
Our Memory, feel that she hath eyes:
Then, why should I be loth to stir?
I feel this place was made for her;
To give new pleasure like the past,   70
Continued long as life shall last.
Nor am I loth, though pleased at heart,
Sweet Highland Girl! from thee to part;
For I, methinks, till I grow old,
As fair before me shall behold,   75
As I do now, the cabin small,
The lake, the bay, the waterfall;
And Thee, the Spirit of them all!

ELEGIAC STANZAS

SUGGESTED BY A PICTURE OF PEELE CASTLE, IN A
STORM, PAINTED BY SIR GEORGE BEAUMONT

I was thy neighbour once, thou rugged Pile!
Four summer weeks I dwelt in sight of thee:
I saw thee every day; and all the while
Thy Form was sleeping on a glassy sea.

So pure the sky, so quiet was the air!   5
So like, so very like, was day to day!
Whene'er I looked, thy Image still was there;
It trembled, but it never passed away.

How perfect was the calm! it seemed no sleep;
No mood, which season takes away, or brings: 10
I could have fancied that the mighty Deep
Was even the gentlest of all gentle Things.

Ah! THEN, if mine had been the Painter's hand,
To express what then I saw; and add the gleam,
The light that never was, on sea or land,   15
The consecration, and the Poet's dream;

I would have planted thee, thou hoary Pile
Amid a world how different from this!
Beside a sea that could not cease to smile;
On tranquil land, beneath a sky of bliss.   20

Thou shouldst have seemed a treasure-house, divine
Of peaceful years; a chronicle of heaven;—
Of all the sunbeams that did ever shine
The very sweetest had to thee been given.

A Picture had it been of lasting ease,   25
Elysian quiet, without toil or strife;
No motion but the moving tide, a breeze,
Or merely silent Nature's breathing life.

1 Peele (or Piel) Castle stands on an island off the Furness peninsula in
Lancashire. Wordsworth stayed at Rampside, opposite Piel Island, in
the summer of 1794.

Such, in the fond illusion of my heart,
Such Picture would I at that time have made: 30
And seen the soul of truth in every part,
A stedfast peace that might not be betrayed.

So once it would have been,—'tis so no more;
I have submitted to a new control:
A power is gone, which nothing can restore;   35
A deep distress hath humanised my Soul.

Not for a moment could I now behold
A smiling sea, and be what I have been:
The feeling of my loss will ne'er be old;
This, which I know, I speak with mind serene.   40

Then, Beaumont, Friend! who would have been the Friend,
If he had lived, of Him whom I deplore,
This work of thine I blame not, but commend;
This sea in anger, and that dismal shore.

O 'tis a passionate Work!—yet wise and well,   45
Well chosen is the spirit that is here;
That Hulk which labours in the deadly swell,
This rueful sky, this pageantry of fear!

And this huge Castle, standing here sublime,
I love to see the look with which it braves,   50
Cased in the unfeeling armour of old time,
The lightning, the fierce wind, and trampling waves.

Farewell, farewell the heart that lives alone,
Housed in a dream, at distance from the Kind!
Such happiness, wherever it be known,   55
Is to be pitied; for 'tis surely blind.

But welcome fortitude, and patient cheer,
And frequent sights of what is to be borne!
Such sights, or worse, as are before me here.—
Not without hope we suffer and we mourn.   60

36 Wordsworth's brother John was drowned in 1805, the year when this poem was written. 41 Sir George Beaumont (1753-1827).

Samuel Taylor Coleridge

1772—1834

THE RIME OF THE ANCIENT MARINER

IN SEVEN PARTS

Facile credo, plures esse Naturas invisibiles quam visibiles in rerum universitate. Sed horum omnium familiam quis nobis enarrabit? et gradus et cognationes et discrimina et singulorum munera? Quid agunt? quae loca habitant? Harum rerum notitiam semper ambivit ingenium humanum, nunquam attigit. Juvat, interea, non diffiteor, quandoque in animo, tanquam in tabula, majoris et melioris mundi imaginem contemplari : ne mens assuefacta hodiernae vitae minutiis se contrahat nimis, et tota subsidat in pusillas cogitationes. Sed veritati interea invigilandum est, modusque servandus, ut certa ab incertis, diem a nocte, distinguamus.—T. BURNET, *Archaeol. Phil.* p. 68.

ARGUMENT

How a Ship having passed the Line was driven by storms to the cold Country towards the South Pole; and how from thence she made her course to the tropical Latitude of the Great Pacific Ocean; and of the strange things that befell; and in what manner the Ancyent Marinere came back to his own Country.

PART ONE

An ancient Mariner meeteth three Gallants bidden to a wedding-feast, and detaineth one.

It is an ancient Mariner,
And he stoppeth one of three.
' By thy long grey beard and glittering eye,
Now wherefore stopp'st thou me?

The Bridegroom's doors are opened wide,   5
And I am next of kin;
The guests are met, the feast is set:
May'st hear the merry din.'

He holds him with his skinny hand,
' There was a ship,' quoth he.   10
' Hold off! unhand me, grey-beard loon! '
Eftsoons his hand dropt he.

12 *Eftsoons:* forthwith.

425

The Wedd-
ing-Guest is
spellbound
by the eye of
the old sea-
faring man,
and con-
strained to
hear his tale.
He holds him with his glittering eye—
The Wedding-Guest stood still,
And listens like a three years' child: 15
The Mariner hath his will.

The Wedding-Guest sat on a stone:
He cannot choose but hear;
And thus spake on that ancient man,
The bright-eyed Mariner.   20

' The ship was cheered, the harbour cleared,
Merrily did we drop
Below the kirk, below the hill,
The Mariner
tells how the
ship sailed
southward
with a good
wind and
fair weather,
till it
reached the
line.
Below the lighthouse top.

The Sun came up upon the left,   25
Out of the sea came he!
And he shone bright, and on the right
Went down into the sea.

Higher and higher every day,
Till over the mast at noon— '   30
The Wedding-Guest here beat his breast,
For he heard the loud bassoon.

The Wedd-
ing-Guest
heareth the
bridal
music; but
the Mariner
continueth
his tale.
The bride hath paced into the hall,
Red as a rose is she;
Nodding their heads before her goes   35
The merry minstrelsy.

The Wedding-Guest he beat his breast,
Yet he cannot choose but hear;
And thus spake on that ancient man,
The bright-eyed Mariner.   40

The ship
driven by a
storm to-
ward the
south pole.
' And now the STORM-BLAST came, and he
Was tyrannous and strong:
He struck with his o'ertaking wings,
And chased us south along.

With sloping masts and dipping prow,   45
As who pursued with yell and blow
Still treads the shadow of his foe,
And forward bends his head,
The ship drove fast, loud roared the blast,
And southward aye we fled.   50

And now there came both mist and snow,
And it grew wondrous cold:
And ice, mast-high, came floating by,
As green as emerald.

The land of
ice, and of
fearful
sounds
where no
living thing
was to be
seen.

And through the drifts the snowy clifts   55
Did send a dismal sheen:
Nor shapes of men nor beasts we ken—
The ice was all between.

The ice was here, the ice was there,
The ice was all around: 60
It cracked and growled, and roared and howled,
Like noises in a swound!

Till a great
sea-bird,
called the
Albatross,
came
through the
snow-fog,
and was
received
with great
joy and
hospitality.

At length did cross an Albatross,
Thorough the fog it came;
As if it had been a Christian soul,   65
We hailed it in God's name.

It ate the food it ne'er had eat,
And round and round it flew.
The ice did split with a thunder-fit;
The helmsman steered us through!   70

And lo! the
Albatross
proveth a
bird of good
omen, and
followeth
the ship as it
returned
northward
through fog
and floating
ice.

And a good south wind sprung up behind;
The Albatross did follow,
And every day, for food or play,
Came to the mariner's hollo!

In mist or cloud, on mast or shroud,   75
It perched for vespers nine;
Whiles all the night, through fog-smoke white,
Glimmered the white Moon-shine.'

The ancient
Mariner
inhospitably
killeth the
pious bird of
good omen.

'God save thee, ancient Mariner!
From the fiends, that plague thee thus!—   80
Why look'st thou so?'—With my cross-bow
I shot the ALBATROSS.

62 *Swound:* swoon, fainting-fit.

PART TWO

The Sun now rose upon the right:
Out of the sea came he,
Still hid in mist, and on the left   85
Went down into the sea.

And the good south wind still blew behind,
But no sweet bird did follow,
Nor any day for food or play
Came to the mariner's hollo!   90

His ship-
mates cry
out against
the ancient
Mariner, for
killing the
bird of good
luck.

And I had done a hellish thing,
And it would work 'em woe:
For all averred, I had killed the bird
That made the breeze to blow.
Ah wretch! said they, the bird to slay,   95
That made the breeze to blow!

But when
the fog
cleared off,
they justify
the same,
and thus
make them-
selves
accomplices
in the crime.

Nor dim nor red, like God's own head,
The glorious Sun uprist:
Then all averred, I had killed the bird
That brought the fog and mist.   100
'Twas right, said they, such birds to slay,
That bring the fog and mist.

The fair
breeze con-
tinues; the
ship enters
the Pacific
Ocean, and
sails north-
ward, even
till it reaches
the Line.

The fair breeze blew, the white foam flew,
The furrow followed free;
We were the first that ever burst   105
Into that silent sea.

The ship
hath been
suddenly
becalmed.

Down dropt the breeze, the sails dropt down,
'Twas sad as sad could be;
And we did speak only to break
The silence of the sea!   110

All in a hot and copper sky,
The bloody Sun, at noon,
Right up above the mast did stand,
No bigger than the Moon.

Day after day, day after day,   115
We stuck, nor breath nor motion;
As idle as a painted ship
Upon a painted ocean.

And the
Albatross
begins to be
avenged.

Water, water, every where,
And all the boards did shrink;   120
Water, water, every where,
Nor any drop to drink.

The very deep did rot: O Christ!
That ever this should be!
Yea, slimy things did crawl with legs   125
Upon the slimy sea.

About, about, in reel and rout
The death-fires danced at night;
The water, like a witch's oils,
Burnt green, and blue and white.   130

A Spirit had
followed
them: one of
the invisible
inhabitants
of this
planet,
neither
departed
souls nor

And some in dreams assuréd were
Of the Spirit that plagued us so;
Nine fathom deep he had followed us
From the land of mist and snow.

angels; concerning whom the learned Jew, Josephus, and the Platonic Constantino-
politan, Michael Psellus, may be consulted. They are very numerous, and there is no
climate or element without one or more.

And every tongue, through utter drought,   135
Was withered at the root;
We could not speak, no more than if
We had been choked with soot.

The ship-
mates, in
their sore
distress,
would fain
throw the
whole guilt
on the
ancient
Mariner: in
sign whereof
they hang
the dead sea-
bird round
his neck.

Ah! well a-day! what evil looks
Had I from old and young!
Instead of the cross, the Albatross   140
About my neck was hung.

PART THREE

There passed a weary time. Each throat
Was parched, and glazed each eye.
A weary time! a weary time!   145
How glazed each weary eye,

When looking westward, I beheld
A something in the sky.

At first it seemed a little speck,
And then it seemed a mist;   150
It moved and moved, and took at last
A certain shape, I wist.

A speck, a mist, a shape, I wist!
And still it neared and neared:
As if it dodged a water-sprite,   155
It plunged and tacked and veered.

With throats unslaked, with black lips baked,
We could nor laugh nor wail;
Through utter drought all dumb we stood!
I bit my arm, I sucked the blood,   160
And cried, A sail! a sail!

With throats unslaked, with black lips baked,
Agape they heard me call:
Gramercy! they for joy did grin,
And all at once their breath drew in,   165
As they were drinking all.

See! see! (I cried) she tacks no more!
Hither to work us weal;
Without a breeze, without a tide,
She steadies with upright keel!   170

The western wave was all a-flame.
The day was well nigh done!
Almost upon the western wave
Rested the broad bright Sun;
When that strange shape drove suddenly   175
Betwixt us and the Sun.

And straight the Sun was flecked with bars,
(Heaven's Mother send us grace!)
As if through a dungeon-grate he peered
With broad and burning face.   180

164 *Gramercy:* exclamation of thankfulness and surprise.

Alas! (thought I, and my heart beat loud)
How fast she nears and nears!
Are those *her* sails that glance in the Sun,
Like restless gossameres?

And its ribs are seen as bars on the face of the setting Sun.

Are those *her* ribs through which the Sun   185
Did peer, as through a grate?
And is that Woman all her crew?
Is that a DEATH? and are there two?
Is DEATH that woman's mate?

The Spectre-Woman and her Death-mate, and no other on board the skeleton ship.

Her lips were red, *her* looks were free,   190
Her locks were yellow as gold:
Her skin was as white as leprosy,
The Night-mare LIFE-IN-DEATH was she,
Who thicks man's blood with cold.

Like vessel, like crew!

Death and Life-in-Death have diced for the ship's crew, and she (the latter) winneth the ancient Mariner.

The naked hulk alongside came,   195
And the twain were casting dice;
' The game is done! I've won! I've won! '
Quoth she, and whistles thrice.

The Sun's rim dips; the stars rush out:
At one stride comes the dark;   200
With far-heard whisper, o'er the sea,
Off shot the spectre-bark.

No twilight within the courts of the Sun.

We listened and looked sideways up!
Fear at my heart, as at a cup,
My life-blood seemed to sip!   205
The stars were dim, and thick the night,
The steersman's face by his lamp gleamed white;
From the sails the dew did drip—
Till clomb above the eastern bar
The hornéd Moon, with one bright star   210
Within the nether tip.

At the rising of the Moon,

One after one, by the star-dogged Moon,
Too quick for groan or sigh,
Each turned his face with a ghastly pang,
And cursed me with his eye.   215

One after another.

His ship-
mates drop
down dead.

Four times fifty living men,
(And I heard nor sigh nor groan)
With heavy thump, a lifeless lump,
They dropped down one by one.

But Life-in-
Death be-
gins her
work on the
ancient
Mariner.

The souls did from their bodies fly,— 220
They fled to bliss or woe!
And every soul, it passed me by,
Like the whizz of my cross-bow!

PART FOUR

The Wedd-
ing-Guest
feareth that
a Spirit is
talking to
him;

' I fear thee, ancient Mariner!
I fear thy skinny hand! 225
And thou art long, and lank, and brown,
As is the ribbed sea-sand.

I fear thee and thy glittering eye,
And thy skinny hand, so brown.'—
Fear not, fear not, thou Wedding-Guest! 230

But the an-
cient Mar-
iner assureth
him of his
bodily life,
and proceed-
eth to relate
his horrible
penance.

This body dropt not down.

Alone, alone, all, all alone,
Alone on a wide wide sea!
And never a saint took pity on
My soul in agony. 235

He despiseth
the creatures
of the calm,

The many men, so beautiful!
And they all dead did lie:
And a thousand thousand slimy things
Lived on; and so did I.

And envieth
that *they*
should live,
and so many
lie dead.

I looked upon the rotting sea, 240
And drew my eyes away;
I looked upon the rotting deck,
And there the dead men lay.

226-7 For the last two lines of this stanza, I am indebted to Mr. Words-
worth. It was on a delightful walk from Nether Stowey to Dulverton,
with him and his sister, in the Autumn of 1797, that this Poem was
planned, and in part composed. (C.)

I looked to heaven, and tried to pray;
But or ever a prayer had gusht,   245
A wicked whisper came, and made
My heart as dry as dust.

I closed my lids, and kept them close,
And the balls like pulses beat;
For the sky and the sea, and the sea and the sky   250
Lay like a load on my weary eye,
And the dead were at my feet.

But the curse liveth for him in the eye of the dead men.

The cold sweat melted from their limbs,
Nor rot nor reek did they:
The look with which they looked on me   255
Had never passed away.

In his loneliness and fixedness he yearneth towards the journeying Moon, and the stars that still sojourn, yet still move onward; and every where the blue sky belongs to them, and is their appointed rest, and their native country and their own natural homes, which they enter unannounced, as lords that are certainly expected and yet there is a silent joy at their arrival.

An orphan's curse would drag to hell
A spirit from on high;
But oh! more horrible than that
Is the curse in a dead man's eye!   260
Seven days, seven nights, I saw that curse,
And yet I could not die.

The moving Moon went up the sky,
And no where did abide:
Softly she was going up,   265
And a star or two beside—

Her beams bemocked the sultry main,
Like April hoar-frost spread;
But where the ship's huge shadow lay,
The charméd water burnt alway   270
A still and awful red.

By the light of the Moon he beholdeth God's creatures of the great calm.

Beyond the shadow of the ship,
I watched the water-snakes:
They moved in tracks of shining white,
And when they reared, the elfish light   275
Fell off in hoary flakes.

Within the shadow of the ship
I watched their rich attire:
Blue, glossy green, and velvet black,
They coiled and swam; and every track   280
Was a flash of golden fire.

245 *Or ever:* before.

Their beauty
and their
happiness.

O happy living things! no tongue
Their beauty might declare:
A spring of love gushed from my heart,
And I blessed them unaware: 285

He blesseth
them in his
heart.

Sure my kind saint took pity on me,
And I blessed them unaware.

The spell
begins to
break.

The self-same moment I could pray;
And from my neck so free
The Albatross fell off, and sank   290
Like lead into the sea.

PART FIVE

Oh sleep! it is a gentle thing,
Beloved from pole to pole!
To Mary Queen the praise be given!
She sent the gentle sleep from Heaven,   295
That slid into my soul.

By grace of
the holy
Mother, the
ancient
Mariner is
refreshed
with rain.

The silly buckets on the deck,
That had so long remained,
I dreamt that they were filled with dew
And when I awoke, it rained.   300

My lips were wet, my throat was cold,
My garments all were dank;
Sure I had drunken in my dreams,
And still my body drank.

I moved, and could not feel my limbs: 305
I was so light—almost
I thought that I had died in sleep,
And was a blessèd ghost.

He heareth
sounds and
seeth strange
sight and
commotions
in the sky
and the
element.

And soon I heard a roaring wind:
It did not come anear;   310
But with its sound it shook the sails,
That were so thin and sere.

The upper air burst into life!
And a hundred fire-flags sheen,
To and fro they were hurried about!   315
And to and fro, and in and out,
The wan stars danced between.

297 *Silly:* poor, helpless.   314 *Sheen:* bright.

And the coming wind did roar more loud,
And the sails did sigh like sedge;
And the rain poured down from one black cloud; 320
The Moon was at its edge.

The thick black cloud was cleft, and still
The Moon was at its side:
Like waters shot from some high crag,
The lightning fell with never a jag,   325
A river steep and wide.

The loud wind never reached the ship,
Yet now the ship moved on!
Beneath the lightning and the Moon
The dead men gave a groan.   330

The bodies
of the ship's
crew are
inspired
and the ship
moves on;

They groaned, they stirred, they all uprose,
Nor spake, nor moved their eyes;
It had been strange, even in a dream,
To have seen those dead men rise

The helmsman steered, the ship moved on;   335
Yet never a breeze up-blew;
The mariners all 'gan work the ropes,
Where they were wont to do;
They raised their limbs like lifeless tools—
We were a ghastly crew.   340

The body of my brother's son
Stood by me, knee to knee:
The body and I pulled at one rope,
But he said nought to me.

'I fear thee, ancient Mariner!'   345
Be calm, thou Wedding-Guest!
'Twas not those souls that fled in pain,
Which to their corses came again,
But a troop of spirits blest:

But not by
the souls of
the men, nor
by dæmons
of earth or
middle air,
but by a
blessed
troop of
angelic
spirits,
sent down
by the
invocation of
the guardian
saint.

For when it dawned—they dropped their arms, 350
And clustered round the mast;
Sweet sounds rose slowly through their mouths,
And from their bodies passed.

Around, around, flew each sweet sound,
Then darted to the Sun;   355
Slowly the sounds came back again,
Now mixed, now one by one.

Sometimes a-dropping from the sky
I heard the sky-lark sing;
Sometimes all little birds that are,   360
How they seemed to fill the sea and air
With their sweet jargoning!

And now 'twas like all instruments,
Now like a lonely flute;
And now it is an angel's song,   365
That makes the heavens be mute.

It ceased; yet still the sails made on
A pleasant noise till noon,
A noise like of a hidden brook
In the leafy month of June,   370
That to the sleeping woods all night
Singeth a quiet tune.

Till noon we quietly sailed on,
Yet never a breeze did breathe:
Slowly and smoothly went the ship,   375
Moved onward from beneath.

The lonesome Spirit from the south-pole carries on the ship as far as the Line, in obedience to the angelic troop, but still requireth vengeance.

Under the keel nine fathom deep,
From the land of mist and snow,
The spirit slid: and it was he
That made the ship to go.   380
The sails at noon left off their tune,
And the ship stood still also.

The Sun, right up above the mast,
Had fixed her to the ocean:
But in a minute she 'gan stir,   385
With a short uneasy motion—
Backwards and forwards half her length
With a short uneasy motion.

Then like a pawing horse let go,
She made a sudden bound:
It flung the blood into my head,   390
And I fell down in a swound.

How long in that same fit I lay,
I have not to declare;
But ere my living life returned,   395
I heard and in my soul discerned
Two voices in the air.

' Is it he? ' quoth one, ' Is this the man?
By him who died on cross,
With his cruel bow he laid full low   400
The harmless Albatross.

The spirit who bideth by himself
In the land of mist and snow,
He loved the bird that loved the man
Who shot him with a bow.'   405

The other was a softer voice,
As soft as honey-dew:
Quoth he, ' The man hath penance done,
And penance more will do.'

PART SIX

FIRST VOICE

'But tell me, tell me! speak again,   410
Thy soft response renewing—
What makes that ship drive on so fast?
What is the ocean doing? '

SECOND VOICE

' Still as a slave before his lord,
The ocean hath no blast;   415
His great bright eye most silently
Up to the Moon is cast—

If he may know which way to go;
For she guides him smooth or grim.
See, brother, see! how graciously   420
She looketh down on him.'

The Polar Spirit's fellow-dæmons, the invisible inhabitants of the element, take part in his wrong; and two of them relate, one to the other, that penance long and heavy for the ancient Mariner hath been accorded to the Polar Spirit, who returneth southward.

FIRST VOICE

'But why drives on that ship so fast,
Without or wave or wind?'

SECOND VOICE

'The air is cut away before,
And closes from behind.   425

Fly, brother, fly! more high, more high!
Or we shall be belated:
For slow and slow that ship will go,
When the Mariner's trance is abated.'

I woke, and we were sailing on   430
As in a gentle weather:
'Twas night, calm night, the moon was high;
The dead men stood together.

All stood together on the deck,
For a charnel-dungeon fitter: 435
All fixed on me their stony eyes,
That in the Moon did glitter.

The pang, the curse, with which they died,
Had never passed away:
I could not draw my eyes from theirs,   440
Nor turn them up to pray.

And now this spell was snapt: once more
I viewed the ocean green,
And looked far forth, yet little saw
Of what had else been seen—   445

Like one, that on a lonesome road
Doth walk in fear and dread,
And having once turned round walks on,
And turns no more his head;
Because he knows, a frightful fiend   450
Doth close behind him tread.

But soon there breathed a wind on me,
Nor sound nor motion made:
Its path was not upon the sea,
In ripple or in shade.   455

It raised my hair, it fanned my cheek
Like a meadow-gale of spring—
It mingled strangely with my fears,
Yet it felt like a welcoming.

Swiftly, swiftly flew the ship,   460
Yet she sailed softly too:
Sweetly, sweetly blew the breeze—
On me alone it blew.

And the
ancient
Mariner be-
holdeth his
native
country.

Oh! dream of joy! is this indeed
The light-house top I see?   465
Is this the hill? is this the kirk?
Is this mine own countree?

We drifted o'er the harbour-bar,
And I with sobs did pray—
O let me be awake, my God!   470
Or let me sleep alway.

The harbour-bay was clear as glass,
So smoothly it was strewn!
And on the bay the moonlight lay,
And the shadow of the Moon.   475

The rock shone bright, the kirk no less,
That stands above the rock:
The moonlight steeped in silentness
The steady weathercock.

And the bay was white with silent light,   480
Till rising from the same,
Full many shapes, that shadows were,
In crimson colours came.

The angelic
spirits leave
the dead
bodies,

And appear
in their own
forms of
light.

A little distance from the prow
Those crimson shadows were: 485
I turned my eyes upon the deck—
Oh, Christ! what saw I there!

Each corse lay flat, lifeless and flat,
And, by the holy rood!
A man all light, a seraph-man,   490
On every corse there stood.

This seraph-band, each waved his hand:
It was a heavenly sight!
They stood as signals to the land,
Each one a lovely light;   495

This seraph-band, each waved his hand,
No voice did they impart—
No voice; but oh! the silence sank
Like music on my heart.

But soon I heard the dash of oars,   500
I heard the Pilot's cheer;
My head was turned perforce away
And I saw a boat appear.

The Pilot and the Pilot's boy,
I heard them coming fast: 505
Dear Lord in Heaven! it was a joy
The dead men could not blast.

I saw a third—I heard his voice:
It is the Hermit good!
He singeth loud his godly hymns   510
That he makes in the wood.
He'll shrieve my soul, he'll wash away
The Albatross's blood.

PART SEVEN

This Hermit good lives in that wood
Which slopes down to the sea.   515
How loudly his sweet voice he rears!
He loves to talk with marineres
That come from a far countree.

He kneels at morn, and noon, and eve—
He hath a cushion plump: 520
It is the moss that wholly hides
The rotted old oak-stump.

The skiff-boat neared: I heard them talk,
' Why, this is strange, I trow!
Where are those lights so many and fair,   525
That signal made but now? '

Approacheth
the ship
with wonder.
' Strange, by my faith! ' the Hermit said—
' And they answered not our cheer!
The planks looked warped! and see those sails,
How thin they are and sere!   530
I never saw aught like to them,
Unless perchance it were

Brown skeletons of leaves that lag
My forest-brook along;
When the ivy-tod is heavy with snow,   535
And the owlet whoops to the wolf below,
That eats the she-wolf's young.'

' Dear Lord! it hath a fiendish look—
(The Pilot made reply)
I am a-feared '—' Push on, push on! '   540
Said the Hermit cheerily.

The boat came closer to the ship,
But I nor spake nor stirred;
The boat came close beneath the ship,
And straight a sound was heard.   545

The ship
suddenly
sinketh.
Under the water it rumbled on,
Still louder and more dread:
It reached the ship, it split the bay;
The ship went down like lead.

The ancient
Mariner is
saved in the
Pilot's boat.
Stunned by that loud and dreadful sound,   550
Which sky and ocean smote,
Like one that hath been seven days drowned
My body lay afloat;
But swift as dreams, myself I found
Within the Pilot's boat.   555

Upon the whirl, where sank the ship,
The boat spun round and round;
And all was still, save that the hill
Was telling of the sound.

535 *Ivy-tod:* ivy-bush.

I moved my lips—the Pilot shrieked 560
And fell down in a fit;
The holy Hermit raised his eyes,
And prayed where he did sit.

I took the oars: the Pilot's boy,
Who now doth crazy go, 565
Laughed loud and long, and all the while
His eyes went to and fro.
' Ha! ha! ' quoth he, ' full plain I see,
The Devil knows how to row.'

And now, all in my own countree, 570
I stood on the firm land!
The Hermit stepped forth from the boat,
And scarcely he could stand.

The ancient Mariner earnestly entreateth the Hermit to shrieve him; and the penance of life falls on him.

' O shrieve me, shrieve me, holy man! '
The Hermit crossed his brow. 575
' Say quick,' quoth he, ' I bid thee say—
What manner of man art thou? '

Forthwith this frame of mine was wrenched
With a woful agony,
Which forced me to begin my tale; 580
And then it left me free.

And ever and anon throughout his future life an agony constraineth him to travel from land to land;

Since then, at an uncertain hour,
That agony returns:
And till my ghastly tale is told,
This heart within me burns. 585

I pass, like night, from land to land;
I have strange power of speech;
That moment that his face I see,
I know the man that must hear me:
To him my tale I teach. 590

What loud uproar bursts from that door!
The wedding-guests are there:
But in the garden-bower the bride
And bride-maids singing are:
And hark the little vesper bell, 595
Which biddeth me to prayer!

O Wedding-Guest! this soul hath been
Alone on a wide wide sea:
So lonely 'twas, that God himself
Scarce seeméd there to be.   600

O sweeter than the marriage-feast,
'Tis sweeter far to me,
To walk together to the kirk
With a goodly company!—

To walk together to the kirk,   605
And all together pray,
While each to his great Father bends,
Old men, and babes, and loving friends
And youths and maidens gay!

And to teach,
by his own
example,
love and
reverence to
all things
that God
made and
loveth.

Farewell, farewell! but this I tell   610
To thee, thou Wedding-Guest!
He prayeth well, who loveth well
Both man and bird and beast.

He prayeth best, who loveth best
All things both great and small;   615
For the dear God who loveth us,
He made and loveth all.

The Mariner, whose eye is bright,
Whose beard with age is hoar,
Is gone: and now the Wedding-Guest   620
Turned from the bridegroom's door.

He went like one that hath been stunned,
And is of sense forlorn:
A sadder and a wiser man,
He rose the morrow morn.   625

FROST AT MIDNIGHT

The Frost performs its secret ministry,
Unhelped by any wind. The owlet's cry
Came loud—and hark, again! loud as before.
The inmates of my cottage, all at rest,
Have left me to that solitude, which suits

Abstruser musings: save that at my side
My cradled infant slumbers peacefully.
'Tis calm indeed! so calm, that it disturbs
And vexes meditation with its strange
And extreme silentness. Sea, hill, and wood,   10
This populous village! Sea, and hill, and wood,
With all the numberless goings-on of life,
Inaudible as dreams! the thin blue flame
Lies on my low-burnt fire, and quivers not;
Only that film, which fluttered on the grate,   15
Still flutters there, the sole unquiet thing.
Methinks, its motion in this hush of nature
Gives it dim sympathies with me who live,
Making it a companionable form,
Whose puny flaps and freaks the idling Spirit   20
By its own moods interprets, every where
Echo or mirror seeking of itself,
And makes a toy of Thought.

                         But O! how oft,
How oft, at school, with most believing mind,
Presageful, have I gazed upon the bars,   25
To watch that fluttering *stranger*! and as oft
With unclosed lids, already had I dreamt
Of my sweet birth-place, and the old church-tower,
Whose bells, the poor man's only music, rang
From morn to evening, all the hot Fair-day,   30
So sweetly, that they stirred and haunted me
With a wild pleasure, falling on mine ear
Most like articulate sounds of things to come!
So gazed I, till the soothing things, I dreamt,
Lulled me to sleep, and sleep prolonged my dreams!   35
And so I brooded all the following morn,
Awed by the stern preceptor's face, mine eye
Fixed with mock study on my swimming book:
Save if the door half opened, and I snatched
A hasty glance, and still my heart leaped up,   40
For still I hoped to see the *stranger's* face,
Townsman, or aunt, or sister more beloved,
My play-mate when we both were clothed alike!

7 Hartley Coleridge (1796-1849).   15 *Only that film:* In all parts of the
kingdom these films are called *strangers* and supposed to portend the
arrival of some absent friend. (C.)

Dear Babe, that sleepest cradled by my side,
Whose gentle breathings, heard in this deep calm,   45
Fill up the interspersèd vacancies
And momentary pauses of the thought!
My babe so beautiful! it thrills my heart
With tender gladness, thus to look at thee,
And think that thou shalt learn far other lore,   50
And in far other scenes! For I was reared
In the great city, pent 'mid cloisters dim,
And saw nought lovely but the sky and stars.
But *thou*, my babe! shalt wander like a breeze
By lakes and sandy shores, beneath the crags   55
Of ancient mountain, and beneath the clouds,
Which image in their bulk both lake and shores
And mountain crags: so shalt thou see and hear
The lovely shapes and sounds intelligible
Of that eternal language, which thy God   60
Utters, who from eternity doth teach
Himself in all, and all things in himself.
Great universal Teacher! he shall mould
Thy spirit, and by giving make it ask.

Therefore all seasons shall be sweet to thee,   65
Whether the summer clothe the general earth
With greenness, or the redbreast sit and sing
Betwixt the tufts of snow on the bare branch
Of mossy apple-tree, while the nigh thatch
Smokes in the sun-thaw; whether the eave-drops fall   70
Heard only in the trances of the blast,
Or if the secret ministry of frost
Shall hang them up in silent icicles,
Quietly shining to the quiet Moon.

George Gordon Noel Byron
(Lord Byron)

1788—1824

BEPPO

A VENETIAN STORY

In this witty, satirical, digressionary narrative (based on a story
he heard in Italy in 1817) Byron discovered the flexible form
which he had been seeking and which he later developed with
great brilliance in *Don Juan*.

> *Rosalind.* Farewell, Monsieur Traveller: Look, you lisp, and wear
> strange suits: disable all the benefits of your own country; be out of love
> with your Nativity, and almost chide God for making you that counten-
> ance you are; or I will scarce think that you have swam in a *Gondola.—As
> You Like It*, Act IV., Scene i.

Annotation of the Commentators.

> That is, *been at Venice*, which was much visited by the young English
> gentlemen of those times, and was *then* what *Paris* is *now*—the seat of all
> dissoluteness.—S.A.

I

'Tis known, at least it should be, that throughout
    All countries of the Catholic persuasion,
Some weeks before Shrove Tuesday comes about,
    The People take their fill of recreation,
And buy repentance, ere they grow devout,   5
    However high their rank, or low their station,
With fiddling, feasting, dancing, drinking, masking,
And other things which may be had for asking.

II

The moment night with dusky mantle covers
    The skies (and the more duskily the better),   10
The Time less liked by husbands than by lovers
    Begins, and Prudery flings aside her fetter;
And Gaiety on restless tiptoe hovers,
    Giggling with all the gallants who beset her;
And there are songs and quavers, roaring, humming,   15
Guitars, and every other sort of strumming.

III

And there are dresses splendid, but fantastical,
  Masks of all times and nations, Turks and Jews,
And harlequins and clowns, with feats gymnastical,
  Greeks, Romans, Yankee-doodles, and Hindoos; 20
All kinds of dress, except the ecclesiastical,
  All people, as their fancies hit, may choose,
But no one in these parts may quiz the Clergy,—
Therefore take heed, ye Freethinkers! I charge ye.

IV

You'd better walk about begirt with briars, 25
  Instead of coat and smallclothes, than put on
A single stitch reflecting upon friars,
  Although you swore it only was in fun;
They'd haul you o'er the coals, and stir the fires
  Of Phlegethon with every mother's son, 30
Nor say one mass to cool the cauldron's bubble
That boil'd your bones, unless you paid them double.

V

But saving this, you may put on whate'er
  You like by way of doublet, cape, or cloak,
Such as in Monmouth-street, or in Rag Fair, 35
  Would rig you out in seriousness or joke;
And even in Italy such places are,
  With prettier name in softer accents spoke,
For, bating Covent Garden, I can hit on
No place that's called ' Piazza ' in Great Britain. 40

VI

This feast is named the Carnival, which being
  Interpreted, implies ' farewell to flesh ':
So call'd, because the name and thing agreeing,
  Through Lent they live on fish both salt and fresh.
But why they usher Lent with so much glee in, 45
  Is more than I can tell, although I guess
'Tis as we take a glass with friends at parting,
In the Stage-Coach or Packet, just at starting.

26 *Smallclothes:* breeches. 30 *Phlegethon:* fiery river in the under-
world of Greek mythology. 35 *Monmouth-street:* in London; was
noted for dealers in second-hand clothes. 39 *Bating:* excepting;
Covent Garden: fruit and flower market-place ('piazza') in London; its
colonnades and galleries were erroneously called piazzas. 41-42
popular etymology. 48 *Packet:* packet-boat.

VII

And thus they bid farewell to carnal dishes,
  And solid meats, and highly spiced ragouts,   50
To live for forty days on ill-dress'd fishes,
  Because they have no sauces to their stews;
A thing which causes many ' poohs ' and ' pishes,'
  And several oaths (which would not suit the Muse),
From travellers accustom'd from a boy   55
To eat their salmon, at the least, with soy;

VIII

And therefore humbly I would recommend
  ' The curious in fish-sauce,' before they cross
The sea, to bid their cook, or wife, or friend,
  Walk or ride to the Strand, and buy in gross   60
(Or if set out beforehand, these may send
  By any means least liable to loss),
Ketchup, Soy, Chili-vinegar, and Harvey,
Or by the Lord! a Lent will well nigh starve ye;

IX

That is to say, if your religion's Roman,   65
  And you at Rome would do as Romans do,
According to the proverb,—although no man,
  If foreign, is obliged to fast; and you
If Protestant, or sickly, or a woman,
  Would rather dine in sin on a ragout—   70
Dine and be d——d! I don't mean to be coarse,
But that's the penalty, to say no worse.

X

Of all the places where the Carnival
  Was most facetious in the days of yore,
For dance, and song, and serenade, and ball,   75
  And Masque, and Mime, and Mystery, and more
Than I have time to tell now, or at all,
  Venice the bell from every city bore,—
And at the moment when I fix my story,
That sea-born city was in all her glory.   80

56 *Soy:* soy-bean sauce.   60 *Strand:* street in the City of London.   63
Chil(l)i: red-pepper; *Harvey:* a pickle (from Harvey Nichol).

XI

They've pretty faces yet, those same Venetians,
   Black eyes, arch'd brows, and sweet expressions still;
Such as of old were copied from the Grecians,
   In ancient arts by modern mimick'd ill;
And like so many Venuses of Titian's 85
   (The best's at Florence—see it, if ye will,)
They look when leaning over the balcony,
Or stepp'd from out a picture by Giorgione,

XII

Whose tints are Truth and Beauty at their best;
   And when you to Manfrini's palace go, 90
That picture (howsoever fine the rest)
   Is loveliest to my mind of all the show;
It may perhaps be also to *your* zest,
   And that's the cause I rhyme upon it so:
'Tis but a portrait of his Son, and Wife, 95
And self; but *such* a Woman! Love in Life!

XIII

Love in full life and length, not love ideal,
   No, nor ideal beauty, that fine name,
But something better still, so very real,
   That the sweet Model must have been the same; 100
A thing that you would purchase, beg, or steal,
   Were't not impossible, besides a shame:
The face recalls some face, as 'twere with pain,
You once have seen, but ne'er will see again;

XIV

One of those forms which flit by us, when we 105
   Are young, and fix our eyes on every face;
And, oh! the Loveliness at times we see
   In momentary gliding, the soft grace,
The Youth, the Bloom, the Beauty which agree,
   In many a nameless being we retrace, 110
Whose course and home we knew not, nor shall know,
Like the lost Pleiad seen no more below.

85 *Titian:* Venetian painter (*c.* 1477/87-1576). 88 *Giorgione:* Venetian painter (*c.* 1476/8-1510). 90 *Manfrini's palace:* The Manfrini Palace collection was later dispersed. 91 *That picture:* formerly known as *Giorgione's Family*, now as *The Tempest*. Giorgione was not married. 112 *Lost Pleiad:* Of the seven Pleiads, daughters of Atlas changed into stars, one (Electra) is generally invisible to the naked eye and known as the 'lost Pleiad'.

A.L.P.

P

XV

I said that like a picture by Giorgione
    Venetian women were, and so they *are*,
Particularly seen from a balcony,   115
    (For beauty's sometimes best set off afar)
And there, just like a heroine of Goldoni,
    They peep from out the blind, or o'er the bar;
And truth to say, they're mostly very pretty,
And rather like to show it, more's the pity!   120

XVI

For glances beget ogles, ogles sighs,
    Sighs wishes, wishes words, and words a letter,
Which flies on wings of light-heel'd Mercuries,
    Who do such things because they know no better;
And then, God knows what mischief may arise,   125
    When Love links two young people in one fetter,
Vile assignations, and adulterous beds,
Elopements, broken vows, and hearts, and heads.

XVII

Shakespeare described the sex in Desdemona
    As very fair, but yet suspect in fame,   130
And to this day from Venice to Verona
    Such matters may be probably the same,
Except that since those times was never known a
    Husband whom mere suspicion could inflame
To suffocate a wife no more than twenty,   135
Because she had a ' Cavalier Servente.'

XVIII

Their jealousy (if they are ever jealous)
    Is of a fair complexion altogether,
Not like that sooty devil of Othello's,
    Which smothers women in a bed of feather,   140
But worthier of these much more jolly fellows,
    When weary of the matrimonial tether
His head for such a wife no mortal bothers,
But takes at once another, or *another's*.

117 *Goldoni:* Carlo Goldoni (1707-93), Italian dramatist. 123 *Mercuries:* messengers. 130 See *Othello*, III. iii. 205-8. 136 *Cavalier(e) Servente:* 'Serving cavalier' and complaisant husband were an Italian institution much commented on by English visitors.

XIX

Didst ever see a Gondola? For fear   145
   You should not, I'll describe it you exactly:
'Tis a long cover'd boat that's common here,
   Carved at the prow, built lightly, but compactly,
Row'd by two rowers, each call'd ' Gondolier,'
   It glides along the water looking blackly,   150
Just like a coffin clapt in a canoe,
Where none can make out what you say or do.

XX

And up and down the long canals they go,
   And under the Rialto shoot along,
By night and day, all paces, swift or slow,   155
   And round the theatres, a sable throng,
They wait in their dusk livery of woe,—
   But not to them do woeful things belong,
For sometimes they contain a deal of fun,
Like mourning coaches when the funeral's done.   160

XXI

But to my story.—'Twas some years ago,
   It may be thirty, forty, more or less,
The Carnival was at its height, and so
   Were all kinds of buffoonery and dress;
A certain lady went to see the show,   165
   Her real name I know not, nor can guess,
And so we'll call her Laura, if you please,
Because it slips into my verse with ease.

XXII

She was not old, nor young, nor at the years
   Which certain people call a ' *certain age*,'   170
Which yet the most uncertain age appears,
   Because I never heard, nor could engage
A person yet by prayers, or bribes, or tears,
   To name, define by speech, or write on page,
The period meant precisely by that word,—   175
Which surely is exceedingly absurd.

154 *Rialto:* bridge in Venice, leading to island of the same name.

XXIII

Laura was blooming still, had made the best
  Of Time, and Time return'd the compliment,
And treated her genteelly, so that, dress'd,
  She look'd extremely well where'er she went;   180
A pretty woman is a welcome guest,
  And Laura's brow a frown had rarely bent;
Indeed, she shone all smiles, and seem'd to flatter
Mankind with her black eyes for looking at her.

XXIV

She was a married woman; 'tis convenient,   185
  Because in Christian countries 'tis a rule
To view their little slips with eyes more lenient;
  Whereas if single ladies play the fool,
(Unless within the period intervenient
  A well-timed wedding makes the scandal cool)   190
I don't know how they ever can get over it,
Except they manage never to discover it.

XXV

Her husband sail'd upon the Adriatic,
  And made some voyages, too, in other seas,
And when he lay in Quarantine for pratique   195
  (A forty days' precaution 'gainst disease),
His wife would mount, at times, her highest attic,
  For thence she could discern the ship with ease:
He was a merchant trailing to Aleppo,
His name Giuseppe, call'd more briefly, Beppo.   200

XXVI

He was a man as dusky as a Spaniard,
  Sunburnt with travel, yet a portly figure;
Though colour'd, as it were, within a tan-yard,
  He was a person both of sense and vigour—
A better seaman never yet did man yard;   205
  And she, although her manners show'd no rigour,
Was deem'd a woman of the strictest principle,
So much as to be thought almost invincible.

192 *Discover:* reveal. 195 *Pratique:* permission to enter port after quarantine. 199 *Aleppo:* city in Syria.

XXVII

But several years elapsed since they had met;
  Some people thought the ship was lost, and some   210
That he had somehow blunder'd into debt,
  And did not like the thought of steering home;
And there were several offer'd any bet,
  Or that he would, or that he would not come;
For most men (till by losing render'd sager)   215
Will back their own opinions with a wager.

XXVIII

'Tis said that their last parting was pathetic,
  As partings often are, or ought to be,
And their presentiment was quite prophetic,
  That they should never more each other see,   220
(A sort of morbid feeling, half poetic,
  Which I have known occur in two or three,)
When kneeling on the shore upon her sad knee
He left this Adriatic Ariadne.

XXIX

And Laura waited long, and wept a little,   225
  And thought of wearing weeds, as well she might;
She almost lost all appetite for victual,
  And could not sleep with ease alone at night;
She deem'd the window-frames and shutters brittle
  Against a daring housebreaker or sprite,   230
And so she thought it prudent to connect her
With a vice-husband, *chiefly* to *protect her*.

XXX

She chose, (and what is there they will not choose,
  If only you will but oppose their choice?)
Till Beppo should return from his long cruise,   235
  And bid once more her faithful heart rejoice,
A man some women like, and yet abuse—
  A Coxcomb was he by the public voice;
A Count of wealth, they said, as well as quality,
And in his pleasures of great liberality.   240

214 *Or . . . or:* either . . . or. 224 Ariadne, princess of Crete, was
deserted by Theseus in Greek mythology. 226 *Weeds:* widows' clothes.

XXXI

And then he was a Count, and then he knew
  Music and dancing, fiddling, French and Tuscan;
The last not easy, be it known to you,
  For few Italians speak the right Etruscan.
He was a critic upon operas, too, 245
  And knew all niceties of sock and buskin;
And no Venetian audience could endure a
Song, scene, or air, when he cried ' seccatura! '

XXXII

His ' bravo ' was decisive, for that sound
  Hush'd ' Academie ' sigh'd in silent awe; 250
The fiddlers trembled as he look'd around,
  For fear of some false note's detected flaw;
The ' Prima Donna's ' tuneful heart would bound,
  Dreading the deep damnation of his ' bah! '
Soprano, Basso, even the Contra-Alto, 255
Wish'd him five fathom under the Rialto.

XXXIII

He patronised the Improvisatori,
  Nay, could himself extemporise some stanzas,
Wrote rhymes, sang songs, could also tell a story,
  Sold pictures, and was skilful in the dance as 260
Italians can be, though in this their glory
  Must surely yield the palm to that which France has;
In short, he was a perfect cavaliero,
And to his very valet seem'd a hero.

XXXIV

Then he was faithful too, as well as amorous; 265
  So that no sort of female could complain,
Although they're now and then a little clamorous,
  He never put the pretty souls in pain;
His heart was one of those which most enamour us,
  Wax to receive, and marble to retain: 270
He was a lover of the good old school,
Who still become more constant as they cool.

---

242 *Tuscan:* Italian. 244 *Etruscan:* the language of Tuscany, regarded as classical form of Italian. 246 *The sock and buskin:* comedy and tragedy. 248 *'Seccatura!':* 'Tiresome, dry stuff!' (Ital.). 250 *Ac(c)ademie:* musical parties (Ital.). 257 *Improv(v)isatori:* impromptu performers (Ital.). 264 Cf. the saying, No man is a hero to his valet.

XXXV

No wonder such accomplishments should turn
  A female head, however sage and steady—
With scarce a hope that Beppo could return,   275
  In law he was almost as good as dead, he
Nor sent, nor wrote, nor show'd the least concern,
  And she had waited several years already;
And really if a man won't let us know
That he's alive, he's *dead*, or should be so.   280

XXXVI

Besides, within the Alps, to every woman,
  (Although, God knows, it is a grievous sin,)
'Tis, I may say, permitted to have *two* men;
  . I can't tell who first brought the custom in,
But ' Cavalier Serventes ' are quite common,   285
  And no one notices nor cares a pin;
And we may call this (not to say the worst)
A *second* marriage which corrupts the *first*.

XXXVII

The word was formerly a ' Cicisbeo,'
  But *that* is now grown vulgar and indecent;   290
The Spaniards call the person a ' *Cortejo*,'
  For the same mode subsists in Spain, though recent;
In short it reaches from the Po to Teio,
  And may perhaps at last be o'er the sea sent:
But Heaven preserve Old England from such courses!   295
Or what becomes of damage and divorces?

XXXVIII

However, I still think, with all due deference
  To the fair *single* part of the creation,
That married ladies should preserve the preference
  In *tête à tête* or general conversation—   300
And this I say without peculiar reference
  To England, France, or any other nation-
Because they know the world, and are at ease,
And being natural, naturally please.

291 *Cortejo:* Cortejo is pronounced Corte*h*o, with an aspirate, according
to the Arabesque guttural. It means what there is as yet no precise
name for in England, though the practice is as common as in any
tramontane country whatever. (B.)   293 *Po . . . Teio:* rivers in Italy
and Portugal.

XXXIX

'Tis true, your budding Miss is very charming,　　　　305
　　But shy and awkward at first coming out,
So much alarm'd, that she is quite alarming,
　　All Giggle, Blush; half Pertness, and half Pout;
And glancing at *Mamma*, for fear there's harm in
　　What you, she, it, or they, may be about,　　　　310
The Nursery still lisps out in all they utter—
Besides, they always smell of bread and butter.

XL

But ' Cavalier Servente ' is the phrase
　　Used in politest circles to express
This supernumerary slave, who stays　　　　315
　　Close to the lady as a part of dress,
Her word the only law which he obeys.
　　His is no sinecure, as you may guess;
Coach, servants, gondola, he goes to call,
And carries fan and tippet, gloves and shawl.　　　　320

XLI

With all its sinful doings, I must say,
　　That Italy's a pleasant place to me,
Who love to see the Sun shine every day,
　　And vines (not nail'd to walls) from tree to tree
Festoon'd, much like the back scene of a play,　　　　325
　　Or melodrame, which people flock to see,
When the first act is ended by a dance
In vineyards copied from the south of France.

XLII

I like on Autumn evenings to ride out,
　　Without being forced to bid my groom be sure　　　　330
My cloak is round his middle strapp'd about,
　　Because the skies are not the most secure;
I know too that, if stopp'd upon my route,
　　Where the green alleys windingly allure,
Reeling with *grapes* red waggons choke the way,—　　　　335
In England 'twould be dung, dust, or a dray.

320 *Tippet:* stole.

XLIII

I also like to dine on becaficas,
  To see the Sun set, sure he'll rise to-morrow,
Not through a misty morning twinkling weak as
  A drunken man's dead eye in maudlin sorrow,
But with all Heaven t'himself; the day will break as   340
  Beauteous as cloudless, nor be forced to borrow
That sort of farthing candlelight which glimmers
Where reeking London's smoky cauldron simmers.

XLIV

I love the language, that soft bastard Latin,   345
  Which melts like kisses from a female mouth,
And sounds as if it should be writ on satin,
  With syllables which breathe of the sweet South,
And gentle liquids gliding all so pat in,
  That not a single accent seems uncouth,   350
Like our harsh northern whistling, grunting guttural,
Which we're obliged to hiss, and spit, and sputter all.

XLV

I like the women too (forgive my folly!),
  From the rich peasant cheek of ruddy bronze,
And large black eyes that flash on you a volley   355
  Of rays that say a thousand things at once,
To the high Dama's brow, more melancholy,
  But clear, and with a wild and liquid glance,
Heart on her lips, and soul within her eyes,
Soft as her clime, and sunny as her skies.   360

XLVI

Eve of the land which still is Paradise!
  Italian Beauty didst thou not inspire
Raphael, who died in thy embrace, and vies
  With all we know of Heaven, or can desire,
In what he hath bequeath'd us?—in what guise   365
  Though flashing from the fervour of the Lyre,
Would *words* describe thy past and present glow,
While yet Canova can create below?

337 *Becaficas:* small edible birds (Ital. *beccafico*). 357 *Dama:* lady.
363 *Raphael:* Italian painter (1483-1520). 368 *Canova:* Antonio
Canova (1757-1822), Italian sculptor.

XLVII

' England! with all thy faults I love thee still,'
  I said at Calais, and have not forgot it;   370
I like to speak and lucubrate my fill;
  I like the government (but that is not it);
I like the freedom of the press and quill;
  I like the Habeas Corpus (when we've got it);
I like a Parliamentary debate,   375
Particularly when 'tis not too late;

XLVIII

I like the taxes, when they're not too many;
  I like a seacoal fire, when not too dear;
I like a beef-steak, too, as well as any;
  Have no objection to a pot of beer;   380
I like the weather, —when it is not rainy,
  That is, I like two months of every year,
And so God save the Regent, Church, and King!
Which means that I like all and every thing.

XLIX

Our standing army, and disbanded seamen,   385
  Poor's rate, Reform, my own, the nation's debt,
Our little riots, just to show we're free men,
  Our trifling bankruptcies in the Gazette,
Our cloudy climate, and our chilly women,
  All these I can forgive, and those forget,   390
And greatly venerate our recent glories,
And wish they were not owing to the Tories.

L

But to my tale of Laura,—for I find
  Digression is a sin, that by degrees
Becomes exceeding tedious to my mind,   395
  And, therefore, may the reader too displease—
The gentle reader, who may wax unkind,
  And caring little for the Author's ease,
Insist on knowing what he means, a hard
And hapless situation for a Bard.   400

369 Cowper, *The Task*, II. 206.   374 *Habeas Corpus:*   The Habeas
Corpus Act of 1679 obliged the jailer to produce the prisoner in Court in
person and certify why he had been imprisoned.

LI

Oh! that I had the art of easy writing
　　What should be easy reading! could I scale
Parnassus, where the Muses sit inditing
　　Those pretty poems never known to fail,
How quickly would I print (the world delighting)   405
　　A Grecian, Syrian, or Assyrian tale;
And sell you, mix'd with western Sentimentalism,
Some samples of the *finest Orientalism*!

LII

But I am but a nameless sort of person,
　　(A broken Dandy lately on my travels)   410
And take for rhyme, to hook my rambling verse on,
　　The first that Walker's Lexicon unravels,
And when I can't find that, I put a worse on,
　　Not caring as I ought for critics' cavils;
I've half a mind to tumble down to prose,   415
But verse is more in fashion—so here goes!

LIII

The Count and Laura made their new arrangement,
　　Which lasted, as arrangements sometimes do,
For half a dozen years without estrangement;
　　They had their little differences, too;   420
Those jealous whiffs, which never any change meant;
　　In such affairs there probably are few
Who have not had this pouting sort of squabble,
From sinners of high station to the rabble.

LIV

But, on the whole, they were a happy pair,   425
　　As happy as unlawful love could make them:
The gentleman was fond, the lady fair,
　　Their chains so slight, 'twas not worth while to break them:
The world beheld them with indulgent air;
　　The pious only wish'd ' the Devil take them! '   430
He took them not; he very often waits,
And leaves old sinners to be young ones' baits.

---

412 *Walker's Lexicon:* John Walker's *Rhyming Dictionary*, first published
1775.

LV

But they were young: Oh! what without our Youth
  Would Love be! What would Youth be without Love!
Youth lends it joy, and sweetness, vigour, truth,   435
  Heart, soul, and all that seems as from above;
But, languishing with years, it grows uncouth—
  One of few things Experience don't improve,
Which is, perhaps, the reason why old fellows
Are always so preposterously jealous.   440

LVI

It was the Carnival, as I have said
  Some six and thirty stanzas back, and so
Laura the usual preparations made,
  Which you do when your mind's made up to go
To-night to Mrs. Boehm's masquerade,   445
  Spectator, or partaker in the show;
The only difference known between the cases
Is—*here*, we have six weeks of ' varnish'd faces.'

LVII

Laura, when dress'd, was (as I sang before)   450
  A pretty woman as was ever seen,
Fresh as the Angel o'er a new inn door,
  Or frontispiece of a new Magazine,
With all the fashions which the last month wore,
  Colour'd, and silver paper leaved between
That and the title-page, for fear the Press   455
Should soil with parts of speech the parts of dress.

LVIII

They went to the Ridotto; 'tis a hall
  Where People dance, and sup, and dance again;
Its proper name, perhaps, were a masqued ball,
  But that's of no importance to my strain;   460
'Tis (on a smaller scale) like our Vauxhall,
  Excepting that it can't be spoilt by rain;
The company is ' mix'd ' (the phrase I quote is
As much as saying they're below your notice);

445 Byron had been reading about the 'splendid masquerade' given by
this widow and millionairess in her London residence in June 1817.
461 *Vauxhall:* Vauxhall Gardens in London, then a popular resort for
pleasure and entertainment.

LIX

For a ' mix'd company ' implies that, save 465
    Yourself and friends, and half a hundred more,
Whom you may bow to without looking grave,
    The rest are but a vulgar set, the bore
Of public places, where they basely brave
    The fashionable stare of twenty score 470
Of well-bred persons, call'd ' *The World;* ' but I,
Although I know them, really don't know why.

LX

This is the case in England; at least was
    During the dynasty of Dandies, now
Perchance succeeded by some other class 475
    Of imitated Imitators:—how
Irreparably soon decline, alas!
    The Demagogues of fashion: all below
Is frail; how easily the world is lost
By Love, or War, and now and then by Frost! 480

LXI

Crush'd was Napoleon by the northern Thor,
    Who knock'd his army down with icy hammer,
Stopp'd by the *Elements*—like a Whaler—or
    A blundering novice in his new French grammar;
Good cause had he to doubt the chance of war, 485
    And as for Fortune—but I dare not d—n her,
Because, were I to ponder to infinity,
The more I should believe in her Divinity.

LXII

She rules the present, past, and all to be yet,
    She gives us luck in lotteries, love, and marriage; 490
I cannot say that she's done much for me yet;
    Not that I mean her bounties to disparage,
We've not yet closed accounts, and we shall see yet
    How much she'll make amends for past miscarriage;
Meantime the Goddess I'll no more importune, 495
Unless to thank her when she's made my fortune.

481 *Thor:* Scandinavian war-god; here, used for the Russian winter.

LXIII

To turn,—and to return;—the Devil take it!
   This story slips for ever through my fingers,
Because, just as the stanza likes to make it,
   It needs must be—and so it rather lingers;   500
This form of verse began, I can't well break it,
   But must keep time and tune like public singers;
But if I once get through my present measure,
I'll take another when I'm next at leisure.

LXIV

They went to the Ridotto ('tis a place   505
   To which I mean to go myself to-morrow,
Just to divert my thoughts a little space
   Because I'm rather hippish, and may borrow
Some spirits, guessing at what kind of face
   May lurk beneath each mask; and as my sorrow   510
Slackens its pace sometimes, I'll make, or find,
Something shall leave it half an hour behind).

LXV

Now Laura moves along the joyous crowd,
   Smiles in her eyes, and simpers on her lips;
To some she whispers, others speaks aloud;   515
   To some she curtsies, and to some she dips,
Complains of warmth, and, this complaint avow'd,
   Her lover brings the lemonade she sips;
She then surveys, condemns, but pities still
Her dearest friends for being dress'd so ill.   520

LXVI

One has false curls, another too much paint,
   A third—where did she buy that frightful turban?
A fourth's so pale she fears she's going to faint,
   A fifth's look's vulgar, dowdyish, and suburban,
A sixth's white silk has got a yellow taint,   525
   A seventh's thin muslin surely will be her bane,
And lo! an eighth appears,—' I'll see no more! '
For fear, like Banquo's kings, they reach a score.

508 *Hippish:* low-spirited.   527-8 See *Macbeth,* IV. i.

LXVII

Meantime, while she was thus at others gazing,
    Others were levelling their looks at her;   530
She heard the men's half-whisper'd mode of praising,
    And, till 'twas done, determined not to stir;
The women only thought it quite amazing
    That, at her time of life, so many were
Admirers still,—but 'Men are so debased—   535
Those brazen Creatures always suit their taste.'

LXVIII

For my part, now, I ne'er could understand
    Why naughty women—but I won't discuss
A thing which is a scandal to the land,
    I only don't see why it should be thus;   540
And if I were but in a gown and band,
    Just to entitle me to make a fuss,
I'd preach on this till Wilberforce and Romilly
Should quote in their next speeches from my homily.

LXIX

While Laura thus was seen and seeing, smiling,   545
    Talking, she knew not why, and cared not what,
So that her female friends, with envy broiling,
    Beheld her airs, and triumph, and all that;
And well-dress'd males still kept before her filing,
    And passing bow'd and mingled with her chat;   550
More than the rest one person seem'd to stare
With pertinacity that's rather rare.

LXX

He was a Turk, the colour of mahogany;
    And Laura saw him, and at first was glad,
Because the Turks so much admire philogyny,   555
    Although their usage of their wives is sad;
'Tis said they use no better than a dog any
    Poor woman, whom they purchase like a pad;
They have a number, though they ne'er exhibit 'em,
Four wives by law, and concubines ' ad libitum.'   560

543 *Wilberforce and Romilly:* William Wilberforce (1759-1833), states-
man and anti-slavery agitator; Sir Samuel Romilly (1757-1818),
criminal law reformer. 555 *Philogyny:* love of women. 558 *Pad:*
horse.

LXXI

They lock them up, and veil, and guard them daily,
   They scarcely can behold their male relations,
So that their moments do not pass so gaily
   As is supposed the case with northern nations;
Confinement, too, must make them look quite palely;   565
   And as the Turks abhor long conversations,
Their days are either pass'd in doing nothing,
Or bathing, nursing, making love, and clothing.

LXXII

They cannot read, and so don't lisp in criticism;
   Nor write, and so they don't affect the Muse;   570
Were never caught in epigram or witticism,
   Have no romances, sermons, plays, reviews,—
In Harams learning soon would make a pretty schism!
   But luckily these Beauties are no ' Blues ';
No bustling *Botherby* have they to show 'em   575
' That charming passage in the last new poem ':

LXXIII

No solemn, antique gentleman of rhyme,
   Who having angled all his life for Fame,
And getting but a nibble at a time,
   Still fussily keeps fishing on, the same   580
Small ' Triton of the minnows,' the sublime
   Of Mediocrity, the furious tame,
The Echo's echo, usher of the school
Of female wits, boy bards—in short, a fool!

LXXIV

A stalking oracle of awful phrase,   585
   The approving ' *Good!* ' (by no means GOOD in law)
Humming like flies around the newest blaze,
   The bluest of bluebottles you e'er saw,
Teasing with blame, excruciating with praise,
   Gorging the little fame he gets all raw,   590
Translating tongues he knows not even by letter,
And sweating plays so middling, bad were better.

574 *Blues:* bluestockings. 574 *Botherbys:* reference to William Sotheby (1757-1833), minor poet and translator. 581 *Triton:* a sea-god of Greek mythology.

LXXV

One hates an author that's *all author*, fellows
  In foolscap uniforms turn'd up with ink,
So very anxious, clever, fine, and jealous,   595
  One don't know what to say to them, or think,
Unless to puff them with a pair of bellows;
  Of Coxcombry's worst coxcombs e'en the pink
Are preferable to these shreds of paper,
These unquench'd snuffings of the midnight taper.   600

LXXVI

Of these same we see several, and of others,
  Men of the World, who know the World like Men,
Scott, Rogers, Moore, and all the better brothers,
  Who think of something else besides the pen;
But for the children of the ' Mighty Mother's,'   605
  The would-be wits, and can't-be gentlemen,
I leave them to their daily ' tea is ready,'
Smug coterie, and literary lady.

LXXVII

The poor dear Mussul*women* whom I mention
  Have none of these instructive pleasant people,   610
And *one* would seem to them a new invention,
  Unknown as bells within a Turkish steeple;
I think 'twould almost be worth while to pension
  (Though best-sown projects very often reap ill)
A missionary author—just to preach   615
Our Christian usage of the parts of speech.

LXXVIII

No Chemistry for them unfolds her gases,
  No Metaphysics are let loose in lectures,
No Circulating Library amasses
  Religious novels, moral tales, and strictures   620
Upon the living manners, as they pass us;
  No Exhibition glares with annual pictures;
They stare not on the stars from out their attics,
Nor deal (thank God for that!) in Mathematics.

603 Sir Walter Scott (1771-1832); Samuel Rogers (1763-1855);
Thomas Moore (1779-1852).

LXXIX

Why I thank God for that is no great matter,   625
   I have my reasons, you no doubt suppose,
And as, perhaps, they would not highly flatter,
   I'll keep them for my life (to come) in prose;
I fear I have a little turn for Satire,
   And yet methinks the older that one grows   630
Inclines us more to laugh than scold, though Laughter
Leaves us so doubly serious shortly after.

LXXX

Oh, Mirth and Innocence! Oh, Milk and Water!
   Ye happy mixtures of more happy days!
In these sad centuries of sin and slaughter,   635
   Abominable Man no more allays
His thirst with such pure beverage. No matter,
   I love you both, and both shall have my praise:
Oh, for old Saturn's reign of sugar-candy!—
Meantime I drink to your return in brandy.   640

LXXXI

Our Laura's Turk still kept his eyes upon her,
   Less in the Mussulman than Christian way,
Which seems to say, ' Madam, I do you honour,
   And while I please to stare, you'll please to stay.'
Could staring win a woman, this had won her,   645
   But Laura could not thus be led astray;
She had stood fire too long and well, to boggle
Even at this Stranger's most outlandish ogle.

LXXXII

The morning now was on the point of breaking,
   A turn of time at which I would advise   650
Ladies who have been dancing, or partaking
   In any other kind of exercise,
To make their preparations for forsaking
   The ball-room ere the Sun begins to rise,
Because when once the lamps and candles fail,   655
His blushes make them look a little pale.

626 *I have my reasons:* Lady Byron's interest in mathematics!   639
The reign of Saturn, a Titan in Greek mythology, was a Golden Age.

LXXXIII

I've seen some balls and revels in my time,
  And stay'd them over for some silly reason,
And then I look'd (I hope it was no crime)
  To see what lady best stood out the season;　　660
And though I've seen some thousands in their prime
  Lovely and pleasing, and who still may please on,
I never saw but one (the stars withdrawn)
Whose bloom could after dancing dare the Dawn.

LXXXIV

The name of this Aurora I'll not mention,　　665
  Although I might, for she was nought to me
More than that patent work of God's invention,
  A charming woman, whom we like to see;
But writing names would merit reprehension,
  Yet if you like to find out this fair *She*,　　670
At the next London or Parisian ball
You still may mark her cheek, out-blooming all.

LXXXV

Laura, who knew it would not do at all
  To meet the daylight after seven hours' sitting
Among three thousand people at a ball,　　675
  To make her curtsey thought it right and fitting;
The Count was at her elbow with her shawl,
  And they the room were on the point of quitting,
When lo! those cursed Gondoliers had got
Just in the very place where they *should not*.　　680

LXXXVI

In this they're like our coachmen, and the cause
  Is much the same—the crowd, and pulling, hauling,
With blasphemies enough to break their jaws,
  They make a never intermitted bawling.
At home, our Bow-street gemmen keep the laws,　　685
  And here a sentry stands within your calling;
But for all that, there is a deal of swearing,
And nauseous words past mentioning or bearing.

665 *Aurora:* Roman goddess of the dawn. 685 *Bow-street gemmen:*
police officers.

LXXXVII

The Count and Laura found their boat at last,
  And homeward floated o'er the silent tide,   690
Discussing all the dances gone and past;
  The dancers and their dresses, too, beside;
Some little scandals eke; but all aghast
  (As to their palace-stairs the rowers glide)
Sate Laura by the side of her adorer,   695
When lo! the Mussulman was there before her!

LXXXVIII

' Sir,' said the Count, with brow exceeding grave,
  ' Your unexpected presence here will make
It necessary for myself to crave
  Its import? But perhaps 'tis a mistake;   700
I hope it is so; and, at once to waive
  All compliment, I hope so for *your* sake;
You understand my meaning, or you *shall*.'
' Sir,' (quoth the Turk), ' 'tis no mistake at all:

LXXXIX

' That Lady is *my wife!* ' Much wonder paints   705
  The lady's changing cheek, as well it might;
But where an Englishwoman sometimes faints,
  Italian females don't do so outright;
They only call a little on their Saints,
  And then come to themselves, almost, or quite;   710
Which saves much hartshorn, salts, and sprinkling faces,
And cutting stays, as usual in such cases.

XC

She said,—what could she say? Why, not a word:
  But the Count courteously invited in
The Stranger, much appeased by what he heard: 715
  ' Such things, perhaps, we'd best discuss within,'
Said he; ' don't let us make ourselves absurd
  In public, by a scene, nor raise a din,
For then the chief and only satisfaction
Will be much quizzing on the whole transaction.'   720

693 *Eke:* also.

XCI

They enter'd, and for coffee call'd—it came,
  A beverage for Turks and Christians both,
Although the way they make it's not the same.
  Now Laura, much recover'd, or less loth
To speak, cries ' Beppo! what's your pagan name?   725
  Bless me! your beard is of amazing growth!
And how came you to keep away so long?
Are you not sensible 'twas very wrong?

XCII

' And are you *really, truly,* now a Turk?
  With any other women did you wive?   730
Is't true they use their fingers for a fork?
  Well, that's the prettiest Shawl—as I'm alive!
You'll give it me? They say you eat no pork.
  And how so many years did you contrive
To—Bless me! did I ever? No, I never   735
Saw a man grown so yellow! How's your liver?

XCIII

' Beppo! that beard of yours becomes you not;
  It shall be shaved before you're a day older:
Why do you wear it? Oh! I had forgot—
  Pray don't you think the weather here is colder?   740
How do I look? You shan't stir from this spot
  In that queer dress, for fear that some beholder
Should find you out, and make the story known.
How short your hair is! Lord! how grey it's grown! '

XCIV

What answer Beppo made to these demands   745
  Is more than I know. He was cast away
About where Troy stood once, and nothing stands;
  Became a slave of course, and for his pay
Had bread and bastinadoes, till some bands
  Of pirates landing in a neighbouring bay,   750
He join'd the rogues and prosper'd, and became
A renegado of indifferent fame.

747 i.e. on the Asiatic shore of the Dardanelles. 749 *Bastinadoes:*
beatings with a stick on the soles of the feet.

XCV

But he grew rich, and with his riches grew so
  Keen the desire to see his home again,
He thought himself in duty bound to do so,   755
  And not be always thieving on the main;
Lonely he felt, at times, as Robin Crusoe,
  And so he hired a vessel come from Spain,
Bound for Corfu: she was a fine polacca,
Mann'd with twelve hands, and laden with tobacco.   760

XCVI

Himself, and much (Heaven knows how gotten!) cash,
  He then embark'd, with risk of life and limb,
And got clear off, although the attempt was rash;
  He said that *Providence* protected him—
For my part, I say nothing—lest we clash   765
  In our opinions:—well—the ship was trim,
Set sail, and kept her reckoning fairly on,
Except three days of calm when off Cape Bonn.

XCVII

They reach'd the Island, he transferr'd his lading,
  And self and live stock to another bottom,   770
And pass'd for a true Turkey-merchant, trading
  With goods of various names, but I've forgot 'em.
However, he got off by this evading,
  Or else the people would perhaps have shot him;
And thus at Venice landed to reclaim   775
His wife, religion, house, and Christian name.

XCVIII

His wife received, the Patriarch re-baptized him,
  (He made the Church a present, by the way;)
He then threw off the garments which disguised him,
  And borrow'd the Count's smallclothes for a day: 780
His friends the more for his long absence prized him,
  Finding he'd wherewithal to make them gay,
With dinners, where he oft became the laugh of them,
For stories—but *I* don't believe the half of them.

759 *Polacca:* three-masted merchant ship of the Mediterranean.
768 *Cape Bon(n):* north-east of Tunis.

Whate'er his youth had suffer'd, his old age 785
  With wealth and talking made him some amends;
Though Laura sometimes put him in a rage,
  I've heard the Count and he were always friends.
My pen is at the bottom of a page,
  Which being finish'd, here the story ends: 790
'Tis to be wish'd it had been sooner done,
But stories somehow lengthen when begun.

THE DREAM

Autobiographical. The poem reflects Byron's boyish infatuation
with Mary Chaworth. The ' hill ' of line 28 is a hill near Annesley
Hall, the Chaworth family residence (line 76) where Byron and
Mary were together in 1803; the ' another ' of line 71 is John
Musters, whom Mary married in 1805; and Byron recalls his
travels in the Levant in 1810 (lines 105-25), his own unfortunate
wedding in 1815 (lines 144-66), Mary's temporary insanity and
separation from her husband in 1816 (lines 167-83), and finally
his own ravaged state of mind in Switzerland where he was
writing the poem in July, 1816.

I
Our life is twofold: Sleep hath its own world,
A boundary between the things misnamed
Death and existence: Sleep hath its own world,
And a wide realm of wild reality,
And dreams in their development have breath, 5
And tears, and tortures, and the touch of Joy;
They leave a weight upon our waking thoughts,
They take a weight from off our waking toils,
They do divide our being; they become
A portion of ourselves as of our time, 10
And look like heralds of Eternity;
They pass like spirits of the past,—they speak
Like Sibyls of the future; they have power—
The tyranny of pleasure and of pain;
They make us what we were not—what they will, 15
And shake us with the vision that's gone by,
The dread of vanish'd shadows—Are they so?

13 *Sibyls:* prophetesses.

Is not the past all shadow?—What are they?
Creations of the mind?—The mind can make
Substance, and people planets of its own   20
With beings brighter than have been, and give
A breath to forms which can outlive all flesh.
I would recall a vision which I dream'd
Perchance in sleep—for, in itself, a thought,
A slumbering thought, is capable of years,   25
And curdles a long life into one hour.

                              II
I saw two beings in the hues of youth
Standing upon a hill, a gentle hill,
Green and of mild declivity, the last
As 'twere the cape of a long ridge of such,   30
Save that there was no sea to lave its base,
But a most living landscape, and the wave
Of woods and corn-fields, and the abodes of men
Scatter'd at intervals, and wreathing smoke
Arising from such rustic roofs;—the hill   35
Was crown'd with a peculiar diadem
Of trees, in circular array, so fix'd,
Not by the sport of nature, but of man:
These two, a maiden and a youth, were there
Gazing—the one on all that was beneath   40
Fair as herself—but the Boy gazed on her;
And both were young, and one was beautiful:
And both were young—yet not alike in youth.
As the sweet moon on the horizon's verge,
The Maid was on the eve of Womanhood;   45
The Boy had fewer summers, but his heart
Had far outgrown his years, and to his eye
There was but one beloved face on earth,
And that was shining on him: he had look'd
Upon it till it could not pass away;   50
He had no breath, no being, but in hers;
She was his voice; he did not speak to her,
But trembled on her words; she was his sight,
For his eye follow'd hers, and saw with hers,
Which colour'd all his objects:—he had ceased   55
To live within himself; she was his life,
The ocean to the river of his thoughts,
Which terminated all: upon a tone,
A touch of hers, his blood would ebb and flow,
And his cheek change tempestuously—his heart   60

Unknowing of its cause of agony.
But she in these fond feelings had no share:
Her sighs were not for him; to her he was
Even as a brother—but no more; 'twas much,
For brotherless she was, save in the name   65
Her infant friendship had bestow'd on him;
Herself the solitary scion left
Of a time-honour'd race.—It was a name
Which pleased him, and yet pleased him not—and why?
Time taught him a deep answer—when she loved   70
Another: even *now* she loved another,
And on the summit of that hill she stood
Looking afar if yet her lover's steed
Kept pace with her expectancy, and flew.

                              III

A change came o'er the spirit of my dream.   75
There was an ancient mansion, and before
Its walls there was a steed caparison'd;
Within an antique Oratory stood
The Boy of whom I spake;—he was alone,
And pale, and pacing to and fro: anon   80
He sate him down, and seized a pen, and traced
Words which I could not guess of; then he lean'd
His bow'd head on his hands, and shook as 'twere
With a convulsion—then arose again,
And with his teeth and quivering hands did tear   85
What he had written, but he shed no tears.
And he did calm himself, and fix his brow
Into a kind of quiet: as he paused,
The Lady of his love re-entered there;
She was serene and smiling then, and yet   90
She knew she was by him beloved,—she knew,
For quickly comes such knowledge, that his heart
Was darken'd with her shadow, and she saw
That he was wretched, but she saw not all.
He rose, and with a cold and gentle grasp   95
He took her hand; a moment o'er his face
A tablet of unutterable thoughts
Was traced, and then it faded, as it came;
He dropp'd the hand he held, and with slow steps
Retired, but not as bidding her adieu,   100
For they did part with mutual smiles; he pass'd
From out the massy gate of that old Hall,

And mounting on his steed he went his way;
And ne'er repass'd that hoary threshold more.

IV

A change came o'er the spirit of my dream.   105
The Boy was sprung to manhood: in the wilds
Of fiery climes he made himself a home,
And his Soul drank their sunbeams: he was girt
With strange and dusky aspects; he was not
Himself like what he had been; on the sea   110
And on the shore he was a wanderer;
There was a mass of many images
Crowded like waves upon me, but he was
A part of all; and in the last he lay
Reposing from the noontide sultriness,   115
Couch'd among fallen columns, in the shade
Of ruin'd walls that had survived the names
Of those who rear'd them; by his sleeping side
Stood camels grazing, and some goodly steeds
Were fasten'd near a fountain; and a man   120
Clad in a flowing garb did watch the while,
While many of his tribe slumber'd around:
And they were canopied by the blue sky,
So cloudless, clear, and purely beautiful,
That God alone was to be seen in Heaven.   125

V

A change came o'er the spirit of my dream.
The Lady of his love was wed with One
Who did not love her better:—in her home,
A thousand leagues from his,—her native home,
She dwelt, begirt with growing Infancy,   130
Daughters and sons of Beauty,—but behold!
Upon her face there was the tint of grief,
The settled shadow of an inward strife,
And an unquiet drooping of the eye,
As if its lid were charged with unshed tears.   135
What could her grief be?—she had all she loved,
And he who had so loved her was not there
To trouble with bad hopes, or evil wish,
Or ill-repress'd affliction, her pure thoughts.
What could her grief be?—she had loved him not,   140
Nor given him cause to deem himself beloved,
Nor could he be a part of that which prey'd
Upon her mind—a spectre of the past.

VI

A change came o'er the spirit of my dream.
The Wanderer was return'd.—I saw him stand   145
Before an Altar—with a gentle bride;
Her face was fair, but was not that which made
The Starlight of his Boyhood;—as he stood
Even at the altar, o'er his brow there came
The self-same aspect, and the quivering shock   150
That in the antique Oratory shook
His bosom in its solitude; and then—
As in that hour—a moment o'er his face
The tablet of unutterable thoughts
Was traced,—and then it faded as it came,   155
And he stood calm and quiet, and he spoke
The fitting vows, but heard not his own words,
And all things reel'd around him; he could see
Not that which was, nor that which should have been—
But the old mansion, and the accustom'd hall,   160
And the remember'd chambers, and the place,
The day, the hour, the sunshine, and the shade,
All things pertaining to that place and hour,
And her who was his destiny, came back
And thrust themselves between him and the light: 165
What business had they there at such a time?

VII

A change came o'er the spirit of my dream.
The Lady of his love:—Oh! she was changed
As by the sickness of the soul; her mind
Had wander'd from its dwelling, and her eyes   170
They had not their own lustre, but the look
Which is not of the earth; she was become
The Queen of a fantastic realm; her thoughts
Were combinations of disjointed things;
And forms, impalpable and unperceived   175
Of others' sight, familiar were to hers.
And this the world calls frenzy; but the wise
Have a far deeper madness—and the glance
Of melancholy is a fearful gift;
What is it but the telescope of truth?   180
Which strips the distance of its fantasies,
And brings life near in utter nakedness,
Making the cold reality too real!

VIII

A change came o'er the spirit of my dream.
The Wanderer was alone as heretofore,   185
The beings which surrounded him were gone,
Or were at war with him; he was a mark
For blight and desolation, compass'd round
With Hatred and Contention; Pain was mix'd
In all which was served up to him, until,   190
Like to the Pontic monarch of old days,
He fed on poisons, and they had no power,
But were a kind of nutriment; he lived
Through that which had been death to many men,
And made him friends of mountains: with the stars   195
And the quick Spirit of the Universe
He held his dialogues; and they did teach
To him the magic of their mysteries;
To him the book of Night was open'd wide,
And voices from the deep abyss reveal'd   200
A marvel and a secret—Be it so.

IX

My dream was past; it had no further change.
It was of a strange order, that the doom
Of these two creatures should be thus traced out
Almost like a reality—the one   205
To end in madness—both in misery.

THE PRISONER OF CHILLON*

SONNET ON CHILLON

Eternal Spirit of the chainless Mind!
    Brightest in dungeons, Liberty! thou art:
    For there thy habitation is the heart—
The heart which love of thee alone can bind;
And when thy sons to fetters are consign'd—

---

191 *Pontic monarch, etc.:* Mithridates had taken so many antidotes that when he tried to poison himself in earnest (63 B.C.) he failed, and had to ask a slave to stab him.

* The Castle of Chillon is at the eastern end of the Lake of Geneva (Lake Leman). François Bon(n)ivard (1496-1570), republican and reformer who tried to free Geneva from the domination of the Duke of Savoy, was imprisoned there from 1530 to 1536.

To fetters, and the damp vault's dayless gloom,
Their country conquers with their martyrdom,
And Freedom's fame finds wings on every wind.
Chillon! thy prison is a holy place,
    And thy sad floor an alter—for 'twas trod,
Until his very steps have left a trace
    Worn, as if thy cold pavement were a sod,
By Bonnivard!—May none those marks efface!
For they appeal from tyranny to God.

ADVERTISEMENT

When this poem was composed, I was not sufficiently aware of the history of Bonnivard, or I should have endeavoured to dignify the subject by an attempt to celebrate his courage and his virtues. With some account of his life I have been furnished, by the kindness of a citizen of that republic, which is still proud of the memory of a man worthy of the best age of ancient freedom:—

'François de Bonnivard, fils de Louis de Bonnivard, originaire de Seyssel et Seigneur de Lunes, naquit en 1496. Il fit ses études à Turin: en 1510 Jean Aimé de Bonnivard, son oncle, lui résigna le Prieuré de St. Victor, qui aboutissait aux murs de Genève, et qui formait un bénéfice considérable...

'Ce grand homme—(Bonnivard mérite ce titre par la force de son âme, la droiture de son cœur, la noblesse de ses intentions, la sagesse de ses conseils, le courage de ses démarches, l'étendue de ses connaissances, et la vivacité de son esprit),—ce grand homme, qui excitera l'admiration de tous ceux qu'une vertu héroïque peut encore émouvoir, inspirera encore la plus vive reconnaissance dans les cœurs des Génévois qui aiment Genève. Bonnivard en fut toujours un des plus fermes appuis: pour assurer la liberté de notre République, il ne craignit pas de perdre souvent la sienne; il oublia son repos; il méprisa ses richesses; il ne négligea rien pour affermir le bonheur d'une patrie qu'il honora de son choix: dès ce moment il la chérit comme le plus zélé de ses citoyens; il la servit avec l'intrépidité d'un héros, et il écrivit son Histoire avec la naïveté d'un philosophe et la chaleur d'un patriote.

'Il dit dans le commencement de son Histoire de Genève, que, *dès qu'il eut commencé de lire l'histoire des nations, il se sentit entraîné par son goût pour les Républiques, dont il épousa toujours les intérêts*: c'est ce goût pour la liberté qui lui fit sans doute adopter Genève pour sa patrie...

'Bonnivard, encore jeune, s'annonça hautement comme le défenseur de Genève contre le Duc de Savoye et l'Evêque...

'En 1519, Bonnivard devient le martyr de sa patrie: Le Duc de Savoye étant entré dans Genève avec cinq cent hommes, Bonnivard craint le ressentiment du Duc; il voulut se retirer à Fribourg pour en éviter les suites; mais il fut trahi par deux hommes qui l'accompagnaient, et conduit par ordre du Prince à Grolée, où il resta prisonnier pendant deux ans. Bonnivard était malheureux dans ses voyages: comme ses malheurs n'avaient point ralenti son zèle pour Genève, il était toujours un ennemi redoutable pour ceux qui la menaçaient, et par conséquent il devait être exposé à leurs coups. Il fut rencontré en 1530 sur le Jura par des voleurs,

qui le dépouillèrent, et qui le mirent encore entre les mains du Duc de
Savoye: ce Prince le fit enfermer dans le Château de Chillon, où il resta
sans être interrogé jusques en 1536; il fut alors délivré par les Bernois,
qui s'emparèrent du Pays de Vaud.

'Bonnivard, en sortant de sa captivité, eut le plaisir de trouver
Genève libre et réformée: la République s'empressa de lui témoigner
sa reconnaissance, et de le dédommager des maux qu'il avait soufferts;
elle le reçut Bourgeois de la ville au mois de Juin, 1536; elle lui donna
la maison habitée autrefois par le Vicaire-Général, et elle lui assigna
une pension de deux cent écus d'or tant qu'il séjournerait à Genève.
Il fut admis dans le Conseil des Deux-Cent en 1537.

'Bonnivard n'a pas fini d'être utile: après avoir travaillé à rendre
Genève libre, il réussit à la rendre tolérante. Bonnivard engagea le
Conseil à accorder [aux ecclésiastiques et aux paysans] un temps suffisant
pour examiner les propositions qu'on leur faisait; il réussit par sa
douceur: on prêche toujours le Christianisme avec succès quand on
le prêche avec charité...

'Bonnivard fut savant: ses manuscrits, qui sont dans la bibliothèque
publique, prouvent qu'il avait bien lu les auteurs classiques Latins,
et qu'il avait approfondi la théologie et l'histoire. Ce grand homme
aimait les sciences, et il croyait qu'elles pouvaient faire la gloire de
Genève; aussi il ne négligea rien pour les fixer dans cette ville naissante;
en 1551 il donna sa bibliothèque au public; elle fut le commencement
de notre bibliothèque publique; et ces livres sont en partie les rares
et belles éditions du quinzième siècle qu'on voit dans notre collection.
Enfin, pendant la même année, ce bon patriote institua la République
son héritière, à condition qu'elle employerait ses biens à entretenir le
collège dont on projetait la fondation.

'Il paraît que Bonnivard mourut en 1570; mais on ne peut l'assurer,
parce qu'il y a une lacune dans le Nécrologe depuis le mois de Juillet,
1570, jusques en 1571.'   [J. Senebier, *Histoire littéraire de Genève*, 1786.]

I

My hair is grey, but not with years,
　Not grew it white
　In a single night,
As men's have grown from sudden fears:
My limbs are bow'd, though not with toil,　　　　　5
　But rusted with a vile repose,
For they have been a dungeon's spoil,
　And mine has been the fate of those
To whom the goodly earth and air
Are bann'd, and barr'd—forbidden fare;　　　　　10
But this was for my father's faith
I suffer'd chains and courted death;
That father perish'd at the stake
For tenets he would not forsake;
And for the same his lineal race　　　　　15
In darkness found a dwelling-place;

We were seven—who now are one,
  Six in youth, and one in age,
Finish'd as they had begun,
  Proud of Persecution's rage;   20
One in fire, and two in field,
Their belief with blood have seal'd,
Dying as their father died,
For the God their foes denied;—
Three were in a dungeon cast,   25
Of whom this wreck is left the last.

II

There are seven pillars of Gothic mould,
In Chillon's dungeons deep and old,
There are seven columns, massy and grey,
Dim with a dull imprison'd ray,   30
A sunbeam which hath lost its way,
And through the crevice and the cleft
Of the thick wall is fallen and left;
Creeping o'er the floor so damp,
Like a marsh's meteor lamp: 35
And in each pillar there is a ring,
  And in each ring there is a chain;
That iron is a cankering thing,
  For in these limbs its teeth remain,
With marks that will not wear away,   40
Till I have done with this new day,
Which now is painful to these eyes,
Which have not seen the sun so rise
For years—I cannot count them o'er,
I lost their long and heavy score   45
When my last brother droop'd and died,
And I lay living by his side.

III

They chain'd us each to a column stone,
And we were three—yet, each alone;
We could not move a single pace,   50
We could not see each other's face,
But with that pale and livid light
That made us strangers in our sight:
And thus together—yet apart,
Fetter'd in hand, but join'd in heart,   55
'Twas still some solace in the dearth
Of the pure elements of earth,

To hearken to each other's speech,
And each turn comforter to each
With some new hope, or legend old,   60
Or song heroically bold;
But even these at length grew cold.
Our voices took a dreary tone,
An echo of the dungeon stone,
   A grating sound, not full and free,   65
   As they of yore were wont to be:
   It might be fancy—but to me
They never sounded like our own.

IV

I was the eldest of the three,
   And to uphold and cheer the rest   70
   I ought to do—and did my best—
And each did well in his degree.
   The youngest, whom my father loved,
Because our mother's brow was given
To him, with eyes as blue as heaven—   75
   For him my soul was sorely moved:
And truly might it be distress'd
To see such bird in such a nest;
For he was beautiful as day—
   (When day was beautiful to me   80
   As to young eagles, being free)—
   A polar day, which will not see
A sunset till its summer's gone,
   Its sleepless summer of long light,
The snow-clad offspring of the sun: 85
   And thus he was as pure and bright,
And in his natural spirit gay,
With tears for nought but others' ills,
And then they flow'd like mountain rills,
Unless he could assuage the woe   90
Which he abhorr'd to view below.

V

The other was as pure of mind,
But form'd to combat with his kind;
Strong in his frame, and of a mood
Which 'gainst the world in war had stood,   95
And perish'd in the foremost rank
   With joy:—but not in chains to pine:
His spirit wither'd with their clank,
   I saw it silently decline—

And so perchance in sooth did mine: 100
But yet I forced it on to cheer
Those relics of a home so dear.
He was a hunter of the hills,
　Had follow'd there the deer and wolf;
　To him his dungeon was a gulf, 105
And fetter'd feet the worst of ills.

VI

　Lake Leman lies by Chillon's walls:
A thousand feet in depth below
Its massy waters meet and flow;
Thus much the fathom-line was sent 110
From Chillon's snow-white battlement,
　Which round about the wave inthrals:
A double dungeon wall and wave
Have made—and like a living grave
Below the surface of the lake 115
The dark vault lies wherein we lay,
We heard it ripple night and day;
　Sounding o'er our heads it knock'd;
And I have felt the winter's spray
Wash through the bars when winds were high 120
And wanton in the happy sky;
　And then the very rock hath rock'd,
　And I have felt it shake, unshock'd,
Because I could have smiled to see
The death that would have set me free. 125

VII

I said my nearer brother pined,
I said his mighty heart declined,
He loathed and put away his food;
It was not that 'twas coarse and rude,
For we were used to hunter's fare, 130
And for the like had little care:
The milk drawn from the mountain goat
Was changed for water from the moat,
Our bread was such as captives' tears
Have moisten'd many a thousand years, 135
Since man first pent his fellow men
Like brutes within an iron den;
But what were these to us or him? .
These wasted not his heart or limb;
My brother's soul was of that mould 140
Which in a palace had grown cold,

A.L.P. Q

Had his free breathing been denied
The range of the steep mountain's side;
But why delay the truth?—he died.
I saw, and could not hold his head,   145
Nor reach his dying hand—nor dead,—
Though hard I strove, but strove in vain,
To rend and gnash my bonds in twain.
He died—and they unlock'd his chain,
And scoop'd for him a shallow grave   150
Even from the cold earth of our cave.
I begg'd them as a boon to lay
His corse in dust whereon the day
Might shine—it was a foolish thought,
But then within my brain it wrought,   155
That even in death his freeborn breast
In such a dungeon could not rest.
I might have spared my idle prayer—
They coldly laugh'd, and laid him there:
The flat and turfless earth above   160
The being we so much did love;
His empty chain above it leant,
Such Murder's fitting monument!

                    VIII
But he, the favourite and the flower,
Most cherish'd since his natal hour,   165
His mother's image in fair face,
The infant love of all his race,
His martyr'd father's dearest thought,
My latest care, for whom I sought
To hoard my life, that his might be   170
Less wretched now, and one day free;
He, too, who yet had held untired
A spirit natural or inspired—
He, too, was struck, and day by day
Was wither'd on the stalk away.   175
Oh, God! it is a fearful thing
To see the human soul take wing
In any shape, in any mood:
I've seen it rushing forth in blood,
I've seen it on the breaking ocean   180
Strive with a swoln convulsive motion,
I've seen the sick and ghastly bed
Of Sin delirious with its dread:

But these were horrors—this was woe
Unmix'd with such—but sure and slow: 185
He faded, and so calm and meek,
So softly worn, so sweetly weak,
So tearless, yet so tender—kind,
And grieved for those he left behind;
With all the while a cheek whose bloom   190
Was as a mockery of the tomb,
Whose tints as gently sunk away
As a departing rainbow's ray;
An eye of most transparent light,
That almost made the dungeon bright,   195
And not a word of murmur—not
A groan o'er his untimely lot,—
A little talk of better days,
A little hope my own to raise,
For I was sunk in silence—lost   200
In this last loss, of all the most;
And then the sighs he would suppress
Of fainting Nature's feebleness,
More slowly drawn, grew less and less:
I listen'd, but I could not hear;   205
I call'd, for I was wild with fear;
I knew 'twas hopeless, but my dread
Would not be thus admonishéd;
I call'd, and thought I heard a sound—
I burst my chain with one strong bound,   210
And rush'd to him:—I found him not,
I only stirr'd in this black spot,
I only lived, *I* only drew
The accursed breath of dungeon-dew;
The last, the sole, the dearest link   215
Between me and the eternal brink,
Which bound me to my failing race,
Was broken in this fatal place.
One on the earth, and one beneath—
My brothers—both had ceased to breathe!   220
I took that hand which lay so still,
Alas! my own was full as chill;
I had not strength to stir, or strive,
But felt that I was still alive—
A frantic feeling, when we know   225
That what we love shall ne'er be so.
   I know not why
   I could not die,

I had no earthly hope—but faith,
And that forbade a selfish death. 230

IX

What next befell me then and there
   I know not well—I never knew—
First came the loss of light, and air,
   And then of darkness too:
I had no thought, no feeling—none— 235
Among the stones I stood a stone,
And was, scarce conscious what I wist,
As shrubless crags within the mist;
For all was blank, and bleak, and grey;
It was not night—it was not day; 240
It was not even the dungeon-light,
So hateful to my heavy sight,
But vacancy absorbing space,
And fixedness—without a place;
There were no stars—no earth—no time— 245
No check—no change—no good—no crime—
But silence, and a stirless breath
Which neither was of life nor death;
A sea of stagnant idleness,
Blind, boundless, mute, and motionless! 250

X

A light broke in upon my brain,—
   It was the carol of a bird;
It ceased, and then it came again,
   The sweetest song ear ever heard,
And mine was thankful till my eyes 255
Ran over with the glad surprise,
And they that moment could not see
I was the mate of misery;
But then by dull degrees came back
My senses to their wonted track; 260
I saw the dungeon walls and floor
Close slowly round me as before,
I saw the glimmer of the sun
Creeping as it before had done,
But through the crevice where it came 265
That bird was perch'd, as fond and tame,
   And tamer than upon the tree;
A lovely bird, with azure wings,

And song that said a thousand things,
   And seem'd to say them all for me!   270
I never saw its like before,
I ne'er shall see its likeness more:
It seem'd like me to want a mate,
But was not half so desolate,
And it was come to love me when   275
None lived to love me so again,
And cheering from my dungeon's brink,
Had brought me back to feel and think.
I know not if it late were free,
   Or broke its cage to perch on mine,   ⁓80
But knowing well captivity,
   Sweet bird! I could not wish for thine!
Or if it were, in wingéd guise,
A visitant from Paradise;
For—Heaven forgive that thought! the while   285
Which made me both to weep and smile—
I sometimes deem'd that it might be
My brother's soul come down to me;
But then at last away it flew,
And then 'twas mortal well I knew,   290
For he would never thus have flown,
And left me twice so doubly lone—
Lone—as the corse within its shroud,
Lone—as a solitary cloud,
   A single cloud on a sunny day,   295
While all the rest of heaven is clear,
A frown upon the atmosphere,
That hath no business to appear
   When skies are blue, and earth is gay.

XI

A kind of change came in my fate,   300
My keepers grew compassionate;
I know not what had made them so,
They were inured to sights of woe,
But so it was:—my broken chain
With links unfasten'd did remain,   305
And it was liberty to stride
Along my cell from side to side,
And up and down, and then athwart,
And tread it over every part;
And round the pillars one by one,   310
Returning where my walk begun,

Avoiding only, as I trod,
My brothers' graves without a sod;
For if I thought with heedless tread
My step profaned their lowly bed,   315
My breath came gaspingly and thick,
And my crush'd heart felt blind and sick.

                        XII
I made a footing in the wall,
    It was not therefrom to escape,
For I had buried one and all   320
    Who loved me in a human shape;
And the whole earth would henceforth be
A wider prison unto me:
No child—no sire—no kin had I,
No partner in my misery;   325
I thought of this, and I was glad,
For thought of them had made me mad;
But I was curious to ascend
To my barr'd windows, and to bend
Once more, upon the mountains high,   330
The quiet of a loving eye.

                        XIII
I saw them—and they were the same,
They were not changed like me in frame;
I saw their thousand years of snow
On high—their wide long lake below,   335
And the blue Rhone in fullest flow;
I heard the torrents leap and gush
O'er channell'd rock and broken bush;
I saw the white-wall'd distant town,
And whiter sails go skimming down;   340
And then there was a little isle,
Which in my very face did smile,
    The only one in view;
A small green isle, it seem'd no more,
Scarce broader than my dungeon floor,   345
But in it there were three tall trees,
And o'er it blew the mountain breeze,
And by it there were waters flowing,
And on it there were young flowers growing,
    Of gentle breath and hue.   350

339 Villeneuve.   341 The Ile de Peilz.

The fish swam by the castle wall,
And they seem'd joyous each and all;
The eagle rode the rising blast,
Methought he never flew so fast
As then to me he seem'd to fly;   355
And then new tears came in my eye,
And I felt troubled—and would fain
I had not left my recent chain;
And when I did descend again,
The darkness of my dim abode   360
Fell on me as a heavy load;
It was as is a new-dug grave,
Closing o'er one we sought to save,—
And yet my glance, too much opprest,
Had almost need of such a rest.   365

                            XIV
It might be months, or years, or days,
    I kept no count, I took no note,—
I had no hope my eyes to raise,
    And clear them of their dreary mote;
At last men came to set me free;   370
    I ask'd not why, and reck'd not where;
It was at length the same to me,
Fetter'd or fetterless to be,
    I learn'd to love despair.
And thus when they appear'd at last,   375
And all my bonds aside were cast,
These heavy walls to me had grown
A hermitage—and all my own!
And half I felt as they were come
To tear me from a second home: 380
With spiders I had friendship made,
And watch'd them in their sullen trade,
Had seen the mice by moonlight play,
And why should I feel less than they?
We were all inmates of one place,   385
And I, the monarch of each race,
Had power to kill—yet, strange to tell!
In quiet we had learn'd to dwell;
My very chains and I grew friends,
So much a long communion tends   390
To make us what we are:—even I
Regain'd my freedom with a sigh.

ODE ON VENICE

This is Byron's other Venice. Written in 1818, a year after the light-hearted *Beppo*, it shows the dark underside of the same city —a city that has become symbolic, in its substitution of pleasure for power, and apathy for vigilance, of the decay of Europe and its need of revolutionary renewal.

I

Oh Venice! Venice! when thy marble walls
  Are level with the waters, there shall be
A cry of nations o'er thy sunken halls,
  A loud lament along the sweeping sea!
If I, a northern wanderer, weep for thee,   5
What should thy sons do?—anything but weep:
And yet they only murmur in their sleep.
In contrast with their fathers—as the slime,
The dull green ooze of the receding deep,
Is with the dashing of the spring-tide foam,   10
That drives the sailor shipless to his home,
Are they to those that were; and thus they creep,
Crouching and crab-like, through their sapping streets.
Oh! agony—that centuries should reap
No mellower harvest! Thirteen hundred years   15
Of wealth and glory turn'd to dust and tears;
And every monument the stranger meets,
Church, palace, pillar, as a mourner greets;
And even the Lion all subdued appears,
And the harsh sound of the barbarian drum,   20
With dull and daily dissonance, repeats
The echo of thy Tyrant's voice along
The soft waves, once all musical to song,
That heaved beneath the moonlight with the throng
Of gondolas—and to the busy hum   25
Of cheerful creatures, whose most sinful deeds
Were but the overbeating of the heart,
And flow of too much happiness, which needs
The aid of age to turn its course apart
From the luxuriant and voluptuous flood   30
Of sweet sensations, battling with the blood.

13 *Sapping:* decaying, crumbling.   19 *The Lion:* the Lion of St. Mark, emblem of Venice.

But these are better than the gloomy errors,
The weeds of nations in their last decay,
When Vice walks forth with her unsoften'd terrors,
And Mirth is madness, and but smiles to slay;   35
And Hope is nothing but a false delay,
The sick man's lightning half an hour ere Death,
When Faintness, the last mortal birth of Pain,
And apathy of limb, the dull beginning
Of the cold staggering race which Death is winning,   40
Steals vein by vein and pulse by pulse away;
Yet so relieving the o'er-tortured clay,
To him appears renewal of his breath,
And freedom the mere numbness of his chain;—
And then he talks of Life, and how again   45
He feels his spirit soaring—albeit weak,
And of the fresher air, which he would seek;
And as he whispers knows not that he gasps,
That his thin finger feels not what it clasps,
And so the film comes o'er him, and the dizzy   50
Chamber swims round and round—and shadows busy,
At which he vainly catches, flit and gleam,
Till the last rattle chokes the strangled scream,
And all is ice and blackness, —and the earth
That which it was the moment ere our birth.   55

II

There is no hope for nations!—Search the page
  Of many thousand years—the daily scene,
The flow and ebb of each recurring age,
  The everlasting *to be* which *hath been*,
  Hath taught us nought, or little: still we lean   60
On things that rot beneath our weight, and wear
Our strength away in wrestling with the air;
For 'tis our nature strikes us down: the beasts
Slaughter'd in hourly hecatombs for feasts
Are of as high an order—they must go   65
Even where their driver goads them, though to slaughter.
Ye men, who pour your blood for kings as water,
What have they given your children in return?
A heritage of servitude and woes,
A blindfold bondage, where your hire is blows.   70
What! do not yet the red-hot ploughshares burn,
O'er which you stumble in a false ordeal,

64 *Hecatombs:* great public sacrifices.

And deem this proof of loyalty the *real*;
Kissing the hand that guides you to your scars,
And glorying as you tread the glowing bars? 75
All that your Sires have left you, all that Time
Bequeaths of free, and History of sublime,
Spring from a different theme! —Ye see and read,
Admire and sigh, and then succumb and bleed!
Save the few spirits who, despite of all, 80
And worse than all, the sudden crimes engender'd
By the down-thundering of the prison-wall,
And thirst to swallow the sweet waters tender'd,
Gushing from Freedom's fountains—when the crowd,
Madden'd with centuries of drought, are loud, 85
And trample on each other to obtain
The cup which brings oblivion of a chain,
Heavy and sore,—in which long yoked they plough'd
The sand,—or if there sprung the yellow grain,
'Twas not for them, their necks were too much bow'd, 90
And their dead palates chew'd the cud of pain:—
Yes! the few spirits—who, despite of deeds
Which they abhor, confound not with the cause
Those momentary starts from Nature's laws,
Which, like the pestilence and earthquake, smite 95
But for a term, then pass, and leave the earth
With all her seasons to repair the blight
With a few summers, and again put forth
Cities and generations—fair, when free—
For, Tyranny, there blooms no bud for thee! 100

III
Glory and Empire! once upon these towers
    With Freedom—godlike Triad! how you sate!
The league of mightiest nations, in those hours
    When Venice was an envy, might abate,
    But did not quench, her spirit—in her fate 105
All were enwrapp'd: the feasted monarchs knew
    And loved their hostess, nor could learn to hate,
Although they humbled—with the kingly few
The many felt, for from all days and climes
She was the voyager's worship;—even her crimes 110
Were of the softer order—born of Love—
She drank no blood, nor fatten'd on the dead,
But gladden'd where her harmless conquests spread;
For these restored the Cross, that from above
Hallow'd her sheltering banners, which incessant 115

Flew between earth and the unholy Crescent,
Which, if it waned and dwindled, Earth may thank
The city it has clothed in chains, which clank
Now, creaking in the ears of those who owe
The name of Freedom to her glorious struggles;   120
Yet she but shares with them a common woe,
And call'd the ' kingdom ' of a conquering foe,
But knows what all—and, most of all, *we* know—
With what set gilded terms a tyrant juggles!

                                IV
The name of Commonwealth is past and gone   125
    O'er the three fractions of the groaning globe;
Venice is crush'd, and Holland deigns to own
    A sceptre, and endures the purple robe;
If the free Switzer yet bestrides alone
His chainless mountains, 'tis but for a time,   130
For Tyranny of late is cunning grown,
And in its own good season tramples down
The sparkles of our ashes. One great clime,
Whose vigorous offspring by dividing ocean
Are kept apart and nursed in the devotion   135
Of Freedom, which their fathers fought for, and
Bequeath'd—a heritage of heart and hand,
And proud distinction from each other land,
Whose sons must bow them at a Monarch's motion,
As if his senseless sceptre were a wand   140
Full of the magic of exploded science—
Still one great clime, in full and free defiance,
Yet rears her crest, unconquer'd and sublime,
Above the far Atlantic!—She has taught
Her Esau-brethren that the haughty flag,   145
The floating fence of Albion's feebler crag,
May strike to those whose red right hands have bought
Rights cheaply earn'd with blood. —Still, still, for ever
Better, though each man's life-blood were a river,
That it should flow, and overflow, than creep   150
Through thousand lazy channels in our veins,
Damm'd like the dull canal with locks and chains,
And moving, as a sick man in his sleep,

122 *'Kingdom'*: the 'Kingdom of Venetian Lombardy', given to the
Emperor of Austria at the Congress of Vienna in 1814. 127-8 *Holland,*
etc.: A 'Kingdom of the Netherlands' was set up in 1814. 144-8 refers
to American naval successes in the war with Britain, 1812-14.   145
Esau-brethren: See *Gen.* xxv.

Three paces, and then faltering: —better be
Where the extinguish'd Spartans still are free,   155
In their proud charnel of Thermopylæ,
Than stagnate in our marsh,—or o'er the deep
Fly, and one current to the ocean add,
One spirit to the souls our fathers had,
One freeman more, America, to thee!   160

Percy Bysshe Shelley

1792—1822

ALASTOR; OR THE SPIRIT OF SOLITUDE

PREFACE

The poem entitled *Alastor* may be considered as allegorical of one of the
most interesting situations of the human mind. It represents a youth
of uncorrupted feelings and adventurous genius led forth by an
imagination inflamed and purified through familiarity with all that is
excellent and majestic, to the contemplation of the universe. He drinks
deep of the fountain of knowledge, and is still insatiate. The magnifi-
cence and beauty of the external world sinks profoundly into the frame
of his conceptions, and affords to their modifications a variety not to be
exhausted. So long as it is possible for his desires to point towards
objects thus infinite and unmeasured, he is joyous, and tranquil, and
self-possessed. But the period arrives when these objects cease to suffice.
His mind is at length suddenly awakened and thirsts for intercourse
with an intelligence similar to itself. He imagines to himself the Being
whom he loves. Conversant with speculations of the sublimest and
most perfect natures, the vision in which he embodies his own imagina-
tions unites all of wonderful, or wise, or beautiful, which the poet, the
philosopher, or the lover could depicture. The intellectual faculties,
the imagination, the functions of sense have their respective requisitions
on the sympathy of corresponding powers in other human beings. The
Poet is represented as uniting these requisitions, and attaching them
to a single image. He seeks in vain for a prototype of this conception.
Blasted by his disappointment, he descends to an untimely grave.

The picture is not barren of instruction to actual men. The Poet's
self-centred seclusion was avenged by the furies of an irresistible passion,
pursuing him to speedy ruin. But that Power which strikes the luminaries
of the world with sudden darkness and extinction, by awakening them
to too exquisite a perception of its influences, dooms to a slow and
poisonous decay those meaner spirits that dare to abjure its dominion.
Their destiny is more abject and inglorious as their delinquency is
more contemptible and pernicious. They who, deluded by no generous

156 *Thermopylæ:* scene of heroic battle between Greeks and invading
Persians, 480 B.C.

error, instigated by no sacred thirst of doubtful knowledge, duped by
no illustrious superstition, loving nothing on this earth, and cherishing
no hopes beyond, yet keep aloof from sympathies with their kind,
rejoicing neither in human joy nor mourning with human grief; these,
and such as they, have their apportioned curse. They languish, because
none feel with them their common nature. They are morally dead.
They are neither friends, nor lovers, nor fathers, nor citizens of the
world, nor benefactors of their country. Among those who attempt to
exist without human sympathy, the pure and tender-hearted perish
through the intensity and passion of their search after its communities,
when the vacancy of their spirit suddenly makes itself felt. All else,
selfish, blind, and torpid, are those unforeseeing multitudes who con-
stitute, together with their own, the lasting misery and loneliness of the
world. Those who love not their fellow-beings live unfruitful lives,
and prepare for their old age a miserable grave.

> " The good die first,
> And those whose hearts are dry as summer dust,
> Burn to the socket! "

December 14, 1815.

> Nondum amabam, et amare amabam, quaerebam quid
> amarem, amans amare.—*Confessions of St. Augustine.**

Earth, ocean, air, belovèd brotherhood!
If our great Mother has imbued my soul
With aught of natural piety to feel
Your love, and recompense the boon with mine;
If dewy morn, and odorous noon, and even,   5
With sunset and its gorgeous ministers,
And solemn midnight's tingling silentness;
If autumn's hollow sighs in the sere wood,
And winter robing with pure snow and crowns
Of starry ice the grey grass and bare boughs;   10
If spring's voluptuous pantings when she breathes
Her first sweet kisses, have been dear to me;
If no bright bird, insect, or gentle beast
I consciously have injured, but still loved
And cherished these my kindred: then forgive   15
This boast, belovèd brethren, and withdraw
No portion of your wonted favour now!

Mother of this unfathomable world!
Favour my solemn song, for I have loved

---

* The motto from St. Augustine reads: 'Not yet was I in love, but I was
in love with loving, I wondered what I might love, being in love with
love.'   2 *Our great Mother:* Nature.

Thee ever, and thee only; I have watched   20
Thy shadow, and the darkness of thy steps,
And my heart ever gazes on the depth
Of thy deep mysteries. I have made my bed
In charnels and on coffins, where black death
Keeps record of the trophies won from thee,   25
Hoping to still these obstinate questionings
Of thee and thine, by forcing some lone ghost
Thy messenger, to render up the tale
Of what we are. In lone and silent hours,
When night makes a weird sound of its own stillness,   30
Like an inspired and desperate alchymist
Staking his very life on some dark hope,
Have I mixed awful talk and asking looks
With my most innocent love, until strange tears
Uniting with those breathless kisses, made   35
Such magic as compels the charmèd night
To render up thy charge: . . . and, though ne'er yet
Thou hast unveiled thy inmost sanctuary,
Enough from incommunicable dream,
And twilight phantasms, and deep noon-day thought,   40
Has shone within me, that serenely now
And moveless, as a long-forgotten lyre
Suspended in the solitary dome
Of some mysterious and deserted fane,
I wait thy breath, Great Parent, that my strain   45
May modulate with murmurs of the air,
And motions of the forests and the sea,
And voice of living beings, and woven hymns
Of night and day, and the deep heart of man.

There was a Poet whose untimely tomb   50
No human hands with pious reverence reared,
But the charmed eddies of autumnal winds
Built o'er his mouldering bones a pyramid
Of mouldering leaves in the waste wilderness:—
A lovely youth,—no mourning maiden decked   55
With weeping flowers, or votive cypress wreath,
The lone couch of his everlasting sleep:—
Gentle, and brave, and generous,—no lorn bard
Breathed o'er his dark fate one melodious sigh:
He lived, he died, he sung, in solitude.   60
Strangers have wept to hear his passionate notes,
And virgins, as unknown he passed, have pined
And wasted for fond love of his wild eyes.

The fire of those soft orbs has ceased to burn,
And Silence, too enamoured of that voice,   65
Locks its mute music in her rugged cell.

By solemn vision, and bright silver dream,
His infancy was nurtured. Every sight
And sound from the vast earth and ambient air,
Sent to his heart its choicest impulses.   70
The fountains of divine philosophy
Fled not his thirsting lips, and all of great,
Or good, or lovely, which the sacred past
In truth or fable consecrates, he felt
And knew. When early youth had passed, he left   75
His cold fireside and alienated home
To seek strange truths in undiscovered lands.
Many a wide waste and tangled wilderness
Has lured his fearless steps; and he has bought
With his sweet voice and eyes, from savage men,   80
His rest and food. Nature's most secret steps
He like her shadow has pursued, where'er
The red volcano overcanopies
Its fields of snow and pinnacles of ice
With burning smoke, or where bitumen lakes   85
On black bare pointed islets ever beat
With sluggish surge, or where the secret caves
Rugged and dark, winding among the springs
Of fire and poison, inaccessible
To avarice or pride, their starry domes   90
Of diamond and of gold expand above
Numberless and immeasurable halls,
Frequent with crystal column, and clear shrines
Of pearl, and thrones radiant with chrysolite.
Nor had that scene of ampler majesty   95
Than gems or gold, the varying roof of heaven
And the green earth lost in his heart its claims
To love and wonder; he would linger long
In lonesome vales, making the wild his home,
Until the doves and squirrels would partake   100
From his innocuous hand his bloodless food,
Lured by the gentle meaning of his looks,
And the wild antelope, that starts whene'er
The dry leaf rustles in the brake, suspend
Her timid steps to gaze upon a form   105

94 *Chrysolite:* name formerly given to green gems such as topaz and
zircon.

More graceful than her own.
                                His wandering step
Obedient to high thoughts, has visited
The awful ruins of the days of old:
Athens, and Tyre, and Balbec, and the waste
Where stood Jerusalem, the fallen towers   110
Of Babylon, the eternal pyramids,
Memphis and Thebes, and whatsoe'er of strange
Sculptured on alabaster obelisk,
Or jasper tomb, or mutilated sphynx,
Dark Æthiopia in her desert hills   115
Conceals. Among the ruined temples there,
Stupendous columns, and wild images
Of more than man, where marble daemons watch
The Zodiac's brazen mystery, and dead men
Hang their mute thoughts on the mute walls around, 120
He lingered, poring on memorials
Of the world's youth, through the long burning day
Gazed on those speechless shapes, nor, when the moon
Filled the mysterious halls with floating shades
Suspended he that task, but ever gazed   125
And gazed, till meaning on his vacant mind
Flashed like strong inspiration, and he saw
The thrilling secrets of the birth of time.

Meanwhile an Arab maiden brought his food,
Her daily portion, from her father's tent.   130
And spread her matting for his couch, and stole
From duties and repose to tend his steps:—
Enamoured, yet not daring for deep awe
To speak her love:—and watched his nightly sleep,
Sleepless herself, to gaze upon his lips   135
Parted in slumber, whence the regular breath
Of innocent dreams arose: then, when red morn
Made paler the pale moon, to her cold home
Wildered, and wan, and panting, she returned.

The Poet wandering on, through Arabie   140
And Persia, and the wild Carmanian waste,

109 *Tyre . . . Ba(a)lbec:* ancient cities in the Lebanon.   112 *Memphis
. . . Thebes:* ancient cities in Lower and Upper Egypt respectively.
119 *The Zodiac's brazen mystery:* in the Temple of Dendera, Upper
Egypt. Without needing an astrolabe, Shelley's friend John F. Newton
believed that 'most ancient and sublime morality was mystically incul-
cated in the most ancient Zodiac.'   139 *Wildered:* bewildered.   141
Carmanian waste: in southern Persia.

And o'er the aërial mountains which pour down
Indus and Oxus from their icy caves,
In joy and exultation held his way;
Till in the vale of Cashmire, far within   145
Its loneliest dell, where odorous plants entwine
Beneath the hollow rocks a natural bower,
Beside a sparkling rivulet he stretched
His languid limbs. A vision on his sleep
There came, a dream of hopes that never yet   150
Had flushed his cheek. He dreamed a veilèd maid
Sate near him, talking in low solemn tones.
Her voice was like the voice of his own soul
Heard in the calm of thought; its music long,
Like woven sounds of streams and breezes, held   155
His inmost sense suspended in its web
Of many-coloured woof and shifting hues.
Knowledge and truth and virtue were her theme,
And lofty hopes of divine liberty,
Thoughts the most dear to him, and poesy,   160
Herself a poet. Soon the solemn mood
Of her pure mind kindled through all her frame
A permeating fire: wild numbers then
She raised, with voice stifled in tremulous sobs
Subdued by its own pathos: her fair hands   165
Were bare alone, sweeping from some strange harp
Strange symphony, and in their branching veins
The eloquent blood told an ineffable tale.
The beating of her heart was heard to fill
The pauses of her music, and her breath   170
Tumultuously accorded with those fits
Of intermitted song. Sudden she rose,
As if her heart impatiently endured
Its bursting burthen: at the sound he turned,
And saw by the warm light of their own life   175
Her glowing limbs beneath the sinuous veil
Of woven wind, her outspread arms now bare,
Her dark locks floating in the breath of night,
Her beamy bending eyes, her parted lips
Outstretched, and pale, and quivering eagerly.   180
His strong heart sunk and sickened with excess
Of love. He reared his shuddering limbs and quelled

143 *Indus:* great river rising from a spur of the Himalayas, in western
Tibet; *Oxus:* now Amu Darya, river rising in the Hindu Kush. 145
Cashmere: Kashmir, state in north India. 163 *Numbers:* verse, rhyth-
mical utterance.

His gasping breath, and spread his arms to meet
Her panting bosom: . . . she drew back a while,
Then, yielding to the irresistible joy,   185
With frantic gesture and short breathless cry
Folded his frame in her dissolving arms.
Now blackness veiled his dizzy eyes, and night
Involved and swallowed up the vision; sleep,
Like a dark flood suspended in its course,   190
Rolled back its impulse on his vacant brain.

Roused by the shock he started from his trance—
The cold white light of morning, the blue moon
Low in the west, the clear and garish hills,
The distinct valley and the vacant woods,   195
Spread round him where he stood. Whither have fled
The hues of heaven that canopied his bower
Of yesternight? The sounds that soothed his sleep,
The mystery and the majesty of Earth,
The joy, the exultation? His wan eyes   200
Gaze on the empty scene as vacantly
As ocean's moon looks on the moon in heaven.
The spirit of sweet human love has sent
A vision to the sleep of him who spurned
Her choicest gifts. He eagerly pursues   205
Beyond the realms of dream that fleeting shade;
He overleaps the bounds. Alas! Alas!
Were limbs, and breath, and being intertwined
Thus treacherously? Lost, lost, for ever lost,
In the wide pathless desert of dim sleep,   210
That beautiful shape! Does the dark gate of death
Conduct to thy mysterious paradise,
O Sleep? Does the bright arch of rainbow clouds,
And pendent mountains seen in the calm lake,
Lead only to a black and watery depth,   215
While death's blue vault, with loathliest vapours hung,
Where every shade which the foul grave exhales
Hides its dead eye from the detested day,
Conduct, O sleep, to thy delightful realms?
This doubt with sudden tide flowed on his heart,   220
The insatiate hope which it awakened, stung
His brain even like despair.
                                        While daylight held
The sky, the Poet kept mute conference

189 *Involved:* rolled round.

With his still soul. At night the passion came,
Like the fierce fiend of a distempered dream.   225
And shook him from his rest, and led him forth
Into the darkness.—As an eagle grasped
In folds of the green serpent, feels her breast
Burn with the poison, and precipitates
Through night and day, tempest, and calm, and cloud,   230
Frantic with dizzying anguish, her blind flight
O'er the wide aëry wilderness: thus driven
By the bright shadow of that lovely dream,
Beneath the cold glare of the desolate night,
Through tangled swamps and deep precipitous dells,   235
Startling with careless step the moonlight snake,
He fled. Red morning dawned upon his flight,
Shedding the mockery of its vital hues
Upon his cheek of death. He wandered on
Till vast Aornos seen from Petra's steep   240
Hung o'er the low horizon like a cloud;
Through Balk, and where the desolated tombs
Of Parthian kings scatter to every wind
Their wasting dust, wildly he wandered on,
Day after day a weary waste of hours,   245
Bearing within his life the brooding care
That ever fed on its decaying flame.
And now his limbs were lean; his scattered hair
Sered by the autumn of strange suffering
Sung dirges in the wind; his listless hand   250
Hung like dead bone within its withered skin;
Life, and the lustre that consumed it, shone
As in a furnace burning secretly
From his dark eyes alone. The cottagers,
Who ministered with human charity   255
His human wants, beheld with wondering awe
Their fleeting visitant. The mountaineer,
Encountering on some dizzy precipice

224-7 The dream-ideal, however beautiful, is destructive unless it can
be related to ordinary life, and this is what the Poet cannot do. T. L.
Peacock, who suggested the title of the poem to Shelley, called Alastor
'a spirit of evil' as well as the spirit of solitude. Although Alastor, or self-
centredness, destroys the Poet, Shelley (unlike the rationalist Peacock)
was more concerned with the loss than with blame. 240 *Aornos:* rock
on the right bank of river Indus, above its junction with river Kabul;
captured by Alexander the Great during his invasion of India. *Petra:*
ancient city in what is now Jordan. 242 *Balk(h):* ancient city in what
is now Afghanistan. 243 Parthia was an ancient kingdom south-east
of the Caspian Sea.

That spectral form, deemed that the Spirit of wind
With lightning eyes, and eager breath, and feet   260
Disturbing not the drifted snow, had paused
In its career: the infant would conceal
His troubled visage in his mother's robe
In terror at the glare of those wild eyes,
To remember their strange light in many a dream   265
Of after-times; but youthful maidens, taught
By nature, would interpret half the woe
That wasted him, would call him with false names
Brother, and friend, would press his pallid hand
At parting, and watch, dim through tears, the path   270
Of his departure from their father's door.

At length upon the lone Chorasmian shore
He paused, a wide and melancholy waste
Of putrid marshes. A strong impulse urged
His steps to the sea-shore. A swan was there,   275
Beside a sluggish stream among the reeds.
It rose as he approached, and with strong wings
Scaling the upward sky, bent its bright course
High over the immeasurable main.
His eyes pursued its flight.—' Thou hast a home,   280
Beautiful bird; thou voyagest to thine home,
Where thy sweet mate will twine her downy neck
With thine, and welcome thy return with eyes
Bright in the lustre of their own fond joy.
And what am I that I should linger here,   285
With voice far sweeter than thy dying notes,
Spirit more vast than thine, frame more attuned
To beauty, wasting these surpassing powers
In the deaf air, to the blind earth, and heaven
That echoes not my thoughts?' A gloomy smile   290
Of desperate hope wrinkled his quivering lips.
For sleep, he knew, kept most relentlessly
Its precious charge, and silent death exposed,
Faithless perhaps as sleep, a shadowy lure,
With doubtful smile mocking its own strange charms.   295

Startled by his own thoughts he looked around.
There was no fair fiend near him, not a sight
Or sound of awe but in his own deep mind.

272 *Chorasmian shore:* delta of the Amu Darya, south of the Aral Sea, or
perhaps here (as it once seems to have been) the Caspian Sea.

A little shallop floating near the shore
Caught the impatient wandering of his gaze.   300
It had been long abandoned, for its sides
Gaped wide with many a rift, and its frail joints
Swayed with the undulations of the tide.
A restless impulse urged him to embark
And meet lone Death on the drear ocean's waste;   305
For well he knew that mighty Shadow loves
The slimy caverns of the populous deep.

The day was fair and sunny, sea and sky
Drank its inspiring radiance, and the wind
Swept strongly from the shore, blackening the waves. 310
Following his eager soul, the wanderer
Leaped in the boat, he spread his cloak aloft
On the bare mast, and took his lonely seat,
And felt the boat speed o'er the tranquil sea
Like a torn cloud before the hurricane.   315

As one that in a silver vision floats
Obedient to the sweep of odorous winds
Upon resplendent clouds, so rapidly
Along the dark and ruffled waters fled
The straining boat.—A whirlwind swept it on,   320
With fierce gusts and precipitating force,
Through the white ridges of the chafèd sea.
The waves arose. Higher and higher still
Their fierce necks writhed beneath the tempest's scourge
Like serpents struggling in a vulture's grasp.   325
Calm and rejoicing in the fearful war
Of wave ruining on wave, and blast on blast
Descending, and black flood on whirlpool driven
With dark obliterating course, he sate:
As if their genii were the ministers   330
Appointed to conduct him to the light
Of those belovèd eyes, the Poet sate
Holding the steady helm. Evening came on,
The beams of sunset hung their rainbow hues
High 'mid the shifting domes of sheeted spray   335
That canopied his path o'er the waste deep;
Twilight, ascending slowly from the east,
Entwined in duskier wreaths her braided locks
O'er the fair front and radiant eyes of day;
Night followed, clad with stars. On every side   340
299 *Shallop:* light open boat. 327 *Ruining:* falling and breaking.

More horribly the multitudinous streams
Of ocean's mountainous waste to mutual war
Rushed in dark tumult thundering, as to mock
The calm and spangled sky. The little boat
Still fled before the storm; still fled, like foam   345
Down the steep cataract of a wintry river;
Now pausing on the edge of the riven wave;
Now leaving far behind the bursting mass
That fell, convulsing ocean. Safely fled—
As if that frail and wasted human form,   350
Had been an elemental god.
                               At midnight
The moon arose: and lo! the ethereal cliffs
Of Caucasus, whose icy summits shone
Among the stars like sunlight, and around
Whose caverned base the whirlpools and the waves ·   355
Bursting and eddying irresistibly
Rage and resound for ever.—Who shall save?—
The boat fled on,—the boiling torrent drove,—
The crags closed round with black and jaggèd arms,
The shattered mountain overhung the sea,   360
And faster still, beyond all human speed,
Suspended on the sweep of the smooth wave,
The little boat was driven. A cavern there
Yawned, and amid its slant and winding depths
Ingulfed the rushing sea. The boat fled on   365
With unrelaxing speed.—' Vision and Love! '
The Poet cried aloud, ' I have beheld
The path of thy departure. Sleep and death
Shall not divide us long! '

                               The boat pursued
The windings of the cavern. Daylight shone   370
At length upon that gloomy river's flow;
Now, where the fiercest war among the waves
Is calm, on the unfathomable stream
The boat moved slowly. Where the mountain, riven,
Exposed those black depths to the azure sky,   375
Ere yet the flood's enormous volume fell
Even to the base of Caucasus, with sound
That shook the everlasting rocks, the mass
Filled with one whirlpool all that ample chasm;
Stair above stair the eddying waters rose,   380
Circling immeasurably fast, and laved
With alternating dash the gnarlèd roots

Of mighty trees, that stretched their giant arms
In darkness over it. I' the midst was left,
Reflecting, yet distorting every cloud, 385
A pool of treacherous and tremendous calm.
Seized by the sway of the ascending stream,
With dizzy swiftness, round, and round, and round,
Ridge after ridge the straining boat arose,
Till on the verge of the extremest curve, 390
Where, through an opening of the rocky bank,
The waters overflow, and a smooth spot
Of glassy quiet 'mid those battling tides
Is left, the boat paused shuddering.—Shall it sink
Down the abyss? Shall the reverting stress 395
Of that resistless gulf embosom it?
Now shall it fall?—A wandering stream of wind,
Breathed from the west, has caught the expanded sail,
And, lo! with gentle motion, between banks
Of mossy slope, and on a placid stream, 400
Beneath a woven grove it sails, and, hark!
The ghastly torrent mingles its far roar,
With the breeze murmuring in the musical woods.
Where the embowering trees recede, and leave
A little space of green expanse, the cove 405
Is closed by meeting banks, whose yellow flowers
For ever gaze on their own drooping eyes,
Reflected in the crystal calm. The wave
Of the boat's motion marred their pensive task,
Which nought but vagrant bird, or wanton wind, 410
Or falling spear-grass, or their own decay
Had e'er disturbed before. The Poet longed
To deck with their bright hues his withered hair,
But on his heart its solitude returned,
And he forbore. Not the strong impulse hid 415
In those flushed cheeks, bent eyes, and shadowy frame
Had yet performed its ministry: it hung
Upon his life, as lightning in a cloud
Gleams, hovering ere it vanish, ere the floods
Of night close over it.
                The noonday sun 420
Now shone upon the forest, one vast mass
Of mingling shade, whose brown magnificence
A narrow vale embosoms. There, huge caves,
Scooped in the dark base of their aëry rocks

395 *The reverting stress:* the force that would draw it back again into the whirlpool.

Mocking its moans, respond and roar for ever. 425
The meeting boughs and implicated leaves
Wove twilight o'er the Poet's path, as led
By love, or dream, or god, or mightier Death,
He sought in Nature's dearest haunt, some bank,
Her cradle, and his sepulchre. More dark 430
And dark the shades accumulate. The oak,
Expanding its immense and knotty arms,
Embraces the light beech. The pyramids
Of the tall cedar overarching, frame
Most solemn domes within, and far below, 435
Like clouds suspended in an emerald sky,
The ash and the acacia floating hang
Tremulous and pale. Like restless serpents, clothed
In rainbow and in fire, the parasites,
Starred with ten thousand blossoms, flow around 440
The grey trunks, and, as gamesome infants' eyes,
With gentle meanings, and most innocent wiles,
Fold their beams round the hearts of those that love,
These twine their tendrils with the wedded boughs
Uniting their close union; the woven leaves 445
Make net-work of the dark blue light of day,
And the night's noontide clearness, mutable
As shapes in the weird clouds. Soft mossy lawns
Beneath these canopies extend their swells,
Fragrant with perfumed herbs, and eyed with blooms 450
Minute yet beautiful. One darkest glen
Sends from its woods of musk-rose, twined with jasmine,
A soul-dissolving odour, to invite
To some more lovely mystery. Through the dell,
Silence and Twilight here, twin-sisters, keep 455
Their noonday watch, and sail among the shades,
Like vaporous shapes half seen; beyond, a well,
Dark, gleaming, and of most translucent wave,
Images all the woven boughs above,
And each depending leaf, and every speck 460
Of azure sky, darting between their chasms;
Nor aught else in the liquid mirror laves
Its portraiture, but some inconstant star
Between one foliaged lattice twinkling fair,
Or painted bird, sleeping beneath the moon, 465
Or gorgeous insect floating motionless,
Unconscious of the day, ere yet his wings

426 *Implicated:* intertwined. 460 *Depending:* hanging.

Have spread their glories to the gaze of noon.
Hither the Poet came. His eyes beheld
Their own wan light through the reflected lines 470
Of his thin hair, distinct in the dark depth
Of that still fountain; as the human heart,
Gazing in dreams over the gloomy grave,
Sees its own treacherous likeness there. He heard
The motion of the leaves, the grass that sprung 475
Startled and glanced and trembled even to feel
An unaccustomed presence, and the sound
Of the sweet brook that from the secret springs
Of that dark fountain rose. A Spirit seemed
To stand beside him—clothed in no bright robes 480
Of shadowy silver or enshrining light,
Borrowed from aught the visible world affords
Of grace, or majesty, or mystery;—
But, undulating woods, and silent well,
And leaping rivulet, and evening gloom 485
Now deepening the dark shades, for speech assuming,
Held commune with him, as if he and it
Were all that was,—only . . . when his regard
Was raised by intense pensiveness, . . . two eyes,
Two starry eyes, hung in the gloom of thought, 490
And seemed with their serene and azure smiles
To beckon him.

    Obedient to the light
That shone within his soul, he went, pursuing
The windings of the dell.—The rivulet
Wanton and wild, through many a green ravine 495
Beneath the forest flowed. Sometimes it fell
Among the moss with hollow harmony
Dark and profound. Now on the polished stones
It danced; like childhood laughing as it went:
Then, through the plain in tranquil wanderings crept, 500
Reflecting every herb and drooping bud
That overhung its quietness.—' O stream!
Whose source is inaccessibly profound,
Whither do thy mysterious waters tend?
Thou imagest my life. Thy darksome stillness, 505
Thy dazzling waves, thy loud and hollow gulfs,
Thy searchless fountain, and invisible course
Have each their type in me: and the wide sky,
And measureless ocean may declare as soon
What oozy cavern or what wandering cloud 510

Contains thy waters, as the universe
Tell where these living thoughts reside, when stretched
Upon thy flowers my bloodless limbs shall waste
I' the passing wind!'

                Beside the grassy shore
Of the small stream he went; he did impress   515
On the green moss his tremulous step, that caught
Strong shuddering from his burning limbs. As one
Roused by some joyous madness from the couch
Of fever, he did move; yet, not like him,
Forgetful of the grave, where, when the flame   520
Of his frail exultation shall be spent,
He must descend. With rapid steps he went
Beneath the shade of trees, beside the flow
Of the wild babbling rivulet; and now
The forest's solemn canopies were changed   525
For the uniform and lightsome evening sky.
Grey rocks did peep from the spare moss, and stemmed
The struggling brook: tall spires of windlestrae
Threw their thin shadows down the rugged slope,
And nought but gnarled roots of ancient pines   530
Branchless and blasted, clenched with grasping roots
The unwilling soil. A gradual change was here,
Yet ghastly. For, as fast years flow away,
The smooth brow gathers, and the hair grows thin
And white, and where irradiate dewy eyes   535
Had shone, gleam stony orbs:—so from his steps
Bright flowers departed, and the beautiful shade
Of the green groves, with all their odorous winds
And musical motions. Calm, he still pursued
The stream, that with a larger volume now   540
Rolled through the labyrinthine dell; and there
Fretted a path through its descending curves
With its wintry speed. On every side now rose
Rocks, which, in unimaginable forms,
Lifted their black and barren pinnacles   545
In the light of evening, and its precipice
Obscuring the ravine, disclosed above,
Mid toppling stones, black gulfs and yawning caves,
Whose windings gave ten thousand various tongues
To the loud stream. Lo ! where the pass expands   550
Its stony jaws, the abrupt mountain breaks,

528 *Windlestrae:* long-stalked species of grass. 546 *Its precipice:* presumably the mountain-walls of the ravine, 'its' being used proleptically.

And seems, with its accumulated crags,
To overhang the world: for wide expand
Beneath the wan stars and descending moon
Islanded seas, blue mountains, mighty streams,   555
Dim tracts and vast, robed in the lustrous gloom
Of leaden-coloured even, and fiery hills
Mingling their flames with twilight, on the verge
Of the remote horizon. The near scene,
In naked and severe simplicity,   560
Made contrast with the universe. A pine,
Rock-rooted, stretched athwart the vacancy
Its swinging boughs, to each inconstant blast
Yielding one only response, at each pause
In most familiar cadence, with the howl   565
The thunder and the hiss of homeless streams
Mingling its solemn song, whilst the broad river,
Foaming and hurrying o'er its rugged path,
Fell into that immeasurable void
Scattering its waters to the passing winds.   570

Yet the grey precipice and solemn pine
And torrent, were not all;—one silent nook
Was there. Even on the edge of that vast mountain,
Upheld by knotty roots and fallen rocks,
It overlooked in its serenity   575
The dark earth, and the bending vault of stars.
It was a tranquil spot, that seemed to smile
Even in the lap of horror. Ivy clasped
The fissured stones with its entwining arms,
And did embower with leaves for ever green,   580
And berries dark, the smooth and even space
Of its inviolated floor, and here
The children of the autumnal whirlwind bore,
In wanton sport, those bright leaves, whose decay,
Red, yellow, or ethereally pale,   585
Rivals the pride of summer. 'Tis the haunt
Of every gentle wind, whose breath can teach
The wilds to love tranquillity. One step,
One human step alone, has ever broken
The stillness of its solitude:—one voice   590
Alone inspired its echoes;—even that voice
Which hither came, floating among the winds,
And led the loveliest among human forms
To make their wild haunts the depository
Of all the grace and beauty that endued   595

Its motions, render up its majesty,
Scatter its music on the unfeeling storm,
And to the damp leaves and blue cavern mould,
Nurses of rainbow flowers and branching moss,
Commit the colours of that varying cheek,   600
That snowy breast, those dark and drooping eyes.

The dim and hornèd moon hung low, and poured
A sea of lustre on the horizon's verge
That overflowed its mountains. Yellow mist
Filled the unbounded atmosphere, and drank   605
Wan moonlight even to fulness: not a star
Shone, not a sound was heard; the very winds,
Danger's grim playmates, on that precipice
Slept, clasped in his embrace.—O, storm of death!
Whose sightless speed divides this sullen night: 610
And thou, colossal Skeleton, that, still
Guiding its irresistible career
In thy devastating omnipotence,
Art king of this frail world, from the red field
Of slaughter, from the reeking hospital,   615
The patriot's sacred couch, the snowy bed
Of innocence, the scaffold and the throne,
A mighty voice invokes thee. Ruin calls
His brother Death. A rare and regal prey
He hath prepared, prowling around the world;   620
Glutted with which thou mayst repose, and men
Go to their graves like flowers or creeping worms,
Nor ever more offer at thy dark shrine
The unheeded tribute of a broken heart.

When on the threshold of the green recess   625
The wanderer's footsteps fell, he knew that death
Was on him. Yet a little, ere it fled,
Did he resign his high and holy soul
To images of the majestic past,
That paused within his passive being now,   630
Like winds that bear sweet music, when they breathe
Through some dim latticed chamber. He did place
His pale lean hand upon the rugged trunk
Of the old pine. Upon an ivied stone
Reclined his languid head, his limbs did rest,   635
Diffused and motionless, on the smooth brink
Of that obscurest chasm;—and thus he lay,
Surrendering to their final impulses

The hovering powers of life. Hope and despair,
The torturers, slept; no mortal pain or fear   640
Marred his repose, the influxes of sense,
And his own being unalloyed by pain,
Yet feebler and more feeble, calmly fed
The stream of thought, till he lay breathing there
At peace, and faintly smiling:—his last sight   645
Was the great moon, which o'er the western line
Of the wide world her mighty horn suspended,
With whose dun beams inwoven darkness seemed
To mingle. Now upon the jaggèd hills
It rests, and still as the divided frame   650
Of the vast meteor sunk, the Poet's blood,
That ever beat in mystic sympathy
With nature's ebb and flow, grew feebler still:
And when two lessening points of light alone
Gleamed through the darkness, the alternate gasp   655
Of his faint respiration scarce did stir
The stagnate night:—till the minutest ray
Was quenched, the pulse yet lingered in his heart.
It paused—it fluttered. But when heaven remained
Utterly black, the murky shades involved   660
An image, silent, cold, and motionless,
As their own voiceless earth and vacant air.
Even as a vapour fed with golden beams
That ministered on sunlight, ere the west
Eclipses it, was now that wondrous frame—   665
No sense, no motion, no divinity—
A fragile lute, on whose harmonious strings
The breath of heaven did wander—a bright stream
Once fed with many-voicèd waves—a dream
Of youth, which night and time have quenched for ever,   670
Still, dark, and dry, and unremembered now.

O, for Medea's wondrous alchemy,
Which wheresoe'er it fell made the earth gleam
With bright flowers, and the wintry boughs exhale
From vernal blooms fresh fragrance! O, that God,   675
Profuse of poisons, would concede the chalice
Which but one living man has drained, who now,
Vessel of deathless wrath, a slave that feels
No proud exemption in the blighting curse

672 *Medea:* enchantress in Greek mythology. 677 *One living man, etc.:*
the Wandering Jew, condemned to travel the earth till Christ's second
coming.

He bears, over the world wanders for ever,   680
Lone as incarnate death! O, that the dream
Of dark magician in his visioned cave,
Raking the cinders of a crucible
For life and power, even when his feeble hand
Shakes in its last decay, were the true law   685
Of this so lovely world! But thou art fled
Like some frail exhalation; which the dawn
Robes in its golden beams,—ah! thou hast fled!
The brave, the gentle, and the beautiful,
The child of grace and genius. Heartless things   690
Are done and said i' the world, and many worms
And beasts and men live on, and mighty Earth
From sea and mountain, city and wilderness,
In vesper low or joyous orison,
Lifts still its solemn voice:—but thou are fled—   695
Thou canst no longer know or love the shapes
Of this phantasmal scene, who have to thee
Been purest ministers, who are, alas!
Now thou art not. Upon those pallid lips
So sweet even in their silence, on those eyes   700
That image sleep in death, upon that form
Yet safe from the worm's outrage, let no tear
Be shed—not even in thought. Nor, when those hues
Are gone, and those divinest lineaments,
Worn by the senseless wind, shall live alone   705
In the frail pauses of this simple strain,
Let not high verse, mourning the memory
Of that which is no more, or painting's woe
Or sculpture, speak in feeble imagery
Their own cold powers. Art and eloquence,   710
And all the shows o' the world are frail and vain
To weep a loss that turns their lights to shade.
It is a woe too ' deep for tears,' when all
Is reft at once, when some surpassing Spirit,
Whose light adorned the world around it, leaves   715
Those who remain behind, not sobs or groans,
The passionate tumult of a clinging hope;
But pale despair and cold tranquillity,
Nature's vast frame, the web of human things,
Birth and the grave, that are not as they were.   720

713 *Too 'deep for tears'*: See Wordsworth's *Ode: Intimations of Immortality*,
line 207. Shelley also quotes Wordsworth in his Preface (*The Excursion*,
I. 500-2).

THE MASK OF ANARCHY

WRITTEN ON THE OCCASION OF THE MASSACRE AT
MANCHESTER

News of the 'Peterloo Massacre' at Manchester on 16th August,
1819, where a ruthless cavalry charge was used to disperse a
meeting of workers and reformers, came to Shelley at a villa near
Leghorn. 'It roused in him,' wrote Mrs. Shelley, 'violent
emotions of indignation and compassion'—perhaps all the
stronger because of his absence from England.

As I lay asleep in Italy
There came a voice from over the Sea,
And with great power it forth led me
To walk in the visions of Poesy.

I met Murder on the way—   5
He had a mask like Castlereagh—
Very smooth he looked, yet grim;
Seven blood-hounds followed him:

All were fat; and well they might
Be in admirable plight,   10
For one by one, and two by two,
He tossed them human hearts to chew
Which from his wide cloak he drew.

Next came Fraud, and he had on,
Like Lord Eldon, an ermined gown;   15
His big tears, for he wept well,
Turned to mill-stones as they fell.

6 *Castlereagh:* Robert Stewart, Viscount Castlereagh (1769-1822),
statesman whose repressive domestic policy was widely regarded as
being responsible for the Peterloo massacre. Shelley expresses the
popular hatred his name evoked.   15 *Eldon:* John Scott, Earl of Eldon
(1751-1838), lawyer and statesman. As Lord Chancellor, Eldon dealt
with wards in Chancery, and had already refused Shelley the right to
bring up his own children Ianthe and Charles. Shelley combines his
attack on Eldon's inhumanity with a reference to what the *Examiner*
newspaper called his 'lachrymose formality'.

And the little children, who
Round his feet played to and fro,
Thinking every tear a gem,   20
Had their brains knocked out by them.

Clothed with the Bible, as with light,
And the shadows of the night,
Like Sidmouth, next, Hypocrisy
On a crocodile rode by.   25

And many more Destructions played
In this ghastly masquerade,
All disguised, even to the eyes,
Like Bishops, lawyers, peers, or spies.

Last came Anarchy: he rode   30
On a white horse, splashed with blood;
He was pale even to the lips,
Like Death in the Apocalypse.

And he wore a kingly crown;
And in his grasp a sceptre shone;   35
On his brow this mark I saw—
'I AM GOD, AND KING, AND LAW!'

With a pace stately and fast,
Over English land he passed,
Trampling to a mire of blood   40
The adoring multitude.

And a mighty troop around
With their trampling shook the ground,
Waving each a bloody sword,
For the service of their Lord.   45

And with glorious triumph, they
Rode through England proud and gay,
Drunk as with intoxication
Of the wine of desolation.

24 *Sidmouth:*   Henry Addington, Viscount Sidmouth (1757-1844),
politician; like Castlereagh, an extreme anti-reformist. His 'Six Acts',
passed after Peterloo, further restricted public assembly and public
oratory.   27 *Masquerade:* the 'mask' (i.e. masque) of the title.   30
Anarchy: misrule, tyranny.   33 See *Rev.* vi. 8.

O'er fields and towns, from sea to sea, 50
Passed the Pageant swift and free,
Tearing up, and trampling down;
Till they came to London town.

And each dweller, panic-stricken,
Felt his heart with terror sicken 55
Hearing the tempestuous cry
Of the triumph of Anarchy.

For with pomp to meet him came,
Clothed in arms like blood and flame,
The hired murderers, who did sing 60
' Thou are God, and Law, and King.

' We have waited weak and lone
For thy coming, Mighty One!
Our purses are empty, our swords are cold,
Give us glory, and blood, and gold.' 65

Lawyers and priests, a motley crowd,
To the earth their pale brows bowed;
Like a bad prayer not over loud,
Whispering—' Thou art Law and God.'—

Then all cried with one accord, 70
' Thou art King, and God, and Lord;
Anarchy, to thee we bow,
Be thy name made holy now! '

And Anarchy, the Skeleton,
Bowed and grinned to every one, 75
As well as if his education
Had cost ten millions to the nation.

For he knew the Palaces
Of our Kings were rightly his;
His the sceptre, crown, and globe, 80
And the gold-inwoven robe.

So he sent his slaves before
To seize upon the Bank and Tower,
And was proceeding with intent
To meet his pensioned Parliament 85

85 *Pensioned:* hireling, bought.
A.L.P.   R

When one fled past, a maniac maid,
And her name was Hope, she said:
But she looked more like Despair,
And she cried out in the air:

' My father Time is weak and gray   90
With waiting for a better day;
See how idiot-like he stands,
Fumbling with his palsied hands!

' He has had child after child,
And the dust of death is piled   95
Over every one but me—
Misery, oh, Misery! '

Then she lay down in the street,
Right before the horses' feet,
Expecting, with a patient eye,   100
Murder, Fraud, and Anarchy.

When between her and her foes
A mist, a light, an image rose,
Small at first, and weak, and frail
Like the vapour of a vale: 105

Till as clouds grow on the blast,
Like tower-crowned giants striding fast,
And glare with lightnings as they fly,
And speak in thunder to the sky,

It grew—a Shape arrayed in mail   110
Brighter than the viper's scale,
And upborne on wings whose grain
Was as the light of sunny rain.

On its helm, seen far away,
A planet, like the Morning's, lay;   115
And those plumes its light rained through
Like a shower of crimson dew.

With step as soft as wind it passed
O'er the heads of men—so fast
That they knew the presence there,   120
And looked,—but all was empty air.

As flowers beneath May's footstep waken,
As stars from Night's loose hair are shaken,
As waves arise when loud winds call,
Thoughts sprung where'er that step did fall.   125

And the prostrate multitude
Looked—and ankle-deep in blood,
Hope, that maiden most serene,
Was walking with a quiet mien:

And Anarchy, the ghastly birth,   130
Lay dead earth upon the earth;
The Horse of Death tameless as wind
Fled, and with his hoofs did grind
To dust the murderers thronged behind.

A rushing light of clouds and splendour,   135
A sense awakening and yet tender
Was heard and felt—and at its close
These words of joy and fear arose

As if their own indignant Earth
Which gave the sons of England birth   140
Had felt their blood upon her brow,
And shuddering with a mother's throe

Had turnèd every drop of blood
By which her face had been bedewed
To an accent unwithstood,—   145
As if her heart cried out aloud:

' Men of England, heirs of Glory,
Heroes of unwritten story,
Nurslings of one mighty Mother,
Hopes of her, and one another;   150

' Rise like Lions after slumber
In unvanquishable number,
Shake your chains to earth like dew
Which in sleep had fallen on you—
Ye are many—they are few.   155

' What is Freedom?—ye can tell
That which slavery is, too well—
For its very name has grown
To an echo of your own.

' 'Tis to work and have such pay   160
As just keeps life from day to day
In your limbs, as in a cell
For the tyrants' use to dwell,

' So that ye for them are made
Loom, and plough, and sword, and spade,   165
With or without your own will bent
To their defence and nourishment.

' 'Tis to see your children weak
With their mothers pine and peak,
When the winter winds are bleak,—   170
They are dying whilst I speak.

' 'Tis to hunger for such diet
As the rich man in his riot
Casts to the fat dogs that lie
Surfeiting beneath his eye;   175

' 'Tis to let the Ghost of Gold
Take from Toil a thousandfold
More than e'er its substance could
In the tyrannies of old.

' Paper coin—that forgery   180
Of the title-deeds, which ye
Hold to something of the worth
Of the inheritance of Earth.

' 'Tis to be a slave in soul
And to hold no strong control   185
Over your own wills, but be
All that others make of ye.

' And at length when ye complain
With a murmur weak and vain
'Tis to see the Tyrant's crew   190
Ride over your wives and you—
Blood is on the grass like dew.

176-83 Or, as William Paterson, founder of the Bank of England, confidently told his shareholders: 'The bank hath profit on the interest of all the moneys which it creates out of nothing.'

'Then it is to feel revenge
Fiercely thirsting to exchange
Blood for blood—and wrong for wrong—   195
Do not thus when ye are strong.

'Birds find rest, in narrow nest
When weary of their wingèd quest;
Beasts find fare, in woody lair
When storm and snow are in the air.   200

'Horses, oxen, have a home,
When from daily toil they come;
Household dogs, when the wind roars,
Find a home within warm doors.

'Asses, swine, have litter spread   205
And with fitting food are fed;
All things have a home but one—
Thou, Oh, Englishman, hast none!

'This is Slavery—savage men,
Or wild beasts within a den   210
Would endure not as ye do—
But such ills they never knew.

'What art thou Freedom? O! could slaves
Answer from their living graves
This demand—tyrants would flee   215
Like a dream's dim imagery:

'Thou art not, as impostors say,
A shadow soon to pass away,
A superstition, and a name
Echoing from the cave of Fame.   220

'For the labourer thou art bread,
And a comely table spread
From his daily labour come
In a neat and happy home.

'Thou art clothes, and fire, and food   225
For the trampled multitude—
No—in countries that are free
Such starvation cannot be
As in England now we see.

' To the rich thou art a check,   230
When his foot is on the neck
Of his victim, thou dost make
That he treads upon a snake.

' Thou art Justice—ne'er for gold
May thy righteous laws be sold   235
As laws are in England—thou
Shield'st alike the high and low.

' Thou art Wisdom—Freemen never
Dream that God will damn for ever
All who think those things untrue   240
Of which Priests make such ado.

' Thou art Peace—never by thee
Would blood and treasure wasted be
As tyrants wasted them, when all
Leagued to quench thy flame in Gaul.   245

' What if English toil and blood
Was poured forth, even as a flood?
It availed, Oh, Liberty.
To dim, but not extinguish thee.

' Thou art Love—the rich have kissed   250
Thy feet, and like him following Christ,
Give their substance to the free
And through the rough world follow thee,

' Or turn their wealth to arms, and make
War for thy belovèd sake   255
On wealth, and war, and fraud—whence they
Drew the power which is their prey.

' Science, Poetry, and Thought
Are thy lamps; they make the lot
Of the dwellers in a cot   260
So serene, they curse it not.

' Spirit, Patience, Gentleness,
All that can adorn and bless
Art thou—let deeds, not words, express
Thine exceeding loveliness.   265

260 *Cot:* cottage.

' Let a great Assembly be
Of the fearless and the free
On some spot of English ground
Where the plains stretch wide around.

' Let the blue sky overhead,   270
The green earth on which ye tread,
All that must eternal be
Witness the solemnity.

' From the corners uttermost
Of the bounds of English coast;   275
From every hut, village, and town
Where those who live and suffer moan
For others' misery or their own,

' From the workhouse and the prison
Where pale as corpses newly risen,   280
Women, children, young and old
Groan for pain, and weep for cold—

' From the haunts of daily life
Where is waged the daily strife
With common wants and common cares   285
Which sows the human heart with tares—

' Lastly from the palaces
Where the murmur of distress
Echoes, like the distant sound
Of a wind alive around   290

' Those prison halls of wealth and fashion,
Where some few feel such compassion
For those who groan, and toil, and wail
As must make their brethren pale—

' Ye who suffer woes untold,   295
Or to feel, or to behold
Your lost country bought and sold
With a price of blood and gold—

' Let a vast assembly be,
And with great solemnity   300
Declare with measured words that ye
Are, as God has made ye, free—

' Be your strong and simple words
Keen to wound as sharpened swords,
And wide as targes let them be,   305
With their shade to cover ye.

' Let the tyrants pour around
With a quick and startling sound,
Like the loosening of a sea,
Troops of armed emblazonry.   310

' Let the charged artillery drive
Till the dead air seems alive
With the clash of clanging wheels,
And the tramp of horses' heels.

' Let the fixèd bayonet   315
Gleam with sharp desire to wet
Its bright point in English blood
Looking keen as one for food.

' Let the horsemen's scimitars
Wheel and flash, like sphereless stars   320
Thirsting to eclipse their burning
In a sea of death and mourning.

' Stand ye calm and resolute,
Like a forest close and mute,
With folded arms and looks which are   325
Weapons of unvanquished war,

' And let Panic, who outspeeds
The career of armèd steeds
Pass, a disregarded shade
Through your phalanx undismayed.   330

' Let the laws of your own land,
Good or ill, between ye stand
Hand to hand, and foot to foot,
Arbiters of the dispute,

' The old laws of England—they   335
Whose reverend heads with age are gray,
Children of a wiser day;
And whose solemn voice must be
Thine own echo—Liberty!

' On those who first should violate   340
Such sacred heralds in their state
Rest the blood that must ensue,
And it will not rest on you.

' And if then the tyrants dare
Let them ride among you there,   345
Slash, and stab, and maim, and hew,—
What they like, that let them do.

' With folded arms and steady eyes,
And little fear, and less surprise,
Look upon them as they slay   350
Till their rage has died away.

' Then they will return with shame
To the place from which they came.
And the blood thus shed will speak
In hot blushes on their cheek.   355

' Every woman in the land
Will point at them as they stand—
They will hardly dare to greet
Their acquaintance in the street.

' And the bold, true warriors   360
Who have hugged Danger in wars
Will turn to those who would be free,
Ashamed of such base company.

' And that slaughter to the Nation
Shall steam up like inspiration,   365
Eloquent, oracular;
A volcano heard afar.

' And these words shall then become
Like Oppression's thundered doom
Ringing through each heart and brain,   370
Heard again—again—again—

' Rise like Lions after slumber
In unvanquishable number—
Shake your chains to earth like dew
Which in sleep had fallen on you—   375
Ye are many—they are few.'

John Keats

1795—1821

LAMIA

Keats's friend Joseph Severn thought the poet was wasting his time on this 'rhymed story about a serpent-girl,' but the poem sends up its own glittering intensity, born of Keats's deep—at times too deep—involvement with its theme of a ruinously delusive passion. The poet's comment on his finished poem, in a letter of September 1819, was: 'I am certain there is that sort of fire in it which must take hold of people in some way—give them either pleasant or unpleasant sensation. What they want is a sensation of some sort.'

PART ONE

Upon a time, before the faery broods
Drove Nymph and Satyr from the prosperous woods,
Before King Oberon's bright diadem,
Sceptre, and mantle, clasp'd with dewy gem,
Frighted away the Dryads and the Fauns   5
From rushes green, and brakes, and cowslip'd lawns,
The ever-smitten Hermes empty left
His golden throne, bent warm on amorous theft:
From high Olympus had he stolen light,
On this side of Jove's clouds, to escape the sight   10
Of his great summoner, and made retreat
Into a forest on the shores of Crete.
For somewhere in that sacred island dwelt
A nymph, to whom all hoofed Satyrs knelt;
At whose white feet the languid Tritons poured   15
Pearls, while on land they wither'd and adored.
Fast by the springs where she to bathe was wont,
And in those meads where sometime she might haunt,
Were strewn rich gifts, unknown to any Muse,
Though Fancy's casket were unlock'd to choose.   20
Ah, what a world of love was at her feet!

1-6 i.e. 'before the nature-spirits of Greek mythology had been dis-
placed by the medieval fairy world ruled by Oberon.'   7 *Hermes:*
Greek messenger-god.   9 *Olympus:*   mountain-abode of Greek gods.
15 *Tritons:* minor Greek sea-gods.

So Hermes thought, and a celestial heat
Burnt from his winged heels to either ear,
That from a whiteness, as the lily clear,
Blush'd into roses 'mid his golden hair,   25
Fallen in jealous curls about his shoulders bare.

From vale to vale, from wood to wood, he flew,
Breathing upon the flowers his passion new,
And wound with many a river to its head,
To find where this sweet nymph prepar'd her secret bed: 30
In vain; the sweet nymph might nowhere be found,
And so he rested, on the lonely ground,
Pensive, and full of painful jealousies
Of the Wood-Gods, and even the very trees.
There as he stood, he heard a mournful voice,   35
Such as once heard, in gentle heart, destroys
All pain but pity: thus the lone voice spake:
' When from this wreathed tomb shall I awake!
' When move in a sweet body fit for life,
' And love, and pleasure, and the ruddy strife   40
' Of hearts and lips! Ah, miserable me! '
The God, dove-footed, glided silently
Round bush and tree, soft-brushing, in his speed,
The taller grasses and full-flowering weed,
Until he found a palpitating snake,   45
Bright, and cirque-couchant in a dusky brake.

She was a gordian shape of dazzling hue,
Vermilion-spotted, golden, green, and blue;
Striped like a zebra, freckled like a pard,
Eyed like a peacock, and all crimson barr'd;   50
And full of silver moons, that, as she breathed,
Dissolv'd, or brighter shone, or interwreathed
Their lustres with the gloomier tapestries—
So rainbow-sided, touch'd with miseries,
She seem'd, at once, some penanced lady elf,   55
Some demon's mistress, or the demon's self.
Upon her crest she wore a wannish fire
Sprinkled with stars, like Ariadne's tiar:
Her head was serpent, but ah, bitter-sweet!
She had a woman's mouth with all its pearls complete: 60
And for her eyes: what could such eyes do there

46 *Cirque-couchant:* lying coiled in circles. 47 *Gordian:* intricately
twisted. 58 *Ariadne's tiar:* constellation formed by Ariadne's crown,
which was given to her by Bacchus when he married her.

But weep, and weep, that they were born so fair?
As Proserpine still weeps for her Sicilian air.
Her throat was serpent, but the words she spake
Came, as through bubbling honey, for Love's sake,   65
And thus; while Hermes on his pinions lay,
Like a stoop'd falcon ere he takes his prey.

'Fair Hermes, crown'd with feathers, fluttering light,
'I had a splendid dream of thee last night:
'I saw thee sitting, on a throne of gold,   70
'Among the Gods, upon Olympus old,
'The only sad one; for thou didst not hear
'The soft, lute-finger'd Muses chaunting clear,
'Nor even Apollo when he sang alone,
'Deaf to his throbbing throat's long, long melodious moan.   75
'I dreamt I saw thee, robed in purple flakes,
'Break amorous through the clouds, as morning breaks,
'And, swiftly as a bright Phœbean dart,
'Strike for the Cretan isle; and here thou art!
'Too gentle Hermes, hast thou found the maid?'   80
Whereat the star of Lethe not delay'd
His rosy eloquence, and thus inquired:
'Thou smooth-lipp'd serpent, surely high inspired!
'Thou beauteous wreath, with melancholy eyes,
'Possess whatever bliss thou canst devise,   85
'Telling me only where my nymph is fled,—
'Where she doth breathe!' 'Bright planet, thou hast said,'
Return'd the snake, 'but seal with oaths, fair God!'
'I swear,' said Hermes, 'by my serpent rod,
'And by thine eyes, and by thy starry crown!'   90
Light flew his earnest words, among the blossoms blown.
Then thus again the brilliance feminine:
'Too frail of heart! for this lost nymph of thine,
'Free as the air, invisibly, she strays
'About these thornless wilds; her pleasant days   95
'She tastes unseen; unseen her nimble feet
'Leave traces in the grass and flowers sweet;
'From weary tendrils, and bow'd branches green,
'She plucks the fruit unseen, she bathes unseen:

63 *Proserpine:* In Sicily, Proserpine was carried off by Pluto to the
Underworld. 67 *Stoop'd:* swooping down. 74 *Apollo:* Greek god of
the sun, poetry, and music. 78 *Phœbean dart:* sunbeam. 81 *Star of
Lethe:* Hermes conducted dead souls into the Underworld, of which
Lethe was one of the rivers. 87 *Planet:* (i) wanderer, messenger,
(ii) Mercury, Roman name of Hermes.

'And by my power is her beauty veil'd   100
'To keep it unaffronted, unassail'd
'By the love-glances of unlovely eyes,
'Of Satyrs, Fauns, and blear'd Silenus' sighs.
'Pale grew her immortality, for woe
'Of all these lovers, and she grieved so   105
'I took compassion on her, bade her steep
'Her hair in weïrd syrops, that would keep
'Her loveliness invisible, yet free
'To wander as she loves, in liberty.
'Thou shalt behold her, Hermes, thou alone,   110
'If thou wilt, as thou swearest, grant my boon!'
Then, once again, the charmed God began
An oath, and through the serpent's ears it ran
Warm, tremulous, devout, psalterian.
Ravish'd, she lifted her Circean head,   115
Blush'd a live damask, and swift-lisping said,
'I was a woman, let me have once more
'A woman's shape, and charming as before.
'I love a youth of Corinth—O the bliss!
'Give me my woman's form, and place me where he is.   120
'Stoop, Hermes, let me breathe upon thy brow,
'And thou shalt see thy sweet nymph even now.'
The God on half-shut feathers sank serene,
She breath'd upon his eyes, and swift was seen
Of both the guarded nymph near-smiling on the green.   125
It was no dream; or say a dream it was,
Real are the dreams of Gods, and smoothly pass
Their pleasures in a long immortal dream.
One warm, flush'd moment, hovering, it might seem
Dash'd by the wood-nymph's beauty, so he burn'd;   130
Then, lighting on the printless verdure, turn'd
To the swoon'd serpent, and with languid arm,
Delicate, put to proof the lythe Caducean charm.
So done, upon the nymph his eyes he bent
Full of adoring tears and blandishment,   135
And towards her stept: she, like a moon in wane,
Faded before him, cower'd, nor could restrain

103 *Silenus:* tipsy old attendant of Bacchus, the Greek wine-god.
114 *Psalterian:* sounding like a psaltery or dulcimer. 115 *Circean:*
temptingly beautiful, like that of Circe in Greek mythology. 119
Corinth: ancient Greek city, on isthmus between Central Greece and the
Peloponnese; a byword for luxury and profligacy. 131 *Printless:* un-
marked by the god's feet. 133 *Caducean:* The caduceus was Hermes's
wand, a rod entwined with two snakes.

Her fearful sobs, self-folding like a flower
That faints into itself at evening hour:
But the God fostering her chilled hand,   140
She felt the warmth, her eyelids open'd bland,
And, like new flowers at morning song of bees,
Bloom'd, and gave up her honey to the lees.
Into the green-recessed woods they flew;
Nor grew they pale, as mortal lovers do.   145

    Left to herself, the serpent now began
To change; her elfin blood in madness ran,
Her mouth foam'd, and the grass, therewith besprent,
Wither'd at dew so sweet and virulent;
Her eyes in torture fix'd, and anguish drear,   150
Hot, glaz'd, and wide, with lid-lashes all sear,
Flash'd phosphor and sharp sparks, without one cooling tear.
The colours all inflam'd throughout her train,
She writh'd about, convuls'd with scarlet pain:
A deep volcanian yellow took the place   155
Of all her milder-mooned body's grace;
And, as the lava ravishes the mead,
Spoilt all her silver mail, and golden brede,
Made gloom of all her frecklings, streaks and bars,
Eclips'd her crescents, and lick'd up her stars: 160
So that, in moments few, she was undrest
Of all her sapphires, greens, and amethyst,
And rubious-argent: of all these bereft,
Nothing but pain and ugliness were left.
Still shone her crown; that vanish'd, also she   165
Melted and disappear'd as suddenly;
And in the air, her new voice luting soft,
Cried, ' Lycius! gentle Lycius! '—Borne aloft
With the bright mists about the mountains hoar
These words dissolv'd: Crete's forests heard no more.   170

    Whither fled Lamia, now a lady bright,
A full-born beauty new and exquisite?
She fled into that valley they pass o'er
Who go to Corinth from Cenchreas' shore;
And rested at the foot of those wild hills,   175
The rugged founts of the Peræan rills,

148 *Besprent:* sprinkled.   151 *Sear:* dry, scorched.   158 *Brede:* reticul-
ation.   163 *Rubious-argent:* ruby-red and silver.   174 *Cenchreas' shore:*
Cenchreae, eastern harbour of Corinth.   176 *Peræan rills:* hot springs
to the north of the isthmus.

And of that other ridge whose barren back
Stretches, with all its mist and cloudy rack,
South-westward to Cleone. There she stood
About a young bird's flutter from a wood,   180
Fair, on a sloping green of mossy tread,
By a clear pool, wherein she passioned
To see herself escap'd from so sore ills,
While her robes flaunted with the daffodils.

Ah, happy Lycius!—for she was a maid   185
More beautiful than ever twisted braid,
Or sigh'd, or blush'd, or on spring-flowered lea
Spread a green kirtle to the minstrelsy:
A virgin purest lipp'd, yet in the lore
Of love deep learned to the red heart's core: 190
Not one hour old, yet of sciential brain
To unperplex bliss from its neighbour pain;
Define their pettish limits, and estrange
Their points of contact, and swift counterchange;
Intrigue with the specious chaos, and dispart   195
Its most ambiguous atoms with sure art;
As though in Cupid's college she had spent
Sweet days a lovely graduate, still unshent,
And kept his rosy terms in idle languishment.

Why this fair creature chose so faerily   200
By the wayside to linger, we shall see;
But first 'tis fit to tell how she could muse
And dream, when in the serpent prison-house,
Of all she list, strange or magnificent:
How, ever, where she will'd, her spirit went;   205
Whether to faint Elysium, or where
Down through tress-lifting waves the Nereids fair
Wind into Thetis' bower by many a pearly stair;
Or where God Bacchus drains his cups divine,
Stretch'd out, at ease, beneath a glutinous pine;   210
Or where in Pluto's gardens palatine
Mulciber's columns gleam in far piazzian line.

179 *Cleone:* Cleona(e), a village between Corinth and Argos. 182
Passioned: marvelled. 191 *Sciential:* knowledgeable, clever. 195 *The
specious chaos:* the attractive but confusing surface of things; *dispart:*
separate. 198 *Graduate:* a graduate undergraduate! *Unshent:* un-
disgraced, irreproachable. 206 *Elysium:* the heaven of Greek mythol-
ogy. 207 *Nereids:* sea-nymphs. 208 *Thetis:* a Nereid, married to
Peleus and loved by Zeus. 211 *Pluto:* Greek god of the Underworld;
palatine: royal. 212 *Mulciber:* Vulcan, Roman god of fire and smithies.

And sometimes into cities she would send
Her dream, with feast and rioting to blend;
And once, while among mortals dreaming thus,   215
She saw the young Corinthian Lycius
Charioting foremost in the envious race,
Like a young Jove with calm uneager face,
And fell into a swooning love of him.
Now on the moth-time of that evening dim   220
He would return that way, as well she knew,
To Corinth from the shore; for freshly blew
The eastern soft wind, and his galley now
Grated the quaystones with her brazen prow
In port Cenchreas, from Egina isle   225
Fresh anchor'd; whither he had been awhile
To sacrifice to Jove, whose temple there
Waits with high marble doors for blood and incense rare.
Jove heard his vows, and better'd his desire;
For by some freakful chance he made retire   230
From his companions, and set forth to walk,
Perhaps grown wearied of their Corinth talk:
Over the solitary hills he fared,
Thoughtless at first, but ere eve's star appeared
His phantasy was lost, where reason fades,   235
In the calm'd twilight of Platonic shades.
Lamia beheld him coming, near, more near—
Close to her passing, in indifference drear,
His silent sandals swept the mossy green;
So neighbour'd to him, and yet so unseen   240
She stood: he pass'd, shut up in mysteries,
His mind wrapp'd like his mantle, while her eyes
Follow'd his steps, and her neck regal white
Turn'd—syllabling thus, ' Ah, Lycius bright,
' And will you leave me on the hills alone?   245
' Lycius, look back! and be some pity shown.'
He did; not with cold wonder fearingly,
But Orpheus-like at an Eurydice;
For so delicious were the words she sung,
It seem'd he had lov'd them a whole summer long: 250
And soon his eyes had drunk her beauty up,
Leaving no drop in the bewildering cup,
And still the cup was full,—while he, afraid

217 *Envious:* competitive. 225 *Egina:* the isle of Ægina in the Saronic
Gulf. 236 *Platonic:* i.e. philosophical. 238 *Drear:* empty, blank.
248 i.e. longingly and with love, as Orpheus gazed back at his wife
Eurydice on their way up from the Underworld.

Lest she should vanish ere his lip had paid
Due adoration, thus began to adore;   255
Her soft look growing coy, she saw his chain so sure:
' Leave thee alone! Look back! Ah, Goddess, see
' Whether my eyes can ever turn from thee!
' For pity do not this sad heart belie—
' Even as thou vanishest so shall I die.   260
' Stay! though a Naiad of the rivers, stay!
' To thy far wishes will thy streams obey:
' Stay! though the greenest woods be thy domain,
' Alone they can drink up the morning rain:
' Though a descended Pleiad, will not one   265
' Of thine harmonious sisters keep in tune
' Thy spheres, and as thy silver proxy shine?
' So sweetly to these ravish'd ears of mine
' Came thy sweet greeting, that if thou shouldst fade
' Thy memory will waste me to a shade:—   270
' For pity do not melt! '—' If I should stay,'
Said Lamia, ' here, upon this floor of clay,
' And pain my steps upon these flowers too rough,
' What canst thou say or do of charm enough
' To dull the nice remembrance of my home?   275
' Thou canst not ask me with thee here to roam
' Over these hills and vales, where no joy is,—
' Empty of immortality and bliss!
' Thou art a scholar, Lycius, and must know
' That finer spirits cannot breathe below   280
' In human climes, and live: Alas! poor youth,
' What taste of purer air hast thou to soothe
' My essence? What serener palaces,
' Where I may all my many senses please,
' And by mysterious sleights a hundred thirsts appease?   285
' It cannot be—Adieu! ' So said, she rose
Tiptoe with white arms spread. He, sick to lose
The amorous promise of her lone complain,
Swoon'd, murmuring of love, and pale with pain.
The cruel lady, without any show   290
Of sorrow for her tender favourite's woe,
But rather, if her eyes could brighter be,
With brighter eyes and slow amenity,
Put her new lips to his, and gave afresh

261 Lycius thinks she may be only a spirit. 265 *Pleiad:* star in the
cluster of the Pleiades. 266-7 alluding to the Platonic (or Pythagorean)
idea of the music of the spheres. 293 *Amenity:* gentleness.

The life she had so tangled in her mesh: 295
And as he from one trance was wakening
Into another, she began to sing,
Happy in beauty, life, and love, and every thing,
A song of love, too sweet for earthly lyres,
While, like held breath, the stars drew in their panting fires. 300
And then she whisper'd in such trembling tone,
As those who, safe together met alone
For the first time through many anguish'd days,
Use other speech than looks; bidding him raise
His drooping head, and clear his soul of doubt,   305
For that she was a woman, and without
Any more subtle fluid in her veins
Than throbbing blood, and that the self-same pains
Inhabited her frail-strung heart as his.
And next she wonder'd how his eyes could miss   310
Her face so long in Corinth, where, she said,
She dwelt but half retir'd, and there had led
Days happy as the gold coin could invent
Without the aid of love; yet in content
Till she saw him, as once she pass'd him by,   315
Where 'gainst a column he leant thoughtfully
At Venus' temple porch, 'mid baskets heap'd
Of amorous herbs and flowers, newly reap'd
Late on that eve, as 'twas the night before
The Adonian feast; whereof she saw no more,   320
But wept alone those days, for why should she adore?
Lycius from death awoke into amaze,
To see her still, and singing so sweet lays;
Then from amaze into delight he fell
To hear her whisper woman's lore so well;   325
And every word she spake entic'd him on
To unperplex'd delight and pleasure known.
Let the mad poets say whate'er they please
Of the sweets of Fairies, Peris, Goddesses,
There is not such a treat among them all,   330
Haunters of cavern, lake, and waterfall,
As a real woman, lineal indeed
From Pyrrha's pebbles or old Adam's seed.

320 *Adonian feast:* feast celebrating the death and resurrection of the
young fertility-god Adonis; plants were tended in baskets, then allowed
to wither and thrown into the sea with images of the god.   329 *Peris:*
fairies in Persian mythology.   333 *Pyrrha's pebbles:* in the Greek flood
legend, Deucalion and Pyrrha re-peopled the earth by throwing pebbles
behind them which became human beings.

Thus gentle Lamia judg'd, and judg'd aright,
That Lycius could not love in half a fright, 335
So threw the goddess off, and won his heart
More pleasantly by playing woman's part,
With no more awe than what her beauty gave,
That, while it smote, still guaranteed to save.
Lycius to all made eloquent reply, 340
Marrying to every word a twinborn sigh;
And last, pointing to Corinth, ask'd her sweet,
If 'twas too far that night for her soft feet.
The way was short, for Lamia's eagerness
Made, by a spell, the triple league decrease 345
To a few paces; not at all surmised
By blinded Lycius, so in her comprized.
They pass'd the city gates, he knew not how,
So noiseless, and he never thought to know.

As men talk in a dream, so Corinth all, 350
Throughout her palaces imperial,
And all her populous streets and temples lewd,
Mutter'd, like tempest in the distance brew'd,
To the wide-spreaded night above her towers.
Men, women, rich and poor, in the cool hours, 355
Shuffled their sandals o'er the pavement white,
Companion'd or alone; while many a light
Flared, here and there, from wealthy festivals,
And threw their moving shadows on the walls,
Or found them cluster'd in the corniced shade 360
Of some arch'd temple door, or dusky colonnade.

Muffling his face, of greeting friends in fear,
Her fingers he press'd hard, as one came near
With curl'd gray beard, sharp eyes, and smooth bald crown,
Slow-stepp'd, and robed in philosophic gown: 365
Lycius shrank closer, as they met and past,
Into his mantle, adding wings to haste,
While hurried Lamia trembled: ' Ah,' said he,
' Why do you shudder, love, so ruefully?
' Why does your tender palm dissolve in dew? '— 370
' I'm wearied,' said fair Lamia: ' tell me who
' Is that old man? I cannot bring to mind
' His features:—Lycius! wherefore did you blind
' Yourself from his quick eyes? ' Lycius replied,
' 'Tis Apollonius sage, my trusty guide 375

375 *Apollonius:* Apollonius of Tyana (b. *c.* 4 B.C.), Pythagorean philosopher and mystic.

' And good instructor; but to-night he seems
' The ghost of folly haunting my sweet dreams.'

While yet he spake they had arrived before
A pillar'd porch, with lofty portal door,
Where hung a silver lamp, whose phosphor glow   380
Reflected in the slabbed steps below,
Mild as a star in water; for so new,
And so unsullied was the marble hue,
So through the crystal polish, liquid fine,
Ran the dark veins, that none but feet divine   385
Could e'er have touch'd there. Sounds Æolian
Breath'd from the hinges, as the ample span
Of the wide doors disclos'd a place unknown
Some time to any, but those two alone,
And a few Persian mutes, who that same year   390
Were seen about the markets: none knew where
They could inhabit; the most curious
Were foil'd, who watch'd to trace them to their house:
And but the flitter-winged verse must tell
For truth's sake, what woe afterwards befel,   395
'Twould humour many a heart to leave them thus,
Shut from the busy world of more incredulous.

PART TWO

Love in a hut, with water and a crust,
Is—Love, forgive us!—cinders, ashes, dust;
Love in a palace is perhaps at last
More grievous torment than a hermit's fast:—
That is a doubtful tale from faery land,   5
Hard for the non-elect to understand.
Had Lycius liv'd to hand his story down,
He might have given the moral a fresh frown,
Or clench'd it quite: but too short was their bliss
To breed distrust and hate, that make the soft voice hiss.   10
Besides, there, nightly, with terrific glare,
Love, jealous grown of so complete a pair,
Hover'd and buzz'd his wings, with fearful roar,
Above the lintel of their chamber door,
And down the passage cast a glow upon the floor.   15

For all this came a ruin: side by side
They were enthroned, in the even tide,

386 *Æolian:* as from an Æolian harp; caused by the wind.

Upon a couch, near to a curtaining
Whose airy texture, from a golden string,
Floated into the room, and let appear   20
Unveil'd the summer heaven, blue and clear,
Betwixt two marble shafts:—there they reposed,
Where use had made it sweet, with eyelids closed,
Saving a tythe which love still open kept,
That they might see each other while they almost slept;   25
When from the slope side of a suburb hill,
Deafening the swallow's twitter, came a thrill
Of trumpets—Lycius started—the sounds fled,
But left a thought a-buzzing in his head.
For the first time, since first he harbour'd in   30
That purple-lined palace of sweet sin,
His spirit pass'd beyond its golden bourn
Into the noisy world almost forsworn.
The lady, ever watchful, penetrant,
Saw this with pain, so arguing a want   35
Of something more, more than her empery
Of joys; and she began to moan and sigh
Because he mused beyond her, knowing well
That but a moment's thought is passion's passing bell.
'Why do you sigh, fair creature?' whisper'd he: 40
'Why do you think?' return'd she tenderly:
'You have deserted me;—where am I now?
'Not in your heart while care weighs on your brow:
'No, no, you have dismiss'd me; and I go
'From your breast houseless: ay, it must be so.'   45
He answer'd, bending to her open eyes,
Where he was mirror'd small in paradise,
'My silver planet, both of eve and morn!
'Why will you plead yourself so sad forlorn,
'While I am striving how to fill my heart   50
'With deeper crimson, and a double smart?
'How to entangle, trammel up and snare
'Your soul in mine, and labyrinth you there
'Like the hid scent in an unbudded rose?
'Aye, a sweet kiss—you see your mighty woes.   55
'My thoughts! shall I unveil them? Listen then!
'What mortal hath a prize, that other men
'May be confounded and abash'd withal,
'But lets it sometimes pace abroad majestical,

24 *Tythe:* tenth part. 32 *Bourn:* limit. 36 *Empery:* dominion. 48
i.e. Venus, goddess of love.

'And triumph, as in thee I should rejoice   60
'Amid the hoarse alarm of Corinth's voice.
'Let my foes choke, and my friends shout afar,
'While through the thronged streets your bridal car
'Wheels round its dazzling spokes.'—The lady's cheek
Trembled; she nothing said, but, pale and meek,   65
Arose and knelt before him, wept a rain
Of sorrows at his words; at last with pain
Beseeching him, the while his hand she wrung,
To change his purpose. He thereat was stung,
Perverse, with stronger fancy to reclaim   70
Her wild and timid nature to his aim:
Besides, for all his love, in self despite,
Against his better self, he took delight
Luxurious in her sorrows, soft and new.
His passion, cruel grown, took on a hue   75
Fierce and sanguineous as 'twas possible
In one whose brow had no dark veins to swell.
Fine was the mitigated fury, like
Apollo's presence when in act to strike
The serpent—Ha, the serpent! certes, she   80
Was none. She burnt, she lov'd the tyranny,
And, all subdued, consented to the hour
When to the bridal he should lead his paramour.
Whispering in midnight silence, said the youth,
'Sure some sweet name thou hast, though, by my truth,   85
'I have not ask'd it, ever thinking thee
'Not mortal, but of heavenly progeny,
'As still I do. Hast any mortal name,
'Fit appellation for this dazzling frame?
'Or friends or kinsfolk on the citied earth,   90
'To share our marriage feast and nuptial mirth?'
'I have no friends,' said Lamia, 'no, not one;
'My presence in wide Corinth hardly known:
'My parents' bones are in their dusty urns
'Sepulchred, where no kindled incense burns,   95
'Seeing all their luckless race are dead, save me,
'And I neglect the holy rite for thee.
'Even as you list invite your many guests;
'But if, as now it seems, your vision rests
'With any pleasure on me, do not bid   100
'Old Apollonius—from him keep me hid.'

76 *Sanguineous:* blood-red. 79-80 Apollo destroyed the Python at the
shrine of Delphi.

Lycius, perplex'd at words so blind and blank,
Made close inquiry; from whose touch she shrank,
Feigning a sleep; and he to the dull shade
Of deep sleep in a moment was betray'd.   105

It was the custom then to bring away
The bride from home at blushing shut of day,
Veil'd, in a chariot, heralded along
By strewn flowers, torches, and a marriage song,
With other pageants: but this fair unknown   110
Had not a friend. So being left alone,
(Lycius was gone to summon all his kin)
And knowing surely she could never win
His foolish heart from its mad pompousness,
She set herself, high-thoughted, how to dress   115
The misery in fit magnificence.
She did so, but 'tis doubtful how and whence
Came, and who were her subtle servitors.
About the halls, and to and from the doors,
There was a noise of wings till in short space   120
The glowing banquet-room shone with wide-arched grace.
A haunting music, sole perhaps and lone
Supportress of the faery-roof, made moan
Throughout, as fearful the whole charm might fade.
Fresh carved cedar, mimicking a glade   125
Of palm and plantain, met from either side,
High in the midst, in honour of the bride:
Two palms and then two plantains, and so on,
From either side their stems branch'd one to one
All down the aisled place; and beneath all   130
There ran a stream of lamps straight on from wall to wall.
So canopied, lay an untasted feast
Teeming with odours. Lamia, regal drest,
Silently paced about, and as she went,
In pale contented sort of discontent,   135
Mission'd her viewless servants to enrich
The fretted splendour of each nook and niche.
Between the tree-stems, marbled plain at first,
Came jasper pannels; then, anon, there burst
Forth creeping imagery of slighter trees,   140
And with the larger wove in small intricacies.
Approving all, she faded at self-will,
And shut the chamber up, close, hush'd and still,

114 *Pompousness:* desire for show.

Complete and ready for the revels rude,
When dreadful guests would come to spoil her solitude. 145

    The day appear'd, and all the gossip rout.
O senseless Lycius! Madman! wherefore flout
The silent-blessing fate, warm cloister'd hours,
And show to common eyes these secret bowers?
The herd approach'd; each guest, with busy brain, 150
Arriving at the portal, gaz'd amain,
And enter'd marveling: for they knew the street,
Remember'd it from childhood all complete
Without a gap, yet ne'er before had seen
That royal porch, that high-built fair demesne; 155
So in they hurried all, maz'd, curious and keen:
Save one, who look'd thereon with eye severe,
And with calm-planted steps walk'd in austere;
'Twas Apollonius: something too he laugh'd,
As though some knotty problem, that had daft 160
His patient thought, had now begun to thaw,
And solve and melt:—'twas just as he foresaw.

    He met within the murmurous vestibule
His young disciple. ' 'Tis no common rule,
' Lycius,' said he, ' for uninvited guest 165
' To force himself upon you, and infest
' With an unbidden presence the bright throng
' Of younger friends; yet must I do this wrong,
' And you forgive me.' Lycius blush'd, and led
The old man through the inner doors broad-spread; 170
With reconciling words and courteous mien
Turning into sweet milk the sophist's spleen.

    Of wealthy lustre was the banquet-room,
Fill'd with pervading brilliance and perfume:
Before each lucid pannel fuming stood 175
A censer fed with myrrh and spiced wood,
Each by a sacred tripod held aloft,
Whose slender feet wide-swerv'd upon the soft
Wool-woofed carpets: fifty wreaths of smoke
From fifty censers their light voyage took 180
To the high roof, still mimick'd as they rose
Along the mirror'd walls by twin-clouds odorous.

155 *Demesne:* property. 160 *Daft:* eluded, thrown off. 172 *Sophist:* ancient Greek teacher of philosophy.

Twelve sphered tables, by silk seats insphered,
High as the level of a man's breast rear'd
On libbard's paws, upheld the heavy gold   185
Of cups and goblets, and the store thrice told
Of Ceres' horn, and, in huge vessels, wine
Come from the gloomy tun with merry shine.
Thus loaded with a feast the tables stood,
Each shrining in the midst the image of a God.   190

   When in an antichamber every guest
Had felt the cold full sponge to pleasure press'd,
By minist'ring slaves, upon his hands and feet,
And fragrant oils with ceremony meet
Pour'd on his hair, they all mov'd to the feast   195
In white robes, and themselves in order placed
Around the silken couches, wondering
Whence all this mighty cost and blaze of wealth could spring.

   Soft went the music the soft air along,
While fluent Greek a vowel'd undersong   200
Kept up among the guests, discoursing low
At first, for scarcely was the wine at flow;
But when the happy vintage touch'd their brains,
Louder they talk, and louder come the strains
Of powerful instruments:—the gorgeous dyes,   205
The space, the splendour of the draperies,
The roof of awful richness, nectarous cheer,
Beautiful slaves, and Lamia's self, appear,
Now, when the wine has done its rosy deed,
And every soul from human trammels freed,   210
No more so strange; for merry wine, sweet wine,
Will make Elysian shades not too fair, too divine.
Soon was God Bacchus at meridian height;
Flush'd were their cheeks, and bright eyes double bright:
Garlands of every green, and every scent   215
From vales deflower'd, or forest-trees branch-rent,
In baskets of bright osier'd gold were brought
High as the handles heap'd, to suit the thought
Of every guest; that each, as he did please,
Might fancy-fit his brows, silk-pillow'd at his ease.   220

   What wreath for Lamia? What for Lycius?
What for the sage, old Apollonius?

185 *Libbard's:* leopard's.   187 *Ceres:* Roman corn-goddess.

Upon her aching forehead be there hung
The leaves of willow and of adder's tongue;
And for the youth, quick, let us strip for him   225
The thyrsus, that his watching eyes may swim
Into forgetfulness; and, for the sage,
Let spear-grass and the spiteful thistle wage
War on his temples. Do not all charms fly
At the mere touch of cold philosophy?   230
There was an awful rainbow once in heaven:
We know her woof, her texture; she is given
In the dull catalogue of common things.
Philosophy will clip an Angel's wings,
Conquer all mysteries by rule and line,   235
Empty the haunted air, and gnomed mine—
Unweave a rainbow, as it erewhile made
The tender-person'd Lamia melt into a shade.

       By her glad Lycius sitting, in chief place,
Scarce saw in all the room another face,   240
Till, checking his love trance, a cup he took
Full brimm'd, and opposite sent forth a look
'Cross the broad table, to beseech a glance
From his old teacher's wrinkled countenance,
And pledge him. The bald-head philosopher   245
Had fix'd his eye, without a twinkle or stir
Full on the alarmed beauty of the bride,
Brow-beating her fair form, and troubling her sweet pride.
Lycius then press'd her hand, with devout touch,
As pale it lay upon the rosy couch: 250
'Twas icy, and the cold ran through his veins;
Then sudden it grew hot, and all the pains
Of an unnatural heat shot to his heart.
'Lamia, what means this? Wherefore dost thou start?
'Know'st thou that man?' Poor Lamia answer'd not.   255
He gaz'd into her eyes, and not a jot
Own'd they the lovelorn piteous appeal:
More, more he gaz'd: his human senses reel:
Some hungry spell that loveliness absorbs;
There was no recognition in those orbs.   260
'Lamia!' he cried—and no soft-toned reply.

224 *Adder's tongue:* kind of fern.   226 *Thyrsus:* ornamental staff
wreathed with ivy and vine, carried by Bacchus and his votaries.
230 *Philosophy:* natural philosophy, i.e. science. In the following
lines Keats is thinking of Newton's experiments with the prism.

The many heard, and the loud revelry
Grew hush; the stately music no more breathes;
The myrtle sicken'd in a thousand wreaths.
By faint degrees, voice, lute, and pleasure ceased;   265
A deadly silence step by step increased,
Until it seem'd a horrid presence there,
And not a man but felt the terror in his hair.
'Lamia!' he shriek'd; and nothing but the shriek
With its sad echo did the silence break.   270
'Begone, foul dream!' he cried, gazing again
In the bride's face, where now no azure vein
Wander'd on fair-spaced temples; no soft bloom
Misted the cheek; no passion to illume
The deep-recessed vision:—all was blight;   275
Lamia, no longer fair, there sat a deadly white.
'Shut, shut those juggling eyes, thou ruthless man!
'Turn them aside, wretch! or the righteous ban
'Of all the Gods, whose dreadful images
'Here represent their shadowy presences,   280
'May pierce them on the sudden with the thorn
'Of painful blindness; leaving thee forlorn,
'In trembling dotage to the feeblest fright
'Of conscience, for their long offended might,
'For all thine impious proud-heart sophistries,   285
'Unlawful magic, and enticing lies.
'Corinthians! look upon that gray-beard wretch!
'Mark how, possess'd, his lashless eyelids stretch
'Around his demon eyes! Corinthians, see!
'My sweet bride withers at their potency.'   290
'Fool!' said the sophist, in an under-tone
Gruff with contempt; which a death-nighing moan
From Lycius answer'd, as heart-struck and lost,
He sank supine beside the aching ghost.
'Fool! Fool!' repeated he, while his eyes still   295
Relented not, nor mov'd; 'from every ill
'Of life have I preserv'd thee to this day,
'And shall I see thee made a serpent's prey?'
Then Lamia breath'd death breath; the sophist's eye,
Like a sharp spear, went through her utterly,   300
Keen, cruel, perceant, stinging: she, as well
As her weak hand could any meaning tell,
Motion'd him to be silent; vainly so,
He look'd and look'd again a level—No!

278 *Ban:* curse. 301 *Perceant:* piercing.

'A serpent!' echoed he; no sooner said,   305
Than with a frightful scream she vanished:
And Lycius' arms were empty of delight,
As were his limbs of life, from that same night.
On the high couch he lay!—his friends came round—
Supported him—no pulse, or breath they found,   310
And, in its marriage robe, the heavy body wound.

"Philostratus. in his fourth book *de Vita Appollonii*, hath a memorable
instance in this kind, which I may not omit, of one Menippus Lycius, a
young man twenty-five years of age, that going betwixt Cenchreas and
Corinth, met such a phantasm in the habit of a fair gentlewoman, which
taking him by the hand, carried him home to her house, in the suburbs
of Corinth and told him she was a Phœnician by birth, and if he would
tarry with her, he should hear her sing and play, and drink such wine as
never any drank, and no man should molest him; but she, being fair and
lovely, would live and die with him, that was fair and lovely to behold.
The young man, a philosopher, otherwise staid and discreet, able to mod-
erate his passions, though not this of love, tarried with her a while to his
great content, and at last married her, to whose wedding, amongst
other guests, came Apollonius; who, by some probable conjectures,
found her out to be a serpent, a lamia; and that all her furniture was,
like Tantalus' gold, described by Homer, no substance but mere illusions.
When she saw herself descried, she wept, and desired Apollonius to be
silent, but he would not be moved, and thereupon she, plate, house,
and all that was in it, vanished in an instant: many thousands took
notice of this fact, for it was done in the midst of Greece."
                    Burton's *Anatomy of Melancholy* Part 3. Sect. 2.
                                Memb. 1. Subs. 1.   (K.)

THE EVE OF SAINT AGNES

I

Saint Agnes' Eve—Ah, bitter chill it was!
The owl, for all his feathers, was a-cold;
The hare limp'd trembling through the frozen grass,
And silent was the flock in woolly fold:
Numb were the Beadsman's fingers, while he told   5
His rosary, and while his frosted breath,

1 *St. Agnes' Eve:* 20th January. St. Agnes, martyred at the age of
thirteen, is the patron of young virgins. 5 *Beadsman:* pensioner whose
duty is to pray for his benefactors; *told:* counted.

Like pious incense from a censer old,
Seem'd taking flight for heaven, without a death,
Past the sweet Virgin's picture, while his prayer he saith.

II

His prayer he saith, this patient, holy man;   10
Then takes his lamp, and riseth from his knees,
And back returneth, meagre, barefoot, wan,
Along the chapel aisle by slow degrees:
The sculptur'd dead, on each side, seem to freeze,
Emprison'd in black, purgatorial rails: 15
Knights, ladies, praying in dumb orat'ries,
He passeth by; and his weak spirit fails
To think how they may ache in icy hoods and mails.

III

Northward he turneth through a little door,
And scarce three steps, ere Music's golden tongue   20
Flatter'd to tears this aged man and poor;
But no—already had his deathbell rung;
The joys of all his life were said and sung:
His was harsh penance on St. Agnes' Eve:
Another way he went, and soon among   25
Rough ashes sat he for his soul's reprieve,
And all night kept awake, for sinners' sake to grieve.

IV

That ancient Beadsman heard the prelude soft;
And so it chanc'd, for many a door was wide,
From hurry to and fro. Soon, up aloft,   30
The silver, snarling trumpets 'gan to chide:
The level chambers, ready with their pride,
Were glowing to receive a thousand guests:
The carved angels, ever eager-eyed,
Star'd, where upon their heads the cornice rests,   35
With hair blown back, and wings put cross-wise on their breasts.

V

At length burst in the argent revelry,
With plume, tiara, and all rich array,
Numerous as shadows haunting faerily
The brain, new stuff'd, in youth, with triumphs gay   40
Of old romance. These let us wish away,
And turn, sole-thoughted, to one Lady there,

37 *Argent:* silver.

Whose heart had brooded, all that wintry day,
On love, and wing'd St. Agnes' saintly care,
As she had heard old dames full many times declare.   45

VI

They told her how, upon St. Agnes' Eve,
Young virgins might have visions of delight,
And soft adorings from their loves receive
Upon the honey'd middle of the night,
If ceremonies due they did aright;   50
As, supperless to bed they must retire,
And couch supine their beauties, lilly white;
Nor look behind, nor sideways, but require
Of Heaven with upward eyes for all that they desire.

VII

Full of this whim was thoughtful Madeline: 55
The music, yearning like a God in pain,
She scarcely heard: her maiden eyes divine,
Fix'd on the floor, saw many a sweeping train
Pass by—she heeded not at all: in vain
Came many a tiptoe, amorous cavalier,   60
And back retir'd; not cool'd by high disdain,
But she saw not: her heart was otherwhere:
She sigh'd for Agnes' dreams, the sweetest of the year.

VIII

She danc'd along with vague, regardless eyes,
Anxious her lips, her breathing quick and short: 65
The hallow'd hour was near at hand: she sighs
Amid the timbrels, and the throng'd resort
Of whisperers in anger, or in sport;
'Mid looks of love, defiance, hate, and scorn,
Hoodwink'd with faery fancy; all amort,   70
Save to St. Agnes and her lambs unshorn,
And all the bliss to be before to-morrow morn.

IX

So, purposing each moment to retire,
She linger'd still. Meantime, across the moors,
Had come young Porphyro, with heart on fire   75
For Madeline. Beside the portal doors,
Buttress'd from moonlight, stands he, and implores
All saints to give him sight of Madeline,

67 *Timbrels:* tambourines. 70 *Amort:* spiritless.

But for one moment in the tedious hours,
That he might gaze and worship all unseen;   80
Perchance speak, kneel, touch, kiss—in sooth such things have
   been.

                          X
He ventures in: let no buzz'd whisper tell:
All eyes be muffled, or a hundred swords
Will storm his heart, Love's fev'rous citadel:
For him, those chambers held barbarian hordes,   85
Hyena foemen, and hot-blooded lords,
Whose very dogs would execrations howl
Against his lineage: not one breast affords
Him any mercy, in that mansion foul,
Save one old beldame, weak in body and in soul.   90

                          XI
Ah, happy chance! the aged creature came,
Shuffling along with ivory-headed wand,
To where he stood, hid from the torch's flame,
Behind a broad hall-pillar, far beyond
The sound of merriment and chorus bland: 95
He startled her, but soon she knew his face,
And grasp'd his fingers in her palsied hand,
Saying, ' Mercy, Porphyro! hie thee from this place:
' They are all here to-night, the whole blood-thirsty race!

                          XII
' Get hence! get hence! there's dwarfish Hildebrand;   100
' He had a fever late, and in the fit
' He cursed thee and thine, both house and land:
' Then there's that old Lord Maurice, not a whit
' More tame for his gray hairs—Alas me! flit!
' Flit like a ghost away.'—' Ah, Gossip dear,   105
' We're safe enough; here in this arm-chair sit,
' And tell me how '—' Good Saints! not here, not here;
' Follow me, child, or else these stones will be thy bier.'

                          XIII
He follow'd through a lowly arched way,
Brushing the cobwebs with his lofty plume,   110
And as she mutter'd ' Well-a—well-a-day! '
He found him in a little moonlight room,

90 *Beldame:* old woman.   105 *Gossip:* godmother.

Pale, lattic'd, chill, and silent as a tomb.
' Now tell me where is Madeline,' said he,
' O tell me, Angela, by the holy loom   115
' Which none but secret sisterhood may see,
' When they St. Agnes' wool are weaving piously.'

XIV

' St. Agnes! Ah! it is St. Agnes' Eve—
' Yet men will murder upon holy days:
' Thou must hold water in a witch's sieve,   120
' And be liege-lord of all the Elves and Fays,
' To venture so: it fills me with amaze
' To see thee, Porphyro!—St. Agnes' Eve!
' God's help! my lady fair the conjuror plays
' This very night: good angels her deceive!   125
' But let me laugh awhile, I've mickle time to grieve.'

XV

Feebly she laugheth in the languid moon,
While Porphyro upon her face doth look,
Like puzzled urchin on an aged crone
Who keepeth clos'd a wond'rous riddle-book,   130
As spectacled she sits in chimney nook.
But soon his eyes grew brilliant, when she told
His lady's purpose; and he scarce could brook
Tears, at the thought of those enchantments cold,
And Madeline asleep in lap of legends old.   135

XVI

Sudden a thought came like a full-blown rose,
Flushing his brow, and in his pained heart
Made purple riot: then doth he propose
A stratagem, that makes the beldame start:
' A cruel man and impious thou art: 140
' Sweet lady, let her pray, and sleep, and dream
' Alone with her good angels, far apart
' From wicked men like thee. Go, go!—I deem
' Thou canst not surely be the same that thou didst seem.'

XVII

' I will not harm her, by all saints I swear,'   145
Quoth Porphyro: ' O may I ne'er find grace
' When my weak voice shall whisper its last prayer,
' If one of her soft ringlets I displace,

117 refers to wool, woven by nuns, from lambs offered as a sacrifice on
St. Agnes' Day. 126 *Mickle:* much. 133 *Brook:* forbear.

'Or look with ruffian passion in her face:
'Good Angela, believe me by these tears;   150
'Or I will, even in a moment's space,
'Awake, with horrid shout, my foemen's ears,
'And beard them, though they be more fang'd than wolves
    and bears.'

XVIII

'Ah! why wilt thou affright a feeble soul?
'A poor, weak, palsy-stricken, churchyard thing,   155
'Whose passing-bell may ere the midnight toll;
'Whose prayers for thee, each morn and evening,
'Were never miss'd.'—Thus plaining, doth she bring
A gentler speech from burning Porphyro;
So woful, and of such deep sorrowing,   160
That Angela gives promise she will do
Whatever he shall wish, betide her weal or woe.

XIX

Which was, to lead him, in close secrecy,
Even to Madeline's chamber, and there hide
Him in a closet, of such privacy   165
That he might see her beauty unespied,
And win perhaps that night a peerless bride,
While legion'd faeries pac'd the coverlet,
And pale enchantment held her sleepy-eyed.
Never on such a night have lovers met,   170
Since Merlin paid his Demon all the monstrous debt.

XX

'It shall be as thou wishest,' said the Dame:
'All cates and dainties shall be stored there
'Quickly on this feast-night: by the tambour frame
'Her own lute thou wilt see: no time to spare,   175
'For I am slow and feeble, and scarce dare
'On such a catering trust my dizzy head.
'Wait here, my child, with patience; kneel in prayer
'The while: Ah! thou must needs the lady wed,
'Or may I never leave my grave among the dead.'   180

158 *Plaining:* complaining. 171 The enchanter Merlin in Celtic mythology is 'monstrous' because his father was the Devil. The 'debt' is paid presumably when he is beguiled and destroyed by Vivien. 173 *Cates:* delicacies. 174 *Tambour frame:* drum-like frame used in embroidery.

XXI

So saying, she hobbled off with busy fear.
The lover's endless minutes slowly pass'd;
The dame return'd, and whisper'd in his ear
To follow her; with aged eyes aghast
From fright of dim espial. Safe at last,   185
Through many a dusky gallery, they gain
The maiden's chamber, silken, hush'd, and chaste;
Where Porphyro took covert, pleas'd amain.
His poor guide hurried back with agues in her brain.

XXII

Her falt'ring hand upon the balustrade,   190
Old Angela was feeling for the stair,
When Madeline, St. Agnes' charmed maid,
Rose, like a mission'd spirit, unaware:
With silver taper's light, and pious care,
She turn'd, and down the aged gossip led   195
To a safe level matting. Now prepare,
Young Porphyro, for gazing on that bed;
She comes, she comes again, like ring-dove fray'd and fled.

XXIII

Out went the taper as she hurried in;
Its little smoke, in pallid moonshine, died: 200
She clos'd the door, she panted, all akin
To spirits of the air, and visions wide:
No uttered syllable, or, woe betide!
But to her heart, her heart was voluble,
Paining with eloquence her balmy side;   205
As though a tongueless nightingale should swell
Her throat in vain, and die, heart-stifled, in her dell.

XXIV

A casement high and triple-arch'd there was,
All garlanded with carven imag'ries
Of fruits, and flowers, and bunches of knot-grass,   210
And diamonded with panes of quaint device,
Innumerable of stains and splendid dyes,
As are the tiger-moth's deep-damask'd wings;
And in the midst, 'mong thousand heraldries,
And twilight saints, and dim emblazonings,   215
A shielded scutcheon blush'd with blood of queens and kings.

198 *Fray'd:* frightened. 216 *Scutcheon:* escutcheon, shield with armorial bearings.

XXV

Full on this casement shone the wintry moon,
And threw warm gules on Madeline's fair breast,
As down she knelt for heaven's grace and boon;
Rose-bloom fell on her hands, together prest,   220
And on her silver cross soft amethyst,
And on her hair a glory, like a saint:
She seem'd a splendid angel, newly drest,
Save wings, for heaven:—Porphyro grew faint:
She knelt, so pure a thing, so free from mortal taint.   225

XXVI

Anon his heart revives: her vespers done,
Of all its wreathed pearls her hair she frees;
Unclasps her warmed jewels one by one;
Loosens her fragrant boddice; by degrees
Her rich attire creeps rustling to her knees: 230
Half-hidden, like a mermaid in sea-weed,
Pensive awhile she dreams awake, and sees,
In fancy, fair St. Agnes in her bed,
But dares not look behind, or all the charm is fled.

XXVII

Soon, trembling in her soft and chilly nest,   235
In sort of wakeful swoon, perplex'd she lay,
Until the poppied warmth of sleep oppress'd
Her soothed limbs, and soul fatigued away;
Flown, like a thought, until the morrow-day;
Blissfully haven'd both from joy and pain: 240
Clasp'd like a missal where swart Paynims pray;
Blinded alike from sunshine and from rain,
As though a rose should shut, and be a bud again.

XXVIII

Stol'n to this paradise, and so entranced,
Porphyro gazed upon her empty dress,   245
And listen'd to her breathing, if it chanced
To wake into a slumberous tenderness;
Which when he heard, that minute did he bless,
And breath'd himself: then from the closet crept,
Noiseless as fear in a wide wilderness,   250
And over the hush'd carpet, silent, stept,
And 'tween the curtains peep'd, where, lo!—how fast she slept.

218 *Gules:* red (heraldic term).   241 *Swart Paynims:* swarthy pagans
(Saracens).

XXIX

Then by the bed-side, where the faded moon
Made a dim, silver twilight, soft he set
A table, and, half anguish'd, threw thereon   255
A cloth of woven crimson, gold, and jet:—
O for some drowsy Morphean amulet!
The boisterous, midnight, festive clarion,
The kettle-drum, and far-heard clarinet,
Affray his ears, though but in dying tone:—   260
The hall door shuts again, and all the noise is gone.

XXX

And still she slept an azure-lidded sleep,
In blanched linen, smooth, and lavender'd,
While he from forth the closet brought a heap
Of candied apple, quince, and plum, and gourd;   265
With jellies soother than the creamy curd,
And lucent syrops, tinct with cinnamon;
Manna and dates, in argosy transferr'd
From Fez; and spiced dainties, every one,
From silken Samarcand to cedar'd Lebanon.   270

XXXI

These delicates he heap'd with glowing hand
On golden dishes and in baskets bright
Of wreathed silver: sumptuous they stand
In the retired quiet of the night,
Filling the chilly room with perfume light.—   275
' And now, my love, my seraph fair, awake!
' Thou art my heaven, and I thine eremite:
' Open thine eyes, for meek St. Agnes' sake,
' Or I shall drowse beside thee, so my soul doth ache.'

XXXII

Thus whispering, his warm, unnerved arm   280
Sank in her pillow. Shaded was her dream
By the dusk curtains:—'twas a midnight charm
Impossible to melt as iced stream:

257 *Morphean:* Morpheus was the Greek god of dreams. 266 *Soother:*
more smooth. 267 *Lucent:* translucent. 269 *Fez:* city in Morocco.
270 Samarcand, city in central Asia (now in the Uzbek S.S.R.), was on
the ancient silk-route from China. 277 *Eremite:* hermit, holy man.

The lustrous salvers in the moonlight gleam;
Broad golden fringe upon the carpet lies: 285
It seem'd he never, never could redeem
From such a stedfast spell his lady's eyes;
So mus'd awhile, entoil'd in woofed phantasies.

XXXIII

Awakening up, he took her hollow lute,—
Tumultuous,—and, in chords that tenderest be, 290
He play'd an ancient ditty, long since mute,
In Provence call'd, ' La belle dame sans mercy: '
Close to her ear touching the melody;—
Wherewith disturb'd, she utter'd a soft moan:
He ceased—she panted quick—and suddenly 295
Her blue affrayed eyes wide open shone:
Upon his knees he sank, pale as smooth-sculptured stone.

XXXIV

Her eyes were open, but she still beheld,
Now wide awake, the vision of her sleep:
There was a painful change, that nigh expell'd 300
The blisses of her dream so pure and deep
At which fair Madeline began to weep,
And moan forth witless words with many a sigh;
While still her gaze on Porphyro would keep;
Who knelt, with joined hands and piteous eye, 305
Fearing to move or speak, she look'd so dreamingly.

XXXV

' Ah, Porphyro! ' said she, ' but even now
' Thy voice was at sweet tremble in mine ear,
' Made tuneable with every sweetest vow;
' And those sad eyes were spiritual and clear: 310
' How chang'd thou art! how pallid, chill, and drear!
' Give me that voice again, my Porphyro,
' Those looks immortal, those complainings dear!
' Oh leave me not in this eternal woe,
' For if thou diest, my Love, I know not where to go.' 315

XXXVI

Beyond a mortal man impassion'd far
At these voluptuous accents, he arose,
Ethereal, flush'd, and like a throbbing star
Seen 'mid the sapphire heaven's deep repose

288 *Woofed:* woven.

Into her dream he melted, as the rose   320
Blendeth its odour with the violet,—
Solution sweet: meantime the frost-wind blows
Like Love's alarum pattering the sharp sleet
Against the window-panes; St. Agnes' moon hath set.

XXXVII

'Tis dark: quick pattereth the flaw-blown sleet: 325
' This is no dream, my bride, my Madeline! '
'Tis dark: the iced gusts still rave and beat:
' No dream, alas! alas! and woe is mine!
' Porphyro will leave me here to fade and pine.—
' Cruel! what traitor could thee hither bring?   330
' I curse not, for my heart is lost in thine,
' Though thou forsakest a deceived thing;—
' A dove forlorn and lost with sick unpruned wing.'

XXXVIII

' My Madeline! sweet dreamer! lovely bride!
' Say, may I be for aye thy vassal blest?   335
' Thy beauty's shield, heart-shap'd and vermeil dyed?
' Ah, silver shrine, here will I take my rest
' After so many hours of toil and quest,
' A famish'd pilgrim,—saved by miracle.
' Though I have found, I will not rob thy nest   340
' Saving of thy sweet self; if thou think'st well
' To trust, fair Madeline, to no rude infidel.

XXXIX

' Hark! 'tis an elfin-storm from faery land,
' Of haggard seeming, but a boon indeed:
' Arise—arise! the morning is at hand;—   345
' The bloated wassaillers will never heed:—
' Let us away, my love, with happy speed;
' There are no ears to hear, or eyes to see,—
' Drown'd all in Rhenish and the sleepy mead:
' Awake! arise! my love, and fearless be,   350
' For o'er the southern moors I have a home for thee.'

XL

She hurried at his words, beset with fears,
For there were sleeping dragons all around,
At glaring watch, perhaps, with ready spears—
Down the wide stairs a darkling way they found.—   355

325 *Flaw-blown:* blown in flurries. 336 *Vermeil:* vermilion. 346
Wassaillers: drinkers, revellers. 349 *Rhenish:* Rhine wine, hock.

In all the house was heard no human sound.
A chain-droop'd lamp was flickering by each door;
The arras, rich with horseman, hawk, and hound,
Flutter'd in the besieging wind's uproar;
And the long carpets rose along the gusty floor.   360

XLI

They glide, like phantoms, into the wide hall;
Like phantoms, to the iron porch, they glide;
Where lay the Porter, in uneasy sprawl,
With a huge empty flaggon by his side:
The wakeful bloodhound rose, and shook his hide,   365
But his sagacious eye an inmate owns:
By one, and one, the bolts full easy slide:—
The chains lie silent on the footworn stones;—
The key turns, and the door upon its hinges groans.

XLII

And they are gone: aye, ages long ago   370
These lovers fled away into the storm.
That night the Baron dreamt of many a woe,
And all his warrior-guests, with shade and form
Of witch, and demon, and large coffin-worm,
Were long be-nightmar'd. Angela the old   375
Died palsy-twitch'd, with meagre face deform;
The Beadsman, after thousand aves told,
For aye unsought for slept among his ashes cold.

Thomas Hood

1799—1845

THE SONG OF THE SHIRT

Printed anonymously in the Christmas number of *Punch*, 1843;
based (with slight variations) on a police report in *The Times*
of 26th October. The comment of a later poet, John Davidson, is
worth quoting: ' It was in the newspapers that Thomas Hood
found the " Song of the Shirt "—in its place the most important

358 *Arras:* tapestry. 376 *Deform:* twisted out of shape. 377 *Aves:*
Hail-Marys.

English poem of the nineteenth century; the " woman in un-
womanly rags plying her needle and thread " is the type of the
world's misery. The " Song of the Shirt " is the most terrible
poem in the English language . . . Poetry will concern itself
with her and hers for some time to come.'

With fingers weary and worn,
   With eyelids heavy and red,
A Woman sat, in unwomanly rags,
   Plying her needle and thread—
      Stitch! stitch! stitch!
In poverty, hunger, and dirt,   5
   And still with a voice of dolorous pitch
She sang the ' Song of the Shirt '!

' Work! work! work!
While the cock is crowing aloof!   10
   And work—work—work,
Till the stars shine through the roof!
  It's O! to be a slave
   Along with the barbarous Turk,
Where woman has never a soul to save,   15
   If this is Christian work!

' Work—work—work
Till the brain begins to swim;
   Work—work—work
Till the eyes are heavy and dim!   20
Seam, and gusset, and band,
     Band, and gusset, and seam,
       Till over the buttons I fall asleep,
    And sew them on in a dream!

' O! Men with Sisters dear!   25
   O! Men! with Mothers and Wives!
It is not linen you're wearing out,
   But human creatures' lives!
     Stitch—stitch—stitch,
   In poverty, hunger, and dirt,   30
Sewing at once, with a double thread,
   A Shroud as well as a Shirt.

'But why do I talk of Death?
　That Phantom of grisly bone,
I hardly fear his terrible shape,   35
　It seems so like my own—
　It seems so like my own,
　Because of the fasts I keep,
Oh! God! that bread should be so dear,
　And flesh and blood so cheap!   40

'Work—work—work!
　My labour never flags;
And what are its wages? A bed of straw,
　A crust of bread—and rags.
That shatter'd roof,—and this naked floor—   45
　A table—a broken chair—
And a wall so blank, my shadow I thank
　For sometimes falling there!

'Work—work—work!
From weary chime to chime,   50
　Work—work—work—
As prisoners work for crime!
　Band, and gusset, and seam,
　Seam, and gusset, and band,
Till the heart is sick, and the brain benumb'd,   55
　As well as the weary hand.

'Work—work—work,
In the dull December light,
　And work—work—work,
When the weather is warm and bright—   60
While underneath the eaves
　The brooding swallows cling
As if to show me their sunny backs
　And twit me with the spring.

'Oh! but to breathe the breath   65
Of the cowslip and primrose sweet—
　With the sky above my head,
And the grass beneath my feet,
For only one short hour
　To feel as I used to feel,   70
Before I knew the woes of want
　And the walk that costs a meal!

'Oh but for one short hour!
    A respite however brief!
No blessed leisure for Love or Hope,   75
    But only time for Grief!
A little weeping would ease my heart,
    But in their briny bed
My tears must stop, for every drop
    Hinders needle and thread!'   80

Seam, and gusset, and band,
Band, and gusset, and seam,
    Work, work, work,
Like the Engine that works by Steam!
A mere machine of iron and wood   85
    That toils for Mammon's sake—
Without a brain to ponder and craze
    Or heart to feel—and break!

With fingers weary and worn,
    With eyelids heavy and red,   90
A Woman sat, in unwomanly rags,
    Plying her needle and thread—
        Stitch! stitch! stitch!
    In poverty, hunger, and dirt,
And still with a voice of dolorous pitch,   95
Would that its tone could reach the Rich!—
    She sang the 'Song of the Shirt'!

Alfred Tennyson
(Lord Tennyson)

1809—1892

THE LADY OF SHALOTT

PART ONE

On either side the river lie
Long fields of barley and of rye,
That clothe the wold and meet the sky;
And thro' the field the road runs by
    To many-tower'd Camelot;   5

86 *Mammon:* idolatrized wealth.
5 *Camelot:* legendary place of King Arthur's court, unidentified.

And up and down the people go,
Gazing where the lilies blow
Round an island there below,
    The island of Shalott.

Willows whiten, aspens quiver,   10
Little breezes dusk and shiver
Thro' the wave that runs for ever
By the island in the river
    Flowing down to Camelot.
Four gray walls, and four gray towers,   15
Overlook a space of flowers,
And the silent isle imbowers
    The Lady of Shalott.

By the margin, willow-veil'd,
Slide the heavy barges trail'd   20
By slow horses; and unhail'd
The shallop flitteth silken-sail'd
    Skimming down to Camelot:
But who hath seen her wave her hand?
Or at the casement seen her stand?   25
Or is she known in all the land,
    The Lady of Shalott?

Only reapers, reaping early
In among the bearded barley,
Hear a song that echoes cheerly   30
From the river winding clearly,
    Down to tower'd Camelot:
And by the moon the reaper weary,
Piling sheaves in uplands airy,
Listening, whispers, ' 'Tis the fairy   35
    Lady of Shalott.'

PART TWO

There she weaves by night and day
A magic web with colours gay.
She has heard a whisper say,
A curse is on her if she stay   40
    To look down to Camelot.

9 *Shalott:* the 'Astolat' of Arthurian legend, an ancient name of Guild-
ford, Surrey. 22 *Shallop:* light open boat.

She knows not what the curse may be,
And so she weaveth steadily,
And little other care hath she,
    The Lady of Shalott.   45

And moving thro' a mirror clear
That hangs before her all the year,
Shadows of the world appear.
There she sees the highway near
    Winding down to Camelot: 50
There the river eddy whirls,
And there the surly village-churls,
And the red cloaks of market girls,
    Pass onward from Shalott.

Sometimes a troop of damsels glad,   55
An abbot on an ambling pad,
Sometimes a curly shepherd-lad,
Or long-hair'd page in crimson clad,
    Goes by to tower'd Camelot;
And sometimes thro' the mirror blue   60
The knights come riding two and two:
She hath no loyal knight and true,
    The Lady of Shalott.

But in her web she still delights
To weave the mirror's magic sights,   65
For often thro' the silent nights
A funeral, with plumes and lights
    And music, went to Camelot:
Or when the moon was overhead,
Came two young lovers lately wed;   70
' I am half sick of shadows,' said
    The Lady of Shalott.

PART THREE

A bow-shot from her bower-eaves,
He rode between the barley-sheaves,
The sun came dazzling thro' the leaves,   75
And flamed upon the brazen greaves
    Of bold Sir Lancelot.

56 *Pad:* leisurely horse.   76 *Greaves:* armour on leg below knee.

A red-cross knight for ever kneel'd
To a lady in his shield,
That sparkled on the yellow field,   80
    Beside remote Shalott.

The gemmy bridle glitter'd free,
Like to some branch of stars we see
Hung in the golden Galaxy.
The bridle bells rang merrily   85
    As he rode down to Camelot:
And from his blazon'd baldric slung
A mighty silver bugle hung,
And as he rode his armour rung,
    Beside remote Shalott.   90

All in the blue unclouded weather
Thick-jewell'd shone the saddle-leather,
The helmet and the helmet-feather
Burn'd like one burning flame together,
    As he rode down to Camelot.   95
As often thro' the purple night,
Below the starry clusters bright,
Some bearded meteor, trailing light,
    Moves over still Shalott.

His broad clear brow in sunlight glow'd;   100
On burnish'd hooves his war-horse trode;
From underneath his helmet flow'd
His coal-black curls as on he rode,
    As he rode down to Camelot.
From the bank and from the river   105
He flash'd into the crystal mirror,
'Tirra lirra,' by the river
    Sang Sir Lancelot.

She left the web, she left the loom,
She made three paces thro' the room,
She saw the water-lily bloom,
She saw the helmet and the plume,
    She look'd down to Camelot.
Out flew the web and floated wide;
The mirror crack'd from side to side;
'The curse is come upon me,' cried   115
    The Lady of Shalott.

PART FOUR

In the stormy east-wind straining,
The pale yellow woods were waning,
The broad stream in his banks complaining,   120
Heavily the low sky raining
    Over tower'd Camelot;
Down she came and found a boat
Beneath a willow left afloat,
And round about the prow she wrote   125
    The Lady of Shalott.

And down the river's dim expanse
Like some bold seër in a trance,
Seeing all his own mischance—
With a glassy countenance   130
    Did she look to Camelot.
And at the closing of the day
She loosed the chain, and down she lay;
The broad stream bore her far away,
    The Lady of Shalott.   135

Lying, robed in snowy white
That loosely flew to left and right—
The leaves upon her falling light—
Thro' the noises of the night
    She floated down to Camelot: 140
And as the boat-head wound along
The willowy hills and fields among,
They heard her singing her last song,
    The Lady of Shalott.

Heard a carol, mournful, holy,   145
Chanted loudly, chanted lowly,
Till her blood was frozen slowly,
And her eyes were darken'd wholly,
    Turn'd to tower'd Camelot.
For ere she reach'd upon the tide   150
The first house by the water-side,
Singing in her song she died,
    The Lady of Shalott.

Under tower and balcony,
By garden-wall and gallery,   155
A gleaming shape she floated by,
Dead-pale between the houses high,
    Silent into Camelot.
Out upon the wharfs they came,
Knight and burgher, lord and dame,   160
And round the prow they read her name,
    The Lady of Shalott.

Who is this? and what is here?
And in the lighted palace near
Died the sound of royal cheer;   165
And they cross'd themselves for fear,
    All the knights at Camelot:
But Lancelot mused a little space;
He said, ' She has a lovely face;
God in his mercy lend her grace,   170
    The Lady of Shalott.'

TITHONUS

One of the situations of tragic decay which fascinated Tennyson.
Eos, the dawn goddess in Greek mythology, loved Tithonus
enough to have him immortalised by Zeus, but forgot to grant
him release from ageing: Tithonus, struldbrug-like, went on
growing old in eternity, wrinkling and shrivelling till he became
little more than a voice of undying regret.

The woods decay, the woods decay and fall,
The vapours weep their burthen to the ground,
Man comes and tills the field and lies beneath,
And after many a summer dies the swan.
Me only cruel immortality   5
Consumes: I wither slowly in thine arms,
Here at the quiet limit of the world,
A white-hair'd shadow roaming like a dream
The ever-silent spaces of the East,
Far-folded mists, and gleaming halls of morn.   10

   Alas! for this gray shadow, once a man—
So glorious in his beauty and thy choice,

Who madest him thy chosen, that he seem'd
To his great heart none other than a God!
I ask'd thee, ' Give me immortality.'   15
Then didst thou grant mine asking with a smile,
Like wealthy men who care not how they give.
But thy strong Hours indignant work'd their wills,
And beat me down and marr'd and wasted me,
And tho' they could not end me, left me maim'd   20
To dwell in presence of immortal youth,
Immortal age beside immortal youth,
And all I was, in ashes. Can thy love,
Thy beauty, make amends, tho' even now,
Close over us, the silver star, thy guide,   25
Shines in those tremulous eyes that fill with tears
To hear me? Let me go: take back thy gift:
Why should a man desire in any way
To vary from the kindly race of men,
Or pass beyond the goal of ordinance   30
Where all should pause, as is most meet for all?

    A soft air fans the cloud apart; there comes
A glimpse of that dark world where I was born.
Once more the old mysterious glimmer steals
From thy pure brows, and from thy shoulders pure,   35
And bosom beating with a heart renew'd.
Thy cheek begins to redden thro' the gloom,
Thy sweet eyes brighten slowly close to mine,
Ere yet they blind the stars, and the wild team
Which love thee, yearning for thy yoke, arise,   40
And shake the darkness from their loosen'd manes,
And beat the twilight into flakes of fire.

    Lo! ever thus thou growest beautiful
In silence, then before thine answer given
Departest, and thy tears are on my cheek.   45

    Why wilt thou ever scare me with thy tears,
And make me tremble lest a saying learnt,
In days far-off, on that dark earth, be true?
' The Gods themselves cannot recall their gifts.'

    Ay me! ay me! with what another heart   50
In days far-off, and with what other eyes
I used to watch—if I be he that watch'd—
The lucid outline forming round thee; saw

The dim curls kindle into sunny rings;
Changed with thy mystic change, and felt my blood   55
Glow with the glow that slowly crimson'd all
Thy presence and thy portals, while I lay,
Mouth, forehead, eyelids, growing dewy-warm
With kisses balmier than half-opening buds
Of April, and could hear the lips that kiss'd   60
Whispering I knew not what of wild and sweet,
Like that strange song I heard Apollo sing,
While Ilion like a mist rose into towers.

    Yet hold me not for ever in thine East:
How can my nature longer mix with thine?   65
Coldly thy rosy shadows bathe me, cold
Are all thy lights, and cold my wrinkled feet
Upon thy glimmering thresholds, when the steam
Floats up from those dim fields about the homes
Of happy men that have the power to die,   70
And grassy barrows of the happier dead.
Release me, and restore me to the ground;
Thou seëst all things, thou wilt see my grave:
Thou wilt renew thy beauty morn by morn;
I earth in earth forget these empty courts,   75
And thee returning on thy silver wheels.

LOCKSLEY HALL

Published 1842. ' " Locksley Hall " is an imaginary place (tho'
the coast is Lincolnshire) and the hero is imaginary. The whole
poem represents young life, its good side, its deficiencies, and its
yearnings. Mr. Hallam said to me that the English people
liked verse in Trochaics, so I wrote the poem in this metre.'
(Tennyson's note)

Comrades, leave me here a little, while as yet 'tis early morn:
Leave me here, and when you want me, sound upon the bugle-
    horn.

'Tis the place, and all around it, as of old, the curlews call,
Dreary gleams about the moorland flying over Locksley Hall;

62 *Apollo:* classical god of the sun, poetry, and music. 63 *Ilion:* Troy.
Legend says its walls were built by Apollo and Poseidon. 71 *Barrows:*
burial-mounds.

Locksley Hall, that in the distance overlooks the sandy tracts,   5
And the hollow ocean-ridges roaring into cataracts.

Many a night from yonder ivied casement, ere I went to rest,
Did I look on great Orion sloping slowly to the West.

Many a night I saw the Pleiads, rising thro' the mellow shade,
Glitter like a swarm of fire-flies tangled in a silver braid.   10

Here about the beach I wander'd, nourishing a youth sublime
With the fairy tales of science, and the long result of Time;

When the centuries behind me like a fruitful land reposed;
When I clung to all the present for the promise that it closed:

When I dipt into the future far as human eye could see;   15
Saw the Vision of the world, and all the wonder that would be.—

In the Spring a fuller crimson comes upon the robin's breast;
In the Spring the wanton lapwing gets himself another crest;

In the Spring a livelier iris changes on the burnish'd dove;
In the Spring a young man's fancy lightly turns to thoughts of
     love.   20

Then her cheek was pale and thinner than should be for one so
     young,
And her eyes on all my motions with a mute observance hung.

And I said, ' My cousin Amy, speak, and speak the truth to me,
Trust me, cousin, all the current of my being sets to thee.'

On her pallid cheek and forehead came a colour and a light,   25
As I have seen the rosy red flushing in the northern night.

And she turn'd—her bosom shaken with a sudden storm of
     sighs—
All the spirit deeply dawning in the dark of hazel eyes—

Saying, ' I have hid my feelings, fearing they should do me wrong;'
Saying, ' Dost thou love me, cousin? ' weeping, ' I have loved thee
     long.'   30

Love took up the glass of Time, and turn'd it in his glowing hands;
Every moment, lightly shaken, ran itself in golden sands.

10 refers to the fine nebulous mass surrounding this star-cluster.

Love took up the harp of Life, and smote on all the chords with
  might;
Smote the chord of Self, that, trembling, pass'd in music out of
  sight.

Many a morning on the moorland did we hear the copses ring, 35
And her whisper throng'd my pulses with the fulness of the Spring.

Many an evening by the waters did we watch the stately ships,
And our spirits rush'd together at the touching of the lips.

O my cousin, shallow-hearted! O my Amy, mine no more!
O the dreary, dreary moorland! O the barren, barren shore! 40

Falser than all fancy fathoms, falser than all songs have sung,
Puppet to a father's threat, and servile to a shrewish tongue!

Is it well to wish thee happy?—having known me—to decline
On a range of lower feelings and a narrower heart than mine!

Yet it shall be: thou shalt lower to his level day by day, 45
What is fine within thee growing coarse to sympathise with clay.

As the husband is, the wife is: thou art mated with a clown,
And the grossness of his nature will have weight to drag thee down.

He will hold thee, when his passion shall have spent its novel force,
Something better than his dog, a little dearer than his horse. 50

What is this? his eyes are heavy: think not they are glazed with
  wine.
Go to him: it is thy duty: kiss him: take his hand in thine.

It may be my lord is weary, that his brain is overwrought:
Soothe him with thy finer fancies, touch him with thy lighter
  thought.

He will answer to the purpose, easy things to understand— 55
Better thou wert dead before me, tho' I slew thee with my hand!

Better thou and I were lying, hidden from the heart's disgrace,
Roll'd in one another's arms, and silent in a last embrace.

Cursed be the social wants that sin against the strength of youth!
Cursed be the social lies that warp us from the living truth! 60

Cursed be the sickly forms that err from honest Nature's rule!
Cursed be the gold that gilds the straiten'd forehead of the fool!

Well—'tis well that I should bluster!—Hadst thou less unworthy
    proved—
Would to God—for I had loved thee more than ever wife was
    loved.

Am I mad, that I should cherish that which bears but bitter
    fruit? 65
I will pluck it from my bosom, tho' my heart be at the root.

Never, tho' my mortal summers to such length of years should
    come
As the many-winter'd crow that leads the clanging rookery home.

Where is comfort? in division of the records of the mind?
Can I part her from herself, and love her, as I knew her, kind? 70

I remember one that perish'd: sweetly did she speak and move:
Such a one do I remember, whom to look at was to love.

Can I think of her as dead, and love her for the love she bore?
No—she never loved me truly: love is love for evermore.

Comfort? comfort scorn'd of devils! this is truth the poet sings, 75
That a sorrow's crown of sorrow is remembering happier things.

Drug thy memories, lest thou learn it, lest thy heart be put to
    proof,
In the dead unhappy night, and when the rain is on the roof.

Like a dog, he hunts in dreams, and thou art staring at the wall,
Where the dying night-lamp flickers, and the shadows rise and
    fall. 80

Then a hand shall pass before thee, pointing to his drunken sleep,
To thy widow'd marriage-pillows, to the tears that thou wilt weep.

Thou shalt hear the ' Never, never,' whisper'd by the phantom
    years,
And a song from out the distance in the ringing of thine ears;

68 *Crow:* rook.   75 *The poet.* Dante (*Inferno*, V. 121-3).

And an eye shall vex thee, looking ancient kindness on thy
 pain. 85
Turn thee, turn thee on thy pillow: get thee to thy rest again.

Nay, but Nature brings thee solace; for a tender voice will cry.
'Tis a purer life than thine; a lip to drain thy trouble dry.

Baby lips will laugh me down: my latest rival brings thee rest.
Baby fingers, waxen touches, press me from the mother's breast. 90

O, the child too clothes the father with a dearness not his due.
Half is thine and half is his: it will be worthy of the two.

O, I see thee old and formal, fitted to thy petty part,
With a little hoard of maxims preaching down a daughter's heart.

' They were dangerous guides the feelings—she herself was not
 exempt— 95
Truly, she herself had suffer'd '—Perish in thy self-contempt!

Overlive it—lower yet—be happy! wherefore should I care?
I myself must mix with action, lest I wither by despair.

What is that which I should turn to, lighting upon days like these?
Every door is barr'd with gold, and opens but to golden keys. 100

Every gate is throng'd with suitors, all the markets overflow.
I have but an angry fancy: what is that which I should do?

I had been content to perish, falling on the foeman's ground,
When the ranks are roll'd in vapour, and the winds are laid with
 sound.

But the jingling of the guinea helps the hurt that Honour feels, 105
And the nations do but murmur, snarling at each other's heels.

Can I but relive in sadness? I will turn that earlier page.
Hide me from my deep emotion, O thou wondrous Mother-Age!

Make me feel the wild pulsation that I felt before the strife,
When I heard my days before me, and the tumult of my life; 110

Yearning for the large excitement that the coming years would
 yield
Eager-hearted as a boy when first he leaves his father's field,

And at night along the dusky highway near and nearer drawn,
Sees in heaven the light of London flaring like a dreary dawn;

And his spirit leaps within him to be gone before him then,   115
Underneath the light he looks at, in among the throngs of men:

Men, my brothers, men the workers, ever reaping something new:
That which they have done but earnest of the things that they
    shall do:

For I dipt into the future, far as human eye could see,
Saw the Vision of the world, and all the wonder that would
    be;   120

Saw the heavens fill with commerce, argosies of magic sails,
Pilots of the purple twilight, dropping down with costly bales;

Heard the heavens fill with shouting, and there rain'd a ghastly
    dew
From the nations' airy navies grappling in the central blue;

Far along the world-wide whisper of the south-wind rushing
    warm,   125
With the standards of the peoples plunging thro' the thunder-
    storm;

Till the war-drum throbb'd no longer, and the battle-flags were
    furl'd
In the Parliament of man, the Federation of the world.

There the common sense of most shall hold a fretful realm in
    awe,
And the kindly earth shall slumber, lapt in universal law.   130

So I triumph'd ere my passion sweeping thro' me left me dry,
Left me with the palsied heart, and left me with the jaundiced
    eye;

Eye, to which all order festers, all things here are out of joint:
Science moves, but slowly slowly, creeping on from point to point:

Slowly comes a hungry people, as a lion creeping nigher,   135
Glares at one that nods and winks behind a slowly-dying fire.

Yet I doubt not thro' the ages one increasing purpose runs,
And the thoughts of men are widen'd with the process of the suns.

What is that to him that reaps not harvest of his youthful joys,
Tho' the deep heart of existence beat for ever like a boy's?   140

Knowledge comes, but wisdom lingers, and I linger on the shore,
And the individual withers, and the world is more and more.

Knowledge comes, but wisdom lingers, and he bears a laden
    breast,
Full of sad experience, moving toward the stillness of his rest.

Hark, my merry comrades call me, sounding on the bugle-
    horn,   145
They to whom my foolish passion were a target for their scorn:

Shall it not be scorn to me to harp on such a moulder'd string?
I am shamed thro' all my nature to have loved so slight a thing.

Weakness to be wroth with weakness! woman's pleasure, woman's
    pain—
Nature made them blinder motions bounded in a shallower
    brain: 150

Woman is the lesser man, and all thy passions, match'd with mine,
Are as moonlight unto sunlight, and as water unto wine—

Here at least, where nature sickens, nothing. Ah, for some retreat
Deep in yonder shining Orient, where my life began to beat;

Where in wild Mahratta-battle fell my father evil-starr'd;— 155
I was left a trampled orphan, and a selfish uncle's ward.

Or to burst all links of habit—there to wander far away,
On from island unto island at the gateways of the day.

Larger constellations burning, mellow moons and happy skies,
Breadths of tropic shade and palms in cluster, knots   of
    Paradise.   160

Never comes the trader, never floats an European flag,
Slides the bird o'er lustrous woodland, swings the trailer from the
    crag;

Droops the heavy-blossom'd bower, hangs the heavy-fruited tree—
Summer isles of Eden lying in dark-purple spheres of sea.

155 *Mahrattas:* race in central India, who had fought wars with the
English.

There methinks would be enjoyment more than in this march of
mind   165
In the steamship, in the railway, in the thoughts that shake
mankind.

There the passions cramp'd no longer shall have scope and
breathing space;
I will take some savage woman, she shall rear my dusky race.

Iron-jointed, supple-sinew'd, they shall dive, and they shall run,
Catch the wild goat by the hair, and hurl their lances in the
sun;   170

Whistle back the parrot's call, and leap the rainbows of the
brooks,
Not with blinded eyesight poring over miserable books—

Fool, again the dream, the fancy! but I *know* my words are wild,
But I count the gray barbarian lower than the Christian child.

I, to herd with narrow foreheads, vacant of our glorious gains, 175
Like a beast with lower pleasures, like a beast with lower pains!

Mated with a squalid savage—what to me were sun or clime?
I the heir of all the ages, in the foremost files of time—

I that rather held it better men should perish one by one,
Than that earth should stand at gaze like Joshua's moon in
Ajalon!   180

Not in vain the distance beacons. Forward, forward let us range,
Let the great world spin for ever down the ringing grooves of
change.

Thro' the shadow of the globe we sweep into the younger day:
Better fifty years of Europe than a cycle of Cathay.

Mother-Age (for mine I knew not) help me as when life begun: 185
Rift the hills, and roll the waters, flash the lightnings, weigh the
Sun.

180 See *Joshua* x. 12. 182 *Grooves:* Tennyson, travelling by the first
train from Liverpool to Manchester on a dark night in 1830, thought the
wheels ran in grooves. 184 *Cathay:* China.

O, I see the crescent promise of my spirit hath not set.
Ancient founts of inspiration well thro' all my fancy yet.

Howsoever these things be, a long farewell to Locksley Hall!
Now for me the woods may wither, now for me the roof-tree
fall.   190

Comes a vapour from the margin, blackening over heath and
holt,
Cramming all the blast before it, in its breast a thunderbolt.

Let it fall on Locksley Hall, with rain or hail, or fire or snow;
For the mighty wind arises, roaring seaward, and I go.

RIZPAH

17—

Based on the story of Mrs. Rooke, an old woman in 18th-century
Brighton whose son was hanged for robbing the mail, and
who went night after night to the gibbet on the Downs and
gradually collected his bones, eventually burying them secretly
in Old Shoreham Churchyard. Her story reminded Tennyson of
Rizpah (*II Sam.* xxi. 8-10).

I
Wailing, wailing, wailing, the wind over land and sea—
And Willy's voice in the wind, ' O mother, come out to me.'
Why should he call me to-night, when he knows that I cannot go?
For the downs are as bright as day, and the full moon stares at
the snow.

II
We should be seen, my dear;   they would spy us out of the
town.   5
The loud black nights for us, and the storm rushing over the
down,
When I cannot see my own hand, but am led by the creak of the
chain,
And grovel and grope for my son till I find myself drenched with
the rain.

190 *Roof-tree:* main beam of a roof.   191 *Holt:* wood.

III

Anything fallen again? nay—what was there left to fall?
I have taken them home, I have number'd the bones, I have
    hidden them all.   10
What am I saying? and what are *you*? do you come as a spy?
Falls? what falls? who knows? As the tree falls so must it lie.

IV

Who let her in? how long has she been? you—what have you
    heard?
Why did you sit so quiet? you never have spoken a word.
O—to pray with me—yes—a lady—none of their spies—   15
But the night has crept into my heart, and begun to darken my
    eyes.

V

Ah—you, that have lived so soft, what should *you* know of the
    night,
The blast and the burning shame and the bitter frost and the
    fright?
I have done it, while you were asleep—you were only made for
    the day.
I have gather'd my baby together—and now you may go your
    way.   20

VI

Nay—for it's kind of you, Madam, to sit by an old dying wife.
But say nothing hard of my boy, I have only an hour of life.
I kiss'd my boy in the prison, before he went out to die.
'They dared me to do it,' he said, and he never has told me a lie.
I whipt him for robbing an orchard once when he was but a
    child—   25
'The farmer dared me to do it,' he said; he was always so wild—
And idle—and couldn't be idle—my Willy—he never could rest.
The King should have made him a soldier he would have been
    one of his best.

VII

But he lived with a lot of wild mates, and they never would let
    him be good;
They swore that he dare not rob the mail, and he swore that he
    would;   30
And he took no life, but he took one purse, and when all was
    done
He flung it among his fellows—I'll none of it, said my son.

VIII

I came into court to the Judge and the lawyers. I told them my
tale,
God's own truth—but they kill'd him, they kill'd him for robbing
the mail.
They hang'd him in chains for a show—we had always borne a
good name— 35
To be hang'd for a thief—and then put away—isn't that enough
shame?
Dust to dust—low down—let us hide! but they set him so high
That all the ships of the world could stare at him, passing by.
God 'ill pardon the hell-black raven and horrible fowls of the air,
But not the black heart of the lawyer who kill'd him and hang'd
him there. 40

IX

And the jailer forced me away. I had bid him my last goodbye;
They had fasten'd the door of his cell. 'O mother!' I heard him
cry.
I couldn't get back tho' I tried, he had something further to say,
And now I never shall know it. The jailer forced me away.

X

Then since I couldn't but hear that cry of my boy that was
dead, 45
They seized me and shut me up: they fasten'd me down on my
bed.
'Mother, O mother!'—he call'd in the dark to me year after
year—
They beat me for that, they beat me—you know that I couldn't
but hear;
And then at the last they found I had grown so stupid and still
They let me abroad again—but the creatures had worked their
will. 50

XI

Flesh of my flesh was gone, but bone of my bone was left—
I stole them all from the lawyers—and you, will you call it a
theft?—
My baby, the bones that had suck'd me, the bones that had
laughed and had cried—
Theirs? O no! they are mine—not theirs—they had moved in
my side.

XII

Do you think I was scared by the bones? I kiss'd 'em, I buried
'em all— 55
I can't dig deep, I am old—in the night by the churchyard wall.
My Willy 'ill rise up whole when the trumpet of judgment 'ill
sound,
But I charge you never to say that I laid him in holy ground.

XIII

They would scratch him up—they would hang him again on the
cursed tree.
Sin? O yes—we are sinners, I know—let all that be, 60
And read me a Bible verse of the Lord's good will toward me—
' Full of compassion and mercy, the Lord '—let me hear it again;
' Full of compassion and mercy—long-suffering.' Yes, O yes!
For the lawyer is born but to murder—the Saviour lives but to
bless.
He'll never put on the black cap except for the worst of the
worst, 65
And the first may be last—I have heard it in church—and the
last may be first.
Suffering—O long-suffering—yes, as the Lord must know,
Year after year in the mist and the wind and the shower and the
snow.

XIV

Heard, have you? what? they have told you he never repented
his sin.
How do they know it? are *they* his mother? are *you* of his kin? 70
Heard! have you ever heard, when the storm on the downs began,
The wind that 'ill wail like a child and the sea that 'ill moan like
a man?

XV

Election, Election and Reprobation—it's all very well.
But I go to-night to my boy, and I shall not find him in Hell.
For I cared so much for my boy that the Lord has look'd into
my care, 75
And He means me I'm sure to be happy with Willy, I know not
where.

62 See *Psalm* lxxxvi. 15. 66 See *Matt.* xix. 30. 73 *Election and Re-
probation:* Calvinist doctrine of divine choice and divine rejection,
destining souls to heaven or to hell.

XVI

And if *he* be lost—but to save *my* soul, that is all your desire:
Do you think that I care for *my* soul if my boy be gone to the fire?
I have been with God in the dark—go, go, you may leave me
    alone—
You never have borne a child—you are just as hard as a stone. 80

XVII

Madam, I beg your pardon! I think that you mean to be kind,
But I cannot hear what you say for my Willy's voice in the
    wind—
The snow and the sky so bright—he used but to call in the dark,
And he calls to me now from the church and not from the gibbet
    —for hark!
Nay—you can hear it yourself—it is coming—shaking the
    walls— 85
Willy—the moon's in a cloud——Good-night. I am going. He
    calls.

Robert Browning

1812—1889

AN EPISTLE
CONTAINING THE STRANGE MEDICAL EXPERIENCE OF
KARSHISH, THE ARAB PHYSICIAN

An oblique, subtle probing of the earliest Christianity, seen
through the puzzled but not unsympathetic eyes of an outsider.
Browning's imaginary Arab doctor meets and talks to Lazarus
in 66 A.D., diagnoses his 'case' (mania subinduced by epilepsy),
but cannot understand the persistence, for over thirty years, of
Lazarus's delusion that he was dead and restored to life.

Karshish, the picker-up of learning's crumbs,
The not-incurious in God's handiwork
(This man's-flesh he hath admirably made,
Blown like a bubble, kneaded like a paste,
To coop up and keep down on earth a space
That puff of vapour from its mouth, man's soul) 5
—To Abib, all-sagacious in our art,

Breeder in me of what poor skill I boast,
Like me inquisitive how pricks and cracks
Befall the flesh through too much stress and strain,   10
Whereby the wily vapour fain would slip
Back and rejoin its source before the term,—
And aptest in contrivance (under God)
To baffle it by deftly stopping such:—
The vagrant Scholar to his Sage at home   15
Sends greeting (health and knowledge, fame with peace)
Three samples of true snakestone—rarer still,
One of the other sort, the melon-shaped,
(But fitter, pounded fine, for charms than drugs)
And writeth now the twenty-second time.   20

My journeyings were brought to Jericho:
Thus I resume. Who studious in our art
Shall count a little labour unrepaid?
I have shed sweat enough, left flesh and bone
On many a flinty furlong of this land.   25
Also, the country-side is all on fire
With rumours of a marching hitherward:
Some say Vespasian cometh, some, his son.
A black lynx snarled and pricked a tufted ear;
Lust of my blood inflamed his yellow balls: 30
I cried and threw my staff and he was gone.
Twice have the robbers stripped and beaten me,
And once a town declared me for a spy;
But at the end, I reach Jerusalem,
Since this poor covert where I pass the night,   35
This Bethany, lies scarce the distance thence
A man with plague-sores at the third degree
Runs till he drops down dead. Thou laughest here!
'Sooth, it elates me, thus reposed and safe,
To void the stuffing of my travel-scrip   40
And share with thee whatever Jewry yields.
A viscid choler is observable
In tertians, I was nearly bold to say;
And falling-sickness hath a happier cure
Than our school wots of: there's a spider here   45
Weaves no web, watches on the ledge of tombs,

17 *Snakestone:* porous stone, regarded as curing snakebite. 28 *Vesp-asian:* Roman emperor (A.D. 9-79) who invaded Palestine A.D. 66. 36 *Bethany:* village near Jerusalem where Lazarus lived. 41 *Jewry:* land of the Jews. 42 *Viscid choler:* ropy bile. 43 *Tertians:* fevers which build up every third (i.e. alternate) day.

Sprinkled with mottles on an ash-grey back;
Take five and drop them . . .but who knows his mind,
The Syrian runagate I trust this to?
His service payeth me a sublimate   50
Blown up his nose to help the ailing eye.
Best wait: I reach Jerusalem at morn,
There set in order my experiences,
Gather what most deserves, and give thee all—
Or I might add, Judæa's gum-tragacanth   55
Scales off in purer flakes, shines clearer-grained,
Cracks 'twixt the pestle and the porphyry,
In fine exceeds our produce. Scalp-disease
Confounds me, crossing so with leprosy—
Thou hadst admired one sort I gained at Zoar—   60
But zeal outruns discretion. Here I end.

    Yet stay: my Syrian blinketh gratefully,
Protesteth his devotion is my price—
Suppose I write what harms not, though he steal?
I half resolve to tell thee, yet I blush,   65
What set me off a-writing first of all.
An itch I had, a sting to write, a tang!
For, be it this town's barrenness—or else
The Man had something in the look of him—
His case has struck me far more than 'tis worth.   70
So, pardon if—(lest presently I lose
In the great press of novelty at hand
The care and pains this somehow stole from me)
I bid thee take the thing while fresh in mind,
Almost in sight—for, wilt thou have the truth?   75
The very man is gone from me but now,
Whose ailment is the subject of discourse.
Thus then, and let thy better wit help all!

    'Tis but a case of mania—subinduced
By epilepsy, at the turning-point   80
Of trance prolonged unduly some three days:
When, by the exhibition of some drug
Or spell, exorcization, stroke of art
Unknown to me and which 'twere well to know,
The evil thing out-breaking all at once   85

50 *Sublimate:* vaporized substance. 55 *Gum-tragacanth:* a thick
mucilage useful in pharmacy and trade. (B.) 57 *Porphyry:* hard stone,
used here for a mortar. 60 *Zoar:* city near Dead Sea. 69 *The Man:*
Lazarus.

Left the man whole and sound of body indeed,—
But, flinging (so to speak) life's gates too wide,
Making a clear house of it too suddenly,
The first conceit that entered might inscribe
Whatever it was minded on the wall   90
So plainly at that vantage, as it were,
(First come, first served) that nothing subsequent
Attaineth to erase those fancy-scrawls
The just-returned and new-established soul
Hath gotten now so thoroughly by heart   95
That henceforth she will read or these or none.
And first—the man's own firm conviction rests
That he was dead (in fact they buried him)
—That he was dead and then restored to life
By a Nazarene physician of his tribe: 100
—'Sayeth, the same bade, ' Rise,' and he did rise.
' Such cases are diurnal,' thou wilt cry.
Not so this figment!—not, that such a fume,
Instead of giving way to time and health,
Should eat itself into the life of life,   105
As saffron tingeth flesh, blood, bones and all!
For see, how he takes up the after-life.
The man—it is one Lazarus a Jew,
Sanguine, proportioned, fifty years of age,
The body's habit wholly laudable,   110
As much, indeed, beyond the common health
As he were made and put aside to show.
Think, could we penetrate by any drug
And bathe the wearied soul and worried flesh,
And bring it clear and fair, by three days' sleep!   115
Whence has the man the balm that brightens all?
This grown man eyes the world now like a child.
Some elders of his tribe, I should premise,
Led in their friend, obedient as a sheep,
To bear my inquisition. While they spoke,   120
Now sharply, now with sorrow,—told the case,—
He listened not except I spoke to him,
But folded his two hands and let them talk,
Watching the flies that buzzed: and yet no fool.
And that's a sample how his years must go.   125
Look, if a beggar, in fixed middle-life,
Should find a treasure,—can he use the same
With straitened habits and with tastes starved small,
And take at once to his impoverished brain
The sudden element that changes things,   130

That sets the undreamed-of rapture at his hand
And puts the cheap old joy in the scorned dust?
Is he not such an one as moves to mirth—
Warily parsimonious, when no need,
Wasteful as drunkenness at undue times?   135
All prudent counsel as to what befits
The golden mean, is lost on such an one:
The man's fantastic will is the man's law.
So here—we call the treasure knowledge, say,
Increased beyond the fleshly faculty—   140
Heaven opened to a soul while yet on earth,
Earth forced on a soul's use while seeing heaven:
The man is witless of the size, the sum,
The value in proportion of all things,
Or whether it be little or be much.   145
Discourse to him of prodigious armaments
Assembled to besiege his city now,
And of the passing of a mule with gourds—
'Tis one! Then take it on the other side,
Speak of some trifling fact,—he will gaze rapt   150
With stupor at its very littleness,
(Far as I see) as if in that indeed
He caught prodigious import, whole results;
And so will turn to us the bystanders
In ever the same stupor (note this point)   155
That we too see not with his opened eyes.
Wonder and doubt come wrongly into play,
Preposterously, at cross purposes.
Should his child sicken unto death,—why, look
For scarce abatement of his cheerfulness,   160
Or pretermission of the daily craft!
While a word, gesture, glance from that same child
At play or in the school or laid asleep,
Will startle him to an agony of fear,
Exasperation, just as like. Demand   165
The reason why—' 'tis but a word,' object—
' A gesture '—he regards thee as our lord
Who lived there in the pyramid alone,
Looked at us (dost thou mind?) when, being young,
We both would unadvisedly recite   170
Some charm's beginning, from that book of his,
Able to bid the sun throb wide and burst
All into stars, as suns grown old are wont.
Thou and the child have each a veil alike
Thrown o'er your heads, from under which ye both   175
A.L.P.   T

Stretch your blind hands and trifle with a match
Over a mine of Greek fire, did ye know!
He holds on firmly to some thread of life—
(It is the life to lead perforcedly)
Which runs across some vast distracting orb   180
Of glory on either side that meagre thread,
Which, conscious of, he must not enter yet—
The spiritual life around the earthly life:
The law of that is known to him as this,
His heart and brain move there, his feet stay here.   185
So is the man perplext with impulses
Sudden to start off crosswise, not straight on,
Proclaiming what is right and wrong across,
And not along, this black thread through the blaze—
' It should be ' baulked by ' here it cannot be.'   190
And oft the man's soul springs into his face
As if he saw again and heard again
His sage that bade him ' Rise ' and he did rise.
Something, a word, a tick o' the blood within
Admonishes: then back he sinks at once   195
To ashes, who was very fire before,
In sedulous recurrence to his trade
Whereby he earneth him the daily bread;
And studiously the humbler for that pride,
Professedly the faultier that he knows   200
God's secret, while he holds the thread of life.
Indeed the especial marking of the man
Is prone submission to the heavenly will—
Seeing it, what it is, and why it is.
'Sayeth, he will wait patient to the last   205
For that same death which must restore his being
To equilibrium, body loosening soul
Divorced even now by premature full growth:
He will live, nay, it pleaseth him to live
So long as God please, and just how God please.   210
He even seeketh not to please God more
(Which meaneth, otherwise) than as God please.
Hence, I perceive not he affects to preach
The doctrine of his sect whate'er it be,
Make proselytes as madmen thirst to do: 215
How can he give his neighbour the real ground,
His own conviction? Ardent as he is—
Call his great truth a lie, why, still the old

177 *Greek fire:* combustible compound including quicklime or nitre,
sulphur, and naphtha.

'Be it as God please' reassureth him.
I probed the sore as thy disciple should: 220
'How, beast,' said I, 'this stolid carelessness
'Sufficeth thee, when Rome is on her march
'To stamp out like a little spark thy town,
'Thy tribe, thy crazy tale and thee at once?'
He merely looked with his large eyes on me.   225
The man is apathetic, you deduce?
Contrariwise, he loves both old and young,
Able and weak, affects the very brutes
And birds—how say I? flowers of the field—
As a wise workman recognizes tools   230
In a master's workshop, loving what they make.
Thus is the man as harmless as a lamb:
Only impatient, let him do his best,
At ignorance and carelessness and sin—
An indignation which is promptly curbed: 235
As when in certain travel I have feigned
To be an ignoramus in our art
According to some preconceived design,
And happed to hear the land's practitioners
Steeped in conceit sublimed by ignorance,   240
Prattle fantastically on disease,
Its cause and cure—and I must hold my peace!

     Thou wilt object—Why have I not ere this
Sought out the sage himself, the Nazarene
Who wrought this cure, inquiring at the source,   245
Conferring with the frankness that befits?
Alas! it grieveth me, the learned leech
Perished in a tumult many years ago,
Accused,—our learning's fate,—of wizardry,
Rebellion, to the setting up a rule   250
And creed prodigious as described to me.
His death, which happened when the earthquake fell
(Prefiguring, as soon appeared, the loss
To occult learning in our lord the sage
Who lived there in the pyramid alone)   255
Was wrought by the mad people—that's their wont!
On vain recourse, as I conjecture it,
To his tried virtue, for miraculous help—
How could he stop the earthquake? That's their way!
The other imputations must be lies: 260

240 *Sublimed:* refined and elevated, made ineffable. 247 *Leech:* doctor.

But take one, though I loathe to give it thee,
In mere respect for any good man's fame.
(And after all, our patient Lazarus
Is stark mad; should we count on what he says?
Perhaps not: though in writing to a leech   265
'Tis well to keep back nothing of a case.)
This man so cured regards the curer, then,
As—God forgive me! who but God himself,
Creator and sustainer of the world,
That came and dwelt in flesh on it awhile!   270
—'Sayeth that such an one was born and lived,
Taught, healed the sick, broke bread at his own house,
Then died, with Lazarus by, for aught I know,
And yet was . . . what I said nor choose repeat,
And must have so avouched himself, in fact,   275
In hearing of this very Lazarus
Who saith—but why all this of what he saith?
Why write of trivial matters, things of price
Calling at every moment for remark?
I noticed on the margin of a pool   280
Blue-flowering borage, the Aleppo sort,
Aboundeth, very nitrous. It is strange!

Thy pardon for this long and tedious case,
Which, now that I review it, needs must seem
Unduly dwelt on, prolixly set forth!   285
Nor I myself discern in what is writ
Good cause for the peculiar interest
And awe indeed this man has touched me with.
Perhaps the journey's end, the weariness
Had wrought upon me first. I met him thus: 290
I crossed a ridge of short sharp broken hills
Like an old lion's cheek-teeth. Out there came
A moon made like a face with certain spots
Multiform, manifold and menacing:
Then a wind rose behind me. So we met   295
In this old sleepy town at unaware,
The man and I. I send thee what is writ.
Regard it as a chance, a matter risked
To this ambiguous Syrian—he may lose,
Or steal, or give it thee with equal good.   300
Jerusalem's repose shall make amends
For time this letter wastes, thy time and mine;

281 *Borage:* herb formerly used as a cordial.

Till when, once more thy pardon and farewell!
   The very God! think, Abib; dost thou think?
So, the All-Great, were the All-Loving too—   305
So, through the thunder comes a human voice
Saying, ' O heart I made, a heart beats here!
' Face, my hands fashioned, see it in myself!
' Thou hast no power nor mayst conceive of mine,
' But love I gave thee, with myself to love,   310
' And thou must love me who have died for thee! '
The madman saith He said so: it is strange.

FRA LIPPO LIPPI

I am poor brother Lippo, by your leave!
You need not clap your torches to my face.
Zooks, what's to blame? you think you see a monk!
What, 'tis past midnight, and you go the rounds,
And here you catch me at an alley's end   5
Where sportive ladies leave their doors ajar?
The Carmine's my cloister: hunt it up,
Do,—harry out, if you must show your zeal,
Whatever rat, there, haps on his wrong hole,
And nip each softling of a wee white mouse,   10
Weke, weke, that's crept to keep him company!
Aha, you know your betters! Then, you'll take
Your hand away that's fiddling on my throat,
And please to know me likewise. Who am I?
Why, one, sir, who is lodging with a friend   15
Three streets off—he's a certain . . . how d'ye call?
Master—a . . . Cosimo of the Medici,
I' the house that caps the corner. Boh! you were best!
Remember and tell me, the day you're hanged,
How you affected such a gullet's-gripe!   20
But you, sir, it concerns you that your knaves
Pick up a manner nor discredit you:
Zooks, are we pilchards, that they sweep the streets
And count fair prize what comes into their net?
He's Judas to a tittle, that man is!   25
Just such a face! Why, sir, you make amends.
Lord, I'm not angry! Bid your hangdogs go

1 *Lippo:* Fra Filippo Lippi (*c.* 1406-69), Italian painter and Carmelite friar. 7 *Carmine:* monastery of friars Del Carmine in Florence. 17 *Cosimo of the Medici:* (1389-1464), wealthy statesman and patron of the arts.

Drink out this quarter-florin to the health
Of the munificent House that harbours me
(And many more beside, lads! more beside!)   30
And all's come square again. I'd like his face—
His, elbowing on his comrade in the door
With the pike and lantern,—for the slave that holds
John Baptist's head a-dangle by the hair
With one hand ('Look you, now,' as who should say)   35
And his weapon in the other, yet unwiped!
·It's not your chance to have a bit of chalk,
A wood-coal or the like? or you should see!
Yes, I'm the painter, since you style me so.
What, brother Lippo's doings, up and down,   40
You know them and they take you? like enough!
I saw the proper twinkle in your eye—
'Tell you, I liked your looks at very first.
Let's sit and set things straight now, hip to haunch.
Here's spring come, and the nights one makes up bands   45
To roam the town and sing out carnival,
And I've been three weeks shut within my mew,
A-painting for the great man, saints and saints
And saints again. I could not paint all night—
Ouf! I leaned out of window for fresh air.   50
There came a hurry of feet and little feet,
A sweep of lute-strings, laughs, and whifts of song,—
Flower o' the broom,
Take away love, and our earth is a tomb!
Flower o' the quince,   55
I let Lisa go, and what good in life since?
Flower o' the thyme—and so on. Round they went.
Scarce had they turned the corner when a titter
Like the skipping of rabbits by moonlight,—three slim shapes,
And a face that looked up . . . zooks, sir, flesh and blood, 60
That's all I'm made of! Into shreds it went,
Curtain and counterpane and coverlet,
All the bed-furniture—a dozen knots,
There was a ladder! Down I let myself,
Hands and feet, scrambling somehow, and so dropped,   65
And after them. I came up with the fun
Hard by Saint Laurence, hail fellow, well met,—
Flower o' the rose,
If I've been merry, what matter who knows?
And so as I was stealing back again   70

47 *Mew:* den, place of hiding or confinement. 67 *Saint Laurence:*
church of San Lorenzo.

To get to bed and have a bit of sleep
Ere I rise up to-morrow and go work
On Jerome knocking at his poor old breast
With his great round stone to subdue the flesh,
You snap me of the sudden. Ah, I see!   75
Though your eye twinkles still, you shake your head—
Mine's shaved—a monk, you say—the sting's in that!
If Master Cosimo announced himself,
Mum's the word naturally; but a monk!
Come, what am I a beast for? tell us, now!   80
I was a baby when my mother died
And father died and left me in the street.
I starved there, God knows how, a year or two
On fig-skins, melon-parings, rinds and shucks,
Refuse and rubbish. One fine frosty day,   85
My stomach being empty as your hat,
The wind doubled me up and down I went.
Old Aunt Lapaccia trussed me with one hand,
(Its fellow was a stinger as I knew)
And so along the wall, over the bridge,   90
By the straight cut to the convent. Six words there,
While I stood munching my first bread that month:
' So, boy, you're minded,' quoth the good fat father
Wiping his own mouth, 'twas refection-time,—
' To quit this very miserable world?   95
' Will you renounce ' . . . ' the mouthful of bread? ' thought I;
By no means! Brief, they made a monk of me;
I did renounce the world, its pride and greed,
Palace, farm, villa, shop and banking-house,
Trash, such as these poor devils of Medici   100
Have given their hearts to—all at eight years old.
Well, sir, I found in time, you may be sure,
'Twas not for nothing—the good bellyful,
The warm serge and the rope that goes all round,
And day-long blessed idleness beside!   105
' Let's see what the urchin's fit for '—that came next.
Not overmuch their way, I must confess.
Such a to-do! They tried me with their books:
Lord, they'd have taught me Latin in pure waste!
Flower o' the clove,   110
All the Latin I construe is, ' amo ' I love!
But, mind you, when a boy starves in the streets
Eight years together, as my fortune was,
Watching folk's faces to know who will fling

73 *Jerome:* St. Jerome (*c.* 347-419/20), Church father.

The bit of half-stripped grape-bunch he desires,   115
And who will curse or kick him for his pains,—
Which gentleman processional and fine,
Holding a candle to the Sacrament,
Will wink and let him lift a plate and catch
The droppings of the wax to sell again,   120
Or holla for the Eight and have him whipped,—
How say I?—nay, which dog bites, which lets drop
His bone from the heap of offal in the street,—
Why, soul and sense of him grow sharp alike,
He learns the look of things, and none the less   125
For admonition from the hunger-pinch.
I had a store of such remarks, be sure,
Which, after I found leisure, turned to use.
I drew men's faces on my copy-books,
Scrawled them within the antiphonary's marge,   130
Joined legs and arms to the long music-notes,
Found eyes and nose and chin for A's and B's,
And made a string of pictures of the world
Betwixt the ins and outs of verb and noun,
On the wall, the bench, the door. The monks looked black. 135
' Nay,' quoth the Prior, ' turn him out, d'ye say?
' In no wise. Lose a crow and catch a lark.
' What if at last we got our man of parts,
' We Carmelites, like those Camaldolese
' And Preaching Friars, to do our church up fine   140
' And put the front on it that ought to be! '
And hereupon he bade me daub away.
Thank you! my head being crammed, the walls a blank,
Never was such prompt disemburdening.
First, every sort of monk, the black and white,   145
I drew them, fat and lean: then, folk at church,
From good old gossips waiting to confess
Their cribs of barrel-droppings, candle-ends,—
To the breathless fellow at the altar-foot,
Fresh from his murder, safe and sitting there   150
With the little children round him in a row
Of admiration, half for his beard and half
For that white anger of his victim's son
Shaking a fist at him with one fierce arm,
Signing himself with the other because of Christ   155
(Whose sad face on the cross sees only this

121 *The Eight:* magistrates who governed Florence.   130 *Antiphonary:*
choir-book.   139 *Camaldolese:* a monastic order.   140 *Preaching Friars:*
order of Dominicans.

After the passion of a thousand years)
Till some poor girl, her apron o'er her head,
(Which the intense eyes looked through) came at eve
On tiptoe, said a word, dropped in a loaf,   160
Her pair of earrings and a bunch of flowers
(The brute took growling), prayed, and so was gone.
I painted all, then cried ' 'Tis ask and have;
' Choose, for more's ready! '—laid the ladder flat,
And showed my covered bit of cloister-wall.   165
The monks closed in a circle and praised loud
Till checked, taught what to see and not to see,
Being simple bodies,—' That's the very man!
' Look at the boy who stoops to pat the dog!
' That woman's like the Prior's niece who comes   170
' To care about his asthma: it's the life! '
But there my triumph's straw-fire flared and funked;
Their betters took their turn to see and say:
The Prior and the learned pulled a face
And stopped all that in no time. ' How? what's here?   175
' Quite from the mark of painting, bless us all!
' Faces, arms, legs and bodies like the true
' As much as pea and pea! it's devil's-game!
' Your business is not to catch men with show,
' With homage to the perishable clay,   180
' But lift them over it, ignore it all,
' Make them forget there's such a thing as flesh.
' Your business is to paint the souls of men—
' Man's soul, and it's a fire, smoke . . . no, it's not . . .
' It's vapour done up like a new-born babe—   185
' (In that shape when you die it leaves your mouth)
' It's . . . well, what matters talking, it's the soul!
' Give us no more of body than shows soul!
' Here's Giotto, with his Saint a-praising God,
' That sets us praising,—why not stop with him?   190
' Why put all thoughts of praise out of our head
' With wonder at lines, colours, and what not?
' Paint the soul, never mind the legs and arms!
' Rub all out, try at it a second time.
' Oh, that white smallish female with the breasts,   195
' She's just my niece . . . Herodias, I would say,—
' Who went and danced and got men's heads cut off!
' Have it all out! ' Now, is this sense, I ask?
A fine way to paint soul, by painting body

189 *Giotto:* (*c.* 1266-1337), Florentine painter. 196 *Herodias:* See
Matt. xiv. 3-11.

So ill, the eye can't stop there, must go further   200
And can't fare worse! Thus, yellow does for white
When what you put for yellow's simply black,
And any sort of meaning looks intense
When all beside itself means and looks nought.
Why can't a painter lift each foot in turn,   205
Left foot and right foot, go a double step,
Make his flesh liker and his soul more like,
Both in their order? Take the prettiest face,
The Prior's niece . . . patron-saint—is it so pretty
You can't discover if it means hope, fear,   210
Sorrow or joy? won't beauty go with these?
Suppose I've made her eyes all right and blue,
Can't I take breath and try to add life's flash,
And then add soul and heighten them threefold?
Or say there's beauty with no soul at all—   215
(I never saw it—put the case the same—)
If you get simple beauty and nought else,
You get about the best thing God invents:
That's somewhat: and you'll find the soul you have missed,
Within yourself, when you return him thanks.   220
'Rub all out!' Well, well, there's my life, in short.
And so the thing has gone on ever since.
I'm grown a man no doubt, I've broken bounds:
You should not take a fellow eight years old
And make him swear to never kiss the girls.   225
I'm my own master, paint now as I please—
Having a friend, you see, in the Corner-house!
Lord, it's fast holding by the rings in front—
Those great rings serve more purposes than just
To plant a flag in, or tie up a horse!   230
And yet the old schooling sticks, the old grave eyes
Are peeping o'er my shoulder as I work,
The heads shake still—' It's art's decline, my son!
'You're not of the true painters, great and old;
'Brother Angelico's the man, you'll find;   235
'Brother Lorenzo stands his single peer:
'Fag on at flesh, you'll never make the third!'
Flower o' the pine,
You keep your mistr . . . manners, and I'll stick to mine!
I'm not the third, then: bless us, they must know!   240
Don't you think they're the likeliest to know,

235 *Brother Angelico:* Fra Angelico (*c.* 1387-1455), painter and Domin-
ican friar. 236 *Brother Lorenzo:* Lorenzo Monaco (*c.* 1370/2-*c.* 1425),
painter and Camaldolensian monk.

They with their Latin? So, I swallow my rage,
Clench my teeth, suck my lips in tight, and paint
To please them—sometimes do and sometimes don't;
For, doing most, there's pretty sure to come   245
A turn, some warm eve finds me at my saints—
A laugh, a cry, the business of the world—
(*Flower o' the peach,*
Death for us all, and his own life for each!)
And my whole soul revolves, the cup runs over,   250
The world and life's too big to pass for a dream,
And I do these wild things in sheer despite,
And play the fooleries you catch me at,
In pure rage! The old mill-horse, out at grass
After hard years, throws up his stiff heels so,   255
Although the miller does not preach to him
The only good of grass is to make chaff.
What would men have? Do they like grass or no—
May they or mayn't they? all I want's the thing
Settled for ever one way. As it is,   260
You tell too many lies and hurt yourself:
You don't like what you only like too much,
You do like what, if given you at your word,
You find abundantly detestable.
For me, I think I speak as I was taught;   265
I always see the garden and God there
A-making man's wife: and, my lesson learned,
The value and significance of flesh,
I can't unlearn ten minutes afterwards.

       You understand me: I'm a beast, I know.   270
But see, now—why, I see as certainly
As that the morning-star's about to shine,
What will hap some day. We've a youngster here
Comes to our convent, studies what I do,
Slouches and stares and lets no atom drop: 275
His name is Guidi—he'll not mind the monks—
They call him Hulking Tom, he lets them talk—
He picks my practice up—he'll paint apace,
I hope so—though I never live so long,
I know what's sure to follow. You be judge!   280
You speak no Latin more than I, belike;
However, you're my man, and you've seen the world

276 *Guidi:* Tommaso Guidi, Florentine painter known as Masaccio
('Hulking Tom') (1401-28); probably Lippi's teacher rather than
pupil.

—The beauty and the wonder and the power,
The shapes of things, their colours, lights and shades,
Changes, surprises,—and God made it all! 285
—For what? Do you feel thankful, ay or no,
For this fair town's face, yonder river's line,
The mountain round it and the sky above,
Much more the figures of man, woman, child,
These are the frame to? What's it all about? 290
To be passed over, despised? or dwelt upon,
Wondered at? oh, this last of course!—you say.
But why not do as well as say,—paint these
Just as they are, careless what comes of it?
God's works—paint any one, and count it crime 295
To let a truth slip. Don't object, ' His works
' Are here already; nature is complete:
' Suppose you reproduce her—(which you can't)
' There's no advantage! you must beat her, then.'
For, don't you mark? we're made so that we love 300
First when we see them painted, things we have passed
Perhaps a hundred times nor cared to see;
And so they are better, painted—better to us,
Which is the same thing. Art was given for that;
God uses us to help each other so, 305
Lending our minds out. Have you noticed, now,
Your cullion's hanging face? A bit of chalk,
And trust me but you should, though! How much more,
If I drew higher things with the same truth!
That were to take the Prior's pulpit-place, 310
Interpret God to all of you! Oh, oh,
It makes me mad to see what men shall do
And we in our graves! This world's no blot for us,
Nor blank; it means intensely, and means good:
To find its meaning is my meat and drink. 315
' Ay, but you don't so instigate to prayer! '
Strikes in the Prior: ' when your meaning's plain
' It does not say to folk—remember matins,
' Or, mind you fast next Friday! ' Why, for this
What need of art at all? A skull and bones, 320
Two bits of stick nailed crosswise, or, what's best,
A bell to chime the hour with, does as well.
I painted a Saint Laurence six months since
At Prato, splashed the fresco in fine style:
' How looks my painting, now the scaffold's down? ' 325

307 *Cullion:* rascal. 323 *Saint Laurence* (d.258), Christian martyr, burnt
on a gridiron. 324 *Prato:* town near Florence.

I ask a brother: ' Hugely,' he returns—
' Already not one phiz of your three slaves
' Who turn the Deacon off his toasted side,
' But's scratched and prodded to our heart's content,
' The pious people have so eased their own   330
' With coming to say prayers there in a rage:
' We get on fast to see the bricks beneath.
' Expect another job this time next year,
' For pity and religion grow i' the crowd—
' Your painting serves its purpose! ' Hang the fools!   335

—That is—you'll not mistake an idle word
Spoke in a huff by a poor monk, God wot,
Tasting the air this spicy night which turns
The unaccustomed head like Chianti wine!
Oh, the church knows! don't misreport me, now!   340
It's natural a poor monk out of bounds
Should have his apt word to excuse himself:
And hearken how I plot to make amends.
I have bethought me: I shall paint a piece
. . . There's for you! Give me six months, then go, see   345
Something in Sant' Ambrogio's! Bless the nuns!
They want a cast o' my office. I shall paint
God in the midst, Madonna and her babe,
Ringed by a bowery flowery angel-brood,
Lilies and vestments and white faces, sweet   350
As puff on puff of grated orris-root
When ladies crowd to church at midsummer.
And then i' the front, of course a saint or two—
Saint John, because he saves the Florentines,
Saint Ambrose, who puts down in black and white   355
The convent's friends and gives them a long day,
And Job, I must have him there past mistake,
The man of Uz (and Us without the z,
Painters who need his patience). Well, all these
Secured at their devotion, up shall come   360
Out of a corner when you least expect,
As one by a dark stair into a great light,
Music and talking, who but Lippo! I!—

346 *Sant' Ambrogio's:* convent in Florence where Lippi painted a
Coronation of the Virgin. 347 *Cast o' my office:* example of my work.
351 *Orris-root:* powdered iris, used as perfume. 354 *Saint John:* the
Baptist, patron saint of Florence. 355 *Saint Ambrose:* (*c.* 340-97),
Church father. 358 See *Job* i. 1. Uz is perhaps Edom, to the south of
Palestine.

Mazed, motionless and moonstruck—I'm the man!
Back I shrink—what is this I see and hear?   365
I, caught up with my monk's-things by mistake,
My old serge gown and rope that goes all round,
I, in this presence, this pure company!
Where's a hole, where's a corner for escape?
Then steps a sweet angelic slip of a thing   370
Forward, puts out a soft palm—' Not so fast! '
—Addresses the celestial presence, ' nay—
' He made you and devised you, after all,
' Though he's none of you! Could Saint John there draw—
' His camel-hair make up a painting-brush?   375
' We come to brother Lippo for all that,
' *Iste perfecit opus!* ' So, all smile—
I shuffle sideways with my blushing face
Under the cover of a hundred wings
Thrown like a spread of kirtles when you're gay   380
And play hot cockles, all the doors being shut,
Till, wholly unexpected, in there pops
The hothead husband! Thus I scuttle off
To some safe bench behind, not letting go
The palm of her, the little lily thing   385
That spoke the good word for me in the nick,
Like the Prior's niece . . . Saint Lucy, I would say.
And so all's saved for me, and for the church
A pretty picture gained. Go, six months hence!
Your hand, sir, and good-bye: no lights, no lights!   390
The street's hushed, and I know my own way back,
Don't fear me! There's the grey beginning. Zooks!

HOW IT STRIKES A CONTEMPORARY

I only knew one poet in my life:
And this, or something like it, was his way.

    You saw go up and down Valladolid,
A man of mark, to know next time you saw.
His very serviceable suit of black   5
Was courtly once and conscientious still,
And many might have worn it, though none did:
The cloak, that somewhat shone and showed the threads,

377 'This man completed the work.' (Lat.) 381 *Hot cockles:* game like
blind-man's-buff. 387 *Saint Lucy:* (281-304), Christian martyr. 3 *Val-
ladolid:* city in Old Castile, Spain. 6 *Conscientious:* scrupulously kept.

Had purpose, and the ruff, significance.
He walked and tapped the pavement with his cane,   10
Scenting the world, looking it full in face,
An old dog, bald and blindish, at his heels.
They turned up, now, the alley by the church,
That leads nowhither; now, they breathed themselves
On the main promenade just at the wrong time: 15
You'd come upon his scrutinizing hat,
Making a peaked shade blacker than itself
Against the single window spared some house
Intact yet with its mouldered Moorish work,—
Or else surprise the ferrel of his stick   20
Trying the mortar's temper 'tween the chinks
Of some new shop a-building, French and fine.
He stood and watched the cobbler at his trade,
The man who slices lemons into drink,
The coffee-roaster's brazier, and the boys   25
That volunteer to help him turn its winch.
He glanced o'er books on stalls with half an eye,
And fly-leaf ballads on the vendor's string,
And broad-edge bold-print posters by the wall.
He took such cognizance of men and things,   30
If any beat a horse, you felt he saw;
If any cursed a woman, he took note;
Yet stared at nobody,—you stared at him,
And found, less to your pleasure than surprise,
He seemed to know you and expect as much.   35
So, next time that a neighbour's tongue was loosed,
It marked the shameful and notorious fact,
We had among us, not so much a spy,
As a recording chief-inquisitor,
The town's true master if the town but knew!   40
We merely kept a governor for form,
While this man walked about and took account
Of all thought, said and acted, then went home,
And wrote it fully to our Lord the King
Who has an itch to know things, he knows why,   45
And reads them in his bedroom of a night.
Oh, you might smile! there wanted not a touch,
A tang of . . . well, it was not wholly ease
As back into your mind the man's look came.
Stricken in years a little,—such a brow   50
His eyes had to live under!—clear as flint
On either side the formidable nose

28 *Fly-leaf ballads:* broadside ballads.

Curved, cut and coloured like an eagle's claw.
Had he to do with A.s surprising fate?
When altogether old B. disappeared   55
And young C. got his mistress,—was't our friend,
His letter to the King, that did it all?
What paid the bloodless man for so much pains?
Our Lord the King has favourites manifold,
And shifts his ministry some once a month;   60
Our city gets new governors at whiles,—
But never word or sign, that I could hear,
Notified to this man about the streets
The King's approval of those letters conned
The last thing duly at the dead of night.   65
Did the man love his office? Frowned our Lord,
Exhorting when none heard—' Beseech me not!
' Too far above my people,—beneath me!
' I set the watch,—how should the people know?
' Forget them, keep me all the more in mind! '   70
Was some such understanding 'twixt the two?

    I found no truth in one report at least—
That if you tracked him to his home, down lanes
Beyond the Jewry, and as clean to pace,
You found he ate his supper in a room   75
Blazing with lights, four Titians on the wall,
And twenty naked girls to change his plate!
Poor man, he lived another kind of life
In that new stuccoed third house by the bridge,
Fresh-painted, rather smart than otherwise!   80
The whole street might o'erlook him as he sat,
Leg crossing leg, one foot on the dog's back,
Playing a decent cribbage with his maid
(Jacynth, you're sure her name was) o'er the cheese
And fruit, three red halves of starved winter-pears,   85
Or treat of radishes in April. Nine,
Ten, struck the church clock, straight to bed went he.

    My father, like the man of sense he was,
Would point him out to me a dozen times;
' 'St—'St,' he'd whisper, ' the Corregidor! '   90
I had been used to think that personage
Was one with lacquered breeches, lustrous belt,
And feathers like a forest in his hat,

74 *Jewry:* Jewish quarter. 76 *Titians:* pictures by the Italian painter
Titian (*c.* 1477/87-1576). 90 *Corregidor:* chief magistrate.

Who blew a trumpet and proclaimed the news,
Announced the bull-fights, gave each church its turn,   95
And memorized the miracle in vogue!
He had a great observance from us boys;
We were in error; that was not the man.

I'd like now, yet had haply been afraid,
To have just looked, when this man came to die,   100
And seen who lined the clean gay garret-sides
And stood about the neat low truckle-bed,
With the heavenly manner of relieving guard.
Here had been, mark, the general-in-chief,
Thro' a whole campaign of the world's life and death,   105
Doing the King's work all the dim day long,
In his old coat and up to knees in mud,
Smoked like a herring, dining on a crust,—
And, now the day was won, relieved at once!
No further show or need for that old coat,   110
You are sure, for one thing! Bless us, all the while
How sprucely we are dressed out, you and I!
A second, and the angels alter that.
Well, I could never write a verse,—could you?
Let's to the Prado and make the most of time.   115

NED BRATTS

From *Dramatic Idyls* (1879). The grotesque, florid, and almost
horrifying raciness of this study in awakened conscience shows
Browning's later manner: let the public like it or—go back to
Bunyan. The poem is based on the story of Old Tod in Bunyan's
Life and Death of Mr. Badman.

'Twas Bedford Special Assize, one daft Midsummer's Day:
A broiling blasting June,—was never its like, men say.
Corn stood sheaf-ripe already, and trees looked yellow as that;
Ponds drained dust-dry, the cattle lay foaming around each flat.
Inside town, dogs went mad, and folk kept bibbing beer   5
While the parsons prayed for rain. 'Twas horrible, yes—but
        queer:
Queer—for the sun laughed gay, yet nobody moved a hand
To work one stroke at his trade: as given to understand

115 *Prado:* promenade of the city.

That all was come to a stop, work and such worldly ways,
And the world's old self about to end in a merry blaze.   10
Midsummer's Day moreover was the first of Bedford Fair,
With Bedford Town's tag-rag and bobtail a-bowsing there.

But the Court House, Quality crammed: through doors ope,
    windows wide,
High on the Bench you saw sit Lordships side by side.
There frowned Chief Justice Jukes, fumed learned Brother
    Small,   15
And fretted their fellow Judge: like threshers, one and all,
Of a reek with laying down the law in a furnace. Why?
Because their lungs breathed flame—the regular crowd forbye—
From gentry pouring in—quite a nosegay, to be sure!
How else could they pass the time, six mortal hours endure   20
Till night should extinguish day, when matters might haply mend?
Meanwhile no bad resource was—watching begin and end
Some trial for life and death, in a brisk five minutes' space,
And betting which knave would 'scape, which hang, from his sort
    of face.

So, their Lordships toiled and moiled, and a deal of work was
    done   25
(I warrant) to justify the mirth of the crazy sun
As this and t'other lout, struck dumb at the sudden show
Of red robes and white wigs, boggled nor answered ' Boh! '
When asked why he, Tom Styles, should not—because Jack Nokes
Had stolen the horse—be hanged: for Judges must have their
    jokes,   30
And louts must make allowance—let's say, for some blue fly
Which punctured a dewy scalp where the frizzles stuck awry—
Else Tom had fleered scot-free, so nearly over and done
Was the main of the job. Full-measure, the gentles enjoyed their
    fun,
As a twenty-five were tried, rank puritans caught at prayer   35
In a cow-house and laid by the heels,—have at 'em, devil may
    care!—
And ten were prescribed the whip, and ten a brand on the cheek,
And five a slit of the nose—just leaving enough to tweak.

Well, things at jolly high-tide, amusement steeped in fire,
While noon smote fierce the roof's red tiles to heart's desire, 40
The Court a-simmer with smoke, one ferment of oozy flesh,
One spirituous humming musk mount-mounting until its mesh

Entoiled all heads in a fluster, and Serjeant Postlethwayte
—Dashing the wig oblique as he mopped his oily pate—
Cried ' Silence, or I grow grease! No loophole lets in air?   45
Jurymen,—Guilty, Death! Gainsay me if you dare! '
—Things at this pitch, I say,—what hubbub without the doors?
What laughs, shrieks, hoots and yells, what rudest of uproars?

Bounce through the barrier throng a bulk comes rolling vast!
Thumps, kicks,—no manner of use!—spite of them rolls at last 50
Into the midst a ball which, bursting, brings to view
Publican Black Ned Bratts and Tabby his big wife too:
Both in a muck-sweat, both . . . were never such eyes uplift
At the sight of yawning hell, such nostrils—snouts that sniffed
Sulphur, such mouths a-gape ready to swallow flame!   55
Horrified, hideous, frank fiend-faces! yet, all the same,
Mixed with a certain . . . eh? how shall I dare style—mirth
The desperate grin of the guess that, could they break from earth,
Heaven was above, and hell might rage in impotence
Below the saved, the saved!

                     ' Confound you! (no offence!) 60
Out of our way,—push, wife! Yonder their Worships be! '
Ned Bratts has reached the bar, and ' Hey, my Lords,' roars he,
' A Jury of life and death, Judges the prime of the land,
Constables, javelineers,—all met, if I understand,
To decide so knotty a point as whether 'twas Jack or Joan 65
Robbed the henroost, pinched the pig, hit the King's Arms with
   a stone,
Dropped the baby down the well, left the tithesman in the lurch,
Or, three whole Sundays running, not once attended church!
What a pother—do these deserve the parish-stocks or whip,
More or less brow to brand, much or little nose to snip,— 70
When, in our Public, plain stand we—that's we stand here,
I and my Tab, brass-bold, brick-built of beef and beer,
—Do not we, slut? Step forth and show your beauty, jade!
Wife of my bosom—that's the word now! What a trade
We drove! None said us nay: nobody loved his life 75
So little as wag a tongue against us,—did they, wife?
Yet they knew us all the while, in their hearts, for what we are
—Worst couple, rogue and quean, unhanged—search near and
   far!

64 *Javelineers:* pikemen who escorted judges at assizes. 78 *Quean:*
woman, wench.

Eh, Tab? The pedlar, now—o'er his noggin—who warned a
    mate
To cut and run, nor risk his pack where its loss of weight   80
Was the least to dread,—aha, how we two laughed a-good
As, stealing round the midden, he came on where I stood
With billet poised and raised,—you, ready with the rope,—
Ah, but that's past, that's sin repented of, we hope!
Men knew us for that same, yet safe and sound stood we!   85
The lily-livered knaves knew too (I've baulked a d——)
Our keeping the " Pied Bull " was just a mere pretence:
Too slow the pounds make food, drink, lodging, from out the
    pence!
There's not a stoppage to travel has chanced, this ten long year,
No break into hall or grange, no lifting of nag or steer,   90
Not a single roguery, from the clipping of a purse
To the cutting of a throat, but paid us toll. Od's curse!
When Gipsy Smouch made bold to cheat us of our due,
—Eh, Tab? the Squire's strong-box we helped the rascal to—
I think he pulled a face, next Sessions' swinging-time!   95
He danced the jig that needs no floor,—and, here's the prime,
'Twas Scroggs that houghed the mare! Ay, those were busy days!

' Well, there we flourished brave, like scripture-trees called bays,
Faring high, drinking hard, in money up to head
—Not to say, boots and shoes, when . . . Zounds, I nearly
    said—   100
Lord, to unlearn one's language! How shall we labour, wife?
Have you, fast hold, the Book? Grasp, grip it, for your life!
See, sirs, here's life, salvation! Here's—hold but out my breath—
When did I speak so long without once swearing? 'Sdeath,
No, nor unhelped by ale since man and boy! And yet   105
All yesterday I had to keep my whistle wet
While reading Tab this Book: book? don't say "book "—they're
    plays,
Songs, ballads, and the like: here's no such strawy blaze,
But sky wide ope, sun, moon, and seven stars out full-flare!
Tab, help and tell! I'm hoarse. A mug or—no, a prayer!   110
Dip for one out of the Book! Who wrote it in the Jail
—He plied his pen unhelped by beer, sirs, I'll be bail!

' I've got my second wind. In trundles she—that's Tab.
" Why, Gammer, what's come now, that—bobbing like a crab

83 *Billet:* stick. 96 *Prime:* best. 97 *Houghed:* hamstrung. 98 See
Psalm xxxvii. 35. 102 *The Book:* Bunyan's *The Pilgrim's Progress.*
114 *Gammer:* old woman (lit. 'grandmother'); *crab:* wild apple.

On Yule-tide bowl—your head's a-work and both your eyes 115
Break loose? Afeard, you fool? As if the dead can rise!
Say—Bagman Dick was found last May with fuddling-cap
Stuffed in his mouth: to choke's a natural mishap!"
" Gaffer, be—blessed," cries she, " and Bagman Dick as well!
I, you, and he are damned: this Public is our hell: 120
We live in fire: live coals don't feel!—once quenched, they learn—
Cinders do, to what dust they moulder while they burn! "

' " If you don't speak straight out," says I—belike I swore—
" A knobstick, well you know the taste of, shall, once more,
Teach you to talk, my maid! " She ups with such a face, 125
Heart sunk inside me. " Well, pad on, my prate-apace! "

' " I've been about those laces we need for . . . never mind!
If henceforth they tie hands, 'tis mine they'll have to bind.
You know who makes them best—the Tinker in our cage,
Pulled-up for gospelling, twelve years ago: no age 130
To try another trade,—yet, so he scorned to take
Money he did not earn, he taught himself the make
Of laces, tagged and tough—Dick Bagman found them so!
Good customers were we! Well, last week, you must know
His girl,—the blind young chit, who hawks about his wares,— 135
She takes it in her head to come no more—such airs
These hussies have! Yet, since we need a stoutish lace,—
' I'll to the jail-bird father, abuse her to his face! '
So, first I filled a jug to give me heart, and then,
Primed to the proper pitch, I posted to their den— 140
Patmore—they style their prison! I tip the turnkey, catch
My heart up, fix my face, and fearless lift the latch—
Both arms a-kimbo, in bounce with a good round oath
Ready for rapping out: no ' Lawks ' nor ' By my troth! '

' " There sat my man, the father. He looked up: what one
feels 145
When heart that leapt to mouth drops down again to heels!
He raised his hand . . . Hast seen, when drinking out the night,
And in, the day, earth grow another something quite
Under the sun's first stare? I stood a very stone.

' " ' Woman! ' (a fiery tear he put in every tone), 150

117 *Fuddling-cap:* drinking cap. 119 *Gaffer:* old man (lit. 'grand-father'). 129 *The Tinker:* John Bunyan (1628-88). 140 *Posted:* hastened. 141 *Patmore:* malapropism for Patmos, a place of solitude or exile, where Bunyan, like St. John, writes a book.

' How should my child frequent your house where lust is sport,
Violence—trade? Too true! I trust no vague report.
Her angel's hand, which stops the sight of sin, leaves clear
The other gate of sense, lets outrage through the ear.
What has she heard!—which, heard shall never be again.   155
Better lack food than feast, a Dives in the—wain
Or reign or train—of Charles! ' (His language was not ours:
'Tis my belief, God spoke: no tinker has such powers.)
' Bread, only bread they bring—my laces: if we broke
Your lump of leavened sin, the loaf's first crumb would
     choke! '   160

' " Down on my marrow-bones! Then all at once rose he:
His brown hair burst a-spread, his eyes were suns to see:
Up went his hands: ' Through flesh, I reach, I read thy soul!
So may some stricken tree look blasted, bough and bole,
Champed by the fire-tooth, charred without, and yet, thrice-
     bound   165
With dreriment about, within may life be found,
A prisoned power to branch and blossom as before,
Could but the gardener cleave the cloister, reach the core,
Loosen the vital sap: yet where shall help be found?
Who says " How save it? "—nor " Why cumbers it the
     ground? "   170
Woman, that tree art thou! All sloughed about with scurf,
Thy stag-horns fright the sky, thy snake-roots sting the turf!
Drunkenness, wantonness, theft, murder gnash and gnarl
Thine outward, case thy soul with coating like the marle
Satan stamps flat upon each head beneath his hoof!   175
And how deliver such? The strong men keep aloof,
Lover and friend stand far, the mocking ones pass by,
Tophet gapes wide for prey: lost soul, despair and die!
What then? " Look unto me and be ye saved! " saith God:
" I strike the rock, outstreats the life-stream at my rod!   180
Be your sins scarlet, wool shall they seem like,—although
As crimson red, yet turn white as the driven snow! " '

' " There, there, there! All I seem to somehow understand
Is—that, if I reached home, 'twas through the guiding hand

156 *Dives:* See *Luke* xvi. 19-31.   157 *Charles:* Charles II (1630-85).
Bratts gets Charles's 'reign' mixed up with 'Charles's Wain', the Great
Bear.   166 *Dreriment:* dismal condition, decay.   168 *Cloister:* en-
closure.   171 *Sloughed about:* covered with diseased tissue.   174 *Marle:*
the burning soil of hell. Cf. Milton, *Paradise Lost,* I. 296   178 *Tophet:*
hell.   180 *Outstreats:* flows out.

Of his blind girl which led and led me through the streets 185
And out of town and up to door again. What greets
First thing my eye, as limbs recover from their swoon?
A book—this Book she gave at parting. 'Father's boon—
The Book he wrote: it reads as if he spoke himself:
He cannot preach in bonds, so,—take it down from shelf 190
When you want counsel,—think you hear his very voice!'

' " Wicked dear Husband, first despair and then rejoice!
Dear wicked Husband, waste no tick of moment more,
Be saved like me, bald trunk! There's greenness yet at core,
Sap under slough! Read, read! "

                  ' Let me take breath, my lords! 195
I'd like to know, are these—hers, mine, or Bunyan's words?
I'm 'wildered—scarce with drink,—nowise with drink alone!
You'll say, with heat: but heat's no stuff to split a stone
Like this black boulder—this flint heart of mine: the Book—
That dealt the crashing blow! Sirs, here's the fist that shook 200
His beard till Wrestler Jem howled like a just-lugged bear!
You had brained me with a feather: at once I grew aware
Christian was meant for me. A burden at your back,
Good Master Christian? Nay,—yours was that Joseph's sack,
—Or whose it was,—which held the cup,—compared with
    mine! 205
Robbery loads my loins, perjury cracks my chine,
Adultery . . . nay, Tab, you pitched me as I flung!
One word, I'll up with fist . . . No, sweet spouse, hold your
    tongue!

' I'm hasting to the end. The Book, sirs—take and read!
You have my history in a nutshell,—ay, indeed! 210
It must off, my burden! See,—slack straps and into pit,
Roll, reach the bottom, rest, rot there—a plague on it!
For a mountain's sure to fall and bury Bedford Town,
" Destruction "—that's the name, and fire shall burn it down!
O 'scape the wrath in time! Time's now, if not too late. 215
How can I pilgrimage up to the wicket-gate?
Next comes Despond the slough: not that I fear to pull
Through mud, and dry my clothes at brave House Beautiful—
But it's late in the day, I reckon: had I left years ago
Town, wife, and children dear . . . Well, Christian did, you
    know!— 220

195 *Slough:* dead tissue. 201 *Just-lugged:* newly baited. 204-5
Joseph's sack, etc.: See *Gen.* xliv. 1-2. 206 *Chine:* spine.

Soon I had met in the valley and tried my cudgel's strength
On the enemy horned and winged, a-straddle across its length!
Have at his horns, thwick—thwack: they snap, see! Hoof and
    hoof—
Bang, break the fetlock-bones! For love's sake, keep aloof
Angels! I'm man and match,—this cudgel for my flail,   225
To thresh him, hoofs and horns, bat's wings and serpent's tail!
A chance gone by! But then, what else does Hopeful ding
Into the deafest ear except—hope, hope's the thing?
Too late i' the day for me to thrid the windings: but
There's still a way to win the race by death's short cut!   230
Did Master Faithful need climb the Delightful Mounts?
No, straight to Vanity Fair,—a fair, by all accounts,
Such as is held outside,—lords, ladies, grand and gay,—
Says he in the face of them, just what you hear me say.
And the Judges brought him in guilty, and brought him out 235
To die in the market-place—St. Peter's Green's about
The same thing: there they flogged, flayed, buffeted, lanced with
    knives,
Pricked him with swords,—I'll swear, he'd full a cat's nine lives,—
So to his end at last came Faithful,—ha, ha, he!
Who holds the highest card? for there stands hid, you see,   240
Behind the rabble-rout, a chariot, pair and all:
He's in, he's off, he's up, through clouds, at trumpet-call,
Carried the nearest way to Heaven-gate! Odds my life—
Has nobody a sword to spare? not even a knife?
Then hang me, draw and quarter! Tab—do the same by her! 245
O Master Worldly-Wiseman . . . that's Master Interpreter,
Take the will, not the deed! Our gibbet's handy close:
Forestall Last Judgment-Day! Be kindly, not morose!
There wants no earthly judge-and-jurying: here we stand—
Sentence our guilty selves: so, hang us out of hand!   250
Make haste for pity's sake! A single moment's loss
Means—Satan's lord once more: his whisper shoots across
All singing in my heart, all praying in my brain,
" It comes of heat and beer! "—hark how he guffaws plain!
" To-morrow you'll wake bright, and, in a safe skin, hug   255
Your sound selves, Tab and you, over a foaming jug!
You've had such qualms before, time out of mind! " He's right!
Did not we kick and cuff and curse away, that night
When home we blindly reeled, and left poor humpback Joe
I' the lurch to pay for what . . . somebody did, you know!   260

227 *Ding:* beat, hammer. 229 *Thrid:* thread, pass through. 236 *St.
Peter's Green:* in front of St. Peter's Church, Bedford.

Both of us maundered then " Lame humpback,—never more
Will he come limping, drain his tankard at our door!
He'll swing, while—somebody . . ." Says Tab, " No, for I'll
    peach! "
" I'm for you, Tab," cries I, " there's rope enough for each! "
So blubbered we, and bussed, and went to bed upon   265
The grace of Tab's good thought: by morning, all was gone!
We laughed—" What's life to him, a cripple of no account? "
Oh, waves increase around—I feel them mount and mount!
Hang us! To-morrow brings Tom Bearward with his bears:
One new black-muzzled brute beats Sackerson, he swears: 270
(Sackerson, for my money!) And, baiting o'er, the Brawl
They lead on Turner's Patch,—lads, lasses, up tails all,—
I'm i' the thick o' the throng! That means the Iron Cage,
—Means the Lost Man inside! Where's hope for such as wage
War against light? Light's left, light's here, I hold light still,   275
So does Tab—make but haste to hang us both! You will? '

I promise, when he stopped you might have heard a mouse
Squeak, such a death-like hush sealed up the old Mote House.
But when the mass of man sank meek upon his knees,
While Tab, alongside, wheezed a hoarse ' Do hang us, please! ' 280
Why, then the waters rose, no eye but ran with tears,
Hearts heaved, heads thumped, until, paying all past arrears
Of pity and sorrow, at last a regular scream outbroke
Of triumph, joy and praise.

                      My Lord Chief Justice spoke,
First mopping brow and cheek, where still, for one that
    budged,   285
Another bead broke fresh: ' What Judge, that ever judged
Since first the world began, judged such a case as this?
Why, Master Bratts, long since, folk smelt you out, I wis!
I had my doubts, i' faith, each time you played the fox
Convicting geese of crime in yonder witness-box—   290
Yea, much did I misdoubt, the thief that stole her eggs
Was hardly goosey's self at Reynard's game, i' feggs!
Yet thus much was to praise—you spoke to point, direct—
Swore you heard, saw the theft: no jury could suspect—
Dared to suspect,—I'll say,—a spot in white so clear: 295
Goosey was throttled, true: but thereof godly fear

263 *Peach:* blab, turn informer. 265 *Bussed:* kissed. 271 *Brawl:* a
round dance. 273 *Iron Cage:* Bunyan's 'man of despair' was shut in an
Iron Cage. 278 *Mote House:* hall of assizes.

Came of example set, much as our laws intend;
And, though a fox confessed, you proved the Judge's friend.
What if I had my doubts? Suppose I gave them breath,
Brought you to bar: what work to do, ere " Guilty, Death,"— 300
Had paid our pains! What heaps of witnesses to drag
From holes and corners, paid from out the County's bag!
Trial three dog-days long! *Amicus Curiæ*—that's
Your title, no dispute—truth-telling Master Bratts!
Thank you, too, Mistress Tab! Why doubt one word you say? 305
Hanging you both deserve, hanged both shall be this day!
The tinker needs must be a proper man. I've heard
He lies in Jail long since: if Quality's good word
Warrants me letting loose,—some householder, I mean—
Freeholder, better still—I don't say but—between 310
Now and next Sessions . . . Well! Consider of his case,
I promise to, at least: we owe him so much grace.
Not that—no, God forbid!—I lean to think, as you,
The grace that such repent is any jail-bird's due:
I rather see the fruit of twelve years' pious reign— 315
Astræa Redux, Charles restored his rights again!
—Of which, another time! I somehow feel a peace
Stealing across the world. May deeds like this increase!
So, Master Sheriff, stay that sentence I pronounced
On those two dozen odd: deserving to be trounced 320
Soundly, and yet . . . well, well, at all events despatch
This pair of—shall I say, sinner-saints?—ere we catch
Their jail-distemper too. Stop tears, or I'll indite
All weeping Bedfordshire for turning Bunyanite! '

So, forms were galloped through. If Justice, on the spur, 325
Proved somewhat expeditious, would Quality demur?
And happily hanged were they,—why lengthen out my tale?—
Where Bunyan's Statue stands facing where stood his Jail.

303 *Dog-days:* maddeningly hot days in late summer; *Amicus Curiæ:* a
friend of the court (Lat.). 316 *Astræa Redux:* 'Justice Returned' (i.e.
at the Restoration in 1660).

Walt Whitman

1819—1892

CROSSING BROOKLYN FERRY

I

Flood-tide below me! I see you face to face!
Clouds of the west—sun there half an hour high—I see you also
   face to face.

Crowds of men and women attired in the usual costumes, how
   curious you are to me!
On the ferry-boats the hundreds and hundreds that cross,
   returning home, are more curious to me than you suppose,
And you that shall cross from shore to shore years hence are more
   to me, and more in my meditations, than you might suppose. 5

II

The impalpable sustenance of me from all things at all hours of
   the day,
The simple, compact, well-join'd scheme, myself disintegrated,
   every one disintegrated yet part of the scheme,
The similitudes of the past and those of the future,
The glories strung like beads on my smallest sights and hearings,
   on the walk in the street and the passage over the river,
The current rushing so swiftly and swimming with me far away, 10
The others that are to follow me, the ties between me and them,
The certainty of others, the life, love, sight, hearing of others.

Others will enter the gates of the ferry and cross from shore to
   shore,
Others will watch the run of the flood-tide,
Others will see the shipping of Manhattan north and west, and
   the heights of Brooklyn to the south and east,   15
Others will see the islands large and small;
Fifty years hence, others will see them as they cross, the sun half
   an hour high,
A hundred years hence, or ever so many hundred years hence,
   others will see them,
Will enjoy the sunset, the pouring-in of the flood-tide, the
   falling-back to the sea of the ebb-tide.

603

III

It avails not, time nor place—distance avails not,　　　　20
I am with you, you men and women of a generation, or ever so
　　many generations hence,
Just as you feel when you look on the river and sky, so I felt,
Just as any of you is one of a living crowd, I was one of a crowd,
Just as you are refresh'd by the gladness of the river and the
　　bright flow, I was refresh'd,
Just as you stand and lean on the rail, yet hurry with the swift
　　current, I stood yet was hurried,　　　　25
Just as you look on the numberless masts of ships and the
　　thick-stemm'd pipes of steamboats, I look'd.

I too many and many a time cross'd the river of old,
Watched the Twelfth-month sea-gulls, saw them high in the air
　　floating with motionless wings, oscillating their bodies,
Saw how the glistening yellow lit up parts of their bodies and
　　left the rest in strong shadow,
Saw the slow-wheeling circles and the gradual edging toward the
　　south,　　　　30
Saw the reflection of the summer sky in the water,
Had my eyes dazzled by the shimmering track of beams,
Look'd at the fine centrifugal spokes of light round the shape of
　　my head in the sunlit water,
Look'd on the haze on the hills southward and south-westward,
Look'd on the vapor as it flew in fleeces tinged with violet,　35
Look'd toward the lower bay to notice the vessels arriving,
Saw their approach, saw aboard those that were near me,
Saw the white sails of schooners and sloops, saw the ships at
　　anchor,
The sailors at work in the rigging or out astride the spars,
The round masts, the swinging motion of the hulls, the slender
　　serpentine pennants,　　　　40
The large and small steamers in motion, the pilots in their
　　pilot-houses,
The white wake left by the passage, the quick tremulous whirl of
　　the wheels,
The flags of all nations, the falling of them at sunset,
The scallop-edged waves in the twilight, the ladled cups, the
　　frolicsome crests and glistening,
The stretch afar growing dimmer and dimmer, the gray walls
　　of the granite storehouses by the docks,　　　　45
On the river the shadowy group, the big steam-tug closely flank'd
　　on each side by the barges, the hay-boat, the belated lighter,

On the neighboring shore the fires from the foundry chimneys
  burning high and glaringly into the night,
Casting their flicker of black contrasted with wild red and yellow
  light over the tops of houses, and down into the clefts of streets.

IV

These and all else were to me the same as they are to you,
I loved well those cities, loved well the stately and rapid river, 50
The men and women I saw were all near to me,
Others the same—others who look back on me because I look'd
  forward to them,
(The time will come, though I stop here to-day, and to-night.)

V

What is it then between us?
What is the count of the scores or hundreds of years between us?

Whatever it is, it avails not—distance avails not, and place avails
  not,   56
I too lived, Brooklyn of ample hills was mine,
I too walk'd the streets of Manhattan island, and bathed in the
  waters around it,
I too felt the curious abrupt questionings stir within me.
In the day among crowds of people sometimes they came upon
  me,   60
In my walks home late at night or as I lay in my bed they came
  upon me,
I too had been struck from the float forever held in solution,
I too had receiv'd identity by my body,
That I was I knew was of my body, and what I should be I knew
  I should be of my body.

VI

It is not upon you alone the dark patches fall,   65
The dark threw its patches down upon me also,
The best I had done seem'd to me blank and suspicious,
My great thoughts as I supposed them, were they not in reality
  meagre?
Nor is it you alone who know what it is to be evil,
I am he who knew what it was to be evil,   70
I too knitted the old knot of contrariety,
Blabb'd, blush'd, resented, lied, stole, grudg'd,
Had guile, anger, lust, hot wishes I dared not speak,
Was wayward, vain, greedy, shallow, sly, cowardly, malignant,
The wolf, the snake, the hog, not wanting in me,   75

The cheating look, the frivolous word, the adulterous wish, not
wanting,
Refusals, hates, postponements, meanness, laziness, none of these
wanting,
Was one with the rest, the days and haps of the rest,
Was call'd by my nighest name by clear loud voices of young
men as they saw me approaching or passing,
Felt their arms on my neck as I stood, or the negligent leaning of
their flesh against me as I sat,   80
Saw many I loved in the street or ferry-boat or public assembly,
yet never told them a word,
Lived the same life with the rest, the same old laughing, gnawing,
sleeping,
Play'd the part that still looks back on the actor or actress,
The same old role, the role that is what we make it, as great as
we like,
Or as small as we like, or both great and small.   85

VII

Closer yet I approach you,
What thought you have of me now, I had as much of you—I laid
in my stores in advance,
I consider'd long and seriously of you before you were born.

Who was to know what should come home to me?
Who knows but I am enjoying this?   90
Who knows, for all the distance, but I am as good as looking at
you now, for all you cannot see me?

VIII

Ah, what can ever be more stately and admirable to me than
mast-hemm'd Manhattan?
River and sunset and scallop-edg'd waves of flood-tide?
The sea-gulls oscillating their bodies, the hay-boat in the twilight,
and the belated lighter?

What gods can exceed these that clasp me by the hand, and with
voices I love call me promptly and loudly by my nighest name
as I approach?   95

What is more subtle than this which ties me to the woman or man
that looks in my face?
Which fuses me into you now, and pours my meaning into you?

We understand then do we not?

What I promis'd without mentioning it, have you not accepted?
What the study could not teach—what the preaching could not
  accomplish is accomplish'd, is it not?   100

IX

Flow on, river! flow with the flood-tide, and ebb with the
  ebb-tide!
Frolic on, crested and scallop-edg'd waves!
Gorgeous clouds of the sunset! drench with your splendor me,
  or the men and women generations after me!
Cross from shore to shore, countless crowds of passengers!
Stand up, tall masts of Mannahatta! stand up, beautiful hills of
  Brooklyn!   105
Throb, baffled and curious brain! throw out questions and
  answers!
Suspend here and everywhere, eternal float of solution!
Gaze, loving and thirsting eyes, in the house or street or public
  assembly!
Sound out, voices of young men! loudly and musically call me
  by my nighest name!
Live, old life! play the part that looks back on the actor or
  actress!   110
Play the old role, the role that is great or small according as one
  makes it!
Consider, you who peruse me, whether I may not in unknown
  ways be looking upon you;
Be firm, rail over the river, to support those who lean idly, yet
  haste with the hasting current;
Fly on, sea-birds! fly sideways, or wheel in large circles high in
  the air;
Receive the summer sky, you water, and faithfully hold it till
  all downcast eyes have time to take it from you!   115
Diverge, fine spokes of light, from the shape of my head, or any
  one's head, in the sunlit water!
Come on, ships from the lower bay! pass up or down, white-sail'd
  schooners, sloops, lighters!
Flaunt away, flags of all nations! be duly lower'd at sunset!
Burn high your fires, foundry chimneys! cast black shadows at
  nightfall! cast red and yellow light over the tops of the houses!

105 *Mannahatta:* Whitman was fond of using what he called 'the
aboriginal name' of Manhattan. 107 Reality is genuinely dissolved in
the flux of appearance; the ferry, a slowly moving vantage-point,
symbolises man's life in the swirl of change, where he wishes he could be
suspended, in and yet not in the flux, for ever. Body, ferry, and city may
decay, but these are the instruments through which the poet sees what is
most real and most lasting.

Appearances, now or henceforth, indicate what you are,   120
You necessary film, continue to envelop the soul,
About my body for me, and your body for you, be hung our
    divinest aromas,
Thrive, cities—bring your freight, bring your shows; ample and
    sufficient rivers,
Expand, being than which none else is perhaps more spiritual,
Keep your places, objects than which none else is more lasting. 125

You have waited, you always wait, you dumb, beautiful ministers,
We receive you with free sense at last, and are insatiate hence-
    forward,
Not you any more shall be able to foil us, or withhold yourselves
    from us,
We use you, and do not cast you aside—we plant you per-
    manently within us,
We fathom you not—we love you—there is perfection in you
    also,   130
You furnish your parts toward eternity,
Great or small, you furnish your parts toward the soul.

Matthew Arnold

1822—1888

SOHRAB AND RUSTUM

The story is found in Firdausi's *Shah-Nameh*, the Persian national
epic. Although the last 18 lines of *Sohrab and Rustum*—one of the
great moments in English poetry, that make you catch your
breath—are in Arnold's most distinctively personal vein, the
poem as a whole draws strength from its use of ancient traditional
material—material of a tested humanity and relevance. ' The
use of the traditional,' Arnold claimed, ' above everything else,
gives to a work that *naïveté*, that flavour of reality and truth, which
is the very life of poetry.'

AN EPISODE

And the first grey of morning fill'd the east,
And the fog rose out of the Oxus stream.
But all the Tartar camp along the stream

2 *Oxus:* now Amu Darya, great river of Central Asia, flowing from the
Hindu Kush to the Aral Sea.

Was hush'd, and still the men were plunged in sleep;
Sohrab alone, he slept not; all night long   5
He had lain wakeful, tossing on his bed;
But when the grey dawn stole into his tent,
He rose, and clad himself, and girt his sword,
And took his horseman's cloak, and left his tent,
And went abroad into the cold wet fog,   10
Through the dim camp to Peran-Wisa's tent.
    Through the black Tartar tents he pass'd, which stood
Clustering like bee-hives on the low flat strand
Of Oxus, where the summer-floods o'erflow
When the sun melts the snows in high Pamere;   15
Through the black tents he pass'd, o'er that low strand,
And to a hillock came, a little back
From the stream's brink—the spot where first a boat,
Crossing the stream in summer, scrapes the land.
The men of former times had crown'd the top   20
With a clay fort; but that was fall'n, and now
The Tartars built there Peran-Wisa's tent,
A dome of laths, and o'er it felts were spread.
And Sohrab came there, and went in, and stood
Upon the thick piled carpets in the tent,   25
And found the old man sleeping on his bed
Of rugs and felts, and near him lay his arms.
And Peran-Wisa heard him, though the step
Was dull'd; for he slept light, an old man's sleep;
And he rose quickly on one arm, and said:—   30
    'Who art thou? for it is not yet clear dawn.
Speak! is there news, or any night alarm?'
    But Sohrab came to the bedside, and said:—
'Thou know'st me, Peran-Wisa! it is I.
The sun is not yet risen, and the foe   35
Sleep; but I sleep not; all night long I lie
Tossing and wakeful, and I come to thee.
For so did King Afrasiab bid me seek
Thy counsel, and to heed thee as thy son,
In Samarcand, before the army march'd;   40
And I will tell thee what my heart desires.

5 *Sohrab:* long-lost son of Rustum, the Persian national hero; serving
with the Tartars.   11 *Peran-Wisa:* Afrasiab's vizier, 'the Nestor of the
Tartars'.   15 *Pamere:* Pamir, high plateau bordered by the ranges of
the Hindu Kush, Himalaya, and Tien Shan.   38 *Afrasiab:* Tartar
chieftain who invaded Persia. Rustum led the Persian armies against
him.   40 *Samarcand:* ancient Tartar capital in what is now Uzbekistan.
    A.L.P.   U

Thou know'st if, since from Ader-baijan first
I came among the Tartars and bore arms,
I have still served Afrasiab well, and shown,
At my boy's years, the courage of a man.   45
This too thou know'st, that while I still bear on
The conquering Tartar ensigns through the world,
And beat the Persians back on every field,
I seek one man, one man, and one alone—
Rustum, my father; who I hoped should greet,   50
Should one day greet, upon some well-fought field,
His not unworthy, not inglorious son.
So I long hoped, but him I never find.
Come then, hear now, and grant me what I ask.
Let the two armies rest to-day; but I   55
Will challenge forth the bravest Persian lords
To meet me, man to man; if I prevail,
Rustum will surely hear it; if I fall—
Old man, the dead need no one, claim no kin.
Dim is the rumour of a common fight,   60
Where host meets host, and many names are sunk;
But of a single combat fame speaks clear.'
    He spoke; and Peran-Wisa took the hand
Of the young man in his, and sigh'd, and said:—
  ' O Sohrab, an unquiet heart is thine!   65
Canst thou not rest among the Tartar chiefs,
And share the battle's common chance with us
Who love thee, but must press for ever first,
In single fight incurring single risk,
To find a father thou hast never seen?   70
That were far best, my son, to stay with us
Unmurmuring; in our tents, while it is war,
And when 'tis truce, then in Afrasiab's towns.
But, if this one desire indeed rules all,
To seek out Rustum—seek him not through fight!   75
Seek him in peace, and carry to his arms,
O Sohrab, carry an unwounded son!
But far hence seek him, for he is not here.
For now it is not as when I was young,
When Rustum was in front of every fray;   80
But now he keeps apart, and sits at home,
In Seistan, with Zal, his father old.
Whether that his own mighty strength at last

42 *Ader-baijan:* Azerbaijan, ancient province of north-west Persia, now
partly in the U.S.S.R.   50 *Rustum:* legendary Persian national hero.
82 *Seistan:* district in what is now south-west Afghanistan.

Feels the abhorr'd approaches of old age,
Or in some quarrel with the Persian King. 85
There go!—Thou wilt not? Yet my heart forebodes
Danger or death awaits thee on this field.
Fain would I know thee safe and well, though lost
To us; fain therefore send thee hence, in peace
To seek thy father, not seek single fights 90
In vain;—but who can keep the lion's cub
From ravening, and who govern Rustum's son?
Go, I will grant thee what thy heart desires.'
    So said he, and dropp'd Sohrab's hand, and left
His bed, and the warm rugs whereon he lay; 95
And o'er his chilly limbs his woollen coat
He pass'd, and tied his sandals on his feet,
And threw a white cloak round him, and he took
In his right hand a ruler's staff, no sword;
And on his head he set his sheep-skin cap, 100
Black, glossy, curl'd, the fleece of Kara-Kul;
And raised the curtain of his tent, and call'd
His herald to his side, and went abroad.
    The sun by this had risen, and clear'd the fog
From the broad Oxus and the glittering sands. 105
And from their tents the Tartar horsemen filed
Into the open plain; so Haman bade—
Haman, who next to Peran-Wisa ruled
The host, and still was in his lusty prime.
From their black tents, long files of horse, they stream'd; 110
As when some grey November morn the files,
In marching order spread, of long-neck'd cranes
Stream over Casbin and the southern slopes
Of Elburz, from the Aralian estuaries,
Or some frore Caspian reed-bed, southward bound 115
For the warm Persian sea-board—so they stream'd.
The Tartars of the Oxus, the King's guard,
First, with black sheep-skin caps and with long spears;
Large men, large steeds; who from Bokhara come
And Khiva, and ferment the milk of mares. 120
Next, the more temperate Toorkmuns of the south,
The Tukas, and the lances of Salore,

101 *Kara-Kul:* near Bokhara; famed for its sheep. 107 *Haman:*
Tartar commander. 113 *Casbin:* Kazvin, ancient city near Elburz
mountain-range. 114 *Elburz:* mountain-range south of the Caspian
Sea. 115 *Frore:* frozen. 119-20 *Bokhara . . . Khiva:* ancient Tartar
cities (and provinces) south of the Aral Sea. 121 *Toorkmuns:* Turk-
mens, a Turkic people now in Soviet Turkmenistan. 122 *Tukas . . .
Salore:* Turkmen tribes of north Persian borders.

And those from Attruck and the Caspian sands;
Light men and on light steeds, who only drink
The acrid milk of camels, and their wells. 125
And then a swarm of wandering horse, who came
From far, and a more doubtful service own'd;
The Tartars of Ferghana, from the banks
Of the Jaxartes, men with scanty beards
And close-set skull-caps; and those wilder hordes 130
Who roam o'er Kipchak and the northern waste,
Kalmucks and unkempt Kuzzaks, tribes who stray
Nearest the Pole, and wandering Kirghizzes,
Who come on shaggy ponies from Pamere;
These all filed out from camp into the plain. 135
And on the other side the Persians form'd;—
First a light cloud of horse, Tartars they seem'd,
The Ilyats of Khorassan; and behind,
The royal troops of Persia, horse and foot,
Marshall'd battalions bright in burnish'd steel. 140
But Peran-Wisa with his herald came,
Threading the Tartar squadrons to the front,
And with his staff kept back the foremost ranks.
And when Ferood, who led the Persians, saw
That Peran-Wisa kept the Tartars back, 145
He took his spear, and to the front he came,
And check'd his ranks, and fix'd them where they stood.
And the old Tartar came upon the sand
Betwixt the silent hosts, and spake, and said:—
'Ferood, and ye, Persians and Tartars, hear! 150
Let there be truce between the hosts to-day.
But choose a champion from the Persian lords
To fight our champion Sohrab, man to man.'
As, in the country, on a morn in June,
When the dew glistens on the pearled ears, 155
A shiver runs through the deep corn for joy—
So, when they heard what Peran-Wisa said,
A thrill through all the Tartar squadrons ran

123 *Attruck:* river Attreck, in north Persia, flowing into the Caspian Sea. 128 *Ferghana:* region of Central Asia, now part of the Kirghiz and Uzbek Soviet Republics. 129 *Jaxartes:* now Syr Darya, great river of Central Asia, flowing from the Tien Shan to the Aral Sea. 131 *Kipchak:* plain north of the Syr Darya. 132 *Kalmucks:* Kalmyks, Mongol nomads found in various parts of Central Asia; *Kuzzaks:* Kazakhs, Turkic nomads now in the Kazakh Soviet Republic. 133 *Kirghizzes:* nomadic Turkic people, now in the Kirghiz Soviet Republic. 138 *Ilyats of Khorassan:* nomads of north-east Persia. 144 *Ferood:* brother of Kai Khosroo (see line 223).

Of pride and hope for Sohrab, whom they loved.
    But as a troop of pedlars, from Cabool,   160
Cross underneath the Indian Caucasus,
That vast sky-neighbouring mountain of milk snow;
Crossing so high, that, as they mount, they pass
Long flocks of travelling birds dead on the snow,
Choked by the air, and scarce can they themselves   165
Slake their parch'd throats with sugar'd mulberries—
In single file they move, and stop their breath,
For fear they should dislodge the o'erhanging snows—
So the pale Persians held their breath with fear.
    And to Ferood his brother chiefs came up   170
To counsel; Gudurz and Zoarrah came,
And Feraburz, who ruled the Persian host
Second, and was the uncle of the King;
These came and counsell'd, and then Gudurz said:—
    ' Ferood, shame bids us take their challenge up,   175
Yet champion have we none to match this youth.
He has the wild stag's foot, the lion's heart.
But Rustum came last night; aloof he sits
And sullen, and has pitch'd his tents apart.
Him will I seek, and carry to his ear   180
The Tartar challenge, and this young man's name.
Haply he will forget his wrath, and fight.
Stand forth the while, and take their challenge up.'
    So spake he; and Ferood stood forth and cried:—
' Old man, be it agreed as thou hast said!   185
Let Sohrab arm, and we will find a man.'
    He spake: and Peran-Wisa turn'd, and strode
Back through the opening squadrons to his tent.
But through the anxious Persians Gudurz ran,
And cross'd the camp which lay behind, and reach'd,   190
Out on the sands beyond it, Rustum's tents.
Of scarlet cloth they were, and glittering gay,
Just pitch'd; the high pavilion in the midst
Was Rustum's, and his men lay camp'd around.
And Gudurz enter'd Rustum's tent, and found   195
Rustum; his morning meal was done, but still
The table stood before him, charged with food—
A side of roasted sheep, and cakes of bread,
And dark green melons; and there Rustum sate
Listless, and held a falcon on his wrist,   200

160 *Cabool:* Kabul, now capital of Afghanistan. 171 *Gudurz and Zoarrah:* leaders of the Persian armies. 172 *Feraburz:* uncle of Kai Khosroo (see line 223).

And play'd with it; but Gudurz came and stood
Before him; and he look'd, and saw him stand,
And with a cry sprang up and dropp'd the bird,
And greeted Gudurz with both hands, and said:—
    'Welcome! these eyes could see no better sight.   205
What news? but sit down first, and eat and drink.'
    But Gudurz stood in the tent-door, and said:—
'Not now! a time will come to eat and drink,
But not to-day; to-day has other needs.
The armies are drawn out, and stand at gaze;   210
For from the Tartars is a challenge brought
To pick a champion from the Persian lords
To fight their champion—and thou know'st his name—
Sohrab men call him, but his birth is hid.
O Rustum, like thy might is this young man's!   215
He has the wild stag's foot, the lion's heart;
And he is young, and Iran's chiefs are old,
Or else too weak; and all eyes turn to thee.
Come down and help us, Rustum, or we lose!'
    He spoke; but Rustum answer'd with a smile:—   220
'Go to! if Iran's chiefs are old, then I
Am older; if the young are weak, the King
Errs strangely; for the King, for Kai Khosroo,
Himself is young, and honours younger men,
And lets the aged moulder to their graves.   225
Rustum he loves no more, but loves the young—
The young may rise at Sohrab's vaunts, not I.
For what care I, though all speak Sohrab's fame?
For would that I myself had such a son,
And not that one slight helpless girl I have—   230
A son so famed, so brave, to send to war,
And I to tarry with the snow-hair'd Zal,
My father, whom the robber Afghans vex,
And clip his borders short, and drive his herds,
And he has none to guard his weak old age.   235
There would I go, and hang my armour up,
And with my great name fence that weak old man,
And spend the goodly treasures I have got,
And rest my age, and hear of Sohrab's fame,
And leave to death the hosts of thankless kings,   240
And with these slaughterous hands draw sword no more.'
    He spoke, and smiled; and Gudurz made reply:—
'What then, O Rustum, will men say to this,

223 *Kai Khosroo:* Khusru I (reigned 531-78), great Persian king and
conqueror.

When Sohrab dares our bravest forth, and seeks
Thee most of all, and thou, whom most he seeks,   245
Hidest thy face? Take heed lest men should say:
Like some old miser, Rustum hoards his fame,
And shuns to peril it with younger men.'
    And greatly moved, then Rustum made reply:—
' O Gudurz, wherefore dost thou say such words?   250
Thou knowest better words than this to say.
What is one more, one less, obscure or famed,
Valiant or craven, young or old, to me?
Are not they mortal, am not I myself?
But who for men of nought would do great deeds?   255
Come, thou shalt see how Rustum hoards his fame!
But I will fight unknown, and in plain arms;
Let not men say of Rustum, he was match'd
In single fight with any mortal man.'
    He spoke, and frown'd; and Gudurz turn'd, and ran   260
Back quickly through the camp in fear and joy—
Fear at his wrath, but joy that Rustum came.
But Rustum strode to his tent-door, and call'd
His followers in, and bade them bring his arms,
And clad himself in steel; the arms he chose   265
Were plain, and on his shield was no device,
Only his helm was rich, inlaid with gold,
And, from the fluted spine atop, a plume
Of horsehair waved, a scarlet horsehair plume.
So arm'd, he issued forth; and Ruksh, his horse,   270
Follow'd him like a faithful hound at heel—
Ruksh, whose renown was noised through all the earth,
The horse, whom Rustum on a foray once
Did in Bokhara by the river find
A colt beneath its dam, and drove him home,   275
And rear'd him; a bright bay, with lofty crest,
Dight with a saddle-cloth of broider'd green
Crusted with gold, and on the ground were work'd
All beasts of chase, all beasts which hunters know.
So follow'd, Rustum left his tents, and cross'd   280
The camp, and to the Persian host appear'd.
And all the Persians knew him, and with shouts
Hail'd; but the Tartars knew not who he was.
And dear as the wet diver to the eyes
Of his pale wife who waits and weeps on shore,   285
By sandy Bahrein, in the Persian Gulf,
Plunging all day in the blue waves, at night,

277 *Dight:* furnished.

Having made up his tale of precious pearls,
Rejoins her in their hut upon the sands—
So dear to the pale Persians Rustum came.   290
  And Rustum to the Persian front advanced,
And Sohrab arm'd in Haman's tent, and came.
And as afield the reapers cut a swath
Down through the middle of a rich man's corn,
And on each side are squares of standing corn,   295
And in the midst a stubble, short and bare—
So on each side were squares of men, with spears
Bristling, and in the midst, the open sand.
And Rustum came upon the sand, and cast
His eyes toward the Tartar tents, and saw   300
Sohrab come forth, and eyed him as he came.
  As some rich woman, on a winter's morn,
Eyes through her silken curtains the poor drudge
Who with numb blacken'd fingers makes her fire—
At cock-crow, on a starlit winter's morn,   305
When the frost flowers the whiten'd window-panes—
And wonders how she lives, and what the thoughts
Of that poor drudge may be; so Rustum eyed
The unknown adventurous youth, who from afar
Came seeking Rustum, and defying forth   310
All the most valiant chiefs; long he perused
His spirited air, and wonder'd who he was.
For very young he seem'd, tenderly rear'd;
Like some young cypress, tall, and dark, and straight,
Which in a queen's secluded garden throws   315
Its slight dark shadow on the moonlit turf,
By midnight, to a bubbling fountain's sound—
So slender Sohrab seem'd, so softly rear'd.
And a deep pity enter'd Rustum's soul
As he beheld him coming; and he stood,   320
And beckon'd to him with his hand, and said:—
  ' O thou young man, the air of Heaven is soft,
And warm, and pleasant; but the grave is cold!
Heaven's air is better than the cold dead grave.
Behold me! I am vast, and clad in iron,   325
And tried; and I have stood on many a field
Of blood, and I have fought with many a foe—
Never was that field lost, or that foe saved.
O Sohrab, wherefore wilt thou rush on death?
Be govern'd! quit the Tartar host, and come   330
To Iran, and be as my son to me,
  288 *Tale:* total.

And fight beneath my banner till I die!
There are no youths in Iran brave as thou.'
   So he spake, mildly; Sohrab heard his voice,
The mighty voice of Rustum, and he saw   335
His giant figure planted on the sand,
Sole, like some single tower, which a chief
Hath builded on the waste in former years
Against the robbers; and he saw that head,
Streak'd with its first grey hairs;—hope filled his soul,   340
And he ran forward and embraced his knees,
And clasp'd his hand within his own, and said:—
   ' O, by thy father's head! by thine own soul!
Art thou not Rustum? speak! art thou not he? '
   But Rustum eyed askance the kneeling youth,   345
And turn'd away, and spake to his own soul:—
   ' Ah me, I muse what this young fox may mean!
False, wily, boastful, are these Tartar boys.
For if I now confess this thing he asks,
And hide it not, but say: *Rustum is here!*   350
He will not yield indeed, nor quit our foes,
But he will find some pretext not to fight,
And praise my fame, and proffer courteous gifts,
A belt or sword perhaps, and go his way.
And on a feast-tide, in Afrasiab's hall,   355
In Samarcand, he will arise and cry:
" I challenged once, when the two armies camp'd
Beside the Oxus, all the Persian lords
To cope with me in single fight; but they
Shrank, only Rustum dared; then he and I   360
Changed gifts, and went on equal terms away."
So will he speak, perhaps, while men applaud;
Then were the chiefs of Iran shamed through me.'
   And then he turn'd, and sternly spake aloud:—
' Rise! wherefore dost thou vainly question thus   365
Of Rustum? I am here, whom thou hast call'd
By challenge forth; make good thy vaunt, or yield!
Is it with Rustum only thou wouldst fight?
Rash boy, men look on Rustum's face and flee!
For well I know, that did great Rustum stand   370
Before thy face this day, and were reveal'd,
There would be then no talk of fighting more.
But being what I am, I tell thee this—
Do thou record it in thine inmost soul:
Either thou shalt renounce thy vaunt and yield,   375
Or else thy bones shall strew this sand, till winds

Bleach them, or Oxus with his summer-floods,
Oxus in summer wash them all away.'
 He spoke; and Sohrab answer'd, on his feet:—
' Art thou so fierce? Thou wilt not fright me so!   380
I am no girl, to be made pale by words.
Yet this thou hast said well, did Rustum stand
Here on this field, there were no fighting then.
But Rustum is far hence, and we stand here.
Begin! thou art more vast, more dread than I,   385
And thou art proved, I know, and I am young—
But yet success sways with the breath of Heaven.
And though thou thinkest that thou knowest sure
Thy victory, yet thou canst not surely know.
For we are all, like swimmers in the sea,   390
Poised on the top of a huge wave of fate,
Which hangs uncertain to which side to fall.
And whether it will heave us up to land,
Or whether it will roll us out to sea,
Back out to sea, to the deep waves of death,   395
We know not, and no search will make us know;
Only the event will teach us in its hour.'
 He spoke, and Rustum answer'd not, but hurl'd
His spear; down from the shoulder, down it came,
As on some partridge in the corn a hawk,   400
That long has tower'd in the airy clouds,
Drops like a plummet; Sohrab saw it come,
And sprang aside, quick as a flash; the spear
Hiss'd, and went quivering down into the sand,
Which it sent flying wide;—then Sohrab threw   405
In turn, and full struck Rustum's shield; sharp rang,
The iron plates rang sharp, but turn'd the spear.
And Rustum seized his club, which none but he
Could wield; an unlopp'd trunk it was, and huge,
Still rough—like those which men in treeless plains   410
To build them boats fish from the flooded rivers,
Hyphasis or Hydaspes, when, high up
By their dark springs, the wind in winter-time
Hath made in Himalayan forests wrack,
And strewn the channels with torn boughs—so huge   415
The club which Rustum lifted now, and struck
One stroke; but again Sohrab sprang aside,
Lithe as the glancing snake, and the club came
Thundering to earth, and leapt from Rustum's hand.

412 *Hyphasis* . . . *Hydaspes:* classical names of the rivers Sutlej and
Jhelum, in the Punjab.

And Rustum follow'd his own blow, and fell 420
To his knees, and with his fingers clutch'd the sand;
And now might Sohrab have unsheathed his sword,
And pierced the mighty Rustum while he lay
Dizzy, and on his knees, and choked with sand;
But he look'd on, and smiled, nor bared his sword, 425
But courteously drew back, and spoke, and said:—
' Thou strik'st too hard! that club of thine will float
Upon the summer-floods, and not my bones.
But rise, and be not wroth! not wroth am I;
No, when I see thee, wrath forsakes my soul. 430
Thou say'st, thou art not Rustum; be it so!
Who art thou then, that canst so touch my soul?
Boy as I am, I have seen battles too—
Have waded foremost in their bloody waves,
And heard their hollow roar of dying men; 435
But never was my heart thus touch'd before.
Are they from Heaven, these softenings of the heart?
O thou old warrior, let us yield to Heaven!
Come, plant we here in earth our angry spears,
And make a truce, and sit upon this sand, 440
And pledge each other in red wine, like friends,
And thou shalt talk to me of Rustum's deeds.
There are enough foes in the Persian host,
Whom I may meet, and strike, and feel no pang;
Champions enough Afrasiab has, whom thou 445
Mayst fight; fight *them*, when they confront thy spear!
But oh, let there be peace 'twixt thee and me! '
He ceased, but while he spake, Rustum had risen,
And stood erect, trembling with rage; his club
He left to lie, but had regain'd his spear, 450
Whose fiery point now in his mail'd right-hand
Blazed bright and baleful, like that autumn-star,
The baleful sign of fevers; dust had soil'd
His stately crest, and dimm'd his glittering arms.
His breast heaved, his lips foam'd, and twice his voice 455
Was choked with rage; at last these words broke way:—
' Girl! nimble with thy feet, not with thy hands!
Curl'd minion, dancer, coiner of sweet words!
Fight, let me hear thy hateful voice no more!
Thou art not in Afrasiab's gardens now 460
With Tartar girls, with whom thou art wont to dance;
But on the Oxus-sands, and in the dance

452 *That autumn-star:* Sirius, supposed to cause pestilence on its ap-
pearance with the sun in July and August.

Of battle, and with me, who make no play
Of war; I fight it out, and hand to hand.
Speak not to me of truce, and pledge, and wine!   465
Remember all thy valour; try thy feints
And cunning! all the pity I had is gone;
Because thou hast shamed me before both the hosts
With thy light skipping tricks, and thy girl's wiles.'
    He spoke, and Sohrab kindled at his taunts,   470
And he too drew his sword; at once they rush'd
Together, as two eagles on one prey
Come rushing down together from the clouds,
One from the east, one from the west; their shields
Dash'd with a clang together, and a din   475
Rose, such as that the sinewy woodcutters
Make often in the forest's heart at morn,
Of hewing axes, crashing trees—such blows
Rustum and Sohrab on each other hail'd.
And you would say that sun and stars took part   480
In that unnatural conflict; for a cloud
Grew suddenly in Heaven, and dark'd the sun
Over the fighters' heads; and a wind rose
Under their feet, and moaning swept the plain,
And in a sandy whirlwind wrapp'd the pair.   485
In gloom they twain were wrapp'd, and they alone;
For both the on-looking hosts on either hand
Stood in broad daylight, and the sky was pure,
And the sun sparkled on the Oxus stream.
But in the gloom they fought, with bloodshot eyes   490
And labouring breath; first Rustum struck the shield
Which Sohrab held stiff out; the steel-spiked spear
Rent the tough plates, but fail'd to reach the skin,
And Rustum pluck'd it back with angry groan.
Then Sohrab with his sword smote Rustum's helm,   495
Nor clove its steel quite through; but all the crest
He shore away, and that proud horsehair plume,
Never till now defiled, sank to the dust;
And Rustum bow'd his head; but then the gloom
Grew blacker, thunder rumbled in the air,   500
And lightnings rent the cloud; and Ruksh, the horse,
Who stood at hand, utter'd a dreadful cry;—
No horse's cry was that, most like the roar
Of some pain'd desert-lion, who all day
Hath trail'd the hunter's javelin in his side,   505
And comes at night to die upon the sand.
The two hosts heard that cry, and quaked for fear,

And Oxus curdled as it cross'd his stream.
But Sohrab heard, and quail'd not, but rush'd on,
And struck again; and again Rustum bow'd   510
His head; but this time all the blade, like glass,
Sprang in a thousand shivers on the helm,
And in the hand the hilt remain'd alone.
Then Rustum raised his head; his dreadful eyes
Glared, and he shook on high his menacing spear, 515
And shouted: *Rustum!*—Sohrab heard that shout,
And shrank amazed; back he recoil'd one step,
And scann'd with blinking eyes the advancing form;
And then he stood bewilder'd; and he dropp'd
His covering shield, and the spear pierced his side. 520
He reel'd, and staggering back, sank to the ground;
And then the gloom dispersed, and the wind fell,
And the bright sun broke forth, and melted all
The cloud; and the two armies saw the pair—
Saw Rustum standing, safe upon his feet,   525
And Sohrab, wounded, on the bloody sand.
    Then, with a bitter smile, Rustum began:—
'Sohrab, thou thoughtest in thy mind to kill
A Persian lord this day, and strip his corpse,
And bear thy trophies to Afrasiab's tent.   530
Or else that the great Rustum would come down
Himself to fight, and that thy wiles would move
His heart to take a gift, and let thee go.
And then that all the Tartar host would praise
Thy courage or thy craft, and spread thy fame,   535
To glad thy father in his weak old age.
Fool, thou art slain, and by an unknown man!
Dearer to the red jackals shalt thou be
Than to thy friends, and to thy father old.'
    And, with a fearless mien, Sohrab replied:—   540
'Unknown thou art; yet thy fierce vaunt is vain.
Thou dost not slay me, proud and boastful man!
No! Rustum slays me, and his filial heart.
For were I match'd with ten such men as thee,
And I were that which till to-day I was,   545
They should be lying here, I standing there.
But that belovéd name unnerved my arm—
That name, and something, I confess, in thee,
Which troubles all my heart, and made my shield
Fall; and thy spear transfix'd an unarm'd foe.   550
And now thou boastest, and insult'st my fate.
But hear thou this, fierce man, tremble to hear:

The mighty Rustum shall avenge my death!
My father, whom I seek through all the world,
He shall avenge my death, and punish thee!'   555
   As when some hunter in the spring hath found
A breeding eagle sitting on her nest,
Upon the craggy isle of a hill-lake,
And pierced her with an arrow as she rose,
And follow'd her to find her where she fell   560
Far off;—anon her mate comes winging back
From hunting, and a great way off descries
His huddling young left sole; at that, he checks
His pinion, and with short uneasy sweeps
Circles above his eyry, with loud screams   565
Chiding his mate back to her nest; but she
Lies dying, with the arrow in her side,
In some far stony gorge out of his ken,
A heap of fluttering feathers—never more
Shall the lake glass her, flying over it;   570
Never the black and dripping precipices
Echo her stormy scream as she sails by—
As that poor bird flies home, nor knows his loss,
So Rustum knew not his own loss, but stood
Over his dying son, and knew him not.   575
   But, with a cold incredulous voice, he said:—
'What prate is this of fathers and revenge?
The mighty Rustum never had a son.'
   And, with a failing voice, Sohrab replied:—
'Ah yes, he had! and that lost son am I.   580
Surely the news will one day reach his ear,
Reach Rustum, where he sits, and tarries long,
Somewhere, I know not where, but far from here;
And pierce him like a stab, and make him leap
To arms, and cry for vengeance upon thee.   585
Fierce man, bethink thee, for an only son!
What will that grief, what will that vengeance be?
Oh, could I live, till I that grief had seen!
Yet him I pity not so much, but her,
My mother, who in Ader-baijan dwells   590
With that old king, her father, who grows grey
With age, and rules over the valiant Koords.
Her most I pity, who no more will see
Sohrab returning from the Tartar camp,
With spoils and honour, when the war is done.   595
But a dark rumour will be bruited up,

592 *Koords:* Kurds, semi-nomadic people of Persia, Turkey, and Iraq.

From tribe to tribe, until it reach her ear;
And then will that defenceless woman learn
That Sohrab will rejoice her sight no more,
But that in battle with a nameless foe,   600
By the far-distant Oxus, he is slain.'
    He spoke; and as he ceased, he wept aloud,
Thinking of her he left, and his own death.
He spoke; but Rustum listen'd, plunged in thought.
Nor did he yet believe it was his son   605
Who spoke, although he call'd back names he knew;
For he had had sure tidings that the babe,
Which was in Ader-baijan born to him,
Had been a puny girl, no boy at all—
So that sad mother sent him word, for fear   610
Rustum should seek the boy, to train in arms.
And so he deem'd that either Sohrab took,
By a false boast, the style of Rustum's son;
Or that men gave it him, to swell his fame.
So deem'd he; yet he listen'd, plunged in thought   615
And his soul set to grief, as the vast tide
Of the bright rocking Ocean sets to shore
At the full moon; tears gather'd in his eyes;
For he remember'd his own early youth,
And all its bounding rapture; as, at dawn,   620
The shepherd from his mountain-lodge descries
A far, bright city, smitten by the sun,
Through many rolling clouds—so Rustum saw
His youth; saw Sohrab's mother, in her bloom;
And that old king, her father, who loved well   625
His wandering guest, and gave him his fair child
With joy; and all the pleasant life they led,
They three, in that long-distant summer-time—
The castle, and the dewy woods, and hunt
And hound, and morn on those delightful hills   630
In Ader-baijan. And he saw that youth,
Of age and looks to be his own dear son,
Piteous and lovely, lying on the sand,
Like some rich hyacinth which by the scythe
Of an unskilful gardener has been cut,   635
Mowing the garden grass-plots near its bed,
And lies, a fragrant tower of purple bloom,
On the mown, dying grass—so Sohrab lay,

634 *Hyacinth:* Cf. the death of the youth Hyacinthus in Greek mythology
—like Sohrab, he was killed unintentionally by the one who loved him
(Apollo).

Lovely in death, upon the common sand.
And Rustum gazed on him with grief, and said:—　　640
  ' O Sohrab, thou indeed art such a son
Whom Rustum, wert thou his, might well have loved.
Yet here thou errest, Sohrab, or else men
Have told thee false—thou art not Rustum's son.
For Rustum had no son; one child he had—　　645
But one—a girl; who with her mother now
Plies some light female task, nor dreams of us—
Of us she dreams not, nor of wounds, nor war.'
  But Sohrab answer'd him in wrath; for now
The anguish of the deep-fix'd spear grew fierce,　　650
And he desired to draw forth the steel,
And let the blood flow free, and so to die—
But first he would convince his stubborn foe;
And, rising sternly on one arm, he said:—
  ' Man, who art thou who dost deny my words?　　655
Truth sits upon the lips of dying men,
And falsehood, while I lived, was far from mine.
I tell thee, prick'd upon this arm I bear
That seal which Rustum to my mother gave,
That she might prick it on the babe she bore.'　　660
  He spoke; and all the blood left Rustum's cheeks,
And his knees totter'd, and he smote his hand
Against his breast, his heavy mailed hand,
That the hard iron corslet clank'd aloud;
And to his heart he press'd the other hand,　　665
And in a hollow voice he spake, and said:—
  ' Sohrab, that were a proof which could not lie!
If thou show this, then art thou Rustum's son.'
  Then, with weak hasty fingers, Sohrab loosed
His belt, and near the shoulder bared his arm,　　670
And show'd a sign in faint vermilion points
Prick'd; as a cunning workman, in Pekin,
Pricks with vermilion some clear porcelain vase,
An emperor's gift—at early morn he paints,
And all day long, and, when night comes, the lamp　　675
Lights up his studious forehead and thin hands—
So delicately prick'd the sign appear'd
On Sohrab's arm, the sign of Rustum's seal.
It was that griffin, which of old rear'd Zal,
Rustum's great father, whom they left to die,　　680
A helpless babe, among the mountain-rocks;
Him that kind creature found, and rear'd, and loved—
679 *Griffin:* fabulous eagle-headed lion.

Then Rustum took it for his glorious sign.
And Sohrab bared that image on his arm,
And himself scann'd it long with mournful eyes, 685
And then he touch'd it with his hand and said:—
  'How say'st thou? Is that sign the proper sign
Of Rustum's son, or of some other man's?'
  He spoke; but Rustum gazed, and gazed, and stood
Speechless; and then he utter'd one sharp cry: 690
O boy—thy father!—and his voice choked there.
And then a dark cloud pass'd before his eyes,
And his head swam, and he sank down to earth.
But Sohrab crawl'd to where he lay, and cast
His arms about his neck, and kiss'd his lips, 695
And with fond faltering fingers stroked his cheeks,
Trying to call him back to life; and life
Came back to Rustum, and he oped his eyes,
And they stood wide with horror; and he seized
In both his hands the dust which lay around, 700
And threw it on his head, and smirch'd his hair,—
His hair, and face, and beard, and glittering arms;
And strong convulsive groanings shook his breast,
And his sobs choked him; and he clutch'd his sword,
To draw it, and for ever let life out. 705
But Sohrab saw his thought, and held his hands,
And with a soothing voice he spake, and said:—
  'Father, forbear! for I but meet to-day
The doom which at my birth was written down
In Heaven, and thou art Heaven's unconscious hand. 710
Surely my heart cried out that it was thou,
When first I saw thee; and thy heart spoke too,
I know it! but fate trod those promptings down
Under its iron heel; fate, fate engaged
The strife, and hurl'd me on my father's spear. 715
But let us speak no more of this! I find
My father; let me feel that I have found!
Come, sit beside me on this sand, and take
My head betwixt thy hands, and kiss my cheeks,
And wash them with thy tears, and say: *My son!* 720
Quick! quick! for number'd are my sands of life,
And swift; for like the lightning to this field
I came, and like the wind I go away—
Sudden, and swift, and like a passing wind.
But it was writ in Heaven that this should be.' 725
  So said he, and his voice released the heart
Of Rustum, and his tears broke forth; he cast

His arms round his son's neck, and wept aloud,
And kiss'd him. And awe fell on both the hosts,
When they saw Rustum's grief; and Ruksh, the horse,   730
With his head bowing to the ground and mane
Sweeping the dust, came near, and in mute woe
First to the one then to the other moved
His head, as if inquiring what their grief
Might mean; and from his dark, compassionate eyes,   735
The big warm tears roll'd down, and caked the sand.
But Rustum chid him with stern voice, and said:—
    ' Ruksh, now thou grievest; but, O Ruksh, thy feet
Should first have rotted on their nimble joints,
Or ere they brought thy master to this field! '   740
    But Sohrab look'd upon the horse and said;—
' Is this, then, Ruksh? How often, in past days,
My mother told me of thee, thou brave steed,
My terrible father's terrible horse! and said,
That I should one day find thy lord and thee.   745
Come, let me lay my hand upon thy mane!
O Ruksh, thou art more fortunate than I;
For thou hast gone where I shall never go,
And snuff'd the breezes of my father's home.
And thou hast trod the sands of Seistan,   750
And seen the River of Helmund, and the Lake
Of Zirrah; and the aged Zal himself
Has often stroked thy neck, and given thee food,
Corn in a golden platter soak'd with wine,
And said: O Ruksh! bear Rustum well!—but I   755
Have never known my grandsire's furrow'd face,
Nor seen his lofty house in Seistan,
Nor slaked my thirst at the clear Helmund stream;
But lodged among my father's foes, and seen
Afrasiab's cities only, Samarcand,   760
Bokhara, and lone Khiva in the waste,
And the black Toorkmun tents; and only drunk
The desert rivers, Moorghab and Tejend,
Kohik, and where the Kalmuks feed their sheep,
The northern Sir; and this great Oxus stream,   765
The yellow Oxus, by whose brink I die.'
    Then, with a heavy groan, Rustum bewail'd:—
' Oh, that its waves were flowing over me!

751 *Helmund:* or Helmand, river flowing into Lake Helmand, Seistan.
752 *Zirrah:* lake in Seistan. 763-4 *Moorghab . . . Tejend . . . Kohik:*
Central Asian rivers to the north of Persia. 765 *Sir:* the Syr Darya.

Oh, that I saw its grains of yellow silt
Roll tumbling in the current o'er my head!'   770
   But, with a grave mild voice, Sohrab replied:—
'Desire not that, my father! thou must live.
For some are born to do great deeds, and live,
As some are born to be obscured, and die.
Do thou the deeds I die too young to do,   775
And reap a second glory in thine age;
Thou art my father, and thy gain is mine.
But come! thou seest this great host of men
Which follow me; I pray thee, slay not these!
Let me entreat for them; what have they done?   780
They follow'd me, my hope, my fame, my star.
Let them all cross the Oxus back in peace.
But me thou must bear hence, not send with them,
But carry me with thee to Seistan,
And place me on a bed, and mourn for me,   785
Thou, and the snow-hair'd Zal, and all thy friends.
And thou must lay me in that lovely earth,
And heap a stately mound above my bones,
And plant a far-seen pillar over all.
That so the passing horseman on the waste   790
May see my tomb a great way off, and cry:
Sohrab, the mighty Rustum's son, lies there,
Whom his great father did in ignorance kill!
And I be not forgotten in my grave.'
   And, with a mournful voice, Rustum replied:—   795
'Fear not! as thou has said, Sohrab, my son,
So shall it be; for I will burn my tents,
And quit the host, and bear thee hence with me,
And carry thee away to Seistan,
And place thee on a bed, and mourn for thee,   800
With the snow-headed Zal, and all my friends.
And I will lay thee in that lovely earth,
And heap a stately mound above thy bones,
And plant a far-seen pillar over all,
And men shall not forget thee in thy grave.   805
And I will spare thy host; yea, let them go!
Let them all cross the Oxus back in peace!
What should I do with slaying any more?
For would that all whom I have ever slain
Might be once more alive; my bitterest foes,   810
And they who were call'd champions in their time,
And through whose death I won that fame I have—
And I were nothing but a common man,

A poor, mean soldier, and without renown,
So thou mightest live too, my son, my son!   815
Or rather would that I, even I myself,
Might now be lying on this bloody sand,
Near death, and by an ignorant stroke of thine,
Not thou of mine! and I might die, not thou;
And I, not thou, be borne to Seistan;   820
And Zal might weep above my grave, not thine;
And say: *O son, I weep thee not too sore,*
For willingly, I know, thou met'st thine end!
But now in blood and battles was my youth,
And full of blood and battles is my age,   825
And I shall never end this life of blood.'
    Then, at the point of death, Sohrab replied:—
' A life of blood indeed, thou dreadful man!
But thou shalt yet have peace; only not now,
Not yet! but thou shalt have it on that day,   830
When thou shalt sail in a high-masted ship,
Thou and the other peers of Kai Khosroo,
Returning home over the salt blue sea,
From laying thy dear master in his grave.'
    And Rustum gazed in Sohrab's face, and said:—   835
' Soon be that day, my son, and deep that sea!
Till then, if fate so wills, let me endure.'
    He spoke; and Sohrab smiled on him, and took
The spear, and drew it from his side, and eased
His wound's imperious anguish; but the blood   840
Came welling from the open gash, and life
Flow'd with the stream;—all down his cold white side
The crimson torrent ran, dim now and soil'd,
Like the soil'd tissue of white violets
Left, freshly gather'd, on their native bank,   845
By children whom their nurses call with haste
Indoors from the sun's eye; his head droop'd low,
His limbs grew slack; motionless, white, he lay—
White, with eyes closed; only when heavy gasps,
Deep heavy gasps quivering through all his frame,   850
Convulsed him back to life, he open'd them,
And fix'd them feebly on his father's face;
Till now all strength was ebb'd, and from his limbs
Unwillingly the spirit fled away,
Regretting the warm mansion which it left,   855
And youth, and bloom, and this delightful world.
    So, on the bloody sand, Sohrab lay dead;
And the great Rustum drew his horseman's cloak

Down o'er his face, and sate by his dead son.
As those black granite pillars, once high-rear'd 860
By Jemshid in Persepolis, to bear
His house, now 'mid their broken flights of steps
Lie prone, enormous, down the mountain side—
So in the sand lay Rustum by his son.

And night came down over the solemn waste, 865
And the two gazing hosts, and that sole pair,
And darken'd all; and a cold fog, with night,
Crept from the Oxus. Soon a hum arose,
As of a great assembly loosed, and fires
Began to twinkle through the fog; for now 870
Both armies moved to camp, and took their meal;
The Persians took it on the open sands
Southward, the Tartars by the river marge;
And Rustum and his son were left alone.

But the majestic river floated on, 875
Out of the mist and hum of that low land,
Into the frosty starlight, and there moved,
Rejoicing, through the hush'd Chorasmian waste,
Under the solitary moon;—he flow'd
Right for the polar star, past Orgunjè, 880
Brimming, and bright, and large; then sands begin
To hem his watery march, and dam his streams,
And split his currents; that for many a league
The shorn and parcell'd Oxus strains along
Through beds of sand and matted rushy isles— 885
Oxus, forgetting the bright speed he had
In his high mountain-cradle in Pamere,
A foil'd circuitous wanderer—till at last
The long'd-for dash of waves is heard, and wide
His luminous home of waters opens, bright 890
And tranquil, from whose floor the new-bathed stars
Emerge, and shine upon the Aral Sea.

861 *Jemshid:* early legendary Persian king, celebrated as the founder of
Persepolis, ancient capital of the Persian empire. 878 *Chorasmian waste:*
region of Khorezm, south of the Amu Darya delta. 880 *Orgunjè:* old
Tartar city between Khiva and the Aral Sea.

George Meredith

1828—1909

THE LARK ASCENDING

He rises and begins to round,
He drops the silver chain of sound,
Of many links without a break,
In chirrup, whistle, slur and shake,
All intervolved and spreading wide,   5
Like water-dimples down a tide
Where ripple ripple overcurls
And eddy into eddy whirls;
A press of hurried notes that run
So fleet they scarce are more than one,   10
Yet changeingly the trills repeat
And linger ringing while they fleet,
Sweet to the quick o' the ear, and dear
To her beyond the handmaid ear,
Who sits beside our inner springs,   15
Too often dry for this he brings,
Which seems the very jet of earth
At sight of sun, her music's mirth,
As up he wings the spiral stair,
A song of light, and pierces air   20
With fountain ardour, fountain play,
To reach the shining tops of day,
And drink in everything discerned
An ecstasy to music turned,
Impelled by what his happy bill   25
Disperses; drinking, showering still,
Unthinking save that he may give
His voice the outlet, there to live
Renewed in endless notes of glee,
So thirsty of his voice is he,   30
For all to hear and all to know
That he is joy, awake, aglow,
The tumult of the heart to hear
Through pureness filtered crystal-clear,
And know the pleasure sprinkled bright   35
By simple singing of delight,
Shrill, irreflective, unrestrained,
Rapt, ringing, on the jet sustained

Without a break, without a fall,
Sweet-silvery, sheer lyrical,   40
Perennial, quavering up the chord
Like myriad dews of sunny sward
That trembling into fulness shine,
And sparkle dropping argentine;
Such wooing as the ear receives   45
From zephyr caught in choric leaves
Of aspens when their chattering net
Is flushed to white with shivers wet;
And such the water-spirit's chime
On mountain heights in morning's prime,   50
Too freshly sweet to seem excess,
Too animate to need a stress;
But wider over many heads
The starry voice ascending spreads,
Awakening, as it waxes thin,   55
The best in us to him akin;
And every face to watch him raised
Puts on the light of children praised,
So rich our human pleasure ripes
When sweetness on sincereness pipes,   60
Though nought be promised from the seas,
But only a soft-ruffling breeze
Sweep glittering on a still content,
Serenity in ravishment.

For singing till his heaven fills,   65
'Tis love of earth that he instils,
And ever winging up and up,
Our valley is his golden cup,
And he the wine which overflows
To lift us with him as he goes: 70
The woods and brooks, the sheep and kine,
He is, the hills, the human line,
The meadows green, the fallows brown,
The dreams of labour in the town;
He sings the sap, the quickened veins;   75
The wedding song of sun and rains
He is, the dance of children, thanks
Of sowers, shout of primrose-banks,
And eye of violets while they breathe;
All these the circling song will wreathe,   80

44 *Argentine:* silvery. 71 *Kine:* cows.

And you shall hear the herb and tree,
The better heart of men shall see,
Shall feel celestially, as long
As you crave nothing save the song.

Was never voice of ours could say   85
Our inmost in the sweetest way,
Like yonder voice aloft, and link
All hearers in the song they drink.
Our wisdom speaks from failing blood,
Our passion is too full in flood,   90
We want the key of his wild note
Of truthful in a tuneful throat,
The song seraphically free
Of taint of personality,
So pure that it salutes the suns,   95
The voice of one for millions,
In whom the millions rejoice
For giving their one spirit voice.

Yet men have we, whom we revere,
Now names, and men still housing here,   100
Whose lives, by many a battle-dint
Defaced, and grinding wheels on flint,
Yield substance, though they sing not, sweet
For song our highest heaven to greet:
Whom heavenly singing gives us new,   105
Enspheres them brilliant in our blue,
From firmest base to farthest leap,
Because their love of Earth is deep,
And they are warriors in accord
With life to serve, and pass reward,   110
So touching purest and so heard
In the brain's reflex of yon bird:
Wherefore their soul in me, or mine,
Through self-forgetfulness divine,
In them, that song aloft maintains,   115
To fill the sky and thrill the plains
With showerings drawn from human stores,
As he to silence nearer soars,
Extends the world at wings and dome,
More spacious making more our home,   120
Till lost on his aërial rings
In light, and then the fancy sings.

Gerard Manley Hopkins

1844—1889

THE WRECK OF THE DEUTSCHLAND

A genuine elegy; a Jesuit priest's verbal gift to God after years of poetic silence; and a manifesto of a new accentual prosody.

To the
happy memory of five Franciscan Nuns
exiles by the Falk* Laws
drowned between midnight and morning of
Dec. 7th, 1875

PART THE FIRST

I

Thou mastering me
God! giver of breath and bread;
World's strand, sway of the sea;
Lord of living and dead;
Thou hast bound bones and veins in me, fastened me flesh,　5
And after it almost unmade, what with dread,
Thy doing: and dost thou touch me afresh?
Over again I feel thy finger and find thee.

II

I did say yes
O at lightning and lashed rod;　　　　　　　　　　10
Thou heardst me truer than tongue confess
Thy terror, O Christ, O God;
Thou knowest the walls, altar and hour and night:
The swoon of a heart that the sweep and the hurl of thee trod
Hard down with a horror of height:　　　　　　　　15
And the midriff astrain with leaning of, laced with fire of stress.

---

* Paul Falk (1827-1900), Prussian statesman and minister of education, helped Bismarck in his policy of subjecting the Catholic Church in Germany to State control.　16 *Stress:* a word specially developed by Hopkins, signifying here the deeply shaking, seizing power of God as received in the soul of man.

633

III

The frown of his face
Before me, the hurtle of hell
Behind, where, where was a, where was a place?
    I whirled out wings that spell   20
And fled with a fling of the heart to the heart of the Host.
My heart, but you were dovewinged, I can tell,
    Carrier-witted, I am bold to boast,
To flash from the flame to the flame then, tower from the grace
    to the grace.

IV

    I am soft sift   25
In an hourglass—at the wall
Fast, but mined with a motion, a drift,
    And it crowds and it combs to the fall;
I steady as a water in a well, to a poise, to a pane,
But roped with, always, all the way down from the tall   30
    Fells or flanks of the voel, a vein
Of the gospel proffer, a pressure, a principle, Christ's gift.

V

    I kiss my hand
To the stars, lovely-asunder
Starlight, wafting him out of it; and   35
    Glow, glory in thunder;
Kiss my hand to the dappled-with-damson west:
Since, tho' he is under the world's splendour and wonder,
    His mystery must be instressed, stressed;
For I greet him the days I meet him, and bless when I under-
    stand.   40

VI

    Not out of his bliss
Springs the stress felt
Nor first from heaven (and few know this)
    Swings the stroke dealt—

20 *That spell:* in that crisis.   23 *Carrier-witted:* like a homing pigeon.
27 *Mined:* undermined.   28 *Combs:* rolls over.   30 *Roped:* i.e. by
streams running down steep hillsides.   31 *Voel:* bare hill (Welsh *y foel*).
The poem was written in North Wales.   39 *Instressed:* distinctively,
inwardly impressed on the feelings.   41 ff. It is not God as the ruler of
heaven who most moves mankind, but God as the suffering Christ.

Stroke and a stress that stars and storms deliver,   45
That guilt is hushed by, hearts are flushed by and melt—
But it rides time like riding a river
(And here the faithful waver, the faithless fable and miss).

VII

It dates from day
Of his going in Galilee;   50
Warm-laid grave of a womb-life grey;
Manger, maiden's knee;
The dense and the driven Passion, and frightful sweat;
Thence the discharge of it, there its swelling to be,
Though felt before, though in high flood yet—   55
What none would have known of it, only the heart, being hard
at bay,

VIII

Is out with it! Oh,
We lash with the best or worst
Word last! How a lush-kept plush-capped sloe
Will, mouthed to flesh-burst,   60
Gush!—flush the man, the being with it, sour or sweet,
Brim, in a flash, full!—Hither then, last or first,
To hero of Calvary, Christ,'s feet—
Never ask if meaning it, wanting , warned of it—men go.

IX

Be adored among men,   65
God, three-numberèd form;
Wring thy rebel, dogged in den,
Man's malice, with wrecking and storm.
Beyond saying sweet, past telling of tongue,
Thou art lightning and love, I found it, a winter and
warm;   70
Father and fondler of heart thou hast wrung:
Hast thy dark descending and most art merciful then.

X

With an anvil-ding
And with fire in him forge thy will
Or rather, rather then, stealing as Spring   75
Through him, melt him but master him still:

56 *Being hard at bay:* with the sympathetic insight of being as Christ was
in his Passion.   58-59 In mortal extremity men will call on, or curse,
their gods.   62 *Brim...full:* brim-full in a flash.   67 *Dogged:* sullenly
obstinate.

Whether at once, as once at a crash Paul,
  Or as Austin, a lingering-out swéet skíll,
    Make mercy in all of us, out of us all
Mastery, but be adored, but be adored King.   80

PART THE SECOND

XI
      ' Some find me a sword; some
        The flange and the rail; flame,
    Fang, or flood ' goes Death on drum,
        And storms bugle his fame.
But wé dream we are rooted in earth—Dust!   85
Flesh falls within sight of us, we, though our flower the same,
    Wave with the meadow, forget that there must
The sour scythe cringe, and the blear share come.

XII
      On Saturday sailed from Bremen,
        American-outward-bound,   90
    Take settler and seamen, tell men with women,
        Two hundred souls in the round—
O Father, not under thy feathers nor ever as guessing
The goal was a shoal, of a fourth the doom to be drowned;
    Yet did the dark side of the bay of thy blessing   95
Not vault them, the millions of rounds of thy mercy not reeve
    even them in?

XIII
      Into the snows she sweeps,
        Hurling the haven behind,
    The Deutschland, on Sunday; and so the sky keeps,
        For the infinite air is unkind,   100
And the sea flint-flake, black-backed in the regular blow,
Sitting Eastnortheast, in cursed quarter, the wind;
    Wiry and white-fiery and whirlwind-swivellèd snow
Spins to the widow-making unchilding unfathering deeps.

77 *Paul:* See *Acts* ix.   78 *Austin:* See the *Confessions* of St. Augustine
(354-430).   88 *Cringe:* bend down; or the word may be being used
transitively; *blear share:* dull blade.   95 *Bay:* architectural as well as
geographical.   96 *Rounds:* turns; *reeve:* gather, haul.   101 *Flint-flake:*
cold, grey, choppy, and spumy.

XIV

She drove in the dark to leeward, 105
She struck—not a reef or a rock
But the combs of a smother of sand: night drew her
Dead to the Kentish Knock;
And she beat the bank down with her bows and the ride of
her keel:
The breakers rolled on her beam with ruinous shock; 110
And canvas and compass, the whorl and the wheel
Idle for ever to waft her or wind her with, these she endured.

XV

Hope had grown grey hairs,
Hope had mourning on,
Trenched with tears, carved with cares, 115
Hope was twelve hours gone;
And frightful a nightfall folded rueful a day
Nor rescue, only rocket and lightship, shone,
And lives at last were washing away:
To the shrouds they took,—they shook in the hurling and horrible
airs. 120

XVI

One stirred from the rigging to save
The wild woman-kind below,
With a rope's end round the man, handy and brave—
He was pitched to his death at a blow,
For all his dreadnought breast and braids of thew: 125
They could tell him for hours, dandled the to and fro
Through the cobbled foam-fleece, what could he do
With the burl of the fountains of air, buck and the flood of the
wave?

XVII

They fought with God's cold—
And they could not and fell to the deck 130
(Crushed them) or water (and drowned them) or rolled
With the sea-romp over the wreck.

107 *Combs:* crest. 108 *Kentish Knock:* sandbank in Thames estuary.
111 *Whorl:* screw-propeller. 112 *Wind:* guide. 117 The predicative
adjectives have almost an exclamatory force. 120 *Shrouds:* rigging.
127 *Cobbled:* patterned like a cobbled road-surface (?), patched (?).
128 *Burl:* spin, whirl; *buck:* arching leap.

Night roared, with the heart-break hearing a heart-broke
    rabble,
The woman's wailing, the crying of child without check—
    Till a lioness arose breasting the babble,   135
A prophetess towered in the tumult, a virginal tongue told.

              XVIII
    Ah, touched in your bower of bone
    Are you! turned for an exquisite smart,
    Have you! make words break from me here all alone,
    Do you!—mother of being in me, heart.   140
O unteachably after evil, but uttering truth,
    Why, tears! is it? tears; such a melting, a madrigal start!
    Never-eldering revel and river of youth,
What can it be, this glee? the good you have there of your own?

              XIX
    Sister, a sister calling   145
    A master, her master and mine!—
    And the inboard seas run swirling and hawling;
    The rash smart sloggering brine
Blinds her; but she that weather sees one thing, one;
    Has one fetch in her: she rears herself to divine   150
    Ears, and the call of the tall nun
To the men in the tops and the tackle rode over the storm's
    brawling.

              XX
    She was first of a five and came
    Of a coifèd sisterhood.
    (O Deutschland, double a desperate name!   155
    O world wide of its good!
But Gertrude, lily, and Luther, are two of a town,
    Christ's lily and beast of the waste wood:
    From life's dawn it is drawn down,
Abel is Cain's brother and breasts they have sucked the same.) 160

136 *Told:* with word-play on *tolled.* 141 *After:* in search of. 147
Hawling: hauling (?), clawing. 148 *Smart:* (i) stinging, (ii) clever,
impudent; *sloggering:* buffeting. 149 *That weather:* during that
weather. 150 *Fetch:* shift, expedient. 154 *Coifèd:* wearing a close-
fitting headdress. 157 *Gertrude:* (c. 1256-c. 1302), German saint and
mystic, lived in convent near Eisleben, Luther's birthplace. *Luther:*
Martin Luther (1483-1546), German reformer and Protestant theo-
logian.

XXI

Loathed for a love men knew in them,
  Banned by the land of their birth,
Rhine refused them. Thames would ruin them;
  Surf, snow, river and earth
Gnashed: but thou art above, thou Orion of light;   165
Thy unchancelling poising palms were weighing the worth,
  Thou martyr-master: in thy sight
Storm flakes were scroll-leaved flowers, lily showers—sweet heaven
was astrew in them.

XXII

Five! the finding and sake
  And cipher of suffering Christ.   170
Mark, the mark is of man's make
  And the word of it Sacrificed.
But he scores it in scarlet himself on his own bespoken,
  Before-time-taken, dearest prizèd and priced—
Stigma, signal, cinquefoil token   175
For lettering of the lamb's fleece, ruddying of the rose-flake.

XXIII

Joy fall to thee, father Francis,
  Drawn to the Life that died;
With the gnarls of the nails in thee, niche of the lance, his
  Lovescape crucified   180
And seal of his seraph-arrival! and these thy daughters
  And five-livèd and leavèd favour and pride,
Are sisterly sealed in wild waters,
To bathe in his fall-gold mercies, to breathe in his all-fire glances.

XXIV

Away in the loveable west,   185
  On a pastoral forehead of Wales,
I was under a roof here, I was at rest,
  And they the prey of the gales;

165 *Orion:* constellation named after the 'huntsman' Orion in Greek
mythology. God has 'hunted' the nuns from their safe retreat in Ger-
many, but for a higher purpose. 166 *Unchancelling:* unwavering (?).
169 *Finding and sake:* emblem and distinguishing mark. 175 *Cinquefoil:*
five-leaved. 177 *Francis:* St. Francis of Assisi (1182-1226), founder of
Franciscan Order. 180 *Lovescape:* 'landscape of love': Christ's five
wounds, reputedly received as stigmata on the body of St. Francis in
1224. 183 *Sealed:* (i) confirmed, (ii) drowned. 186-7 at St. Beuno's
College, St. Asaph, north Wales.

She to the black-about air, to the breaker, the thickly
Falling flakes, to the throng that catches and quails   190
    Was calling ' O Christ, Christ, come quickly ':
The cross to her she calls Christ to her, christens her wild-worst
Best.

XXV

    The majesty! what did she mean?
    Breathe, arch and original Breath.
Is it love in her of the being as her lover had been?   195
    Breathe, body of lovely Death.
They were else-minded then, altogether, the men
Woke thee with a *we are perishing* in the weather of Gen-
nesareth.
    Or is it that she cried for the crown then,
The keener to come at the comfort for feeling the combating
keen?   200

XXVI

    For how to the heart's cheering
    The down-dugged ground-hugged grey
    Hovers off, the jay-blue heavens appearing
    Of pied and peeled May!
Blue-beating and hoary-glow height; or night, still higher, 205
With belled fire and the moth-soft Milky Way,
    What by your measure is the heaven of desire,
The treasure never eyesight got, nor was ever guessed what for the
hearing?

XXVII

    No, but it was not these.
    The jading and jar of the cart,   210
    Time's tasking, it is fathers that asking for ease
    Of the sodden-with-its-sorrowing heart,
Nor danger, electrical horror; then further it finds
The appealing of the Passion is tenderer in prayer apart:
    Other, I gather, in measure her mind's   215
Burden, in wind's burly and beat of endragonèd seas.

190 *Catches and quails:* catches the breath and daunts the courage.
195 'Is she eager to suffer and be a sacrifice, as Christ was?' 197-8 See
Matt. viii. 23-27. 200 'Is she eager to be in heaven after the strife of
earth?' 206 *Belled fire:* a difficult phrase; may refer to blossom, or to
stars (perhaps an echo of Shakespeare's 'stelled fires' in *King Lear*).
210-14 'Asking for relief belongs rather to sufferers in the daily round;
eagerness to emulate the divine sacrifice comes rather in moments of
lonely meditation.'

XXVIII

But how shall I . . . make me room there:
Reach me a . . . Fancy, come faster—
Strike you the sight of it? look at it loom there,
Thing that she . . . there then! the Master,   220
Ipse, the only one, Christ, King, Head:
He was to cure the extremity where he had cast her;
Do, deal, lord it with living and dead;
Let him ride, her pride, in his triumph, despatch and have done
with his doom there.

XXIX

Ah! there was a heart right   225
There was single eye!
Read the unshapeable shock night
And knew the who and the why;
Wording it how but by him that present and past,
Heaven and earth are word of, worded by?—   230
The Simon Peter of a soul! to the blast
Tarpeian-fast, but a blown beacon of light.

XXX

Jesu, heart's light,
Jesu, maid's son,
What was the feast followed the night   235
Thou hadst glory of this nun?—
Feast of the one woman without stain.
For so conceivèd, so to conceive thee is done;
But here was heart-throe, birth of a brain,
Word, that heard and kept thee and uttered thee outright.   240

XXXI

Well, she has thee for the pain, for the
Patience; but pity of the rest of them!
Heart, go and bleed at a bitterer vein for the
Comfortless unconfessed of them—

---

218 *Fancy:* imagination. 221 *Ipse:* himself (Lat.). 226 *Single eye:*
Cf. *Matt.* vi. 22. 227 'Saw the meaning of that chaotic, testingly-
terrible night.' 231 *Simon Peter of a soul:* The nun, in her natural fear,
is like Simon Peter who called on Christ to save him from drowning
(*Matt.* xiv. 30). 232 *Tarpeian-fast, etc.:* Yet she is also as steadfast as
the Tarpeian Rock of ancient Rome, and a glorious example for all to
see. 235 Feast of the Immaculate Conception of the Blessed Virgin
Mary, 8 December. 238 The nun, who is also a virgin, also 'conceives'
Christ when she calls on him.

No not uncomforted: lovely-felicitous Providence   245
Finger of a tender of, O of a feathery delicacy, the breast
     of the
          Maiden could obey so, be a bell to, ring of it, and
Startle the poor sheep back! is the shipwrack then a harvest, does
     tempest carry the grain for thee?

XXXII

          I admire thee, master of the tides,
          Of the Yore-flood, of the year's fall;   250
     The recurb and the recovery of the gulf's sides,
          The girth of it and the wharf of it and the wall;
Stanching, quenching ocean of a motionable mind;
Ground of being, and granite of it: past all
          Grasp God, throned behind   255
Death with a sovereignty that heeds but hides, bodes but abides;

XXXIII

          With a mercy that outrides
          The all of water, an ark
     For the listener; for the lingerer with a love glides
          Lower than death and the dark;   260
A vein for the visiting of the past-prayer, pent in prison,
The-last-breath penitent spirits—the uttermost mark
          Our passion-plungèd giant risen,
The Christ of the Father compassionate, fetched in the storm of
     his strides.

XXXIV

          Now burn, new born to the world,   265
          Double-naturèd name,
     The heaven-flung, heart-fleshed, maiden-furled
          Miracle-in-Mary-of-flame,
Mid-numbered He in three of the thunder-throne!
Not a dooms-day dazzle in his coming nor dark as he
     came;   270
          Kind, but royally reclaiming his own;
A released shower, let flash to the shire, not a lightning of fire
     hard-hurled.

250 *Yore-flood:* Noah's flood.   253 *Ocean of a motionable mind:* God can
control and steady our restless minds as he does the sea.   256 *Bodes:*
foreshadows uncertainly.   260 i.e. into Purgatory.   262 *Uttermost
mark:* sinners nearest despair, at the limit of God's mercy.

xxxv
Dame, at our door
Drowned, and among our shoals,
Remember us in the roads, the heaven-haven of the
Reward: 275
Our King back, oh, upon English souls!
Let him easter in us, be a dayspring to the dimness of us,
be a crimson-cresseted east,
More brightening her, rare-dear Britain, as his reign rolls,
Pride, rose, prince, hero of us, high-priest,
Our hearts' charity's hearth's fire, our thoughts' chivalry's throng's
Lord. 280

John Davidson

1857—1909

THIRTY BOB A WEEK

From *Ballads and Songs* (1894). 'Davidson had a great theme,
and also found an idiom which elicited the greatness of the
theme, which endowed this thirty-bob-a-week clerk with a dignity
that would not have appeared if a more conventional poetic
diction had been employed. The personage that Davidson
created in this poem has haunted me all my life, and the poem is
to me a great poem for ever.' (T. S. Eliot)

I couldn't touch a stop and turn a screw;
And set the blooming world a-work for me,
Like such as cut their teeth—I hope, like you—
On the handle of a skeleton gold key;
I cut mine on a leek, which I eat it every week; 5
I'm a clerk at thirty bob as you can see.

But I don't allow it's luck and all a toss;
There's no such thing as being starred and crossed;
It's just the power of some to be a boss,
And the bally power of others to be bossed: 10
I face the music, sir; you bet I ain't a cur;
Strike me lucky if I don't believe I'm lost!

275 *Roads:* sheltered anchorage. 277 *Easter:* rise in the east (with
word-play on Easter). 10 *Bally:* slang euphemism for *bloody* (cf. also
blooming, line 72).

For like a mole I journey in the dark,
    A-travelling along the underground
From my Pillar'd Halls and broad Suburbean Park,   15
    To come the daily dull official round;
And home again at night with my pipe all alight,
    A-scheming how to count ten bob a pound.

And it's often very cold and very wet,
    And my missis stitches towels for a hunks;   20
And the Pillar'd Halls is half of it to let—
    Three rooms about the size of travelling trunks.
And we cough, my wife and I, to dislocate a sigh,
    When the noisy little kids are in their bunks.

But you never hear her do a growl or whine,   25
    For she's made of flint and roses, very odd;
And I've got to cut my meaning rather fine,
    Or I'd blubber, for I'm made of greens and sod:
So p'r'aps we are in Hell for all that I can tell,
    And lost and damn'd and served up hot to God.   30

I ain't blaspheming, Mr. Silver-tongue;
    I'm saying things a bit beyond your art:
Of all the rummy starts you ever sprung,
    Thirty bob a week's the rummiest start!
With your science and your books and your the'ries about
    spooks,   35
    Did you ever hear of looking in you heart?

I didn't mean your pocket, Mr., no:
    I mean that having children and a wife,
With thirty bob on which to come and go,
    Isn't dancing to the tabor and the fife: 40
When it doesn't make you drink, by Heaven! it makes you think,
    And notice curious items about life.

I step into my heart and there I meet
    A god-almighty devil singing small,
Who would like to shout and whistle in the street,   45
    And squelch the passers flat against the wall;
If the whole world was a cake he had the power to take,
    He would take it, ask for more, and eat it all.

20 *Hunks:* stingy employer.   40 *The tabor and the fife:* drums and flutes.

And I meet a sort of simpleton beside,
   The kind that life is always giving beans;
With thirty bob a week to keep a bride
   He fell in love and married in his teens:
At thirty bob he stuck; but he knows it isn't luck:
   He knows the seas are deeper than tureens.   50

And the god-almighty devil and the fool   55
   That meet me in the High Street on the strike,
When I walk about my heart a-gathering wool,
   Are my good and evil angels if you like.
And both of them together in every kind of weather
   Ride me like a double-seated bike.   60

That's rough a bit and needs its meaning curled.
   But I have a high old hot 'un in my mind—
A most engrugious notion of the world,
   That leaves your lightning 'rithmetic behind:
I give it at a glance when I say ' There ain't no chance,   65
   Nor nothing of the lucky-lottery kind.'

And it's this way that I make it out to be:
   No fathers, mothers, countries, climates—none;
Not Adam was responsible for me,
   Nor society, nor systems, nary one: 70
A little sleeping seed, I woke—I did, indeed—
   A million years before the blooming sun.

I woke because I thought the time had come;
   Beyond my will there was no other cause;
And everywhere I found myself at home,   75
   Because I chose to be the thing I was;
And in whatever shape of mollusc or of ape
   I always went according to the laws.

I was the love that chose my mother out;
   I joined two lives and from the union burst;   80
My weakness and my strength without a doubt
   Are mine alone for ever from the first:
It's just the very same with a difference in the name
   As ' Thy will be done.' You say it if you durst!

50 *Giving beans:* punishing. 63 *Engrugious:* egregious, remarkable
(malapropism).

They say it daily up and down the land   85
    As easy as you take a drink, it's true;
But the difficultest go to understand,
    And the difficultest job a man can do,
Is to come it brave and meek with thirty bob a week,
    And feel that that's the proper thing for you.   90

It's a naked child against a hungry wolf;
    It's playing bowls upon a splitting wreck;
It's walking on a string across a gulf
    With millstones fore-and-aft about your neck;
But the thing is daily done by many and many a one;   95
    And we fall, face forward, fighting, on the deck.

Rudyard Kipling

1865—1936

McANDREW'S HYMN

Lord, Thou hast made this world below the shadow of a dream,
An', taught by time, I tak' it so—exceptin' always Steam.
From coupler-flange to spindle-guide I see Thy Hand, O God—
Predestination in the stride o' yon connectin'-rod.
John Calvin might ha' forged the same—enorrmous, certain,
    slow—   5
Ay, wrought it in the furnace-flame—*my* ' Institutio.'
I cannot get my sleep to-night; old bones are hard to please;
I'll stand the middle watch up here—alone wi' God an' these
My engines, after ninety days o' race an' rack an' strain
Through all the seas of all Thy world, slam-bangin' home again. 10
Slam-bang too much—they knock a wee—the crosshead-gibs are
    loose,
But thirty thousand mile o' sea has gied them fair excuse. . . .
Fine, clear an' dark—a full-draught breeze, wi' Ushant out o'
    sight,
An' Ferguson relievin' Hay. Old girl, ye'll walk to-night!

87 *Go:* case, thing. 4 *Connectin(g)-rod:* rod connecting piston or cross-
head to the crank in a reciprocating engine; its lunging movement is
a sort of 'stride'. 6 *Institutio:* Calvin's *Christianae Religionis Institutio*
(1536). 11 *Crosshead-gibs:* brass bearing surfaces let into the bar at the
end of the piston-rod. 13 *Ushant:* island off Finistère, the north-west
tip of France. The ship is steaming into the English Channel, making
for Plymouth.

His wife's at Plymouth. . . . Seventy—One—Two—Three since
    he began—   15
Three turns for Mistress Ferguson . . . and who's to blame the
    man?
There's none at any port for me, by drivin' fast or slow,
Since Elsie Campbell went to Thee, Lord, thirty years ago.
(The year the *Sarah Sands* was burned. Oh, roads we used to tread,
Fra' Maryhill to Pollokshaws—fra' Govan to Parkhead!)   20
Not but they're ceevil on the Board. Ye'll hear Sir Kenneth say:
' Good morrn, McAndrew! Back again? An' how's your bilge
    to-day? '
Miscallin' technicalities but handin' me my chair
To drink Madeira wi' three Earls—the auld Fleet Engineer
That started as a boiler-whelp—when steam and he were low. 25
I mind the time we used to serve a broken pipe wi' tow!
Ten pound was all the pressure then—Eh! Eh!—a man wad drive;
An' here, our workin' gauges give one hunder sixty-five!
We're creepin' on wi' each new rig—less weight an' larger power;
There'll be the loco-boiler next an' thirty mile an hour!   30
Thirty an' more. What I ha' seen since ocean-steam began
Leaves me na doot for the machine: but what about the man?
The man that counts, wi' all his runs, one million mile o' sea:
Four time the span from earth to moon. . . . How far, O Lord,
    from Thee
That wast beside him night an' day? Ye mind my first typhoon? 35
It scoughed the skipper on his way to jock wi' the saloon.
Three feet were on the stokehold-floor—just slappin' to an' fro—
An' cast me on a furnace-door. I have the marks to show.
Marks! I ha' marks o' more than burns—deep in my soul an'
    black,
An' time like this, when things go smooth, my wickudness comes
    back.   40
The sins o' four an' forty years, all up an' down the seas,
Clack an' repeat like valves half-fed. . . . Forgie's our trespasses!
Nights when I'd come on deck to mark, wi' envy in my gaze,
The couples kittlin' in the dark between the funnel-stays;
Years when I raked the Ports wi' pride to fill my cup o' wrong— 45
Judge not, O Lord, my steps aside at Gay Street in Hong-Kong!
Blot out the wastrel hours of mine in sin when I abode—
Jane Harrigan's an' Number Nine, The Reddick an' Grant Road!

15 *Seventy, etc.:* revolutions of the crank-shaft per minute (engine speed).
19 The year 1857. 20 districts of Glasgow, going from north to south
and from west to east. 36 *Scoughed:* buffeted, knocked over (?); *jock:*
joke, banter. 44 *Kittlin':* cuddling.

An' waur than all—my crownin' sin—rank blasphemy an' wild.
I was not four and twenty then—Ye wadna judge a child?   50
I'd seen the Tropics first that run—new fruit, new smells, new air—
How could I tell—blind-fou wi' sun—the Deil was lurkin' there?
By day like playhouse-scenes the shore slid past our sleepy eyes;
By night those soft lasceevious stars leered from those velvet skies,
In port (we used no cargo-steam) I'd daunder down the streets—   55
An ijjit grinnin' in a dream—for shells an' parrakeets,
An' walkin'-sticks o' carved bamboo an' blowfish stuffed an' dried—
Fillin' my bunk wi' rubbishry the Chief put overside.
Till, off Sambawa Head, Ye mind, I heard a land-breeze ca',
Milk-warm wi' breath o' spice an' bloom: ' McAndrew, come awa'! '   60
Firm, clear an' low—no haste, no hate—the ghostly whisper went,
Just statin' eevidential facts beyon' all argument:
' Your mither's God's a graspin' deil, the shadow o' yoursel',
' Got out o' books by meenisters clean daft on Heaven an' Hell.
' They mak' him in the Broomielaw, o' Glasgie cold an' dirt,   65
' A jealous, pridefu' fetich, lad, that's only strong to hurt.
' Ye'll not go back to Him again an' kiss His red-hot rod,
' But come wi' Us ' (Now, who were *They*?) ' an' know the Leevin' God,
' That does not kipper souls for sport or break a life in jest,
' But swells the ripenin' cocoanuts an' ripes the woman's breast.'   70
An' there it stopped—cut off—no more—that quiet, certain voice—
For me, six months o' twenty-four, to leave or take at choice.
'Twas on me like a thunderclap—it racked me through an' through—
Temptation past the show o' speech, unnameable an' new—
The Sin against the Holy Ghost? . . . An' under all, our screw.   75

That storm blew by but left behind her anchor-shiftin' swell.
Thou knowest all my heart an' mind, Thou knowest, Lord, I fell—
Third on the *Mary Gloster* then, and first that night in Hell!

---

55 *Daunder:* wander. 58 *Chief:* chief engineer. 59 *Sambawa Head:* Sumbawa is an island in the Indonesian archipelago, east of Java. 65 *Broomielaw:* dockside street in Glasgow. 75 See *Matt.* xii. 24-32. 78 *Third:* third engineer.

Yet was Thy Hand beneath my head, about my feet Thy Care—
Fra' Deli clear to Torres Strait, the trial o' despair,   80
But when we touched the Barrier Reef Thy answer to my
    prayer! . . .
We dared na run that sea by night but lay an' held our fire,
An' I was drowsin' on the hatch—sick—sick wi' doubt an' tire:
' *Better the sight of eyes that see than wanderin' o' desire!* '
Ye mind that word? Clear as our gongs—again, an' once
    again,   85
When rippin' down through coral-trash ran out our moorin'-
    chain:
An', by Thy Grace, I had the Light to see my duty plain.
Light on the engine-room—no more—bright as our carbons burn.
I've lost it since a thousand times, but never past return!

       ·   ·   ·   ·   ·

Obsairve! Per annum we'll have here two thousand souls
    aboard—   90
Think not I dare to justify myself before the Lord,
But—average fifteen hunder souls safe-borne fra' port to port—
I *am* o' service to my kind. Ye wadna blame the thought?
Maybe they steam from Grace to Wrath—to sin by folly led—
It isna mine to judge their path—their lives are on my head. 95
Mine at the last—when all is done it all comes back to me,
The fault that leaves six thousand ton a log upon the sea.
We'll tak' one stretch—three weeks an' odd by ony road ye
    steer—
Fra' Cape Town east to Wellington—ye need an engineer.
Fail there—ye've time to weld your shaft—ay, eat it, ere ye're
    spoke;   100
Or make Kerguelen under sail—three jiggers burned wi' smoke!
An' home again—the Rio run: it's no child's play to go
Steamin' to bell for fourteen days o' snow an' floe an' blow.
The bergs like kelpies overside that girn an' turn an' shift
Whaur, grindin' like the Mills o' God, goes by the big South
    drift.   105

80 *Deli:* port in north Sumatra; *Torres Strait:* in the South Pacific,
between New Guinea and Australia. 81 *Barrier Reef:* great coral reef
off east coast of Australia. 83 *Tire:* fatigue. 84 Cf. *Eccles.* vi. 9. 88
Carbons: lamps. 99 *Wellington:* capital of New Zealand. 100 *Shaft:*
connecting engine to propeller. 101 *Kerguelen:* remote volcanic island
in southern Indian Ocean; *jiggers:* small sails. 102 *Rio:* Rio de Jan-
eiro, in Brazil. 103 *Steamin' to bell:* standing by at the engines for the
belled orders from the bridge. 104 *Kelpies:* water-monsters in Scottish
folklore; *girn:* fret, cry.

(Hail, Snow and Ice that praise the Lord. I've met them at their work,
An' wished we had anither route or they anither kirk.)
Yon's strain, hard strain, o' head an' hand, for though Thy Power brings
All skill to naught, Ye'll understand a man must think o' things.
Then, at the last, we'll get to port an' hoist their baggage clear—   110
The passengers, wi' gloves an' canes—an' this is what I'll hear:
' Well, thank ye for a pleasant voyage. The tender's comin' now.'
While I go testin' follower-bolts an' watch the skipper bow.
They've words for every one but me—shake hands wi' half the crew,
Except the dour Scots engineer, the man they never knew.   115
An' yet I like the wark for all we've dam'-few pickin's here—
No pension, an' the most we'll earn's four hunder pound a year.
Better myself abroad? Maybe. *I'd* sooner starve than sail
Wi' such as call a snifter-rod *ross* . . . French for nightingale.
Commeesion on my stores? Some do; but I cannot afford   120
To lie like stewards wi' patty-pans. I'm older than the Board.
A bonus on the coal I save? Ou ay, the Scots are close,
But when I grudge the strength Ye gave I'll grudge their food to *those.*
(There's bricks that I might recommend—an' clink the firebars cruel.
No! Welsh—Wangarti at the worst—an' damn all patent fuel!)   125
Inventions? Ye must stay in port to mak' a patent pay.
My Deeferential Valve-Gear taught me how that business lay.
I blame no chaps wi' clearer heads for aught they make or sell.
I found that I could not invent an' look to these as well.
So, wrestled wi' Apollyon—Nah!—fretted like a bairn—   130
But burned the workin'-plans last run, wi' all I hoped to earn.
Ye know how hard an Idol dies, an' what that meant to me—
E'en tak' it for a sacrifice acceptable to Thee. . . .
Below there! Oiler! What's your wark? Ye find it runnin' hard?
Ye needn't swill the cup wi' oil—this isn't the Cunard!   135

112 *Tender:* small vessel coming from shore.   113 *Follower-bolts:* The follower is the plug or 'gland' of the steam-tight chamber through which the piston-rod passes. 115 *Dour:* severe, uncommunicative. 119 *Snifter-rod:* Both *snifter-rod* and its French name *rossignol* refer to the sound of air being controlled by a valve.   121 *Patty-pans:* baking-dishes for pies and pasties. The reference is to dishonest indents for new stores. 122 *Close:* saving. 124 *Clink:* clog (with clinker from patent-fuel bricks). 125 *Wangarti:* coal from Wangarti in New South Wales. 130 *Apollyon:* the Devil. 135 *Cunard:* renowned steamship line.

Ye thought? Ye are not paid to think. Go, sweat that off again!
Tck! Tck! It's deeficult to sweer nor tak' The Name in vain!
Men, ay, an' women, call me stern. Wi' these to oversee,
Ye'll note I've little time to burn on social repartee.
The bairns see what their elders miss; they'll hunt me to an'
    fro,   140
Till for the sake of—well, a kiss—I tak' 'em down below.
That minds me of our Viscount loon—Sir Kenneth's kin—the chap
Wi' Russia-leather tennis-shoon an' spar-decked yachtin'-cap.
I showed him round last week, o'er all—an' at the last says he:
'Mister McAndrew, don't you think steam spoils romance at
    sea?'   145
Damned ijjit! I'd been doon that morn to see what ailed the
    throws,
Manholin', on my back—the cranks three inches off my nose.
Romance! Those first-class passengers they like it very well,
Printed an' bound in little books; but why don't poets tell?
I'm sick of all their quirks an' turns—the loves an' doves they
    dream—   150
Lord, send a man like Robbie Burns to sing the Song o' Steam!
To match wi' Scotia's noblest speech yon orchestra sublime
Whaurto—uplifted like the Just—the tail-rods mark the time.
The crank-throws give the double-bass, the feed-pump sobs an'
    heaves,
An' now the main eccentrics start their quarrel on the sheaves: 155
Her time, her own appointed time, the rocking link-head bides,
Till—hear that note?—the rod's return whings glimmerin'
    through the guides.
They're all awa'! True beat, full power, the clangin' chorus
    goes
Clear to the tunnel where they sit, my purrin' dynamoes.
Interdependence absolute, foreseen, ordained, decreed,   160
To work, Ye'll note, at ony tilt an' every rate o' speed.
Fra' skylight-lift to furnace-bars, backed, bolted, braced an'
    stayed,
An' singin' like the Mornin' Stars for joy that they are made;

143 *Spar-decked:* suitable for the upper deck. 146 *Throws:* measured movement of crank-arms. 153 *Tail-rods:* continuation of piston-rods through back cover of cylinder; they steady the piston and so in a sense 'mark time'. 154 *Feed-pump:* pump supplying boiler with water. 155 *Eccentrics:* mechanism that converts rotating to reciprocating motion: its metal discs are mounted out of centre and so 'quarrelling' in their relative motions; *sheaves:* the discs of the eccentrics. 156-7 The eccentrics and their rods operate a slide-valve through a 'link', the position of which determines the rotation of the engine. 157 *Whings:* pounds, swings. 163 Cf. *Job* xxxviii. 7.

While, out o' touch o' vanity, the sweatin' thrust-block says:
' Not unto us the praise, or man—not unto us the praise! '   165
Now, a' together, hear them lift their lesson—theirs an' mine:
' Law, Orrder, Duty an' Restraint, Obedience, Discipline! '
Mill, forge an' try-pit taught them that when roarin' they arose,
An' whiles I wonder if a soul was gied them wi' the blows.
Oh for a man to weld it then, in one trip-hammer strain,   170
Till even first-class passengers could tell the meanin' plain!
But no one cares except mysel' that serve an' understand
My seven thousand horse-power here. Eh, Lord! They're grand
   —they're grand!
Uplift am I? When first in store the new-made beasties stood,
Were Ye cast down that breathed the Word declarin' all things
   good?   175
Not so! O' that warld-liftin' joy no after-fall could vex,
Ye've left a glimmer still to cheer the Man—the Arrtifex!
That holds, in spite o' knock and scale, o' friction, waste an' slip,
An' by that light—now, mark my word—we'll build the Perfect
   Ship.
I'll never last to judge her lines or take her curve—not I.   180
But I ha' lived an' I ha' worked. Be thanks to Thee, Most High!
An' I ha' done what I ha' done—judge Thou if ill or well—
Always Thy Grace preventin' me. . . .
                  Losh! Yon's the ' Stand-by ' bell.
Pilot so soon? His flare it is. The mornin'-watch is set.
Well, God be thanked, as I was sayin', I'm no Pelagian yet.   185
Now I'll tak' on. . . .
   'Morrn, Ferguson. Man, have ye ever thought
What your good leddy costs in coal? . . . I'll burn 'em down to port.

164 *Thrust-block:* block transmitting propeller thrust to ship hull.
165 Cf. *Psalm* cxv. 1. 168 *Try-pit:* testing-pit for new engines. 169
Whiles: at times. 170 *Trip-hammer:* massive machine-hammer
worked by a tripping device. 177 *Ar(r)tifex:* artificer (Lat.). 178
Knock: thumping noise in cylinder; *scale:* hard furry deposit in boiler;
slip: propeller slip. 183 *Preventin':* going ahead of. 185 *Pelagian:*
one who disbelieves in original sin. Perhaps McAndrew might expect to
become one, as he is a *pelagian* in another sense: an inhabitant of the
open sea.

William Butler Yeats

1865—1939

MEDITATIONS IN TIME OF CIVIL WAR

'I live in a mediaeval Tower in the West of Ireland, beside a
bridge that may be blown up any night.' 'Perhaps there is nothing
so dangerous to a modern state, when politics take the place of
theology, as a bunch of martyrs. A bunch of martyrs (1916)
were the bomb and we are living in the explosion.' (Yeats, from
two letters of 1922, when he was writing the poem.)

I

ANCESTRAL HOUSES

Surely among a rich man's flowering lawns,
Amid the rustle of his planted hills,
Life overflows without ambitious pains;
And rains down life until the basin spills,
And mounts more dizzy high the more it rains   5
As though to choose whatever shape it wills
And never stoop to a mechanical
Or servile shape, at others' beck and call.

Mere dreams, mere dreams! Yet Homer had not sung
Had he not found it certain beyond dreams   10
That out of life's own self-delight had sprung
The abounding glittering jet; though now it seems
As if some marvellous empty sea-shell flung
Out of the obscure dark of the rich streams,
And not a fountain, were the symbol which   15
Shadows the inherited glory of the rich.

Some violent bitter man, some powerful man
Called architect and artist in, that they,
Bitter and violent men, might rear in stone
The sweetness that all longed for night and day,   20
The gentleness none there had ever known;
But when the master's buried mice can play,
And maybe the great-grandson of that house,
For all its bronze and marble, 's but a mouse.

653

O what if gardens where the peacock strays　　　　25
With delicate feet upon old terraces,
Or else all Juno from an urn displays
Before the indifferent garden deities;
O what if levelled lawns and gravelled ways
Where slippered Contemplation finds his ease　　　　30
And Childhood a delight for every sense,
But take our greatness with our violence?

What if the glory of escutcheoned doors,
And buildings that a haughtier age designed,
The pacing to and fro on polished floors　　　　35
Amid great chambers and long galleries, lined
With famous portraits of our ancestors;
What if those things the greatest of mankind
Consider most to magnify, or to bless,
But take our greatness with our bitterness?　　　　40

II

MY HOUSE

An ancient bridge, and a more ancient tower,
A farmhouse that is sheltered by its wall,
An acre of stony ground,
Where the symbolic rose can break in flower,
Old ragged elms, old thorns innumerable,　　　　45
The sound of the rain or sound
Of every wind that blows;
The stilted water-hen
Crossing stream again
Scared by the splashing of a dozen cows;　　　　50

A winding stair, a chamber arched with stone,
A grey stone fireplace with an open hearth,
A candle and written page.
Il Penseroso's Platonist toiled on
In some like chamber, shadowing forth　　　　55
How the daemonic rage
Imagined everything.
Benighted travellers

27 *Juno:* wife and counterpart of Jupiter in Roman mythology; repre-
sented as attended by peacocks. 41 *Ancient tower:* Yeats had bought
this Norman tower, Thoor Ballylee in Galway, in 1915. 54 See
Milton's *Il Penseroso*, lines 85 ff.

From markets and from fairs
Have seen his midnight candle glimmering.   60

Two men have founded here. A man-at-arms
Gathered a score of horse and spent his days
In this tumultuous spot,
Where through long wars and sudden night alarms
His dwindling score and he seemed castaways   65
Forgetting and forgot;
And I, that after me
My bodily heirs may find,
To exalt a lonely mind,
Befitting emblems of adversity.   70

III
MY TABLE

Two heavy trestles, and a board
Where Sato's gift, a changeless sword,
By pen and paper lies,
That it may moralise
My days out of their aimlessness.   75
A bit of an embroidered dress
Covers its wooden sheath.
Chaucer had not drawn breath
When it was forged. In Sato's house,
Curved like new moon, moon-luminous,   80
It lay five hundred years.
Yet if no change appears
No moon; only an aching heart
Conceives a changeless work of art.
Our learned men have urged   85
That when and where 'twas forged
A marvellous accomplishment,
In painting or in pottery, went
From father unto son
And through the centuries ran   90
And seemed unchanging like the sword.
Soul's beauty being most adored,
Men and their business took
The soul's unchanging look;

72 *Sato:* a Japanese, co-member of a secret society, who gave the sword
to Yeats in America in 1920. The sword symbolises both ancestral
tradition and the life of action.

For the most rich inheritor,   95
Knowing that none could pass Heaven's door
That loved inferior art,
Had such an aching heart
That he, although a country's talk
For silken clothes and stately walk,   100
Had waking wits; it seemed
Juno's peacock screamed.

IV

MY DESCENDANTS

Having inherited a vigorous mind
From my old fathers, I must nourish dreams
And leave a woman and a man behind   105
As vigorous of mind, and yet it seems
Life scarce can cast a fragrance on the wind,
Scarce spread a glory to the morning beams,
But the torn petals strew the garden plot;
And there's but common greenness after that.   110

And what if my descendants lose the flower
Through natural declension of the soul,
Through too much business with the passing hour,
Through too much play, or marriage with a fool?
May this laborious stair and this stark tower   115
Become a roofless ruin that the owl
May build in the cracked masonry and cry
Her desolation to the desolate sky.

The Primum Mobile that fashioned us
Has made the very owls in circles move;   120
And I, that count myself most prosperous,
Seeing that love and friendship are enough,
For an old neighbour's friendship chose the house
And decked and altered it for a girl's love,
And know whatever flourish and decline   125
These stones remain their monument and mine.

119 *The Primum Mobile:* the 'first moving thing' (Lat.); in the Ptole-
maic astronomy, the outer sphere which carried with it all the spheres
of the stars, planets, and sun.

V

THE ROAD AT MY DOOR

An affable Irregular,
A heavily-built Falstaffian man,
Comes cracking jokes of civil war
As though to die by gunshot were   130
The finest play under the sun.

A brown Lieutenant and his men,
Half dressed in national uniform,
Stand at my door, and I complain
Of the foul weather, hail and rain,   135
A pear-tree broken by the storm.

I count those feathered balls of soot
The moor-hen guides upon the stream,
To silence the envy in my thought;
And turn towards my chamber, caught   140
In the cold snows of a dream.

VI

THE STARE'S NEST BY MY WINDOW

The bees build in the crevices
Of loosening masonry, and there
The mother birds bring grubs and flies.
My wall is loosening; honey-bees,   145
Come build in the empty house of the stare.

We are closed in, and the key is turned
On our uncertainty; somewhere
A man is killed, or a house burned,
Yet no clear fact to be discerned: 150
Come build in the empty house of the stare.

127 *Irregular:* an Irish Republican, one of those who opposed the
British Treaty of 1921 which provided for the partition of Ulster and
gave the new Irish Free State not full independence but Dominion
status. 132 *Lieutenant:* i.e. of the National Army; supporter of the
Treaty during the Civil War of 1922. 146 *Stare:* starling.

A barricade of stone or of wood;
Some fourteen days of civil war;
Last night they trundled down the road
That dead young soldier in his blood: 155
Come build in the empty house of the stare.

We had fed the heart on fantasies,
The heart's grown brutal from the fare;
More substance in our enmities
Than in our love; O honey-bees,   160
Come build in the empty house of the stare.

VII
I SEE PHANTOMS OF HATRED AND OF THE HEART'S
FULLNESS AND OF THE COMING EMPTINESS

I climb to the tower-top and lean upon broken stone,
A mist that is like blown snow is sweeping over all,
Valley, river, and elms, under the light of a moon
That seems unlike itself, that seems unchangeable,   165
A glittering sword out of the east. A puff of wind
And those white glimmering fragments of the mist sweep by.
Frenzies bewilder, reveries perturb the mind;
Monstrous familiar images swim to the mind's eye.

' Vengeance upon the murderers,' the cry goes up,   170
' Vengeance for Jacques Molay.' In cloud-pale rags, or in lace,
The rage-driven, rage-tormented, and rage-hungry troop,
Trooper belabouring trooper, biting at arm or at face,
Plunges towards nothing, arms and fingers spreading wide
For the embrace of nothing; and I, my wits astray   175
Because of all that senseless tumult, all but cried
For vengeance on the murderers of Jacques Molay.

Their legs long, delicate and slender, aquamarine their eyes,
Magical unicorns bear ladies on their backs.
The ladies close their musing eyes. No prophecies,   180
Remembered out of Babylonian almanacs,
Have closed the ladies' eyes, their minds are but a pool
Where even longing drowns under its own excess;
Nothing but stillness can remain when hearts are full
Of their own sweetness, bodies of their loveliness.   185

171 *Jacques Molay:* (1228-1314), last of the grand masters of the Knights
Templars, burned at the stake in Paris for refusing to admit the papal
charges against his Order.

The cloud-pale unicorns, the eyes of aquamarine,
The quivering half-closed eyelids, the rags of cloud or of lace,
Or eyes that rage has brightened, arms it has made lean,
Give place to an indifferent multitude, give place
To brazen hawks. Nor self-delighting reverie,   190
Nor hate of what's to come, nor pity for what's gone,
Nothing but grip of claw, and the eye's complacency,
The innumerable clanging wings that have put out the moon.

I turn away and shut the door, and on the stair
Wonder how many times I could have proved my worth   195
In something that all others understand or share;
But O! ambitious heart, had such a proof drawn forth
A company of friends, a conscience set at ease,
It had but made us pine the more. The abstract joy,
The half-read wisdom of daemonic images,   200
Suffice the ageing man as once the growing boy.

Robert Frost

1875—1963

PAUL'S WIFE

To drive Paul out of any lumber camp
All that was needed was to say to him,
' How is the wife, Paul?—and he'd disappear.
Some said it was because he had no wife,
And hated to be twitted on the subject;   5
Others because he'd come within a day
Or so of having one, and then been jilted;
Others because he'd had one once, a good one,
Who'd run away with someone else and left him;
And others still because he had one now   10
He only had to be reminded of,—
He was all duty to her in a minute:
He had to run right off to look her up,
As if to say, ' That's so, how is my wife?
I hope she isn't getting into mischief.'   15
No one was anxious to get rid of Paul.
He'd been the hero of the mountain camps
Ever since, just to show them, he had slipped
The bark of a whole tamarack off whole,

19 *Tamarack:* American larch.

As clean as boys do off a willow twig   20
To make a willow whistle on a Sunday
In April by subsiding meadow brooks.
They seemed to ask him just to see him go,
' How is the wife, Paul? ' and he always went.
He never stopped to murder anyone   25
Who asked the question. He just disappeared—
Nobody knew in what direction,
Although it wasn't usually long
Before they heard of him in some new camp,
The same Paul at the same old feats of logging.   30
The question everywhere was why should Paul
Object to being asked a civil question—
A man you could say almost anything to
Short of a fighting word. You have the answers.
And there was one more not so fair to Paul: 35
That Paul had married a wife not his equal.
Paul was ashamed of her. To match a hero,
She would have had to be a heroine;
Instead of which she was some half-breed squaw.
But if the story Murphy told was true,   40
She wasn't anything to be ashamed of.

You know Paul could do wonders. Everyone's
Heard how he thrashed the horses on a load
That wouldn't budge until they simply stretched
Their rawhide harness from the load to camp.   45
Paul told the boss the load would be all right,
' The sun will bring your load in '—and it did—
By shrinking the rawhide to natural length.
That's what is called a stretcher. But I guess
The one about his jumping so's to land   50
With both his feet at once against the ceiling,
And then land safely right side up again,
Back on the floor, is fact or pretty near fact.
Well, this is such a yarn. Paul sawed his wife
Out of a white-pine log. Murphy was there,   55
And, as you might say, saw the lady born.
Paul worked at anything in lumbering.
He'd been hard at it taking boards away
For—I forget—the last ambitious sawyer
To want to find out if he couldn't pile   60
The lumber on Paul till Paul begged for mercy.
They'd sliced the first slab off a big butt log,
49 *Stretcher:* tall story.   62 *Butt:* thick trunk near root.

And the sawyer had slammed the carriage back
To slam end on again against the saw teeth.
To judge them by the way they caught themselves 65
When they saw what had happened to the log,
They must have had a guilty expectation
Something was going to go with their slambanging.
Something had left a broad black streak of grease
On the new wood the whole length of the log 70
Except, perhaps, a foot at either end.
But when Paul put his finger in the grease,
It wasn't grease at all, but a long slot.
The log was hollow. They were sawing pine.
'First time I ever saw a hollow pine. 75
That comes of having Paul around the place.
Take it to hell for me,' the sawyer said.
Everyone had to have a look at it,
And tell Paul what he ought to do about it.
(They treated it as his.) 'You take a jack-knife, 80
And spread the opening, and you've got a dug-out
All dug to go a-fishing in.' To Paul
The hollow looked too sound and clean and empty
Ever to have housed birds or beasts or bees.
There was no entrance for them to get in by. 85
It looked to him like some new kind of hollow
He thought he'd *better* take his jack-knife to.
So after work that evening he came back
And let enough light into it by cutting
To see if it was empty. He made out in there 90
A slender length of pith, or was it pith?
It might have been the skin a snake had cast
And left stood up on end inside the tree
The hundred years the tree must have been growing.
More cutting and he had this in both hands, 95
And, looking from it to the pond near by,
Paul wondered how it would respond to water.
Not a breeze stirred, but just the breath of air
He made in walking slowly to the beach
Blew it once off his hands and almost broke it. 100
He laid it at the edge where it could drink.
At the first drink it rustled and grew limp.
At the next drink it grew invisible.
Paul dragged the shallows for it with his fingers,
And thought it must have melted. It was gone. 105
And then beyond the open water, dim with midges,
Where the log drive lay pressed against the boom,

It slowly rose a person, rose a girl,
Her wet hair heavy on her like a helmet,
Who, leaning on a log looked back at Paul.   110
And that made Paul in turn look back
To see if it was anyone behind him
That she was looking at instead of him.
Murphy had been there watching all the time,
But from a shed where neither of them could see him.   115
There was a moment of suspense in birth
When the girl seemed too water-logged to live,
Before she caught her first breath with a gasp
And laughed. Then she climbed slowly to her feet,
And walked off talking to herself or Paul   120
Across the logs like backs of alligators,
Paul taking after her around the pond.

Next evening Murphy and some other fellows
Got drunk, and tracked the pair up Catamount,
From the bare top of which there is a view   125
To other hills across a kettle valley.
And there, well after dark, let Murphy tell it,
They saw Paul and his creature keeping house.
It was the only glimpse that anyone
Has had of Paul and her since Murphy saw them   130
Falling in love across the twilight mill-pond.
More than a mile across the wilderness
They sat together halfway up a cliff
In a small niche let into it, the girl
Brightly, as if a star played on the place,   135
Paul darkly, like her shadow. All the light
Was from the girl herself, though, not from a star,
As was apparent from what happened next.
All those great ruffians put their throats together,
And let out a loud yell, and threw a bottle,   140
As a brute tribute of respect to beauty.
Of course the bottle fell short by a mile,
But the shout reached the girl and put her light out.
She went out like a firefly, and that was all.

So there were witnesses that Paul was married,   145
And not to anyone to be ashamed of.
Everyone had been wrong in judging Paul.
Murphy told me Paul put on all those airs

124 *Catamount:*   not identified.   126 *Kettle valley:*   corrie, circular
hollow in hills.

About his wife to keep her to himself.
Paul was what's called a terrible possessor. 150
Owning a wife with him meant owning her.
She wasn't anybody else's business,
Either to praise her, or so much as name her,
And he'd thank people not to think of her.
Murphy's idea was that a man like Paul 155
Wouldn't be spoken to about a wife
In any way the world knew how to speak.

THE AXE-HELVE

I've known ere now an interfering branch
Of alder catch my lifted axe behind me.
But that was in the woods, to hold my hand
From striking at another alder's roots,
And that was, as I say, an alder branch. 5
This was a man, Baptiste, who stole one day
Behind me on the snow in my own yard
Where I was working at the chopping-block,
And cutting nothing not cut down already.
He caught my axe expertly on the rise, 10
When all my strength put forth was in his favor,
Held it a moment where it was, to calm me,
Then took it from me—and I let him take it.
I didn't know him well enough to know
What it was all about. There might be something 15
He had in mind to say to a bad neighbor
He might prefer to say to him disarmed.
But all he had to tell me in French-English
Was what he thought of—not me, but my axe;
Me only as I took my axe to heart. 20
It was the bad axe-helve someone had sold me—
'Made on machine,' he said, ploughing the grain
With a thick thumbnail to show how it ran
Across the handle's long drawn serpentine,
Like the two strokes across a dollar sign. 25
'You give her one good crack, she's snap raght off.
Den where's your hax-ead flying t'rough de hair?'
Admitted; and yet, what was that to him?

'Come on my house and I put you one in
What's las' awhile—good hick'ry what's grow crooked. 30

De second growt' I cut myself—tough, tough! '

Something to sell? That wasn't how it sounded.

' Den when you say you come? It's cost you nothing.
To-naght? '

          As well to-night as any night.

Beyond an over-warmth of kitchen stove   35
My welcome differed from no other welcome.
Baptiste knew best why I was where I was.
So long as he would leave enough unsaid,
I shouldn't mind his being overjoyed
(If overjoyed he was) at having got me   40
Where I must judge if what he knew about an axe
That not everybody else knew was to count
For nothing in the measure of a neighbor.
Hard if, though cast away for life with Yankees,
A Frenchman couldn't get his human rating!   45

Mrs. Baptiste came in and rocked a chair
That had as many motions as the world:
One back and forward, in and out of shadow,
That got her nowhere; one more gradual,
Sideways, that would have run her on the stove   50
In time, had she not realized her danger
And caught herself up bodily, chair and all,
And set herself back where she started from.
' She ain't spick too much Henglish—dat's too bad.'

I was afraid, in brightening first on me,   55
Then on Baptiste, as if she understood
What passed between us, she was only feigning.
Baptiste was anxious for her; but no more
Than for himself, so placed he couldn't hope
To keep his bargain of the morning with me   60
In time to keep me from suspecting him
Of really never having meant to keep it.

Needlessly soon he had his axe-helves out,
A quiverful to choose from, since he wished me
To have the best he had, or had to spare—   65
Not for me to ask which, when what he took
Had beauties he had to point me out at length

To insure their not being wasted on me.
He liked to have it slender as a whipstock,
Free from the least knot, equal to the strain　70
Of bending like a sword across the knee.
He showed me that the lines of a good helve
Were native to the grain before the knife
Expressed them, and its curves were no false curves
Put on it from without. And there its strength lay　75
For the hard work. He chafed its long white body
From end to end with his rough hand shut round it.
He tried it at the eye-hole in the axe-head.
'Hahn, hahn,' he mused, ' don't need much taking down.'
Baptiste knew how to make a short job long　80
For love of it, and yet not waste time either.

Do you know, what we talked about was knowledge?
Baptiste on his defence about the children
He kept from school, or did his best to keep—
Whatever school and children and our doubts　85
Of laid-on education had to do
With the curves of his axe-helves and his having
Used these unscrupulously to bring me
To see for once the inside of his house.
Was I desired in friendship, partly as some one　90
To leave it to, whether the right to hold
Such doubts of education should depend
Upon the education of those who held them?

But now he brushed the shavings from his knee
And stood the axe there on its horse's hoof,　95
Erect, but not without its waves, as when
The snake stood up for evil in the Garden,—
Top-heavy with a heaviness his short,
Thick hand made light of, steel-blue chin drawn down
And in a little—a French touch in that.　100
Baptiste drew back and squinted at it, pleased;
' See how she's cock her head! '

John Masefield

b. 1878

THE *WANDERER*

All day they loitered by the resting ships,
Telling their beauties over, taking stock;
At night the verdict left my messmates' lips,
' The *Wanderer* is the finest ship in dock.'

I had not seen her, but a friend, since drowned,   5
Drew her, with painted ports, low, lovely, lean,
Saying, ' The *Wanderer*, clipper, outward bound,
The loveliest ship my eyes have ever seen—

' Perhaps to-morrow you will see her sail.
She sails at sunrise ': but the morrow showed   10
No *Wanderer* setting forth for me to hail;
Far down the stream men pointed where she rode,

Rode the great trackway to the sea, dim, dim,
Already gone before the stars were gone.
I saw her at the sea-line's smoky rim   15
Grow swiftly vaguer as they towed her on.

Soon even her masts were hidden in the haze
Beyond the city, she was on her course
To trample billows for a hundred days;
That afternoon the norther gathered force,   20

Blowing a small snow from a point of east.
' Oh, fair for her,' we said, ' to take her south.'
And in our spirits, as the wind increased,
We saw her there, beyond the river mouth,

Setting her side-lights in the wildering dark,   25
To glint upon mad water, while the gale
Roared like a battle, snapping like a shark,
And drunken seamen struggled with the sail.

4 The *Wanderer* was launched in Liverpool in 1891 and was sunk at the
mouth of the Elbe in 1907. Many legends of its unluckiness were
current. 25 *Wildering:* perplexing.

While with sick hearts her mates put out of mind
Their little children left astern, ashore,   30
And the gale's gathering made the darkness blind,
Water and air one intermingled roar.

Then we forgot her, for the fiddlers played,
Dancing and singing held our merry crew;
The old ship moaned a little as she swayed.   35
It blew all night, oh, bitter hard it blew!

So that at midnight I was called on deck
To keep an anchor-watch: I heard the sea
Roar past in white procession filled with wreck;
Intense bright frosty stars burned over me,   40

And the Greek brig beside us dipped and dipped,
White to the muzzle like a half-tide rock,
Drowned to the mainmast with the seas she shipped;
Her cable-swivels clanged at every shock.

And like a never-dying force, the wind   45
Roared till we shouted with it, roared until
Its vast vitality of wrath was thinned,
Had beat its fury breathless and was still.

By dawn the gale had dwindled into flaw,
A glorious morning followed: with my friend   50
I climbed the fo'c's'le-head to see; we saw
The waters hurrying shorewards without end.

Haze blotted out the river's lowest reach;
Out of the gloom the steamers, passing by,
Called with their sirens, hooting their sea-speech;   55
Out of the dimness others made reply.

And as we watched, there came a rush of feet
Charging the fo'c's'le till the hatchway shook.
Men all about us thrust their way, or beat,
Crying, " The *Wanderer*! Down the river! Look! "   60

I looked with them towards the dimness; there
Gleamed like a spirit striding out of night,
A full-rigged ship unutterably fair,
Her masts like trees in winter, frosty-bright.

38 *Anchor-watch:* watch duty while ship lies at anchor. 49 *Flaw:*
gusts of wind.

Foam trembled at her bows like wisps of wool;　　65
She trembled as she towed. I had not dreamed
That work of man could be so beautiful,
In its own presence and in what it seemed.

" So, she is putting back again," I said.
" How white with frost her yards are on the fore! "　　70
One of the men about me answer made,
" That is not frost, but all her sails are tore,

" Torn into tatters, youngster, in the gale;
Her best foul-weather suit gone." It was true,
Her masts were white with rags of tattered sail　　75
Many as gannets when the fish are due.

Beauty in desolation was her pride,
Her crowned array a glory that had been;
She faltered tow'rds us like a swan that died,
But although ruined she was still a queen.　　80

" Put back with all her sails gone," went the word;
Then, from her signals flying, rumour ran,
" The sea that stove her boats in killed her third;
She has been gutted and has lost a man."

So, as though stepping to a funeral march,　　85
She passed defeated homewards whence she came
Ragged with tattered canvas white as starch,
A wild bird that misfortune had made tame.

She was refitted soon: another took
The dead man's office; then the singers hove　　90
Her capstan till the snapping hawsers shook;
Out, with a bubble at her bows, she drove.

Again they towed her seawards, and again
We, watching, praised her beauty, praised her trim,
Saw her fair house-flag flutter at the main,　　95
And slowly saunter seawards, dwindling dim;

And wished her well, and wondered, as she died,
How, when her canvas had been sheeted home,
Her quivering length would sweep into her stride,
Making the greenness milky with her foam.　　100
83 *Third:* third mate. 90 *Hove:* pushed.

But when we rose next morning, we discerned
Her beauty once again a shattered thing;
Towing to dock the *Wanderer* returned,
A wounded sea-bird with a broken wing.

A spar was gone, her rigging's disarray   105
Told of a worse disaster than the last;
Like draggled hair dishevelled hung the stay,
Drooping and beating on the broken mast.

Half-mast upon her flagstaff hung her flag;
Word went among us how the broken spar   110
Had gored her captain like an angry stag,
And killed her mate a half-day from the bar.

She passed to dock upon the top of flood.
An old man near me shook his head and swore:
" Like a bad woman, she has tasted blood—   115
There'll be no trusting in her any more."   ·

We thought it truth, and when we saw her there
Lying in dock, beyond, across the stream,
We would forget that we had called her fair,
We thought her murderess and the past a dream.   120

And when she sailed again, we watched in awe,
Wondering what bloody act her beauty planned,
What evil lurked behind the thing we saw,
What strength was there that thus annulled man's hand,

How next its triumph would compel man's will   125
Into compliance with external Fate,
How next the powers would use her to work ill
On suffering men; we had not long to wait.

For soon the outcry of derision rose,
" Here comes the *Wanderer*! " the expected cry.   130
Guessing the cause, our mockings joined with those
Yelled from the shipping as they towed her by.

She passed us close, her seamen paid no heed
To what was called; they stood, a sullen group,
Smoking and spitting, careless of her need,   135
Mocking the orders given from the poop.

107 *Stay:* supporting rope.

Her mates and boys were working her; we stared.
What was the reason of this strange return,
This third annulling of the thing prepared?
No outward evil could our eyes discern.　　　　140

Only like one who having formed a plan
Beyond the pitch of common minds, she sailed,
Mocked and deserted by the common man,
Made half divine to me for having failed.

We learned the reason soon; below the town　　145
A stay had parted like a snapping reed,
" Warning," the men thought, " not to take her down."
They took the omen, they would not proceed.

Days passed before another crew would sign.
The *Wanderer* lay in dock alone, unmanned,　　150
Feared as a thing possessed by powers malign,
Bound under curses not to leave the land.

But under passing Time fear passes too;
That terror passed, the sailors' hearts grew bold.
We learned in time that she had found a crew　　155
And was bound out and southwards as of old.

And in contempt we thought, " A little while
Will bring her back again, dismantled, spoiled.
It is herself; she cannot change her style;
She has the habit now of being foiled."　　　　160

So when a ship appeared among the haze,
We thought, " The *Wanderer* back again "; but no,
No *Wanderer* showed for many, many days,
Her passing lights made other waters glow.

But we would often think and talk of her,　　　165
Tell newer hands her story, wondering, then,
Upon what ocean she was *Wanderer*,
Bound to the cities built by foreign men.

And one by one our little conclave thinned,
Passed into ships and sailed and so away,　　　170
To drown in some great roaring of the wind,
Wanderers themselves, unhappy fortune's prey.

And Time went by me making memory dim,
Yet still I wondered if the *Wanderer* fared
Still pointing to the unreached ocean's rim, 175
Brightening the water where her breast was bared.

And much in ports abroad I eyed the ships,
Hoping to see her well-remembered form
Come with a curl of bubbles at her lips
Bright to her berth, the sovereign of the storm. 180

I never did, and many years went by,
Then, near a Southern port, one Christmas Eve,
I watched a gale go roaring through the sky,
Making the caldrons of the clouds upheave.

Then the wrack tattered and the stars appeared, 185
Millions of stars that seemed to speak in fire;
A byre cock cried aloud that morning neared,
The swinging wind-vane flashed upon the spire.

And soon men looked upon a glittering earth,
Intensely sparkling like a world new-born; 190
Only to look was spiritual birth,
So bright the raindrops ran along the thorn.

So bright they were, that one could almost pass
Beyond their twinkling to the source, and know
The glory pushing in the blade of grass, 195
That hidden soul which makes the flowers grow.

That soul was there apparent, not revealed,
Unearthly meanings covered every tree,
That wet grass grew in an immortal field,
Those waters fed some never-wrinkled sea. 200

The scarlet berries in the hedge stood out
Like revelations but the tongue unknown;
Even in the brooks a joy was quick: the trout
Rushed in a dumbness dumb to me alone.

All of the valley was aloud with brooks; 205
I walked the morning, breasting up the fells,
Taking again lost childhood from the rooks,
Whose cawing came above the Christmas bells.

I had not walked that glittering world before,
But up the hill a prompting came to me, 210
" This line of upland runs along the shore:
Beyond the hedgerow I shall see the sea."

And on the instant from beyond away
That long familiar sound, a ship's bell, broke
The hush below me in the unseen bay. 215
Old memories came: that inner prompting spoke.

And bright above the hedge a seagull's wings
Flashed and were steady upon empty air.
" A Power unseen," I cried, " prepares these things;
Those are her bells, the *Wanderer* is there." 220

So, hurrying to the hedge and looking down,
I saw a mighty bay's wind-crinkled blue
Ruffling the image of a tranquil town,
With lapsing waters glittering as they grew.

And near me in the road the shipping swung, 225
So stately and so still in such great peace
That like to drooping crests their colours hung,
Only their shadows trembled without cease.

I did but glance upon those anchored ships.
Even as my thought had told, I saw her plain; 230
Tense, like a supple athlete with lean hips,
Swiftness at pause, the *Wanderer* come again—

Come as of old a queen, untouched by Time,
Resting the beauty that no seas could tire,
Sparkling, as though the midnight's rain were rime, 235
Like a man's thought transfigured into fire.

And as I looked, one of her men began
To sing some simple tune of Christmas Day;
Among her crew the song spread, man to man,
Until the singing rang across the bay; 240

And soon in other anchored ships the men
Joined in the singing with clear throats, until
The farm-boy heard it up the windy glen,
Above the noise of sheep-bells on the hill.

Over the water came the lifted song—   245
Blind pieces in a mighty game we swing;
Life's battle is a conquest for the strong;
The meaning shows in the defeated thing.

Wallace Stevens

1879—1955

SUNDAY MORNING

I

Complacencies of the peignoir, and late
Coffee and oranges in a sunny chair,
And the green freedom of a cockatoo
Upon a rug mingle to dissipate
The holy hush of ancient sacrifice.   5
She dreams a little, and she feels the dark
Encroachment of that old catastrophe,
As a calm darkens among water-lights.
The pungent oranges and bright, green wings
Seem things in some procession of the dead,   10
Winding across wide water, without sound.
The day is like wide water, without sound,
Stilled for the passing of her dreaming feet
Over the seas, to silent Palestine,
Dominion of the blood and sepulchre.   15

II

Why should she give her bounty to the dead?
What is divinity if it can come
Only in silent shadows and in dreams?
Shall she not find in comforts of the sun,
In pungent fruit and bright, green wings, or else   20
In any balm or beauty of the earth,
Things to be cherished like the thought of heaven?
Divinity must live within herself:
Passions of rain, or moods in falling snow;
Grievings in loneliness, or unsubdued   25
Elations when the forest blooms; gusty

1 *Peignoir*: dressing-gown.   7 *That old catastrophe:* Christ's crucifixion,
or religion in general. It is Sunday morning, but the lady prefers her
'sunny chair' to the pew she cannot believe in.
    A.L.P.   Y

Emotions on wet roads on autumn nights;
All pleasures and all pains, remembering
The bough of summer and the winter branch.
These are the measures destined for her soul.   30

III

Jove in the clouds had his inhuman birth.
No mother suckled him, no sweet land gave
Large-mannered motions to his mythy mind.
He moved among us, as a muttering king,
Magnificent, would move among his hinds,   35
Until our blood, commingling, virginal,
With heaven, brought such requital to desire
The very hinds discerned it, in a star.
Shall our blood fail? Or shall it come to be
The blood of paradise? And shall the earth   40
Seem all of paradise that we shall know?
The sky will be much friendlier then than now,
A part of labour and a part of pain,
And next in glory to enduring love,
Not this dividing and indifferent blue.   45

IV

She says, ' I am content when wakened birds,
Before they fly, test the reality
Of misty fields, by their sweet questionings;
But when the birds are gone, and their warm fields
Return no more, where, then, is paradise? '   50
There is not any haunt of prophecy,
Nor any old chimera of the grave,
Neither the golden underground, nor isle
Melodious, where spirits gat them home,
Nor visionary south, nor cloudy palm   55
Remote on heaven's hill, that has endured
As April's green endures; or will endure
Like her remembrance of awakened birds,
Or her desire for June and evening, tipped
By the consummation of the swallow's wings.   60

V

She says, ' But in contentment I still feel
The need of some imperishable bliss.'
Death is the mother of beauty; hence from her,
Alone, shall come fulfilment of our dreams
And our desires. Although she strews the leaves   65

Of sure obliteration on our paths,
The path sick sorrow took, the many paths
Where triumph rang its brassy phrase, or love
Whispered a little out of tenderness,
She makes the willow shiver in the sun   70
For maidens who were wont to sit and gaze
Upon the grass, relinquished to their feet.
She causes boys to pile new plums and pears
On disregarded plate. The maiden taste
And stray impassioned in the littering leaves.   75

VI

Is there no change of death in paradise?
Does ripe fruit never fall? Or do the boughs
Hang always heavy in that perfect sky,
Unchanging, yet so like our perishing earth,
With rivers like our own that seek for seas   80
They never find, the same receding shores
That never touch with inarticulate pang?
Why set the pear upon those river-banks
Or spice the shores with odours of the plum?
Alas, that they should wear our colors there,   85
The silken weavings of our afternoons,
And pick the strings of our insipid lutes!
Death is the mother of beauty, mystical,
Within whose burning bosom we devise
Our earthly mothers waiting, sleeplessly.   90

VII

Supple and turbulent, a ring of men
Shall chant in orgy on a summer morn
Their boisterous devotion to the sun,
Not as a god, but as a god might be,
Naked among them, like a savage source.   95
Their chant shall be a chant of paradise,
Out of their blood, returning to the sky;
And in their chant shall enter, voice by voice,
The windy lake wherein their lord delights,
The trees, like serafin, and echoing hills   100
That choir among themselves long afterward.
They shall know well the heavenly fellowship
Of men that perish and of summer morn.
And whence they came and whither they shall go
The dew upon their feet shall manifest.   105

VIII

She hears, upon that water without sound,
A voice that cries, ' The tomb in Palestine
Is not the porch of spirits lingering.
It is the grave of Jesus, where he lay.'
We live in an old chaos of the sun,   110
Or old dependency of day and night,
Or island solitude, unsponsored, free,
Of that wide water, inescapable.
Deer walk upon our mountains, and the quail
Whistle about us their spontaneous cries;   115
Sweet berries ripen in the wilderness;
And, in the isolation of the sky,
At evening, casual flocks of pigeons make
Ambiguous undulations as they sink,
Downward to darkness, on extended wings.   120

William Carlos Williams

1883-1963

TRACT

I will teach you my townspeople
how to perform a funeral—
for you have it over a troop
of artists—
unless one should scour the world—   5
you have the ground sense necessary.

See! the hearse leads.
I begin with a design for a hearse.
For Christ's sake not black—
nor white either—and not polished!   10
Let it be weathered—like a farm wagon—
with gilt wheels (this could be
applied fresh at small expense)
or no wheels at all:
a rough dray to drag over the ground.   15

112 *Island solitude:* the world, unvisited by God.

Knock the glass out!
My God—glass, my townspeople!
For what purpose? Is it for the dead
to look out or for us to see
how well he is housed or to see   20
the flowers or the lack of them—
or what?
To keep the rain and snow from him?
He will have a heavier rain soon:
pebbles and dirt and what not.   25
Let there be no glass—
and no upholstery phew!
and no little brass rollers
and small easy wheels on the bottom—
my townspeople what are you thinking of?   30

A rough plain hearse then
with gilt wheels and no top at all.
On this the coffin lies
by its own weight.
        No wreaths please—   35
especially no hot house flowers.
Some common memento is better,
something he prized and is known by:
his old clothes—a few books perhaps—
God knows what! You realize   40
how we are about these things
my townspeople—
something will be found—anything
even flowers if he had come to that.
So much for the hearse.   45

For heaven's sake though see to the driver!
Take off the silk hat! In fact
that's no place at all for him—
up there unceremoniously
dragging our friend out to his own dignity!   50
Bring him down—bring him down!
Low and inconspicuous! I'd not have him ride
on the wagon at all—damn him—
the undertaker's understrapper!
Let him hold the reins   55
and walk at the side
and inconspicuously too!

Then briefly as to yourselves:
Walk behind—as they do in France,
seventh class, or if you ride   60
Hell take curtains! Go with some show
of inconvenience; sit openly—
to the weather as to grief.
Or do you think you can shut grief in?
What—from us? We who have perhaps   65
nothing to lose? Share with us
share with us—it will be money
in your pockets.
          Go now
I think you are ready.

BURNING THE CHRISTMAS GREENS

Their time past, pulled down
cracked and flung to the fire
—go up in a roar

All recognition lost, burnt clean
clean in the flame, the green   5
dispersed, a living red,
flame red, red as blood wakes
on the ash—

and ebbs to a steady burning
the rekindled bed become   10
a landscape of flame

At the winter's midnight
we went to the trees, the coarse
holly, the balsam and
the hemlock for their green   15

At the thick of the dark
the moment of the cold's
deepest plunge we brought branches
cut from the green trees

to fill our need, and over   20
doorways, about paper Christmas
bells covered with tinfoil
and fastened by red ribbons

we stuck the green prongs,
in the windows hung   25
woven wreaths and about pictures
the living green. On the

mantle we built a green forest
and among those hemlock
sprays put a herd of small   30
white deer as if they

were walking there. All this!
and it seemed gentle and good
to us. Their time past,
relief! The room bare. We   35

stuffed the dead grate
with them upon the half burntout
log's smoldering eye, opening
red and closing under them

and we stood there looking down.   40
Green is a solace
a promise of peace, a fort
against the cold (though we

did not say so) a challenge
above the snow's   45
hard shell. Green (we might
have said) that, where

small birds hide and dodge
and lift their plaintive
rallying cries, blocks for them   50
and knocks down

the unseeing bullets of
the storm. Green spruce boughs
pulled down by a weight of
snow—Transformed!   55

Violence leaped and appeared.
Recreant! roared to life
as the flame rose through and
our eyes recoiled from it.

In the jagged flames green   60
to red, instant and alive. Green!
those sure abutments . . . Gone!
lost to mind

and quick in the contracting
tunnel of the grate   65
appeared a world! Black
mountains, black and red—as

yet uncolored—and ash white,
an infant landscape of shimmering
ash and flame and we, in   70
that instant, lost

breathless to be witnesses,
as if we stood
ourselves refreshed among
the shining fauna of that fire.   75

Ezra Pound

b. 1885

NEAR PERIGORD

From *Lustra* (1916). A character-study of Bertran de Born, the Provençal troubadour who flourished in the last quarter of the 12th century. Essentially the poem asks a question: were the love-poems of this restless warrior-poet really love-poems, or was war his mistress, and each song he sent his minstrel to sing in neighbouring castles a mere device for espionage?

> *A Perigord, pres del muralh*
> *Tan que i puosch'om gitar ab malh.**

You'd have men's hearts up from the dust
And tell their secrets, Messire Cino,
Right enough? Then read between the lines of Uc St. Circ,
Solve me the riddle, for you know the tale.

* The motto, from a poem by Bertran de Born, Pound translates else-where as: 'At Perigord near to the wall/Aye, within a mace throw of it.'
2 *Cino:* fictitious character. 3 *Uc St. Circ:* (*fl. c.* 1210-53), Provençal troubadour and biographer.

Bertrans, En Bertrans, left a fine canzone: 5
'Maent, I love you, you have turned me out.
The voice of Montfort, Lady Agnes' hair,
Bel Miral's stature, the viscountess' throat,
Set all together, are not worthy of you. . . .'
And all the while you sing out that canzone,   10
Think you that Maent lived at Montaignac,
One at Chalais, another at Malemort
Hard over Brive—for every lady a castle,
Each place strong.

       Oh, *is* it easy enough?   15
Tairiran held hall in Montaignac,
His brother-in-law was all there was of power
In Perigord, and this good union
Gobbled all the land, and held it later for some hundred years.
And our En Bertrans was in Altafort,   20
Hub of the wheel, the stirrer-up of strife,
As caught by Dante in the last wallow of hell—
The headless trunk ' that made its head a lamp,'
For separation wrought out separation,
And he who set the strife between brother and brother   25
And had his way with the old English king,
Viced in such torture for the ' counterpass '.
How would you live, with neighbours set about you—
Poictiers and Brive, untaken Rochecouart,
Spread like the finger-tips of one frail hand;   30
And you on that great mountain of a palm—
Not a neat ledge, not Foix between its streams,
But one huge back half-covered up with pine,
Worked for and snatched from the string-purse of Born—
The four round towers, four brothers—mostly fools: 35

5 *Bertrans:* Bertran de Born (1135/40?-*c.* 1207), Provençal troubadour
and warrior. *Born* is a region in south-west France (Landes). *En* is an
honorific title—'Sir'. *Canzone:* song resembling madrigal. (Ital.)
6 *Maent:* the Lady Maent (or Maeut) de Montignac. 7-8 Other great
ladies of Provence are compared, and dismissed. 11-12 *Mont(a)ignac*
... *Chalais* ... *Malemort:* strongholds in and near Périgord. 13 *Brive:*
town in the old province of Limousin, south central France. 16
Tairiran: Maent's husband. 18 *Perigord:* Périgord, former province
of south central France (Dordogne). 20 *Altafort:* Hautefort, Bertran's
castle in Périgord. 22-23 See Dante, *Inferno*, XXVIII. 118-42.
25-26 Bertran stirred up strife between the English king Henry II
(1133-89) and his four sons, Henry, Richard Cœur-de-Lion, Geoffrey,
and John. 27 *Viced:* held, secured; *counterpass:* Dante's *contrapasso*,
retribution. 29 *Poictiers* ... *Rochecouart:* towns in west central France.
32 *Foix:* town in south of France, at foot of Pyrenees.

What could he do but play the desperate chess,
And stir old grudges?
   ' Pawn your castles, lords!
Let the Jews pay.'
   And the great scene—   40
(That, maybe, never happened!)
   Beaten at last,
Before the hard old king:
   ' Your son, ah, since he died
My wit and worth are cobwebs brushed aside 45
In the full flare of grief. Do what you will.'

 Take the whole man, and ravel out the story.
He loved this lady in castle Montaignac?
The castle flanked him—he had need of it.
You read to-day, how long the overlords of Perigord, 50
The Talleyrands, have held the place; it was no transient fiction.
And Maent failed him? Or saw through the scheme?

 And all his net-like thought of new alliance?
Chalais is high, a-level with the poplars.
Its lowest stones just meet the valley tips 55
Where the low Dronne is filled with water-lilies.
And Rochecouart can match it, stronger yet,
The very spur's end, built on sheerest cliff,
And Malemort keeps its close hold on Brive,
While Born, his own close purse, his rabbit warren, 60
His subterranean chamber with a dozen doors,
A-bristle with antennæ to feel roads,
To sniff the traffic into Perigord.
And that hard phalanx, that unbroken line,
The ten good miles from there to Maent's castle, 65
All of his flank—how could he do without her?
And all the road to Cahors, to Toulouse?
What would he do without her?

 ' Papiol,
Go forthright singing—Anhes, Cembelins. 70
There is a throat; ah, there are two white hands;

40-46 *The great scene, etc.*: apocryphal scene between Henry II and
Bertran after the young Henry had died and Bertran (who supported
him) had been driven out of his castle by Richard.   51 *Talleyrands:*
ancient noble family in Périgord. 56 *Dronne:* river in Périgord.
67 *Cahors:* town in south-west France, between Limoges and Toulouse.
69 *Papiol:* Bertran's jongleur or wandering minstrel, who was sent to
sing his songs before Anhes, Cembelins, and other ladies.

There is a trellis full of early roses,
And all my heart is bound about with love.
Where am I come with compound flatteries—
What doors are open to fine compliment? '   75
And every one half jealous of Maent?
He wrote the catch to pit their jealousies
Against her; give her pride in them?

Take his own speech, make what you will of it—
And still the knot, the first knot, of Maent?   80

   Is it a love poem? Did he sing of war?
Is it an intrigue to run subtly out,
Born of a jongleur's tongue, freely to pass
Up and about and in and out the land,
Mark him a craftsman and a strategist?   85
(St. Leider had done as much as Polhonac,
Singing a different stave, as closely hidden.)
Oh, there is precedent, legal tradition,
To sing one thing when your song means another,
' *Et albirar ab lor bordon*—— '   90
Foix' count knew that. What is Sir Bertrans' singing?
Maent, Maent, and yet again Maent,
Or war and broken heaumes and politics?

II
   End fact. Try fiction. Let us say we see
En Bertrans, a tower-room at Hautefort,   95
Sunset, the ribbon-like road lies, in red cross-light,
Southward toward Montaignac, and he bends at a table
Scribbling, swearing between his teeth; by his left hand
Lie little strips of parchment covered over,
Scratched and erased with *al* and *ochaisos*.   100
Testing his list of rhymes, a lean man? Bilious?
With a red straggling beard?
And the green cat's-eye lifts towards Montaignac.

---

77 *Catch:* song, but also suggesting a trap. 86 *St. Leider, etc.:* Guillem
de St.-Leidier paid court to the Marchioness of Poulignac by disguising
his love-songs and getting her husband, by a beautiful irony, to sing
them to her. 90 Pound elsewhere translates this line from 'the sar-
donic Count of Foix' as ' And sing not all they have in mind.' 93
Heaumes: helmets (Fr.). 100 *Al . . . ochaisos:* rhyme-endings in Bert-
ran's poem *Dompna soissenbuda*, already referred to at lines 6-9 and 69-75.

Or take his ' magnet ' singer setting out,
Dodging his way past Aubeterre, singing at Chalais   105
  In the vaulted hall,
Or, by a lichened tree at Rochecouart
Aimlessly watching a hawk above the valleys,
Waiting his turn in the mid-summer evening,
Thinking of Aelis, whom he loved heart and soul . . .   110
To find her half alone, Montfort away,
And a brown, placid, hated woman visiting her,
Spoiling his visit, with a year before the next one.
Little enough?
Or carry him forward. ' Go through all the courts,   115
My Magnet,' Bertrans had said.

  We came to Ventadour
In the mid love court, he sings out the canzon,
No one hears save Arrimon Luc D'Esparo—
No one hears aught save the gracious sound of compliments. 120
Sir Arrimon counts on his fingers, Montfort,
Rochecouart, Chalais, the rest, the tactic,
Malemort, guesses beneath, sends word to Cœur-de-Lion:
The compact, de Born smoked out, trees felled
About his castle, cattle driven out!   125
Or no one sees it, and En Bertrans prospered?

  And ten years after, or twenty, as you will,
Arnaut and Richard lodge beneath Chalus:
The dull round towers encroaching on the field,
The tents tight drawn, horses at tether   130
Farther and out of reach, the purple night,
The crackling of small fires, the bannerets,
The lazy leopards on the largest banner,
Stray gleams on hanging mail, an armourer's torchflare
Melting on steel.   135

  And in the quietest space
They probe old scandals, say de Born is dead;
And we've the gossip (skipped six hundred years).

104 *Magnet:* the jongleur who is to catch—what? 105 *Aubeterre:* town
on river Dronne. 110-11 *Aelis . . . Montfort:* Cf. line 7. 117 *Ventadour:*
Maria of Ventadour was Maent's sister. Arrimon, Richard's friend and
Bertran's enemy, guesses the hidden military significance of the song,
and moves to forestall Bertran. 128 *Arnaut:* Arnaut Daniel (*fl. c.*
1180-1210), Provençal troubadour, in an imaginary scene with Richard
before the assault on the castle of Châlus in Limousin (1199).

Richard shall die to-morrow—leave him there
Talking of *trobar clus* with Daniel.   140
And the ' best craftsman ' sings out his friend's song,
Envies its vigour . . . and deplores the technique,
Dispraises his own skill?—That's as you will.
And they discuss the dead man,
Plantagenet puts the riddle: ' Did he love her? ' 145
And Arnaut parries: ' Did he love your sister?
True, he has praised her, but in some opinion
He wrote that praise only to show he had
The favour of your party; had been well received.'
' You knew the man.'   150
   ' *You* knew the man.'
' I am an artist, you have tried both métiers.'
' You were born near him.'
   ' Do we know our friends? '
' Say that he saw the castles, say that he loved Maent! ' 155
' Say that he loved her, does it solve the riddle? '
 End the discussion, Richard goes out next day
And gets a quarrel-bolt shot through his vizard,
Pardons the bowman, dies,

   Ends our discussion. Arnaut ends 160
' In sacred odour '—(that's apocryphal!)
And we can leave the talk till Dante writes:
Surely I saw, and still before my eyes
Goes on that headless trunk, that bears for light
Its own head swinging, gripped by the dead hair, 165
And like a swinging lamp that says, ' Ah me!
I severed men, my head and heart
Ye see here severed, my life's counterpart.'

Or take En Bertrans?

---

140 *Trobar clus:* difficult poetry, poetry requiring a key; the more esoteric of the two modes of Provençal verse-writing, opposed to *trobar clar*, or clear, open poetry. 141 *Best craftsman:* Dante called Arnaut Daniel a 'better craftsman' than the Italian poet Guido Guinizelli (*c.* 1230/40-76); he acknowledged both as his masters. See *Purgatorio*, XXVI. 117. 145 *Plantagenet:* the royal line, begun with Henry II in 1154, to which Richard belonged. 152 *Métier:* trade, profession (Fr.). 158 *Quarrel-bolt:* square-headed bolt used with crossbow. 163-8 See *Inferno*, XXVIII. 118-42.

III

Ed eran due in uno, ed uno in due ;
Inferno, XXVIII, 125

Bewildering spring, and by the Auvezere   170
Poppies and day's eyes in the green émail
Rose over us; and we knew all that stream,
And our two horses had traced out the valleys;
Knew the low flooded lands squared out with poplars,
In the young days when the deep sky befriended.   175
    And great wings beat above us in the twilight,
And the great wheels in heaven
Bore us together . . . surging . . . and apart . . .
Believing we should meet with lips and hands,
    High, high and sure . . . and then the counter-thrust: 180
' Why do you love me? Will you always love me?
But I am like the grass, I cannot love you.'
Or, ' Love, and I love and love you,
And hate your mind, not *you*, your soul, your hands.'

    So to this last estrangement, Tairiran!   185

    There shut up in his castle, Tairiran's,
She who had nor ears nor tongue save in her hands,
Gone—ah, gone—untouched, unreachable!
She who could never live save through one person,
She who could never speak save to one person,   190
And all the rest of her a shifting change,
A broken bundle of mirrors . . . !

Thomas Stearns Eliot

b. 1888

GERONTION*

A monologue, though hardly a portrait, of an old man whose ' dry
thoughts ' are concerned more with the spiritually ' dry season ' he
lives in than with the decay of his own vigour. In the perspective

---

170 Auvezere: river in Périgord. 171 *Day's eyes:* daisies; *émail:*
enamel (Fr.).
* 'Little old man' (Gk.).

of 1920, Gerontion sees as little hope in the modern dilutions and falsifications of Christianity as in the brief heroic outburst of modern history. No hero himself, he is tempted to welcome the disintegration of society, as confirming his latent pessimism.

> *Thou hast nor youth nor age*
> *But as it were an after dinner sleep*
> *Dreaming of both.*
> [SHAKESPEARE, Measure for Measure, III. i]

Here I am, an old man in a dry month,
Being read to by a boy, waiting for rain.
I was neither at the hot gates
Nor fought in the warm rain
Nor knee deep in the salt marsh, heaving a cutlass,   5
Bitten by flies, fought.
My house is a decayed house,
And the jew squats on the window sill, the owner,
Spawned in some estaminet of Antwerp,
Blistered in Brussels, patched and peeled in London.   10
The goat coughs at night in the field overhead;
Rocks, moss, stonecrop, iron, merds.
The woman keeps the kitchen, makes tea,
Sneezes at evening, poking the peevish gutter.
                  I an old man,   15

A dull head among windy spaces.

Signs are taken for wonders. ' We would see a sign! '
The word within a word, unable to speak a word,
Swaddled with darkness. In the juvescence of the year
Came Christ the tiger   20

In depraved May, dogwood and chestnut, flowering judas,
To be eaten, to be divided, to be drunk
Among whispers; by Mr. Silvero

1-2 based on a passage in A. C. Benson's *Edward FitzGerald* (1905). FitzGerald's remark about the 'cursed inactivity' of the 19th century is also relevant. 3 *Hot gates:* refers perhaps to the heroically defended pass of Thermopylae (480 B.C.). 9 *Estaminet:* café, tavern (Fr.). 12 *Stonecrop:* low creeping plant growing on rocks; *merds:* dung. 17-19 based on a passage in a sermon by Lancelot Andrews (1555-1626). 19 *Juvescence:* presumably for *juvenescence*, early youth. 20 *The tiger:* i.e. beautiful but dangerous, a symbol of latent power sheathed in the soft and gentle. Cf. line 48. 21 based on a passage in *The Education of Henry Adams* (1907): this rank spring growth with its 'passionate depravity' came to symbolize for Adams the pullulating chaos of history. *Dogwood* is a tree with white or pink flowers, *floweriug judas* a tree with purple flowers.

With caressing hands, at Limoges
Who walked all night in the next room;   25
By Hakagawa, bowing among the Titians;
By Madame de Tornquist, in the dark room
Shifting the candles; Fräulein von Kulp
Who turned in the hall, one hand on the door. Vacant shuttles
Weave the wind. I have no ghosts,   30
An old man in a draughty house
Under a windy knob.

After such knowledge, what foregiveness? Think now
History has many cunning passages, contrived corridors
And issues, deceives with whispering ambitions,   35
Guides us by vanities. Think now
She gives when our attention is distracted
And what she gives, gives with such supple confusions
That the giving famishes the craving. Gives too late
What's not believed in, or if still believed,   40
In memory only, reconsidered passion. Gives too soon
Into weak hands, what's thought can be dispensed with
Till the refusal propagates a fear. Think
Neither fear nor courage saves us. Unnatural vices
Are fathered by our heroism. Virtues   45
Are forced upon us by our impudent crimes.
These tears are shaken from the wrath-bearing tree.

The tiger springs in the new year. Us he devours. Think at last
We have not reached conclusion, when I
Stiffen in a rented house. Think at last   50
I have not made this show purposelessly
And it is not by any concitation
Of the backward devils.
I would meet you upon this honestly.
I that was near your heart was removed therefrom   55
To lose beauty in terror, terror in inquisition.
I have lost my passion: why should I need to keep it
Since what is kept must be adulterated?
I have lost my sight, smell, hearing, taste and touch:
How should I use them for your closer contact?   60

23 *Mr. Silvero, etc.:* The names in this passage suggest modern cosmo-
politan rootlessness.   24 *Limoges:* city in France, famed for its porcelain
and enamel.   26 *Titians:* pictures by Titian (*c.* 1477/87-1576), Italian
painter.   52-53 *Concitation of the backward devils:* stirring up the lusts and
fears of the past.   54 *You:* left undefined. 'A woman' and 'Christ'
have been suggested.

These with a thousand small deliberations
Protract the profit of their chilled delirium,
Excite the membrane, when the sense has cooled,
With pungent sauces, multiply variety
In a wilderness of mirrors. What will the spider do,　　65
Suspend its operations, will the weevil
Delay? De Bailhache, Fresca, Mrs. Cammel, whirled
Beyond the circuit of the shuddering Bear
In fractured atoms. Gull against the wind, in the windy straits
Of Belle Isle, or running on the Horn,　　70
White feathers in the snow, the Gulf claims,
And an old man driven by the Trades
To a sleepy corner.

　　　　　　　　　　　　　Tenants of the house,
Thoughts of a dry brain in a dry season.　　75

BURNT NORTON

Burnt Norton is a country house in Gloucestershire which Eliot
visited in 1934. The poem is the first of the group of *Four Quartets*
(1936-42). It is a fine evocation of the search for something
permanent or timeless within the flux of experience, whether in
life (the 'moment in the rose-garden') or in art (the 'Chinese
jar'). A certain quietism and fear of the daily plight (seen in
the passage describing the London Underground) are qualified
by the poet's admission that 'only through time time is
conquered.'

τοῦ λόγου δ' ἐόντος ξυνοῦ ζώουσιν
οἱ πολλοὶ ὡς ἰδίαν ἔχοντες φρόνησιν.

1. p. 77. Fr. 2.

ὁδὸς ἄνω κάτω μία καὶ ὡυτή.*

1. p. 89. Fr. 60.

Diels: *Die Fragmente der Vorsokratiker*
(Herakleitos).

67 The international names suggest a decadent Europe as well as the
more general dissolution of the world. 68 *Bear:* constellation of Ursa
Major. 70 *Belle Isle:* island between Newfoundland and Labrador;
the Horn: Cape Horn, southernmost point of South America. 71 *The
Gulf:* the Gulf of Mexico, or the Gulf Stream. 72 *Trades:* winds
blowing from north or south towards equator.
* The double epigraph reads: 'The Law is universal, but most people
live as if they had wisdom of their own.' 'The way up and the way down
are one.'

I

Time present and time past
Are both perhaps present in time future,
And time future contained in time past.
If all time is eternally present
All time is unredeemable.   5
What might have been is an abstraction
Remaining a perpetual possibility
Only in a world of speculation.
What might have been and what has been
Point to one end, which is always present.   10
Footfalls echo in the memory
Down the passage which we did not take
Towards the door we never opened
Into the rose-garden. My words echo
Thus, in your mind.   15
                    But to what purpose
Disturbing the dust on a bowl of rose-leaves
I do not know.
                    Other echoes
Inhabit the garden. Shall we follow?   20
Quick, said the bird, find them, find them,
Round the corner. Through the first gate,
Into our first world, shall we follow
The deception of the thrush? Into our first world.
There they were, dignified, invisible,   25
Moving without pressure, over the dead leaves,
In the autumn heat, through the vibrant air,
And the bird called, in response to
The unheard music hidden in the shrubbery,
And the unseen eyebeam crossed, for the roses   30
Had the look of flowers that are looked at.
There they were as our guests, accepted and accepting.
So we moved, and they, in a formal pattern,
Along the empty alley, into the box circle,
To look down into the drained pool.   35
Dry the pool, dry concrete, brown edged,
And the pool was filled with water out of sunlight,
And the lotos rose, quietly, quietly,
The surface glittered out of heart of light,
And they were behind us, reflected in the pool.   40
Then a cloud passed, and the pool was empty.
Go, said the bird, for the leaves were full of children,

34 *Box:* evergreen shrub.

Hidden excitedly, containing laughter.
Go, go, go, said the bird: human kind
Cannot bear very much reality.   45
Time past and time future
What might have been and what has been
Point to one end, which is always present.

II

Garlic and sapphires in the mud
Clot the bedded axle-tree.   50
The trilling wire in the blood
Sings below inveterate scars
Appeasing long forgotten wars.
The dance along the artery
The circulation of the lymph   55
Are figured in the drift of stars
Ascend to summer in the tree
We move about the moving tree
In light upon the figured leaf
And hear upon the sodden floor   60
Below, the boarhound and the boar
Pursue their pattern as before
But reconciled among the stars.

At the still point of the turning world. Neither flesh nor
  fleshless;
Neither from nor towards; at the still point, there the dance
  is,   65
But neither arrest nor movement. And do not call it fixity,
Where past and future are gathered. Neither movement from nor
  towards,
Neither ascent nor decline. Except for the point, the still point,
There would be no dance, and there is only the dance.
I can only say, *there* we have been: but I cannot say where. 70
And I cannot say, how long, for that is to place it in time.
The inner freedom from the practical desire,
The release from action and suffering, release from the inner
And the outer compulsion, yet surrounded
By a grace of sense, a white light still and moving,   75
Erhebung without motion, concentration
Without elimination, both a new world
And the old made explicit, understood

49 *Garlic and sapphires:* images of the coarse and the flashy in temporal
experience. 76 *Erhebung:* exaltation (Ger.).

In the completion of its partial ecstasy,
The resolution of its partial horror.   80
Yet the enchainment of past and future
Woven in the weakness of the changing body,
Protects mankind from heaven and damnation
Which flesh cannot endure.
                              Time past and time future   85
Allow but a little consciousness.
To be conscious is not to be in time
But only in time can the moment in the rose-garden,
The moment in the arbour where the rain beat,
The moment in the draughty church at smokefall   90
Be remembered; involved with past and future.
Only through time time is conquered.

                                 III
Here is a place of disaffection
Time before and time after
In a dim light: neither daylight   95
Investing form with lucid stillness
Turning shadow into transient beauty
With slow rotation suggesting permanence
Nor darkness to purify the soul
Emptying the sensual with deprivation   100
Cleansing affection from the temporal.
Neither plenitude nor vacancy. Only a flicker
Over the strained time-ridden faces
Distracted from distraction by distraction
Filled with fancies and empty of meaning   105
Tumid apathy with no concentration
Men and bits of paper, whirled by the cold wind
That blows before and after time,
Wind in and out of unwholesome lungs
Time before and time after.   110
Eructation of unhealthy souls
Into the faded air, the torpid
Driven on the wind that sweeps the gloomy hills of London,
Hampstead and Clerkenwell, Campden and Putney,

90 *Smokefall:* either (i) evening, or (ii) a gust of pollen ('smoke') shaken
from a churchyard yew-tree. 97-98 The illusion of something un-
moving (like a beautiful shadow cast in brilliant sunshine), counter-
pointed against our knowledge that it is moving and indeed vanishing,
sharpens appreciation. 104 *Distracted, etc.:* prevented from going mad
by e.g. studying the advertisements in the Underground. 111 *Eructa-
tion:* belching.

Highgate, Primrose and Ludgate. Not here 115
Not here the darkness, in this twittering world.
Descend lower, descend only
Into the world of perpetual solitude,
World not world, but that which is not world,
Internal darkness, deprivation 120
And destitution of all property,
Desiccation of the world of sense,
Evacuation of the world of fancy,
Inoperancy of the world of spirit;
This is the one way, and the other 125
Is the same, not in movement
But abstention from movement; while the world moves
In appetency, on its metalled ways
Of time past and time future.

IV

Time and the bell have buried the day, 130
The black cloud carries the sun away.
Will the sunflower turn to us, will the clematis
Stray down, bend to us; tendril and spray
Clutch and cling?
Chill 135
Fingers of yew be curled
Down on us? After the kingfisher's wing
Has answered light to light, and is silent, the light is still
At the still point of the turning world.

V

Words move, music moves
Only in time; but that which is only living 140
Can only die. Words, after speech, reach
Into the silence. Only by the form, the pattern,
Can words or music reach
The stillness, as a Chinese jar still 145
Moves perpetually in its stillness.
Not the stillness of the violin, while the note lasts,

---

125 *The other:* i.e. the *Erhebung* of line 76, the *plenitude* of line 102.
These are contrasted with *descent* (line 107) and *vacancy* (line 102).
128 *Appetency:* desire. 137-8 *The kingfisher's wing, etc.:* The bright flash
of the flying kingfisher is an image of the suddenness and evanescence of
beauty, which is a 'message' that may never be repeated and therefore
must be seized, though it is only one of the ways into reality. 145 Cf.
Keats's Grecian urn, the 'silent form' that can 'tease us out of thought'.

Not that only, but the co-existence,
Or say that the end precedes the beginning,
And the end and the beginning were always there   150
Before the beginning and after the end.
And all is always now. Words strain,
Crack and sometimes break, under the burden,
Under the tension, slip, slide, perish,
Decay with imprecision, will not stay in place,   155
Will not stay still. Shrieking voices
Scolding, mocking, or merely chattering,
Always assail them. The Word in the desert
Is most attacked by voices of temptation,
The crying shadow in the funeral dance,   160
The loud lament of the disconsolate chimera.

The detail of the pattern is movement,
As in the figure of the ten stairs.
         Desire itself is movement
         Not in itself desirable;   165
         Love is itself unmoving,
         Only the cause and end of movement,
         Timeless, and undesiring
         Except in the aspect of time
         Caught in the form of limitation   170
         Between un-being and being.
         Sudden in a shaft of sunlight
         Even while the dust moves
         There rises the hidden laughter
         Of children in the foliage   175
         Quick now, here, now, always—
         Ridiculous the waste sad time
         Stretching before and after.

148-52 Cf. the time theories of J. W. Dunne, which were much discussed
about this period (*An Experiment with Time*, 1927; *The New Immortality*,
1938). 158 *The Word in the desert:* prophet or hermit, or Christ himself.
161 *Chimera:* bogy; hybrid monster seen in hallucination. Cf. Bosch's
painting *The Temptation of St. Anthony*. 163 the 'ladder of contempla-
tion' in St. John of the Cross, the Spanish mystic (1542-91). See *The
Dark Night of the Soul*, II. xvii-xix.

Isaac Rosenberg

1890—1918

DEAD MAN'S DUMP

The plunging limbers over the shattered track
Racketed with their rusty freight,
Stuck out like many crowns of thorns,
And the rusty stakes like sceptres old
To stay the flood of brutish men   5
Upon our brothers dear.

The wheels lurched over sprawled dead
But pained them not, though their bones crunched,
Their shut mouths made no moan.
They lie there huddled, friend and foeman,   10
Man born of man, and born of woman,
And shells go crying over them
From night till night and now.

Earth has waited for them,
All the time of their growth   15
Fretting for their decay:
Now she has them at last!
In the strength of their strength
Suspended—stopped and held.

What fierce imaginings their dark souls lit?   20
Earth! have they gone into you!
Somewhere they must have gone,
And flung on your hard back
Is their soul's sack
Emptied of God-ancestralled essences.   25
Who hurled them out? Who hurled?

None saw their spirits' shadow shake the grass,
Or stood aside for the half used life to pass
Out of those doomed nostrils and the doomed mouth,
When the swift iron burning bee   30
Drained the wild honey of their youth.

1 *Limbers:* fore-parts of gun-carriages.

What of us who, flung on the shrieking pyre,
Walk, our usual thoughts untouched,
Our lucky limbs as on ichor fed,
Immortal seeming ever?   35
Perhaps when the flames beat loud on us,
A fear may choke in our veins
And the startled blood may stop.

The air is loud with death,
The dark air spurts with fire,   40
The explosions ceaseless are.
Timelessly now, some minutes past,
These dead strode time with vigorous life,
Till the shrapnel called ' An end! '
But not to all. In bleeding pangs   45
Some borne on stretchers dreamed of home,
Dear things, war-blotted from their hearts.

Maniac Earth! howling and flying, your bowel
Seared by the jagged fire, the iron love,
The impetuous storm of savage love.   50
Dark Earth! dark Heavens! swinging in chemic smoke,
What dead are born when you kiss each soundless soul
With lightning and thunder from your mined heart,
Which man's self dug, and his blind fingers loosed?

A man's brains splattered on   55
A stretcher-bearer's face;
His shook shoulders slipped their load,
But when they bent to look again
The drowning soul was sunk too deep
For human tenderness.   60

They left this dead with the older dead,
Stretched at the cross roads.

Burnt black by strange decay
Their sinister faces lie,
The lid over each eye,   65
The grass and coloured clay
More motion have than they,
Joined to the great sunk silences.

34 *Ichor:* fluid in Greek gods' veins.

Here is one not long dead;
His dark hearing caught our far wheels,   70
And the choked soul stretched weak hands
To reach the living word the far wheels said,
The blood-dazed intelligence beating for light,
Crying through the suspense of the far torturing wheels
Swift for the end to break   75
Or the wheels to break,
Cried as the tide of the world broke over his sight.

Will they come? Will they ever come?
Even as the mixed hoofs of the mules,
The quivering-bellied mules,   80
And the rushing wheels all mixed
With his tortured upturned sight.
So we crashed round the bend,
We heard his weak scream,
We heard his very last sound,   85
And our wheels grazed his dead face.

Hugh MacDiarmid
(Christopher Murray Grieve)

b. 1892

STONY LIMITS

(IN MEMORIAM: CHARLES DOUGHTY, 1843-1926)

From the volume of the same title, published 1934. MacDiarmid
wrote of this book: 'Stony Limits was written in the Shetland
Isles, where I lived for a number of years . . . and most of the
poems in it reflect the effect upon me of Northern light and the
geology of the Shetland landscape. In its use of scientific
terminology this book anticipates the subsequent development of
my work.' Geology was one of Doughty's keenest interests.

Under no hanging heaven-rooted tree,
Though full of mammuks' nests,
Bone of old Britain we bury thee
But heeding your unspoken hests

2 *Mammuks:* fictitious birds.

Naught not coeval with the Earth   5
And indispensable till its end
With what whom you despised may deem the dearth
Of your last resting-place dare blend.
Where nature is content with little so are you
So be it the little to which all else is due.   10

Nor in vain mimicry of the powers
That lifted up the mountains shall we raise
A stone less of nature's shaping than of ours
   To mark the unfrequented place.
You were not filial to all else   15
Save to the Dust, the mother of all men,
And where you lie no other sign needs tells
(Unless a gaunt shape resembles you again
In some momentary effect of light on rock)
But your family likeness to all her stock.   20

Flowers may be strewn upon the grave
   Of easy come easy go.
Fitly only some earthquake or tidal wave
O'er you its red rose or its white may throw
But naught else smaller than darkness and light   25
—Both here, though of no man's bringing!—
And as any past time had been in your sight
Were you now from your bed upspringing,
Now or a billion years hence, you would see
Scant difference, eyed like eternity.   30

How should we have anything to give you
   In death who had nothing in life,
Attempting in our sand-riddles to sieve you
Who were with nothing but the sheer elements rife?
Anchor of truth, facile as granite you lie,   35
A plug suspended in England's false dreams.
Your worth will be seen by and by,
Like God's purpose in what men deem their schemes,
Nothing ephemeral can seek what lies in this ground
Since nothing can be sought but the found.   40

The poem that would praise you must be
Like the glass of some rock, sleek brown, crowded

17 'No other sign is needed to tell where you lie.' Poet's grammar.
36 *Plug:* cylindrical rock-mass plugging extinct volcano.

With dark incipient crystal growths, we see;
Or a glimpse of Petavius may have endowed it
With the tubular and dumb-bell-shaped inclusions surrounded 45
  By the broad reaction rims it needs.
I have seen it in dreams and know how it abounded
—Ah! would I could find in me like seeds!—
As the north-easterly garden in the lunation grows,
A spectacle not one man in ten millions knows. 50

I belong to a different country than yours
And none of my travels have been in the same lands
Save where Arzachel or Langrenus allures
Such spirits as ours, and the Straight Wall stands,
But crossing shear planes extruded in long lines of ridges, 55
Torsion cylinders, crater rings, and circular seas
And ultra-basic xenoliths that make men look midges
Belong to my quarter as well, and with ease
I too can work in bright green and all the curious interference
Colours that under crossed nicols have a mottled appearance. 60

Let my first offering be these few pyroxenes twinned
On the orthopinacoid and hour-glass scheme,
Fine striæ, microline cross-hatchings, and this wind
Blowing plumes of vapour forever it would seem
From cone after cone diminishing sterile and grey 65
In the distance; dun sands in ever-changing squalls;
Crush breccias and overthrusts; and such little array
Of Geology's favourite fal-de-lals
And demolitions and entrenchments of weather
As any turn of my eyes brings together. 70

44, 53 *Petavius . . . Arzachel . . . Langrenus:* large mountain-rings on the moon, each containing smaller craters. 45 *Inclusions:* foreign matter in minerals. 49 *Lunation:* time of full moon, with reference to the apparent surface changes sometimes observed through a telescope in the north-east quadrant of the moon. 53 See 44. 54 *Straight Wall:* a remarkable 60-mile-long geological fault on the moon. 55 *Shear planes:* parallel planes displaced, one being thrust over another in the same direction. 56 *Torsion cylinders:* forms of metamorphic rock caused by crustal rolling (?). 57 *Ultra-basic xenoliths:* alien fragments in igneous rock. It is presumably their age rather than their size that makes 'men look midges'. 60 *Nicols:* prisms of Iceland spar. 61 *Pyroxenes:* group of minerals: metasilicates of calcium, magnesium, iron, etc. 62 *Orthopinacoid:* form of crystal with two faces parallel to the ortho-axis and the vertical axis. 63 *Striæ:* streaks, scratches. 67 *Crush breccias:* rocks consisting of angular fragments; *overthrusts:* reversed geological faults resulting in horizontal thrust of one rock-mass over another.

I know how on turning to noble hills
And stark deserts happily still preserved
For men whom no gregariousness fills
With the loneliness for which they are nerved
—The lonely at-one-ment with all worth while—   75
I can feel as if the landscape and I
Became each other and see my smile
In the corners of the vastest contours lie
And share the gladness and peace you knew,
—The supreme human serenity that was you!   80

I have seen Silence lift his head
And Song, like his double, lift yours,
And know, while nearly all that seems living is dead,
You were always consubstantial with all that endures.
Would it were on Earth! Not since Ezekiel has that faw sun
     ringed   85
A worthier head: red as Adam you stood
In the desert, the horizon with vultures black-winged,
And sang and died in this still greater solitude
Where I sit by your skull whose emptiness is worth
The sum of almost all the full heads now on Earth   90
—By your roomy skull where most men might well spend
Longer than you did in Arabia, friend!

Hart Crane

1899—1932

VOYAGES

I

Above the fresh ruffles of the surf
Bright striped urchins flay each other with sand.
They have contrived a conquest for shell shucks,
And their fingers crumble fragments of baked weed
Gaily digging and scattering.   5

And in answer to their treble interjections
The sun beats lightning on the waves,
The waves fold thunder on the sand;
And could they hear me I would tell them:

85 *Ezekiel:* Doughty, like the Hebrew prophet, has left his 'Prophetic
Books'. *Faw:* shimmering.   3 *Shell shucks:* pieces of sea-shell.

O brilliant kids, frisk with your dog,   10
Fondle your shells and sticks, bleached
By time and the elements; but there is a line
You must not cross nor ever trust beyond it
Spry cordage of your bodies to caresses
Too lichen-faithful from too wide a breast.   15
The bottom of the sea is cruel.

                          II
And yet this great wink of eternity,
Of rimless floods, unfettered leewardings,
Samite sheeted and processioned where
Her undinal vast belly moonward bends,   20
Laughing the wrapt inflections of our love;

Take this Sea, whose diapason knells
On scrolls of silver snowy sentences,
The sceptred terror of whose sessions rends
As her demeanors motion well or ill,   25
All but the pieties of lovers' hands.

And onward, as bells off San Salvador
Salute the crocus lustres of the stars,
In these poinsettia meadows of her tides,—
Adagios of islands, O my Prodigal,   30
Complete the dark confessions her veins spell.

Mark how her turning shoulders wind the hours,
And hasten while her penniless rich palms
Pass superscription of bent foam and wave,—
Hasten, while they are true,—sleep, death, desire,   35
Close round one instant in one floating flower.

Bind us in time, O Seasons clear, and awe.
O minstrel galleons of Carib fire,
Bequeath us to no earthly shore until
Is answered in the vortex of our grave   40
The seal's wide spindrift gaze toward paradise.

18 *Leewardings:* wind-sheltered passages. 19 *Samite:* rich silk fabric.
20 *Undinal:* an *undine* is a fabulous water-sprite. 22 *Diapason:* full
harmony. 27 *Bells off San Salvador:* alludes to the legend of a sunken
city off the island of San Salvador in the Bahamas. 29 *Poinsettia:*
bright Mexican flower. 30 *Adagios of islands:* 'The reference is to the
motion of a boat through islands clustered thickly, the rhythm of the
motion, etc.' (C.)

III

Infinite consanguinity it bears—
This tendered theme of you that light
Retrieves from sea plains where the sky
Resigns a breast that every wave enthrones;   45
While ribboned water lanes I wind
Are laved and scattered with no stroke
Wide from your side, whereto this hour
The sea lifts, also, reliquary hands.

And so, admitted through black swollen gates   50
That must arrest all distance otherwise,—
Past whirling pillars and lithe pediments,
Light wrestling there incessantly with light,
Star kissing star through wave on wave unto
Your body rocking!
                and where death, if shed,   55
Presumes no carnage, but this single change,—
Upon the steep floor flung from dawn to dawn
The silken skilled transmemberment of song;

Permit me voyage, love, into your hands . . .

IV

Whose counted smile of hours and days, suppose   60
I know as spectrum of the sea and pledge
Vastly now parting gulf on gulf of wings
Whose circles bridge, I know, (from palms to the severe
Chilled albatross's white immutability)
No stream of greater love advancing now   65
Than, singing, this mortality alone
Through clay aflow immortally to you.

All fragrance irrefragibly, and claim
Madly meeting logically in this hour
And region that is ours to wreathe again,   70
Portending eyes and lips and making told
The chancel port and portion of our June—

Shall they not stem and close in our own steps
Bright staves of flowers and quills to-day as I

58 *Transmemberment:* reincarnation. 68 *Irrefragibly:* irresistibly
(Crane's conflation of *irrefragably* and *irrefrangibly*). 72 *Chancel port and
portion:* allotted haven of communion.

Must first be lost in fatal tides to tell?   75
In signature of the incarnate word
The harbor shoulders to resign in mingling
Mutual blood, transpiring as foreknown
And widening noon within your breast for gathering
All bright insinuations that my years have caught   80
For islands where must lead inviolably
Blue latitudes and levels of your eyes,—

In this expectant, still exclaim receive
The secret oar and petals of all love.

                                   V
Meticulous, past midnight in clear rime,   85
Infrangible and lonely, smooth as though cast
Together in one merciless white blade—
The bay estuaries fleck the hard sky limits.

—As if too brittle or too clear to touch!
The cables of our sleep so swiftly filed,   90
Already hang, shred ends from remembered stars.
One frozen trackless smile . . . What words
Can strangle this deaf moonlight? For we

Are overtaken. Now no cry, no sword
Can fasten or deflect this tidal wedge,   95
Slow tyranny of moonlight, moonlight loved
And changed . . . ' There's

Nothing like this in the world,' you say,
Knowing I cannot touch your hand and look
Too, into that godless cleft of sky   100
Where nothing turns but dead sands flashing.

'—And never to quite understand!' No,
In all the argosy of your bright hair I dreamed
Nothing so flagless at this piracy.

                                              But now
Draw in your head, alone and too tall here.   105
Your eyes already in the slant of drifting foam;
Your breath sealed by the ghosts I do not know:
Draw in your head and sleep the long way home.

86 *Infrangible:* inviolable.

VI

Where icy and bright dungeons lift
Of swimmers their lost morning eyes,   110
And ocean rivers, churning, shift
Green borders under stranger skies,

Steadily as a shell secretes
Its beating leagues of monotone,
Or as many waters trough the sun's   115
Red kelson past the cape's wet stone;

O rivers mingling toward the sky
And harbor of the phœnix' breast—
My eyes pressed black against the prow,
—Thy derelict and blinded guest   120

Waiting, afire, what name, unspoke,
I cannot claim: let thy waves rear
More savage than the death of kings,
Some splintered garland for the seer.

Beyond siroccos harvesting   125
The solstice thunders, crept away,
Like a cliff swinging or a sail
Flung into April's inmost day—

Creation's blithe and petalled word
To the lounged goddess when she rose   130
Conceding dialogue with eyes
That smile unsearchable repose—

Still fervid covenant, Belle Isle,
—Unfolded floating dais before
Which rainbows twine continual hair—   135
Belle Isle, white echo of the oar!

The imaged Word, it is, that holds
Hushed willows anchored in its glow.
It is the unbetrayable reply
Whose accent no farewell can know.   140

116 *Kelson:* inner keel fitted over a ship's floor-timbers to bind them to the keel. 125 *Siroccos:* hot oppressive winds from Africa. 133 *Belle Isle:* island between Newfoundland and Labrador.

Wystan Hugh Auden

b. 1907

SPAIN 1937

Yesterday all the past. The language of size
Spreading to China along the trade-routes; the diffusion
    Of the counting-frame and the cromlech;
Yesterday the shadow-reckoning in the sunny climates.

Yesterday the assessment of insurance by cards,   5
The divination of water; yesterday the invention
    Of cart-wheels and clocks, the taming of
Horses; yesterday the bustling world of navigators.

Yesterday the abolition of fairies and giants;
The fortress like a motionless eagle eyeing the valley,   10
    The chapel built in the forest;
Yesterday the carving of angels and of frightening gargoyles.

The trial of heretics among the columns of stone;
Yesterday the theological feuds in the taverns
    And the miraculous cure at the fountain;   15
Yesterday the Sabbath of Witches. But to-day the struggle.

Yesterday the installation of dynamos and turbines;
The construction of railways in the colonial desert;
    Yesterday the classic lecture
On the origin of Mankind. But to-day the struggle.   20

Yesterday the belief in the absolute value of Greek;
The fall of the curtain upon the death of a hero;
    Yesterday the prayer to the sunset,
And the adoration of madmen. But to-day the struggle.

As the poet whispers, startled among the pines   25
Or, where the loose waterfall sings, compact, or upright
    On the crag by the leaning tower:
' O my vision. O send me the luck of the sailor.'

3 *Cromlech:* prehistoric stone monument. 16 *Sabbath:* midnight
meeting.

And the investigator peers through his instruments
At the inhuman provinces, the virile bacillus   30
    Or enormous Jupiter finished:
' But the lives of my friends. I inquire, I inquire.'

And the poor in their fireless lodgings dropping the sheets
Of the evening paper: ' Our day is our loss. O show us
    History the operator, the   35
Organizer, Time the refreshing river.'

And the nations combine each cry, invoking the life
That shapes the individual belly and orders
    The private nocturnal terror:
' Did you not found once the city state of the sponge,   40

' Raise the vast military empires of the shark
And the tiger, establish the robin's plucky canton?
    Intervene. O descend as a dove or
A furious papa or a mild engineer: but descend.'

And the life, if it answers at all, replies from the heart   45
And the eyes and the lungs, from the shops and squares of the
    city:
    ' O no, I am not the Mover,
Not to-day, not to you. To you I'm the

' Yes-man, the bar-companion, the easily-duped:
I am whatever you do; I am your vow to be   50
    Good, your humorous story;
I am your business voice; I am your marriage.

' What's your proposal? To build the Just City? I will.
I agree. Or is it the suicide pact, the romantic
    Death? Very well, I accept, for   55
I am your choice, your decision: yes, I am Spain.'

Many have heard it on remote peninsulas,
On sleepy plains, in the aberrant fishermen's islands,
    In the corrupt heart of the city;
Have heard and migrated like gulls or the seeds of a flower.   60

They clung like burrs to the long expresses that lurch
Through the unjust lands, through the night, through the alpine
    tunnel;
    They floated over the oceans:
They walked the passes: they came to present their lives.

On that arid square, that fragment nipped off from hot   65
Africa, soldered so crudely to inventive Europe,
    On that tableland scored by rivers,
Our fever's menacing shapes are precise and alive.

To-morrow, perhaps, the future: the research on fatigue
And the movements of packers; the gradual exploring of all
    the   70
    Octaves of radiation;
To-morrow the enlarging of consciousness by diet and breathing.

To-morrow the rediscovery of romantic love;
The photographing of ravens; all the fun under
    Liberty's masterful shadow;   75
To-morrow the hour of the pageant-master and the musician.

To-morrow, for the young, the poets exploding like bombs,
The walks by the lake, the winter of perfect communion;
    To-morrow the bicycle races
Through the suburbs on summer evenings: but to-day the
    struggle.   80

To-day the inevitable increase in the chances of death;
The conscious acceptance of guilt in the fact of murder;
    To-day the expending of powers
On the flat ephemeral pamphlet and the boring meeting.

To-day the makeshift consolations; the shared cigarette;   85
The cards in the candle-lit barn and the scraping concert,
    The masculine jokes; to-day the
Fumbled and unsatisfactory embrace before hurting.

The stars are dead; the animals will not look:
We are left alone with our day, and the time is short and   90
    History to the defeated
May say Alas but cannot help or pardon.

Charles Olson

b. 1910

THE LORDLY AND ISOLATE SATYRS

Olson's 'projective' or 'open' verse, where as he says 'form is
never any more than an extension of content,' attempts to develop
an objectivity in the line of Pound and Williams—a movement
away from 'lyrical interference of the individual as ego' in the
general direction of the larger epic or dramatic forms. In this
poem, written 1956, the implied comparison between the sudden
appearance of a band of young motorcyclists on a beach and the
disturbing irruption of satyrs in some ancient glade is used
to show the power of physical presence, of figures in a land-
scape, even when no act of communication with these figures is
involved.

The lordly and isolate Satyrs—look at them come in
on the left side of the beach
like a motorcycle club! And the handsomest of them,
the one who has a woman, driving that snazzy
convertible   5
          Wow, did you ever see even in a museum
such a collection of boddisatvahs, the way
they come up to their stop, each of them
as though it was a rudder
the way they have to sit above it   10
and come to a stop on it, the monumental solidity
of themselves, the Easter Island
they make of the beach, the Red-headed Men

---

1 *Isolate:* isolated. 4 *Snazzy:* smart and flashy. 7 *Boddisatvahs:* In
Buddhism, *bodhisattvas* are persons who voluntarily postpone their
private Nirvana or spiritual perfection in order to help others towards
enlightenment. (Sanskrit) Although the term is being used with some
irony, the irony is not complete. Such Buddhist references are frequent
in American 'beat' poetry of the 1950s. 12 *Easter Island:* Pacific island
famed for its huge stone figures. Their history is unknown.

These are the Androgynes,
the Fathers behind the father, the Great Halves   15

Or as that one was, inside his pants, the Yiddish poet
a vegetarian. Or another—all in his mouth—a snarl
of the Sources. Or the one I loved most, who once,
once only, let go the pain, the night he got drunk,
and I put him to bed, and he said, Bad blood.   20

Or the one who cracks and doesn't know
that what he thinks are a thousand questions are suddenly
a thousand lumps thrown up where the cloaca
again has burst: one looks into the face and exactly as suddenly
it isn't the large eyes and nose but the ridiculously small mouth 25
which you are looking down as one end of

—as the Snarled Man
is a monocyte.

Hail the ambiguous Fathers, and look closely
at them, they are the unadmitted, the club of Themselves,   30
weary riders, but who sit upon the landscape as the Great
Stones. And only have fun among themselves. They are
the lonely ones

Hail them, and watch out. The rest of us,
on the beach as we had previously known it, did not know   35
there was this left side. As they came riding in from the sea
—we did not notice them until they were already creating
the beach we had not known was there—but we assume
they came in from the sea. We assume that. We don't know.

14-28 Various comparisons emphasise the ambiguous image the motor-
cyclists present: like the ancient satyrs, they seem both less and more
than human. They are mixed-up ('snarled'), narcissistic ('monocytes'—
single cells), they combine masculine strength with elaborate self-
decoration and seem wedded to their machines ('androgynes'—men-
women), but they transmit a mysterious energy ('fathers behind the
father'). 21 *Cracks:* starts speaking, breaks the mask. 23 *Cloaca:*
sewer. 31-32 *Great Stones:* e.g. the Easter Island monoliths.

In any case the whole sea was now a hemisphere,   40
and our eyes like half a fly's, we saw twice as much. Every-
thing opened, even if the newcomers just sat, didn't,
for an instant, pay us any attention. We were as we had been,
in that respect. We were as usual, the children were being fed pop
and potato chips, and everyone was sprawled as people are   45
on a beach. Something had happened but the change
wasn't at all evident. A few drops of rain
would have made more of a disturbance.

There we were. They, in occupation of the whole view
in front of us and off to the left where we were not used to look. 50
And we, watching them pant from their exertions, and talk to each
    other,
the one in the convertible the only one who seemed to be circulat-
    ing.
And he was dressed in magnificent clothes, and the woman with
    him
a dazzling blond, the new dye making her hair a delicious
streaked ash. She was as distant as the others. She sat in her flesh
    too.   55

These are our counterparts, the unknown ones.

They are here. We do not look upon them as invaders. Dimen-
    sionally

they are larger than we—all but the woman. But we are not
    suddenly

small. We are as we are. We don't even move, on the beach.

It is a stasis. Across nothing at all we stare at them.   60
We can see what they are. They don't notice us. They have
    merely
and suddenly moved in. They occupy our view. They are between
    us
and the ocean. And they have given us a whole new half of the
    beach.

60 *Stasis:* moment of fixity and stillness.

As of this moment, there is nothing else to report.
It is Easter Island transplanted to us. With the sun, and a
warm   65
summer day, and sails out on the harbour they're here, the Con-
temporaries. They have come in.

Except for the stirring of the leader, they are still
catching their breath. They are almost like scooters the way
they sit there, up a little, on their thing. It is as though   70
the extra effort of it tired them the most. Yet that just there
was where their weight and separateness—their immensities—
lay. Why they seem like boddisatvahs. The only thing one noticed
is the way their face breaks when they call across to each other.
Or actually speak quite quietly, not wasting breath. But the
face   75
loses all containment, they are fifteen year old boys at the moment
they speak to each other. They are not gods. They are not even
stone.
They are doubles. They are only Source. When they act like us
they go to pieces. One notices then that their skin
is only creased like red-neck farmers. And that they are all   80
freckled. The red-headed people have the hardest time
to possess themselves. Is it because they were over-
fired? Or why—even to their beautiful women—do the red ones
have only that half of the weight?

We look at them, and begin to know. We begin to see 85
who they are. We see why they are satyrs, and why one half
of the beach was unknown to us. And now that it is known,
now that the beach goes all the way to the headland we thought
we were huddling ourselves up against, it turns out it is the
same. It is the beach. The Visitors—Resters—who, by being
there,   90
made manifest what we had not known—that the beach fronted
wholly
to the sea—have only done that, completed the beach.

The difference is
we are more on it. The beauty of the white of the sun's light, the
blue the water is, and the sky, the movement on the painted
lands-   95

78 *Doubles . . . Source:* They may look like gods, but anything godlike
about them is only a reaction they may cause, not an inherent possession.
82-83 *Over-fired:* i.e. like potter's clay.

cape, the boy-town the scene was, is now pierced with angels and
with fire. And winter's ice shall be as brilliant in its time as
life truly is, as Nature is only the offerer, and it is we
who look to see what the beauty is.

These visitors, now stirring   100
to advance, to go on wherever they do go restlessly never com-
    pleting
their tour, going off on their motorcycles, each alone except for
the handsome one, isolate huge creatures wearing down nothing as
they go, their huge third leg like carborundum, only the vault
of their being taking rest, the awkward boddhas   105

We stay. And watch them
gather themselves up. We have no feeling except love. They are
    not
ours. They are of another name. These are what the gods are.
    They
look like us. They are only in all parts larger. But the size is
only different. The difference is, they are not here, they are
    not   110
on this beach in this sun which, tomorrow, when we come to swim,
will be another summer day. They can't talk to us. We have no
    desire
to stop them any more than, as they made their camp, only
    possibly
the woman in the convertible one might have wanted to be
    familiar
with. The Leader was too much as they.   115

They go. And the day

103-4 *Huge . . . carborundum:* man and machine seen as a single moving
unit, the motorcycle as an extension of the human body (like the hoofs
and tail of the satyr).   105 *Boddhas:* bodhisattvas, probably with a pun
on 'bodies' or 'buddies'.

Dylan Thomas

1914—1953

OVER SIR JOHN'S HILL

Over Sir John's hill,
The hawk on fire hangs still;
In a hoisted cloud, at drop of dusk, he pulls to his claws
And gallows, up the rays of his eyes the small birds of the bay
And the shrill child's play   5
Wars
Of the sparrows and such who swansing, dusk, in wrangling
   hedges.
And blithely they squawk
To fiery tyburn over the wrestle of elms until
The flash the noosed hawk   10
Crashes, and slowly the fishing holy stalking heron
In the river Towy below bows his tilted headstone.

Flash, and the plumes crack,
And a black cap of jack-
Daws Sir John's just hill dons, and again the gulled birds hare   15
To the hawk on fire, the halter height, over Towy's fins,
In a whack of wind.
There
Where the elegiac fisherbird stabs and paddles
In the pebbly dab-filled   20
Shallow and sedge, and ' dilly dilly ' calls the loft hawk,
' Come and be killed,'
I open the leaves of the water at a passage
Of psalms and shadows among the pincered sandcrabs prancing
And read, in a shell,   25
Death clear as a buoy's bell:
All praise of the hawk on fire in hawk-eyed dusk be sung,

1 *Sir John's hill:* near Laugharne, in South Wales. 9 *Tyburn:* place of
execution: the hawk is seen as the hangman of the small birds. 12
Towy: river in Wales. 21 *Loft:* raised aloft.

When his viperish fuse hangs looped with flames under the brand
Wing, and blest shall
Young   30
Green chickens of the bay and bushes cluck, ' dilly dilly,
Come let us die.'
We grieve as the blithe birds, never again, leave shingle and elm,
The heron and I,
I young Æsop fabling to the near night by the dingle   35
Of eels, saint heron hymning in the shell-hung distant

Crystal harbour vale
Where the sea cobbles sail,
And wharves of water where the walls dance and the white cranes
    stilt.
It is the heron and I, under judging Sir John's elmed   40
Hill, tell-tale the knelled
Guilt
Of the led-astray birds whom God, for their breast of whistles,
Have mercy on,
God in his whirlwind silence save, who marks the sparrows hail, 45
For their souls' song.
Now the heron grieves in the weeded verge. Through windows
Of dusk and water I can see the tilting whispering
Heron, mirrored, go,
As the snapt feathers snow,   50
Fishing in the tear of the Towy. Only a hoot owl
Hollows, a grassblade blown in cupped hands, in the looted elms
And no green cocks or hens
Shout
Now on Sir John's hill. The heron, ankling the scaly   55
Lowlands of the waves,
Makes all the music; and I who hear the tune of the slow,
Wear-willow river, grave,
Before the lunge of the night, the notes on this time-shaken
Stone for the sake of the souls of the slain birds sailing.   60

28 *Fuse:* track, swoop; *brand:* torch like, ardent.   38 cobbled street
reflected in the water. Cf. the 'dancing walls' of line 39.

Robert Lowell

b. 1917

THE QUAKER GRAVEYARD IN NANTUCKET

(FOR WARREN WINSLOW, DEAD AT SEA)

From *Lord Weary's Castle* (1946). Deliberate echoes of *Lycidas* challenge comparison with Milton's elegy, but Lowell's more tense, violent, and comfortless poem is a witness to a very individual mind. The tenseness is not surprising: Lowell, who became a Catholic convert in 1940, is meditating on a graveyard in the stronghold of his New England Puritan ancestors.

Let man have dominion over the fishes of the sea and the fowls of the air and the beasts and the whole earth, and every creeping creature that moveth upon the earth.

I

A brackish reach of shoal off Madaket,—
The sea was still breaking violently and night
Had steamed into our North Atlantic Fleet,
When the drowned sailor clutched the drag-net. Light
Flashed from his matted head and marble feet,   5
He grappled at the net
With the coiled, hurdling muscles of his thighs:
The corpse was bloodless, a botch of reds and whites,
Its open, staring eyes
Were lustreless dead-lights   10
Or cabin-windows on a stranded hulk
Heavy with sand. We weight the body, close
Its eyes and heave it seaward whence it came,
Where the heel-headed dogfish barks its nose
On Ahab's void and forehead; and the name   15
Is blocked in yellow chalk.
Sailors, who pitch this portent at the sea
Where dreadnoughts shall confess
Its heel-bent deity,
When you are powerless   20

1 *Madaket:* on Nantucket Island, Massachusetts. 10 *Dead-lights:* porthole shutters.

To sand-bag this Atlantic bulwark, faced
By the earth-shaker, green, unwearied, chaste
In his steel scales: ask for no Orphean lute
To pluck life back. The guns of the steeled fleet
Recoil and then repeat   25
The hoarse salute.

II

Whenever winds are moving and their breath
Heaves at the roped-in bulwarks of this pier,
The terns and sea-gulls tremble at your death
In these home waters. Sailor, can you hear   30
The Pequod's sea wings, beating landward, fall
Headlong and break on our Atlantic wall
Off 'Sconset, where the yawing S-boats splash
The bellbuoy, with ballooning spinnakers,
As the entangled, screeching mainsheet clears   35
The blocks: off Madaket, where lubbers lash
The heavy surf and throw their long lead squids
For blue-fish? Sea-gulls blink their heavy lids
Seaward. The winds' wings beat upon the stones,
Cousin, and scream for you and the claws rush   40
At the sea's throat and wring it in the slush
Of this old Quaker graveyard where the bones
Cry out in the long night for the hurt beast
Bobbing by Ahab's whaleboats in the East.

III

All you recovered from Poseidon died   45
With you, my cousin, and the harrowed brine
Is fruitless on the blue beard of the god,
Stretching beyond us to the castles in Spain,
Nantucket's westward haven. To Cape Cod
Guns, cradled on the tide,   50
Blast the eelgrass about a waterclock
Of bilge and backwash, roil the salt and sand

23 *Orphean lute:* Orpheus descended to Hades, to win back by means of his music his dead wife Eurydice. 31 *Pequod:* name of whaling-ship in Herman Melville's novel *Moby Dick* (1851). 33 *'Sconset:* Siasconset, on Nantucket Island; *S-boats:* type of racing yacht. 34 *Spinnakers:* large triangular sails on racing yachts, used for running before the wind. 35 *Mainsheet:* rope extending the mainsail. 37 *Squids:* artificial bait. 44 *Ahab:* captain of the *Pequod.* 45 *Poseidon:* Greek sea-god. 51 *Eelgrass:* seaweed with grass-like leaves. 52 *Roil:* stir, mix.

Lashing earth's scaffold, rock
Our warships in the hand
Of the great God, where time's contrition blues   55
Whatever it was these Quaker sailors lost
In the mad scramble of their lives. They died
When time was open-eyed,
Wooden and childish; only bones abide
There, in the nowhere, where their boats were tossed   60
Sky-high, where mariners had fabled news
Of IS, the whited monster. What it cost
Them is their secret. In the sperm-whale's slick
I see the Quakers drown and hear their cry:
" If God himself had not been on our side,   65
If God himself had not been on our side,
When the Atlantic rose against us, why,
Then it had swallowed us up quick."

IV

This is the end of the whaleroad and the whale
Who spewed Nantucket bones on the thrashed swell   70
And stirred the troubled waters to whirlpools
To send the Pequod packing off to hell:
This is the end of them, three-quarters fools,
Snatching at straws to sail
Seaward and seaward on the turntail whale,   75
Spouting out blood and water as it rolls,
Sick as a dog to these Atlantic shoals:
Clamavimus, O depths. Let the sea-gulls wail

For water, for the deep where the high tide
Mutters to its hurt self, mutters and ebbs.   80
Waves wallow in their wash, go out and out,
Leave only the death-rattle of the crabs,
The beach increasing, its enormous snout
Sucking the ocean's side.
This is the end of running on the waves;   85
We are poured out like water. Who will dance
The mast-lashed master of Leviathans
Up from this field of Quakers in their unstoned graves?

62 *IS, the whited monster:* the white whale, Moby Dick, which 'is' but
remains elusive and uncaught; allegorically, in Ahab's view, the blank
destructiveness of the universe, seen as a concentrated 'existence'.
63 *Slick:* smooth oily patch on water. 78 *Clamavimus:* 'We have cried
out.' (Lat.)

V

When the whale's viscera go and the roll
Of its corruption overruns this world   90
Beyond tree-swept Nantucket and Wood's Hole
And Martha's Vineyard, Sailor, will your sword
Whistle and fall and sink into the fat?
In the great ash-pit of Jehoshaphat
The bones cry for the blood of the white whale,   95
The fat flukes arch and whack about its ears,
The death-lance churns into the sanctuary, tears
The gun-blue swingle, heaving like a flail,
And hacks the coiling life out: it works and drags
And rips the sperm-whale's midriff into rags,   100
Gobbets of blubber spill to wind and weather,
Sailor, and gulls go round the stoven timbers
Where the morning stars sing out together
And thunder shakes the white surf and dismembers
The red flag hammered in the mast-head. Hide,   105
Our steel, Jonas Messias, in Thy side.

VI

OUR LADY OF WALSINGHAM

There once the penitents took off their shoes
And then walked barefoot the remaining mile;
And the small trees, a stream and hedgerows file
Slowly along the munching English lane,   110
Like cows to the old shrine, until you lose
Track of your dragging pain.
The stream flows down under the druid tree,
Shiloah's whirlpools gurgle and make glad
The castle of God. Sailor, you were glad   115
And whistled Sion by that stream. But see:

Our Lady, too small for her canopy,
Sits near the altar. There's no comeliness
At all or charm in that expressionless
Face with its heavy eyelids. As before,   120
This face, for centuries a memory,
Non est species, neque decor,

91 *Wood's Hole:* place on the Cape Cod coast, opposite Martha's
Vineyard. 92 *Martha's Vineyard:* neighbouring island to Nantucket.
94 *Ash-pit of Jehoshaphat:* valley of God's judgement (see *Joel* iii. 2).
98 *Swingle:* flail, or the working part of one. 114 *Shiloah:* reservoir near
Jerusalem. 122 'There is neither beauty nor elegance.' (Lat.)

Expressionless, expresses God: it goes
Past castled Sion. She knows what God knows,
Not Calvary's Cross nor crib at Bethlehem   125
Now, and the world shall come to Walsingham.

                                    VII
The empty winds are creaking and the oak
Splatters and splatters on the cenotaph,
The boughs are trembling and a gaff
Bobs on the untimely stroke   130
Of the greased wash exploding on a shoal-bell
In the old mouth of the Atlantic. It's well;
Atlantic, you are fouled with the blue sailors,
Sea-monsters, upward angel, downward fish:
Unmarried and corroding, spare of flesh   135
Mart once of supercilious, wing'd clippers,
Atlantic, where your bell-trap guts its spoil
You could cut the brackish winds with a knife
Here in Nantucket, and cast up the time
When the Lord God formed man from the sea's slime   140
And breathed into his face the breath of life,
And blue-lung'd combers lumbered to the kill.
The Lord survives the rainbow of His will.

John Wain

b. 1925

A SONG ABOUT MAJOR EATHERLY

The book (Fernand Gigon's *Formula for Death—The Atom Bombs
and After*) also describes how Major Claude R. Eatherly, pilot of
the aircraft which carried the second bomb to Nagasaki, later
started having nightmares. His wife is quoted as saying: "He often
jumps up in the middle of the night and screams out in an inhuman
voice which makes me feel ill: 'Release it, release it.' "
    Major Eatherly began to suffer brief periods of madness, says
Gigon. The doctors diagnosed extreme nervous depression, and
Eatherly was awarded a pension of 237 dollars a month.

126 *Walsingham:* town in Norfolk; its shrine was a centre of pilgrimage.

This he appears to have regarded 'as a premium for murder, as a payment for what had been done to the two Japanese cities.' He never touched the money, and took to petty thievery, for which he was committed to Fort Worth prison.

Report in *The Observer*, August, 1958. (W.)

I

Good news. It seems he loved them after all.
His orders were to fry their bones to ash.
He carried up the bomb and let it fall.
And then his orders were to take the cash,

A hero's pension. But he let it lie.   5
It was in vain to ask him for the cause.
Simply that if he touched it he would die.
He fought his own, and not his country's wars.

His orders told him he was not a man:
An instrument, fine-tempered, clear of stain,   10
All fears and passions closed up like a fan:
No more volition than his aeroplane.

But now he fought to win his manhood back.
Steep from the sunset of his pain he flew
Against the darkness in that last attack.   15
It was for love he fought, to make that true.

II

To take life is always to die a little: to stop
any feeling and moving contrivance, however ugly,
unnecessary, or hateful, is to reduce by so much the total
of life there is. And that is to die a little.   20

To take the life of an enemy is to help him,
a little, towards destroying your own. Indeed, that is why
we hate our enemies: because they force us to kill them.
A murderer hides the dead man in the ground:
but his crime rears up and topples on to the living,   25
for it is they who now must hunt the murderer,
murder him, and hide him in the ground: it is they
who now feel the touch of death cold in their bones.

Animals hate death. A trapped fox will gnaw
through its own leg: it is so important to live   30
that he forgives himself the agony,
consenting, for life's sake, to the desperate teeth
grating through bone and pulp, the gasping yelps.

That is the reason the trapper hates the fox.
You think the trapper doesn't hate the fox?   35
But he does, and the fox can tell how much.
It is not the fox's teeth that grind his bones,
It is the trapper's. It is the trapper, there,
Who keeps his head down, gnawing, hour after hour.

And the people the trapper works for, they are there too,   40
heads down beside the trap, gnawing away.
Why shouldn't they hate the fox? Their cheeks are smeared
with his rank blood, and on their tongues his bone
being splintered, feels uncomfortably sharp.

So once Major Eatherly hated the Japanese.   45

III

Hell is a furnace, so the wise men taught.
The punishment for sin is to be broiled.
A glowing coal for every sinful thought.

The heat of God's great furnace ate up sin,
Which whispered up in smoke or fell in ash: 50
So that each hour a new hour could begin.

So fire was holy, though it tortured souls,
The sinner's anguish never ceased, but still
Their sin was burnt from them by shining coals.

Hell fried the criminal but burnt the crime,   55
Purged where it punished, healed where it destroyed:
It was a stove that warmed the rooms of time.

No man begrudged the flames their appetite.
All were afraid of fire, yet none rebelled.
The wise men taught that hell was just and right.   60

'The soul desires its necessary dread:
Only among the thorns can patience weave
A bower where the mind can make its bed.'

Even the holy saints whose patient jaws
Chewed bitter rind and hands raised up the dead   65
Were chestnuts roasted at God's furnace doors.

The wise men passed. The clever men appeared.
They ruled that hell be called a pumpkin face.
They robbed the soul of what it justly feared.

Coal after coal the fires of hell went out.   70
Their heat no longer warmed the rooms of time,
Which glistened now with fluorescent doubt.

The chilly saints went striding up and down
To warm their blood with useful exercise.
They rolled like conkers through the draughty town.   75

Those emblematic flames sank down to rest,
But metaphysical fire can not go out:
Men ran from devils they had dispossessed,

And felt within their skulls the dancing heat
No longer stored in God's deep boiler-room.   80
Fire scorched their temples, frostbite chewed their feet.

That parasitic fire could race and climb
More swiftly than the stately flames of hell.
Its fuel gone, it licked the beams of time.

So time dried out and youngest hearts grew old.   85
The smoky minutes cracked and broke apart.
The world was roasting but the men were cold.

Now from this pain worse pain was brought to birth,
More hate, more anguish, till at last they cried,
'Release this fire to gnaw the crusty earth: 90

Make it a flame that's obvious to sight
And let us say we kindled it ourselves,
To split the skulls of men and let in light.

Since death is camped among us, wish him joy,
Invite him to our table and our games. 95
We cannot judge, but we can still destroy.'

And so the curtains of the mind were drawn.
Men conjured hell a first, a second time:
And Major Eatherly took off at dawn.

IV

Suppose a sea-bird, 100
its wings stuck down with oil, riding the waves
in no direction, under the storm-clouds, helpless,
lifted for an instant by each moving billow
to scan the meaningless horizon, helpless,
helpless, and the storms coming, and its wings dead, 105
its bird-nature dead:
                    Imagine this castaway,
loved perhaps, by the Creator, and yet abandoned,
mocked by the flashing scales of the fish beneath it,
who leap, twist, dive, as free of the wide sea 110
as formerly the bird of the wide sky,
now helpless, starving, a prisoner of the surface,
unable to dive or rise:
                this is your emblem.
Take away the bird, let it be drowned 115
in the steep black waves of the storm, let it be broken
against rocks in the morning light, too faint to swim:
take away the bird, but keep the emblem.

It is the emblem of Major Eatherly,
who looked round quickly from the height of each wave, 120
but saw no land, only the rim of the sky
into which he was not free to rise, or the silver
gleam of the mocking scales of the fish diving
where he was not free to dive.

Men have clung always to emblems, 125
of tokens of absolution from their sins.
Once it was the scapegoat driven out, bearing
its load of guilt under the empty sky
until its shape was lost, merged in the scrub.

Now we are civilized, there is no wild heath. 130
Instead of the nimble scapegoat running out
to be lost under the wild and empty sky,
the load of guilt is packed into prison walls,
and men file inward through the heavy doors.

But now that image, too, is obsolete.   135
The Major entering prison is no scapegoat.
His penitence will not take away our guilt,
nor sort with any consoling ritual:
this is penitence for its own sake, beautiful,
uncomprehending, inconsolable, unforeseen.   140
He is not in prison for his penitence:
it is no outrage to our law that he wakes
with cries of pity on his parching lips.
We do not punish him for cries or nightmares.
We punish him for stealing things from stores.   145

O, give his pension to the storekeeper.
Tell him it is the price of all our souls.
But do not trouble to unlock the door
and bring the Major out into the sun.
Leave him: it is all one: perhaps his nightmares   150
grow cooler in the twilight of the prison.
Leave him; if he is sleeping, come away.
But lay a folded paper by his head,
nothing official or embossed, a page
torn from your notebook, and the words in pencil.   155
Say nothing of love, or thanks, or penitence:
say only 'Eatherly, we have your message.'

Christopher Logue

b. 1926

THE STORY OF
TWO GENTLEMEN AND THE GARDENER
or
HOW TO PROVE THE SUN

One Spring, the old Philosopher, feeling his bones
To be almost dry, wished to retire. For sixty years
His search after truth had been constant.
But standing at the door is hard. And because
The leaders of his country were speaking again
About loyalty and sacrifice, the old Philosopher knew   5
Misery was on the way; and to spend a year or two,
At rest, in the palace gardens, he must hurry.

He cleaned his shoes. Then, carrying his necessaries—
That is to say, almost nothing—he walked   10
Just one last time among men and streets
He had never understood, towards the huge iron gates,
And showed his references. They asked him to wait.
Later, as he had given no trouble to the authorities,
Had been thankful for small mercies, patient,   15
Confining his efforts to logic, god, or similar affairs
Not of great interest to his neighbours, he was admitted.

The ladies in waiting washed the old Philosopher
And gave him a change of clean linen. One said:
Tell us why you have come to the palace gardens?   20
—What will you do among the lawns and statues?
These were questions he had anticipated. First,
I shall talk to my nephew the Poet, he answered.
Luckier than me, he is still young, and has lived
Herein since passing his examination. Second,   25
I shall die. As for why I am here, is it not true
That the pawns are nearest the Queen?

And he passed out of sight round a mulberry tree.

That night, while reading softly to each other
From the books they had written, these gentlemen   30
Agreed to walk in the gardens after lunch each day
Considering their works by talk and talk about.
If Monday was given over to Rhyme, then, Tuesday
Was reserved for Logic, Choice, Necessity and Doubt.
So it was decided. The old Philosopher was glad   35
At getting such good terms. He unpacked his bundle,
And went to sleep.

And on the seventh day it fell
For the old Philosopher to lead the talk.
High on the palace steps they met, above them   40
The white sun; and arm in arm they glided down
Over the thousand-year-old lawn
Between stone lords and naked ladies till
The old man sat his nephew by a green
And shady place, with their backs against   45
The garden wall. Consider, he began,
The Sun . . . but then over the wall they heard a girl
Sing in a high voice:

I sent my lover a writ and a shilling,
For his fare to wherever we could meet,   50
He had been faithless, I must forgive him,
He did not come, I cannot sleep.
  And if he does not come to me
  This Mary will be forced to lie
  Down and die for want of him   55
  And for want of the golden city.

And the old Philosopher didn't mind, well,
Not much, and said: Good, good . . . the Sun—

My lover came along by heel and toe
All the way to me from Jericho,   60
Now you goose and now you gander
Lift your four grey wings together,
  Fly this loving baker's daughter
  And her man across the river
  Or their love will surely die   65
  For the want of the golden city.

Good. Good . . . the old man said . . . As we began, the Sun—

I'm giving you girls a secret to keep,
When a rogue kisses you, count your teeth,
He will be faithless, you must forgive him,   70
When the grey wings lift, fly with them.
  And if to you a child is born,
  Nurse him well poor little worm,
  Foster him till all three die
  For the want of the golden city.   75

Nephew, may we move on? This sun is hot, and time—
Soft stone—is passing by the things we have to say.
How did the tune go? asked the boy who carried
The old Philosopher's books. Well enough to be remembered,
The Poet said, before the boy carrying his slate   80
Had the chance to sing to his companion.

Nephew, the Sun . . . How can we be sure it's truly . . .
Sun. And, if it truly is, is truly there?

And if, Uncle, the Sun is truly there today
How can we know it is the sun that we saw yesterday?   85

O, Nephew—if tomorrow it comes up, what certainty
Is there it is the sun that warms us now? Alas,
The nourishment of doubt is endless. And fed by doubt
The relatives put up their feet for forty winks.

Permit me, Sirs . . . a voice behind them said . . . To be of use.   90
And opening their eyes they saw the Gardener.
Many times I have watched you . . . he went on . . . Recommend,
Suggest, enquire, read out loud, note down, get mad—
Sometimes it rained and I could eavesdrop, yet
All the while among these green things you turned grey.   95
Today, behind the rose tree there, I saw your troubles
Plain. And now, if you desire, I will clear up the matter.

Then, as they were courteous men,
They asked the Gardener to speak but cautioned him
That speculations identical—but more complex—than these   100
Had lasted them for years and years. Begin . . . they said.
So the Gardener told them how the Sun is round,
Is gold is vast is life is beautiful
And useful, far, adored, old, constant,
And they would spin round it seventy times   105
Or less, seeing as that the age was hard,
And how the Sun was rich, perpetual, generous . . .

And so forth.

He spoke for hours about the Sun.
At length the old Philosopher held up his hand: 110
If we agreed with all you say, my friend,
Nothing is changed. Our doubt, our doubt,
Your proof, no proof. And the Sun is going in
Despite your eloquence. The point stays moot.
A moment, Sirs. My proof . . . the Gardener said . . .   115
Is only half complete. Would you come back,
Tomorrow, say—and let me finish? Yes?

Next day, this time at dawn, the four of them
Waited, a little cold inside, until the Gardener showed.
Now . . . said the old Philosopher . . . Conclude.   120
So the Gardener told them how the Sun is round,
Is gold is vast is life is beautiful
And useful, far, adored, old, constant—
Stop! . . the Poet said . . . All this we heard before.

Indeed . . . the Gardener said . . . Before I can conclude,   125
First you must prove yourselves to be
The Gentlemen whom I saw yesterday. Tell me,
How else can I be truly sure you are
Those who heard the opening of the proof?

May I go back and hear that singing girl?   130
Asked the boy who carried the Poet's slate.
Does it cost much to be a gardener?
Asked the boy with the old Philosopher's books.
Gentlemen . . . the Gardener said . . . As I have done
This little much for you, what can you do for me?   135
But, come—by your long noses I can tell
On your hands are four green thumbs.

Allen Ginsberg

b. 1926

AMERICAN CHANGE

Published 1961. Poetry tends to build up towards high art,
rhetoric, irony, sophistication, the abstract; and then by a
necessary and often violent reaction it returns towards speech,
life, and directness. Ginsberg, rejecting the complexly imaged but
often cold and unurgent tradition of modern American 'academic'
poetry, rediscovered some of the virtues of spontaneity and of the
spoken language, of (as he says) 'rhythm of actual speech &
rhythm prompted by direct transcription of visual & other
mental data . . . The problem has been to communicate the
very spark of life, and not some opinion about that spark.'

    The first I looked on, after a long time far from home in
mid Atlantic on a summer day
Dolphins breaking the glassy water under the blue sky,
    a gleam of silver in my cabin, fished up out of my jangling
new pocket of coins and green dollars
    —held in my palm, the head of the feathered indian, old
Buck-Rogers eagle eyed face, a gash of hunger in the cheek
    gritted jaw of the vanished man begone like a Hebrew
with hairlock combed down the side— O Rabbi Indian   5

4 *Buck Rogers:* one of the first American film cowboys; he portrayed
himself on the screen.

What visionary gleam 100 years ago on Buffalo prairie under
the molten cloud shot sky, "the same clear light 10,000 miles
in all directions"
 but now with all the violin music of Vienna, gone into the
great slot machine of Kansas City, Reno—
 The coin seemed so small after vast European coppers thick
francs, leaden pesetas, lira endless and heavy,
 a miniature primeval memorialized in 5c. nickel candystore
nostalgia of the redskin, dead on silver coin,
 with shaggy buffalo on reverse, hump-backed little tail
incurved, head butting against the rondure of Eternity,   10
 cock forelock below, bearded shoulder muscle folded below
muscle, head of prophet, bowed,
 vanishing beast of Time, hoar body rubbed clean of wrinkles
ridiculous buffalo— Go to New York.

Dime next I found, Minerva, sexless cold & chill, ascending
goddess of money— and was it the wife of Wallace Stevens,
truly?
 and now from the locks flowing the miniature wings of speedy
thought,
 executive dyke, Minerva, goddess of Madison Avenue, forgotten
useless dime that can't buy hot dog, dead dime—   15

Then we've George Washington, less primitive, the snubnosed
quarter, smug eyes and mouth, some idiot's design of the sexless
Father,
 naked down to his neck, a ribbon in his wig, high forehead, Roman
line down the nose, fat cheeked, still showing his falsetooth ideas—
O Eisenhower & Washington— O Fathers— No movie star
dark beauty— O thou Bignoses—

---

7 *Kansas City:* city in Missouri. *Reno:* city in Nevada. 10 *Rondure:*
swelling curve. 13 *Dime:* coin=one tenth of a dollar, or 10 cents.
Minerva: Roman goddess of wisdom, patroness of trading. *Wallace
Stevens:* the American poet, who was vice-president of a large insurance
company and was sometimes taunted with his devotion to the world of
business and finance. 14 Minerva is said to have sprung from the
head of Jupiter. 15 *Dyke:* masculine woman. *Madison Avenue:* street
in New York famed as centre of advertising business. 16 *Washington:*
George Washington, first President of U.S.A. 1789-97 (1732-99).
Quarter: coin=one quarter of a dollar, or 25 cents. 17 *Eisenhower:*
Dwight D. Eisenhower, U.S. President 1953-61 (1890-).

Quarter, remembered quarter, 40c. in all— What'll you buy me
when I land— one icecream soda?—
poor pile of coins, original reminders of the sadness, forgotten
money of America—
nostalgia of the first touch of those coins, American change,   20
the memory in my aging hand, the same old silver reflective
there,
the thin dime hidden between my thumb and forefinger
All the struggles for those coins, the sadness of their reappearance
my reappearance on those fabled shores
and the failure of that Dream, that Vision of Money reduced to
this haunting recollection   •   25
of the gas lot in Paterson where I found half a dollar gleaming.
in the grass—

I have a $5 bill in my pocket— it's Lincoln's sour black head
moled wrinkled, forelocked too, big eared, flags of announce-
ment flying over the bill, stamps in green and spiderweb black,
   long numbers in racetrack green, immense promise, a girl, a hotel,
a busride to Albany, a night of brilliant drunk in some faraway
corner of Manhattan
   a stick of several teas, or paper or cap of Heroin, or a $5 strange
present to the blind.
   Money money, reminder, I might as well write poems to you—
dear American money— o statue of Liberty I ride enfolded in
my money in my mind to you— and last   30

   Ahhh! Washington again, on the Dollar, same poetic black print,
dark words, The United States of America, innumerable
numbers
   R956422481 One Dollar This Certificate Is Legal Tender
(tender!) for all debts public and private
   My God My God why have you forsaken me
   Ivy Baker Priest Series 1935F

26 *Gas lot:* petrol station. *Paterson:* city in New Jersey. 27 *Lincoln:*
Abraham Lincoln, U.S. President 1861-65 (1809-65). 28 *Albany:*
capital city of state of New York. *Manhattan:* borough of New York
City. 29 *Stick . . . teas:* marijuana or similar narcotic cigarette. *Cap:*
capsule. 30 *Statue of Liberty:* in New York harbour. 33 See *Matt.*
xxvii. 46. Cf. lines 37, 39. Ginsberg's poetry is much concerned with
the theme of the distortion or weakening of the original American
ideal of liberty, especially in the oppressive period of distrust follow-
ing the Second World War. 34 the Treasury signature and year of
issue.

and over, the Eagle, wild wings outspread, halo of the Stars
encircled by puffs of smoke & flame—   35
a circle the Masonic Pyramid, the sacred Swedenborgian Dollar
America, bricked up to the top, & floating surreal above
the triangle of holy outstaring Eye sectioned out of the aire, shin-
ing
light emitted from the eybrowless triangle— and a desert of
cactus scattered all around, clouds afar,
this being the Great Seal of our Passion, Annuit Coeptes, Novis
Ordo Seclorum,
the whole surrounded by green spiderwebs designed by T-
Men to prevent foul counterfeit—   40

ONE.

35 The reverse side of the note contains representations of the obverse
and reverse of the Great Seal of the U.S. The eagle and the constel-
lation (on obverse of seal) are the American national emblem and the
symbol of the independent states of the union respectively. 36-39
imagery and mottoes on reverse of Great Seal. 'The Pyramid signifies
strength and duration. The eye over it and the motto allude to the
many signal interpositions of providence in favour of the American
cause . . . and the words under it signify the beginning of the new
American Era.' (C. Thomson, Secretary of Congress, 1782) *Sweden-
borgian:* Emanuel Swedenborg (1688-1772), scientist and mystical
theologian, announced a new era in which the world had essentially
been changed and turned in a new spiritual direction. The unfinished
brick pyramid on the American seal also suggests a mystical upward
development—towards the triangle containing God's eye. *Surreal:* in-
congruous and disturbing. *Passion:* (i) suffering, (ii) intense hope.
Annuit Coeptes: for *Annuit Cœptis*, 'he [i.e. God] has prospered our under-
takings'. *Novis Ordo Seclorum:* for *Novus Ordo Seclorum,* 'a new order of the
ages'. 40 *T-Men:* special agents of U.S. Treasury Department.

INDEX

733

Rommel, A., 457
Romulo, C., 241
Ronan, T., C-49
"Rondine", 565
Ronga, L., 592
Rongen, B., 813
RONSARD PRIZE, 949
Rooke, D., 25
Roos, E. de, 51
Rooth, E., 471
Samuel ROS PRIZE, 619
Rosa, G.T., 103, 231, 677
LA ROSA D'ORO, 840
Ramon ROSA PRIZE, 950
Rosales, C., 191
Rosales, L., 845
Max ROSE PRIZE, 951
ROSEGGER PRIZE, C-10
Peter ROSEGGER PRIZE, 952
Roselle-Bordoy, G., 844
Rosen, S.N., 1031, B-137
Ross, B., C-77
Victor ROSSEL PRIZE, 953
Rosset, A., 949
Rossi, C-15
Rossi, A.M., 878, 1097
Rossi, P., 816
Rossi, V.G., 103, 1118
Rossino, G., 266
Rosso, R., 901
Rost, N., 874
Rostand, J., 11, 621, 852
Rotkovic, R., 768
Rostock, Rad des Bezirkes, 181
Rostworowski, C-20
Léopold ROSY PRIZE, 954
Rotary Club di Padova e di
    Venezia, 245
Roth, E., 406, 774
Rothman, Mrs. M.E., 204
Rotter, F., 642
Rotterdam Society for Public
    Utility, 955
Rotterdamse Kunststichting, 124
"ROTTERDAMSE NUTS" PRIZE,
    955
Rougemont, D. de, 299
Rouget, P., 858
Rouquette, M., 359
Rousseau, I., 449
Rousseau, P., 787
Rousseaux, A., 183, B-54
Roussel, R., 563
Rousselet, 470

Rousselof, J., 61, 327
Rousset, D., 924
Roussev, H., 312
Roux, F. de, 924
Rouzh, I., 193
Rovigo, C-15
Rowohlt Verlag, Ernest, 407
Roy, G., 381
Roy, H. van, 465
Roy, J., 8, 359, 416, 763,
    863, 924
Royal Netherlands Academy of
    Sciences, C-18
Royal Netherlands Association of
    Editors, 478
Royal Spanish Academy See
    Real Academia Español
Royal Society of Literature
    (United Kingdom), 137, 1082,
    1083
Rozas Larrain, C., 687
Rozhdestvnsky, R., C-26
Ruanda-Urundi, C-39
Rubén Morales, J., 758
Rubinstein, J., 643A
Rubió, J.I., 562
Rubio, R., 756
Rubio de Juan, M., 764
Rubow, P., 55
Rudahigwa--King of Ruanda, 262
Rudigoz, R., 1079
Rudnicka, H., 886
Rudnicki, A., 900
Rudolf, L., 455
Rudolph, J., 679
Rueda, S., 719
Rueda Medina, G., 655
Rueda Iberico, Ediciones, 712
Ruehmkorf, P., 597
Ruet, N., 722
Rugeles, M.F., 1108
Ruiz Albéniz, V., 715
Ruiz Castillo, 1029
Juan RUIZ DE ALARCÓN PRIZE,
    956
Ruiz Garcia, E., C-64
Ruiz Guiñazú, A., 644
Rulfo, J., 1131
Rumania. Council of Ministers
    957, 960
    Institute for Cultural Relations
    with Foreign Countries,
    C-22
RUMANIAN ACADEMY PRIZES,

Terzakis, A., 484
Tesini, G., C-15
Testa, C., 103
Testori, G., 901
Teuber, A., 406
Tet Toe, 196, 983
Teuffenbach, I., 560
"TEXTE UND ZEICHEN" NOVEL
 PRIZE, C-10
Tha, Shwegaing, 983
THAI LITERARY AWARDS, C-62
THAILAND ROYAL INSTITUTE OF
 ARTS AND SCIENCES ESSAY
 CONTEST, 1057
Thakin Ba Thaung, 196
Tharaud, J. and J., 8, 481
Thaw, U Ba, 983
Concepcion de THAYLHARDAR
 PRIZE, 564
Theater--Awards for Writing
 for See Drama
Theiner-Haffner, G., 560 (2)
Thelen, A.V., 403
Themba, D.L., 326
Themelis, Y., 484
Theodorakopoulos, I., 484
Theodorescu, C., 960
Theodorescu, R., 958
Theotokas, G., 484
Theurillat, H., 882
Thiago de Melo, 825
Thibaudeau, J., 384
Thibault, J.A., 806
Thiele, C., 682
Thierry, M.-P., 84
Thin, Mg, 983
Thin, Sagaing U Po, 983
13 NOVEMRI NAGRADA, 817
Thiry, M., 84, 760
Thiry, R., 84
Thoby-Marcelin, P., 494
Thomas, A., 1137
Thomas, D., 367, 585
Thomas, H., 381, 739, 939
Thomas, I., 1123
Thomas, L., 909
Thomas, M., 654
Thomas, R., 909
Thompson, J., 682
Thompson, S.H., 282
Thomsen, G.R., 369
Thorrez-Bodet, J., 49
THREE CROWNS LITERARY
 PRIZE, 1058

Thurk, H., 338
Thury, Z., 83
Thurzó, G., 83
Ti, Thuriya Kan, 983
Tiakhonov, M., 1032
Tic, N., 957, 1119 (2)
Tichy, A., 93, 1121
Tick, S., 908
Tiemeijer, H., 51
Tiempo, C., 191
Tiempo, E.K., 494, 943
Tiempo, E.L., 870 (2)
Nestor de TIERE PRIZE, 1059
Tierlinck, H., 332
TIERRA DEL FUEGO BEST
 BOOK OF THE YEAR, 1060,
 and 234
Tijeras, E., 583
Tillard, P., 453, 685
Tillich, P., 417, 476
Timar, M., 1050
"Times," Manila, B-160
"Times of India. Directory and
 Yearbook", B-161
Tin, Man, 983
Tin Lin, 1032
Tindall, N.B., 86
Ting Ling, 1032
Tinoco, B., 776
Tipping, E.W., 1137
Tismi, A., 167
TIRSO DE MOLINO PRIZE,
 1061
TOBAR PRIZE, 1062
Toaka, N., 781
Tobino, M., 1041, 1106
Tocantins, L., 776
Todorov, A., 312
Todorovic, G., 167
Todorovski, G., 817
Toe, Tet, 196, 983
Tofanelli, A., 1118
Toita, K., 781
Tokuda, S., 631
Tolkien, J.R.R., 568
Tollens Fund, 598, 1063
TOLLENS PRIZE, 1063
Tolluoglu, M., 71
Tolnai, G., 83
Tolstoi, A.N., 1032 (2)
Tolstoy, A., 1032
Leo TOLSTOY MEMORIAL
 PRIZE, 1064
Toma, A., 960

Vrettos, S., 622
Vriend, J.J., 124
Vries, A.H. de, 449
Vries, Hendrik, de, 309, 547, 1099
Vries, T. de, 1127 (2)
Vries, W. de, 333
Vriesland, V.E. van, 49, 542, 547
"Vrije Woord", 67
Vring, G. von der, 406, 774, 799
Vroman, L., 1099
Vrugt, J.P. See Blaman, A.
Vucetic, S., 275
Vuco, A., 805, 1164
Vujcic-Lazovska, I., 275
Vukovic, M.T., B-165
Vulliamu, L., 758
Vuyk, B., 1099

Wachter, L. de, C-4
Wadman, A., 611
Wagenaar-Nolthenius, H., 51
Wagenfeld, K., 325
Waggerl, K.H., 94, 1037
Wägner, E., 804
Wagner, J., 875
Wahlstrom & Widstrand, 849
Wai, Min Yu, 983
Waif, W., 465
Walberg, P., 969
Waldburger, F., 481
Waldeck, H.S., 94
Walder, F., 481
Waldinger, E., 1124
Waldmann, D., 990
Wales Eisteddfod, 349
Walgrave, J.W., 1149
William Gaston WALKLEY
    AWARDS FOR AUSTRALIAN
    JOURNALISM, 1137
Wallenius, K.M., 394
Wallis, R., 796
Walloon Provinces, Belgium, 446
Walpole, H., juror--36
Walravens, J., 646, C-4
Walser, M., 491, 531
Walsh, R.J., 191
Waltari, M.T., 392, 395
Waltari, S., 601
Walter, B., 774
Walter, H., 500
Walter, O.F., 1106

Waltz, J., 359
Walz, W., 625
Wandira, A., 1153
Wang Lan, 238
Wang Ping-Ling, 238
Wang Ting-chun, 236
Wangenheim, G. von, 339, 1145
WAR AGAINST FASCISM
    MEDAL, 1138
Warmond, B., 203, 449
Warner, J.V., 88
Wärnlof, A.L., 539
Warren, H., 1099
Warren, R.P., 439
WARSAW CITY PRIZE, 1139
WARSAW CITY PRIZE FOR
    YOUNG POETS, 1140
Warsaw Creative Youth Club,
    1140, 1141
Warsaw Liberation, 1139
Warsaw Municipal Council, 1139,
    1140
WARSAW STUDENT AND YOUTH
    AWARD FOR YOUNG POETS,
    1141
Warsaw's Atheneum Theatre, 647
Warsinsky, W., 368
Warszawski Klub Tworczy Mlodych,
    1140, 1141
Waser, M., 1172
Wasilevska, W.L., 1032 (2)
Wassing, A., 1044
Wast, H., 64, C-64, C-65
Wat, A., 818
Watanabe, Kazuo, 1158
Watanabe, Kieko, 781
Waterhouse, E.G., 471
Watkins, G., 90, 487
Watters, E., 445, 582
G.J. WATTUMULL AWARDS, 1142
Wattumull Foundation, 1142
WATTUMULL PRIZE, 1142
Wawra, K., 93, 642
Wazyk, A., 885
Webb, F., 682
Webster, E., 25
Wedding, A., 474
"Week End Mail", 1137
"Weekly Information News,"
    Yugoslavia, 805
Wegner, W., 140
Wehner, J.M., 774
Weid, M., 94
Weidenfeld & Nicolson, 407